HELLENISTIC ATHENS

HELLENISTIC ATHENS

AN HISTORICAL ESSAY

BY

WILLIAM SCOTT FERGUSON

NEW YORK

Howard Fertig

1969

First published in 1911

Howard Fertig, inc. edition 1969

Published by arrangement with Macmillan & Co. Ltd.
acting for the Executors of the author

Library of Congress Catalog Card Number: 68-9652

PRINTED IN THE UNITED STATES OF AMERICA
BY NOBLE OFFSET PRINTERS, INC.

TO

THE MEMORY OF MY FATHER

DONALD FERGUSON

PREFACE

A CONNECTED history of Athens during the Hellenistic period does not exist. The nearest approach to one may be obtained by combining Gaetano de Sanctis's *Contributi alla Storia Atheniese della Guerra Lamiaca alla Guerra Cremonidea* (1893) with the *History of Athens from 229 to 31 B.C.*, written in his own language by the Russian scholar, Sergius Shebelew (1898). But apart from the obvious inaccessibility of these works to the English reader, they do not, even when taken together, cover the entire period; and, while each was excellent in its own time, neither is any longer adequate from the standpoint of either the specialist or the reader at large. The present book, therefore, aims to fill a conspicuous gap in historical literature.

It has many shortcomings, doubtless, and some of them are probably inexcusable; but it is perhaps pardonable for the author to say, what the specialist knows in advance, that others are due to the character of the sources from which the narrative is drawn. He had to deal with a considerable body of official documents, dateless except in an approximate way, and an inconsiderable body of literary notices, also weak in chronological coherence. The chronology had first to be established; then the general lines of development to be perceived and drawn. In both of these tasks he has received great help from the works of other students, as the footnotes show; but overmuch had still to be done by himself.

The author has aimed to trace the general movement of Athenian affairs from the death of Alexander the Great in 323 B.C. to the sack of Athens by Sulla in 86 B.C. This has been at times a bold undertaking, and the book abounds in weak bridges thrown over broad chasms; but it seemed best to make the venture. The specialist will not be misled thereby—the guarded phraseology being, it is hoped, his sufficient danger-signals — while an unbroken passage is absolutely necessary for readers of general history, should any pass this way. The author trusts that nothing essential has been omitted in the text; but he has tried to relegate to the footnotes everything that has simply evidential value, and to the scientific journals all detailed arguments and investigations. For this he hopes that the hypothetical general reader will be grateful: the specialist is asked to regard the book in the context of the author's pamphlets and articles cited below[1] and of the other literature listed in the general bibliography.

We owe it as a duty to the greatness of Athens, says Freeman, to study the story of her miserable fall. This statement may be correct in its recognition of an obligation, but it implies a judgment which, though widely shared, is undoubtedly premature and probably unjust. In any case, the problem has taken such a different form

[1] Appendix I. p. 470.

since Freeman wrote that no one would now think of
approaching a book on Hellenistic Athens to discover
the secret of Athenian decline. Most historians, we
venture to think, will now agree that the battle of
Chaeronea (338 B.C.) simply put an end to an *interregnum* on land and the battle of Amorgos (322 B.C.) to
an *interregnum* on sea ; that the fate of Athens was
settled by the Peloponnesian War, and the fate of Greece
by this struggle and that which followed between Sparta
and its allies. Certainly, whoever believes with Freeman
that history is first of all past politics must no longer
look for the supreme crisis in Athenian affairs after
Alexander's time. Thenceforth he will be interested
mainly in what is perhaps the central theme of Hellenism
—the gradual transformation of a lot of little city-states
into municipalities of large territorial empires. This
process may be observed from two standpoints : (1)
that of the organizing powers — Alexander and his
successors, Aratus and the various Leagues, Rome ; (2)
that of the cities transformed. Of these, none had a
more eventful and individual experience than Athens.
Hence this special study of its history.

On the other hand, history is not all past politics.
Or, to put the matter differently, politics are unintelligible when considered apart from other manifestations of national activity. Certainly, the significance
of Athens during the Hellenistic period was due mainly
to its being recognized as the centre of the finest Greek
culture. Pre-eminence in this respect was generally
accorded to it until the middle of the second century
B.C. Then came the last great crisis in Athenian life
—a fresh start, which destroyed old character and

cost the living Athenians the esteem of the world.
Thereafter, the city was cherished for its memories
alone.   The changes in culture and in reputation, however, as well as the previous decay of civic autonomy,
were consummated by the play of forces working without as well as within Athens ; hence it has been
necessary to describe not simply developments peculiar
to that city, but also, though of course in a sketchy
way, the larger Hellenistic movements by which it was
repelled or attracted.

In his entire work, and in particular in the phase of it
just stated, the author has been much helped by the
historians of Hellenism in general.   Of his indebted-
ness to J. Beloch he is especially conscious.   To him
and to his other critics of the past, J. Kirchner of
Berlin, J. Sundwall of Helsingfors, W. Kolbe of Rostock,
and P. Roussel of the French School in Athens, he begs
to make grateful acknowledgment of services received.
With all their contentions he could not agree ; but he
hopes they will themselves see that he has neglected
nothing which they have written.   The kindness and
resourcefulness of A. Wilhelm of Vienna are so pro-
verbial that no one who has an interest in Greek inscriptions will be surprised that the author is under
obligations to him both for his published works and for
data communicated privately.   He wishes, therefore, to
thank him, and at the same time to thank Th. Reinach
of Paris, F. Dürrbach of Toulouse, and A. C. Johnson
of the American School in Athens, for giving advance
information in regard to unpublished documents.

The book—such as it is—was written in pleasant
places—among the hills which look through the Golden

Gate upon the Pacific; among the elms which used to shade the simple home of Harvard University; in Italy at the foot of the Alps and in the sight of those lesser mountains which watched the Roman armies march forth to achieve the empire of the world. To librarians and others in Berkeley, Cambridge, Turin, and Rome, the author is grateful for many courtesies; and he would like particularly to remember President B. I. Wheeler of the University of California, and President R. S. Woodward of the Carnegie Institution of Washington, to whose co-operative good-will and generosity he owes a year's leisure from the exacting duties of college instruction.

CONTENTS

CHAPTER I

CHAPTER II

CHAPTER III

CHAPTER IV

CHAPTER V

CHAPTER VI

CHAPTER VII

CONTENTS

CHAPTER VIII

CHAPTER IX

CHAPTER X

CHAPTER I

THE FIRST STRUGGLES FOR INDEPENDENCE

'Ελλὰs μέν ἐστι μία, πόλεις δὲ πλείονες.
POSEIDIPPUS (Koch, iii. p. 345, No. 28).

ἐκ δὲ τοῦ λέγειν τε καὶ
ἑτέρων ἀκούειν καὶ θεωρῆσαι . .
κατὰ μικρὸν ἀεί, φασί, φύονται φρένες.
PHILEMON (Koch, ii. p. 511, No. 103).

IN Greece liberal institutions were acclimated for the
first time in the history of mankind. In conjunction
with them a culture was developed more passionately
artistic and more keenly intellectual, more many-sided
and human in its interests than in any other country.
The intelligence which created it created simultaneously constitutional government; in fact, the freedom
and intensity of public life in old Greece formed the most
influential condition of her spiritual achievements. For
her eminence in art, literature, and philosophy was
attained, not by the unaided efforts of solitary genius,
nor yet alone by the upward movement of the masses;
but her uniqueness resulted from peculiar opportunities for the working together of these two forces. It
was this co-operation which made progress not only
swift and direct, but also continuous and vital. The
finest poetry and the noblest art, however individual
in character and attribution, always appeared as the
outcome of a popular interest, or as the inevitable
consequence of a social custom. Thus no one can view
understandingly the sculptures of Praxiteles who does
not see at the same time a host of stone-cutters making
the Attic grave monuments and an army of obscure

1

artists making the Attic vases, both working in haste, but with extraordinary sureness of touch and delicacy of feeling.   Nor can one comprehend Sophocles or Aristophanes apart from the Attic theatre, alive with men who were for the greater part ex-performers, and hence both appreciative and critical.   Who can think of Homer, Sappho, or Herodotus without their eager audiences, or of Socrates without his group of listeners and disputants on the street corner ?   Undeniably, the spiritual achievements of the ancient Greeks were due in large part to the intimacy of their life as citizens, to the smallness and compactness of the city-state.

And yet the city-state was the cause of manifold ills.   By its very nature it condemned the country to a multiplicity of political units, and thus forbade the formation of a single nation ; for the permanent union of two city-states was possible only through an arrangement which did violence to the integrity of one of them.   The germ of disunion was thus inherent in every alliance ; hence the weakness of the Spartan and Athenian empires ; and, after the Peloponnesian War had laid prostrate Athens—the only city-state qualified for national supremacy—it was this native inability to unite which caused the rapid shifting of centres of influence in the fourth century B.C.   But the consequence of political instability was civil war, since, in the absence of union, peace among such a group of states was possible only when the strength of all remained unchanged or increased proportionately, or when each one was completely isolated from the others. The first of these conditions might conceivably have been fulfilled, though it never was fulfilled ; but the realization of the second, though assumed in the political science of Plato and Aristotle, was altogether visionary. Men must first destroy Homer and carry the waters of the Mediterranean over his memory, and then destroy commerce and learn to do without iron, or copper, or tin, or grain, or slaves, or some other indispensable commodity.   The penalty of isolation was barbarism. Yet the penalty for intermingling was civil war, and for hundreds of years prior to the rise of Macedon, war had succeeded war, with effects the more disastrous the more through advance of civilization the humour for fighting diminished, and its hardships to individuals increased. It would be ridiculous to affirm that this long series of civil wars promoted the development of culture. Still, it had not been a fatal retardent, and there is no sufficient reason to believe that its continuance would have forced Greece to abandon her liberal institutions, dependent as these were upon the maintenance of the city-states.

Moreover, there had been sedition *within* the Greek cities from time immemorial, and when the factional wars ceased entirely, as in the later Hellenistic days, internal peace followed, but it was the peace of a graveyard. The strong ferment of a city life, which was at the same time national in its interests and responsibilities, had kept the civic mass in ceaseless motion, and quick and complete were the changes by which public law was made to accord with fluctuations in economic and social conditions. That is to say, the march of progress in Greece was accompanied by revolutions, by the turbulent rush of institutions to express altered facts as soon as the alterations were recognized. In most of the small and least progressive states the change was from oligarchy to democracy, and from democracy back to oligarchy, the revolution being occasioned by the tendency of land—the chief or only wealth—to fall unendingly into the hands of a smaller and smaller number of citizens, whose position became thereby more and more precarious, till finally the masses broke out in revolt, cancelled debts, and redistributed property. In the larger and more progressive cities, on the other hand, the development of commerce and industry, with their corollaries, banking, shipping, and retail trade, not only diverted the energies of men from the acquisition of land to the acquisition of capital, and thus helped to preserve a class of small farmers, but it also increased the complexity of social life, and, to a corresponding degree, the stability of public institutions.

The equilibrium of classes served to stave off revolutions; while the presence of a middle class in the background, made up largely of agriculturists, could never be ignored by extremists. It was a steadying influence in every-day politics, and an arbiter in the event of a crisis. Accordingly, in cities like Athens during the fourth century B.C., the rich and the poor were never squarely pitted against each other, with the result that neither gained a decisive superiority over its opponents, and that for several generations violent constitutional changes were lacking.[1] However much the rich might protest and intrigue, the state continued to recognize the obligations of wealth. It met many of its normal expenditures by collecting income-taxes, and many others by putting specific tasks upon the shoulders of the rich men in turn; while it devoted its surplus revenues to giving bonuses to citizens who had not the means of performing worthily their civic duties. There is no denying that the burdens of the wealthy were severe, but they brought some compensations with them. The Athenians, like all democrats, were very susceptible to the influence of money, and they made it a point, despite democratic theory—which, by means of election by lot, indemnity for time given to the public, and rotation of office, aimed to secure the succession of all citizens to offices—to give their magistracies largely to men of means.[2] To be sure, the positions usually involved only unimportant routine duties, but the wealthy did not despise them: love of distinctions was too deeply ingrained for that. Still, they resented bitterly the financial demands put upon them, and were often in negotiation with the public enemy with a view to bettering their constitutional position. The democrats of the city held them constantly under suspicion. Through the fact that the general assembly was held in Athens, and that the city

---

[1] See, on this point particularly, Francotte, *L'Industrie dans la Grèce ancienne*, ii. 312 ff.

[2] That this was the case in the time of Demosthenes has been shown by Sundwall, "Epigraphische Beiträge zur social-politischen Geschichte Athens im Zeitalter des Demosthenes," *Klio*, Beiheft i. 4.

population was distributed over all ten voting districts, and that absent voters were not counted, the multitude resident in the capital ordinarily controlled the decision of the Athenians; and for largely the same reasons—the inability of those resident at a distance from the place of meeting to perform public services profitably—the same elements controlled the courts also. In the hands of the urban and suburban multitude, then, the real decision of Athenian affairs rested, and between it, composed in large part of citizens of moderate means[1] and in still larger part of the poor, and the men of wealth already referred to, there was waged an irregular class war. The rich had private means of carrying on the struggle: the democrats sent their adversaries to the jury courts, and kept their lives and property constantly in danger. This was not a healthy condition of the commonwealth; but it was not a new one, and, moreover, it was the successor, after the wonderful, but abnormal, age of empire, of an even less tolerable state of affairs. Class struggles had not prevented extraordinary progress in the past: why should they do so in the future? They had, at times, created a liberal or reactionary tyrant; but they were more often the regulator of popular institutions than the destroyer of them. Struggles of this sort were destructive of property, undoubtedly, but the material prosperity of Athens had not been ruined by them, and Greece, as a whole, maintained a higher standard of living in the fourth century B.C. than ever before.[2]

Had the Greek city-states been in possession of the whole world they might have continued to thrive in spite of the civil and class wars with which they were harassed. Unfortunately for them this was not the case. They had repulsed the attack of the Persian king, and during the glorious epoch of the Athenian empire they had held him permanently in check; but they had been unable to conquer Asia, and of late their ancient

[1] Demades was the leader of this faction (Beloch, *Die attische Politik seit Perikles*, 249 f.).
[2] Beloch, *Griechische Geschichte*, ii. 339, 613.

foe had given victory to whichever side he had aided in the civil war, and in this way had moulded Greek politics to his will. They had been unable to penetrate into the interior of Macedon or Italy, or to do more than to defend themselves against Carthage. They had thus let peoples grow strong on all sides of them, of which those were most to be feared which, like Macedon and Italy, had maintained the military spirit of barbarians while enjoying the benefits of intimate intercourse with the highest civilization of the Greek cities.

It was in the domain of foreign politics that the Greek city-state experienced failure. But failure here was fatal; for it meant the destruction of the city-state itself —the fine, sensitive mother of Greek freedom and life.

The bankruptcy of the city-state was proclaimed from the housetops by the treaty of Antalcidas[1] in 387/6 B.C., which, by a peculiar irony of fate, made the autonomy of all Greek cities the fundamental article in a definite settlement of national disputes. But this autonomy was qualified by a destructive condition: it conceded to the king of the Persians the decision in matters of peace and war with other states. In this way the suzerainty of Persia was established, and, despite various efforts, the city-states of Greece were unable to shake it off. What they failed to do Philip of Macedon accomplished after many years of persistent effort; but he substituted for Persian dictation the suzerainty of his own country, which, given the monarchical organization of Macedon, meant his own personal suzerainty. Philip was a Greek in language, race, and culture, and his expulsion of the Persian was thus a vindication of national independence; but to the democratic city-states of Greece his supremacy was abhorrent because he was a king, because he was near enough and energetic enough to manage their foreign affairs, because he had allied himself with the aristo-cratic opposition in various states, because he made a nation master of Greece which was not its equal in civilization, — which, in fact, was ranked among the

---

[1] Kärst, *Geschichte des hellenistischen Zeitalters*, i. 31 f.

barbarians,—and finally, because he had achieved his
position by violence. The incarnation of opposition to
Philip was Demosthenes, the Athenian. Demosthenes
fought for a cause which was already lost. The freedom
of the city-states was formally annulled six years before
he was born. He thus placed his city in deadly peril
for the first of many times, not, as he and it believed,
with any prospect of gaining complete liberty, but with
the sole possible issue of getting a new master for an
old one. The most that his energy, enthusiasm, and
eloquence accomplished was to put Athens once more
in the forefront of Greek politics—all to no purpose,
however; and it is a moot-point whether the sea-power
of Athens or the clemency of the victor saved his city
from destruction in 338 B.C., and again three years later.

For the fifteen years between 338 and 323 B.C.
Athens had a taste of municipal life; and, seeing that
Demosthenes and his generation were alive, we are not
surprised that she found it bitter. For many years
she had no ground for complaint as to the attitude of
Philip and Alexander in her regard. For not only did
they refrain from restricting the internal freedom of the
Athenians, but they left them at liberty to choose their
friends and enemies as they themselves saw fit. Still,
it was understood that certain politicians were in touch
with Macedon, and this knowledge was sufficient to secure
for them a respectful hearing in the public meetings.
From them Athens received advice on foreign affairs.
Thus it came about that Phocion, Aeschines, and in the
later days of Alexander's reign, Demetrius of Phalerum
were influential in the city alongside of Demosthenes,
Demades, and Lycurgus. A sort of coalition government was inaugurated, the aristocrats attending to
foreign, the democrats to home politics : rather, both
agreeing, out of deference to the political convictions
of Phocion and his clientèle, and to the wishes of the
Macedonian king, to avoid all foreign complications.
The objects of the two groups were altogether different.
To men like Aeschines[1] and Demetrius the full import

---

[1] Aeschines, *In Ctes.* 133 ff. ; Beloch, ii. 655 f.

of Alexander's work was understood, and out of the rise
of Macedon to the dominion of the world they drew the
conclusion that the only safe policy for Athens was
to attach herself loyally to the side of the victor, and
to leave to Tyché the deposition of the Macedonians
in the event of their misusing the goods confided to
them.[1]   Lycurgus and Demosthenes were not so cold-
blooded and not so far-seeing.   They refused to accept
the battle of Chaeronea as the Armageddon of Athenian
imperialism; and since the majority of the Athenians
was with them, they used the situation to prepare for a
reopening of the struggle.[2]   Hence these democratic
leaders, at the same time that they attended in Periclean
fashion to the beautifying of the city, gave supreme
care to arrangements for war, and to the management
of finance.   It was at this time that the Panathenaic
stadium, the *gymnasium* in Lyceum, and many another
structure was built, and it was now that the marble
Dionysiac theatre in Athens, and the *deigma* and stone
dockyards in the Piraeus were completed.[3]   Place was
made for three hundred and seventy-two warships.   In
about 338 B.C. a system of universal conscription was
introduced.   Something similar had existed for centuries
in the case of that part of the population which served
as heavy-armed infantry, but now every Athenian
ephebe was drafted into barracks at the Piraeus, and,
after a year of training in tactics, archery, and the use
of spear and catapult, he was provided with a lance and
shield and put for the term of another year[4] into service

---

[1] Demetrius of Phalerum, *Frg.* 19; *FHG.* ii. 368.

[2] For the *Restorationspolitik* of this period see, in particular, Wilamowitz,
Aristoteles und Athen, i. 351 ff.

[3] For the work of Lycurgus see [Plut.] *Lives of the Ten Orators*,
841 D; *IG.* ii. 240 (Ditt. *Syll.*² 168); and Beloch, iii. 1. 56 ff., and especially
n. 4.

[4] Aristotle, *Const. of Athens*, 42. 3.   That the ephebate was radically
reconstructed at *ca.* 335 B.C. was first observed by Wilamowitz, *op. cit.* i. 191 ff.,
353 ff. (cf. Beloch, ii. 614).   The absence of any such formal organization in
earlier times has been further demonstrated by Bryant, *Harvard Studies in
Classical Philology*, xviii. 79 ff.   Still, it is inconceivable that the young men
eligible for hoplite service in Athens were not trained for war prior to 338 B.C.
(cf. Ed. Meyer, *Gesch. d. Alt.* iv. 56).   It has been suggested that these and
these alone were trained prior to Chaeronea (Gilbert, *Gk. Const. Antiq.* 315;
Girard, *Epheboi* in Daremberg-Saglio; Beloch, *Klio*, v. 351; Sundwall, *Acta
Soc. Scien. Fennicae*, xxxiv. 4. 22).   That seems reasonable.

in the frontier forts, which were modernized for his reception. A mole thrown across the entrance to the inner harbour sufficed, along with the new dockyards and the new ephebe garrisons, to make the Piraeus reasonably safe from surprise or siege. Thus one inadequacy in the Cononian system of defence was removed. Another was inherent in the material out of which the walls were then constructed—bricks. Hence stone was substituted for it wherever practicable, and in order to prevent the great rams, then first employed in attacking fortified places, from being moved freely up to the walls, a ditch was dug in front of them at exposed places and protected by a palisade.[1]

At about the same time a further step was taken in the reconstruction of the war department, and as a continuation of the policy already inaugurated of detailing a special general to command the army of attack and another to command the army of reserve, specific duties were given to three more of the ten generals, the rest being still reserved for emergencies. Henceforth one general had charge of the hoplites, and in the event of a foreign expedition the hoplite-general was commander-in-chief. Another was designated for home defence, and for all campaigns fought on Attic soil. Two were in command of the garrisons in the Piraeus, and the fifth had to do with naval preparations.[2] And not simply was this reorganization carried through, but the people were authorized to choose their generals from all the citizens without any reference whatever to tribal representation.[3] The lesson had thus been learned that the Athenian militia was too amateurish, that a divided responsibility was often no responsibility at all, and that no consideration of local politics should exclude the best

---

[1] Frickenhaus, *Athens Mauern im IV. Jahrhundert v. Chr.*, Diss., Bonn, 1905, p. 46.

[2] Aristotle, *Const. of Athens*, 61. 1 ; cf. *Klio*, 1909, p. 314 ff. The detailing of two generals to the Piraeus commands was doubtless a consequence of stationing the ephebes there.

[3] Sundwall, *Epigr. Beitr.* 19 ff. It may be observed in this connexion that in some year between 374/3 and 341/0 B.C. this same change was made in the case of the Delian Amphictyones (*Class. Review*, 1901, p. 38, and *BCH.*, 1884, p. 394 n. 7).

available man from military command—a tardy lesson, but a valuable one.

Eubulus had given Athens a regular finance department for the first time, and had placed certain commissioners of the theoric fund in control of all expenditures.[1] For a time after 338 B.C. the supremacy of this board was threatened by the treasurership of military funds which was created in 347/6 B.C., possibly on the initiative of Demosthenes;[2] but its vital connexion with all receipts and outlays speedily regained for it the chief control, and it was probably as a member of this commission for one period, and its "boss" during eleven others, that Lycurgus dominated Athenian finance from 338 to 326 B.C.[3] The total revenues of the city in 346 B.C. had been only four hundred talents.[4] Since then the expenses had been increased enormously. The pay of the ephebes now amounted to forty talents annually, and very large sums were disbursed for public buildings and festivals. This proves a proportionately large increase of revenues, and, in fact, they were trebled within twenty years,[5] an increase, however, which was partly offset by the loss in the purchasing power of money. Lycurgus was a very skilful financier, and, since the era of peace promoted the commerce and industry of Athens, the prosperity of private individuals was equal to that of the public. Still the unpopularity of the Macedonian régime showed conclusively that politics are independent of economics.

---

[1] Aeschines, *In Ctes.* 25.

[2] Fränkel, *Zur Gesch. d. attisch. Finanzverwaltung; hist. u. philol. Aufsätze Ernst Curtius gewidmet*, 37 ff. ; Sundwall, Ἐφ. Ἀρχ., 1909, p. 207 f.

[3] Of course Lycurgus was a member of various boards of public works during this time, but as such he could not have increased the revenues. His activity as finance minister, like that of Pericles, Cleon, Eubulus, Demetrius of Phalerum, Eurycleides, was extra-official. See Gilbert, *op. cit.* 245 ff., and below, Appendix II. The view that any or all of these financial offices were held for four years at a stretch is probably incorrect.

[4] Theopompus in *Berl. Klass. Texte*, i. (Didymus, i. 8. 58 ff.) ; cf. Stahelin, *Klio*, 1905, p. 147. If [Plut.] *Vita Lycurg.* 842 F is to be trusted, the revenues prior to 338 B.C. were 600 talents, which Lycurgus doubled. In [Plut.] *Lives of the Ten Orators*, 852 B, he is said, however, to have spent 18,900 talents in twelve years, or an average of 1575 per year.

[5] Spangenberg, *De Athen. publicis institutis aetate Macedonum commutatis*, Diss., Halle, 1884, p. 13 ; cf. below, ii. 58, n. 3.

Meanwhile the active mind of Alexander had elaborated a system of government for the world which lay at his feet. His cardinal idea was to reserve for himself the supreme and absolute directive of ecumenical affairs, and to parcel up the world for local administration, the fusion of discordant races, and the diffusion of Greek culture, into a multitude of city-states, which, out of regard for ancient sentiment and the most authoritative political theory, had to be free and self-governing. The reign of law in public and private business, the participation of all citizens in politics, and abundant opportunity for the rapid interchange of ideas and accomplishments—all the priceless legacies, in fact, of Greek experience—were thus to be retained. The great problem was to conciliate civic freedom and autonomy with the dominating and controlling position of Alexander, which, as past disorders had proved, was essential for the future peace and prosperity of the world. This problem Alexander solved with genuine Greek audacity and thoroughness by requiring that every city should enrol him among its gods. Henceforth he would be, of course, omnipotent in political matters, but, like the fourth century B.C. Greek gods, neither lawless nor destitute of an ethical nature.

For Alexander to demand deification involved in the case of Athens no stretching of his rights as overlord ; but the granting of it cancelled the agreement into which he had entered with it and the other states in Greece at the congress of Corinth in 335 B.C. This consequence was, perhaps, not obvious at the time the question was debated in the Athenian assembly.[1] At any rate, it was on religious grounds that Lycurgus, Pytheas, and others, among whom at the outset was Demosthenes, opposed the innovation. They would have no gods, they protested, except the traditional ones. Demades, however, urged the *demos* "to have a care lest in guarding heaven it lose earth," and Demosthenes,

---

[1] Hypereides, *Contra Dem.* xxxi. (p. 19, Blass[3]); Dinarch. *Contra Dem.* 94 ; Val. Max. vii. 2, ext. 13 ; Timaeus in Polybius, xii. 12 b ; cf. *Lives of the Ten Orators*, 842 D, and Plut. *Political Precepts*, 8 (p. 804). See especially Ed. Meyer, *Kleine Schriften*, 301 ff., 330 ff.

changing sides, dissuaded it from a "rivalry with Alexander for the honours of the celestial world." " Let us recognise him," he said, "as the son of Zeus, or for all I care, as the son of Poseidon if he prefers it." Since the Athenian aristocrats were doubtless in favour of the proposal, and the accredited leaders of the democrats thus supported them, the coalition government bore down all opposition in Athens, and Alexander was admitted into the Attic Olympus as a new Dionysus (324 B.C.).[1] The world was ringing with the discovery in India of Nysa, famous in Dionysiac story, and the triumphal march of Alexander through Asia was likened to the mythical procession of the youthful Thracian god. A son of the supreme deity the king-god had to be; who of the children of Zeus was more suited than Dionysus? [2]

The Athenians deified Alexander contemptuously and in anger, and in this spirit legalized despotism. That a constitutional absolutism was the result they perhaps did not observe clearly, but events moved rapidly in the world at that time. For Alexander at once violated the Corinthian conventions, and ordered the reinstatement of exiles everywhere in the Greek world.[3] Only in this way could his realm be rid of homeless and lawless men. The king of Macedon had had no right to thrust his hand into the city-states, but the god Alexander was a native of every town, and entitled, not simply to be heard, but also to be obeyed. Athens was unwilling to restore its exiles, for that involved the relinquishing of Samos, from which Athenian cleruchs had driven the native population; but Demosthenes was influential enough to prevent an immediate refusal. Negotiations were started, and the

---

[1] Athen. vi. 251 B; Dinarch. *loc. cit.*; Hypereides, *loc. cit.*; Diog. Laert. vi. 63; cf. Beloch, iii. 1. 50.

[2] The identification thus made was of profound influence upon the subsequent treatment of the Dionysiac motive in Greek vase-painting, and it set the Ptolemaic and Seleucid successors of Alexander to work manufacturing Dionysiac traits in their own careers. It was with Dionysus also that Athens equated Mithradates Eupator and Mark Antony. Cf. P.-W. v. 1039 ff.; *Klio*, 1901, pp. 58, 70, 67, n. 5 f., 83, n. 2; Preller, *Griech. Myth.*[4] i. 704. 5.

[3] For this and the Harpalus incident see Beloch, iii. 1. 59 ff.

matter dragged along. To be unable to resent this
seeming infraction of their sovereign rights chagrined
the Athenians deeply, but fresh humiliation followed.
In the same year Harpalus, the runaway treasurer of
Alexander, appeared off the Piraeus with thirty ships,
six thousand soldiers, and seven hundred talents, and
requested admission. With such an ally Alexander
must be defied or never. Demosthenes, however, with
a moderation which is a strong testimonial to the genius
of Alexander, succeeded in having Harpalus excluded,
and even when the fugitive treasurer returned to Athens
as a suppliant, without troops or ships but with his
money, he found only a temporary asylum. Despite
her pride in being the traditional refuge of the exiled
and oppressed, the city could not refuse to listen to the
demand for his surrender, which was promptly made.
The best she could do was to detain Harpalus and his
gold, and appeal from Philoxenus—the treasury official
sent in pursuit of him—to Alexander himself. After a
while it was found that Harpalus had escaped, and that
one-half of the treasure had been abstracted and spent
before his departure. A great scandal occurred. The
Areopagus was appointed a special commission to inquire
into the disappearance of the money. It reported that
three hundred and fifty talents had been distributed by
Harpalus among the leading democratic politicians of
Athens, and that Demosthenes himself had received
twenty of them. The men designated by the Areopagus
were then tried before the jury courts. The facts were
hard to discover; but the plea of Demosthenes, that he
had used the money for public purposes, was weak; and
the prosecutors, of whom the most aggressive were new
or more extreme radicals, like Stratocles of Diomeia, or
Hypereides, roused the people by accusing him of over-
friendliness and consideration for Alexander. Lycurgus
was already dead. Demades disdained to defend himself,
and paid the fine imposed, but lost all political influence.
Demosthenes was found guilty; and, through inability to
meet the fine of fifty talents, went as an exile to Aegina.
The coalition government was thus dismembered, and

Phocion and Demetrius of Phalerum had no longer democratic colleagues. It was clear that only the direct interference of Alexander could prevent the complete ascendancy of the most violent members of the anti-Macedonian party.

At this point, word arrived that Alexander was dead. It was not fully credited at first. Demades affirmed that if it were true the whole world would stink from the carcass.[1] None the less, preparations for a revolt were made. One-half of the treasure of Harpalus, which was still on the Acropolis, formed the nucleus of a war fund, and Leosthenes was sent quietly to Taenarum to secure the services of the soldiers who had their rendezvous there, especially the six thousand who had returned from Asia with Harpalus. When the death of the great king was known to be a fact, secession was agreed upon, despite the protests of Phocion, the aristocratic, and Demades, the democratic leader of the propertied classes. Common cause was made with the Aetolians, who, through refusing to reinstate the exiles, were already in difficulties with Alexander; and a proclamation was issued to all Greece calling upon the cities everywhere to form a Hellenic League for the overthrow of the Macedonian suzerainty. The appeal was well answered. Leosthenes, who had received arms and money from Athens, marched north, and occupied the pass at Thermopylae. The Phocians, Locrians, and all the lesser peoples in the vicinity of Mt. Oeta, as well as the Aetolians and various Thessalian cities, joined his standards. He then returned to Boeotia to effect a juncture with the Athenians, who, leaving three regiments for the defence of Attica under Phocion the home-general, had crossed the frontier with the other seven containing five thousand men. In addition, they took with them five hundred horse and two thousand mercenaries. The two forces united, and defeated an army made up of the Macedonian garrison of the Cadmia, together with the Boeotians, whose loyalty Alexander had secured by giving them the

[1] Plut. *Phocion*, 22.

property of the Thebans.   Then the whole army entered Thessaly.[1]

Antipater, the Macedonian regent, had with him only thirteen thousand foot, six hundred cavalry, and one hundred and ten ships.   None the less he started for Greece in the autumn of 323 B.C., hoping to check the uprising before it got well started.   His army, however, was insufficient.   The Thessalians generally went over to the Greeks, and their adhesion gave Leosthenes such a superiority that in the battle which ensued Antipater was defeated, and forced to throw himself into the fortress of Lamia.   There he stood a siege.   The revolt now spread to Euboea, Acarnania, Epirus, and Leucas, as well as to the Peloponnesus, where Argos, and the cities in the Argolid generally, together with Elis and Messene, joined the Greek confederacy, while Corinth, Megalopolis, Achaea, and Sparta remained Macedonian or neutral. Throughout the winter the siege of Lamia continued. Antipater was at one time ready to negotiate for peace, but Leosthenes would listen to nothing but an unconditional surrender.   This the Macedonian refused, and his chances improved when, not long afterwards, Leosthenes was slain in a skirmish.   The hope of the regent was that reinforcements would come from Asia. In this he was not disappointed.   Leonnatus, satrap of Hellespontine Phrygia, started for Greece in the spring of 322 B.C., and after enlisting troops *en route* entered Thessaly for the relief of Lamia with over twenty thousand foot and twenty-five hundred horse.   The Greeks, under the command of Antiphilus, an Athenian, raised the siege of Lamia, and marched to meet Leonnatus. They had over twenty thousand infantry, and thirty-five hundred cavalry.   It was essential for them to deal with the two Macedonian armies separately, and in this they succeeded.   The Thessalian cavalry gained a signal victory over that of Leonnatus, and in the conflict the Macedonian leader lost his life.   This determined the

---

[1] For the Hellenic War see Diod. xvii. 111, xviii. 9 ff. ; Plut. *Phocion*, 23 ff. ; Paus. i. 25. 4 ff. ; cf. i. 1. 3, iv. 28. 3, v. 4. 9, vii. 6. 6 ; Justin, xiii. 5. 9 ff. ; *IG*. ii. 182. 249 (Ditt. *Syll.*[2] 180), cf. *GGA.*, 1903, p. 786 ; Hypereides, *Epitaph.* 10 ff. ; Suidas, *s.v.* "Lamia," "Leosthenes."   Cf. Beloch, iii. 1. 71 ff.

Macedonian infantry to retreat to inaccessible ground, where they maintained themselves till the following day, when Antipater arrived with his army. The superiority of the Greek cavalry was so decisive, however, that Antipater did not risk a second engagement, but withdrew out of danger by keeping to rough districts.

The revolt of the Greeks had now grown into a Hellenic War, and this was, in fact, the contemporary designation of this struggle. At its start Demosthenes had been in exile, but he had aided in winning allies in the Peloponnesus, and in consideration of this service the Athenian state paid his fine and he returned home. A warship conveyed him from Aegina to the Piraeus, and there the magistrates and the entire population greeted him with the utmost enthusiasm. He was the old Demosthenes again, not the cautious statesman of the coalition time; but the day of his return—" the proudest day of his whole life "—preluded the final catastrophe in the great tragedy of Athenian democracy. The initial successes of the Greeks on the land might have been decisive had their naval operations been more fortunate. It was essential for ultimate victory that the fleet of Antipater should be crushed before reinforcements could arrive from Cyprus and Phoenicia, and that the Asiatic armies should be prevented from crossing into Europe. To what extent these objects were feasible we do not know. Certainly neither was accomplished. At first the Greeks seem to have used their naval superiority simply to win recruits for their alliance, and the only enterprise of which we have knowledge for the year 323 B.C. was the capture of Styra in Euboea by Phaedrus of Sphettus, the old Athenian general.[1] But they did not ignore the strategical need of guarding the Hellespont; for in the next year, when reinforcements were in motion to join Antipater, a Greek fleet under the command of the Athenian admiral Euetion was in

---

[1] Ditt. *Syll.*² 213, n. 1; Strabo, x. 1. 6, p. 446; cf. Niese, *Gesch. d. griech. u. maked. Staaten*, i. 207; *IG.* ii. 5. 270 (Ditt. *Syll.*² 187); 'Εφ. 'Αρχ., 1900, p. 147, No. 5 (Wilhelm, *Beiträge zur griech. Inschriftenkunde*, no. 46).

position near Abydus. It was, however, defeated
disastrously in a battle in the straits, doubtless by the
hundred and ten ships of Antipater, and only part of it
succeeded in reaching the Piraeus in safety. Thereupon
the control of the sea and of the entire situation was
lost.[1] A second army, under the command of Craterus,
was already on its way from Asia when Leonnatus was
defeated. It consisted of six thousand Macedonian
veterans, whom Alexander had dismissed shortly before
his death, and to it were joined four thousand new
recruits, fifteen hundred cavalry, and Persian archers
and slingers. At the same time one hundred and thirty
ships were added to Antipater's fleet, which had
probably withdrawn south after its victory in the
Hellespont; so that in the final campaign of the war
the numerical superiority, both by land and sea, rested
with the Macedonians. Naturally the Athenians had
done their best to repair their losses. Of ships they
had no lack, since upwards of four hundred of them
had lain in the Piraeus at the opening of the struggle;
the shortage was in crews. Hence a call was issued for
volunteers, and in response to it, as we learn by chance,
one metic furnished as many as twelve sailors. None
the less the lead of the Macedonians was not overcome.
Accordingly Euetion with only one hundred and
seventy vessels met Cleitus with two hundred and forty
near Amorgos, and was defeated and perhaps cut off
from a retreat to the Piraeus. The control of the sea
passed definitely into the hands of the enemy; and
" with right," says Beloch, " might the Macedonian
admiral, Cleitus, compare himself with the sea-god,
Poseidon; for he had won the greatest battle which
was fought on the Aegean Sea since Salamis. And
more than that; it was a decision of importance in

---

[1] *IG.* ii. 194. This fragment Dr. A. S. Johnson, of the American School in
Athens, very kindly informs me is probably to be joined to *IG.* ii. 229 (321–18
B.C.). A new inscription of the year 302 B.C., which Dr. Johnson will publish
soon in the *Amer. Jour. of Arch.*, localizes the defeat of the Athenians near
Abydus. Ditt. *Syll.*² 266, cf. Wilhelm, GGA. 1903, p. 792; *IG.* ii. 270.
Diodorus (xviii. 15) begins his account of the naval operations after the defeat
of the Greeks in the Hellespont, but betrays the reference which his authority
had made to this incident by alluding to two sea-fights.

universal history, for on this day the Attic dominion of the sea was borne to the grave, and with it the political greatness of Athens." [1]　The engagement on land could not be deferred any longer.　Antiphilus, with twenty‑five thousand foot and thirty‑five hundred cavalry, met Antipater at Crannon, in Thessaly, with forty thousand infantry, three thousand archers, and five thousand horse.[2]　Again, the Thessalian cavalry won a victory, but it was more than offset by the defeat of the infantry.　The losses on either side, one hundred and thirty of the victors, five hundred of their opponents, were trivial, but the battle was none the less decisive.　It was a clear augury of Macedonian success, and with the memory of the sack of Thebes still fresh in their minds, the Greeks concluded to ask for peace before it was too late.　Antipater refused to deal with the Hellenic League, but offered to arrange terms with the cities individually. These, thereupon, opened negotiations separately, and one after another abandoned the alliance until Athens and the Aetolians stood alone.　In the meanwhile there had been an anti-Greek movement in Boeotia, probably when the reinforcements from Asia began to arrive in Thessaly, whereupon the three regiments left behind in Athens for the defence of the country had clamoured to be led out for its suppression ; but Phocion had refused to cross the frontiers unless his army were reinforced by all the citizens who, because of old age, were excused from active service.　This led to the expedition being abandoned.[3]　Later on, Attica was itself exposed to attack ; for, probably after the victory at Amorgos, Cleitus had landed troops at Rhamnus, which, under the command of Micion, proceeded to ravage the *paralia.* These Phocion met energetically and defeated, their leader being among the slain.[4]　The fiasco in Thessaly

---

[1] Beloch, iii. 1. 75 ff.　Cf. de Sanctis, *Studi di storia antica*, ii. 3 ff.　See on the battle of Amorgos, Plut. *Demetr.* 11 ; Tyche of Alex. ii. 5 ; Jacoby, *Das Marmor Parium*, 21 (*IG.* xii. 5. 1, 444 cxiv.).　Fischer (Diod. iv. 342. 11) sticks by Diodorus, who puts the decisive battle off the Echinades islands.

[2] On 7th of Metageitnion (July) 322 B.C.　Plut. *Cam.* 19 ; cf. *Dem.* 28.　For a reference to the Panathenaea of the preceding month see *JHS.*, 1908, p. 308 ; cf. below, iii. 128, n. 2.

[3] Plut. *Phocion*, 25.

[4] *Ibid.* ; cf. Droysen, *Geschichte des Hellenismus*, ii.² 1. 69.

now changed the whole situation. Fifty thousand victorious Macedonians—more, perhaps, than any ruler of that country led into action either before or after— pressed forward towards the frontiers of Attica, while the irresistible fleet of Cleitus lay within sight of Sunium. In these circumstances a blockade meant starvation into surrender, so that Athens, too, must yield. The citizens hurried to reinstate Demades, who, because of three motions adjudged illegal, had been deprived of civic rights in 323 B.C., and to send him together with Demetrius of Phalerum to interview Antipater.[1] The invasion was stopped, but the terms of Antipater were those of Leosthenes less than a year earlier—uncon- ditional surrender. Athens was forced to accept, and the city was at the mercy of the regent. Demosthenes, Hypereides, Aristonicus of Marathon, Himeraeus of Phalerum, and others, who had nothing but severity to expect, fled from the city. The rest tried conciliation, and Phocion, Demades, and Xenocrates, the head of the Academy, were sent to secure the best terms possible. The philosopher was received with scant courtesy, and doubtless had little influence upon the issue of the embassy,[2] but this was soon forgotten, and it was not long before the president of the Academy was the most natural person for Athens to entrust with a critical mission. We do not know what were the interests represented by Xenocrates which failed to obtain due consideration in the deliberations of Antipater and the Athenians. Certainly, those supported by Phocion and Demades were not neglected. In fact, the regent accepted their point of view almost *in toto*—that a constitutional change was necessary, which should place the city in the secure control of the propertied classes. He

---

[1] Demetr. Περὶ ἑρμηνείας, 289 ; cf. Schäffer, *Demosthenes und seine Zeit*, iii. 354, and de Sanctis, 14.

[2] Plut. *Phocion*, 27 ; Diog. Laert. iv. 9 ; Crönert, *Kolotes und Menedemos*, 67 ff. κεχειροτονημένους [διαψη]φίσασθαι λέγειν αὐτὸν [ἐν πρώτ]οις καὶ διὰ τὴν ἡλι[κίαν καὶ] διὰ τὴν περὶ τοὺς λό[γους ἄσκ]ησιν · τὸν δὲ Ξενο[κράτην, ὡς] εἰώθει διαπε[ραίνεσθαι] πρὸς θέσιν ἐν Ἀ[καδημείαι], τὸν αὐτὸν τρό[πον διεξέρχ]εσθαι καὶ τὸ[ν λόγον πρὸς τὸ]ν Ἀντίπα[τρον ὑπὲρ τῆς πόλεως οὐ δε]ξαμέ[νου δὲ ἀποτυχεῖν. Cf. Sudhaus, *Philodems Rhetorik*, ii. 173. Demetrius of Phalerum seems to have said in his *Politics* that Xenophanes failed through being no ῥήτωρ. Crönert, 68 f.

differed simply in insisting that more than an abolition
of the radical democracy was necessary for this purpose,
and, despite the protests of Phocion, he maintained the
necessity of putting a Macedonian garrison in the Piraeus.
On this point he was firm, but he went so far in friendliness as to reserve the question of the Athenian evacuation
of Samos for the decision of the two kings who were
the nominal heirs of Alexander. This proved adverse
to Athens,[1] and the Samians returned home after forty-
three years of exile. Oropus was lost to Athens, probably
at the same time, but otherwise Athenian territory was
left intact.

On the 22nd of Boedromion (August) 322 B.C.
Menyllus, a Macedonian officer, led a body of soldiers into
the Piraeus, and stationed them on Munychia, the hill-fort
which dominated the harbour of Athens. Three weeks
later the men who had misled the city into the insurrection were all dead—condemned by the Athenians, hunted
down by Archias, an agent of Antipater. Hypereides,
Aristonicus, and Himeraeus were found in the temple
of Aeacus at Aegina, Demosthenes in that of Poseidon in
Celauria. The first three were decoyed out and slain,
but the great orator and agitator anticipated assassination by taking poison. He may have stooped to unworthy
means in carrying on war against Macedon : the honesty
of his convictions no one should doubt. He may have
lacked political insight : courage he certainly possessed.
That he was a great artist and a powerful speaker his
most bitter enemies never denied or doubted. They did
not expect the courtesies of modern debate in a controversy where the lives of the participants and those of
their friends were forfeit on failure to convince the
common people. His death is no evidence of his
inferiority in his profession, for he fought with emotions
and ideas against swords. "Had but the strength of
thy arm, Demosthenes, equalled thy spirit," ran a contemporary epigram, "never would Greece have sunk
under the foreigner's yoke."

---

[1] Perdiccas got the blame for insisting on the evacuation, Diog. Laert. x. 1.
The costs of the war were debited to the Athenians, but payment was not
insisted upon. See below, i. 27.

His conviction in Athens was the work of Antipater
and the aristocratic leaders, for the garrison in Munychia
had sufficed to intimidate the populace, and put the
propertied classes in control of the government in
August 322 B.C.[1] Among the ten generals there were
some who, like Phocion, were ready to take orders from
the new authorities. The election of a new set was
accordingly unnecessary,[2] and it was seemingly at this
time that Thymochares of Sphettus, son of the Phaedrus
who had been one of the generals in 323 B.C., took the
command of the fleet for the rest of the year. The
remnant of the Athenian navy was put freely at the
disposal of Antipater, and it was, doubtless, at his
request that the people sent Thymochares in the spring
of 321 B.C. to co-operate with Antigonus in the maritime
war which was then being conducted near Cyprus as
part of the general struggle begun in this year between
the regent Perdiccas and the satraps. The Athenian
admiral had the good fortune to fall in with and capture
the command of Hagnon of Teus, a famous fop whom
Alexander had once found wearing silver nails in his
boots.[3] This was a memorable success, but it did not
bring universal joy to the Athenians; for, under Antipater's influence, the control of affairs in the city had
come so completely into the hands of the aristocratic
faction that Demades, the leader of the propertied
democrats, had entered into negotiations with Perdiccas
in the hope of gaining from him a larger measure of

[1] Phocion is said to have been responsible for the κατάλυσις τῶν νόμων at
this time, Diod. xviii. 66. 5 ; cf. below, i. 24, n. 5.

[2] de Sanctis (5) takes the view that the old generals were discharged.
Generals could be deprived of their office by an adverse vote of the people
during any prytany. The consequence of this ἀποχειροτονία, which, as Sandys
(Const. of Athens, 227, n. on § 2) has observed, "must have been instituted
with special reference to military officials," was that the suspended generals
had to stand trial before a jury (Arist. Const. of Athens, 43. 4, 61. 2), and it
was in this way that Phocion and his companions were tried in the course of
the year 319/8 B.C. (see below, i. 32). However, we have no evidence that
this was done in 322 B.C. It is easier to believe that the son of Phaedrus
was regularly elected in the beginning of 322/1 B.C. and retained in office till
the end, than elected among the aristocrats in the middle of the year. In
JHS., 1908, p. 308, moreover, an inscription is published from which we learn
that a cavalry officer who had gained a victory at the Panathenaea of 322 B.C.
was re-elected in 321/0 B.C. (cf. below, iii. 128, n. 2).

[3] IG. ii. 331. 5 (Ditt. Syll.[2] 213). This passage is misdated by Dittenberger.
Plut. Alex. 40.

popular freedom. The discomfiture and death of Perdiccas frustrated this plan (May-June 321 B.C.), so that it was in a narrow, aristocratic spirit that the Athenian constitution was remodelled at the end of the year 322/1 B.C.[1]

The propertied classes were established definitely in power. This was done by disqualifying all Athenians who did not own property to the value of two thousand *drachmae*,[2] that is to-day, about twelve thousand men,[3] or four-sevenths of the entire citizen population. This measure, which left only nine thousand men in possession of the franchise, at once restricted the vote to those hitherto liable for hoplite service,[4] and created a new class in Athens, one lacking the *ius suffragii et honorum*, but differing from the metics through having the *ius conubii et commerci*.[5] It emptied the jury-courts,[6] and reduced by four-sevenths the corps of ephebes. The disfranchisement extended also to those upon whom the citizenship had been conferred by special vote of the ecclesia,[7] and a little later it was prescribed that henceforth the decision of the popular assembly in favour of a grant of citizenship should be ratified, not, as was hitherto the practice, by a second meeting of six thousand citizens, but by a panel of jurors, as in the case of a new law.[8] Doubtless the courts were also invoked to settle disputes as to the possession, or lack, of the property qualification by native-born Athenians. Election by lot was abolished at the same time, and election from

---

[1] de Sanctis, 5 ; *Cornell Studies*, vii. 34. That the change of government occurred at the end of 322/1 B.C. is also shown by the fact that in 321/0 B.C. the Piraeus relet the Paralia, Almyris, Theseum, καὶ τἄλλα τεμένη ἅπαντα (among which are one of Schoenus and a Thesmophorion) for a period of ten years. To the victors belonged the spoils—rather an end was put to a reign of graft.

[2] Diod. xviii. 18. 4.

[3] The number 12,000 was ascertained by subtracting the 9000 registered citizens from the total of 21,000 ascertained at the census of Demetrius of Phalerum.

[4] Sundwall, *Acta*, 3 ff.

[5] They were rated with the citizens in the census returns referred to.

[6] Suidas, *s.v.* "Demades": οὗτος κατέλυσε τὰ δικαστήρια καὶ τοὺς ῥητορικοὺς ἀγῶνας.

[7] *IG*. ii. 5. 231*b* (Ditt. *Syll.*[2] 161, 163).

[8] *IG*. ii. 229. 223 ; ii. 5. 229*c* ; cf. *Klio*, 1905, p. 172, and Gilbert, *op. cit.* 185, n. 2. See below, iii. 130, n. 4. Later we find the law-courts in question called "the public law-courts."

and by all qualified citizens was substituted for it.[1]
The rotation of offices among the tribes ceased in so far
as the chief-clerkship and the priesthood of Asclepius
were concerned, and doubtless also wherever else it had
been applied.[2]   The distribution of surpluses to the
common folk, and payments for attending the meetings
of the ecclesia, for jury service, and perhaps also for
holding offices, were suspended now that the poor had
no citizen status to maintain.   It was at this time
probably that the commission in charge of the theoric
fund was abolished, and the facts squared with the
institution in that an officer took its place, deputed by
name, as well as function, to superintend the administration.[3]   It may further be surmised that this substitution
was only part of a general reorganization of the management of finance ;[4] for the receivers-general (*apodectae*)
do not appear afterwards in the Athenian documents.[5]
At the same time,[6] in all probability, the treasurership
of military funds was abolished.[7]   Now that Athens had
ceased to have a foreign policy it ceased to have need
of an organization for handling army moneys.   Besides,
this office had been created in view of a Macedonian
war, and had been used during the past sixteen years to
prepare for the struggle which had now failed so disastrously.   What more natural than that the Macedonians should dispense with it and that the oligarchs

---

[1] The proof of this is found in the standing of the men who obtained the
offices.   It is, however, implied in the statement of Diodorus (xviii. 18. 4) that
those who had 2000 *drachmae* were made κυρίους τοῦ πολιτεύματος καὶ τῆς
χειροτονίας.

[2] See below, i. 24. n. 6.

[3] Pollux, viii. 113 ὁ δὲ ἐπὶ τῆς διοικήσεως αἱρετὸς ἦν ἐπὶ τῶν προσιόντων καὶ
ἀναλισκομένων.

[4] Köhler (*IG*. ii. 719) once suggested that the treasurers of the other gods
were also abolished at this time ; and this may still prove to be the case.   See
Bannier, *Rhein. Mus.*, 1910, p. 19 f. ; *ibid.*, 1911, p. 45.

[5] They are mentioned for the last time in *IG*. ii. 811 (323/2 B.C.) ; cf. P.-W.
i. 2818.

[6] The treasury of the senate was subsequently in charge of one official in
place of two.   Gilbert, *op. cit.* 271, n. 3.   The single *tamias* appears in
276/5 B.C. (*IG*. 329).

[7] The ταμίας τῶν στρατιωτικῶν is not attested for the period 323/2-307 B.C.
From *IG*. ii. 270 we learn of the existence of a military fund, which Fränkel
(*op. cit.* 44) has brought into connexion with this official, between 347/6 and
323/2 B.C.   After 323/2 B.C. payment into it ceased.   Of course this may also
have occurred without the office being abolished.

should restore the financial system of Eubulus ? Henceforth one officer, the superintendent of the administration, was to receive and distribute all revenues and
control the action of all the spending departments.
Reserves were to be deposited, as of old, along with
the sacred treasures, in the custody of the treasurers of
Athena on the Acropolis. Never before had there been
such an effective centralization of Athenian finance.[1]

The committee of ten *astynomi*, five of whom had
served in the city and five in the Piraeus, was also
abolished, and its duties added to those of the ten
agoranomi.[2] The *eleven* were dispensed with altogether,
and their duties of summary imposition of justice upon
" evil-doers " were transferred to the Areopagus ;[3] while
their duties as keepers of the state prison were henceforth performed by eleven men specifically called
desmophylaces or gaolers.[4] The so-called prytany-
secretary, who had had general charge of the publication and preservation of the public decrees,—activities
diminished greatly by the " discharge of the demos," [5]—
was found unnecessary, and his duties were accordingly
divided between two subordinates, the controller (*anagrapheus*) and the secretary of the senate. Of these
the former was raised in rank to an annual public
official, and delegated to supervise the work of the ten
senators who served in the latter capacity, each for the
term of a prytany. He may also have had some control
over legislation.[6]

The theory of government underlying the changes
of which the few noted are typical—that the leisure,
independence, and self-interest, which the ownership of
property entailed, and the intelligence which a superior

---

[1] See below, Appendix II.

[2] *IG.* ii. 5. 192c. 17 (Ditt. *Syll.*[2] 500) ἐπειδὴ δὲ καὶ ἡ τῶν ἀστυνόμων ἐπι-
μέλεια προστέτακται τοῖς ἀγορανόμοις.

[3] Pollux, viii. 102 ; cf. *Klio*, 1911, p. 272.

[4] Sundwall, *Acta*, 14, n. 6, in emendation of Tod, *Annual of the British
School at Athens*, ix. 156.

[5] The sum of the charges made later against Phocion and his companions
was : ὅτι οὗτοι παραίτιοι γεγένηνται μετὰ τὸν Λαμιακὸν πόλεμον τῆς τε δουλείας
τῇ πατρίδι καὶ τῆς καταλύσεως τοῦ δήμου καὶ τῶν νόμων, Diod. xviii. 66. 5 ; cf.
Beloch, iii. 1. 79 and n. 4.

[6] *Cornell Studies*, vii. 41 ; cf. Wilhelm, *Österr. Jahreshefte*, 1908, p. 95.

education promoted, gave to the upper class a right
both to determine the general policy and to attend to
the administration of a state[1]—was the one popularly
attributed to Solon; and it was, in fact, according to his
laws that the oligarchy professed to govern.[2]   The
realization of this principle involved the discharge of
the *demos* and the reservation of the active and public
rights of citizenship to nine thousand Athenians.   The
recognition of fitness as the sole qualification for office
was incompatible with the use of the lot and mechanical
rotation among the tribes as means of distributing
offices.   Hence the lot and the official order were
abolished.   The discharge of the *demos* involved a great
reduction in the number of offices and officers, as well
as the abandonment of the important democratic
principle that no man should be permitted to hold a
senatorship more than twice or an ordinary office more
than once in his lifetime.   With twenty-one thousand
citizens it must have been difficult to obtain the two
hundred and fifty new senators and the scores of new
allotted magistrates required each year;[3] for the number

---

[1] The government between 322 and 318 B.C. is referred to in a decree passed
in 318/17 B.C. (*IG*. ii. 5. 231*b*; Ditt. *Syll.*[2] 163) as: οἱ ἐν τῆι ὀλι(γ)αρχίαι
πολιτευόμε[νοι].

[2] Diod. xviii. 18. 5.   Sundwall (*Acta*, 5; cf. de Sanctis, *Atthis*, 231) calls
attention to the fact that 2000 *drachmae* of property was in effect the qualification for admission to the *zeugite* class; and that 9000 citizens corresponded
closely to the number of those who, through registration in the three upper
classes of Solon, were eligible for hoplite service in the fourth century B.C.

[3] There must have been *ca.* 20 new officials annually if the same group of
twice *ca.* 400 men exchanged offices till each had died or had held positions in
his thirtieth year and in every second year thereafter for his natural lifetime.
There was, of course, no such monopoly of magistracies.   In fact, it is very
doubtful if many persons held office for more than two or three terms (the
Prosopographia has few who are known to have held office so often), since the
lot gave an even chance of election to all of those who were eligible; hence we
must triple or quadruple the twenty to get the normal number of magistrates
needed annually.   However, for this computation we can work with only the
absolute minimum.   Areopagites, *diaetetae*, and *dicasts* could be at the same
time officers; but it is probable that, as in the constitution proposed in 411
B.C., senators were *ipso facto* excluded from holding allotted magistracies.
Naturally, the lot prevented many senators from being re-elected for the second
term allowed; so that 250 is also the absolute theoretical minimum only.   We
may, however, affirm with safety that the Athenian offices and senatorships
could not be filled at all unless over 300 eligibles reached the age of thirty every
year.   If a prohibition against duplication existed for the *deme* offices, and if
it was also forbidden to hold a public office or senatorship along with a *deme*
office, the absolute minimum would have to be doubled; but it seems improbable that these restrictions existed.

of men annually attaining their thirtieth year out of such a total was less than six hundred.[1] It may indeed have been because of this difficulty that we find some of the colleges of ten—particularly those for which there existed a special property qualification—short two or three members in various years in the fourth century B.C.[2] With nine thousand citizens the problem[3] was insoluble; for such a population can have yielded an annual crop of less than two hundred and fifty men in their thirtieth year. Hence, as we have seen, offices were doubled up, abolished, and transferred from a Board to a single magistrate. Nothing else was possible, and we must also assume that repeated tenure of senator-ships, and probably also of magistracies, was legalized.

It is improbable that many of the disfranchised citizens left Athens. That Antipater had meant to

[1] $\frac{1}{41}$ (512), if as in France; $\frac{1}{34}$ (619), if as in the United States. Or if the average age at entering was ten years later (thirty-five to forty-four) $\frac{1}{46}$ (456), if as in France; $\frac{1}{42}$ (500), if as in the United States. Of course, the maximum of those theoretically available must be reduced considerably to allow for the existence of ἄτιμοι, of those disqualified every year by absence from Attica on official or private business, and of those who were employed year after year in the subordinate salaried administrative positions. Also, a considerable margin had to be allowed for accidental shortages of the crop of citizens in particular years. The tendency must have been for men to assume office soon after passing the qualifying age—thirty; and Demosthenes, for example, was senator at thirty-four.

[2] For a shortage in the number of the treasurers of Athena, see *Ath. Mitt.*, 1908, p. 202, and Ἐφ. Ἀρχ., 1909, p. 204 ff.; in the number of the *amphictyones* in Delos, Ditt. *Syll.*[2] 86 ; cf. *Class. Rev.*, 1901, p. 38 ff.

[3] It is stated most definitely in the data as to the offices given in Aristotle's *Const. of Athens*, and in the following passages : οὐδ' ἀρχὴν καταστήσω ὥστ' ἄρχειν ὑπεύθυνον ὄντα ἑτέρας ἀρχῆς . . . · οὐδὲ δὶς τὴν αὐτὴν ἀρχὴν τὸν αὐτὸν ἄνδρα, οὐδὲ δύο ἀρχὰς ἄρξαι τὸν αὐτὸν ἐν τῷ αὐτῷ ἐνιαυτῷ (Dicast's oath in Dem. *C. Timocrat.* 150). ἄρχειν δὲ τὰς μὲν κατὰ πόλεμον ἀρχὰς ἔ[ξεσ]τι πλεονάκις, τῶν δ' ἄλλων οὐδεμίαν, πλὴν βουλεῦσαι δίς (Aristotle, *op. cit.* 62. 3). The elections took place some time prior to the end of each civil year (Aristotle, *op. cit.* 44. 4 for the military offices ; for the others, *IG.* ii. Add. 489b ; cf. ii. 416) ; so that no *interregnum* was imposed by the *docimasia*. The outgoing magistrate, on the other hand, was not free from the *euthynia* till some time after he had laid down his office. An interval of three days after his account was audited was also prescribed (Aristotle, *op. cit.* 48. 4). Apparently a month was ordinarily required for the judicial proceedings (*Klio*, 1904, p. 5 f.), and he was allowed the same interval in which to present his account (Harpocr. *s.v.* λογισταί). Hence it must have been exceptionable for a man to hold two routine offices in succession. How the generals came to serve for year after year we do not know ; cf. Wilamowitz, *Phil. Untersuch.* i. 59 ff. ; Gilbert, *op. cit.* 224, n. 2 ; Ed. Meyer, *Gesch. d. Alt.* iv. 320. Out of 9000 males over nineteen years of age France would have 220 in any annual group of those between twenty-five and thirty-four ; the United States, 265. France would have 196 in any similar group of those between thirty-five and forty-four ; the United States, 213.

force the Aetolians to migrate from their mountains into central Asia Minor is probable; but that he actually deported the Attic outcasts into Thrace is disproved by their presence in their own country five years later. Since violence was not used, the opportunity given them to join in colonizing Thrace can have appealed to those alone who had nothing to abandon and who had no hòpe of a restoration.   These were apparently not numerous in Attica, but it is likely that they formed the great majority of the cleruchs who had been ejected from their lots in Samos.[1]   Had only nine thousand citizens remained in Athens, it is thinkable that Antipater might have withdrawn the garrison from the Piraeus, as he had agreed to do; but with eight or ten thousand men there eager for a change, Phocion, who was the head of the government and held the office of hoplite-general, refused even to ask the regent for its removal, and induced him not to demand the war indemnity, upon the payment of which the withdrawal of the troops was conditional.[2]   His colleague, Demades, who headed the propertied democrats, and who, because of four successful interventions with the Macedonian rulers, had come to overestimate his own influence, adopted zealously the popular cause.[3]   The Macedonian garrison was a constant humiliation to patriotic Athenians, and there was obviously a strong minority among the citizens which desired to see it depart.   The propertied classes, accordingly, were divided into two groups on this question, and Demades finally took his son, Demeas, with him, and went to press upon the regent the evacuation of Munychia.   His agitation was dangerous; for it could not be doubtful that the withdrawal of the garrison would be followed by an attack upon the privileges of the nine thousand, and the restoration of the anti-Macedonian democracy.

[1] Diodorus (xviii. 18. 4) says: οὗτοι μὲν οὖν ὄντες πλείους τῶν μυρίων καὶ δισχιλίων μετεστάθησαν ἐκ τῆς πατρίδος.   This, however, is Diodorus's misinterpretation of his source.

[2] Plut. *Phocion*, 30. 5.

[3] He proposed and carried decrees rewarding foreigners for services rendered to Athenians who had fought against Antipater at Abydus and Amorgos. *IG.* ii. 193, 194, 229.

Accordingly the dominant faction, which sought at all hazards to preserve the goodwill of Antipater and the Macedonians,[1] put forward Deinarchus, a Corinthian, and a close friend of Phocion,[2] to accuse Demades before Cassander, who had taken his father's place during the last illness of the old regent. There was nothing in itself objectionable in the demand of Demades; hence the charge could concern his motives alone. These, however, were proved to be treasonable by the evidence of the letters, written by him to Perdiccas in 322/1 B.C., which had been found when Perdiccas was overthrown. And, indeed, had the mind of Cassander not been poisoned in advance, it is hard to understand his treatment of the Athenian ambassadors, for he had both Demades and his son executed.[3]

Shortly afterwards (319 B.C.), Antipater died, having designated Polyperchon, an old Macedonian general, as regent of the empire, and his son, Cassander, *chiliarch*. The latter wished for the possession of Macedon, and sought to obtain it through the support of Antigonus of Phrygia, who challenged Polyperchon's title to the regency. He accordingly went to Asia to secure troops and a navy, but before doing so—in fact, before the death of Antipater was known—he succeeded in having Menyllus relieved of the command of the garrison in Munychia, and Nicanor, a devoted partisan of himself, put in his stead.[4] Ptolemy of Egypt joined Antigonus.

---

[1] Wilhelm, *Österr. Jahreshefte*, 1908, p. 90.

[2] Not the orator. Plut. *Phocion*, 33.

[3] Arrian, *De succ. Alex.* 14 f. ; Diod. xviii. 48 (where Antipater is said to have put Demades to death) ; Plut. *Phocion*, 30 (where the letters are said to have been to Antigonus—a change made because Perdiccas was dead in 319 B.C.) ; *id.*, *Dem.* 31 ; Suidas, *s.v.* "Demades" ; cf. Athen. xiii. 591 F. The reasons given by de Sanctis (7) for rejecting this story are insufficient. The agitation of Demades and the accusation of Deinarchus need the compromising letters as a complement. There was time for the letters to have been sent between the occupation of Munychia in 322 and the death of Perdiccas in 321 B.C. Niese (i. 233) accepts the letters as genuine. Beloch (iii. 1. 98, n. 2) follows de Sanctis. The time was winter or spring of 320/19 B.C. Reusch, *Hermes*, 1880, p. 342 ff.

[4] The adopted son and son-in-law of Aristotle. Heberdey, *Festschrift für Th. Gomperz*, 412 ff. ; Wilamowitz, *Arist. u. Athen*, i. 315, 337, 368. He is called *agonothetes* in Plut. *Phocion*, 31, for the year 319 B.C. ; but this is only a descriptive, not a technical term. P.-W. i. 874 ; Unger, *Sitz. d. Akad. München*, 1878, i. 422 ; Köhler, *Ath. Mitt.*, 1879, p. 328 ; Capps, *Amer. Journ. Arch.*, 1900, p. 85, n. 1.

The Greek cities, moreover, were mainly in the control of oligarchies whom Antipater had established, and these now transferred their allegiance to his son. Self-preservation thus forced Polyperchon to extend the hand to the democrats and, accordingly, he issued an edict in the name of the imbecile king, Philip Arrhidaeus, to the following effect:[1] "Seeing that our forefathers have in many ways benefited the Greeks, we desire to continue their policy and to make clear to all the goodwill we have towards them. Some time ago, when Alexander departed from men, and the kingdom devolved upon us, we thought it our duty to establish everywhere the peace and government which our father Philip had maintained, and sent communications to this effect to all the cities. But when it resulted, through our being far away, that certain misguided Greek states waged war upon the Macedonians, and were subdued by our generals, they suffered many hardships. Set these down to the credit of our generals (*i.e.* Antipater). We, for our part, out of regard for our original policy, hereby ordain for you peace, the constitutions of the days of Philip and Alexander, and the liberties which were conferred by the edicts formerly issued by them. We also restore those dispossessed or exiled by our generals during the period which has elapsed since Alexander crossed into Asia, and command that they receive back all their property, and be admitted to citizenship without violence and without reviving old sores. We hereby annul all enactments of a contrary tenor, except such as apply to those exiled legally for murder or impiety. Let not, however, the faction of Polyaenetus, banished from Megalopolis for high treason, be restored, nor the exiles of Amphissa, Tricca, Pharcadon, or Heracleia; but all others shall be re-admitted before the thirtieth of Xandicus. Should it appear, however, that Philip or Alexander made arrangements to their own detriment, let such matters be brought to our attention in order that we may apply the remedies, and thus benefit ourselves and the

---

[1] Diod. xviii. 56. 5.

cities. The Athenians shall have all else as in the time of Philip and Alexander, but the Oropians shall retain Oropus. Samos we give to Athens, since our father, Philip, gave it to her. Let all the Greeks pass a resolution that no one shall wage war or do aught against us under penalty of exile or confiscation of property both for himself and his family. We command that you confer about these and other matters with Polyperchon. Do you, as we have already requested, obey him; for we shall not forget those who fail to comply with any of our messages."

This proclamation,[1] which was probably issued in the fall of 319 B.C., made the position of Phocion and the aristocrats extremely difficult. After the end of Xandicus (March 318 B.C.), their privileges were to be annulled automatically by the king's edict; that is to say, by the same authority by which they had been established two years earlier. But in the six months still to elapse something might be done. Nicanor, who on his arrival had come to an understanding with Phocion, and at his suggestion had given games in Athens at considerable personal expense, besides otherwise conciliating the people,[2] sought to win the sympathy of the city for Cassander. He now met the general clamour that he should evacuate Munychia as soon as possible, by asking for a few days' respite, on the pledge that he sought to promote the best interest of the city; and it was only after a personal effort to bring the Athenian senate round to his view of the situation had almost cost him his life that he began to add a few soldiers every night to his garrison so as finally to be able to defend his post against attacks. The Athenians suspected his sincerity, and despite the

---

[1] Beloch (iii. 1. 102, n. 2) thinks the edict not quite complete as we have it, since the clause relating to the withdrawal of the garrison to which Diodorus refers in xviii. 64. 5 is omitted. But in this latter case what the ambassadors sent by Athens to Nicanor, demanded on the strength of the proclamation, was not the removal of the garrison, but autonomy. The proclamation did *not* touch on the matter of the garrisons—advisedly doubtless. The precise date of the edict is unknown, but in February 318 B.C. the Athenians were already in negotiations with Polyperchon. Wilhelm, *Österr. Jahreshefte*, 1908, p. 88.

[2] Plut. *Phocion*, 31 ; cf. Köhler, *Ath. Mitt.*, 1885, p. 235.

aristocratic control of the executive, which was thus friendly to Cassander, the popular party mastered the government,[1] and sent ambassadors to the king and Polyperchon, asking them for aid in carrying out the programme of democratic restoration ; while at the same time they held frequent public meetings [2] to deliberate upon a war with Nicanor, and passed a resolution, on the motion of Philomelus of Lamptrae, requiring all the citizens to arm and put themselves at the disposal of Phocion. To this Phocion paid no heed, so that the Athenians were unable to do anything till Nicanor had increased his force sufficiently to enable him to seize the walls of the Piraeus and the fortifications of the harbour. This was too much for their endurance, and accordingly they forced Phocion and two others [3] to remonstrate with Nicanor, and to request him to obey the command of the king in the matter of their autonomy. The commandant referred them to Cassander : as a good soldier he must await orders from the general who had appointed him. Nor did the receipt of a letter from Olympias—who he understood was to assume the regency in the interest of her grandson — commanding him, greatly to the joy of the Athenians, to relinquish the Piraeus and Munychia, lead him to do more than to make further promises.

In this way the winter passed, but in March (318 B.C.) Alexander, the son of Polyperchon, entered Attica with an army to drive out Nicanor, as it seemed

---

[1] The fact that the ecclesia was controlled by the friends of Polyperchon and democracy—the party which Demades had led, probably—even before the reinstatement of the exiles, is obvious both from Plutarch (*Phocion*, 32) and from the inscription published by Wilhelm (*Österr. Jahreshefte*, 1908, p. 88). On the other hand, that the administration was aristocratic, and hence adverse to an unconditional surrender to Polyperchon, is clear from the inability of the populace to act except through Phocion, and from the fact that the secretary of the senate for even the seventh prytany (February, 318 B.C.) was Aphobetus of Cothocidae, brother or son of Aeschines (Wilhelm, *op. cit.* p. 89).

[2] No less than seven decrees of this year are extant, in part at least (Wilhelm, *loc. cit.* 82 ff.).

[3] Conon, son of Timotheus of Anaphlystus, and Clearchus, son of Nausicles of Aegilia ; Diod. xviii. 64. 5, and, for the whole circumstances, Droysen, ii. 1. 215 ff.

to the Athenians, to seize the Piraeus for himself, as it proved, and as Phocion and his friends secretly urged. Negotiations, from which the Athenians were excluded then followed between Nicanor and Alexander. The Athenians concluded that they were being humbugged, and, as the last of Xandicus had now arrived, they took matters into their own hands.[1] The thousands of men who had been disfranchised were again entitled to exercise the rights of citizens, and, as was natural, they immediately dominated the popular assembly. They dismissed all the magistrates, and appointed a new set from among the convinced democrats.[2] At least one of the old officers, the eponymous archon, Apollodoros, was re-elected, and the senate was not disturbed. The example of the aristocrats in 322 B.C., moreover, was followed in that all detailed changes in the magistracies were deferred till the opening of the new year.[3] The old generals were at once suspended, and Phocion and his associates were thus called upon to give an accounting for their conduct in office.[4] They had been in collusion with Nicanor and Alexander, of that there could be no doubt. Phocion had, in fact, connived at the escape of Nicanor from the trap which Dercylus, the home general, had set for him when he had come in person to negotiate with the Athenian senate. He had closed his eyes to the preparations which were being made by Nicanor for the seizure of the Piraeus, and his ears both to the expostulations of his fellow-citizens and to a

---

[1] Unger (*Philol.*, 1878, p. 451 f.), on the basis of *IG*. ii. 299b, plus Add. p. 414, determined that the revolution took place in the middle of 319/8 B.C., about three months before the last of Xandicus ; cf. Beloch, iii. 1. 103 ; iii. 2. 191. Wilhelm has, however, shown, by a masterly interpretation of several new fragmentary decrees of this year (*Österr. Jahreshefte*, 1908, pp. 82-100), that this is an error, and that the outbreak took place after the 30th of Elaphebolion, and before the 20th of Munychion, *i.e.* at the last of Xandicus, as Diodorus (xviii. 64 ff.; cf. 56. 5) implies. de Sanctis (11, n. 2) had already noticed the chronological difficulties of Unger's view.

[2] Thus Epicurus—subsequently one of those directly responsible for the death of Phocion—was elected *anagrapheus* for the rest of the year (Wilhelm, *loc. cit.* 92 ; cf. below, i. 34, n. 4).

[3] Even the office of *anagrapheus* remained in existence till the end of 319/8 B.C. It was abolished at the beginning of 318/7 B.C. (*IG*. ii. 5. 231b ; Ditt. *Syll.*2 163).

[4] See Diod. xviii. 64 ff.; Plut. *Phocion*, 31-38 ; Nepos, *Phocion*, 3-4, for the circumstances of Phocion's downfall.

formal resolution calling the people to arms under his command.   He had tried to bring about an understanding between Nicanor and Alexander with a view to the retention of a Macedonian garrison in Munychia, and the maintenance of an oligarchy in Athens [1]—all, perhaps, for the good of the city, but for the disadvantage of the democracy now in power.   Phocion thought it wise to leave Athens, and, since he had lost the confidence of Nicanor through acting for Alexander in the crisis, he was obliged to put himself under the protection of the latter, from whom he had reason to expect gratitude.   However, he made a fatal mistake. Demetrius of Phalerum, Callimedes the Crab, Charicles, and others who, perhaps, had remained aloof from the intrigue with Alexander, escaped to Nicanor in the Piraeus, and were safe.   Polyperchon, who had now no hope of winning Athens except by conciliating the democrats, and whose proclamation must lack effect elsewhere, if he were seen to be dallying with the oligarchs in Athens, gave to Phocion and his companions only a farcical hearing, at the end of which he expressed his conviction that they were guilty of high-treason.   He, however, shirked the responsibility of passing judgment, and, at the request of Hagnonides of Pergase, the leader of the Athenian democrats, who had come to Polyperchon in Phocis to present the charges against the oligarchs, he ordered Cleitus to take them in chains to Athens.[2]   They were to be tried where their crimes had been committed.   This was equivalent to a death sentence.   None the less, Phocion tried to make a defence before the confused mob, which, upon his arrival, swarmed into the theatre to pronounce the verdict.   He had been general of Athens for forty-five years,[3] and though his treason to the democrats was manifest, there was much that he could urge in extenuation.   He probably could have divulged matters embarrassing to Polyperchon had he been given an opportunity to make a full statement, either when

---

[1] Nepos, *Phocion*, 2 f. ; Niese, i. 241 ff. ; de Sanctis, 11.
[2] Plut. *Phocion*, 33.   [3] *Ibid.* 8 ; cf. Kirchner, *PA.* ii. 15,076.

brought before the king, or now before the Athenians.[1] Accordingly, his voice was drowned in the clamour of interruptions, and no heed was paid even to his generous plea for his companions. They had for judges men whom they had treated for three years as almost beyond the pale of organized society.[2] Hence they were all alike condemned to death, and on the 19th of Munychion (April) they drank the deadly hemlock.[3] Those who had escaped to Nicanor were included in the sentence, but not in its execution.[4]

Not long after the death of Phocion, Cassander sailed into the Piraeus with thirty-five ships and four thousand soldiers which he had received from Antigonus. His arrival relieved the tension of Nicanor's position, and this able and faithful soldier, leaving the walls and harbour defences of the Piraeus as well as the Long Walls leading to Athens,[5] to the care of his master, concentrated his own troops within Munychia.[6] Polyperchon had lost his opportunity. With the army with which he now entered Attica, twenty thousand Macedonian infantry, four thousand allied foot, one thousand cavalry, and sixty-five elephants, he might have overwhelmed Nicanor, had he come in person when he sent his son Alexander. Now he could do nothing. To storm the Piraeus was out of the question. His enemy could get provisions by sea more easily than he could by land, and to draw upon Attica was simply to exhaust more speedily the quite inadequate supplies of Athens. He could merely leave his son with a detachment to aid in the protection of the Athenians, and seek to retrieve

[1] The indictment seems to have charged him with the aristocratic revolution of 322 B.C. (Diod. xviii. 66. 5). An inquiry into the negotiations of 319/8 B.C. would have been dangerous to Alexander and Polyperchon, perhaps. Cf. de Sanctis, 11.

[2] Wilamowitz, *op. cit.* i. 362 : "Man wird angesichts des Elends der Masse über die grauenvollen Zuckungen der nächsten Jahre milder urteilen."

[3] See the piteous story of his death in Plut. *Phocion*, 36, and Diod. xviii. 67. For the short interval—nineteen days—between his fall and his execution see Wilhelm, *Österr. Jahreshefte*, 1908, p. 93.

[4] Hagnonides of Pergase (de Sanctis, 10), Glaucippus the son of Hypereides, Epicurus, and Demophilus were those whom public opinion held chiefly responsible for the death of Phocion. The comrades of Phocion were Nicocles, Tydippus, Hegemon, and Pythocles (de Sanctis, 11).

[5] Paus. i. 25. 5.   [6] Diod. xviii. 68.

his mistake elsewhere. We do not need to follow him in his disastrous attack on Megalopolis, nor to describe the ultimate discomfiture of Eumenes, his brilliant ally in Asia. Cassander at once seized Aegina, and attacked Salamis, but before he could master the Salaminians, who defended themselves manfully,[1] Polyperchon was able to bring a fleet together and come to the rescue of the island. The magnitude of the loss of the Piraeus was now apparent, for Cassander simply withdrew within its impregnable harbour, and despite the great naval superiority of Polyperchon, the latter could do him no harm.[2]

Not simply was Polyperchon repulsed at Megalopolis, but he suffered a complete disaster on sea also. The scene of naval operations had been transferred to the Propontis, whither Nicanor took the ships of Cassander shortly after the repulse at Salamis, and whither Cleitus had followed him with the whole fleet of Polyperchon. It was at the end of the Bosporus near Byzantium that the two navies came into contact, that of Nicanor being now one hundred and thirty warships strong. In the engagement which followed, the hero of Amorgos won, but at dawn of the following day Antigonus, who had taken personal command of the remnant of his fleet, found the ships of the victor beached, and, attacking them simultaneously by land and sea, took or destroyed almost all of them. The blow was a fatal one for Polyperchon, and the collapse of his power involved that of the Athenian democracy.[3]

In the fall of 318 B.C.[4] Nicanor returned in triumph to the Piraeus with his irresistible fleet, and Salamis was unable to maintain itself[5] longer. Hagnonides of Pergase remained in control of the government in Athens for only about nine months,[6] but during that time he stained his hands with the blood of Phocion, and would have done the like with that of Theophrastus, whom he accused of impiety, had he not soon lost

---

[1] It was possibly at this time that Leon fell (*IG.* ii. 2719); cf. Wilhelm, *Österr. Jahreshefte*, 1909, p. 135. [2] Diod. xviii. 69.

[3] Diod. xviii. 72; Polyaenus, iv. 6. 8. [4] Beloch, iii. 2, § 86.

[5] Paus. i. 25. 6; cf. below, iii. 117, n. 2. [6] See below, i. 36, n. 5.

the confidence of the people. He, doubtless, cared little for the religious views of the Peripatetic, but for his political opinions and affiliations, as a good democrat, he could entertain nothing but hatred. Was not Nicanor, who had done Athens so much harm, the adopted son and son-in-law of the teacher of Theophrastus?[1] The school of Aristotle was, in fact, a centre of aristocratic influence, and the ideas it disseminated as to the best state, and the society from which its Athenian members were mainly recruited, made it doubly objectionable to the democrats. None the less, Hagnonides obtained barely one-fifth of the votes of the Areopagus when the trial of Theophrastus occurred.[2] The occupation of the Piraeus by the enemy had cut off the natural transmarine supplies for a large part of the Athenian population. Still, Attica was able to provide war rations for those within the city. In the winter of 318 B.C., however, Alexander, who commanded the troops of Polyperchon in this neighbourhood, withdrew to join his father in Macedon, and in the spring of the year Cassander seized Panacton and mastered the open country.[3] This meant ultimate starvation, and it was speedily followed by the raising of a voice in the popular assembly for the opening of negotiations with Cassander.[4] A moment of excitement ensued, but the good sense of the people prevailed, and it was unanimously agreed to send an embassy to him. Nothing could have suited Cassander better. His aim was the Macedonian crown, not the coercion of Athens, and, hence, terms were easily arranged.[5] To him one thing alone was of essential importance—the establishment of a government in Athens which was friendly to himself. The working out of the details he left to Demetrius of Phalerum, who was recommended to him by his stead-

[1] See above, i. 28, n. 4.
[2] Diog. Laert. v. 37 ; Aelian, *Var. hist.* viii. 12 ; cf. below, iii. 104 ff., for a renewal of the attack on Theophrastus. For the jurisdiction of the Areopagus in cases of impiety see Diog. Laert. ii. 101, 116, and P.-W. *s.v.* " Asebeia."
[3] Paus. i. 25. 6. [4] Diod. xviii. 74.
[5] Later than the 1st of Poseideon (November 318 B.C. ; cf. *Class. Phil.*, 1908, p. 386), as *IG.* ii. 5. 231*b* shows. Early in the spring of 317 B.C., doubtless, before Cassander set out for Macedon (Beloch, iii. 2. 191).

fastness in 319/8 B.C., and by his conspicuous personal qualities. Demetrius, accordingly, effected an agreement with the party within the city.[1] The Athenians were to have possession of their city and country, of their revenues, of their navy (of which not much was now left), and of everything else that belonged to them with the exception of Munychia, which Cassander was to retain until he had finished the war with Polyperchon. They were, however, to exclude from citizenship all who possessed less than one thousand *drachmae* of property, and entrust the supervision of the government to one person, who should be an Athenian citizen, but whom Cassander should designate.[2] His choice was Demetrius himself. In this way Athens came again into the control of a timocracy, but it was a less narrow one than in 322 B.C. Some were disfranchised, doubtless, but apparently not more than a few thousands, and it was probably out of these that the colony which was sent to Carthage in 309 B.C. was mainly composed;[3] so that Demetrius, ignoring the events of 318 B.C., was able to claim at a later time that he had restored the democracy in Athens. Had the rest been free to follow their own inclinations, their policy in the next few years would have been very different from what it was. The citizens were bound by the neighbouring Macedonian garrison, and its control of the harbour, to give a respectful hearing to all suggestions of which Demetrius of Phalerum was either the mouthpiece or the originator. Hence there was good reason for the opinion, popularly held, that the city was in the hands of a tyrant.

[1] *IG.* ii. 584.
[2] Diod. xviii. 74 καταστῆσαι δ' ἐπιμελητὴν τῆς πόλεως ἕνα ἄνδρα 'Αθηναῖον ὃν ἂν δόξῃ Κασσάνδρῳ.   [3] Diod. xx. 40. 5.

CHAPTER II

THE RÉGIME OF DEMETRIUS OF PHALERUM

'Εχθαίρω τὸ ποίημα τὸ κυκλικόν, οὐδὲ κελεύθῳ
χαίρω, τίς πολλοὺς ὧδε καὶ ὧδε φέρει·
μισῶ καὶ περίφοιτον ἐρώμενον, οὔτ' ἀπὸ κρήνης
πίνω· σικχαίνω πάντα τὰ δημόσια.

CALLIMACHUS (Mackail, *Select Epigrams*, iv. 31).

PHANOSTRATUS of Phalerum had two sons, Himeraeus and Demetrius,[1] of whom the first was a democrat and an anti-Macedonian, the other an aristocrat and a supporter of Phocion. Since Demetrius had come under the influence of Aristotle and Theophrastus, we naturally suppose that it was he who chose his party on purely personal grounds. Both were youths of more than ordinary capacity, and they were so closely identified with the policies of their respective parties that before they were thirty-five they had been in turn condemned to death by their political opponents. Himeraeus had died with Hypereides in 322 B.C.,[2] while Demetrius was one of the ambassadors who arranged the terms of surrender which called for his brother's death. He played a leading part in the oligarchic government of the following three years, but, wiser than Phocion, he did not desert Nicanor, the son-in-law of Aristotle, to whom, through friendship with Theophrastus, he was doubtless attached by a personal tie, and thus he escaped the death penalty which was imposed upon him in 318 B.C.

NOTE.—The author is indebted in this chapter to his friend Professor Henry W. Prescott, of the University of Chicago, for valuable criticisms and suggestions. Naturally this does not imply a joint responsibility for anything contained in it.

[1] Kirchner, *PA.*, 7578, 3455, where complete references are given.
[2] See above, i. 20.

He was brought into contact with Cassander during the following winter, and to this he owed his nomination to the dangerous office of political dictator and Macedonian agent in Athens.[1]

Demetrius of Phalerum was at once a political idealist and a practical politician—as are most republican states-men. The former trait he owed in large measure to his education. Theophrastus had been his teacher,[2] and through him he had come to believe in the Aristotelian creed that the essence of politics consisted in fostering the middle classes.[3] He had been taught that men were not born fully equipped for citizenship, as democratic theory upheld, but had to be selected and moulded for the most elementary civic duties; and, through holding these ideas, he came inevitably to co-operate with the leaders of the aristocratic faction. He conceived it to be his duty as reformer to put the best elements in power, but to base the state on so broad a citizenship that it was supported by an actual majority of the people;[4] and as lawgiver, to prevent the economic ruin of the citizens by legis-lating against expenditures for luxurious or other unwise purposes.

It seems unlikely that any alteration in the magis-tracies was made on the establishment of the régime of Demetrius, or at the end of the year 318/7 B.C. ; for the constitutional changes noticeable occurred later and at different times. All that was done at the start was to limit the franchise to possessors of one thousand *drachmae*, to substitute for election by lot and rotation of offices among the tribes election by show of hands

---

[1] Ἱμεραίου τοῦ ἀδελφοῦ ἀναιρεθέντος ὑπ' Ἀντιπάτρου αὐτὸς μετὰ Νικάνορος διέτριβεν, αἰτίαν ἔχων ὡς τὰ ἐπιφάνεια τοῦ ἀδελφοῦ θύων (Athen. xii. 542 E). Demetrius appears first in 324 B.C. (Diog. Laert. v. 75). He was still alive in 283 B.C., and probably for some years afterwards, and he did not die a natural death (Diog. Laert. v. 78 ; cf. Cic. *Pro Rabirio*, 23). His grandson was over thirty years of age in 262/1 B.C. (see below, iv. 183). Hence he was born at *ca.* 350 B.C. Ostermann, *De Demetrii Phalerei vita*, Diss., Herzfeld, 1847, p. 11.

[2] Diog. Laert. v. 75 ; Strabo, ix. 398 ; Cic. *De leg.* iii. 14, *De offic.* i. 1, *De fin.* v. 54 ; Suidas, *s.v.*

[3] Wilamowitz, *op. cit.* i. 362 f. ; Martini in P.-W. iv. 2827 f. ; Beloch, iii. 1. 152.

[4] Accordingly, the property qualification for the franchise was set at 1000 *drachmae*, not at 2000 as in 321 B.C.

from among all the citizens,[1] and to empower Demetrius
to revise the laws. This was a task quite to the taste
of a pupil of Theophrastus, whose work on the *Laws*
was as epoch-making as that of Aristotle on *Politics*, and
the revision of Demetrius, which for the first time put
into effect the conclusions reached by contemporary
students of comparative law, and was based particularly
upon the investigations of his teacher,[2] secured for him
a momentary renown and a lasting reputation ; in fact, a
place along with Theseus or Draco and Solon as the
third *nomothetes* of the Athenians.[3]

Demetrius was anything but a rigorist in the conduct
of his own life. He was now about thirty-five years of
age, and a strikingly handsome man. He laid so much
stress upon an effective appearance that he blondined
his hair, and cultivated an extreme elegance of manner.[4]
He was fond of social pleasures, and his dinners, drinking-
parties, and *liaisons* with beautiful courtesans were
matters of common knowledge and conversation.[5] His
relations with his boy-lover Theognis were notorious,
and it speaks more for his personal attractiveness than
for the character of at least certain young Athenians
that they envied his favourite and sought, by obtruding
their charms upon his notice as he took his afternoon
walk on Tripod Street, to obtain for themselves his
place. That he seduced men's wives, corrupted their
sons, and played fast and loose with public moneys, was
alleged by his enemies—with how much truth it is

[1] This substitution had been made in 321 B.C., but the restoration of 318 B.C.
had occurred in the meanwhile. This had also reimposed the old disability as
to holding a civil office twice or a senatorship three times. Demetrius,
seemingly, did not change back.

[2] See *Klio*, xi. (1911), p. 268 ff.

[3] Syncellus, 521 Δημήτριος ὁ Φαληρεὺς ἐγνωρίζετο τρίτος νομοθέτης ᾿Αθήνησιν.
The Parian marble (Jacoby, 22) puts this legislation in 317/6 B.C. See also
Ditt. *Syll.*[2] 164, which Wilhelm (*GGA.*, 1898, p. 223) has successfully restored
[νόμους] ἔθ[η]κεν καλ[λίστους]. This also makes the code practically the first
achievement of Demetrius after obtaining power. Cf. below, ii. 43, n. 2. For
the work of Theophrastus on the *Laws* see the important article by Dareste,
" Le Traité des lois de Théophraste," in *Revue de législation française et étrangère*,
1870–71, p. 262 ff.

[4] Duris in Athen. xii. 542 D (*FHG.* ii. 475) ; Aelian, *Var. hist.* ix. 9 ; cf.
Martini in P.-W. iv. 2822 ; Beloch, iii. 1. 154.

[5] Duris, *loc. cit.* ; Diyllus in Athen. xiii. 593 f. (*FHG.* ii. 361) ; Hegesander
in Athen. iv. 167 D (*FHG.* iv. 415) ; cf. below, iv. 183. Favorinus and Didymus
in Diog. Laert. v. 76.

impossible to say.[1] But though an Epicurean by
instinct, and often self-indulgent, he was never attracted
by the mere naturalism of vice, and there was nothing
gross and coarse about his pleasures.   How a man of
such a disposition could plan a campaign of moral
reform it is difficult to imagine, and, in fact, we have no
reason for believing that he had any such thing in mind.
On the other hand, an *élégant* like Demetrius could not
but be disgusted at the licence of the Athenian rabble—
the lack of respect of the young for the old, of the
common for those in authority ; the impertinence of the
slaves and the offensive displays of the parvenus and
vain women ;[2] in a word, at the results of the democratic
theory which had sought, so far as possible, to permit
men ζῆν ὥς τις βούλεται.   The backing of a Macedonian
garrison was necessary, but with it Demetrius did not
hesitate to impose, for the first time in nearly three
hundred years, a set of sumptuary laws upon uncon-
ventional, liberty- and pleasure-loving Athens.[3]   By
prohibiting the excessive indulgence of various tastes,
moreover, he thought it possible to lessen private
extravagances, and thus improve the economic condition
of the citizens.

The natural feeling of grief for the dead had called
forth in the Greek Middle Ages a display of pomp
and anguish at funerals equally offensive to good taste
and to democratic sentiment.   Solon had, accordingly,
sought to check such abuses by legislation.   His laws
became ineffectual at the same time with the Areopagus,
which had been empowered to enforce them, and during
the latter half of the fifth and the entire fourth century
B.C. there had been an ever-increasing rivalry between
Athenian families to keep alive the memory of their
dead by wonderfully beautiful, but ruinously costly,
grave monuments.   A man's burial often required a

---

[1] Carystius in Athen. xii. 542 ; cf. Phaedrus, v. 1, and Droysen, ii. 2. 107.

[2] Of this licence there is abundant evidence in the New Comedy.   Two
slaves might stop a citizen and solicit, almost as a right, his decision in a
matter of dispute between them (Menander, *Epitr.* 1 ff.).

[3] See, however, Duris, *loc. cit.* : ὁ τοῖς ἄλλοις τιθέμενος θεσμοὺς Δημήτριος
καὶ τοὺς βίους τάττων ἀνομοθέτητον ἑαυτῷ τὸν βίον κατεσκεύαζεν.

greater outlay of money than did many years of his life.[1] This Demetrius, like his master Theophrastus, found objectionable and accordingly remedied. No such extravagances were to be allowed in the future, and the terraces and retaining walls in the Cerameicus, which had served to set apart plots for the use, glorification, and ruination of various families, were in some cases taken down, and forbidden altogether for the future.[2] It was a severe blow to Attic art; for the Athenian tombstones, unlike those in the Campo Santo at Genoa, to which a similar vanity has given rise, were models of ethical restraint and of simple grace, and their prohibition destroyed in part the private demand for sculptures. None the less, solvent citizens were of more value to Athens than beautiful sepulchres. Scope was still left for seemly piety, since the law of Demetrius allowed the erection of a round column, a simple slab, or a graceful vase, but nothing more elaborate or more expensive.[3] It likewise forbade extravagant displays at funerals, and required that burial take place before daybreak.[4] Another provision limited to thirty the number of guests at marriages, dinner-parties, and similar private festivities;[5] another forbade women to make other than a modest appearance abroad;[6] and had we the entire code, or any considerable fraction of it, we should doubtless find many of a similar tenor. All of these enactments disclose an interest in the material welfare of the propertied classes of Attica, for which he had chief

---

[1] Böckh, *Staatshaushaltung der Athener*, i.[3] 146. For the family character of these monuments, and the work of Demetrius in closing this period of activity in the Cerameicus, see A. Brückner, *Ath. Mitt.*, 1908, p. 193, and *Der Friedhof am Eridanos*. This measure was probably a Peripatetic prescription, *Klio*, xi. (1911), p. 269.

[2] Cicero (*loc. cit.* below) alludes to the *amplitudines sepulcrorum, quas in Ceramico videmus*—the meaning of which has been discovered by A. Brückner, *op. cit.* 25 ff.

[3] Cic. *De leg.* ii. 64-66 "funerum sepulchrorumque magnificentiam sumptumque minuit. sepulchris autem novis finivit modum; nam super terrae tumulum noluit quidquam statui nisi columellam tribus cubitis ne altiorem aut mensam aut labellum et huic procurationi certum magistratum praefecerat."

[4] Spangenberg, *op. cit.* 13.

[5] Philochorus, vii. (*FHG*. i. 408) in Athen. vi. 245 c.

[6] See below, ii. 46, n. 1.

regard. One important section of the new code was thus made up of the sumptuary laws,[1] and in it the spirit of the teaching of Theophrastus was clearly manifested. The same was the case with another—that dealing with real property. What Theophrastus had urged upon the ideal legislator—the public registration of all transfers—Demetrius did not indeed enact, but he took other measures to accomplish the same purpose, and thereby reduce the embarrassing uncertainty which often existed in Athens as to the titles or liabilities of property. What his remedies were we cannot say definitely, but perhaps it was required that the originals of all contracts involving the testamentary disposition, sale, donation, or mortgaging of houses or land should be dated precisely and deposited with reliable third parties. Certainly the copies published during the next decade or two in Attica and in the cleruchies exhibited significant changes in these particulars. His aim here, which was obviously to protect business men in making investments, was accordingly consistent with his general policy. In other respects the nature of the revision is not known. The entire code was promulgated in the year 316/5 B.C.[2] It superseded, not simply the existing laws, but probably also such decrees as had been passed to cover cases where the laws were inapplicable, or not sufficiently explicit. This done, Demetrius had to arrange for the observance of the new code. Chronic violations were to be anticipated from two quarters, firstly from wilful magistrates and the whimsical popular assembly. To be sure there was already a means established for checking lawlessness of this kind. A magistrate was bound to give a strict accounting for his acts both monthly to the auditors of the senate, and at the expiry of his annual term before special Boards of magistrates and a jury court. This scrutiny was intended particularly to ensure honesty in the administration of public funds, and we do not hear that Demetrius

---

[1] Beloch (iii. 1. 152, n. 3) minimizes unduly the weight of this part of the work of Demetrius.   [2] See *Klio*, xi. (1911), p. 265.

changed it in any particular. Even more rigorous, perhaps, was the summary executive and judicial procedure (*eisangelia*) devised not simply against public men who were lawless, disloyal, or dishonest, but also against private citizens accused of similar offences. There can be no doubt that it had been much abused of late, particularly by Lycurgus, who had prosecuted his adversaries by means of it with great ferocity. This method of control Demetrius did not abolish, for the state continued to need an effective safeguard against political offenders; but he raised the minimum of jurors competent to decide such cases from one thousand to fifteen hundred[1]—a change all the more significant in view of the disfranchisement of the poor. It helped to prevent the predominance of any but the aristocratic party in the courts which were wont to render verdicts on political grounds. The responsibility for an illegal decree, moreover, had been from of old fastened upon the mover of it, and the famous *graphe paranomon* had transferred the decision as to his guilt or innocence to the jury courts. In other words, final action upon a proposal was suspended till a judicial decision had been reached as to its legality. This worked no serious injury when local questions were involved; though a large body of ordinary citizens, whose judgment was subject to political or other influences quite foreign to the case, was not the best conceivable party to settle problems of constitutional law. Where, however, the questions required prompt diplomatic or military action, nothing could be more harmful. The remedy for these evils was taken by Demetrius from the repertory of Aristotle.[2] He established a committee of seven *nomophylaces*,[3] or guardians of the laws, who were doubtless chosen by election from all the citizens, and whose prestige was strengthened by their being given the insignia of priests, and prominent positions at religious festivals

---

[1] *Lex Cantabr.* Nauck, p. 350 ; cf. Spangenberg, *op. cit.* 17.
[2] Arist. *Politics*, iv. 11. 9, 12. 8, vi. 5. 13 ; cf. P.-W. iv. 2828.
[3] See *Klio*, xi. (1911), p. 271 ff.

and processions. "They compelled the magistrates to use the laws," says Philochorus, "and took their seats with the presiding officers at the meetings of the ecclesia and senate to prevent anything being done to the detriment of the city." We have no means of ascertaining the effect of this innovation, unless the paucity of decrees published during the next ten years is. attributable to this cause; but it is difficult to imagine how Demetrius could have devised a less ob-jectionable method of controlling effectively the popular assembly. The guardians of the laws had the main ele-ments of strength which had led to the aggrandizement of the ephors at Sparta, and it is easy to understand that the Board was abolished on the restoration of the democracy in 307 B.C. It had probably been monopolized by the aristocratic friends of Demetrius.

The second quarter from which chronic violations of the new code were to be anticipated was from private citizens, to whom its most striking feature, the series of sumptuary enactments, was likely to be very objectionable. A new magistracy was, apparently, demanded for its enforcement. Again the recommenda-tions of Aristotle were adopted,[1] and a Board of *gynaeconomi*, or "regulators of women," was con-stituted.[2] Despite their name, their duties were as

[1] Aristotle, *Pol.* iv. 12. 9, vi. 5. 13 ; Martini, P.-W. iv. 2828.

[2] Philochorus, *Frg.* 143 ; Timocles (Koch, *Comicorum Atticorum fragmenta*, ii. 465. 32) and Menander (Koch, iii. 78. 272) in Athen. vi. 245 B ; Plautus, *Aulul.* 498 ff. :—

> nulla igitur dicat : equidem dotem ad te adtuli
> maiorem multo quam tibi erat peculia.
> enim mihi quidem aequomst purpuram atque aurum dari,
> ancillas, mulos, muliones, pedisequos,
> salutigerulos pueros, vehicla qui vehar.
> *Euc.*   ut matronarum hic facta pernovit probe
> moribus praefectum mulierum hunc factum velim.

Idem, Most. 941, where there is a reference to the *gynaeconomi* in the words : "Nisi forte factu's praefectus novos, qui res alienas procures, quaeras, videas, audias." Cf. Fredershausen's interpretation (*De iure Plautino et Terentiano*, Diss., Gött. 1906, p. 53). Cf. also Hüffner (*De Plauti comoediarum exemplis Atticis quaest. max. chronol.*, Diss., Gött. 1894, pp. 61, 65) ; [Plato], *Axiochus*, 367'A ; cf. below, iii. 129, n. 1 ; Menander, *Fab. inc.* i. 9 ; Cic. *De leg.* iii. 66, quoted above, ii. 42, n. 3 ; Thalheim, P.-W. ii. 632, ii. 1529. Thalheim here admits a late extension of the jurisdiction of the Areopagus ; cf. Wilamowitz, *op. cit.* ii. 188. It had this enlarged jurisdiction in 318 B.C. ; see above, i. 36 ; Martini, P.-W. iv. 2826 ; Spangenberg, *op. cit.* 11 ; Böckh, *Kleine Schriften*, v. 421 ff ; Philippi, *Areopag und Epheten*, 308 ; Meier und Schömann (Lipsius),

extensive as the laws themselves, and they accordingly looked in at banquets, counted guests, examined sepulchral monuments, checked debauchery, and made general inquisition into the private life of citizens. Their title, however, was not inappropriate, since no small part of their work was to prevent the extravagances of women in the matter of dress, servants, and equipages—at least to stop them from appearing in public with garments of purple and ornaments of gold, in fancy carriages drawn by mules or horses and accompanied by coachmen, lackeys, pages, and maids ; for such displays seem to have been prohibited by the legislation of Demetrius.[1] The *gynaeconomi* had full authority to impose fines, but the larger questions involved in the sumptuary laws, and in all probability any judicial decisions, were reserved for the Areopagus,[2] to which the old censorial powers were thus in part restored. This was as Isocrates and men of his way of thinking had advocated ;[3] and so influential did the Areopagus become that Demetrius took an early opportunity to abandon the generalship for a year, and by taking the archonship in its stead to qualify for membership in it.

So far as we can judge from the few sections known to us, the so-called sumptuary laws of Demetrius took cognisance of acts regulated by fashion and not by ingrained social custom. In other words, they dealt with practical problems, and the legislation had all the

i. 108 ff. ; Wachsmuth, *Die Stadt Athen*, ii. 1. 390, n. 2 ; de Sanctis, 4. de Sanctis puts the establishment of the *gynaeconomi* in 321 B.C. ; Busolt, *Griech. Staatsalter.* 190.

[1] Plautus, *Aulul.* 498 ff. ; cf. above, ii. 45, n. 2. That Plautus reflects Attic usage here is obvious. It is also clear from Aristotle (*Pol.* iv. 12. 9, p. 1300, vi. 5. 13, p. 1323) that the purpose of the *gynaeconomi* was primarily to regulate the ἔξοδοι of the women. Phylarchus (Athen. xii. 521 B) mentions a Syracusan law which prescribed : τὴν ἐλευθέραν μὴ ἐκπορεύεσθαι ἡλίου δεδυκότος ἐὰν μὴ μοιχευθησομένην, ἐκωλύετο δὲ καὶ ἡμέρας ἐξιέναι ἄνευ τῶν γυναικονόμων, ἀκολουθούσης αὐτῇ μιᾶς θεραπαινίδος. The regulations issued by the *gynaeconomi* are probably meant, not the consultation of the officials on each occasion. Lycurgus had introduced a law at Athens forbidding women to go ἐπὶ ζεύγους in the procession to Eleusis at the time of the Mysteries ὅπως μὴ ἐλαττῶνται αἱ δημοτικαὶ ὑπὸ τῶν πλουσίων. [Plut.], *Lives of the Ten Orators*, 842 A. Aelian, *Var. hist.* xiii. 24.

[2] Philochorus, *Frg.* 143 (*FHG.* i. 408) ; Menander, *Fab. inc.* i. 9 ; [Plato], *Axiochus*, 367 A. Cf. above, i. 36, ii. 45, n. 2 ; below, iii. 129, n. 1.

[3] Isocrates, *Areopagiticus*, 36 ff.

more hope of success in that it co-operated with a natural inclination to avoid unnecessary expenditures— an inclination which was reinforced before many years had passed, by the economic decay of Athens.[1] It was not till one hundred and fifty years later that a faint beginning was made with a larger outlay on grave monuments, and the law which regulated their form was not abrogated then or for a long time afterwards.[2]

Technically, Demetrius was *epimeletes*,[3] or super-intendent of the state. That is to say, he occupied in Athens the same position which the Athenian high-commissioners had occupied in the cleruchies on Lemnos,[4] a position, moreover, which did not disqualify him from holding a regular office at the same time ; and for year after year he was elected general of Athens,[5] and, in

---

[1] For the work of Demetrius in relieving paupers see Plut. *Aristides*, 27. For his interest in the welfare of citizens see Polybius, xii. 13. 10.

[2] See below, vii. *ca.* 286.

[3] He is called ἐπιστάτης by Strabo (ix. 398) and by Diodorus (xx. 45. 5) where, however, we have simply : οὗτος μὲν οὖν ἔτη δέκα τῆς πόλεως ἐπιστατήσας ἐξέπεσεν. Polybius (xii. 13. 9) speaks of him as προστάτης, but this is simply as προστάτης τοῦ δήμου.

The only place in which the formal title of Demetrius is to be expected is in Diodorus, xviii. 74. 3, where the terms of the convention made between Athens and Cassander in 317 B.C. are given. It is there said : συνέθεντο . . . καταστῆσαι δ᾿ ἐπιμελητὴν τῆς πόλεως ἕνα ἄνδρα Ἀθηναῖον ὃν ἂν δόξῃ Κασσάνδρῳ . . . οὗτος δὲ παραλαβὼν τὴν ἐπιμέλειαν τῆς πόλεως ἦρχεν εἰρηνικῶς καὶ πρὸς τοὺς πολίτας φιλανθρώπως. The same title is used again in Diodorus, xx. 45. 2 Διονύσιος ὁ καθεστάμενος ἐπὶ τῆς Μουνυχίας φρούραρχος καὶ Δημήτριος ὁ Φαληρεὺς ἐπιμελητὴς τῆς πόλεως γεγενημένος ὑπὸ Κασσάνδρου. Cf. Paus. i. 25. 6 ; Plut. *Demetr.* 8 ; Athen. xii. 542 F.

The advantage of being *epimeletes* was that an *epimeleia* could be combined with any regular office. It was, moreover, as uninvidious and colourless a title as that of *princeps* in Rome. Nor was it foreign to Macedonian experience, since it was with this title that Hieronymus of Cardia subsequently governed Thebes for Demetrius Poliorcetes (Plut. *Demetr.* 39). Moreover, Cassander himself put Megalopolis under an *epimeletes* only two years later (Diod. xix. 64. 1).

It is, of course, possible that *epimeletes* (or *epistates*) is descriptive and not technical. In this case the only official designation of Demetrius is *strategus* ; cf. below, n. 5. On the other hand, it is highly improbable, both in itself and because of the terms of the treaty with Cassander, that Demetrius was destitute of a constitutional, and hence defined, position in the Macedonian state. According to the later usage of the Seleucid, Ptolemaic, Attalid, Macedonian, and Rhodian empires (Holleaux, *BCH.*, 1893, p. 52 ff. ; Cardinali, *Il Regno di Pergamo*, 237 f. ; Ditt. *OGIS.* 254 ; *IG.* xii. 5. 2, 1061) the holder of such a position in an autonomous city was normally called *epistates.* Hence Strabo and Diodorus, in designating Demetrius *epistates*, interpret his position correctly, but do not aim at antiquarian precision. His real title is preserved to us only in the treaty.

[4] Michel, *Recueil des inscr. grecques*, 160, 161.

[5] At the time of *IG.* ii. 1217 (Ditt. *Syll.*[2] 165) Demetrius was in his fourth generalship. This was probably 314/3 B.C. See *JHS.*, 1910, p. 193. In 309/8

all probability, hoplite-general, or commander-in-chief. He is accused of having neglected the Athenian army, and this charge is probably correct in that Demetrius admitted to the ephebe corps, and through it to the citizen army, not all the free inhabitants, as had earlier been the case, but only those who had the citizenship.[1] But this innovation can hardly have been unwise or unpopular. It freed the poorer classes from the severe obligation of giving two years of their lives to other than industrial pursuits : and that military training was regarded as a hardship, we have ample proof in the falling away of the ephebe corps when service in it was made voluntary. The militia was thus reduced in strength, but the superintendent probably increased, rather than diminished, the number of the mercenaries in the employ of the state.[2] At the opening of his régime he maintained a fleet of at least twenty warships.[3] It was a small squadron in comparison with that kept ready for action ten years earlier; but the battle of Amorgos had come in the interval, and there were only two alternatives at this time—a fleet capable of ruling the sea, and one sufficient for suppressing piracy and the wanton attacks of the other independent city-states. The first, Demetrius wisely regarded as beyond the financial and military capacity of Athens, while towards

---

B.C. he was archon, but in 308/7 B.C. he was again general (Polyaenus, iv. 7. 6). We have no information as to the office he held in 313/2-310/9 B.C., but the war then in progress (see below, ii. 51 ff.) makes it altogether probable that he was also general.

The inscription published in Ditt. *Syll.*[2] 164 is a decree of the *deme* Aexone in honour of Demetrius. It reads : καὶ εἰ[ρήνην κατηργάσατο ᾿Α]θηναίοις καὶ τεῖ χώ[ραι, καὶ . . . . αἱρ]εθεὶς ὑπὸ τοῦ δήμ[ου - - νόμους] ἔθ[η]κεν καλ[λίστους. Cf. Wilhelm, *GGA.*, 1898, p. 223, n. 3. Since he obtained the office designated in the lacuna at the hands of the *demos*, it was not the one to which he was appointed by Cassander in accordance with the convention quoted above. Hence, even if ἐπιμελητής is a possible restoration, as Wilhelm (*GGA.*, 1903, p. 784) affirms, it is not so acceptable as that given by de Sanctis (15), στρατηγός, since, if the inscription belongs to 314/3 B.C., Demetrius must really have been general in 317/6 B.C., the year of his legislation. On the other hand, νομοθέτης is also possible, but I am inclined to think that if his position as codifier of the laws was involved he would have been designated ἀναγραφεὺς τῶν νόμων.

[1] Duris in Athen. xii. 542 c (*FHG.* ii. 475). στρατιῶται is used by Duris, but it is hardly technical. Martini (P.-W. iv. 2822, 2824) disputes the truth of the charge of Duris. For the matter of the ephebes see Sundwall, *Acta*, 22 ff. Cf. below, iii. 128, and de Sanctis, 4, n. 5.

[2] Diod. xx. 45. 2.

[3] See the passage of Diodorus cited in ii. 51, n. 3 below.

the latter he was favourably disposed because of his general predilection for peace.[1]

The understanding with Cassander was essential for the maintenance of Demetrius in Athens, and yet it was the cause of most of his difficulties. He joined hands cheerfully in the restoration of Thebes in 316 B.C.; and, considering the circumstances under which the city was destroyed nineteen years before, we are not surprised to learn that the walls were rebuilt for the most part by the Athenians.[2] Co-operation in this undertaking was popular in Athens, but it was otherwise with the great struggle with Antigonus, which began in the following year; for this ruler, after his victory over Eumenes, drove Seleucus out of Babylon, and disclosed the ambition of restoring the unity of Alexander's empire. In the prosecution of this purpose he began the conquest of Phoenicia in the spring of 315 B.C., and not long afterwards issued a declaration in favour of the independence and autonomy of the Greeks.[3] The promise of assistance, implicit in this pronouncement, encouraged the Athenians on Lemnos (and Imbros) to free themselves from the control of Demetrius and Cassander, which, doubtless, had been accompanied by restrictions upon popular freedom in the cleruchy similar to those existent in the metropolis. Accordingly, they cut themselves loose from the mother city in the spring or early summer of 314 B.C.[4] Athens was concerned at the loss

---

[1] An expedition led by Thymochares of Sphettus against the pirate Glaucetes in 315/4 B.C. is referred to in *IG.* ii. 331 (Ditt. *Syll.*[2] 213. 10); cf. also Plautus, *Bacchides*, 279 ff.; *Menaechmi*, 344.

[2] Diod. xix. 54. 1 ff.   [3] *Ibid.* xix. 58. 1, 61. 3.

[4] The time results from Diod. xix. 56. 4, 58. 1 ff., 66 ff.; cf. Beloch, iii. 1. 126, n. 3. Asander, satrap of Caria, gave the Athenians ships and money for their needs (Wilhelm, *Annual of the British School in Athens*, vii. 156). In return he was rewarded with praise, citizenship, maintenance in the *prytaneum*, and an equestrian statue, in January 313 B.C. Hence the service was rendered in 314 B.C. at the latest. He probably came to Greece to get the troops which Cassander put at the disposal of Prepelaus and him in the fall of 314 B.C., and, while on his way back to Caria, joined Aristotle in his first attack on Lemnos. In 315/14 B.C., on the other hand, Thymochares of Sphettus had charge of the Athenian fleet (Ditt. *Syll.*[2] 213. 10). Hence the year of the expedition to Lemnos was 314/13 B.C. It is also under the archonship of Nicodorus (314/13 B.C.) that Diodorus mentions the enterprise.

As is well known, the Delian *hieropoei* let the lands of the temple entrusted to their care for ten-year periods. One of these began in the archonship of Sosisthenes (*BCH.*, 1903, p. 64 ff.; cf. *BCH.*, 1905, p. 438 ff.), which, according

of her colony, Macedon at its junction to Antigonus;
hence, at the request of Cassander, Demetrius at once
despatched his fleet to Lemnos under the command of a
certain Aristotle. The twenty Athenian ships, together
with an Egyptian squadron under Seleucus, after failing
to intimidate the Lemnians into abandoning Antigonus,
landed troops, devastated the country, and blockaded
the city closely. This done, Seleucus sailed away to
Cos, whereupon Dioscorides, who had been sent, after
the fall of Tyre in 314 B.C., to the aid of the islanders
with the main fleet of Antigonus, took advantage of the
isolation of Aristotle to fall upon him with irresistible
force.[1] The Athenian ships were mostly[2] captured,
crews and all, and Lemnos was lost to Athens.[3] Imbros
was equally involved in the disaster,[4] for the democrats
were beyond doubt a majority among the Athenians
there, as on Lemnos, and, for that matter, in the capital
itself, and they inclined towards Antigonus for the same
reason that their opponents held to Cassander—that
upon his assistance depended their control of the island.
Delos, where Demetrius had gained a chariot race,
perhaps as late as the spring of 314 B.C.,[5] broke away
from Athens at the same time.[6] It had been retained
hitherto by force; now the Delians took charge of their
own affairs, and of the administration of the temple of

---

to my chronology (*JHS.*, 1910, p. 192 ff.), coincides with 253 B.C. The first
ten-year period, however, did not begin till some time in the neighbourhood of
300 B.C. See Dürrbach, *BCH.*, 1911, pp. 19, and especially 31, n. 2. Between
then and 314 B.C. three periods of irregular lengths elapsed, one of which was
of five years duration and another seemingly of four. The liberation of Delos
may, none the less, be dated with certainty in 314 B.C.; for this conclusion is
altogether independent of the Delian archon-list, since we now know (*IG.*, xii.
8. 18) that the island was still Athenian in July 314 B.C. See below, v. 189, n. 1.

[1] Diod. xix. 68. 3 ff.   [2] *IG.* ii. 268.
[3] Some time between 314 and 307 B.C. *IG.* xii. 8. 7 was passed.
[4] During the period of independence which followed (314–307) *IG.* xii. 8.
47-48 were passed. Imbros retained the Attic *demes* unchanged, and rounded
out the cleruch government by establishing offices identical with those in
Athens. Thus, in *IG.* xii. 8. 47, an Imbrian *polemarch*, designated by lot, is
mentioned. From *IG.* xii. 8. 48 we may infer that soldiers from Imbros fought
with Antigonus in the wars.   [5] See above, ii. 47, n. 5.
[6] For the date see Homolle, *Les Archives de l'intendance sacrée à Delos* (*Bibl.
des écoles françaises*, 49) 34 ; cf. above, ii. 49, n. 4 ; *BCH.*, 1905, p. 434 ff., where
the temple records for the first year of the Delian administration are published ;
1907, p. 208 ff., and 1911, p. 17 ff. Dürrbach's view, however, that the
League of the Islanders existed from 314 B.C. is hardly proven ; cf. *JHS.*, 1910,
p. 200. 51.

Apollo, which gave to the island its chief value.   The new régime immediately cancelled all contracts made by the *amphictyones* with Athenian citizens, and these were probably expelled altogether.   Athens was not to regain Delos for one hundred and forty-eight years.

We have no means of measuring the impression which the loss of Lemnos, Imbros, and Delos produced in Athens, but it was, doubtless, very great,[1] and, without the knowledge of Demetrius, word was sent to Antigonus requesting him to come and free the city.[2]   In the early half of the following year (313 B.C.) a half-hearted effort for peace was made by Cassander and Antigonus, but after a conference at the Hellespont the two generals separated to renew the struggle.   Cassander went to Greece with a powerful army and thirty ships, and began the siege of Oreus, on the island of Euboea.[3]   Two fleets of Antigonus, one hundred and twenty strong, came to its rescue, and burned four of Cassander's vessels, and nearly destroyed the whole of them.   The main fleet of Cassander had, apparently, made its rendezvous at the Piraeus.   At any rate, the Athenian citizens were compelled to man their vessels and to start, under the leadership of Thymochares of Sphettus,[4] with their allies to the aid of Cassander.   Their arrival apparently destroyed the naval superiority of Antigonus, since he lost four ships in the skirmish which followed ; and, accordingly, he sent Polemaeus with a second fleet of one hundred and fifty ships, on which were five thousand infantry and five hundred cavalry, to draw Cassander from Oreus by threatening Chalcis.   The manœuvre was successful ; for Cassander, though he had forced all his allies present at Oreus, except the Athenians, to disembark and join in the siege operations,[5] was unable to capture the place before the risk of losing Chalcis became so great that he withdrew to meet Polemaeus, who,

[1] Perhaps *IG*. ii. 1217 (Ditt. *Syll.*[2] 165) was dedicated almost immediately after the Panathenaea of July 314 B.C., since, if it came later, there would be some unhappiness in mentioning the Delia.

[2] Diod. xix. 78. 4.   [3] *Ibid.* xix. 75. 7.

[4] He succeeded Aristotle, and was thus in a position to lead the expedition in 313/12 B.C.   [5] *IG*. ii. 331 (Ditt. *Syll.*[2] 213. 15).

thereupon, beached his ships and secured himself behind fortifications thrown up on the continental side of the Euripus.[1] Antigonus then displayed the point of his chief offensive.[2] He recalled his fleet from Greece (313 B.C.), and by threatening to cross the Hellespont with his main army, forced Cassander to return to Macedon. This Cassander did, but on the way he took Oropus and Boeotia. Polemaeus, who had remained behind in Europe with an army, now (fall of 313 B.C.) had a free hand; and since he came, as it seemed, to liberate the Greeks, not to give them a new master, he achieved a series of important successes. Chalcis came into his hands; he reconquered Oropus, won over Carystus and Eretria, and marched into Attica. The Athenians were in collusion with him, and when he drew near, they forced Demetrius to make a truce, and send an embassy to secure admission for the city into the League of which Antigonus was the head.[3] Since Boeotia, Phocis, and Locris were then overrun by Polemaeus, and it was expected that Antigonus would attack Macedon in person in the following spring (312 B.C.)—after having secured his rear against Ptolemy of Egypt by leaving his son, afterwards surnamed Poliorcetes, with some twenty thousand men in Syria—we may be sure that Demetrius of Phalerum spent an anxious winter in Athens.[4] We do not need to narrate here how the inability of Demetrius Poliorcetes to cope with Ptolemy in the spring of 312 B.C., and his defeat at Gaza, ruined the plans of Antigonus. The invasion of Europe was abandoned; the general of Antigonus in the Peloponnesus lost confidence in his master and revolted. Polemaeus was forced to spend the year 312 B.C. in trying to check this defection, and Cassander

[1] Diod. xix. 77. 5 ; cf. Beloch, iii. 1. 130.
[2] Kromayer, *Hist. Zeitsch.* c. p. 50.   [3] Diod. xix. 78. 4.
[4] It occurred to me that the government of Demetrius irregularly intercalated a month in this year with a view to preventing a change of magistrates in this unsettled time ; cf. the table given in *Class. Phil.*, 1908, p. 386. Sund-wall, however (*Öfversigt af Finska Vetenskaps-Societetens Förhandlingar*, lii. 1909-1910, Afd. B, No. 3, p. 17), by a new restoration of the prescript of *IG.* ii. 236, makes 313/12 B.C. an ordinary, and not an intercalary year ; and an un-published inscription in the possession of Kirchner (*Berl. phil. Woch.*, 1910, p. 1332) shows him to be right.

was able to retrieve, at least morally, his position in
Greece. The negotiations of Demetrius of Phalerum
with Antigonus thus came to nothing; and since it was
now apparent that Antigonus was unable to subdue the
other generals, and it was unnecessary for them to
destroy him, a general peace was easily arranged in
311 B.C.[1]

During the following four years (311–307 B.C.) we
know of no conflict in which Athens took part; nor, in
spite of various threatening incidents, did anything
occur to affect seriously the relations of the generals.
Cassander, indeed, murdered the young king Alexander,
and connived at the death of his bastard brother Heracles,
but the shock thereby given to public opinion was more
than balanced by the removal of all rival claimants to
the throne of Macedon. Thus for four years Athens had
complete peace. There was none to question seriously
the political supremacy of Demetrius of Phalerum, and
the gradual strengthening of Cassander's position suppressed the unrest manifest in the city in 314 and
313 B.C. The appointment of the regent, in the first
instance, had not been followed by the persecution of
his political opponents, and, so far as we are aware, no
distinguished Athenians were forced into exile at that
time. A general amnesty was obviously one of the
conditions arranged in 317 B.C., and to it Demetrius
adhered strictly. There is nothing in the character of
Cassander to suggest that he was the advocate of gentle-
ness and moderation ; and there was much in the recent
experience of the Athenian aristocrats and moderates to
make them clamorous for revenge. The relatives and
friends of those executed in 318 B.C. were indisposed to
let bygones be bygones; but the most they could get
was the satisfaction of seeing the murderers of Phocion
overtaken by private calamities. They could not even
get the sentence against their old leader rescinded. The
amnesty was, doubtless, the work of Demetrius himself,
and after having advised clemency in the crisis, he would
not tolerate harshness in the sequel ; hence Demochares,

---

[1] Ditt. *OGIS*. 5 ; cf. Diod. xix. 105. 3.

the nephew of Demosthenes, Stratocles of Diomeia, and other prominent democrats remained in Athens with their party. Nor did the correspondence with Antigonus and Polemaeus inaugurate a reign of terror, but the Phalerian was mild, urbane, and conciliatory as before. The foreign storms seemed over and the Athenians generally reconciled to the domestic situation. So untroubled, in fact, had the political horizon become in 309 B.C. that Demetrius ventured to lay down the generalship, which he had probably held hitherto,[1] and to take in its stead the archonship. This was, doubtless, with a view to carrying out reforms in the institutions with which this office was connected most intimately. Possibly it was during his archonship that he made an enumeration of the people,[2] the first recorded instance of a complete census in the history of Greece ; at any rate, it was probably in the period of security which followed the peace of 311 B.C. that this was done. It was discovered that there were in Attica twenty-one thousand citizens and ten thousand foreign residents, or, including their families, from one hundred to one hundred and twenty-five thousand persons. The returns for the slave population have not come down to us,[3] but the number of slaves perhaps equalled the total of citizens and aliens combined. This represents a total population of about two hundred or two hundred and

---

[1] See above, ii. 47, n. 5.

[2] Ctesicles in Athen. vi. 272 B (*FHG.* iv. 375) ἐξετασμὸν - - τῶν κατοι-κούντων τὴν ᾿Αττικήν. Martini (P.-W. iv. 2827) refuses to fix upon an exact date.

[3] See below, ii. 64, n. 8. The traditional figure (Ctesicles, *loc. cit.*) is 400,000 (οἰκετῶν δὲ μυριάδας μ´), which has been proved over and over again to be false ; cf. Ed. Meyer, *Forsch. zur alten Geschichte*, ii. 185 ff. ; Beloch, *Bevölk. der griech. röm. Welt*, 84, 4 ff., 57 ff. In 321/18 B.C. there were but 9000 citizens. What could they have done against 400,000 slaves ? The conditions in Athens would have been far worse than in Sparta, since the Helots never numbered the half of 400,000, and they were not let move about at pleasure like the slaves in Attica. The Athenian slaves never impeded the free action of Athens abroad. Wilamowitz (*op. cit.* ii. 208) interprets the 21,000 as *epitime Athener über 30 Jahre* : Beloch (*op. cit.* 57 ; cf. Meyer, *op. cit.* ii. 168) as all Athenian citizens—those disfranchised in 317 B.C. as well as those left with the franchise—over eighteen years of age. Beloch has strengthened his interpretation materially by a consideration of the army put by Athens into the Hellenic War (Diod. xviii. 11. 3) and of the number of ephebes listed in *IG.* ii. 5. 563b, and 251b. See *Klio*, 1905, p. 349 ff. ; Sundwall, *Acta*, 22 ff.

fifty thousand.[1]   The most important work of Demetrius
as archon,[2] however, was the abolition of the *leiturgies*, or
semi-voluntary public services demanded of the wealthy
men in the state.   Hitherto the expense of providing
choruses for the Dionysia, Lenaea, and Thargelia had
fallen upon individuals ; and as archon, Demetrius had
the duty of nominating three of the richest men available in all Athens to provide funds for the tragic
choruses, and of seeing to it that the tribes, acting singly
or in pairs, presented the twenty-five rich men needed to
finance the presentation of comedies and the dithyrambic
contests of men and boys.[3]   For such a task he had
objections on principle, since the *choregia* laid a heavy
burden upon the men of substance in the community,
upon those whose preservation was the pivotal point in
his statecraft.   Apart from the heavy outlay needed for
providing and training the choruses, there fell upon the
victorious *choregus* the expense of erecting a monument
for the prize tripod, an extra which, in the picturesque
phrasing of Demetrius,[4] was " not the consecration of
victory, but the libation for a dissipated fortune, and
the cenotaph of an abandoned home." Accordingly, he
altered the whole institution, and transferred to the
state the cost of all the choruses.[5]   A similar step had
been taken elsewhere already, notably in the case of the
Dionysiac procession.   Its *epimeletae,* or superintendents,
had once had to pay the cost out of their own pockets,
but in Aristotle's time [6] they received one hundred *minae*
from the state for this object.   Demetrius went farther
in the same direction, and abolished the *choregia*

---

[1] Beloch (iii. 1. 306) makes the population of the city of Athens at this time *ca.* 100,000 ; that of Attica and its cleruchies (Scyros, Lemnos, Imbros, Samos, and the Thracian Chersonese) in the middle of the fourth century B.C. he computes at from 300,000 to 400,000 ; cf. below, viii. *ca.* 315 f.

[2] Duris, *FHG.* ii. 475.   There is, unfortunately, no ancient report extant as to the time or circumstances of this reform.

[3] Aristotle, *Const. of Athens*, 56. 2 ff.

[4] Plut. *Whether the Athenians were more eminent in war or wisdom*, 5 οὐκ ἀνάθημα τῆς νίκης, ὡς Δημήτριός φησιν, ἀλλ' ἐπίσπεισμα τῶν ἐκκεχυμένων βίων καὶ τῶν ἐκλελοιπότων κενοτάφιον οἴκων.   Cf. Köhler, *Rhein. Mus.*, 1898, p. 492.

[5] See Köhler, *loc. cit.*, and *Ath. Mitt.*, 1878, p. 240 ; Reisch, *De musicis Graecorum certaminibus*, 81 ff. and P.-W. i. 874 ; cf. Martini, P.-W. iv. 2825. There were *choregi* in 317/16 B.C., *IG.* ii. 5. 584*b* ; cf. Capps, *Amer. Jour. Arch.*, 1900, p. 85, n. 1.   [6] Aristotle, *Const. of Athens*, 56. 4.

altogether.   Henceforth a public official, *agonothetes* by
title, was to be elected annually to make the preparations for the Dionysiac contests, and to expend the
moneys to be given therefor out of the public funds.[1]
The work which the various *choregi* had been obliged to
perform the *agonothetes* was the better in a position to
care for, in that the choruses had ceased to be an integral
part of the comedies, and perhaps also of the tragedies.
Hence they need not have been in each case a new composition.   Being at best merely musical and orchestral
interludes, less careful training of the performers was
required ; and since, as will be explained later, this work
was now attended to by professional artists, the concern
of public officials for their training was simply interference.   Accordingly, from the administrative point of
view, the abolition of the *choregi* was quite a simple
matter.   Nor did the reform of Demetrius stop there.
The objections valid in the case of the *choregia* of the
Dionysiac festivals were applicable to the *choregia* of
the Panathenaea, Hephaestia, and, in fact, wherever there
were public contests supported by private enterprise.[2]
The archon had not simply charge of the celebration of
the Dionysia and Thargelia, but he had also some duties
in connexion with the Panathenaea.[3]   Hence Demetrius
was able, without unduly stretching his prerogatives, to
make alterations here also.   With 312/11 B.C. our
series of Panathenaic vases—a fourth-century B.C. revival
of the otherwise abandoned sixth-century black-figured
style—ceases.   This kind of prize was given at the
Great Panathenaea of 310 B.C., but not subsequently.[4]

---

[1] Sundwall, *Acta*, 15 ff.

[2] See Gilbert, *op. cit.* 360 ; Aristotle, *Const. of Athens*, 57. 1 ; *IG.* ii. 553 ;
P.-W. iii. 2418.   [3] Aristotle, *op. cit.* 60. 2.

[4] See now von Brauchitsch, *Die panathenaïschen Preisamphoren*, and for a
complete list of the dated *amphorae* thus far found, Robinson, *Amer. Jour.
Arch.*, 1910, p. 425.   Of the twenty-four in the catalogue fifteen are dated in the
first years of the Olympiad, six in the second, and three in the fourth.   The
archons for the years in which the Great Panathenaea took place were not at
all interested in the vases, those for the following years relatively little, while
those for the years next thereafter are responsible for almost two-thirds of all
the vases extant.   The olive crop for the Great Panathenaic years was, of
course, not harvested at the time the fête was held.   There are no vases extant
for the Great Panathenaea of 358, 354, 342, and 314 B.C.   All other of these
fêtes between 374 and 310 are represented.

The contest of Homeric rhapsodists Demetrius removed
from the Panathenaea and added to the Dionysia, so that
henceforth a branch of the Attic gild of Dionysiac artists
made the epos its specialty ; [1] and it seems probable
that the *athlothetae,* who had hitherto conducted the
Panathenaea, were superseded at this time by an
agonothetes, who, in addition, defrayed with state money
the expense for the Panathenaic choruses hitherto met
by private citizens. [2] Moreover, it devolved upon his
colleague, the king-archon, to nominate a group of rich
men to meet the cost of running the *gymnasia* and
managing the torch-races, which formed an important
part of five or six Athenian festivals. [3] This was a
burden which Aristotle had represented as oppressive
and objectionable ; [4] hence, it was natural for Demetrius
to remove it. At any rate, when these services are
referred to in our records subsequently, [5] they are
rendered by one official who holds a regular annual
magistracy, and, doubtless, administered some public
funds. [6]

The reform of the national festivals thus relieved
the men of means in Attica of a heavy tax, and by
making the fêtes a charge upon the consolidated
revenues, and by extending over a period of years the
outlay hitherto demanded in a lump sum, it prevented
the burden from weighing so heavily upon individuals.
In fact, it is altogether unlikely that the subsidies

[1] Athen. xiv. 620 B τοὺς δὲ νῦν Ὁμηριστὰς ὀνομαζομένους πρῶτος εἰς τὰ θέατρα
παρήγαγε Δημήτριος ὁ Φαληρεύς. Cf. Susemihl, *Gesch. d. griech. Literatur in
der Alexandrinerzeit,* i. 137, n. 681 ; Ostermann, *op. cit.* 43 ; below, vii. *ca.* 290.

[2] The *athlothetae* appear for the last time in our records in 320/19 B.C. (*IG.*
ii. 5. 192c ; Ditt. *Syll.*[2] 500). These officials, who served for four years at a
stretch (Aristotle, *op. cit.* 60. 1), may have held office for 314/13–310/9 B.C.
and have functioned for the last time in July 310 B.C. Cf. *Klio,* 1908, p. 345 ff.
To what the lexicographical notice (ἀγωνοθέτης ὁ ἐν τοῖς σκηνικοῖς· ἀθλοθέτης ὁ ἐν
τοῖς γυμνικοῖς *Lex. Cantab.* in Nauck, *Lex. Vindobonense,* 330 ; cf. Zonar. *Lex.*
19 ; Ammon. Valck. 4 ; *Lex. Bekk.* 333. 28 ; Photius, Suidas, *s.v.* "agonothetes."
Hesychius is slightly different) refers, I do not know. Sundwall thinks that
Demetrius instituted one *agonothetes* for all the fêtes, and that it was not till
229 (rather 232) B.C. that others were established. See, however, *Klio,* 1908,
p. 345 ff.

[3] Arist. *Const. of Athens,* 57. 1.

[4] *Politics,* v. 7. 11, p. 1309 a.

[5] *IG.* ii. 5. 614b (Ditt. *Syll.*[2] 192) 53. (240/39 B.C.) ; Teles (Hense[2]) 50.
(*ca.* 240 B.C.) ; Ἐφ. Ἀρχ., 1897, p. 42 ff., No. 13 (224/3 B.C.).

[6] See Daremberg et Saglio, *s.v.* "Lampadedromia," "Gymnasiarchia."

granted to the new magistrates occasioned any increase
of taxation, for they were first made at approximately
the same time that the theoric distributions and pay
for *ecclesiastic* duties seem to have been abolished :
and, what was more important, they were granted first
after Athens had ceased to have a great navy to build
and keep in repair. In fact, the abolition of the *choregia*
followed closely after, if it did not actually accompany,
the abolition of the *trierarchia*,[1] which by means of
the *symmory*-system had placed the chief burden for
the maintenance of the fleet upon the same class which
benefited through being relieved of the cost of the
festivals. The reduction of the fleet from three hundred
to less than thirty ships lowered the state's outlay to a
corresponding degree, so that much more than a shifting
of the incidence of taxation was involved. The whole
reform meant the lifting of a terrible incubus from the
backs of the propertied classes.[2]

Demetrius was fortunate in that the peace of the
country and the ebb and flow of its commerce were
hardly disturbed during the ten years of his régime.
The revenues were thus ample for the greatly reduced
expenditure. They reached, according to Duris of
Samos,[3] the total of twelve hundred talents annually ;
in other words, Demetrius raised, without the incentive
of a prospective war, and despite the prostration of a
great military reverse, the same amount as Lycurgus
had collected. It is thus probable that the public and
private wealth of the country was greater in 308 B.C.
than at any time since Aegospotami. In fact, the
prosperity of Attica under Demetrius is admitted by

---

[1] See *Klio*, 1909, p. 317. Theophrastus (*Characters*, xxvi. 6) makes the
oligarch of 319/17 B.C. (for the date see Cichorius in *Theophrasts Charactere,
herausg. v. der philol. Gesellschaft zu Leipzig*, lvii. ff. and Beloch, iii. 2. 364 f.)
say : πότε παυσόμεθα ὑπὸ τῶν λειτουργιῶν καὶ τῶν τριηραρχιῶν ἀπολλύμενοι ; That
his wish was part of the oligarchic programme is likely in this case as in that of
his other *dictum* : ἢ τούτους δεῖ ἢ ἡμᾶς οἰκεῖν τὴν πόλιν. We do not know how
the tetreremes in the possession of Athens in 306 B.C. were handled. They
were apparently destroyed by Cassander in 304 B.C. Subsequently, the city had
merely the shadow of a navy. See below, iv. 158, n. 3 ; v. *ca.* 211 ; vi. *ca.* 272 ;
vii. *ca.* 282.

[2] Daremberg et Saglio, *s.v.* "Leitourgia."

[3] Athen. xii. 542 C (Aelian, *Var. hist.* ix. 9) ; cf. Köhler, *Rhein. Mus.*, 1898,
p. 492, n. 1, and Beloch, iii. 1. 152, n. 2. See above, i. 10.

his most bitter enemies.[1]   Business was active, prices
good, and the supplies of food abundant.   Accordingly,
the regent had funds for a large variety of projects.   It
did not enter into his political programme to glorify
Athens by erecting great public buildings, as Pericles
and Lycurgus had done : his whole legislation was, in
fact, a protest against such extravagances.[2]   Still, he
was not illiberal,[3] and he stood personally in intimate
contact with the high and luxurious culture of his time.
He had the sporting interests of his people, and was
pleased when his horses were victorious in the national
races.[4]   He entertained in regal fashion, and kept open
house[5] for the frail beauties of the Athenian *demimonde*.
His love for magnificence was displayed in the wonderful
Dionysiac procession which he arranged while archon in
308 B.C. ;[6] and his passion for public distinctions—his
pleasure in the numerous crowns and statues offered to
him by the Athenians—was so notorious, that a comic
poet affirmed that he had accepted a statue for every
day of the year.[7]   He thus laid himself open to the
charge of extravagance and of bringing his own legislation into discredit; but it has often been the privilege
and pride of a government to discourage private luxury
while insisting that the public prestige be maintained
without regard to the cost.   Demetrius was indifferent
to the claims of imperial greatness, but he desired Athens
to remain the best place in which men of the world, as
well as of art, science, and letters, could live.   He was
himself an orator of the first rank—the last of the great

---

[1] Demochares in Polybius, xii. 13. 9 ff. (*FHG.* ii. 448) ; Duris in Athen. xii.
542 c (*FHG.* ii. 475) ; cf. Diog. Laert. v. 75.   We learn by a mere accident
that when the Carthaginian navy entered the harbour of Syracuse in 311 B.C.
at the opening of the war with Agathocles, one or more Athenian merchant-
ships were lying at anchor there (Diod. xix. 103. 4).   At the same time, Zeno
of Citium came to Athens with a cargo.   See below, iv. 185, n. 5, and von
Arnim, *Stoic. vet. frag.* i. 3 f.   [2] Cic. *De offic.* ii. 60.

[3] Diog. Laert. v. 75 προσόδοις καὶ κατασκευαῖς ηὔξησε τὴν πόλιν.   A portico
was built by Philo at Eleusis (Vitr. vii. *praef.* 17, *IG.* ii. 834c ; cf. Larfeld,
Handbuch der griech. Epigraphik, ii. 1. 173).   There is nothing to suggest
that Demetrius was close with the public money.   See Plut. *Aristid.* 27.

[4] *IG.* ii. 1217.   [5] Duris, *loc. cit.*

[6] Duris, *loc. cit.* ; cf. Pfuhl, *De Athen. pompis sacr.*, Berlin, 1900, p. 77. 25.

[7] Pliny, *Nat. hist.* xxxiv. 27 ; Nonius, 528 ; Diog. Laert. v. 75 ; cf. Nepos,
Milt. vi. 4 ; Strabo, ix. 398 ; Plut. *Pol. Precepts*, 820 E ; *IG.* ii. 1217 ; Wachsmuth, *Die Stadt Athen*, i. 611 ; Martini, P.-W. iv. 2820 ; Beloch, iii. 1. 154, n. 5.

Attic orators, according to Quintilian,[1] the most learned of them, according to Cicero.[2] He was elegant in his diction, as in his pleasures and clothing—a subtle debater, rather than a passionate public speaker.[3] He was also a man of marked scholarly interests, and was able to associate with his court the most important men of letters in Athens. The great comedian, Menander, was his friend, and to this in part, perhaps, the dramatist owed his unpopularity with the masses,[4] as he certainly did the narrowness of his escape from death or exile when Demetrius was expelled in 307 B.C.[5] Xenophanes, the Academician, was the colleague of Demetrius on an embassy in 322 B.C.,[6] and for another philosopher, Theodorus the atheist, the Phalerian secured an acquittal when he was on trial for impiety.[7] He had thus a general friendship for scientists, but there can be no doubt that his scholarly sympathies were most deeply involved in the institution and activities of his teacher, Theophrastus. Theophrastus was a metic, and hence not in a position to acquire property in Attica. Accordingly, he could not follow the example of Plato,[8] even if he had had the means to do so, and buy a lot of land upon which to establish his school. Hence Demetrius came to his assistance, and the state gave special permission[9] for the association, of which Theophrastus was the head, to purchase a garden in which to erect dwelling-houses, porticoes—from which came its name, the Peripatos—honorary statues, and a shrine of the Muses, which was decorated with an altar, images of the goddesses,

[1] *Inst. orat.* x. 1. 80.

[2] Brutus, 37 ; cf. *De orat.* ii. 95 ; *De rep.* ii. 1.

[3] Cic. *De offic.* i. 3 "disputator subtilis orator parum vehemens, dulcis tamen." Cf. Crönert, *Kolotes*, 45 f., and Kuiper, "De diatribe quadam immerito vindicato Demetrio Phalereo" in *Feestbundel Prof. Boot.*, Leiden, 1901, p. 169 ff., against the view of Blass (*Att. Bereds.*[2] iii. 2. 344 ff.) and Norden (*Ant. Kunstprosa*, i. 127 ff.) that Demetrius was the founder of Asianism.

[4] Phaedrus, v. 1. He gained his first city victory in the year 316/15 B.C., according to the *Parian Chronicle*, and only 8 in all out of a possible of over 100 (Beloch, iii. 1. 513). The victories probably belong to 316/15–308/7 and 301/0–297/6 B.C.

[5] See below, iii. 101, n. 4.   [6] See above, i. 19.

[7] Diog. Laert. ii. 101 ; cf. Kirchner, *PA.* i. p. 228.

[8] Wilamowitz, *Antigonus von Karystos*, 279 ff.

[9] Diog. Laert. v. 39 ; cf. Wilamowitz, *op. cit.* 267. He was doubtless given the rights of ἔγκτησις.

and dedicatory offerings.   The circle of students became,
therewith, a religious club devoted to the service of the
Muses, and the second of the great Attic schools was
legally established and endowed.   At its head was a
life-long officer, who disposed of the property by will to
the successor whom he directly, or indirectly, designated.
It had its priests for the cult of its patron saints, the
Muses; and the older members (*presbyters*) took turns
at proctering the lectures, and arranging for the monthly
dinners.   The control of the school was in the hands of
the life-long superintendent and the *presbyters*.   The
pupils had the privileges of the institution, but could
not hold the higher offices, and were required to contribute one and one-half *drachmae* per month for the
communal dinner.   To this, distinguished visitors or
benefactors of the school might come as guests on the
invitation of the superintendent.   Such was the organization of the primitive universities in Athens.   Like
those of the Middle Ages of Europe—Bologna and Paris,
for example—they were essentially educational gilds.[1]

It is unquestionable that Demetrius was anxious to
make himself popular with his fellow-citizens.   Hence
the studied amiability of his manners, and the profusion
of his public and private hospitality.   But it was a
vain effort.   The very lavishness of his entertaining
and the magnitude of his personal expenditures offended
the sentiment of the populace, and emphasized the fact
that through him it had lost the privileges of self-
government.   His ostentation betrayed constantly the
tyranny.   Nor was this all.   He secured peace and
prosperity, beyond a doubt, but it was at the sacrifice
of Athenian independence; and the neglect of the
fleet,[2] whatever its economic advantages might be,
destroyed all prospect of future liberty, and made
Athens of less value as an ally to friendly powers.
That the city should be permanently in bondage to
Macedon, however, was pleasing only to a small circle

---

[1] For this organization see Wilamowitz, *loc. cit.*, and below, v. *ca.* 215 ff.
[2] For the thirty tetreremes which served with Demetrius Poliorcetes in
306 B.C. see below, iii. 112, n. 5.

of radical aristocrats who had the full confidence of
Demetrius. Furthermore, he had muzzled the popular
assembly ; and his abolition of tribal activities [1] tended
to lessen the participation of the public in politics—both
changes being to the grave disadvantage of democracy.
Consequently, he was regarded both as a tyrant and as
the head of an oligarchy, and the only thing that kept
him in power was the presence in the Piraeus of
Cassander's garrison, and Dionysius, its commandant.[2]

The democrats in Athens had long since abandoned
all correspondence with Polyperchon, whose weak and
unprincipled conduct had brought him into discredit
with everybody ; but they had found a more hopeful
champion in Antigonus. Antigonus had not only proclaimed the freedom of all the Greek cities, but he had
been active for several years in putting his proclamation
into effect. He estimated highly the strength of public
opinion in Greece,[3] and, wherever his arms were victorious,
foreign garrisons, if present, had been thrown out, and
the citizens given charge of their own affairs. That
meant, ordinarily, the restoration of democratic government. The Athenians were thus led, on general grounds,
to look towards him as a deliverer; and, moreover, they
could not forget that only the mischance at Gaza in
312 B.C. had come between them and the liberty which
seemed so near. Antigonus was well aware of the
situation in Athens, and the unexecuted provision of
the peace of 311 B.C., that all the Greek cities should
be free, gave him a constant pretext to drive Demetrius
of Phalerum and Dionysius out of Attica. But for four
years he refused to avail himself of it. However, seeing
that in 308 B.C. Ptolemy of Egypt "freed" Andros,
Corinth, and Sicyon without provoking a universal war,
Antigonus concluded that the time was ripe for inter-

[1] Cf. Wilamowitz, *GGA.*, 1906, p. 614, n. 1, and especially above i.
9, ii. 39.

[2] Between 317 and 307 B.C. there were two Macedonian agents in Athens,
the commandant of the Athenian garrison, and the Athenian political adviser.
When Athens was under Macedonian control subsequently, there was only one
official, who, at first a foreigner but later an Athenian, combined both offices.
He was called στρατηγός (*IG.* ii. 5. 591b). Dionysius, on the other hand, was
simply φρούραρχος.   [3] Ditt. *OGIS.* 5 ; cf. Beloch, iii. 1. 131.

fering in Athens.   Accordingly, he fitted out an expedition of two hundred and fifty ships in the spring of 307 B.C., and put it under the command of his son, Demetrius Poliorcetes,[1] with instructions to liberate Greek cities, and especially to free Athens.   The preparations were made with such secrecy that the young admiral arrived quite unexpectedly off the Piraeus, and, through finding the chain of the harbour undrawn, he was able to sail with twenty ships into the heart of this city[2] without meeting resistance.   A herald then made proclamation from the fleet, explaining the purpose of its coming, whereupon the moment a landing was made the soldiers of Poliorcetes were joined by the citizens in the Piraeus.   Dionysius abandoned the town, but withdrew to his fort on Munychia: Demetrius of Phalerum did likewise, but Athens itself was his destination. There, however, he found nothing but enthusiasm for the son of Antigonus, and the best that he could accomplish was to have himself appointed one of an embassy to obtain from his namesake a guarantee of the city's autonony.   This was easily secured, and along with it a safe escort for himself to Thebes, where he had reason to expect gratitude because of his zeal for its restoration. His most intimate friends likewise left the city, whereupon the democracy was at once restored.

For the moment Dionysius was left blockaded in Munychia while Demetrius Poliorcetes departed to seize Megara.   On his return, about two months later, the fort in the Piraeus was captured by storm, and razed to the ground, and Dionysius himself taken prisoner.   This done, Demetrius Poliorcetes paid his first visit to Athens.[3] His arrival was made the occasion of a great popular demonstration.   For his part, he announced to the assembled people his determination to restore to them the Piraeus, and to leave them free to govern themselves

[1] Associated with him was his more experienced cousin Telesphorus ; cf. below, iii. 101, n. 4.

[2] With twenty ships, according to Polyaenus, iv. 7. 6, the rest having been left in ambush behind Sunium ; cf. Diod. xx. 45 f. ; Plutarch (*Demetr.* 8) mentions 250 ships.   His arrival took place on the 25th of Thargelion (*ca.* June 10th) 307 B.C.

[3] For the chronology of these incidents see below, iii. 96, n. 1-2, and 101, n. 2.

as they saw fit. For their part, the Athenians, on the
motion of Stratocles of Diomeia, voted to erect gold
statues of Antigonus and Demetrius beside those of the
tyrannicides Harmodius and Aristogeiton; to crown each
with a crown worth two hundred talents; to erect for
them an altar where Demetrius first stepped from his
chariot on entering Athens, and to worship them with
annual games,—the Antigonia and Demetria,—a procession, and a sacrifice, as the Saviour Gods; to weave
their likenesses with those of the other gods into the
peplos given in 306/5 B.C., and every fourth year
thereafter to Athena; to confer upon them the title of
king, and to make them the eponymous heroes of two new
tribes, to be named the Antigonis and Demetrias.[1]   At
the same time, but at the suggestion of Demetrius,
according to Plutarch,[2] instructions were given to the
ambassadors who were sent to announce the content of
this decree to Antigonus, that they should ask him for
one hundred and fifty thousand *medimni* of grain and
timber for building one hundred war-ships.   Lemnos
had been free since 314 B.C., and she at once joined the
mother city.   Imbros was, however, in the possession of

---

[1] What happened at this time is stated best by Diod. xx. 46. He omits the
conferring of the regal title; cf. below, iii. 107, n. 4; Plutarch (*Demetr.* 10) agrees
in the main, but he enlarges on the regal title, and inserts a false account of
the substitution of the eponymous archon by the priest of the Soteres.   Then
in §§ 12 and 13 he completes the topic by enumerating the honours which were
conferred upon Demetrius at later times, or foisted on him sportively or
maliciously by the Attic playwrights.   The annual games were, doubtless, called
Demetria and Antigonia.   The Demetria in Athens are mentioned in Plut.
Demetr. 12, and in Duris, *Frg.* 31 (*FHG.* ii. 477) γινομένων δὲ τῶν Δημητρίων
Ἀθήνησιν ἐγράφετο ἐπὶ τοῦ προσκηνίου ἐπὶ τῆς οἰκουμένης ὀχούμενος. They probably
alternated with the Antigonia.   Plutarch (*loc. cit.*) has a record of the substitution of the Dionysia by the Demetria, and, since, from the fragment of
Duris just quoted, it appears that the Demetria were celebrated in the theatre,
they may have accompanied and eclipsed the Dionysia.   Hence, too, the divine
disfavour with the way the Dionysia were celebrated (Plut. *Demetr.* 12).   Being
gods, the ambassadors to them were of course *theori*, and they seem to have
had their sacred triremes, Antigonis and Demetrias (Photius, *s.v.* "Paralus").   A
contest of *paeanes* for Antigonus and Demetrius, in which Hermocles of Cyzicus
won first place, is mentioned by Philochorus (Athen. xv. 697 A; *FHG.* i., *Frg.*
145; cf. Susemihl, ii. 518).   Divine honours, consisting of a sacrifice, *agon*,
procession, and fête (θυσία, ἀγών, στεφανηφορία, πανήγυρις), had been given to
Antigonus at Scepsis prior to 311 B.C.   In 311 B.C., when his suzerainty over
the free cities of Asia was definitely settled, he received, in addition, that part of
the outfit of a god which required a permanent and irrevocable outlay of money
—a *temenos*, altar, and idol (Ditt. *OGIS.* 6, n. 6).   For the statues of the *Soteres*
in Athens see *IG.* ii. 3, 1400.   [2] Demetr. 10.

Antigonus, but he now withdrew his garrison and handed the island over to the Athenians.[1] It may be surmised that Scyros became Athenian at the same time or a little later, since its inhabitants were Athenians like those of Lemnos and Imbros,[2] and had thus a right to be allowed to join the mother country because of the general policy of Antigonus that all Greek cities should be free.[3] This same consideration governed the fate of Delos. Since it did not wish to form part of Athens, Antigonus could not consistently coerce it. It was, of course, equally impossible to restore Samos and Oropus to Athens. Still, all the communities of Athenians were again united, all were freed from foreign garrisons and governors, and, though they had two new gods who were less unreal and more imperious than the Olympians, they had as yet nothing but help and kindness to expect from them. Hence they accepted with genuine satisfaction the congratulations which poured in upon them from all quarters of the Greek world.[4]

The battle of Amorgos and the anti-imperialistic policy of Demetrius of Phalerum contributed much towards what the opening up of the East and the establishment of the new monarchical states had made inevitable—the loss of economic and political power and prestige on the part of Athens. The political decay made itself obvious first, for of this there could be no concealment; while the ten years of peace and military relaxation tended to obscure the shifting of commerce

[1] Diodorus (xx. 46. 4-5) mentions only the restoration of Imbros, because Lemnos was not in the hands of Antigonus at the time. Lemnos was Athenian in 305/4 B.C. (Ditt. *Syll.*[2] 181).

[2] Cf. Meyer, *Gesch. d. Alt.* v. 8. The small islands between Scyros and Magnesia,—Icos, Peparathos, and Sciathos,—though given later on to Athens, were inhabited by Chalcidians, not Athenians. The *demos* of Peparathos gave a crown to Athens in *ca.* 307/6 B.C. (*IG.* ii. 731-732), as did the *demos* of Myrina, Tenedos, Miletus, as well as Ephesus, Colophon, and some place on the Pontus. Athens at this time voted a crown to Lysimachus of Thrace—in return for favours, doubtless. Possibly he had allied himself with Antigonus after Ptolemy and Cassander came to friendly terms with one another in 308 B.C.

[3] For Scyros see Graindor, *Histoire de l'île de Skyros*, 67 ff. According to Graindor (75 f.) the inscription published in Ditt. *Syll.*[2] 383 with the archon Athenion—a Scyrian magistrate—belongs in all probability to the first half of the third century B.C. Fredrich, however, dissents, and on the basis of the lettering, which he has himself studied, he dates it in *ca.* 150 B.C. *IG.* xii. 8, 666 and p. 176.   [4] See above, ii. 65, n. 2.

from the Piraeus to Rhodes, Alexandria, and the eastern cities generally ; and the enormous amount of silver and gold put into circulation through the dissipation of the temple treasures of Persia helped to give a fictitious appearance of prosperity. The corresponding increase in the world's commerce prevented any such rapid rise of prices as had accompanied the breaking down of the temple hoardings in Greece in the latter part of the fifth and the early half of the fourth centuries B.C., but on the whole there was an elevation rather than a lowering of prices.[1] At the time of Pericles two obols were reckoned sufficient for the nourishment of a man. They are still regarded as barely adequate, but only to furnish starvation rations,[2] while the daily indemnity for public services was now three times that amount.[3] The contemporary comedies are filled with complaints as to the cost of fish, flesh, and all kinds of food products.[4] And, in fact, the price of wheat—and probably also of meat—was now two and three times what it had been at the beginning of the century.[5] Naturally there was a corresponding rise in wages,[6] and a mason now received nine obols where he had earlier received only three. The increase brought hard times to those whose incomes did not advance with the cost of living, and particularly to the poor among them ; so that in the contemporary comedy old people are represented as suffering and even perishing from hunger,[7] and men were forced to indent themselves and their children to work to all intents and purposes as slaves till they had paid off debts which they had contracted

[1] See Beloch, ii. 355 ff. ; Westermann, *Class. Phil.* 1910, p. 215.

[2] Menander, *Fab. inc.* ii. 13. Two obols instead of one were now given by the state for the maintenance of citizens who could not work (Beloch, i. 468, n. 2).   [3] See Francotte, *op. cit.* i. 326 ; Beloch, ii. 358.

[4] Alexis in Koch, ii. 16, 76, 78, 125, 126, 200 ; also Theoph. *Char.* iii. 3, xxiii. 5, and for expensive clothing, xxiii. 8. As a matter of fact, the highest prices known to have been given in Attica for cattle and sheep were those paid at Eleusis in 329 B.C. The former averaged 400, the latter 30 *drachmae* (*IG.* ii. 5. 834*b*, ll. 77 f. ; cf. Barbogallo, *Riv. di stor. antica*, 1908, p. 308 ff.).

[5] Corsetti, *Studi di storia antica*, ii. 68 ff.

[6] Jevons, *JHS.*, 1895, p. 239 ff.

[7] Menander, *Periceir.*, 6 ff. ; *Heros*, 27 ff. ; *Georgus*, where the son of Myrrhine is working for Cleaenetus because of the poverty of his mother.

to keep body and soul together.[1] The reforms of Demetrius of Phalerum aggravated the distress, for to many loss of citizenship meant loss of occupation; hence there was a political point in the advice tendered by the comedian Timocles that he should busy himself in trying to discover who of the poor lacked bread rather than who of the rich had too many guests to dinner.[2] Under these circumstances the tendency to emigrate was strong. We learn particularly of a large exodus of the Athenian poor to Cyrene, where Ophelas was organizing his ill-fated expedition for the conquest and exploitation of the Carthaginian empire.[3] Nor was the cost of living enhanced for the poor alone. The yearly hire of a courtesan is fixed in the New Comedy at from twenty to forty *minae*,[4] or fifteen times the auction price of female slaves in 415 B.C.[5] This was, of course, a special price; still, Planesium in the *Curculio* of Plautus had been bought while a mere child for ten *minae* and sold while an attractive young girl for thirty,[6] while thirty, forty, fifty, and even sixty *minae* are commonly mentioned in the comedies as prices paid for handsome female prisoners of war.[7] This represents the one extreme. The other is found in the five *minae* per head arranged between Demetrius Poliorcetes and the Rhodians as the price to be paid for the slaves taken in the course of the siege of 305/4 B.C., and in the ten *minae* fixed on the same occasion as the ransom of the prisoners of war;[8] for this was a wholesale rate and in a glutted market. Since the *apophora*, or net earnings,[9] of a skilled slave were two or three obols per day a generation earlier, it was, doubtless, at least an obol per day higher on the average in 310 B.C.; so that, at the

---

[1] Menander, *Heros*, 30 ff.   [2] Athen. vi. 245.   [3] Diod. xx. 40. 5 ff.
[4] Menander, *Fab. inc.* ii. 10 f.; Plautus, *Asin.* 230. For the relation which prevailed between rent and price in Italy at the time of the Renascence see Rodocanachi, *La Femme italienne a l'époque de la Renaissance*, 216 ff., 222. A man paid as much for three or four years' use of a slave as the purchase price of an ordinary slave.
[5] Ditt. *Syll.*[2] 38.   [6] 491, 528.
[7] Plautus, *Epidic.* 705, 646, 466 ff.; *Most.* 300; Terence, *Phormio*, 557; *Adelphi*, 191, 223, 742. Sixty *minae* were given for boys and girls to serve in the court of Ptolemy I. (Joseph. *Antiq. of the Jews*, xii. 4. 9).
[8] Diod. xx. 84. 6.   [9] P.-W. ii. 174.

current rate of interest for such an investment, twenty per cent, a capital of from five to seven *minae* was involved.[1]

At the time of Isaeus less than one talent was accounted a sufficient dowry.[2] Now the comic poets, with exaggeration for stage effect, of course, put it at three or four talents.[3] The households with which the comedians deal are, it is clear, those of rich men. To their regular equipment belonged at least one maid and one man servant.[4] They seem to have been run without much regard to cost. The women dressed richly and spent freely for cosmetics, personal adornments, and other articles of luxury.[5] Dinner-parties were given with the assistance of professional cooks and caterers, who were too great artists to be handicapped by considerations of economy.[6] The men flung away thirty

---

[1] Beloch (ii. 358) is inclined to fix 5 *minae* as the average value of a slave, but it is perhaps a little higher ; cf. Böckh, *Staatsh.*[2] i. 85 ff., where the data are given most completely ; but no account is taken of the rise of prices in the fourth century B.C.   He notes (88, cf. Frankel, *ibid.* ii. 19 *) that from $4\frac{1}{2}$ to 9 Attic *minae* are the normal prices of male and female slaves in the Delphian emancipation documents, and that the Romans sold by Hannibal in Achaea were ransomed at the rate of 5 *minae* apiece—again the wholesale rate (Livy, xxxiv. 50).   On the other hand (Polybius, vi. 58), Hannibal offered to ransom the Romans captured at Cannae for 3 *minae* each.   This was about the price of slaves in Italy in the fourteenth century.   In the fifteenth the price had doubled (Rodocanachi, *op. cit.* 217).   It was 35 to 40 florins in the one and *ca.* 80 florins in the other.   Occasionally the price there also rose to 800 florins ($1750) or 85 *minae*.   For the rate of interest in Athens see Böckh, 156 ff., and Billeter, *Gesch. des Zinsfusses*, 10 ff.

[2] Böckh (i. 84), on the basis of Isaeus, viii. 35, says that 40 *minae* was the dowry of a man of slender means : his house was mortgaged for only 10 *minae*. In Isaeus, xi. 40, a dowry of 20 *minae* is mentioned.   The man left a fortune of $5\frac{1}{2}$ talents ; he received from his father 46 *minae* (Böckh, i. 145).   From Dem., *C. Boeot.* p. 1009. 28, we learn that the dowry of the mother of Mantitheus was one talent.   From Dem., *C. Aphob.* p. 822. 27. 4 ff., it appears that the mother of Demosthenes, who received 14 talents from his father, had a dowry of 50 *minae* ; she was to have had 80 *minae* on her re-marriage to Aphobus.

[3] Menander, *Fab. inc.* ii. 8, *Periceir.* 437.   The dowry given by Demochares to his daughter Hippocleia (Ditt. *Syll.*[2] 819) sustained a second mortgage of unknown value in addition to a first of one talent.   Talents of a dowry are mentioned in Theophr. *Char.* xxviii. 4.

[4] The *hegemon* Polemon (*Periceir.*) has Doris and Sosias, and others whom Sosias (176) calls ἱερόσυλα θηρία.   Pheidias (?) has Plangon and Davus (*Heros*). Demeas (*Samia*) has an old freedwoman and Parmenon.   Charisius (*Epitr.*) has the nurse Sophrone and Onesimus ; Cleaenetus (*Georgus*) has Davus and the μειράκιον, as well as the οἰκέται καὶ βάρβαροι, who till his farm ; and the like is the case in Plautus and Terence.   The duties of a maid are set forth in Plautus, *Mercator*, 395 ff. ; cf. Rodocanachi, *op. cit.* 227.

[5] See above, ii. 45, n. 2.

[6] Menander, *Samia*, 71 ff.   See especially Rankin, *The Rôle of the* μάγειροι *in the Life of the Ancient Greeks.*

and forty *minae* for "pleasure women," with some
expostulations of course, but with no apparent impair-
ment of fortune. There was thus the appearance of
much wealth in Athens between 317 and 307 B.C., and,
despite her loss of political and military significance,
there was still no city quite so important. "It was,"
Antigonus affirmed, "the beacon tower of the world
whence alone the fame of men was flashed to the ends
of the earth."[1] To be praised and known there was the
highest ambition of generals, artists, and literary men.
Alexander had sent it three hundred panoplies taken
from the Persians at the battle of the Granicus.[2]
Seleucus forwarded to it a tiger probably captured in
India,[3] and showed it other courtesies.[4] Ophelas of
Cyrene married an Athenian wife.[5] Athens was
suggested to Olympias, Alexander's mother, as the most
suitable place for her residence,[6] and Ptolemy of Egypt
did it the highest honour by seeking to make Alexandria,
his new capital, a second Athens;[7] whereupon Antigonus,
not to be outdone, moved Athenians to his kingdom and
with them founded Antigoneia, which he destined to be
the capital of the world.[8] Athens itself would have
been the chief jewel in the crown of any monarch; hence
its possession was the primary object of Cassander,
Polyperchon, and Demetrius in their campaigns in
Greece. It was to Athens that scholars flocked, for
from there came the new views of life—the new determinations of the values of human activities, which
formed the subjects of discussion among educated men
everywhere in the ancient world; hence to it went men
like Philemon, Diphilus, and Apollodorus the comedians,
to say nothing of Deinarchus the orator and the multitude
of students of science and philosophy registered in the
Athenian schools. Nor was the eminence of Athens
more conspicuous in the world of letters than it was in

---

[1] Plut. *Demetr.* 8.
[2] Arrian, i. 16. 7 ; Diod. xvii. 21. 2 ; Plut. *Alex.* 16.
[3] Philemon in Koch, ii. 490. 47 ; Alexis in Koch, ii. 372. 204.
[4] Gellius, *N.A.* vii. 17.
[5] Diod. xx. 40. 5 ; Plut. *Demetr.* 14. [6] Diod. xix. 51. 2.
[7] See below, iv. 170. [8] See below, iii. 112.

the world of pleasure.[1]   The playwrights of the Middle
Comedy may have been animated with a remnant of the
old Aristophanic indignation when they turned upon the
Athenian *demi-monde* and singled out its most conspicuous beauties for the public denunciation which it
was no longer safe to level at the politicians.   If so, the
courtesans had good reason to be grateful to their
enemies, for through the attacks made upon them on
the stage they became at once known the whole world
over.   Physical charms were of course not wanting to
the women in whose lax salons the fashionable youth
of Athens loitered, and in fact the attraction of the
hetaerae was then as always primarily voluptuous and
sensual.   Still, more than personal beauty is needed to
explain the commanding position which the Athenian
courtesans now obtained, for the city became to the
Hellenistic potentates what Miletus and the Ionian
towns had once been to the Lydians and the Persians
—the most popular source of their supply of " pleasure
women."   In the eyes of these men the wit, intelligence,
and refinement which came from life in Athens [2] were
advantages which added greatly to the value of their
possessions.[3]   Hence the marvellous career of Thais,
mistress of Alexander and of Ptolemy—to whom she
bore several children ; of Lamia,[4] at whose feet Demetrius
Poliorcetes lay for many years ; Pythonice and Glycera,
who went to Babylon to Harpalus, Alexander's treasurer ;
and of scores of other less notable courtesans.[5]   By this
exodus Athens lost many famous beauties, but to take
the place of those who went off with the officers to Asia,
others came from elsewhere in Greece, and Samian,
Andrian, Sicyonian, Rhodian and other women displayed
their charms on the streets and squares of Athens.

---

[1] For the rest of this chapter see Oeri, " Die attische Gesellschaft in der
neueren Komödie der Griechen " (*Sammlung gemeinverständ. wissensch. Vorträge*,
Neue Folge, xii. 275) ; and for certain parts of it, Legrand, " Daos, tableau de
la comédie grecque pendant la période dite nouvelle " (*Annales de l'université de
Lyon*, 1910).
[2] Plautus, *Menaechmi*, 353 ff. " Sternite lectos, incendite odores : munditia
inlecebra animost amantum.   Amanti amoenitas malost, nobis lucrost."
[3] Athen. xiii. 576 E.   [4] Jacobs, *Vermischte Schriften*, iv. 523 ff.
[5] Beloch, iii. 1. 430.

There was, perhaps, no business more capitalistic in its organization [1] and international in its scope than the traffic in courtesans, so that, despite its losses, the Athenian *demi-monde* maintained its lead and its reputation.

In Macedon, where city life was not so prevalent as in Greece, society had retained up to Alexander's age much of the old-time Homeric simplicity. The court of Philip II. was not marked by great elegance and refinement, but to it belonged Olympias; and where such an imperious and self-willed woman reigned, her sex must have enjoyed a freedom and consideration not possible in Athens. It was, however, on the model of the Macedonian court that the officers of Alexander ordered their households; and when Eastern customs were considered, they were the customs of the Persian and Egyptian monarchies, where the queen and the queen-mother were always potent personages, and hence they could but strengthen Macedonian tendencies to give to women social and political importance. The influence of a court is always far-reaching, and in this case it accelerated a movement, of which the Greek courtesans had been hitherto the leaders, for the emancipation of women. The age of the *diadochi* is thus marked by great social changes, especially in the new capitals, but also in other parts of the Hellenistic world. [2] The whole East was filled with the confusion incident to a great immigration. In hundreds of places new cities were being formed into which colonists flocked, or were drawn, not simply from every part of the Greek world, but also from the localities adjacent to each foundation. From the Danube to Ethiopia, from the Aegean to the Himalayas, the land seethed with the unrest of changing political, social, and racial relations. A Macedonian

---

[1] For the *leno* and his operations see especially Plautus, *Curculio*, 494 ff., where his profession and that of the banker are compared. Leo (*Plaut. Forsch.* 126) remarks: "Die neue Komödie hat in immer steigendem Masse ihre Erfindungen aus dem Verkehr der attischen Jugend mit den Hetaeren geschöpft, die in das neue Athen aus allen Teilen der hellenischen Welt zusammenströmten, wie zur Zeit der ἀρχαία die Sophisten."

[2] See Helbig, *Untersuch. über die campanische Wandmalerei*, 190 ff. ; Beloch, iii. 1. 425 ff. ; and on the other side Rohde, *Griech. Roman*,[2] 59 ff.

who took an Egyptian, a Greek who took a Syrian,
woman to wife must devise a new set of conventions for
the performance of their social duties. An Athenian
girl installed in a new home in Elephantine or in
Antioch was dependent upon her own resources to a
much greater degree than was one who remained at
home surrounded by her kinsmen and within easy reach
of her natural guardian. She must be given freedom
of access to the courts and personal right to hold
property, without which she would be entirely at the
mercy of her husband. In other words, her parents
were bound to see that privileges were guaranteed to
her in the marriage contract which they would not think
of demanding for their daughters who married their
neighbours' sons. The instability of life, the enormous
increase of opportunity to move from one place to
another, made new safeguards of the home, that is to
say, of the wife and mother, advisable.[1] The consequence
was that everywhere in the Hellenistic world the old
rules of society were being abandoned, and new ones, of
which a marked characteristic was an enlargement of
woman's liberties, were being formed to take their place.
There had been no such occasion for the creation of a new
social régime since the seventh century B.C.[2] In Athens,
as for that matter in the cities of old Greece generally,
the causes of social change just enumerated were not
directly operative. A royal family did not exist there ;
the city was not dependent for its prosperity upon its
attractiveness to immigrants ; there was no new contact
with foreign races. Hence it is the influence of the
hetaerae upon the structure of Athenian society, and
the reaction of the new world upon the old, that we have
to consider and, if possible, measure at this point. The
Athens with which we are to deal is, of course, the
Athens of the New Comedy,[3] and it is upon the

[1] See particularly the marriage contract from Elephantine of the year
311/0 B.C. published by Rubensohn in *Elephantine-Papyri*, 18 ff.
[2] A similar opportunity came with the founding of the European colonies
in North America.
[3] For a careful consideration of the New Comedy as a literary or dramatic
production see the work of Legrand cited above, ii. 70, n. 1.

fragments of this literature in the first place, and, by way of corroborating information there obtained, upon the Latin adaptations of it in the second place, that we are mainly dependent for knowledge of these matters.

The abolition of the *theorica* had perhaps some influence upon the character of Athenian comedy. Hitherto the daily wage of an ordinary labourer had been paid to all citizens who attended the theatre, so that even the poorest, and in fact especially the poorest, were among its regular patrons.[1] Nothing, of course, excluded them between 321 and 307 B.C., but they no longer obtained an indemnity for the time which the theatre took from remunerative work. Hence it is easily intelligible that in the audiences to which Menander made his first successful appeals the men of substance and education in the community formed a much larger proportion than heretofore, and secured a corresponding increase of influence. At this time education meant primarily philosophical education, and to every man of cultivation the ideas current in the schools were familiar. That they should be appropriated by the stage was in these circumstances inevitable ; and, in fact, whether approved of by the comedians or disapproved, they *did* enter into the plays in scores of suitable or intentionally unsuitable characters and connexions.[2] The attitude of the comedians to the doctrines of the philosophers was in some cases one of hostility. Thus the old master Alexis, whose dramatic career began before 350 B.C.,[3] and whose spirit had been determined during democratic days, seems to have ridiculed and denounced the school-men.[4] On the other hand, the new master Menander— the pupil of Theophrastus, the friend of Demetrius of Phalerum, the poet of the aristocrats—was no less saturated with the ideas of the philosophers than Euripides had been with those of the Sophists, and ethical reflection took a place in his comedies which is defensible artistically only in consideration of the

[1] Ed. Meyer, *Gesch. d. Alt.* iii. 573.
[2] Ranke Fr., *Periplecomenus sive de Epicuri, Peripateticorum, Aristippi placitorum apud poetas comicos vestigiis*, Diss., Marburg, 1900.
[3] See below, iv. 171, n. 1.   [4] Ribbeck, *Alazon*, 77 f.

interest and attainment of the select Athenian audiences
to which they were presented.   Menander was, of course,
in thus far caviare to the many, and accordingly failed
of contemporary popularity; but it was in the maxims
in which he put the moral and religious reflection of the
first thinkers of his age that it lived on in the consciousness of men of cultivation in after times—such was the
simplicity and aptness of his phrasing, and the ease and
natural grace of his diction.[1]

The writers of the so-called Middle Comedy seem,
as already stated, to have assailed the courtesans with
special animus.   The *bête noire* of their successors was
the professional soldier.   To run off to the wars—to
Cilicia or Asia or somewhere else in the East—is a
threat which was at this time directed at the father of
many a wayward lad, and the contrast is many times
drawn in the plays between a life of idleness and
pleasure in Athens and the constant dangers and hardships of the camp, march, and battlefield.   The temptation
to be gone was apparently not often the prospect of a
new home.   It was, when not merely relief from paternal
control, the pay and the plunder which drew young
Athenians into Asia; and it is chiefly with veterans
who have returned enriched with spoils or commissioned
to get recruits for new campaigns that the comedians
deal.[2]   Athens itself maintained a considerable detachment of mercenaries, and during the periods of Macedonian
occupation others in the service of the suzerain were at
home in Attica.   In such a corps almost every country
in the world might on occasion be represented.[3]   Such
men had, of course, much to tell of the new world and
its wonders, of their own exploits and those of their
generals.   They had souvenirs to display, gold to
squander, and gorgeous uniforms in which to set off
their figures.[4]   Consequently they were dangerous rivals

[1] von Arnim, "Kunst und Weisheit in den Komödien Menanders," *Neue
Jahrb.*, 1910, p. 241 ff.
[2] Wollner, *Die auf das Kriegswesen bezüglichen Stellen bei Plautus und
Terentius*, Progr., Landau, 1892-1901.
[3] *IG.* ii. 963 ; cf. below, vi. *ca.* 250 f.
[4] Wollner, *op. cit.* ; Ribbeck, *Alazon*, 30 ff.

of the young civilians in the favour of the courtesans.
Prone to bluster, quick to anger, wont to use straight-
forward, if somewhat unsophisticated and at times
brutal, methods to attain their objects, they inspired
mingled feelings of contempt, ridicule, fear, and hatred
in the minds of the *jeunesse dorée* of Athens. The real
impression they created lies behind the caricature of
them which appears in the comedies.[1] There they are
at once braggards and cowards, despite their experience,
slow-minded and gullible, and coarse and brutal with
women despite all their attempts at gallantry.[2] Seldom,
as in the *Periceiromene* of Menander, does a touch of
sympathy enter into the delineation of them. With
them, however, came doubtless many a breeze from the
world of Asiatic adventure into the quiet, set life of
Athens.

The Old Attic Comedy had gratified unblushingly
and with undeniable vigour the natural man's enjoyment
of obscenity, but the Athenian world had grown strait-
laced since the days of Aristophanes, so that a much
more advanced sense of decency had helped to drive the
comedians to other sources of amusement.[3] In abandoning this fruitful field they doubtless made a concession
to the taste of the educated men who now set the
fashion, and it seems clear that Menander, the chief
among the new playwrights, wrote with them chiefly in
mind. For this reason also, perhaps, homosexuality
ceased to be a matter of frequent comment and insinua-
tion in the New Comedy—a literary fact to which it has
been surmised that a reality corresponded, granted the
now general passion for forming sentimental relations
with individuals of the opposite sex.[4] However that

---

[1] In all probability Xenophon might have appeared on the stage at this
time as a *miles gloriosus*. [2] Menander, *Periceir*. 65 f.

[3] The absence of the verb πέρδομαι is significant of the change : also the
paucity of unmentionable jokes.

[4] Cf. Becker, *Charikles ; zweiter Excurse zur fünften Scene*, ii. 230. See,
however, Athen. xii. 542 D, and Bethe, "Die dorische Knabenliebe," *Rh. Mus.*,
1907, p. 438 ff. The latter claims that moral opposition to *paederastia* was
first offered by the sophists. Since Demetrius of Phalerum and Demetrius
Poliorcetes, Demochares, Arcesilaus, and Zeno practised it, the abstinence of the
New Comedy in this particular (Plut. *Symp*. vii. 8. 3, p. 712c) is very remarkable.
How little shame was involved in homosexuality in early Greek times is

may be, the old Athenian candour, in dealing with matters of sex, still persisted. Women were recognized as free personalities, not treated, like the contemporary Hebrew women, as if they were destitute of all but animal natures, and men expressed a very real regard for their feelings and rights, at least in the plays of Menander ; but sexual desires and relations were talked about with even greater frankness and greater lack of a sense of shame than they were in England prior to the Puritan movement.[1] The Greeks were never steeled by asceticism and a northern climate to the suppression of their natural passions ; hence in Menander's play[2] Charisius could make Pamphile, whom he found straying by night from the company of women with whom she was celebrating the Tauropolia, the victim of his brutal lust without the slightest fear of lynching ; but the offence he had committed was done during intoxication, and on coming to a realization of the fact that he had brought shame upon a girl of good parentage, the young man was overwhelmed with remorse.[3] Not the act, but the social consequences caused his repentance, seemingly. At the same time, his relation towards his wife was one of genuine love, and it was her affection for him which led her to pardon in his case the indulgence of which

made clear by the following rock inscription from Thera (*IG.* xii. 3. 537): [τὸν δεῖνα] ναὶ τὸν Δελφίνιον h[ο?] Κρίμων τε(ί)δε ὦῖπhε, παῖδα Βαθυκλέος, ἀδελφhεὸ[ν δὲ τοῦ δεῖνος], if this has been interpreted correctly by Bethe. Cf., however, the objections of Semenov and Ruppersberg, *Rh. Mus.*, 1911, p. 146 ff.

[1] Philemon, Koch, ii. 479 ; Timocles, Koch, ii. 461. 22 ; Phoenicides, Koch, ii. 334. The great revolution in the sense of decency which Taine (*Voyage en Italie,*[2] i. 138 ; cf. Navarre, *Utrum mulieres Athenienses scaenicos ludos spectaverint necne,* 66) connects with *l'avènement du pantalon*—erroneously, no doubt—had no parallel in Greek antiquity. The sexual relations were always a piquant topic, but it was not tabooed in polite conversation among men and women. Everywhere, both within the houses and without them, and especially at religious festivals, were to be seen the αἰδοῖα, which were used in ceremonies of all kinds. The cock found by the French at Delos (*Acad. inscr. C.R.,* 1904, p. 729), and the gigantic *phallus* borne in the celebrated procession of Ptolemy Philadelphus, show how different was the Greek sense of decency from ours (cf. P.-W. vi. 2011). Hence much was possible without the least sense of shame which would be nowadays intolerable.

[2] Lefebvre, *Fragments d'un manuscrit de Ménander,* Cairo, 1907, and better, van Leeuwen, *Menandri quatuor fab.*[2], 1908. New editions by A. Koerte and E. Capps (*Four Plays of Menander,* 1910) have recently appeared. I cite from the Teubner text by Koerte.

[3] *Epitr.* 255, 459 ff. ; cf. Terence, *Adelphi.* 469 "persuasit nox, amor, vinum, adulescentia : humanumst." Plautus, *Aulul.* 794 "ego me iniuriam fecisse filiae fateor tuae Cereris vigiliis per vinum atque impulsu adulescentiae."

she was herself thought guilty.[1] Menander could even create a character who would apply to men the same standard of purity demanded of women.[2]

The scenes of comedies were always laid in the street. So long as this remained the case, respectable women—the wives, and, above all, the marriageable daughters, of citizens—could take little part in the dramatic action.[3] A very serious limitation was thereby imposed upon the playwrights,[4] but it was an inevitable limitation, so long as the play was to be a mirror of social and not of domestic life. Men and women could not mingle on the stage in a way which was impossible on the streets and squares of Athens. Of course, women might go on errands to the market, or to tend the sick,[5] though this was in the main a privilege of which only poor[6] and elderly women availed themselves.[7] When young and attractive girls and matrons of good families went out, it was in a waggon, or with one or more duennas;[8] and loitering, strolling, or other than a modest carriage was fatal to character. But this was as it always had been, and such appearances gave no opportunity for men and women to become acquainted.[9] From a marriage feast women could not be excluded, but at other banquets they did not appear, and it is obvious that there was no relaxation of conventions at weddings. Accordingly, a play which dealt with the social life of Athens could take none but the courtesan for its heroine; and for this reason we cannot use the data of the New Comedy to reconstruct more than the life with which it deals—the border life in which *monde* and *demi-monde* met, the life in public which was not

---

[1] *Epitr.* 487 ff.   [2] *Ibid.*; cf. Plautus, *Mercator*, 817 ff.

[3] Cf. Wilamowitz, *Neue Jahrb.* 1908, p. 54; Becker, *Charikles*, iii. 265.

[4] For the devices employed to escape from it see Legrand, *Daos*, 434 ff.

[5] Becker, *Charikles*, iii. 272.

[6] Aristotle, *Pol.* iv. 15, p. 1300, vi. 8, p. 1323.

[7] Hypereides in Stobaeus, lxxiv. 33 δεῖ τὴν ἐκ τῆς οἰκίας ἐκπορευομένην ἐν τοιαύτῃ καταστάσει εἶναι τῆς ἡλικίας, ὥστε τοὺς ἀπαντῶντας πυνθάνεσθαι μὴ τίνος ἐστὶ γυνή, ἀλλὰ τίνος μήτηρ;

[8] For the disadvantages of having a pretty maid see Plautus, *Mercator*, 405 ff.

[9] Becker, *loc. cit.* 266; Naevius, *Frg. trag.* 7 (*Danae* of Euripides) "desubito famam tollunt, si quam solam videre in via." Plautus, *Mercator*, 821 "uxor virum si clam domo egressast foras, viro fit causa, exigitur matrimonio."

political or commercial. The real private life of most citizens was closed to the drama.[1]

For this reason the courtesan has the leading female part in the New Comedy, and the plays are full of the wooing and pranks of hard-hearted or soft-hearted adventuresses. Some of these are beyond redemption, but in them the playwrights and their patrons had least interest; those are the favourites who comport themselves in such a fashion that, when they are subsequently found to be of citizen parentage, they can become the wives of their citizen lovers without difficulty; and even the incorrigible Habrotonon in the *Epitrepontes* becomes tender in her womanly fondness for children,[2] while Chryseis, the concubine of Demeas in the *Samia*, held a high place in her master's esteem, and enjoyed a social consideration far superior to that of the common prostitutes,[3] for whom a scorn is at times expressed almost modern in its cruelty.[4]

Young women in Athens were apparently so closely secluded that a seduction in the New Comedy is ordinarily a rape,[5] or the outcome of a religious festival

---

[1] Savage, *The Athenian Family*, Diss., Baltimore, 1907. A few passages will suffice to show the extent of the permissible here. Menander, Koch, iii. 546 :

> τοὺς τῆς γαμετῆς ὅρους ὑπερβαίνεις, γύναι,
> τὴν αὐλίαν · πέρας γὰρ αὔλειος θύρα
> ἐλευθέρᾳ γυναικὶ νενόμιστ' οἰκίας ·
> τὸ δ' ἐπιδιώκειν εἴς τε τὴν ὁδὸν τρέχειν,
> ἔτι λοιδορουμένην, κυνός ἐστ' ἔργον, 'Ρόδη.

Cf. *ibid.* Koch, iii. 484. The κακόλογος of Theophrastus (*Char.* xxviii.)—a really evil person—in slandering a man, says that his mother was a Thracian lady, but that in Thrace noble ladies ἐκ τῆς ὁδοῦ τοὺς παριόντας συναρπάζουσι . . καὶ αὐταὶ τὴν θυρὰν τὴν αὔλειον ὑπακούουσι. Cf. *ibid.* iv. 12. Menander, Koch, iii. 566 :

> χαλεπόν, Παμφίλη,
> ἐλευθέρᾳ γυναικὶ πρὸς πόρνην μάχη ·
> πλείονα κακουργεῖ, πλείον' οἶδ', αἰσχύνεται
> οὐδέν, κολακεύει μᾶλλον.

Cf. the sonnet composed by Antonio Pucci on the subject, *Le Schiave hanno vantaggio in ciascun atto* (Hauvette, *Journ. des savants*, 1907, p. 543, n. 2). Menander, Koch, iii. 438 :

> τρέφει δὲ χωρίς, ὡς ἐλευθέραν πρέπει.

[2] *Epitr.* 249.   [3] *Samia*, 162 ff.   [4] *Ibid.* 175 ff.
[5] See above, ii. 71, n. 2 ; Caecilius, *Titthe*, cited by Nonius, *s.v. gravidavit* Plautus, *Trucul.* 828 ; Terence, *Hecyra*, 570 ff. How the seduction of Plangon in the *Samia* and of Myrrhine's daughter in the *Georgus* of Menander was effected, we do not know.

where, especially when nocturnal rites were celebrated, the two sexes mingled in a way perilous to virtue.[1] The impetuous lover in the *Periceiromene* of Menander has a chance to meet the lady whom he admires and near whom he lives only by surprising her when she comes to the door to despatch a maid on an errand.[2] It is clear from the plot of the *Phasma* that the males of two adjoining houses did not know by sight the women of each other's family.[3] The *liaisons* in Menander's plays of Laches and Myrrhine, Moschion and Plangon, Pheidias and Plangon, Polemon and Glycera, Demeas and Chryseis, Charisius and Habrotonon, do not warrant the conclusion that general sexual licence existed. Rather do they disclose the prevalence in Athens of two proprieties—one for the wives and daughters of citizens, the other for the rest of the women. It is the odd relation of Moschion and Plangon, two persons of citizen status, that makes the *Samia* of Menander possible, and the problem which this relation presented serves to disclose the social stigma placed upon the illicit intercourse of free men and women. In fact, the Attic law seems to have imposed the death penalty upon a man guilty of seduction or rape[4]—a law which is regularly ignored in the comedy. The soldier Polemon is bound to marry his mistress Glycera, to whom he is so ardently attached that he is furiously jealous, and, after a quarrel, humbly repentant, as well as proof against the seductions of other women—the moment she is found

---

[1] Aelian, *Anim.* vii. 19 τὰ μίκρα μειράκια τὰ τοῦ Μενάνδρου ἐν ταῖς παννυχίσιν ἀκόλαστα. Menander, Koch, iii. 404, and Gellius, *NA.* ii. 23. 15 "filia hominis pauperis in pervigilio vitiata est : ea res clam patrem fuit," etc. *Ibid.* Koch, iii. 558 Διονυσίων μὲν ἦν πομπή κτλ. Cf. Plautus, *Cist.* 91 ; Theocr. ii. 66 ; Xenoph. Ephes. *Anth. et Habrocom.* i. 2-3 ; Cic. *De leg.* ii. 14-15 ; Dinarch. i. 23 Θεμίστιον δὲ τὸν Ἀφιδναῖον διότι τὴν Ῥοδίαν κιθαριστρίαν ὕβρισεν Ἐλευσινίοις θανάτῳ ἐζημιώσατε. Menander, *Epitr.* 254 ff. (at the Tauropolia) ; *ibid.* Koch, iii. 494 (at the Panathenaea) ; *ibid.* Koch, iii. 134 ; cf. Aelian, *Épist.* xv. (at a fête of Pan) ; cf. also Ribbeck, *Abh. d. säch. Gesell., phil.-hist. Klasse*, x. 13 ; Rapp, *Rhein. Mus.*, 1872, pp. 1-12 ; Navarre, *op. cit.* 39 f. ; Meineke, iv. 694 ; Leo, *Plaut. Forsch.* 143, where a number of instances from Euripides, *Auge* (fête of Athena), *Ion* (fête of Dionysus) and *Aeolus* are given.   [2] 32 ff.

[3] Menander, Koch, iii. p. 143 ; Koerte, *Menandrea*, 201 ff.

[4] Dinarch. i. 23 ; cf. Thonissen, *Droit pénal de la république athénienne*, 336. [Dem.], *In Neaer.* 65 ; Terence, *Eun.* 967 ff. ; Lipsius, *Das attische Recht*, ii. 1. 429 ff. ; cf., however, 435.

to be of free birth ; and he is, in fact, eager to do so.[1]
That this esoteric propriety has sorry implications for
the treatment of slave women is of course to be
conceded, and it appears that even the wife of a slave
might be exposed to the lust of her master, though
regard not simply for his own property, but also for the
personality of his slaves and the wishes of his wife,
conditioned the use of this prerogative of ownership [2]—
for against other men the law gave ample protection [3]—
so that married slaves might have their own home,
property, children, and practical independence even in
the eye of the law,[4] being free from their master's
control [5] so long as they paid their *apophora*, or
personal rent, regularly. It is a flagrant offence to the
family for a married man to keep a mistress.[6] To the
unmarried and the widowed another code applied,[7] and
there can be no doubt that the society of Menander
recognized concubinage as legitimate in their case in a
way in which modern society does not [8]—though the
facts never vary much.[9] On the other hand, the factor
which determined the formation of such a relation
was not ownership, but inclination—mutual inclination frequently—and its rupture was little short of a
scandal.[10]

An illegitimate birth brought with it, to the mother,
slavery at her father's option, to the family, disgrace ;
and concealment was imperative. The method employed

[1] Menander, *Periceir.* 52 ff., 224 ff., 254 ff., 400 ff.
[2] Plautus, *Casina.* The scene in Plautus, *Bacchides*, 830 ff., shows that the Attic law protected the wife of a foreigner.
[3] Lipsius, *op. cit.* ii. 1. 426 ff.
[4] *Papyr. grecs de Lille*, i. 2. 127. Part of the Attic law, in effect in Egypt, provided μηθενὶ ἐξέστω σώματα πωλεῖν [ἐπ'] ἐξαγωγῇ, μηδὲ στίζειν, μηδ[ὲ] μα[στ]ί[ζε]ιν . .
[5] See Menander, *Epitr.* 50, 159 ff. A man did not always look upon emancipation as a pleasant alternative ; cf. Menander, *Heros*, 21 ff. ; *ibid.* Koch, iii. 110 ; Plautus, *Casina*, 293 ; *Epid.* 726 ff. It might bring starvation. To a girl it seems to have been always desirable.
[6] Becker, *Charikles*, iii. 279. See also the marriage contract of 311 B.C. published in *Elephantine-Papyri*, 18 ff.
[7] Cf. *e.g.* Menander, *Samia* and *Periceir.*
[8] [Dem.], *In Neaer.* 122 τὰς μὲν γὰρ ἑταίρας ἡδονῆς ἕνεκ' ἔχομεν, τὰς δὲ παλλακὰς τῆς καθ' ἡμέραν θεραπείας τοῦ σώματος, τὰς δὲ γυναῖκας τοῦ παιδοποιεῖσθαι γνησίως καὶ τῶν ἔνδον φύλακα πιστὴν ἔχειν.
[9] Ed. Meyer, *Gesch. d. Alt.* i. 1³. 18, *Kleine Schriften*, 190.
[10] Menander, *Samia*, 190 ff.

was exposure, for which, however, the less odious
alternative existed of giving the child to another,
ordinarily, a more humble family—one belonging to a
different walk in life.[1] The exposure was made in the
hope, in which all concerned may not have concurred,
that somebody else would take and rear the child ;
since otherwise it would not have been exposed at daybreak and in a place of public resort, and the jewels,
clothing, or other marks of identification attached to
the babe would have had no meaning ; [2] and while, of
course, the argument from silence is obviously dangerous
in this connexion, it must be mentioned that no one
seems to have passed by helpless infants. The finder
might be embarrassed by the possession of a babe, but
he had no motive to conceal its existence, and he might
dispose of it openly to whosoever might care to take it.[3]
When this, too, was impossible there was nothing to
prevent him from exposing it again. The exposure of
other than illegitimate children was thus not unheard of,
at any rate in the case of females, where, indeed, it was
probably quite common ; [4] but for a father to abandon a

[1] Menander, *Heros*, Prol. 2.
[2] The συνεκτιθέμενα were such as might help to identify the father, if he were
unknown. van Leeuwen, Menander, *Epitr.* 187 ; cf. A. Körte, *Ber. d. säch.
Gesell., phil.-hist. Klasse*, 1908, p. 164. The view of Glotz ("L'Exposition des
enfants" in his *Études sociales et juridiques sur l'antiquité grecque*, 199 ff.) is that
they were not γνωρίσματα, but amulets. This is a conjecture pure and simple.
Moreover, Glotz seems to me to exaggerate the extent of exposure at Athens.
The *Prosopographia* shows clearly that more than one son was commonly raised,
and the New Comedy, that the exposure of a boy required the explanation of
special circumstances (see below, ii. 82, n. 1). The anxiety of Syriscus in the
Épitrepontes to obtain the female child which Davus had found, is inadequately
motived if exposed girls—to say nothing of boys—were to be found at any
moment, and when called upon to cite precedents of fortunate identifications of
exposed children, Syriscus (*Épitr.* 108 ff.) has resort to literature and mythology,
not to contemporary experience. Nor are the arguments adduced to prove that
most of the exposed children perished, conclusive. It is true that their fate, if
taken up, was slavery, and in the case of girls, the brothel (Terence, *Heauton.*
640), but it is also true that, being native Greeks, their value for this purpose
was doubtless considerable. Hence it was profitable to raise them. The
a priori argument thus falls to the ground. The point against the frequency
of raising waifs, drawn from the fact that the law gave the child without
compensation to the parent, on subsequent identification (cf. Plautus, *Curculio*,
490) has no real value. It was open to the finder ordinarily to destroy the
proofs of parentage. Hence the positive evidence, which favours the view
taken in the text (Glotz, 202 ff.), is the only real evidence we possess.
[3] See the *Epitr.* 33 ff.
[4] Poseidippus, *Hermaphroditus, Frg.* 11 (Koch, iii. 338) :

> υἱὸν τρέφει πᾶς κἂν πένης τις ὢν τύχῃ,
> θυγατέρα δ᾽ ἐκτίθησι κἂν ᾖ πλούσιος.

boy was justifiable only on the score of extreme poverty.[1]
It would be absurd to affirm from general considerations
of social structure that women in Athens were without
influence in family life ; and, indeed, the evidence to
the contrary is overwhelming.[2] Of course, the comic
tendency to caricature is accountable for much exaggeration, but the fact stands out clearly that in the house
the wife was often a power to be reckoned with—a
power which probably was more influential in keeping
ladies from conversing on the streets and squares, or
appearing to receive their husbands' guests, or obtruding
themselves in any way upon public notice, than was
male prejudice. In fact, the home seems to have been
the wife's castle, and the husband to have been sometimes surprisingly ignorant of what was going on there.[3]

Marriage required the participation of the father or
guardian in the contracting of it, so that an elopement

---

[1] Menander, *Periceir.* 381 f. :

ἡγησάμην δὴ πτωχὸν ὄντα παιδία
τρέφειν ἀβούλου παντελῶς ἀνδρὸς τρόπον.

The exposure is here motived by the sudden poverty of the father and the death
in childbed of the mother of the abandoned twins.

[2] Menander, Koch, iii. 302 :

οὗτος μακάριος ἐν ἀγορᾷ νομίζεται ·
ἐπὰν δ' ἀνοίξῃ τὰς θύρας, τρισάθλιος,
γυνὴ κρατεῖ πάντων, ἐπιτάττει, μάχετ' ἀεί.

Naturally the Comedy makes the *dotata* the typical tyrant (cf. Plautus, *Aulul.*
475 ff., where the question of a rich man's marrying a poor girl is debated) ;
she had the means of making a dissolute husband mind his *p*'s and *q*'s. The
evil of marrying without a dowry was not simply prospective lack of influence
(Plautus, *Aulul.* 534), but the instability of the home, since divorce was easier
(Menander, *Periceir.* 24 ; Plautus, *Trinum.* 684 ff.). It is easy, however, to
see from these very instances that the bond was stronger than the dowry :
cf. also Menander, *Epitr.* 499, where Pamphile is made to affirm the view of
matrimony which the Stoa inculcated, and which is set forth in the *Digest*,
23. 2. 1 "nuptiae sunt coniunctio maris et feminae et consortium omnis vitae,
divini et humani iuris communicatio." In Menander (Koch, iii. 325) the value
even of a rich wife is recognized :

ἐλθόντ' εἰς νόσον
τὸν ἔχοντα ταύτην ἐθεράπευσεν ἐπιμελῶς,
ἀτυχοῦντι συμπαρέμεινεν, ἀποθανόντα τε
ἔθαψε, περιέστειλεν οἰκείως · ὅρα
εἰς ταῦθ', ὅταν λυπῇ τι τῶν καθ' ἡμέραν.

One of the most horrible things that could be said of a man was this : τῇ γὰρ
αὐτοῦ γυναικὶ τάλαντα εἰσενεγκαμένῃ προῖκα, ἐξ οὗ παιδίον αὐτῷ γεννᾷ, τρεῖς
χαλκοῦς εἰς ὄψον δίδωσι καὶ τῷ ψυχρῷ λούεσθαι ἀναγκάζει τῇ τοῦ Ποσειδῶνος
ἡμέρᾳ (Theoph. *Char.* xxviii. 4).
[3] The instances in the Comedy where a pregnancy is far advanced, and even
a child born without the husband or the father being aware of the situation,
must have had some relation to real conditions.

was impossible, and the consent of the parent or his substitute obligatory.[1] In fact, the structure of society was such that the arrangement of a marriage was necessarily the affair of the parents. It was apparently difficult enough for fathers to get their daughters safely married,[2] and with the candour which everywhere marks Attic speech—which, in fact, is accountable for many modern misjudgments of Greek life and thought—the idea that daughters are a great evil is freely expressed in the New Comedy,[3] though here, too, there is doubtless much exaggeration for comic effect. They had little chance to attract suitors by their personal charms, though love at sight seems to have been common among the impressionable youth of Athens ; the *Geschlechtstriebe* found easy and respectable satisfaction elsewhere ;[4] children had ceased to be indispensable, and were no longer generally desired ;[5] so that marriage—apart from personal inclination, which could not always be ignored or prevented[6]—was ordinarily a matter of household *oeconomy* and of business, into which the question of a dowry entered largely.[7] Three or four talents[8] are

---

[1] Plautus, *Aulul.* 793. See in general Ledl, *Wiener Stud.*, 1908, p. 11 ff.
[2] Menander, Koch, iii. 65. 102.
[3] *Ibid.* iii. 60 :

> εὐδαιμονία τοῦτ' ἐστὶν υἱὸς νοῦν ἔχων ·
> ἀλλὰ θυγάτηρ κτῆμ' ἐστὶν ἐργῶδες πατρί.

[4] Menander, Koch, iii. 566, and see above, ii. 80, n. 8.
[5] *Ibid.* 656 :

> οὐκ ἔστιν οὐδὲν ἀθλιώτερον πατρός,
> πλὴν ἕτερος ἂν ᾖ πλειόνων παίδων πατήρ.

Ibid. 649 :

> τὸ γυναῖκ' ἔχειν εἶναί τε παίδων, Παρμένων,
> πατέρα μερίμνας τῷ βίῳ πολλὰς φέρει.

Cf. also 418, 648, 650, 651 ; Theophr. *Char.* xvii. 7.

[6] In fact, the New Comedy has many young men who follow their inclination into matrimony—often by forbidden ways, to be sure, but still in ways open in life doubtless ; cf. Menander, Koch, iii. 532, where an abused husband (?) protests vigorously against the fashion of taking wives without inspection, and adds : περιάξω τὴν ἐμαυτοῦ θυγατέρα τὴν πόλιν ὅλην. Cf. also iii. 885 ἐγάμησεν ἣν ἐβουλόμην ἐγώ.

[7] The case against matrimony is stated by the *alter Aristippus*, Periplecomenus in Plautus's *Miles*, 626 ff. Ranke (*Periplecomenus, sive de Epicuri, Peripateticorum, Aristippi placitorum apud poetas comicos vestigiis*, Diss., Marburg, 1900, p. 65 ff.) compares this passage with the precipitate of Theophrastus's Περὶ γάμου, which lies in Hieronymus, *Adv. Jov.* i. 313 (Migne) (cf. Bock, *Aristoteles, Theophrastus, Seneca de matrimonio*), and concludes that the comedian was simply the first of many writers to reproduce the philosopher's argumentation.   [8] See above, ii. 68, n. 3.

mentioned in the New Comedy as the sums lost to a
well-to-do father with each daughter—as the sums
which made the new household a partnership out of
which the husband could withdraw or be ejected only
with severe economic loss to himself—out of which the
wife's father could not withdraw his daughter on due
provocation, except with her consent.[1] Divorce was
probably not common in Athens at the time of the New
Comedy, and it may be doubted whether unhappy
marriages were more frequent then than now.[2] The
evidence for a clear opinion on these points is not to be
found in the plays, or, for that matter, anywhere in the
extant sources. There is, indeed, much grumbling at
the awkward consequences of knowing nothing about
the disposition and character of a wife until after the

---

[1] This is proved by Menander, *Epitr.* 464 ff., in favour of the view of Wyse
and Goligher (*Hermathena*, xiv. 190 ff.). Despite his desire to save the dowry
of his daughter Pamphile, Smicrines was unable to take her home with him.
His plan in 538 ff. was to carry her off by violence (Capps, *Amer. Jour. Phil.*,
1908, p. 420, n. 3).

[2] Menander, Koch, iii. 647 :

οἰκεῖον οὕτως οὐδέν ἐστιν, ὦ Λάχης,
ἐὰν σκοπῇ τις, ὡς ἀνήρ τε καὶ γυνή.

Family life is, in general, dependent upon the character of individuals ;
hence, too diversified for easy description. Still, the pressure of society makes
itself felt even within the harem, so that some uniformity is reached. It is
none of our business to deal with private life as such in this book ; hence it
is merely to direct attention to the realities as against, on the one hand, the mis-
leading candour of Attic speech, and, on the other, the deceptive idealism of
Christian ethics, that we append the following analysis of family conditions in
Italian towns of the fifteenth and sixteenth centuries B.C. (Rodocanachi, *op. cit.*,
as summarized by Hauvette in *Jour. des savants*, 1907, p. 543 f.) :

"Poètes et artistes de la Renaissance ne nous présentent de la femme
qu'une image idéale ; il faudrait, en regard, tracer un tableau exact de ce
qu'était sa condition réelle dans la famille et dans la société. Le contraste
serait pénible. C'est une minorité de femmes qui fut appelée alors à jouer un
rôle en vue ; les autres végétaient, étouffaient à l'ombre des grands murs où
les retenaient leurs absorbantes fonctions de mères de famille. La plupart
mouraient à la peine : épouser quatre et jusqu'à cinque femmes, l'une après
l'autre, sans préjudice des concubines, — car cette humiliation n'était pas
épargnée aux épouses, même sous le toit conjugal,—en avoir quelque trente
enfants, tant légitimes que bâtards, quitte à n'en élever que cinque ou six,
n'était pas exceptionnel parmi les bourgeois florentins du XVe siècle : ces pères
de famille semaient la mort autour d'eux. À cette dure vie, le cœur des
femmes s'endurcissait, et lorsque l'appât du plaisir les sollicitait, comment
beaucoup n'y auraient-elles pas cédé ? Comment ia pauvre instruction qu'elles
recevaient les en aurait-elle défendues ? Les moralistes et les conteurs se
sont beaucoup indignés, ou amusés, de leurs déportements ; mais, objets de
convoitises grossières et souvent d'entreprises odieuses, pour tout appui elles
n'obtenaient que la sévérité des hommes. L'Arioste dénonce avec force
l'impunité dont pouvait jouir l'insulteur d'une jeune fille ; et lorsque les lois
sur l'adultère étaient appliquées, c'était parfois à la femme seule. Il y a un

marriage ; [1] and there can be little doubt that Athens was stirred by the movements introduced from the *demi-monde*, and from without for the freer intercourse of men and women in society. But it is equally indubitable that public opinion, at least among the upper classes, was opposed to them. In fact, Demetrius of Phalerum made an effort to keep in control such women as forgot their sex and place, and accordingly empowered the board of *gynaeconomi* to prevent the wives or daughters of citizens from going out without a maid or a carriage, or at night—regulations by no means new,[2] but in need of more than public opinion for their enforcement, and, doubtless, capable of enforcement now that the poorer people were excluded from the citizenship.[3] This magistracy hardly outlasted the downfall of its author ; but it is probable that the public opinion which gave it its chief power of repression was strengthened by the scandals which accompanied the establishment of the court of Demetrius Poliorcetes in Athens.[4] Certainly the writings of Plato, in which equality of the sexes had been advocated, now brought fierce attacks upon the Academy ;[5] and we may be certain that Zeno's *Polity*, in which differences of sex were ignored altogether, simply added fuel to the fire of reaction.[6] Hence the emancipation of women made slow, if any, progress in Athens. It was, in fact, an unfriendly territory for the social innovations of Hellenism, and we can still trace in the few fragments of the contemporary literature which

---

fond de vérité tragique dans l'action bouffonne de la *Mandragore* : la vertu d'une honnête femme trahie par tous, par son marie, par sa mère, par son confesseur."

[1] Cf. *e.g.* Menander, Koch, iii. 532 ; Hieronymus, *loc. cit.*

[2] They belonged, in fact, to the laws of Solon (Plut. *Solon*, 21).

[3] Aristotle, *Pol.* iv. 15 = p. 1300 παιδονόμος δὲ καὶ γυναικονόμος καὶ εἴ τις ἄλλος ἄρχων κύριός ἐστι τοιαύτης ἐπιμελείας ἀριστοκρατικόν, δημοκρατικὸν δ' οὐ· πῶς γὰρ οἷόν τε κωλύειν ἐξιέναι τὰς τῶν ἀπόρων ; vi. 8 = p. 1323 τούτων δ' ἔνιαι φανερῶς εἰσιν οὐ δημοτικαὶ τῶν ἀρχῶν, οἷον γυναικονομία καὶ παιδονομία· τοῖς γὰρ ἀπόροις ἀνάγκη χρῆσθαι καὶ γυναιξὶ καὶ παισὶν ὥσπερ ἀκολούθοις διὰ τὴν ἀδουλίαν.

[4] See below, iii. 111, 119.   [5] See below, iii. 106.

[6] Wendland, *Hellenistisch-römische Kultur*, 16 ff. It is not, of course, denied that Zeno's teaching worked ultimately for a further emancipation of women. The doctrine of the Stoa was affirmed on the Attic stage by Menander in the *Epitrepontes* ; cf. above, ii. 82, n. 2. The year of this play is not known, but Koerte (*Menandrea*, xxvi.) is probably right in assigning it to the poet's maturity.

have been preserved to us the huge mass of scorn and
abuse which was heaped upon the few ladies who studied
in the garden with Epicurus, and upon the zealots who
joined the Cynics in their vagabond life.[1] Philemon
probably reflects the popular sentiments of his time
more truly than Menander does. The dramatic conventions imposed the same restrictions upon them both ;
so that we necessarily find the same general kind of life
delineated—the same lack of faith in women[2] and the
same absence of worthy ideals. To Philemon life has
no lasting satisfactions : evil predominates.[3] It has no
clear meaning or purpose : it is sustained by no religious
hope of any kind. The gods are there, and by them
oaths are taken and sacrifices are offered, but they are
there simply as old finery which we do not like to
destroy, but for which we have no further use.[4] They
no longer enter into the thoughts of men, and whether
one wills to believe in them, or wills to disbelieve in
them, makes little difference in the life of individuals.[5]
That is dependent largely upon natural endowment,[6]
but much also upon chance.[7] There is no sure guide,
and time alone can solve the riddles of life and existence.[8]
There was nothing in the *Zeitgeist* to make old age
tolerable, and for its approach the Athenians of the New
Comedy seem to have only a feeling of terror. Death
was preferable to the loss of power and of capacity to
enjoy. These are ideas of frequent occurrence in the
fragments of Philemon, the favourite comedian of his
age, and they doubtless reflect, in addition to a popular
view, the experience of a life which, in its unusual compass,
saw his adopted country afflicted again and again with

---

[1] Wilamowitz, *Griech. Literatur*, 91.
[2] Koch, ii. 198, 236.   [3] *Ibid.* 28, 158.
[4] Greenough, *Harvard Studies in Clas. Phil.* x. 141 ff., with whose general
conclusions, however, I cannot agree. Cf. Reitzenstein, *GGA.*, 1908, p. 781 f.
[5] Koch, ii. 118*ab*, p. 515 (cf. 166) :

> θεὸν νόμιζε καὶ σέβου, ζήτει δὲ μή·
> πλεῖον γὰρ οὐδὲν ἄλλο τοῦ ζητεῖν ἔχεις.
> εἶτ' ἔστιν, εἶτ' οὐκ ἔστιν μὴ βούλου μαθεῖν,
> ὡς ὄντα τοῦτον καὶ πάροντ' ἀεὶ σέβου.

[6] *Ibid.* 89. 170 ; cf. Menander, *Epitr.* 544 ff.
[7] Koch, ii. 10, 53, 137. On the rôle played by chance in dramatic technique
see Legrand, *Daos*, 392 ff.   [8] Koch, ii. 149, 192, 204, 235*a* (?), 240 (?).

the misery of wars, sieges, and revolutions—all to no purpose.

The religious attitude of Philemon is not peculiarly his. The deities of the Athenians were associated in thinking and in cult with a decaying social and political order, so that its fate was bound to affect theirs. Every instinct of the people, however, prompted the conservation of institutions which bore the impress of all that was most glorious in the past of Athens. The majority did not despair of the city-state, even though it was hard to understand the ways of its gods. Hence there could be no abandoning the ancient festivals and usages. On the contrary, they must be the more scrupulously adhered to because of the strong undercurrent of doubt and wonder. It was, accordingly, not an accident that the popular party, on recovering the government in 307 B.C., acknowledged their spiritual kinship to Lycurgus of Butadae ; for his pietism and fanaticism for archaizing harmonized with a general tendency.[1] It was his spirit which manifested itself in the persecution of Theophrastus for impiety, the expulsion of Theodorus the atheist, and the attempted regulation of the schools of philosophy.[2] Nor were Demetrius of Phalerum and his set children of a different creed despite their enlightenment and their hostility to democracy. Was not their professed objection to popular government its being a relatively late and dangerous innovation ? They accordingly revived, in addition to a limited franchise, the Areopagus, *nomophylaces*, and much besides. They sought to check social change by the sumptuary laws and the supervision of the public life of women. Their leader was, of course, not a religious conservative, for it was he who gave classic expression to the Hellenistic idea of Tyche,[3] and elevated this capricious goddess into the place of Zeus and his colleagues. No one had emancipated himself more completely from the common superstitions. Still,

---

[1] See below, iii. 102 ; cf. Beloch, ii. 612.

[2] See above, i. 35 f. ; Beloch, iii. 1. 432 ; below, iii. 104 ff.

[3] Demetr. *Frg.* 19 : *FHG.* ii. 368. His work Περὶ τύχης is preserved in substance in Plutarch's *Consolation to Apollonius* ; cf. Bury, *The Ancient Greek Historians*, 200 ff.

he was not indifferent to the struggle which now raged
between the orgiastic foreign worships and the old public
cults. He might write the hymn-book of Serapis for
Ptolemy in Alexandria, but to adhere to the same
policy in Athens meant to uphold the official worships.[1]
That educated public opinion, which became dominant
in Athens under his government, was hostile to the
new religious associations which were being formed at
this time is indicated by the scorn of Demosthenes,[2]
the sneers of Theophrastus,[3] and the whole drift of
Epicureanism,[4] as well as by their prohibition in the
Laws of Plato,[5] and their caricature in many of the
plays of Menander.[6] Still, the state was definitely committed to their legality, so that despite the refusal of
the senate in 333/2 B.C. to grant or reject the application of the merchants of Citium for permission to establish
a shrine of Aphrodite Urania in the Piraeus, the people,
on the motion of Lycurgus, bowed to the precedents
adduced, and gave the permit as desired.[7] The most
that Athens could do was to regulate the foreign cults,
and it was for suborning young women, not for impiety,
that action was brought against the famous courtesan
Phryne, who had formed in Athens a dissolute club for
the worship of the Thracian god Isodaetes, while it was
for poisoning and working charms that the priestesses
Ninos and Theoris were condemned, the latter on the
suit of Demosthenes.[8] The regulation adopted was that
the consent of the state should be obtained by every
association desirous of owning a shrine on Attic territory,[9]
and to require, as the people of the Piraeus did, that
when religious meetings were held, chapels were
dedicated, or purifications were effected in public
temene, the priest or priestess should of necessity be
present.[10] The great difficulty was that there was in
Athens one alien and more than two slaves for every

---

[1] Poland, *Gesch. des griech. Vereinswesens*, 519.   [2] *De cor.* 257 ff.
[3] *Char.* xvi., xxvii.   [4] Kaerst, *op. cit.* ii. 1. 246.   [5] x. 910.
[6] Kaerst, *loc. cit.* 245, n. 2.   [7] *IG.* ii. 168.
[8] Beloch, ii. 5 ff.   [9] See below, ix. *ca.* 352.
[10] *IG.* ii. 573b [ὅπως ἂν μηδ]εὶς ἀφέτους ἀφιεῖ μηδὲ θιά[σους] συνάγει μηδὲ
ἱερὰ ἐνιδρεύω[ντα]ι μηδὲ καθαρμοὺς ποιῶσιν μηδ[ὲ] πρὸς τοὺς βωμοὺς μηδὲ τὸ μέγαρον
προσίωσιν ἄνευ τῆς ἱερέας. See also below, iii. 105 f.

two persons of citizen status, so that the price of social and religious purity was eternal vigilance. The law thrust all bastards ruthlessly down into the disfranchised or servile class, and imposed the severest penalties upon inter-marriage with foreigners and fraudulent claims of citizenship.[1] The whole increase of illicit connexions went thus to augment the outcasts, and in this harsh way social contamination was prevented.[2] It was, however, quite impossible to deny to the aliens and slaves the practice of their peculiar religions, just as it was impossible to prevent lawless relations between citizens and foreign women; but this had consequences of the most serious character. Not only did Athens possess a vast population in which, through its lack of education, both old superstitions lingered and new ones festered, but it had also in its lower classes, and especially in the wives and daughters of citizens, to whose education little care was given, ever-present agencies for the trans-mission upwards of religious ideas and observances, however primitive or crass they might be.[3] The citadel of Athenian enlightenment was ever in a state of siege, and just because of the heroic efforts of the intellectual leaders to propagate indifference or unbelief among the defenders, harmony of view was destroyed, and the struggle of philosophic sects took its place. Out of the past and the present, moreover, came a multitude of quiet voices insinuating the comfort and delight of spiritual surrender.[4] It was not an accident that

---

[1] [Dem.] 59. 16-17, 52 ; Aristot. *Const. of Athens*, 42 ; cf. Wyse, *The Speeches of Isaeus*, 273 ff.

[2] See now on this entire question Ledl, "Das attische Bürgerrecht und die Frauen," *Wiener Stud.*, 1907, pp. 173 ff., 1908, pp. 1 ff., and 173 ff.

[3] Plautus, *Miles*, 691 ff. ; cf. Ranke, *op. cit.* 83. See Theophr. *Char.* xvi. 12, where the Leipzig editors quote Strab. vii. 297 αὗται δὲ καὶ τοὺς ἄνδρας προκαλοῦνται πρὸς τὰς ἐπὶ πλέον θεραπείας τῶν θεῶν καὶ ἑορτὰς καὶ ποτνιασμούς · σπάνιον δ' εἴ τις ἀνὴρ καθ' αὑτὸν ζῶν εὑρίσκεται τοιοῦτος.

[4] Nothing could interpret better the condition of the Athenians than *Bishop Blougram's Apology* :

> Just when we are safest, there's a sunset-touch,
> A fancy from a flower-bell, some one's death,
> A chorus-ending from Euripides,—
> And that's enough for fifty hopes and fears
> As old and new at once as nature's self,
> To rap and knock and enter in our soul,
> Take hands and dance there, a fantastic ring,
> Round the ancient idol, on his base again.

Stoicism, which strove to rescue religious faith, was first taught in Athens at this time.

Menander created characters lacking in ideals, bent upon "common pleasure in youth and upon common gain in old age,"[1] and without more than ludicrous enthusiasms; but this does not mean as much for his contemporaries in general. It means simply that such characters existed. Any other sort of men would have been ridiculous on the comic stage, and, however much comedy and tragedy may have approximated in type in his time, Menander was still a comedian by profession.[2] Earnestness of purpose, delicacy of feeling, and sturdiness in doing what is right, one may find in Menander —witness Syriscus in the *Epitrepontes* and Glycera in the *Periceiromene*;[3] and one may also find these qualities applauded there, but it is hardly an accident that in the instances cited they are exemplified in slaves. In general, they are foreign to the amused seriousness of the poet, and we know of nothing to substantiate the view that they were common and natural in the plays of his more popular rivals.

The New Comedy shows us institutions characteristic of life in cities—lodging-houses in charge of " skippers,"[4] brothels open on the side streets, panders and procuresses, caterers, cooks, *parasites*, and the various ministrants of low pleasures.[5] It brings into connexion with this apparatus of debauchery young men of the best families who are sowing their wild oats, and old men whose roving fancy is stronger than the fear of their wives or who are conniving at the intrigues of their sons or friends.[6] The nearest it can come to a love relation prior to matrimony is to make the heroine the daughter of a citizen mother, begotten ordinarily in a lawless

---

[1] Wilamowitz, *Griech. Literatur*, 130.

[2] This consideration is overlooked by Mahaffy (*Greek Life and Thought*, 125 ff.) in his diatribe on Attic society at the time of the New Comedy; cf. also *Athenaeum*, 1908, ii. 136.

[3] *Epitr.* 76 ff. ; *Periceir.* 27 ff.   [4] *Naucleri*; cf. Harpocr. *s.v.*

[5] Alexis, Koch, ii. 329. 98 ; Plautus, *Menaechmi*, 338.

[6] It is significant for the general attitude that Moschion in Menander's *Periceir.* thinks that his mother is making it easy for him to carry on the intrigue with Glycera ; cf. Plautus, *Asinaria*, 64 ff.

way, exposed but saved, and hence brought on to the
stage as a courtesan.[1]   With her a young man becomes
infatuated to the alarm of his father ; the recognition
ensues, and the parents give their sanction to the union.
This, or something similar, forms the web into which
are set the characters which the Attic writers of this
age loved to draw.

The kind of plot selected speaks volumes for the
absence of social intercourse among young men and
women of citizen status, as well as for the interest of
the playgoers in the affairs of lovers ; but it is altogether
misinterpreted when it is construed to imply that rape,
seductions, illegitimate births, and exposures of children
were of everyday occurrence in Athenian society.   They
could happen, of course, since otherwise the New Comedy
would not have been a mirror of life at all ; but no one
would think of arguing from the poets' use of recognitions
of the sort described that an Athenian might expect to
find a daughter in any brothel.   We might as fairly conclude that all brothers-in-law among the Mohammedans
were seducers, because in the Arabian folk-tales of the
Chaste Wife it is her husband's brother who always
appears first in that rôle.   It cannot be denied, however,
that the plots are stereotyped, and from the modern
point of view lacking in originality.   They differ from
one another merely as the old Greeks liked things of
the same kind to differ—as one Apollo or Aphrodite
statue differed from another—as each Ionic temple had
individuality.   Like nature, the classic Greeks were
ever " careful of the type " but " careless of the single
life " ; and that the New Comedy belongs, as a whole,
to the Hellenic and not to the Hellenistic world is
proved also by the uniformity, not to say monotony, of
the characters with which it deals.   They have finely
shaded differences, of course, but they are commonly far
less individuals than types of individuals.   The conventional or traditional—be it derived from the stage,

---

[1] The *Periceiromene* differs from the *Epitrepontes* and the *Heros* in that the
heroine is born in matrimony, but exposed through poverty ; cf. Koerte, *loc.
cit.*   In the *Georgus* and the *Samia* a citizen girl is involved ; cf. above, ii. 79.

or the feeling of the audience, or the habit of the artist —imposed severe limits within which alone the comedian had full freedom of invention. In fact, what had once been a wise regulation of progress had now degenerated into a manner. In the domain of science the subordination of the species to the genus represented sound method still, and in Theophrastus's *History of Plants* it achieved a notable triumph over nature at this very time;[1] but to literature it now stood as a theological doctrine does to religion.

Out of a common interest in types came the farmer and the *parasite*, the stern and the good-natured father, the pleasure-seeking son, the intriguing slave, the pert courtesan, the miser, the swaggering soldier, the compliant nurse, the indulgent mother, and the tyrannous wife of the New Comedy, as well as the thirty *Characters* of Theophrastus. Neither seeks the good and the noble, but only the weak, ludicrous, and common. Not much of the background of life is given, but now and then we get a glimpse of a country-house with its carts and wagons,[2] or a street with a crowd of roisterers or of lawless soldiers;[3] under cover of the night, a hold-up, rape, or murder; a rustic indifferent to the artistic wonders of Athens but agape on the square as a fine ox goes by;[4] a lover serenading his mistress;[5] a flatterer or a bore sticking close to his victim;[6] a superstitious fellow prostrate on his knees before the smooth fetich stones by the roadside, or hurrying with wife and children to the sea to take a purificatory bath;[7] groups of rich men about the banking tables in the agora;[8] a showman or juggler on the square giving a popular entertainment and squabbling with the bystanders for the admission fee;[9] fathers sitting with their boys at a festival, or putting their children to sleep by telling them stories;[10]

---

[1] Beloch, iii. 1. 452, 485.   [2] Plautus, *Aulul.* 505 :

> Nunc quoquo venias plus plaustrorum in aedibus
> Videas quam ruri quando ad villam veneris.

[3] Menander, *Periceir.* 71 ; *ibid.* 276 ff.   [4] Theophr. *Char.* iv. 8.
[5] *Ibid.* xii. 3.   [6] *Ibid.* ii., iii.   [7] *Ibid.* xvi. 5, 11.
[8] *Ibid.* v. 7 ; cf. Wachsmuth, *Stadt Athen*, ii. 1. 460, 492 f.
[9] Theophr. *Char.* vi. 4, xxvii. 7.   [10] *Ibid.* ix. 5, xxx. 6, vii. 8.

an agitator haranguing in strident tones the passers to and fro on a street corner ;[1] a good-natured or truckling guest letting himself be mauled by his host's children ;[2] picnics galore of phratries, *demesmen,* and acquaintances ;[3] salesmen of fish, meat, nuts, flowers, perfumes, flute-girls ;[4] loungers munching nuts on the sly, stealing a hot bath, snatching a sausage, or throwing in an extra bone or piece of meat when making a purchase ;[5] slaves of both sexes, foreigners and citizens of all sorts and stations busy with domestic or foreign business, or jostling and talking in the streets, squares, and porticoes —the whole farrago of Attic life. Unfortunately, we rarely get more than a glimpse.

Taken as a whole, the New Comedy and the *Characters* of Theophrastus probably admit us only to what was least worthy in the life of Athens at the end of the fourth and the beginning of the third century B.C. —the relaxation of the rich youth of Athens on being freed at length from the intolerable financial and military burdens of imperialism. We see, moreover, citizens at their play, not at their work ; for the ordinary occupations of men were now, as ever in antiquity, unfit subjects for serious art. To conclude that citizens did not work at all is absurd, for four-sevenths of their entire body had property worth less than twenty *minae.* That is to say, a house (3-10 *minae*)[6] and two or three acres of land (10-12 *minae*),[7] or a house and furnishings and one or two slaves,[8] were hardly within their reach. The return from twenty *minae,* however advantageously employed, cannot have yielded more than three *minae* annually (15 per cent)—enough, perhaps, to support a family of two, but only in a very shabby way.[9] All

---

[1] Theophr. *Char.* vi. 7.   [2] *Ibid.* v. 5.
[3] *Ibid.* xxx. 16, x. 11, xv. 7, xvii. 9, xxii. 9, xxx. 4.
[4] *Ibid.* vi. 9, xi. 7.   [5] *Ibid.* xi. 4, ix. 8, 4.
[6] Böckh, *Staatsh.*[2] i. 84 ; cf. ii. 17.*   [7] *Ibid.* i. 79 f. ; cf. ii. 16.*
[8] See above, ii. 68, 85, n. 3.
[9] Böckh, *op. cit.* i. 141 ; cf. ii. 32* f.   One hundred and seventy-five *drachmae* per year were given to each (or 350 for every two) of the seventeen temple slaves employed on the building operations at Eleusis at this time (*IG.* ii. 834*b*, Col. i. 5, 42 ; Col. ii. 5 ; *IG.* ii. 5. 834*b*, 40) for their maintenance. Four obols per day were allowed the archons εἰς σίτησιν (Aristotle, *Const. of Athens,* 62. 2). This would require 487 *drachmae* per year for a man and his wife—more than he could

with less than twenty *minae* must have worked with their own hands for the support of their families; and few of those with more could raise a family, provide a dowry for their daughters, and spending money for their sons, without giving their personal attention to business. And in fact, as already remarked, in the background of the New Comedy and the *Characters* we get frequent glimpses of men of wealth who frequent the banks [1] and the shipping docks,[2] who seek bargains for the products of their estates,[3] go abroad on business trips,[4] and thus manifest an absorbing interest in money-making.

The Athenian majority lacked clear ideas, but not definite ideals. From the latter it drew the power of self-control it exhibited in several political crises,[5] and the vigour of the resistance it made time and again against overwhelming military odds.[6] If it did not bear, it at least nurtured the stern creed of Zeno and the kindly agnosticism of Epicurus. It reaffirmed under great provocation the right of everybody to freedom of thought;[7] protested, though lamely and ineffectually, against the deification of kings;[8] produced martyrs to the cause of virtue,[9] and stood for the old, when the new was fashionable and popular, against what it regarded as the contamination of language, customs, and institutions.[10]

---

raise with a capital of 2000 *drachmae*, if none of it went to pay rent or were invested in a dwelling-house. He might buy three slaves and obtain *apophorae* amounting to perhaps 9 obols per day, but there was a great likelihood that the slaves would be idle part of the time each year (Francotte, *op. cit.* ii. 3 ff.); besides, he had to face the grave risk of their dying, being sick, running away, or becoming incapable of further work. He had thus to put aside a large part of the annual earnings to replace his capital. Hence it is doubtful if in this way he could net 3 *minae* per year on his investment.

[1] Theophr. *Char.* v. 7 ; Plautus, *Asinar.* 116.

[2] Theophr. *Char.* xxxiii. 2 (this whole *Character* is significant for its revelation of the ideals of rich people) ; Plautus, *Bacchides*, 235 ff., *Mercator*, 255 ff.—from which it is clear that the big ships lay at anchor in the Piraeus at some distance from the shore, as at present. They had to be reached with the aid of *lembi*.   [3] *Ibid.* iv. 15 ; cf. Plautus, *Asinar.* 333.

[4] See Diod. xix. 103. 4 ; cf. above, ii. 59, n. 1 ; Terence, *Hecyra*, 171-5 ; Plautus, *Bacchides*, 243. 388, *Most.* 440, *Merc.* 11, and especially 71 ff. ; Menander, *Georgus*, 6. The whole subject is treated by Knapp in *Class. Phil.*, 1907, pp. 19 ff., 281 ff.   [5] See above, i. 31 ; below, iii. 110.

[6] See below, iii. 95 ; notes 1-5.   [7] See below, iii. 107.

[8] See above, i. 11, and below, iii. 123.   [9] Plut. *Demetr.* 24.

[10] For the reaction against Attic culture see Wilamowitz, *Sitzb. d. Berl. Akad.*, 1904, p. 640 ; and *Griech. Literatur*, 83 ff.

CHAPTER III

THE DEMOCRATIC RESTORATION AND THE RULE OF
THE MODERATES

φιλοσοφίαν καινὴν γὰρ οὗτος φιλοσοφεῖ,
πεινῆν διδάσκει καὶ μαθητὰς λαμβάνει.
εἷς ἄρτος, ὄψον ἰσχάς, ἐπιπιεῖν ὕδωρ.

PHILEMON in *Philosophers* (Koch, ii. 85, p. 502).

THE coming of Demetrius Poliorcetes opened a new era of internal and external conflict for Athens, which continued almost without intermission for forty-six years. Seven times the government changed hands,[1] and on as many occasions the constitution was in some degree altered. Three different parties,[2] with different political ideas and traditions, strove for the mastery, and as often as a change came, the foreign policy of Athens was reversed. Four times the institutions were modified, and a new government established, through the violent intervention of a foreign prince.[3] Three uprisings were bloodily suppressed,[4] and the city sustained four blockades,[5] all with equal heroism, but twice unsuccessfully. Athens was rarely the initiator of trouble in this long period of disaster, but she seldom escaped being drawn into the struggles which others had precipitated.

The elections and the beginning of the new year intervened between the seizure of the Piraeus in June[6]

---

[1] 307, 303, 301, 294, 276, 266, 261 B.C.
[2] Whom we may call the radical democrats, the moderates, and the aristocrats, with an imperialistic, neutral, and pro-Macedonian foreign policy respectively.   [3] 303, 294, 276, 261 B.C.
[4] 303, 295, and 287/6 B.C.   [5] 304, 296-4, 287, 265-1 B.C.
[6] Plut. *Demetr.* 8 πέμπτῃ φθίνοντος Θαργηλιῶνος, *ca.* June 10th ; cf. *Class. Phil.* iii. 386.

307 B.C., and the triumphal entry of Demetrius Poliorcetes into the city about two months later. It was
in June that the democracy was re-established. The
popular assembly was opened at that time to all citizens,
and it entered at once upon the task of governing; but
the magistracies established by Demetrius of Phalerum
to which objection was taken were, doubtless, not
abolished till the beginning of the year 307/6 B.C., when
such detailed changes in the offices as seemed advisable
were made.[1]   Then, on the arrival of Demetrius
Poliorcetes about a month later (August 307 B.C.), the
two new tribes were created,[2] after which a reconstruction of the senate became necessary.   Its number was
increased from five hundred to six hundred, and its
prytanies from ten to twelve. The innovation was a
commendable one, for it brought about a coincidence
between the prytany period and the month, and thus
did away, for a short time only, however, with the
discrepancy between the official and the calendar
divisions of the year. The new tribes were given the
first and second places in the official order, and provided
with *demes*, prytanies, and officials when established.
The introduction occasioned a reorganization of the
Attic municipalities. *Demes* were taken from the old
tribes in such a way that equality of population in all
the tribes resulted, care being given, furthermore, that
the new tribes should have adequate representation from
the city, coast, and uplands. That is to say, the

[1] This is suggested by the fact that the priest of Asclepius for 307/6 B.C.
was apparently taken from Erechtheis—the first tribe in the official order.   Had
a new priest been appointed in Thargelion, it is conceivable that the priest for
307/6 B.C. would have been from Aegeis.

[2] This we know for three reasons : (1) Because the priest of Asclepius was
chosen at the beginning of 307/6 B.C. from Erechtheis, not from Antigonis, as
would have been the case had the two new tribes been in existence at that time
("Priests of Asklepios," *Univ. Cal. Publ., Class. Phil.* i. 132, 141.   Note 15 is to
be corrected.)   (2) Because the first prytany of 307/6 B.C. had thirty-six days,
just as if the year was to have had but ten prytanies ; whereas the following
four prytanies had thirty days each (Beloch, *Klio*, i. 413 ; Kirchner, *Sitz. d.
Berl. Akad.* 1910, 982).   (3) Because the creation of the tribes was coincident
with the arrival of Demetrius Poliorcetes in Athens, which is everywhere
represented as having taken place during the archonship of Anaxicrates (Plut.
Demetr. 10 ; Parian Chronicle, Jacoby, 23 ; Diod. xx. 45 ; Diony. Hal. *De
Dinarch.* 650. 5. 633. 16, 634. 9. 636. 10, 639. 3), *i.e.* after the beginning of
307/6 B.C.   The Parian Chronicle puts the first advent of Demetrius in 308/7 B.C.,
the capture of Munychia, however, in 307/6 B.C.

opportunity was chosen to restore the equilibrium between the tribes and between the sectional interests of Attica, which had been established by Cleisthenes in 508 B.C., but disturbed by the natural growth and shifting of population during the following two hundred years.[1] The enlargement of the Senate increased unnecessarily the cost of administration, but it ensured still further the participation in public life of practically all the citizens. Almost every Athenian must, henceforth, have been a senator for at least one of the two terms allowed by law. For even if men entered the Senate as early in their lives as possible, and were senators for two years in succession : that is to say, if they were senators during their thirtieth and thirty-first years, there were less than six hundred citizens available for three hundred places. If, on the other hand, they entered regularly at thirty-five or forty, and were re-elected for their second term ten years later, the number of men cannot have exceeded the number of places by more than a hundred. Since this latter arrangement was, doubtless, closer to the normal ; since, moreover, many of the citizens were content with being a senator for one term only, the circumstances must have been quite peculiar which allowed a man to escape this office altogether.[2] Twelve tribes involved twelve regiments of both horse and foot and twelve *taxiarchs* and *phylarchs*,[3] but they did not require more than ten generals,[4] or more than two *hipparchs*. They required, in other words, that those officials be increased in

---

[1] See on this point Bates, *Cornell Studies*, viii. 6 ff., and especially Kirchner, *Rhein. Mus.*, 1904, 294 ff. ; also Sundwall, *Klio*, Beiheft, i. 4. 88 ff. The work by Shebelew on the composition of the new Attic *phylae* (*Stephanos in Honour of Sokolow*, St. Petersburg, 1895) I have been unable to use.

[2] In this computation it is assumed that Athens had 21,000 citizens still. The census which yielded this number was probably taken after the despatch of the colonists to Thrace, but before the departure of the settlers to Carthage and Antigoneia. The emigration from Athens, of which these three instances are typical, probably did much more than offset the natural increase of population ; hence we are prepared to find the number of ephebes considerably less in 305/4 B.C. than thirty years earlier. This shrinkage, not a change in the organization, explains the slight falling off which Sundwall (*Acta*, 22 ff.) has noted. It is probable, therefore, that after 306/5 B.C. Athens had, for a time at least, somewhat less than 21,000 citizens. Sundwall's data suggest, in fact, that they numbered about 15,000.

[3] Colin, *BCH.*, 1906, p. 240, n. 2.   [4] See *Klio*, 1909, p. 314 ff.

number by the addition of two members whose duties, like those of the *sophronistae, parasiti* (?), *sitonae,*[1] concerned the tribes directly. The rest, like the nine archons, were probably left unchanged. We may observe in this conservatism a reasonable disinclination to augment the number of paid officials, but it had another aspect as well. The individual members of Boards of ten were henceforth representatives of the whole people, not, as earlier, of the several tribes; for from this time forward the tribe ceased to nominate or to secure one of its own members for each public committee. The tribe was thus reduced still more in political importance,[2] while the state was able to command the services of the men who, wherever resident or registered, were best qualified for office—the democratic theory that all men were equally qualified being thus tacitly abandoned. The weight of this change was, however, lessened seriously by the fact that committees of ten had been reduced to a minimum in 321 B.C. If restored in 318 B.C., the restoration was but ephemeral, and it seems unlikely that they were restored

---

[1] *IG.* ii. 5. 251*b* ; cf. Sundwall, *Klio,* 1906, p. 330, and *Acta,* 22 ff. Diodorus, brother of Diphilus of Sinope (Koch, ii. p. 420, 2. 23-30), says :

τὸν Ἡρακλέα τιμῶσα λαμπρῶς ἡ πόλις
ἐν ἅπασι τοῖς δήμοις θυσίας ποιουμένη,
εἰς τὰς θυσίας ταύτας παρασίτους τῷ θεῷ
οὐ πώποτ᾽ ἀπεκλήρωσεν, οὐδὲ παρέλαβεν
εἰς ταῦτα τοὺς τυχόντας, ἀλλὰ κατέλεγεν
ἐκ τῶν πολίτων δώδεκ᾽ ἄνδρας ἐπιμελῶς
ἐκλεξαμένη τοὺς ἐκ δύ᾽ ἀστῶν γεγονότας,
ἔχοντας οὐσίας, καλῶς βεβιωκότας.

For the date of this reference to twelve *parasites,* see Capps, *Amer. Jour. Arch.,* 1900, p. 83 ; cf. Wilhelm, *Urk. dram. Aufführ.* 59 ff. According to Francotte (*Mélanges Nicole,* 135 ff.), *sitonae* were created only when the state needed to take special measures to provision the city. With them a *tamias* was associated. They were in existence during the Four Years' War (*IG.* ii. 252, ii. 5. 252*d,* ii. 348, 353 ?) ; for some years before, and during 283/2 B.C. (*IG.* ii. 5. 614*c* ; Ditt. *Syll.*[2] 505) ; in *ca.* 230/29 B.C. (*IG.* ii. 335) ; in 175/4 B.C. (*IG.* ii. 5. 435*b*) ; and if our record were not so grievously defective, we should probably hear of their existence at a good many points in between. They were chosen by popular election. In a country which, like Attica, did not raise grain for more than one-half of its population (Francotte, *loc. cit.*), and which was not infrequently in hostile relations with the lords of the sea, or was unable for other reasons to secure a regular and abundant importation of food-stuffs, the office of the *sitonae* was often an onerous and responsible one. It is clear that the Athenians always lived in close proximity to starvation (cf. above, ii. 66 ; below, vi. *ca.* 262, viii. *ca.* 312). Another Board of twelve members is found in Wilhelm, *Beiträge,* p. 66.

[2] See above, i. 9, 23, ii. 55 ; cf. *Klio,* 1909, p. 322.

in 307 B.C. at all; for, though it was a democracy which then assumed power, it was a democracy to whose direct traditions belonged a simplification and strengthening of the magistracy, and between 346 and 323 B.C. much had already been done in this direction.[1] The democracy of 307 B.C. set aside the *gynaeconomi* and the *nomophylaces* and re-established the treasurership of military funds,[2] but it did not re-establish the *leiturgies*, nor did it abrogate the laws regarding funerals, or the *agonothesia*, or the general superintendency of the administration.[3] *Astynomi* reappeared; but, like the *agoranomi*, we find subsequently only two of them, one each for Athens and the Piraeus,[4] and there was no restoration of the *eleven* at all, the Areopagus being left in possession of jurisdiction over malefactors. A much less radical and consistent democracy came thus into being—one which took account of the training and natural aptitude of certain citizens for executive work, and gave such freedom to a relatively small group of magistrates that it took a place henceforth near the ecclesia as a second power in the state. The *leiturgies* remained abolished, but it proved easier to legislate them out of existence than to eradicate the popular expectation that the rich should make special outlays for the public good. Resort was, accordingly, had to general subscriptions and property taxes whenever crises occurred, and the budget was seemingly made out with the possibility in mind of raising emergency funds in this way; but a less unpopular method was devised of enabling larger expenditures under normal circumstances. This was to confer the magistracies upon rich men, in the expectation that they would use their wealth to supplement the public funds put at their disposal. The *leiturgies* were thus in a fashion renewed, but their oppressiveness to individuals was greatly reduced by the neglect of the navy and the cessation of tribal competitions, as well as

---

[1] See below, iii. 102, and above, i. 9.

[2] *IG.* ii. Add. 737. Habron of Butadae was military treasurer in 306/5 and Philip of Acharnae in 305/4 B.C. See above, i. 23, n. 7.

[3] See below, Appendix II.

[4] *IG.* ii. 5, 314c; cf. Ditt. *Syll.*[2] 500, n. 6; Wilhelm, *Beiträge*, No. 68.

by the state's assumption of expenses which had been earlier left entirely to private citizens. Such donations, moreover, could be obtained only at an important sacrifice of democratic susceptibilities; for to obtain them, the populace had to give these offices to the propertied classes, which thus secured an influence more fairly proportionate to their public obligations.   It gave them, however, with a restriction which was at once a boon and a disability to rich public men; for no individual was allowed to hold the same magistracy twice, however much he should want it or the populace should want him to have it.   Prior to 321/20 B.C. three alone of the magistracies, those of the superintendent of springs, the treasurer of military funds, and the committee on theoric expenditures, had belonged to this category — of offices filled by popular election, yet tenable for one term only.   Now it was enlarged considerably; for in it remained the superintendent of springs, doubtless, and the military treasurer now restored, while into it had come seemingly the general superintendent of the administration, the *agonothetae*, and the *gymnasiarch*—the officials upon whose shoulders had been placed the onus of spending the public moneys earlier handled by the theoric committee.   Of these, the general superintendent of the administration occupied the position of greatest strategic strength in that he controlled the entire governmental service.   It was he who gave to the finances of Athens such unity of management as they subsequently possessed, and through his hands passed the pay of the magistrates, senators, jurors, and soldiers, as well as the indemnities given for time spent in the ecclesia and the appropriations made for the purchase and distribution of grain: for, as already stated, he took the place of the *apodectae* also. Like them he seems to have had no treasury, or unlike them one in which only the surpluses were kept; but he had to be consulted by the treasurer of the grain moneys, the treasurer of the military funds, and doubtless also by all those in charge of spending departments. The control of this office was bound to be one of the most important objects of party struggle in Athenian politics in the third century B.C.[1]

The democrats were in no hurry to start judicial proceedings against Demetrius of Phalerum and his partisans. They did not do so when the ex-dictator escaped to Thebes, nor yet when the new year began, or when Demetrius Poliorcetes entered Athens. But when the question of Athenian autonomy had been decided definitely, accusations were entered against the members of the deposed government.[2] The guilt of the accused was unquestionable; they had overturned the democracy beyond a doubt, and the penalty was prescribed by law, so that the court had simply to render the verdict. It was uncommonly mild. Those who stood trial were declared innocent, and only those who had fled were condemned to death. The sentence was incapable of execution, but all the statues of Demetrius of Phalerum were destroyed with the exception of one, which, at the request of Poliorcetes, who probably saw to it also that no blood was shed in the crisis, was left upon the Acropolis.[3] Menander was in danger of being brought to trial, but was saved by the intercession of Telesphorus, a cousin of Poliorcetes.[4] Deinarchus, the orator, was less fortunate. Fearing, as he explained later, the envy which had arisen because of his wealth, he fled to Chalcis.[5] Thus a brilliant social group was dispersed, and much lost permanently to Athens that was soundest in her public life.[6]

The most influential personage in the city during the following period was Stratocles of Diomeia. A decidedly

---

[1] See below, Appendix II.

[2] The time results from the following passage of Philochorus (Dion. Hal. De Dinarch. 3; FHG. i. Frg. 144) τοῦ γὰρ 'Αναξικράτους ἄρχοντος εὐθὺ μὲν ἡ τῶν Μεγαρέων πόλις ἑάλω· ὁ δὲ Δημήτριος, ὁ κατελθὼν ἐκ τῶν Μεγάρων, κατεσκευάζετο τὰ πρὸς τὴν Μουνυχίαν, καὶ τὰ τείχη κατασκάψας ἀπέδωκε τῷ δήμῳ. ὕστερον δὲ εἰσηγγέλθησαν πολλοὶ <τῶν> πολιτῶν, ἐν οἷς καὶ Δημήτριος ὁ Φαληρεύς. τῶν δὲ εἰσαγγελθέντων, οὓς μὲν οὐκ ὑπομείναντας τὴν κρίσιν ἐθανάτωσαν τῷ ψήφῳ, οὓς δὲ ὑπακουσάντας ἀπέλυσαν.
Demetrius Poliorcetes was in Athens at the time the sentence was passed upon Demetrius of Phalerum; Favorinus, below, n. 3.

[3] Favorinus in Diog. Laert. v. 77.

[4] Diog. Laert. v. 79. 80. Telesphorus was not a cousin of Demetrius of Phalerum; cf. Beloch, iii. 1. 126, n. 3, iii. 2. 89.

[5] Dion. Hal. De Dinarch. 2. p. 634.   [6] Ibid.

unpleasant picture has survived to us of this man. He
was loose in his personal habits, and his relations with
the courtesan Phylacium—a very ordinary prostitute,
if an obscure passage in Athenaeus[1] is to be trusted
—were the talk of the town. Cleon, we are told by
Plutarch,[2] was his political model, and in the popular
assembly he in turn flattered and flouted the majority.
He outdid every one else in waiting on the nod of
Demetrius Poliorcetes,[3] and yet maintained the appearance of being the servant of the common folk. He left
behind him a lasting reputation as an orator, and,
doubtless, was an effective public speaker.[4] Personally
he had little in common with the uncompromising
democrat and rigorist, Lycurgus of Butadae; but the
name of the Eteobutad was one to conjure with in
Athens at this time, and to identify itself with his clear-
cut policy was an important asset to a new government.
This advantage Stratocles sought to gain by presenting
to the people a memorial, which is preserved to us both
in the literary and lapidary tradition,[5] of the public
services of Lycurgus, and by requesting for him the
grant of an honorary statue. The epoch of the
coalition government had been especially conspicuous
for its brilliant financial administration and the construction of magnificent public works—departments for
which Lycurgus had assumed direct and personal
responsibility. Hence it was peculiarly appropriate
that the control first (307/6 B.C.) of the general administration,[6] and then (306/5 B.C.), when the war was on, of
military funds, should be entrusted to Habron of
Butadae, Lycurgus' son.[7] Nor did he fail to meet the
high expectations of his father's admirers, but won an
enviable reputation for skilful finance. Stratocles had
been himself a democratic member of the government

---

[1] xiii. 596 F ; cf. Plut. *Amator.* 750 F. ; *Demetr.* 11.
[2] *Demetr.* 11 ; *Pol. Precepts*, 798 E.
[3] *Demetr.* 12. 24. 26 ; Diod. xx. 46.
[4] Blass, *Att. Bered.* iii. 2.² 95.
[5] [Plut.], *Lives of the Ten Orators*, 852 A ff. ; Ditt. *Syll.*² 168 ; *IG.* ii. 240.
[6] *IG.* ii. 167. 36 ; cf. below, Appendix II.
[7] Ditt. *Syll.*² 181. 31. For the fame of his work in these offices see [Plut.],
Lives of the Ten Orators, 843 A ; cf. Kirchner, *PA.* 15.

of 335/23 [1] B.C., and Habron the heir of one of its democratic leaders. The greatest of the group of popular
leaders of the past generation was now represented
by Demochares of Leuconoe, the son of Demosthenes' sister. He was already over forty years of age,[2]
but during the past fifteen of them there had been
little place in public life for a kinsman of the great
orator. His subsequent career was checkered, and he
spent almost half of it in exile; but in 307 B.C., the
elements dominant in Athens were those which had prepared for war with Macedon during Alexander's lifetime
and had completely mastered the government on his
death. With these Demochares was in entire sympathy,
and he threw himself energetically into the task of
reviving the power and political influence of Athens,
and at the same time of destroying everything hostile
to a democratic government. In spite of Chaeronea
and Crannon he upheld stoutly the imperialistic policy
of his uncle. 'Demetrius of Phalerum plumed himself,
forsooth, on the increased prosperity of the city, but
what praise did he deserve therefor not due to any
banausic tax-jobber? And at what a price the riches
had been purchased! The state had been dragged
across the stage of great and noble actions, like a donkey
in the play. It had abandoned the leadership to others.
And a fine set of laws this blondined Solon had drawn
up. Let them be revised at once.'[3] A revision of the
law code was, accordingly, begun.[4] *Nomothetae*[5] were

---

[1] See above, i. 13. [2] Kirchner, *PA*, 3716.
[3] Polybius, xii. 13. 9 ff. ; *FHG*. ii. 448. 2.
[4] The revision of the law code was a tedious undertaking, since the findings
of the legislative committee were subject to actions of illegality. Hence, as in
410-404 B.C. and in 403-399 B.C. (Ed. Meyer, *Gesch. d. Alt.* v. 215 ff.), a period
of several years was necessary to bring the task to completion. In 304/3 B.C.
the work was still in progress, and Euchares of Conthyle was praised for publishing the sections rearranged in that year (*IG*. ii. 258).
[5] Alexis (Athen. xiii. 610 E : Koch, ii. 327. 94) :

> τοῦτ' ἐστὶν 'Ακαδήμεια, τοῦτο Ξενοκράτης.
> πόλλ' ἀγαθὰ δοῖεν οἱ θεοὶ Δημητρίῳ
> καὶ τοῖς νομοθέταις, διότι τοὺς τὰς τῶν λόγων,
> ὥς φασι, δυνάμεις παραδιδόντας τοῖς νέοις
> ἐς κόρακας ἐρρίφασιν ἐκ τῆς 'Αττικῆς.

Cf. Wilamowitz, *Antigonus*, 195 ff. The proposal of Sophocles is called a νόμος
by Pollux (ix. 42) and Diogenes Laertius (v. 38). The *graphē paranomon*

chosen to sit in judicial form upon the new proposals.
One, made by a certain Sophocles of Sunium, was a
measure like in spirit and conception to the indictment
preferred against Socrates.   It forbade any one of the
philosophers to conduct a school without the express
permission of the senate and people of Athens.[1]   This
was a plausible, and, as it seemed, a timely proposition.
There were two schools of philosophy in Athens at this
moment, one of which had been chartered for more than
two generations—that of Plato ; while the other, as we
have seen, was organized under the régime of Demetrius
of Phalerum.   The second was the institution especially
assailed,[2] since out of its midst had come the Phalerian
himself.   Theophrastus, its leader, was intimately associated with the oligarchic government, and had been
already tried on a criminal charge during the last period
of democratic fervour ; its founder had been a Macedonian
subject, the tutor of Alexander and the confidant of
Philip.   Its antecedents were thus disloyal and aristocratic, while its influence was, doubtless, similar, and
thousands of pupils came under the dangerous teaching
of Theophrastus.   In fact, the Peripatetic school was
closely identified in popular thinking with the recent
tyranny, and many of those who had fled on its overthrow had been of this philosophic persuasion.   The
nomothetae were convinced, and the proposal of
Sophocles became law, whereupon Theophrastus left
Athens.   The full import of the innovation may have
been realized only gradually.   Philosophy had indeed
been an aristocratic movement from its very inception.
It had been recognized as dangerous to democratic
principles from the time of Alcibiades and Critias,
while "the greatest crime in Athenian history" had

was admissible in the case of a *nomos* which had been enacted by the *nomothetae*, as well as in the case of a *psephisma* (Goodwin, *Demosthenes' De Corona*,
316 ff.).   The procedure followed by the *nomothetae* in enacting a *nomos* was,
in fact, almost identical with that of the ecclesia.   See 'Εφ. 'Αρχ., 1910, p. 1 f. ;
Journal des Savants, 1902, pp. 177 ff.

[1] Pollux, ix. 42 ; Diog. Laert. v. 38.   Athenaeus (xiii. 610 F) erroneously
calls it a *psephisma*.

[2] This has been shown by Wilamowitz, *op. cit.* 195 ff.   There is no excuse
for what is found in *Neue Jahrbücher*, 1906, p. 684.

been committed in defending democracy against the
aristocratic tendency of the teaching of Socrates. And
yet there was a widespread conviction in Athens that
Socrates, Plato, and Aristotle were the jewels in the
city's crown of honour, and that upon the continued
presence of their schools depended in large part the
cultural supremacy of Athens. Baser motives may have
actuated others. The reputation of Theophrastus and
Polemon attracted crowds of foreigners to the city
whose presence was of material advantage to many
interests. Finally, there was a technical difficulty in
the way of the legislation. It was possible to bring
action against an individual teacher, but no special law
was required for his conviction if he was a malefactor.
In this case, not an individual, but an institution was
assailed, and the institution was one of the most
venerable in the *patria* of Athens. The school of
Theophrastus was a religious club dedicated to the
service of the Muses,[1] and to molest it was an impiety,
forbidden by an existing enactment. For a law of
Solon himself had established the utmost freedom of
association for religious or other purposes. Thus the
ancient document ran : " Should the *demos*, brotherhoods, *orgeones*, *gennetae*, messmates, burial unions,
thiasotae, or men setting out for piracy or trade, make
agreements with one another, they shall be binding
unless forbidden by public statutes." [2] Nor, in fact,
had the Athenians interfered with the right of individuals
to organize in clubs for any of these purposes. Hitherto
the state had merely controlled the acquisition by them
of Attic real property, their use of religious enclosures,
temples, shrines, or altars, and their privileges in similar
matters of obvious public concern. What their members
did or taught they had to answer for as individuals.[3]
Now, on the other hand, the state proposed to investi-

---

[1] Wilamowitz, *op. cit.* 263 ff. (*Excurs.* 2 : *Die rechtliche Stellung der
Philosophenschulen*).

[2] Gaius, *Digest*, 47. 22. 4 ἐὰν δὲ δῆμος ἢ φράτερες ἢ ὀργεῶνες ἢ γεννηταὶ ἢ
σύσσιτοι ἢ ὁμόταφοι ἢ θιασῶται ἢ ἐπὶ λείαν οἰχόμενοι ἢ εἰς ἐμπορίαν, ὅ τι ἂν τούτων
διαθῶνταί <τινες> πρὸς ἀλλήλους, κύριον εἶναι ἐὰν μὴ ἀπαγορεύῃ δημόσια γράμματα.
" Das letzte ist schwerlich die authentische Fassung," adds Wilamowitz (278),
whose text I have quoted.   [3] See above, ii. 88 f.

gate the *ulterior* purpose of each association, existent
or contemplated,—the *immediate* motive being, of
course, always unimpeachable,—and to make the right
to organize dependent upon the findings.   Henceforth, a
club formed without permission was bound to be illegal,
since every aggregate might in form worship the
Muses, but in reality teach philosophy.   And who
knew to what else the government of the day might
eventually object if its right to suppress philosophic
unions were unchallenged ?   Other similar associations,
such as those formed in the service of the oriental
deities, might be investigated next.

The old law of Solon was thus in substance cancelled by the new law of Sophocles.   Hence Philon, an
Athenian member of the Peripatetic school, had good
ground for indicting its author on the charge of proposing an unconstitutional measure.   This he did in the
spring or early summer of 306 B.C., after the departure
from Athens of Demetrius Poliorcetes, in all probability.[1]
No less than Demochares pled for the defendant, and
the general tenor of his argument is still determinable.
The legal point was, doubtless, evaded, if our meagre
report is at all trustworthy, and abuse was heaped upon
the philosophers indiscriminately.[2]   'Socrates a good
soldier—as readily make a spear of savory.   Aristotle
betrayed his native city, Plato and Xenocrates turned
out rascally pupils—men notorious for their ill-gotten
wealth, and their impious and disreputable manner of
living.   Look at Callippus of Syracuse, Euaeon of
Lampsacus, and Timaeus of Cyzicus—all treacherous
and tyrannical rulers.   Look at Chaeron of Pellene,
who drove out the worthiest citizens, gave their property
to their slaves, and established a community of marriage
in which the wives of his victims were forced to give
their favours promiscuously—a fine product   of the

---

[1] In March 306 B.C. (time of Dionysia) the philosophers were still in exile.
The law was doubtless rescinded before the coming of Epicurus to Athens, *i.e.*
before the end of 307/6 B.C.   Its abrogation, therefore, followed close upon the
departure of Demetrius Poliorcetes, whose personal interest in its enactment is,
perhaps, vouched for by the passage of Alexis quoted above, iii. 103, n. 5.   Otherwise, Wilamowitz, 189.   [2] Athen. xi. 509.

beautiful *Republic* and the lawless *Laws*. The Academy stands condemned by its fruits ; so that even if the law of Sophocles disturbs Plato's brood while seeking to destroy the Peripatetic nest of traitors, the state will obtain the more benefit.' The pleader must not be held responsible for all the vituperation in his plea, for scurrility was generally characteristic of Attic oratory, and Demochares had good precedents for the attempt to rouse to the utmost the passions and prejudices of the jurymen, in order to obscure the weakness of his arguments. But the law was entirely against him ; so that Philon won his case, and Sophocles was fined five talents, whereupon Theophrastus returned to Athens.[1] The decision was a famous one, and its consequences far reaching. Freedom of association[2] was thereby finally established in Athens, and the attempt was never again made to interfere with the organization of the philosophic schools. Immediately after the condemnation of Sophocles, Epicurus came from Lampsacus and established the Garden in Athens.[3]

Upon the arrival of Demetrius, as already mentioned, the Athenians had given to him and his father the title of king.[4] Since the murder of the young Alexander in

---

[1] Diog. Laert. v. 38.

[2] Freedom of thought, it should be observed, is quite another matter. Indirectly, however, it was involved in the decision.

[3] Diog. Laert. x. 2. In the early summer of 306 B.C., according to von Arnim's precise calculation in P.-W. vi. 1. 134 ; cf. below, iv. 173 f.

[4] Plut. *Demetr.* 10 πρῶτοι μὲν γὰρ ἀνθρώπων ἀπάντων τὸν Δημήτριον καὶ 'Αντίγονον βασιλεῖς ἀνηγόρευσαν. Diodorus (xx. 46. 2) says nothing of this, and in xx. 53. 2, like Plutarch in §§ 18 and 19, he makes Antigonus assume the regal title after the battle of Salamis in 306 B.C. Demetrius became king at the same time. We cannot confirm the accuracy of Plutarch's report ; for in the Attic documents we have no case of the use of the title king in their connexion before the last day of the month Munychion of 306/5 B.C. (April 305 B.C.) ; cf. *IG.* ii. 247 ; *IG.* ii. 737 (Ditt. *Syll.*[2] 181. 29) ; here the item was entered ἐνάτῃ φθίνοντος of Scirophorion, but the document was not drafted till later. *IG.* ii. 238 belongs, not to 307/6 B.C. but to 305/4 B.C. Sundwall, *Acta*, 11 ; *IG.* ii. 239 is dateless. On the other hand, it is rash to set Plutarch aside because of the two passages from plays of Alexis (Athen. xiii. 610 ; cf. Wilamowitz, *op. cit.* 195 ff. ; Koch, ii. 336. 111. ; cf. Kaibel, P.-W. i. 1469) which were presented in 307/5 B.C. ; for the omission in them of the title βασιλεύς (in the second it is given to Antigonus but not to Demetrius) is paralleled by its omission in *IG.* ii. 737 (Ditt. *Syll.*[2] 181) l. 7 (ἐνάτῃ φθίνοντος of Munychion), which was inscribed at the same time as *ibid.* l. 29, in which there is a reference to Antigonus and Demetrius as βασιλεῖς. The regal title is thus lacking on the ἐνάτῃ φθίνοντος and present on the last day of Munychion 305 B.C., about eight months after the battle of Salamis.

310/9 B.C. there had been no central kingship in the
world.[1] In 307 B.C. it was revived, and, to the disgust
of republicans of those and later ages, revived by the
people which stood most conspicuously for liberal
institutions. This, however, is but a superficial view
of the matter; for Antigonus, the Macedonian, recreated
the kingship, or at least aspired to do so : Athens merely
gave him his title. Their action was, doubtless, meant
to please, but though it helped to clear the air, it
involved for Antigonus the awkwardness of a premature
disclosure of plans. Accordingly, he did not accept the
title immediately; for to take it would have been to
acknowledge publicly what his ambition had long since
led his rivals to suspect, that he intended, not to assert
his independence of the central government, as did the
other captains, but to re-establish in his own person the
unity of Alexander's empire. By conferring the title
of king, however, Athens, the metropolis of the Greek
world, recognized him as the legitimate successor of the
great Alexander. This was an event, aside from its
momentary inconvenience, of the greatest political
importance to Antigonus. To Athens, too, it was not
without conceivable advantages. There were, doubtless,
many Greek cities which preferred autonomy under a
distant monarch to the same status under the eye of a
neighbouring satrap. Perhaps, also, the acceptance of
Antigonus as king would help to end the civil war,
which, it seemed, must otherwise continue interminably,
to the prostration of liberty and commerce—things dear
to Athens at all times. There were thus reasons of
policy for this act. The Athenians, however, conferred
godhood upon their benefactor also,[2] and thereby, it
is affirmed, brought back into European usage an
institution which, to their immortal glory, the Greeks
had been the first to expel from universal acceptance.[3]

[1] Of course, there continued to be kings in Amathus, Tyre, Sparta, Epirus,
and many other places ; but there had ceased to be a "king of kings."
[2] Plut. *Demetr.* 10 ; Diod. xx. 46. 2 ; cf. von Prott, *Rhein. Mus.*, 1898,
p. 460 ff. Cardinali, *Studi di storia antica*, vi. 139 ff., and the other literature
cited by him on p. 145.
[3] See in this connexion the remarks of Gilbert Murray, *The Rise of the
Greek Epic*, 129—where, however, the Hellenistic kingship is misunderstood.

The charge is in any case a formidable one ; for in after ages the attribution of divinity to a king was destined to confer upon a political order not simply some of the authority—a benefit in times of anarchy—but also some of the harmful immutability of a religious institution. But it seems unlikely that the Athenians had any freedom of choice; for Alexander had made godhood simply an attribute of universal kingship, and although since his death, as, for that matter, before the rise of Macedon, it had been bestowed upon men who lacked the regal title, it was none the easier to give the kingship without it. The two were, in fact, inseparably connected in the thinking of the best Greeks; and the organic relation of absolute monarchy and godhood had been taught to his pupils by Aristotle a generation earlier, and demonstrated to the reading world in a striking passage of his *Politics*.[1] The great advantage of deification was that it gave the king, with whose real creation Athens had nothing whatever to do, a legal personality in a democratic community, and made it easier for staunch republicans to accept the patronage of one in the position of Demetrius. It had, accordingly, its juristic *raison d'être* : it was, in fact, the only known device for combining a complex of free cities into a territorial state monarchically organized. Moreover, we must not charge the originators of deification with all the evils which it produced later on. Many generations were still to come and go, and many evils had yet to befall Greece and break the spirit of its people, before men had sunk so low that they stood in awe, traitors to the cause of human dignity, before the god-kings whom they themselves had created. The Greek world was, in the main, as yet uninfluenced by the conception of God popular in the East—a being, male or female, omnipotent, eternal, universal, living apart from the world, and separated from men by a vast chasm ; who, however, had the habit of taking human shape in order

---

[1] iii. 13, p. 1284 a. The connexion has been set forth with similar precision by the greatest of modern jurists, Th. Mommsen (*Staatsrecht*, ii.³ 755). The genesis of deification has been recently sketched by "the master of those who know" among living historians of antiquity, Ed. Meyer (*Kleine Schriften*, 285 ff.).

to perform miracles, utter prophecies, and reveal a peculiar *regimen* or peculiar ideas, on the acceptance of which depended immortality, prosperity, happiness, and remission of sin. Thus, the monarchs of 307 B.C. neither received nor expected a religious veneration not then accorded to the ancient deities of Greece; and so little of it did these obtain, so generally were they the subjects of jests, denial, contumely, and belittlement, that it is difficult to see what addition of dignity apotheosis could confer upon a king. Genuine religious sentiment was at its lowest ebb at this time; Olympus, it was affirmed, was entirely populated with departed kings, rulers, and other benefactors, and the masses were thus accustomed to deities of all kinds and characters already. Nevertheless, it could hardly be maintained that Demetrius Poliorcetes appeared well in the rôle of a divinity. At heart he was a Macedonian nobleman, young, handsome, generous, but autocratic and impulsive. He had come early to the consciousness of his own powers, and already in 307 B.C. deferred to nothing except to the judgment of his stronger-minded father. He took a mediaeval delight in war, but the game was with him the chief thing, the object of effort being secondary. After victory came enjoyment—self-gratification; and where could one enjoy more richly than in Athens? It was there that he spent the winter of 307 B.C., and seeing that the life in the city had still much of the old democratic *abandon*, we can easily imagine that he found it pleasant. The young man was passionately devoted to fair women and handsome boys; and where could beautiful, intelligent, and complaisant *hetaerae* be found, if not in the home of Thais, Phryne, Pythonice, Glycera, and their like? He was already the husband of Phila, the noble daughter of Antipater, a woman older than himself, and the victim of a political union. But conjugal fidelity was not a Macedonian virtue. There lived at this time in Athens the beautiful widow, Euthydice, the daughter of Miltiades of Laciadae, and a descendant of Miltiades and Cimon.[1] In 309/8 B.C. her

---

[1] Diod. xx. 40. 5; Plut. *Demetr.* 14.

first husband, Ophelas, lord of Cyrene, had been foully
murdered before the walls of Carthage by his ally,
Agathocles of Syracuse, and Euthydice with her offspring [1] had thereupon returned home to rise within two
years to be the consort of another prince. She was,
obviously, not an ordinary person. A son [2] borne by
her to Demetrius we hear of later, but, like the
Chalcidian woman with whom Antiochus the Great
consoled himself during his winter in Europe, Euthydice
disappears from history upon her second union. We are
told that this marriage gave great joy to the Athenians,
but our informant, the sober Plutarch, remarks that it
was in reality not much of a compliment, seeing that
Demetrius had intimate relations with many courtesans,
and also with many free ladies at the same time. He
seems to have approved of the expulsion of the
Peripatetics,[3] but to have disapproved of the extremes
to which the people went in branding the Phalerian and
his friends—a difference in keeping with his character,
for he was both an enthusiastic believer in the Athenian
democracy, and an exponent of knightly courtesy towards
the vanquished.

In accordance with the instructions received from
his father he had to content himself for the present
with the liberation of Athens, and in view of his own
return to Asia, to give attention to the formation of a
confederacy of the Greek cities which were willing to
co-operate with the Athenians against Macedon. It
was sufficient for the purpose of Antigonus to start
anew in this way an agitation in favour of himself in
all the Greek cities located in the provinces of his
adversaries. The next step was to become undisputed
master of the sea, which meant to crush Ptolemy of

---

[1] The subsequent appearance of the name Ophelas in this family (Kirchner,
PA. 5547) shows that she brought at least one child back to Athens with her.
She came honestly by her spirit of enterprise, since her father Miltiades led out
a colony from Athens in 325/4 B.C. (*IG.* ii. 809 ; Ditt. *Syll.*[2] 153) probably to
Adria at the mouth of the Po river. Did he also serve as *oecist* for the colony
which went with Ophelas to Carthage in 309 B.C. (Diod. xx. 40. 5 ; cf. above,
ii. 67) ? It was at this time that his daughter married the lord of Cyrene.

[2] Named Corrhagus after his paternal grandfather ; Plut. *Demetr.* 53.

[3] See above, iii. 101, n. 2.

Egypt. Accordingly, he recalled Demetrius, who left Athens in the spring of 306 B.C., accompanied by many settlers[1] for the city, Antigoneia on the Orontes, which Antigonus founded in this year to serve as the new capital of the world. Demetrius then assumed command of the fleet, which, in the following three years, took a leading part in the great campaigns against Egypt and Rhodes.[2] In the meanwhile Athens had to stand the brunt of the Four Years' War, as the struggle was called, which was carried on by her with Cassander between the first and the second appearance of Demetrius Poliorcetes in Greece (307-304 B.C.).[3] It was to relieve the immediate distress, rather than to provision the city for a siege— for the European enemy was weak on the sea—that Antigonus sent one hundred and fifty thousand *medimni* of grain to Athens in 307/6 B.C. ;[4] but the simultaneous gift of timber for one hundred ships was, doubtless, part of the military preparation for the struggle. Some of the material probably arrived in the fall of 307 B.C., for already in the spring of 306 B.C. thirty swift-sailing tetreremes were ready for action.[5] They went, however, with Demetrius to Cyprus ; for defence against an attack by land was the real problem of Athens. It was not simply that the walls of the city were in need of repair in many places, but that they had become generally antiquated. The progress which had been made of late in the art of besieging cities was enormous, for Dionysius

---

[1] Pausanias of Damascus, *Frg.* 4 (*FHG.* iv. 469) ὁ δὲ Σέλευκος μετὰ τὸ καταστρέψαι τὴν Ἀντιγονείαν ἐποίησε μετοικῆσαι τοὺς Ἀθηναίους εἰς ἣν ἔκτισε πόλιν Ἀντιόχειαν τὴν μεγάλην τοὺς οἰκοῦντας τὴν Ἀντιγονείαν, οὕστινας ἦν ἐκεῖ ἐάσας Ἀντίγονος μετὰ Δημητρίου υἱοῦ αὐτοῦ, καὶ ἄλλους δὲ ἄνδρας Μακεδόνας, τοὺς πάντας ἄνδρας ϛϛ̅.

[2] It was an Athenian architect named Epimachus who built for him the famous *helepolis* used at the siege of Rhodes, *Vitr.* x. 16. 4.

[3] Ladek, *Wien. Stud.* xiii. 63 ff. de Sanctis seems still disposed to defend his location of this war in the period between 294 and 288 B.C. (*Studi di storia antica*, ii. 29. 50 ff. ; *Klio*, 1909, p. 7), but I can see no reason whatever to disturb Plutarch. The Athenians certainly took part in the attack on the Piraeus in 307 (Diod. xx. 45. 3), which year, along with 306, 305, and 304 B.C., makes a four years' period in which they were fighting continuously. Cassander, to be sure, again menaced Attica in 301 B.C., but there is no evidence that actual fighting ensued. See also Beloch, iii. 2. 374 ff.

[4] Diod. xx. 46. 4 ; cf. above, iii. 98, n. 1.

[5] Diod. xx. 50. 3. Had these thirty warships been in the harbour of Athens on its capture by Poliorcetes a year earlier, they could hardly have failed of mention in Diodorus or Plutarch, especially since Demetrius arrived with only twenty ships. (See above, ii. 63, n. 2.)

of Syracuse, and Philip and Alexander of Macedon, had revolutionized siege operations and thereby altered the problem of defence. Something had been done to meet the changed requirements between 338 and 322 B.C., but there was still much room for improvement.[1] Movable towers had been invented, from which missiles could be thrown down upon defenders on the walls, if protected only by a breastwork. This must be prevented. Accordingly the breastwork on the top of the wall was raised,[2] apertures being left at suitable intervals, and a covered gangway was constructed all along the circuit of the wall, the roof, which sloped outwards, being supported on the inside by stout pillars placed at intervals of seven feet. It seems that the ditch and palisade, which had been placed in front of the wall at exposed points in 337 B.C., were put again in readiness, and the walls themselves strengthened by substituting stone for brick in places where, through neglect, breaches had appeared. Athens was thereby converted into a fortress of the best modern type. The work was begun in 307/6 B.C. The wall was divided into sections, and each was given to a contractor, who was responsible for the labour, and had to complete the work according to definite specifications, and to the satisfaction of an elected architect. The reconstruction cost large sums of money, but the enthusiasm of the restored democracy was not diminished by this consideration. In 307/6 B.C. direct property taxes were authorized,[3] and citizens, metics, and foreigners came forward with generous contributions.[4] The city, however, had need of other things

---

[1] See above, i. 9.

[2] *IG.* ii. 167, published in Wachsmuth, *Stadt Athen*, ii., vi. ff. Habron was ὁ ἐπὶ τῇ διοικήσει ; this clinches the date of the document. Cf. Frickenhaus, *Die Mauern Athens im 4. Jhrh.* 29 f. Frickenhaus gives a new and improved text. "The Roofed Gallery on the Walls of Athens," is the title of a good article by Caskey in *Amer. Jour. Arch.*, 1910, p. 298 ff.

[3] *IG.* ii. 270, and ii. 5. p. 77 (Ditt. *Syll.*[2] 187. 29), and especially *IG.* ii. 413.

[4] *Ibid.* In 306/5 B.C. the towers of the southern wall were being constructed. For the contributions see *IG.* ii. 252 and 5. 252d (in and prior to 305/4 B.C.) ; 253 and 246 (from the people of Colophon ; cf. Wilhelm, *Urk. dram. Aufführ.* 238) ; 254 (donation of some talents of silver) ; 259. 251 (a service which earned for Asclepiades of Byzantium a statue to cost 3000 *drachmae* and a crown to cost 1000 more, as well as expenses in connexion therewith of still 180) ; 413 (see below, p. 114, n. 1).

than walls. Arms, armour, missiles, and catapults were
required,[1] and it was in providing these that Demochares
of Leuconoe made good by executive efficiency the
reverse sustained in the law-courts.[2] At the same time
special pains were taken to stock the city adequately
with provisions.[3] All this made Athens a power to be
reckoned with once more, but she was still by no means
a match for Macedon. Accordingly, she sent Olympiodorus [4] by sea, the land route being blocked by the enemy,
to arrange joint action with the Aetolians, the persistent
foes of Cassander, and the old friends of Athens. The
legate was successful in his mission, and the united
efforts of the two peoples repulsed the attack made by
Cassander on Athens in the late summer of 306 [5] B.C.
Hegesias was general in this year.[6] In the one following,
the command passed over to Olympiodorus. The position
of Athens had improved markedly in the meanwhile,
chiefly because Cassander was obliged by the great
victory of Demetrius at Salamis, and the grave peril of
Ptolemy, to keep his main army in reserve for the war
in Asia. But Athens, too, could act more energetically,
since more timber for warships and one hundred and
fifty talents of money had arrived from Antigonus, and
the military treasurer and the Areopagus, upon the
shoulders of which rested the general charge of the
financial preparations, had raised other sums at home.[7]

---

[1] *IG.* ii. 250. 733. 734. 413 (Wilhelm, *GGA.*, 1903, p. 793), where it is said
of Euenides of Phaselis : καὶ νῦν εἰς τοὺς καταπάλτας νευρὰς ἐπέδωκεν.
[2] [Plut.], *Lives of the Ten Orators*, 851 D ; cf. *IG.* ii. 733b.
[3] See above, iii. 98, n. 1.
[4] Paus. i. 26. 3.
[5] *IG.* ii. 249. Wilhelm (*GGA.*, 1898, p. 222) and Dittenberger (*Syll.*[2]
184, n. 5) refer the attack here mentioned to this year also. *IG.* ii. 272.
[6] *IG.* ii. 733b. 13 and Ditt. *Syll.*[2] 187. 32.
[7] *IG.* ii. 737 ; Ditt. *Syll.*[2] 181. 7 ff. ; (April 305 B.C.) ; *ibid.* 28 ff. and
32 ff. (June 305 B.C.). Demetrius also sent 1200 suits of armour from the
spoils of the victory of Salamis (Plut. *Demetr.* 17). An echo of the jubilation
in Athens at this time is still perceptible through a fragment of Alexis
(Koch, ii. 336):

> τοὺς τρεῖς δ' ἔρωτος προσαποδώσεις ὕστερον·
> ἕν' Ἀντιγόνου τοῦ βασιλέως νίκης καλῶς,
> καὶ τοῦ νεανίσκου κύαθον Δημητρίου.
> φέρε τὸν τρίτον - -
> Φίλας Ἀφροδίτης· κτλ.

This passage has been referred correctly by Kaibel (P.-W. i. 1469) to Antigonus
Monophthalmus, Demetrius Poliorcetes, and Phila—the latter's wife. Had

Her diplomatic strength was thus much enhanced, so that Demochares induced Boeotia, which had probably joined Cassander on his approach in 306 B.C.,[1] to cease hostilities, consent to a truce, and eventually enter into an alliance with his country. This opened the way into Phocis,[2] where Cassander was being detained by the necessity of reducing Elatea before advancing farther. Here Olympiodorus, at the head of the Greek army, met him, and, in co-operation with the Elateans, forced him

---

the reference been to Antigonus Gonatus, Phila his wife, and Demetrius their son, the order of the names must have been different. Besides, the equation of Phila with Aphrodite was natural for the wife of Poliorcetes, but hardly for the wife of Gonatus (see below, v. 190, n. 3). Moreover, the ascription of the reference to the latter triad is possible only on the untenable hypothesis (Bergk, *Rhein. Mus.*, 1880, p. 260 ff.) that it was an interpolation made in the play of Alexis after his death. The shrine erected at Thria in Attica by Adeimantus, a courtier of Poliorcetes (Strabo, xiii. 589, Athen. vi. 253 A), was in honour of Phila Aphrodite, *i.e.* the wife of Poliorcetes. Hence Dionysius, son of Tryphon (time of Augustus), errs in confusing her with the wife of Gonatus. (The same confusion is found in Suidas, *s.v.* "Aratus of Soli.") That it was erected in 305 B.C. is made probable by the passage from Alexis quoted above, since the cult name and the shrine doubtless belong together, and also by a consideration of the matrimonial adventures of Demetrius. He married Deidamia in 303 B.C., and "ordered" Ptolemais a few years after ; cf. Wilamowitz, *Antigonus*, 199, n. 21. It is likely that Phila was in Athens between 307/6 and 306/5 B.C., though she seems to have been in Lycia or Cilicia in the following year (Ditt. *Syll.*[2] 183, n. 2). What happened to her on the arrival of Deidamia, who, of course, was quite a different person from Euthydice, Lamia, etc., and with whom her husband's relations were quite different from those entertained with the doughty Cratesipolis (Plut. *Demetr.* 9), and the runaway Lanassa (Plut. *Pyrrhus*, 10), we do not know ; but her children were put with their grandmother in Cyprus (Plut. *Demetr.* 35. 38). Deidamia stayed in Athens till 301 B.C., when she was escorted to Magara. She bore Demetrius a son named Alexander, probably after 301 B.C., who was brought up in Egypt (Plut. *Demetr.* 53), but she died in *ca.* 299 B.C., while on her way to join her husband in Asia (Plut. *Demetr.* 32). Phila had in the meanwhile joined Demetrius (*ibid.*). Now, in *ca.* 299/8 B.C., she returned to Macedon to her brother Cassander, as a missionary, seemingly, on her husband's behalf ; but perhaps in consequence of her inability to effect a reconciliation between Demetrius and Cassander, the former turned towards Egypt, and was promised the hand of Ptolemais, the king's daughter. Then came the acquisition of Macedon, to which Phila was in a sense the heiress (Plut. *Demetr.* 37), the reinstatement of Phila, her suicide in 288 B.C., and Demetrius's union with her niece Ptolemais, of which Demetrius the Fair was the fruit (*ibid.* 46. 53). From this sketch it is clear that only in 307/5 or in 294/0 B.C. could a temple be erected to Phila in Athens —the period prior to Phila's first divorce being, however, the preferable one.

[1] From the fact that Demetrius of Phalerum went to Boeotia in 307 B.C., Beloch infers that the country was hostile to Demetrius Poliorcetes at this time ; but Demetrius had private reasons for going to Thebes (see above, ii. 49), and, moreover, he went with the consent of Poliorcetes. The *koinon* of the Boeotians was friendly to Athens in March 306 B.C., since it was crowned at the Dionysia of the year of Anaxicrates (*IG.* ii. 736).

[2] That the war was drawn off to a distance from Athens is clear from the fact that the catapults, missiles, etc., were stored away in the temple at this time (*IG.* ii. 733, 734, and *Klio*, 1909, p. 319 f.).

to retreat beyond Thermopylae.[1] Thus far the Athenians had been successful, but in the next year the whole situation was changed. The Aetolians, Phocians, and Boeotians no longer prosecuted the war with vigour, if they took part in it at all. Indeed, it seems clear from the military operations of 304 B.C. that Boeotia had joined hands with Cassander again.[2] Probably the defeat of Antigonus and Demetrius in Egypt, and the loss of prestige they sustained through their apparent inability to capture Rhodes, which, taken together, meant the failure of their effort to master the whole empire, cost them their friends in Greece, and enabled Cassander to throw all his troops into the Hellenic war. Since, at the same time, the Greek cities, garrisoned by Ptolemaic troops, notably Corinth, came by surrender into his possession, and the allies of Antigonus and Demetrius in the Peloponnesus seceded to Polyperchon,[3] Athens was left alone, and experienced disaster after disaster. Phyle and Panacton, and the passes which they dominated, fell into the enemy's hands;[4] but, perhaps, the most important new factor in the war was the fleet which Cassander brought into action in 304 B.C., and by means of which he defeated and captured the navy of Athens. There were Salaminians among his prisoners. These he liberated without ransom, and this evidence of goodwill towards the islanders, together with the grave peril in which they found themselves, induced them, despite the fact that their city had been fortified anew in the preceding two years,[5] to surrender Salamis

---

[1] Beloch (iii. 1. 170, n. 3) puts this incident in 301 B.C. Pausanias (x. 18. 7 ; 34. 3) got his knowledge of it from the bronze statue of Olympiodorus which the grateful Elateans erected at Delphi, the inscription of which seems not to have contained a date. Certainly the relief of Elatea must belong to 305 B.C., or to the period after the return of Demetrius from Rhodes, *i.e.* to 301 B.C. Beloch's reasons for rejecting 305 B.C. have no value—the chief being derived from a misinterpretation of the decree in honour of Demochares (cf. iii. 2. 374 ff.). After 303/2 B.C. Demochares was in exile (see below, iii. 122) ; hence 305 B.C. is the only possible date. Besides, there was no such permanent relief of Elatea possible in 301 B.C., as the erection of the statue to Olympiodorus demands.

[2] Otherwise the rapid advance of Cassander to the Attic frontier is inexplicable.

[3] Beloch, iii. 1. 164.   [4] Plut. *Demetr.* 23.

[5] Ἐφ. Ἀρχ., 1900, p. 148. The lettering of this decree of the soldiers in garrison at Sunium is like that of *IG.* ii. 270 (302/1 B.C.) or 297 (299/8 B.C.).

into Cassander's hands.[1] Aeschetades, the Athenian general in charge of the island, was blamed for this disaster, and was condemned to death by the Athenians, while those Salaminians who were responsible for the transition to Cassander, and who established on the island a new state, were subsequently expelled.[2] Attica was now open to attack from sea and land, and for the first time in a hundred years a foreign army set itself down to the siege of the city.[3] The catapults and missiles had not been idle on the Acropolis for more than a year.

It was apparent that the fall of Athens would be only a question of time and hunger, if the city were left to itself. Hence urgent requests were made of Demetrius that he should come to its relief.[4] Rhodes was as yet unconquered, but the prospects of success there were not improving. Accordingly, it was given an honourable peace, and Demetrius started for Greece with his army and a fleet of three hundred and thirty ships. He landed at Aulis in Boeotia, and forced Cassander to retreat by threatening the communications of his army. Boeotia and Phocis thereupon fell into his hands, while the fleet of his adversary probably sought safety in Corinth, whence also it may have come. A land engagement took place south of Thermopylae in which Cassander was defeated, whereupon Heracleia, the key of the pass, was lost, and Cassander was deserted by six thousand of his Macedonian troops. With this, the campaign of 304 B.C. ended, and the victor recaptured Phyle,

---

Lines 2 ff. (-ελλην-) may refer to 323/2 B.C. (cf. Ditt. *Syll.*[2], 187, 18); lines 14 ff. to 306/5 or 305/4 B.C.; and lines 21 ff. to 305/3 B.C. Cf. also Wilhelm, *Beiträge*, 57 ff.

[1] Polyaenus, iv. 11. 1; cf. Beloch, iii. 1. 164, n. 3.

[2] Paus. i. 35. 2. Niese (i. 244. 4; 247, n. 1) dates this incident in 317 B.C. (cf. Kirchner, *PA.* 322), but it was thought by Pausanias to be distinct from the events of this year as described by him in i. 25. 6. Beloch (iii. 1. 164, n. 3) errs in referring the two passages to 304 B.C.; see above, i. 35. Athens had no fleet when Salamis was captured in 317 B.C.; when she had a fleet, in 318 B.C., the Salaminians repulsed the attack of Cassander (Diod. xviii. 69). It was probably at this time that the grave *stele* of Leon and Leaina (see above, i. 35, n. 1) was used to receive a decree of the Salaminians in which τὸ]ν ταμία[ν τὸν τὴν δ]ευ[τέραν? τετράμηνον ταμιεύοντα is mentioned. Wilhelm, *Österr. Jahreshefte*, 1909, p. 135.

[3] Beloch, iii. 1. 164.   [4] *IG.* ii. 238 (305/4 B.C.; Sundwall, *Acta*, 11).

Panacton, and Salamis, and handed them back to the Athenians.[1] Thus was concluded the Four Years' War.[2]

The powerful army of Demetrius, and the crews of his three hundred and thirty warships, were doubtless quartered in Athens and the Piraeus during the winter of 304/3 B.C.—a circumstance to be remembered when passing judgment upon the spiritless conduct manifested by the Athenians on this occasion. The young king was by this time fully alive to the material advantages of apotheosis. There was a trait in his character not dissimilar to that manifested by Caligula when in ordering his own cultus he prescribed that the sacrifices should consist of flamingos, peacocks, heathcocks, guinea-fowl, pheasants, and like gorgeous or toothsome birds. There could be no doubt that the temples were the most commodious and attractive residences in all Greek cities; nor was Diogenes the Cynic the only Hellene who had discovered how refreshing they were in the hot Greek summers. On his way to Athens, Demetrius had taken up quarters in the shrine of Apollo during his stay on Delos. Now he occupied the Parthenon,[3] and this audacious use of the great temple—the St. Peter's of Athens—he justified by the unanswerable observation that, with deification, he had become the younger brother of Athena. Certainly he could find no other justification. The concubines in his train were numerous, and at this time an elderly adventuress, Lamia by name—a fascinating woman, whose doings were bruited abroad in contemporary court gossip, and in the pornographic literature of that and later ages—was able to exert a

---

[1] Plut. *Demetr.* xxiii. [2] Prior to December of 304 B.C.

[3] Teles (Hense[2]), 8. 4 ; cf. *JHS.*, 1910, p. 193. For this winter in Athens see in general Plut. *Demetr.* 23, 24, 26, and for Lamia, 27. Plutarch attaches this digression on Demetrius's misbehaviour to a remark made à propos of the collection of tribute from Athens for Lamia's toilet, which is alleged to have taken place in 303 B.C. ; but her entertaining must have occurred during the one winter Demetrius spent in Athens after her capture at the battle of Salamis. The incident of the tribute is timeless and placeless. *Frg.* 81 of the comedian Antiphanes probably belongs to a play produced in this year (Wilhelm, *Urk. dram. Aufführ.* 57 f.). The collocation of τοῦ γλυκυτάτου βασιλέως (Demetrius) and τῆς σεμνῆς θεᾶς (Athena) suits the situation at the time of the Dionysia or Lenaea of 304/3 B.C. admirably. It was then that Demetrius issued the notable series of gold staters described by Seltman (*Num. Chron.*, 1909, p. 267, No. 3), on which was stamped the head of Athena with his own features.

dominating influence upon him. There were orgies in the Maiden's shrine which astonished the pleasure-loving Athenians.[1] The wives, sons, and daughters of the citizens were exposed to the capricious lust of the rough Macedonian baron, and the least scandalous scenes witnessed on the Acropolis were those in which the king's *hetaerae* played the leading parts. But all through the winter the round of gaiety continued. Lamia's banquets, according to a current witticism, took cities by storm as irresistibly as the battering-rams of Demetrius. His Athenian partisans shared in this debauchery, some from inclination, we may be sure, and some with simulated acquiescence. The government was, indeed, under great obligations to the prince, and honours of all sorts were conferred upon him and his courtiers—deification and worship upon strumpets and minions, and civic privileges upon unworthy favourites.[2] Demetrius saw nothing but servility on all sides, according to Demochares, and was constrained to remark upon the paucity of worthy men among the Athenians.[3] In fact, there existed widespread discontent at his arrogance, and intense indignation at the shameless cringing of Stratocles and his associates, as was made clear after the departure of the king, when, during his triumphal march through the Peloponnesus, the Athenians were left for a while to themselves.

The government established in 307 B.C. had long since ceased to be harmonious. There had probably

---

[1] Philippides (Plut. *Demetr.* 26) says, in regard to Stratocles :

ὁ τὴν ἀκρόπολιν πανδοκεῖον ὑπολαβὼν
καὶ τὰς ἑταίρας εἰσαγαγὼν τῇ Παρθένῳ.

[2] Demochares, *FHG.* ii. 449 ; cf. Plut. *Demetr.* 24 ; *IG.* ii. 5. 264d (Ditt. *Syll.*[2] 173), which Wilhelm (*GGA.*, 1903, p. 785) has shown to have been passed in 303/2 B.C. ; ii. 243 (Ditt. *Syll.*[2] 179), 419 ; cf. Wilhelm, *GGA.*, 1903, p. 792 ; ii. 415 : cf. Wilhelm, *loc. cit.* In July 302 B.C. the decree in praise of Nicon of Abydus referred to above, i. 17, n. 1, was passed. At the moment, Abydus was fighting for Antigonus against Lysimachus.

[3] *FHG.* ii. 449. Demochares here very cleverly makes Poliorcetes, father of Antigonus who was the regent of Athens at the time he was writing, endorse the condemnation he passed upon Stratocles and his followers. What Demetrius really thought is, of course, another matter. The view taken of Stratocles and his adherents in the *Histories* of Demochares thus agrees with that expressed by his son Laches in regard to those who had exiled his father— they were destroyers of the *demos*. Cf. below, iv. 173.

never been much sympathy between Stratocles and Demochares, for Stratocles had been prominent among the prosecutors of Demosthenes in the Harpalus case,[1] while Demochares had, doubtless, as in 322 B.C., when Antipater demanded the public men responsible for the Hellenic War,[2] done his utmost in his uncle's defence. Demochares was working for an ideal democracy, and for a free and imperial Athens, whereas Stratocles was content to rule as the vicegerent of Poliorcetes. The course of events had accordingly brought it about that his position was almost identical with that of Demetrius of Phalerum whom he had succeeded. There were political fanatics in Athens at this time—men in whom devotion to party left no room for any other loyalty, or understanding for anybody else's views, and Demochares was their leader. In this spirit he had assailed the philosophers. That the attack failed was probably due, in part at least, to the indifference or hostility of those who were democrats from self-interest rather than from conviction, and of those whose democracy was tempered by experience as well as by philosophic criticism. In the spirit of *intransigentism* also Glaucippus, the son of Hypereides, brought a *graphe paranomon* in January of 304 B.C. against Meidias, the son of Demosthenes's old opponent, for proposing that public recognition be given to the services of Phocion. It is significant that the motion of Meidias was passed in the ecclesia in the first instance, and equally significant that the son of Hypereides failed to impress his views upon the jury courts, especially since in 304 B.C. the Athenian democracy was again at war with Macedon as at the time when Phocion was executed. In this case too the influence of the indifferent, and, in particular, of the moderate, democrats was probably decisive. The remains of Phocion, which had been cast out of Attica in 318 B.C., were now brought back and publicly buried, and a statue was erected in his honour at the state's expense.[3]

---

[1] See above, i. 13.
[2] [Plut.], *Lives of the Ten Orators*, 847 D.
[3] *Ibid.* 850 B; cf. Schäffer, *Philol.*, 1854, p. 165; Kirchner, *PA.* 2987; Diod. xviii. 67. 6; Nepos, *Phocion*, iv. 4.

The irreconcilable democrats were thus beaten a second time, but it was again in a matter in which the moderates supported Stratocles. In 303 B.C., however, as already intimated, a more serious crisis came.[1] The campaign of Demetrius in the Peloponnesus had been brilliantly successful, and on coming thereby into possession of the greater part of Greece south of Thermopylae he had con'voked at the Isthmus a Hellenic Congress which elected him suzerain of Greece and commander-in-chief of the national forces. The League formed by Philip and renewed by Alexander was thus re-established, and into it, of course, Athens entered.[2] An old constitutional question which the death of Alexander the Great had left unsolved was thereupon raised again—as to the rights of the suzerain to interfere in the internal problems of the several cities constituting the League. Philip had reserved to himself none, and prior to his assumption of divinity Alexander had possessed none either. Philip Arrhidaeus, at the instigation of Poly-perchon, had expressly restored the status which existed before Alexander's crossing into Asia ; so that the Athenians in 303 B.C. had some reason for believing that the formation anew of the Corinthian confederation was equivalent to a declaration of their internal liberty. Accordingly, when the jury courts condemned Cleomedon, a notable partisan of Demetrius, to a fine of fifty talents, and the king, through affection for the delinquent's graceless son, interfered and the verdict was quashed, a popular outburst occurred, and for a time the faction of Stratocles lost control of the rudder. A decree was passed prohibiting any citizen from soliciting the inter-vention of Demetrius in the domestic affairs of the city. The suzerain made it at once clear that he construed his position as that of the god Alexander, not as that of the

---

[1] Plut. *Demetr.* 24. For the time see *Klio*, 1905, 173 ff. The bitterness of the struggle which accompanied this uprising is obvious from the abuse showered upon Demochares by Archedicus the comic poet, for which see Polybius xii. 13 ; and by Democleides, a demagogue of the faction of Stratocles. Timaeus incorporated it in his history (Book 38), inadvisedly, as Polybius (*loc. cit.*) proved. Beloch's transfer (iii. 2, 375 f.) of this crisis to 291/0 B.C. seems to me reckless.

[2] *IG.* ii. 5. 264c.

generalissimo Philip, and bringing pressure to bear upon Athens, he re-established the ascendancy of Stratocles and his following. These, thereupon, dealt summarily with the authors of the sedition. Some were executed, others banished, and among those who left the city on this occasion was Demochares of Leuconoe. The will of Demetrius was then formally voted to be decisive in all matters, both secular and religious.[1] He thereupon proclaimed his ambition of taking the place of Alexander's son by marrying this unfortunate youth's promised bride Deidamia, the sister of Pyrrhus, at a national festival at Argos and in the presence of delegates from all Greece. Then in the following spring he made full use of the absolute power which had been conferred upon him in Athens; for he requested that he should be admitted at the wrong time and without the necessary preliminary initiation into the august Eleusinian Mysteries. The calendar at Athens was flexible enough, in all reason, and it was not difficult to intercalate a month when it seemed good to the majority to do so; for the *demos*, not the astronomers, ruled the city.[2] Still it was a rather outrageous *tour de force* by which Stratocles humoured the whim of Demetrius without violating too much popular superstition. The month of Munychion (April 302 B.C.) was declared to be Anthesterion (February) and the Little Mysteries were celebrated. It was then decreed to be Boedromion (September), and the initiation was completed. It was for this reason, doubtless, that Munychion was called by the wags in Athens Demetrius's month.[3]

After this Demetrius sailed to Thessaly to wrest it and Macedon from Cassander, while his new queen, Deidamia, was left to the hospitality of the Athenians. We do not need to follow him in his career in the north,

---

[1] Plut. *Demetr.* 24.

[2] *Class. Phil.* iii. 386 ff., and especially Kirchner, *Sitz. d. Berl. Akad.* 1910, p. 982 ff., where it is shown that the archon irregularly intercalated a month in 307/6 B.C. and again and again during the following two centuries.

[3] Plut. *Demetr.* 12, where in connexion with the first stay of Poliorcetes in Athens over winter (307/6 B.C.), a lot of dateless incidents are gathered together. Several of them look like witticisms of the comic stage, and in this light Grote (xii. 386, n. 1) regarded the alleged juggling with the months. Diodorus (xx. 110) mentions only the irregularity of the initiation.

but note simply that he conquered part of Thessaly in 302 B.C., and was in a position to settle matters finally with Cassander when recalled by his father to join in the great campaign which ended for them with total defeat at Ipsus in the late summer of 301 B.C. We restrict our attention to the doings of Athens. The departure of Demetrius in 302 B.C. was not followed by open revolt, but public opinion expressed itself forcibly and fearlessly. The New Comedy did not eschew politics altogether. Archedicus had assailed Demochares in the most scurrilous fashion, and Alexis had evinced enthusiasm at both the banishment of the philosophers and the great victory won by Demetrius at Salamis in Cyprus in 306 B.C.[1] The most effective rôle of comedy had always been opposition, and it now attacked the government of Stratocles. Stratocles, it appears, threatened to muzzle the playwrights on the pretext that they were aiding the aristocratic faction, as the moderates were called, who now formed the chief opposition to the official democracy. The most vigorous spokesman of the stage at this time was Philippides of Cephale, a comedian of note, who at the Lenaea or Dionysia of 301 B.C. assailed Stratocles for bringing the vengeance of the gods upon Athens. In the preceding July, it seems, the mast and the *peplos* had been torn away by the wind while the ship to which they were attached was being borne in the Panathenaic procession, and simultaneously a disastrous hailstorm had destroyed grapes and grain in Attica. For this, said Philippides, Stratocles was accountable through having given to men the honours due to gods. Such irreverent behaviour, he affirmed, not the reproaches of the comedians, was bringing the democracy into discredit,[2] and he went

---

[1] See above, iii. 103, n. 5 ; 114, n. 7 ; 121, n. 1.

[2] Plut. *Demetr.* 12, and for its date and interpretation, *Klio*, 1905, p. 163, n. 2. The injury to the ship can have occurred only in 306/5 or 302/1 B.C. The earlier date is excluded because the repairs were not made till 299/8 B.C. (*IG.* ii. 314 ; Ditt. *Syll.*² 197), *i.e.* for the Panathenaea of 298/7 B.C. Besides, it is probable that the verse quoted by Plutarch (*Demetr.* 26), ὁ τὸν ἐνιαυτὸν συντεμὼν εἰς μῆν' ἕνα, as well as those quoted above, iii. 119, n. 1, belong to the same general indictment of Stratocles, *i.e.* to the same play. The play, accordingly, followed 302 B.C., *i.e.* it belongs to the spring of 301 B.C. To it belong, also, probably, the verses quoted in Plut. *Demetr.* 12 and *Amator.* 750 F ; cf. Frantz, *Hermes*, 1900, p. 671.

on in vigorous style to denounce his trifling with the
calendar, his turning the Parthenon into a public-house,
and his defiling the Virgin by procuring courtesans for
the tenant of her shrine. His audacity seemingly led him
so far as to bring Stratocles himself together with his
mistress, Phylacium, on the stage. After this attack
Philippides probably thought himself unsafe in the city.
It is likely, moreover, that he had no sympathy with the
party which stood to assume the government should
Stratocles fall. At any rate, he betook himself to the
camp of Lysimachus of Thrace,[1] subsequently the most
bitter enemy of Demetrius, whither, in all probability,
Demochares had gone before him.[2]

The situation in Athens now became extremely critical;
for, on the withdrawal of Demetrius to Asia, Cassander
had again invaded Greece. He made an unsuccessful
attack on Argos; hence he must have mastered central
Greece with little difficulty, and thus come into a
position to proceed at any moment to the siege of
Athens. The connexion of the city with the sea was
thus of vital importance, for it was from the sea that
relief must come. Hence the work of repairing the Long
Walls and the fortifications of the Piraeus was pushed
energetically with funds raised at home and abroad.[3]
Unaided, Athens could not struggle with Cassander;
that the Four Years' War had made clear. What,
then, was to be done when the news arrived that the
allies of Cassander had gained a complete victory at
Ipsus, and that Antigonus was dead and Demetrius a
fugitive?

The only safety lay in a change of government,[4] for
which, moreover, the internal conditions were ripe; for
the democratic leaders (307-301 B.C.), like the oligarchic
of the preceding decade, had come into complete discredit with the people through what the world-situation
made necessary—the formation of tolerable relations

---

[1] *IG.* ii. 314 and ii. 5, p. 85 (Ditt. *Syll.*[2] 197. 10 ff.).
[2] See below, iv. 137, n. 6.
[3] *IG.* ii. 5. 371c, which, as Köhler has seen, must refer to this time.
[4] For this change of government see *Klio*, 1905, p. 155 ff., and Ed. Meyer,
ibid. 180 ff.

with the contemporary great powers. Each had in turn offended public opinion by invoking monarchical inter- ference in support of its own government. Now the Athenians were again at liberty to choose their advisers, but they could not return to those whom the arrival of Demetrius Poliorcetes in 307 B.C. had caused them to dismiss and send into exile. The internal situation was thus favourable for the moderates—for those who advo- cated the old ideal of a government based upon the substantial elements in the state, upon a party composed of men who wished to see the *demos* curbed, but not through outside interference. Accordingly, in the late summer of 301 B.C., the partisans of this political creed, Phaedrus of Sphettus, Philippides of Paeania, Lachares of unknown *deme* and parentage, and others whose names are lost, mastered the government. Demetrius of Phalerum was living in exile, perhaps in Thebes,[1] ready to return when the occasion offered itself, when the balance should incline in favour of Cassander. Deinarchus the orator was in Chalcis, hoping that time would obscure his sycophancy, that his oligarchic friends would obtain power, or that the influence of Theo- phrastus would work his recall, and others of the same party were waiting for a chance to regain their property and political importance ; but for these the moderates had no use, and they were all left in exile. On the other hand, they could not admit to their ranks democrats from conviction and inheritance, men who were bound to oppose any change in the existing democratic institu- tions, and who had not yet learned that Athens was too weak to grasp at empire. Particularly objectionable were those who had opposed Stratocles, and had, there- fore, escaped the disgrace of their party ; for such men

---

[1] It is generally assumed that he remained in Thebes till the death of Cassander in 297 B.C. (Diod. xx. 45. 4 ; Diog. Laert. v. 78 ; cf. Strabo, ix. 398 ; Cic. *De fin.* v. 54 ; Syncell. 521. 13). To what Polyaenus (iii. 15) refers is not clear ; cf. Droysen (ii. 2. 317, n. 2), who, however, gives no authorities for his view. Certainly, Cassander cannot have protected him from Poliorcetes in Thebes in 304–301 B.C. ; but it was from Athens, not from Poliorcetes, that Demetrius of Phalerum had to fear. With the death of Cassander ended the prospects of his return to power in Athens ; so he went to Egypt to begin a new career.

would be dangerous to the new government. Hence, Demochares and Philippides, the comedian, were not allowed to return to Athens.

Queen Deidamia was the guest of the Athenians. It was far from their intention to outlaw Demetrius Poliorcetes, and for this reason they left his statue, tribe, deification, and other honours unmolested;[1] but the presence in the city of his queen committed the government to his cause, which was contrary to its interest and wishes. Accordingly, she was escorted to Megara with the courtesy and pomp befitting her rank, and, at the same time, an embassy was sent to Demetrius announcing to him and to the world in general the new foreign policy of the state.[2] Athens was to have no entangling relations with any of the kings. She affirmed her intention of preserving the strictest neutrality. By withdrawing from international politics, entering none of the contemporary alliances, and avoiding all occasion for outside interference, the government hoped to preserve the country from all but the most wanton and odious attacks. This Phaeacian policy was not a novelty. It had an inherent attraction for doctrinaires and dilettanti in politics; for those who thought so well of human nature as to believe that, if Athens wished political isolation, she had only to ask for it; that others, to whom she would be a priceless possession, would disinterestedly leave her alone. Theramenes had been among the first to uphold doctrines of this sort, in

---

[1] The statues of Antigonus and Demetrius appear in 295/4 B.C. (*IG.* ii. 300). The priest of the Soteres was still in existence in 289 B.C. Plut. *Demetr.* 46 καὶ τόν τε Δίφιλον, ὃς ἦν ἱερεὺς τῶν Σωτήρων ἀναγεγραμμένος, ἐκ τῶν ἐπωνύμων ἀνεῖλον, ἄρχοντας αἱρεῖσθαι πάλιν, ὥσπερ ἦν πάτριον, ψηφισάμενοι. Moreover, it is not stated explicitly that the office was abolished at this time. The Soteres were still worshipped in Athens in 235/4 B.C. (Kirchner, *Klio*, 1908, p. 487 f.). The attention paid to the cult probably depended upon the relations with Macedon at the time; so that in *IG.* ii. 431 (212/11 B.C.) the Soteres are omitted where they are mentioned in *Klio*, 1908, p. 487. The cult itself was not abolished, in all likelihood, till 200 B.C. (see below, vi. *ca.* 277). The tribe of Demetrius and that of his father remained in existence till 201 B.C. Upon their maintenance that of the Soteres depended. How long the Antigonia and Demetria lasted we do not know precisely; but from *IG.* ii. 5. 614*b*, we learn that Demetria were re-established in 240/39 B.C., which implies the cessation of this fête much earlier. It was probably abolished in 289/8 B.C., and there is no evidence extant for the subsequent existence of Antigonia.

[2] Plut. *Demetr.* 30.

so far, at least, as their domestic bearing was concerned, and Xenophon and Isocrates had lent their authority and eloquence to the promulgation of them.[1] They had come to clearer and clearer formulation through the statecraft of Eubulus, Aeschines, and Phocion, and the latter, as we have just seen, was now their honoured martyr. They were finally realised for a short time in 301-296 B.C., and again on two later occasions in the third century (276-266 and 229-224 B.C.) ; but their realization and subsequent maintenance depended upon the existence of a balance of power in the ancient world, upon an equilibrium of forces like to that which has worked in recent times for the preservation of the small states in Europe. Thus in 301 B.C. Demetrius Poliorcetes was unable to coerce his rebellious city ; nor was the coalition of powers which won the battle of Ipsus in a better position to compel her submission, for on the morrow of the victory it broke into its elements, and a new series of moves and countermoves began, the upshot of which was that Poliorcetes was admitted to the league, and that a serious effort was made to maintain the *status quo* by judicious matrimonial alliances and a temporary cessation of political rivalry.[2] Each ruler feared to jeopardise his belongings by striving for more. It was for this interval that the neutral government remained in power in Athens.

To a state which depended for its independence upon the goodwill of its neighbours great armaments seemed an expensive and unnecessary burden. The abandonment of an aggressive foreign policy made preparations for attack senseless. This was the view taken by the moderates in 301 B.C. Hence they made a profound change in the whole life of the people in that they abandoned conscription as a system of national defence, and instituted in its stead volunteer service.[3] Henceforth the fighting force of Athens consisted ordinarily of twelve select bodies of both infantry and

---

[1] Ed. Meyer, *Klio*, 1905, p. 180.
[2] *Ibid.* 182.
[3] *Priests of Asklepios*, 162 ff., 170 ; Sundwall, *Acta*, 22 ff.

cavalry,[1] and of detachments of paid mercenaries.[2]   It
was no longer necessary for all, or, as prior to 338 B.C.,
the propertied young men of Attica to gather in the
Piraeus and the frontier forts for training and service in
the art of war ; and, the compulsion being removed, the
ephebe registration fell from about eight hundred[3] to
about thirty.   The corps of ephebes was, thereafter, composed of young men of good families ; and while it
remained like the cavalry, a source of civic pride and an
ornament to religious processions, it became almost a
negligible military factor.[4]   The organization was reduced,
the twelve *sophronistae* and one of the two *paedotribae*
being dispensed with.[5]   The *cosmetes*, or rector, needed
no assistants for so few pupils, but the staff of trainers
was retained, and military instruction in all its branches
was given as before.   The term of service, however, was
reduced to one year, and instead of living in barracks in
the Piraeus and the frontier forts, the ephebes spent
their year in Athens.   This made it possible to add
instruction in the liberal sciences to the strictly technical
course in tactics, archery, and the use of the javelin and
catapult.   The young men who volunteered to enter the
military school were also expected or required to attend
the lectures of the philosophers, and those who did not
become cadets had now their eighteenth and nineteenth

---

[1] The ἐπίλεκτοι, who appear in *IG.* ii. 323 at the time of the Celtic migration
and in the games of the second century B.C.   See *IG.* ii. 444, 445, 446.

[2] Technically στρατιῶται.   The word ξένοι appears in the inscriptions of
this period to designate a part of the mercenaries only (*IG.* ii. 331. 25, ii. 5.
614*b* ; Wilhelm, *Beiträge*, 59, No. 46 ; and *JHS.*, 1908, p. 308).   In the last
inscription, line 11, ἵππαρχος or φύλαρχος should be substituted for what the
editor has restored στρατηγός, which has one letter too many.   The πάλιν of
line 11 shows that the position which brought the officer into connexion
with the ξένοι was, as in the preceding year, a cavalry command.   For the
ἀνθιππασία see Ditt. *Syll.*[2] 200.   It formed part of the Panathenaic games.
Since the archon for the following year was Archippus (321/20 B.C.), the date of
the inscription is Ol. 114. 3 (322/21 B.C.).   The Archippus of 318/17 B.C. is
excluded by the requirement that the preceding year be Panathenaic.   The
corps of ξένοι could apparently be put under the command of a *hipparch* or
general as the circumstances demanded.   It probably contained cavalry as well
as infantry.   Similarly, Pleistarchus at about this time τῆς ἵππου Κασσάνδρου
καὶ τοῦ ξενικοῦ τὴν ἀρχὴν ἀδελφὸς ὢν ἐπετέτραπτο (Paus. i. 15. 1).   The ξένοι in
the New Comedy are of course the foreign mercenaries.   These existed in considerable numbers till 229 B.C.   See below, vi. *ca.* 251 notes, and above, ii. 74.

[3] Accepting Sundwall's careful estimate, *Acta*, 24 f.

[4] It might, however, be used in a crisis, as in 283/82 B.C.   See below, iv. 153.

[5] Aristot. *Const. of Athens* 42. 2 f.

years free to complete their general education.[1]   There was thus an increased demand for instruction in physics, metaphysics, and, above all, in practical ethics, and it can hardly be accidental that immediately afterwards Zeno, a Semite from Citium, who had been a student in Athens since 311/0 B.C., opened his own school.[2]   He had been a business man in his younger days, and in the choice of a site for his establishment he did not belie his training; for instead of retiring to a garden in the suburbs, as his three most serious competitors had done, he began giving his lectures in the Stoa Poicile, a portico facing the great piazza of Athens;[3] and, in fact, he seems to have reached the ephebes in quite a special way.[4]

The supremacy of the moderates necessitated constitutional changes, for it was not likely that a state, organized so cleverly to ensure the domination of the majority, would entrust its affairs indefinitely to the

[1] Wilamowitz (*Antigonus*, 295, n. 6) has paralleled [Plato], *Axiochus*, 366 E, and the diatribe of Crates reproduced by Teles (Hense,[2] 49 f.).   Both set forth in detail the course of study of an Athenian boy, and both are doubtless derived from a common source.   This must have been written before 301 B.C. ; for in the *Axiochus* we have mention of the formal registration among the ephebes (ἐπειδὰν δ᾽ εἰς τοὺς ἐφήβους ἐγγραφῇ, κοσμητὴς καὶ φόβος χειρῶν ; cf. *Priests of Asklepios*, 163, n. 82) ; of the Lyceum and the Academy alone, and of the *sophronistae*.   The source of the *Axiochus* was, further, written in all probability prior to 307 B.C. ; cf. καὶ τὴν ἐπὶ τοὺς νέους αἵρεσιν τῆς ἐξ Ἀρείου πάγου βουλῆς, which points to 317-307 B.C. as a more definite date.   All of this the writer of the *Axiochus* left unchanged.   On the other hand, Teles, who lived in *ca.* 238 B.C., in restating the same arguments, which he attributes to Crates, left unmentioned arrangements foreign to his own time.   The familiarity of Crates with Athenian institutions of the time of Demetrius of Phalerum and his introduction of the Athenian curriculum into his diatribe show—what his relation to Zeno suggests (see below, iv. 185, n. 5)—that the cynic Plato lived in Athens at this time.

[2] In the archonship of Clearchus (301/0 B.C.) ; cf. Beloch (Crönert), iii. 2. 39, 471.

[3] Judeich, *Topographie von Athen*, 299 ff.

[4] Thus in the honorary decree referred to below (iv. 187) it is said that below διετέλεσε καὶ τοὺς εἰς σύστασιν αὐτῷ τῶν νέων πορευομένους παρακαλῶν ἐπ᾽ ἀρετὴν καὶ σωφροσύνην παρώρμα πρὸς τὰ βέλτιστα.   Of the decree two copies were to be made and set up on stone, one in the Academy and the other in the Lyceum ; upon which Wilamowitz remarks : "an den beiden Orten, wo der Staat seine Epheben erziehen liess, mahnte nun die öffentliche Anerkennung der σωφροσύνη die Jugend zur Nachahmung.   Ein Psephisma σωφροσύνης ἕνεκα ist genau so singulär wie die Wahl der Gymnasien als Aufstellungsort."   Cf. Diog. Laert. vii. 169 (Κλεάνθην) ἡγούμενόν τε τῶν ἐφήβων ἐπί τινα θέαν ὑπ᾽ ἀνέμου παραγυμνωθῆναι καὶ ὀφθῆναι ἀχίτωνα· ἐφ᾽ ᾧ κρότῳ τιμηθῆναι ὑπ᾽ Ἀθηναίων.   See von Arnim, *op. cit.* i. 140. 622, from which it is clear that Sphaerus, the pupil of Zeno, aimed to reach the ephebes at Sparta ; cf. Plut. *Cleon*, 2, and von Arnim, ii. 3. 3*a*. A statue of Chrysippus stood in the Ptolemaeum, the new rendezvous of the Athenian ephebes (Paus. i. 17. 2) ; see below, vi. 260.

guidance of a minority.   The *demos* had to be disarmed.
This was accordingly done.   How, we do not know
completely, but our defective records enable us to
detect a reconstruction of the financial administration,
and the substitution of elected for allotted magistrates.
Subsequent to this epoch, at any rate, we miss
various officials who had earlier been of importance
in finance, notably the treasurer of the *demos*, while
an elected officer, the *exetastes*, or inspector, makes
his appearance to co-operate with the *trittyarchs* in
controlling various public moneys.[1]   In 297/6 B.C. a
further change was effected, and the general superintendent of the administration was given charge of the
state treasury, from which disbursements were made
for legislative and diplomatic purposes.[2]   At the same
time, probably, the treasurers of Athena were abolished,[3]
and their duties, at least in so far as the custody of
munitions of war, which were regularly stored in the
temples, were concerned, appear to have been attended
to afterwards by one of the ten generals specially
detailed for the preparation and preservation of military
machines and stores.   Probably a law of citizenship
similar to that of 321 B.C., though less rigorous in its
demand of a property qualification, was passed; certainly
the same method was employed—judicial control[4]—to
prevent the people from bestowing its civic privileges
upon unworthy persons, such as the favourites of
Demetrius Poliorcetes had often been.   How seriously
the position of the populace was impaired by all these
changes we can judge only from the result.

Among the moderates Lachares seems to have been
the most energetic man, and he is referred to by our

[1] *IG.* ii. 297 (299/8 B.C.) ; cf. 'Εφ. 'Αρχ., 1900, p. 133.
[2] *IG.* ii. 300, ii. 5. 300*b* (295/4 B.C.) ; cf. *Klio*, 1905, p. 171, and Westermann, *Class. Phil.*, 1910, p. 212 f.
[3] Köhler, *Zeitsch. f. Num.*, 1898, p. 15.   They appear in 300/299 B.C.
and probably also in 299/8 B.C. (*IG.* ii. 612), while the new generalship ἐπὶ
τὴν παρασκευήν, for which see *Klio*, 1909, p. 320, is in existence at the beginning
of 296/5 B.C. (*IG.* ii. 331 ; Ditt. *Syll.*[2] 213. 21 f.).
[4] *IG.* ii. 300 (cf. Larfeld, *op. cit.* 790), as interpreted by *IG.* ii. 229 (322/1–
319/8 B.C.).   *IG.* ii. 243 (306–301 B.C.) shows that the reference to the law-courts
was not existent continuously from 319/8 B.C. forward.   An unpublished decree,
probably of the year 289/8 B.C. (see below, iv. 147, n. 1), shows that the courts
for this purpose were called τὰ δημόσι[α] δι[καστή]ρ[ια].

authorities as the leader of the government.[1] His personal supremacy was further enhanced by a confidential arrangement into which he entered with Cassander, the purport of which was, perhaps, not revealed till later.[2] In 301 B.C. Cassander was satisfied with the exclusion of Demetrius, and at once made a peace with the new government.[3] Later he gave it his active support.[4] In fact, he had no alternative, since to continue the war would have forced Athens back into the hands of Demetrius, who was lord of the sea still, as well as of Megara, Corinth, and Argos. Moreover, since he could not count on the assistance of his allies now that Antigonus was crushed, he preferred not to fight it out with Demetrius single-handed. A similar regard for Cassander saved Athens from a war with Demetrius, whom, moreover, the Athenians had conciliated by handing over to him the ships which he had left in the Piraeus. It was to Lysimachus of Thrace that the enemies of Demetrius, who were at the same time enemies of Cassander, had gone; but he, too, remained friendly to the new government. In 301 B.C. he sent home certain Athenians whom Demetrius and Antigonus had kept captive in Asia — probably as hostages; and two years later he forwarded to Athens ten thousand *medimni* of grain, and a mast and a sail for the Panathenaic *peplos*.[5] By this time Seleucus and Ptolemy had become the allies of Demetrius and Lysimachus respectively, so that they too were probably not wanting in cordiality toward Athens.[6] Neutrality as a foreign policy seemed thus a brilliant success. But in 298/7 B.C. Cassander died, and his oldest son, Philip, followed him to the grave in four months. His other sons, two foolish young men,

---

[1] Paus. i. 25. 7 ; cf. *Klio*, 1905, p. 163, n. 1, p. 183, n. 1.

[2] Paus. *loc. cit.*

[3] *Marmor Parium* (Jacoby), 24, where the entry under the year 301/0 B.C., 'Αθηναῖοι δὲ Κασ-, can mean only the formation of a peace.

[4] *IG.* ii. 297 (Ditt. *Syll.*[2] 188).

[5] Ditt. *Syll.*[2] 197. 10 ff. ; cf. *Klio*, 1905, p. 163, n. 2.

[6] The work of Shtchukarew (*Journ. of the Ministry of Public Instruction*, St. Petersburg, 1889) on the archons of Athens between 300 and 265 B.C., and that of Sokolow on the same subject (*Collected Writings*, § xix., 1910. Russian), I have been unable to use.

Alexander and Antipater, quarrelled over the succession.
This changed the situation completely. The strong,
careful man who for nineteen years had stood as ruler
of Macedon in the centre of the tangled diplomacy
and the vast combinations by which the division of
Alexander's empire was perpetuated had found no
worthy successor, and in two places his absence was felt
immediately, in Athens and in Syria. In Athens dissatisfaction with the constitutional changes, chagrin on
the part of the extremists at their loss of power, and
dissensions among the governing faction now culminated
in an attack upon Lachares, who was suspected of
having been Cassander's tool, and the city broke out in
open sedition.[1] In Syria, Seleucus pressed Demetrius
for the surrender of the best parts of his kingdom,
while Demetrius saw in the anarchy in Macedon an
opportunity to make good by conquests in Europe
prospective losses in Asia. Accordingly he sought to
strike while the iron was hot in Macedon, and civil war
was rife in Athens; hence in 296 B.C. he sailed for
Greece, Athens being his objective point. When he
arrived off the coast of Attica a storm scattered his fleet
and destroyed many of his ships. A large number of
sailors and soldiers lost their lives, but Demetrius
escaped, and after collecting the fragments of his army
he made an attack on the city. It was beaten off with
ease. Consequently he had to wait for reinforcements;
and, while using the interval for an incursion into the
Peloponnesus, he was wounded before the walls of
Messene, and thus forced to make a further delay.
Upon his recovery he returned to Attica, and Eleusis
fell into his hands. Rhamnus was likewise occupied,
and the country lying between these two places was
devastated. In the meanwhile the sedition in Athens
had reached the natural outcome, for Lachares had
strengthened his position through an alliance with the
Boeotians, and upon the approach of danger had drawn
the reins of government more tightly.[2] The institutions

---

[1] Plut. *Demetr.* 33 f. ; Paus. i. 25. 7.
[2] Plut. *loc. cit.* ; Paus. *loc. cit.*

of 301 B.C. were not modified, but a new assignment of
the magistracies was made (spring of 295 B.C.).[1] The
senate was discharged and a new one appointed in its
place, from which we may perhaps infer that it had
favoured the popular movement. The eponymous
archon, Nicias, was re-elected—a step so obviously
expedient that no comment upon it is necessary. The
re-election of a general is, however, significant—significant of the worth of Lachares, since the general elected
was an honourable man like Phaedrus of Sphettus.[2]
Lachares was prepared for defection. He crushed his
opponents within the city, not without bloodshed,[3] and
made himself, in fact, dictator of Athens. The dis-
affected remnants, thereupon, withdrew to the Piraeus,
and formed themselves into a separate body-politic
there.[4] This made it possible for Demetrius to concentrate his forces upon the city proper, but an assault was
not to be thought of, and, indeed, was not necessary,
for starvation could do the work as well and better.[5]
Demetrius crucified the owner and pilot of a merchant
ship, which was caught while running the blockade, and
thus deterred others from trying to introduce supplies
stealthily. Provisions ran short. Barley sold at forty
drachmae per *medimnus* and wheat at three hundred,
twenty and sixty times the normal price, so that the
distress soon became acute. Epicurus put his school
on rations, and counted out the few beans which had
to suffice for the daily sustenance of each member.
Plutarch tells a horrible story of a struggle between
a father and son for the possession of a dead mouse.
Lachares set a worthy example of unselfishness, and
cheerfully shared the privations of his troops.[6] When
money ran short in the public chests, he did not spare
the religious dedications, but melted down the precious

---

[1] *IG.* ii. 299 ; cf. Beloch, iii. 2. 197 f. For the maintenance of the republican
institutions see *IG.* ii. 299 and ii. 5. 299c ; cf. *Klio*, 1905, p. 160.

[2] *IG.* ii. 331. 21 ff ; cf. Wilamowitz, *Antigonus*, 238.

[3] Paus. i. 29. 10.

[4] Inferred by de Sanctis (27, n. 4) from *IG.* ii. 300, and Polyaenus, iv.
7. 5. Beloch (iii. 1. 225, n. 1) assents, but Kolbe (*Ath. Mitt.*, 1905, p. 87, n. 1)
dissents. [5] For the siege see Plut. *Demetr.* 33 f.

[6] Koch, iii. 357 ; Wilamowitz, *Antigonus*, 200.

objects preserved in the temples, and thus supplemented the silver coins with an issue of gold.[1] This ensured the fidelity of his soldiers, but it did not give them bread. The city stood loyally by Lachares, but the Piraeus was in the possession of the democrats. These did not desire the state to fall into the hands of Demetrius, but they were willing to go so far as to co-operate with him for their own restoration. The king was, doubtless, ready with promises, and by this means got armour and weapons from the Piraeus for one thousand of his troops.[2] In the city this dealing with the enemy was viewed as treason, and a decree was passed imposing the death penalty upon any one who should raise the question of a peace or conference with Demetrius.[3] The spirit of the defenders was thus dauntless, but, as the months went by, the situation grew more and more intolerable. The only hope was that relief would come from without, and of this there were great expectations, for the rivals of Demetrius had thrown themselves upon his Asiatic empire, and Ptolemy had sent, not his daughter as he had agreed, but the fleet which he had been strengthening quietly since 306 B.C., with instructions to seize Cyprus first and then proceed through the islands [4] to the relief of Athens. There was a joyful moment in the city when the one hundred and fifty Egyptian ships hove in sight off Aegina, but the jubilation was short-lived. The navy of Demetrius proved twice as powerful, and upon its appearance in full strength, the admiral of Ptolemy withdrew without risking an engagement. This settled the fate of Athens. Lachares escaped in disguise to his friends in Boeotia, and the city opened its gates to Demetrius. The entrance of the king was impressive, and the citizens were con-

---

[1] Paus. i. 29. 16 ; cf. Köhler, *Zeitsch. f. Num.*, 1898, p. 10 ff. At p. 15, n. 1, he says: "Die anderweitig sich findende Angabe, Lachares habe das Gold der Parthenos-Statue geraubt, beruht wahrscheinlich auf einer missverstandenen Phrase." The phrase referred to is found in the *Areopagites* of Demetrius (Koch, iii. 357) : γυμνὴν Ἀθηνᾶν τότ' ἐποίησε Λαχάρης.

[2] Polyaenus, iv. 7. 5. There is possibly a reference to this co-operation with the Piraeus in Paus. i. 25. 8.

[3] Plut. *Demetr.* 34.

[4] It was at this time that he laid the basis for the subsequent domination of Egypt in the Aegean Sea (see below, iv. 151, n. 5).

voked in the theatre to meet him (spring of 294 B.C.).[1]
What his pleasure was, no one knew till he stepped
forward in the theatre and addressed the assembly.
Then it was obvious that his mood was merciful. He
bore the city no ill-will for its desertion, for this had
been the fault, not of the state, but of the oligarchic
faction ; and the resistance had been due, not to the
best men of the city—had they not gone to the Piraeus?
—but to Lachares, the sacrilegious tyrant. It remained
simply to restore the government of Stratocles, and to
abolish the limitations imposed upon popular rights in
301 B.C. This Demetrius announced to be his intention,
and at the same time he relieved the distress in the
city by a gift of one hundred thousand *medimni* of
grain. The rest of the king's programme was then
disclosed. Dromocleides of Sphettus, a close associate
of Stratocles, interrupted the applause by moving that
the Piraeus and Munychia be handed over to the king.
In view of the attitude of the harbour-town during the
siege, there was, doubtless, no need of the troops of
Demetrius in the theatre to explain the passage of this
resolution, but it was not so easy to give it effect. The
party in the Piraeus resisted, and it was only after a
siege had begun that a reconciliation was effected and
the garrison of Demetrius admitted.[2] The iron hand
which put the rudder in the feeble grasp of Stratocles
was then displayed, when Demetrius seized the city end
of the Long Walls also, and secured it by fortifications
thrown up on the Museum hill.[3] The situation of 317-
307 B.C. was thus restored, and it was only in the
personnel and traditions of the dominant party that the
status of the city differed from what it had been at the
time of Demetrius of Phalerum.

[1] *IG.* ii. 300. [2] Polyaenus, iv. 7. 5.
[3] Plut. *Demetr.* 34 ; Paus. i. 25. 8.

CHAPTER IV

THE CRUSHING OF ATHENS BETWEEN MACEDON AND EGYPT

ἐγὼ Πτολεμαίου τοῦ βασιλέως τέτταρα
χυτρίδι' ἀκράτου τῆς τ' ἀδελφῆς προσλαβὼν
τῆς τοῦ βασιλέως ταῦτ', ἀπνευστί τ' ἐκπιὼν
ὡς ἄν τις ἥδιστ' ἴσον ἴσῳ κεκραμένον,
καὶ τῆς ὁμονοίας, διὰ τί νῦν μὴ κωμάσω
ἄνευ λυχνούχου πρὸς τὸ τηλικοῦτο φῶς ;

ALEXIS, 244 (Koch, ii. p. 386).

ATHENS surrendered in the spring of 294 B.C., and in the following July[1] the democratic institutions entered into operation. Some of the offices abolished in 301 B.C. were not restored. Thus the treasurer of the *demos* appears no more in the Athenian documents. Others were adapted to the new situation. Thus the official in charge of the general administration was given a number of colleagues.[2] The abolition of the treasurership of the *demos* may have made this enlargement advisable, but the substitution of a committee for a single magistrate, especially for one who, like the official in charge of the general administration between 301 and 294 B.C., had become unduly strong,[3] was a logical democratic procedure, and, had we the means of knowing, we should probably find that the restoration of the extreme democracy was accompanied by a similar multiplication of officers in other departments. Possibly the treasurers of Athena would have been re-established, had their charge not become a sinecure through the fact that Lachares had denuded the temples

---

[1] *Klio*, 1905, p. 172, n. 5. [2] *Ibid.* 170. [3] *Ibid.* 171, n. 3.

of their precious objects during the siege.[1] Besides, the days of temple finance were long since past, and this Board of treasurers had been needed because the temples were banks as well as places of deposit for ex-votos. Now they contained nothing which a caretaker could not safeguard. One democratic step the new government did not venture to take : it did not restore the system of national conscription.[2] To do so would have evoked a military display offensive to Demetrius, and could have been viewed by him only as a threat. Besides, while the régime of 294 B.C. was democratic in its leanings, it included men who had belonged to the moderate party. The relations produced between the leaders of the rival factions by the recent calamities were proclaimed officially, when Stratocles came forward in 294 B.C. and moved a vote of thanks for the many services rendered to Athens by Philippides of Paeania.[3] Phaedrus, too, notwithstanding that he had been faithful to Lachares at the time of the *coup d'état*, was retained in no less a position than the generalship of home defence.[4] Even more important was the adhesion of Olympiodorus, who attained the archonship in the year following the restoration.[5] There was thus a general disposition on the part of the democrats who followed Stratocles and believed in Demetrius to let bygones be bygones. The extreme partisans, however, were not forgiven. The former dictator, Demetrius of Phalerum, was now in Egypt, and his fellow-exiles were scattered. Demochares was probably in Thrace all this while,[6] and apart from the

---

[1] Paus. i. 29. 16 ; cf. Köhler, *Zeitsch. f. Num.*, 1898, p. 15, n. 1.
[2] *Priests of Asklepios*, 166.   [3] *IG.* ii. 302.
[4] *Class. Phil.*, 1907, p. 308 ff.   [5] *IG.* ii. 302.
[6] This conclusion is based upon two arguments. 1. The silence in regard to the place of exile in the honorary degree passed by the Athenians on the motion of his son in 271/0 B.C. ([Plut.], *Lives of the Ten Orators*, 850 F). This is inexplicable except on the assumption that it was the kingdom of Lysimachus. Apart from the fact that Lysimachus was the mortal personal enemy of Demetrius Poliorcetes, it would have been bad policy for one asking a favour of a community under the suzerainty of Antigonus to emphasize the connexion of Demochares with the father of the rival of Antigonus to the throne of Macedon (*Klio*, 1905, p. 380 ff.). 2. The influence which Demochares possessed in Thrace after his return from exile. It was to Lysimachus and Antipater, his son-in-law, alone that Demochares made a personal application

fact that a protégé of Lysimachus was naturally an enemy of Demetrius, his own quarrel with Demetrius was mortal. Besides, he could not exist in Athens alongside of Stratocles.

There can be no doubt that the mass of the Athenian people was disappointed grievously with the action of Demetrius; for the garrison in the Museum gave the lie to all assertions that Athens was free and autonomous, and the figure of Athena Promachus, which Demetrius put upon his silver coins,[1] showed that he regarded Athens as his Greek capital. Yet it was for liberty and self-government that the democracy existed, for these ends that it drew vitality from its glorious past. The question in 294 B.C. was, therefore, not how long the democracy could maintain itself against the oligarchy of the moderate or extreme sort, but how long it could maintain friendly relations with its suzerain. The situation became acute speedily; for in the year of his conquest of Athens, Demetrius came by a series of peculiar accidents into possession of the throne of Macedon,[2] and thereby associated with himself all the detestation which two generations of struggle had created in the minds of Attic democrats against that country and its rulers. The gravest menace to the freedom of Athens came thus to be its foretime liberator, and, just as in 307 B.C., so in 294 B.C., any distant king was more acceptable to the *demos* than its nearest neighbour. It is possible that the death of Stratocles occurred in 293 B.C.; at any rate he disappears from public life at this time, and the government came more and more into the hands of those whom Demetrius regarded as his political enemies. His time had been occupied fully in Macedon during the year of his accession in putting his house in order,

---

for funds (see below, iv. 146). Possibly he went to Macedon first and thence to Thrace along with Antipater. In this way his encounter with Philip (Seneca, *De ira*, iii. 23; cf. Droysen, ii. 2. 249, n. 2), the rival of Antipater, would find an explanation, as well as the interest of Antipater in the Athenian uprising. Cf. also Polybius, xii. 13. 8, where we learn that Demochares had made bitter attacks upon the regent Antipater.

[1] See Seltman, *Num. Chron.*, 1909, p. 271, Nos. 8, 10; cf. 273 and *JHS.*, 1910, p. 196, n. 36.   [2] Plut. *Demetr.* 36 f.

but in 293 B.C. he was ready to round out his dominions in Greece. Boeotia was not yet his, but it yielded on his arrival, revolted, however, when a Spartan army came to its assistance, but gave way again when Demetrius forced the Spartans to retreat. It was still treated with clemency, but Thebes, its capital, was put under the dictatorship of the historian, Hieronymus of Cardia, and a Macedonian garrison was laid in the Cadmia. The ruler of Macedon was thus becoming rapidly the master of Greece ; and what was even more serious, the ruler in question had been, along with his father, king of the world, and was known to cherish still the ambition of crushing those monarchs who, forsooth, called themselves kings too, but who were really only rebellious satraps.[1] Demetrius must be met in Greece itself : that was clear to at least Ptolemy of Egypt, who had succeeded Cassander in the rôle of champion of states' rights. He had tried to rescue Athens in 295/4 B.C., but at that time his fleet had been too weak. He had established Pyrrhus in Epirus to watch Demetrius from that quarter.[2] That his hand came again into play in the fall of 292 B.C.[3] is hardly dubitable, for at this moment, while Demetrius was engaged in Thrace in an effort to steal the kingdom of Lysimachus, Thebes revolted a second time, and Athens entered into negotiations with Egypt. With the subjugation of Thebes we are not concerned directly here. Antigonus, the son of Demetrius and Phila, called away

---

[1] Plut. *Demetr.* 25. 41 f. ; cf. above, ii. 64, n. 1 ; below, iv. 148. Demetrius showed by externals that he had his father's ambition of becoming heir to Alexander's kingship.

[2] Plut. *Pyrrh.* 5.

[3] From 293/2 B.C. onward, as is well known, no list of Athenian archons is extant. That used for chronological purposes in this book is constructed in *Cornell Studies*, x., *Gött. gel. Anz.*, 1900, p. 433 ff. (Kirchner), and *Univ. of Calif. Publ.*; *Class. Phil.* i. (cited as *Priests of Asklepios*), 131 ff. Kolbe's substitute for part of it (*op. cit.* below, iv. 142, n. 1) has been rejected for adequate reasons by Kirchner (*Berl. phil. Woch.*, 1909, pp. 845 ff.) and Pomtow (*ibid.*, 1910, p. 1096). See also *Deutsche Literaturzeitung*, 1910, p. 1953, and below, iv. 182, n. 1. The calendar cycle in use at this time is now pretty definitely established (see Sundwall, *op. cit.* above ii. 52, n. 4) ; but Kirchner (see above, iii. 122, n. 2) has shown that it was violated too frequently to be of assistance in making chronological determinations. For Pomtow's new dating of Polyeuctus (277/6 B.C.) and Hieron (276/5 B.C.), which, if accepted, would put Philocrates in 270/69 instead of 268/7 B.C., and Eubulus out of his place in 276/5 B.C., see below, iv. 164, n. 1.

from the lecture-room of Zeno, whom he admired devotedly, and from the arms of the beautiful Athenian courtesan, Demo, made his entry into history by defeating the Boeotians in the open field.[1] Upon the arrival of his father with the Macedonian army, the siege of Thebes was begun. Pyrrhus, Ptolemy's protégé, sought to create a diversion by invading Thessaly, but Demetrius expelled him without withdrawing his troops from the leaguer of Thebes, and after a long and obstinate resistance the city was taken by storm (291 B.C.). In the meanwhile a crisis had come in Athens. We can easily understand that on becoming king of Macedon Demetrius found himself in a sense the recognized head of the party in Greece which had looked to Philip, Alexander, Antipater, and Cassander for leadership. Its members, however, had been harried and oppressed by his own earlier supporters in the Greek cities, and many of them were now fugitives. Hence he was in a position at once to rid Greece of a source of faction and to obtain a new group of adherents for himself simply by ordering a restoration of exiles. This he accordingly did in 292 B.C.,[2] so that Deinarchus the orator and others of those banished in 307 B.C. re-established themselves in Athens.[3] It is possible that the restoration of similar elements, followed by an unsuccessful attempt on their part to seize the government, had caused the revolt in Boeotia.

---

[1] His intimacy with Zeno antedates 277/6 B.C. when he called the Stoic to Pella ; hence it must belong between 294 and 289 B.C. His son by Demo (Athen. xiii. 578 A; cf. Diog. Laert. vii. 36) fought in his campaign in the Peloponnesus against Pyrrhus in 273/2 B.C. (Plut. *Pyrrh.* 34)—hence must have been born prior to 289 B.C. That Antigonus was sowing his wild oats at this time is also clear from Athen. iii. 101 E ; iv. 128 ; cf. Wilamowitz, *Antigonus,* 203, n. 27.

[2] The date is still uncertain. For against the arguments urged in *Class. Phil.,* 1906, p. 313 ff. ; 1907, p. 305 ff. in favour of 292/1 B.C. for the death of Menander and the archonship of Philippus, in which the exiles returned to Athens, the fact that the thirty-second year of Ptolemy Soter's reign—with which Philippus is equated—was actually 293/2 B.C. and not 292/1 B.C. (Rubensohn, "Elephantine-papyri" in *Ägypt. Urk. aus d. Museen in Berlin,* Sonderheft, 22 ff. ; cf. Bouché-Leclercq, *Acad. inscr. C.R.,* 1908, p. 142 ff., and below, iv. 170, n. 3) must be placed. But since the Egyptian-Macedonian year began at the fall equinox and the Attic at the summer solstice, the summer of 292 B.C. belongs to the Egyptian-Macedonian year 293/2 B.C. and the Attic year 292/1 B.C. ; so that the point is still open.

[3] Dion. Hal. *De Dinarch.* 634.

Athens certainly was full of speculation as to the
meaning and probable outcome of the return of its
exiles. Omens appeared to attest the interest of the
Athenian gods, and the seer, Philochorus, was called
upon to interpret them. He found in them no menace
to the popular government, and, doubtless, cheered
the spirits of many an anxious democrat. The restoration of the oligarchs was accompanied by no constitutional changes,[1] but it was clear that the *émigrés*
were meant to be a thorn in the side of the existing
government—a centre of agitation, and, if need be, a
new tool for carrying through in Athens the will of the
king. This was apparently well understood in Athens ;
so that the constitutionalists had to look abroad for a
new protector. Hence Phaedrus of Sphettus was sent on
a mission to the court of Alexandria. A gift of corn
and money from Ptolemy Soter sealed the understanding
reached between him and Athens ;[2] but Phaedrus convinced himself that the time was not ripe for an outbreak.

Shortly after the fall of Thebes another crisis
occurred in Athens. In the spring of 290 B.C.
Demetrius followed a chance to wound Pyrrhus, and at
the same time to indulge his natural bent for an amatory
adventure. Lanassa, the daughter of Agathocles of
Syracuse, abandoned her husband, the young Epirote
king, and offered her hand and her possessions—notably
the rich and important islands of Corcyra and Leucas,
which had been her dowry—to the handsome Macedonian
ruler. Demetrius, accordingly, left his realm to take
care of itself, and went to seize Lanassa and her islands.
A point of departure was thereby won for a western
expedition, should the hope of gaining Italy, Sicily,
and Carthage prove stronger than the allurements of
the East. But in the meanwhile he was sacrificing
vital interests nearer home, for the Aetolians took
advantage of his absence to seize Delphi and to ravage
his dominions far and near.[3] Their plundering ex-

---

[1] Philochorus in Dion. Hal. *loc. cit.* 637.
[2] *IG.* ii. 331 ; cf. Kirchner, *PA.* 13963.
[3] See Hiller von Gärtringen, P.-W. iv. 2568.

peditions reached as far as Attica, where there was a
danger, which the old friendliness of Athens and Aetolia
augmented, that their appearance would lead to an
outbreak against its careless lord.[1] To forestall such
a catastrophe the oligarchs in the city, acting doubtless
in concert with the Macedonian garrisons, seem to have
had a design to master the government and put an
end to popular liberty altogether, but the moderate
elements, whose leader, Phaedrus of Sphettus, was
hoplite-general for this year, succeeded in preventing
both sets of extremists from putting their plans into
effect.[2] It was at this same time, moreover, that Zenon,
the commander of some Egyptian cruisers stationed in
the Aegean Sea, acting doubtless under instructions
from Alexandria, far from seizing, actually escorted
the grain ships bound for the Piraeus.[3] Athens was

---

[1] Probably the reference in lines 30 ff. of *IG*. ii. 331 (Ditt. *Syll.*[2] 213)
is to a disposition on the part of the Athenians to join the Aetolians and
Ptolemy at this time. A political crisis is doubtless meant, in which the
advice of Phaedrus was sound. Beloch and Kolbe (*Die attischen Archonten*,
23, 64 ; *Abhand. d. Gött. Gesellschaft*, Neue Folge, x. 4), who date the archon
Cimon in 292/1 B.C., refer it to a disposition to join in the revolt of Thebes in
this year. But this is less likely (*Class. Phil.*, 1907, p. 306). We do not
know whether Attic territory was menaced at that time or not, whereas we
have contemporary evidence that in 291/0 B.C. the Aetolians threatened to
plunder Attica (see below, iv. 143). The passage is followed closely by the
excision in line 40, in which the incidents of 289/7 B.C. were alluded to ;
and this in turn by the excision in lines 42-44, where the circumstances of
the understanding reached with Antigonus in 287/6 B.C. were referred to.
The excision of lines 47-52 then dealt with the relations of Athens to
Antigonus during the war of 283 B.C. Ptolemy and Antigonus were friendly
in 275 B.C., when the entire decree was prepared ; this explains the inclusion
of the embassy to Egypt in 292/1 B.C. The career of Phaedrus,—a moderate
throughout,—his commendation in 275 B.C., and the reason for each excision
become clear if the chronology used in the above analysis of the decree
is accepted.

[2] Putting the archon Cimon in 291/0 B.C., which may be done even if
Philippus is dated in 293/2 B.C. From *IG*. ii. 331, 30 ff., it is clear that in
Cimon's archonship Attic territory was menaced and a domestic sedition
occurred. The view of the incident taken in the text explains the rôle
which Phaedrus played.

[3] *IG*. ii. 5. 309*b* (Ditt. *Syll.*[2] 193. 11 ff.) ἐπειδὴ Ζή[νων καθεστηκ]ὼς ὑπὸ
τοῦ βασιλέως Πτολ[εμαίου ἐπὶ τῶν ἀ]φράκτων εὔνους ὢν δ[ι]ατε[λεῖ κοινῆι τε τῶι]
δήμωι καὶ ἰδίαι ἑκάστωι Ἀ[θηναίων ἐνδεικν]ύμενος οἷς ἂν περιτυ[γχάνηι καὶ λέγων
κ]αὶ πράττων ἀγαθὸν ὅ τι [δύναται ὑπὲρ τῆς] πόλεως. ἐπιμελεῖται δὲ [καὶ τῆς
κομιδῆς το]ῦ σίτου τῶι δήμωι, ὅπως ἀ[ν ἀσφαλέστατα δια]κομίζηται, συναγωνι-
ζό[μενος τῆι τοῦ δήμ]ου σωτηρίαι. This decree was passed in Hecatombaeon
(July) 290 B.C. It has been interpreted correctly by Bouché-Leclercq (*Hist.
des Lagides*, iv. 302): "D'après l'inscription précitée, la flotte égyptienne
commandée par Zénon aurait été envoyée *avant* le soulèvement d'Athènes."
Cf. *Klio*, 1905, p. 178, and Ditt. *OGIS*. ii. 773. For the Athenian nesiarchs
who in the fourth century B.C. preceded the Egyptian of the third, and had

thus being solicited to a revolt and provisioned for a siege.

It was in September (Boedromion) of 290 B.C. that Demetrius reached Athens on his return from Leucas and Corcyra.[1] His arrival was timed to coincide with the celebration of the Eleusinian Mysteries, and when the population went forth, as usual, with hymns and dancing, they associated Demeter and Demetrius in their adoration.[2] Possibly the king met the procession, which, with a strange mixture of reverence and ribaldry, conducted Iacchus to Eleusis. " The king comes," they sang, " light-hearted as befits a god, fair and laughing, yet majestic withal in his circle of courtiers, he the sun, they the stars : hail ! child of mighty Poseidon and of Aphrodite. The other gods are a long way off, or have no ears, or no existence, or take no care of us, but thee we see face to face—a true god, not one of wood or stone. To thee we pray : first, dear lord, give us peace, for that thou canst. The Sphinx, that pest, not of Thebes alone, but of all Greece, who starting like her of old from his rocky seat snatches us and bears us away, resistance futile—the Aetolian, I mean, plunderer of his neighbour, and now of us, take thou in hand thyself. Else, find some Oedipus who shall hurl down this Sphinx or make it harmless." The song thus suited the occasion and the merry mood of Demetrius. It must not be taken too seriously : the puns betray its frivolity.[3] It adroitly blends supplication wi'ch admonition, and, possibly, apologizes for the inertness of the Athenians during the nuptial trip of Demetrius. The thing made a great sensation, and was sung thereafter at banquets, drawing forth the indignation of the austere Demochares and the curiosity of the sensational Duris.[4] Athenaeus marshals it among the classic examples of flattery, and it increased the disgust with

---

charge of the παραπομπὴ τοῦ σίτου, see Dem. xviii. 73, *IG.* ii. 5. 196, Antiphanes in Athen. viii. 342 E, and especially Wilhelm, *Urk. dram. Aufführ.* 248.

[1] Athen. vi. 253 C.   See below, iv. 144, n. 2.

[2] Plut. *Demetr.* 12.

[3] See ἀληθινόν and λίθινον ; Σφίγγα and σπίγγον—a little inoffensive bird.

[4] Demochares, *Frg.* 4 (*FHG.* ii. 449) ; Duris, *Frg.* 30 (*FHG.* ii. 476).

which Grote[1] threw down his pen at the end of his great panegyric on the Athenian democracy.

This was in September. In October[2] the Pythia was due. Since this festival had been celebrated last, in 294 B.C., the conduct of the games had passed, upon the seizure of Delphi, into the hands of the Aetolians, a people whose reputation was none too good, and who, moreover, were the enemies of the Macedonian king. Demetrius showed his disregard for ancient usages, and at the same time protested against the Aetolian annexation of Delphi, by celebrating the Pythia of 290 B.C. in his Greek capital, Athens. This done he left the city, and it was never his privilege to enter its gates again, for the following year of his reign was filled with wars—with the invasion of Aetolia and Epirus, with Pyrrhus's victory over Pantauchus and inroad into Macedon, with Demetrius's final defeat of Pyrrhus and the truce with which the struggle ended;[3] then in the winter of 289/8 B.C. Athens revolted.

The government had been well aware that it existed simply on tolerance, and that on the first opportunity the restored oligarchs were to take its place. Hence preparations for secession were quietly made, and in the early summer of 289 B.C., perhaps at the time of the successes of Pyrrhus, Philippides, the comedian, who stood in a confidential relation to Lysimachus of Thrace, and Demochares, a privileged person at the court of the same monarch, and whose following in Athens was considerable, and whose adhesion lent to the liberty movement the authority of a weighty name, were recalled from exile.[4] In other words, in 289 B.C. Athens

[1] *History of Greece*, xii. 384-393.

[2] For the month see *Class. Phil.*, 1907, p. 307, n. 1. That the Pythia came in the fourth month of the Attic year in the third century B.C. is further proven by the fact that it was celebrated in or about the Coan month Panamos (*Acad. inscr. C.R.*, 1904, p. 172), which, according to Paton (*Inscriptions of Cos*, 327 ff.), was the last month of the year, and hence came just before the autumnal equinox; and by the further fact that Charmion, son of Eumaridas, a *theorus* from Cydonia εἰς Δελφούς, obviously on his way to the Pythia, stopped at Athens in the third month of the year (*IG*. ii. 5. 385c).

[3] Plut. *Demetr.* 41-43; *Pyrrhus*, 7. 10.

[4] *Klio*, 1905, p. 176 ff.; *ibid.* 163, n. 2. A new committee on general administration was elected in July 290 B.C. in the archonship of Diocles. It is possible that Demochares was put into it in anticipation of his return; for

came to a similar understanding with Lysimachus to that reached with Ptolemy two years and a half earlier. The garrison in the Museum was then approached. It consisted of mercenary troops to whom the cause was of trifling importance, and, accordingly, it was not difficult for the Athenians to secure the sympathy and assistance of a large number of them. The commander, Spintharus, seems to have remained faithful to Demetrius, but his lieutenant, Strombichus, and the detachment of which he had charge, were won over. They agreed to join the Athenians in an attack upon the fort which they were appointed to guard.[1] It was thus a simple matter to drive the " accursed Macedonians," as Epicurus [2] called them, out of the city. Olympiodorus led the assault upon the Museum; the traitorous Strombichus fought with him against his commander, and it cost Athens only thirteen lives to rid itself of its foreign garrison.[3] Demochares followed up this success by dislodging the Macedonians from Eleusis,[4] but all efforts to capture the

---

even if he had been exiled formally in 303 B.C., the decree had been cancelled in the archonship of Philippus, so that he was again a citizen. But there are two other possibilities : (1) that Demochares returned to Athens between the first and the end of July 290 B.C. ; (2) that he was elected to the committee for 289/8 B.C. Of these, the latter is altogether the most likely. See below, Appendix II.

[1] *IG.* ii. 317 (Ditt. *Syll.*[2] 198).

[2] Usener, *Epicurea,* 133 ; the archon is Euthius (287/6 B.C.) not Isaeus (288/7) ; cf. Crönert, *Kolotes,* 54, n. 259, and for an allusion to an Epicurean during the siege of 296/4 B.C. (?) *ibid.* 174.

[3] Paus. i. 26. 1 f. ; 29. 13. The information of Pausanias in regard to Olympiodorus was obviously obtained from an honorary decree, and the dedicatory inscriptions of honorary statues ; cf. i. 25. 2 ; 26. 3.

[4] Eleusis was regained before 283/2 B.C. (*IG.* ii. 614c ; cf. Kirchner, *GGA.,* 1900, p. 439, § 4), and doubtless before 288/7 B.C.—the time of the *agon* instituted by Philippides to Demeter and Core (*IG.* ii. 314 ; Ditt. *Syll.*[2] 197. 44) ; before Munychion (April) 288 B.C., according to Lattermann (*Klio,* 1906, p. 165 ff.), who has shown that *IG.* ii. 5. 1054d p. 234 (Ditt. *Syll.*[2] 538), which is dated in the archonship of Diotimus, belongs to 289/8 B.C. ; in which case Athens resumed work, suspended apparently for some time, in the Eleusinian precinct.

Of the four issues of copper money recognized by Cavaignac ("Les Monnaies d'Eleusis," *Revue numismatique,* 1908, p. 311 ff.) as belonging to periods of Eleusinian independence, one is dated by him in 403 B.C., and another in 287-285/4 B.C. ; the other two are left dateless. Eleusis was Athenian from 289/8 B.C. onward ; hence this period is excluded. The possible eras of Eleusinian independence are 318/7 B.C. ; 304 B.C.—while Cassander was besieging Athens ; 296-294 B.C.—from the time Poliorcetes captured Eleusis (Plut. *Demetr.* 33) till the fall of Athens, and perhaps till the capture of Eleusis by Demochares in 289/8 B.C. ; 265-261 B.C.—during the Chremonidean War, when Eleusis was certainly not in the possession of the Athenians.

Two of the three issues doubtless belong to 296–(294)289/8 B.C., and 265–

Piraeus and the frontier posts were fruitless. Athens, however, was free.[1] But that the war would stop at this point no Athenian had ever imagined. It was well understood that a concerted attack on Macedon had been arranged between Pyrrhus and Lysimachus for the spring of 288 B.C., and that at the same time the great fleet of Ptolemy was to make its appearance in the Aegean Sea ; but in the meanwhile, and until the allies had brought the war to a successful termination, Athens must face a siege, which had to be all the more dreaded in that the insurrection had failed to put it in possession of its harbour. The city, therefore, required to be stocked with money, and, above all, with provisions ; for who had forgotten the horrors of Lachares' defence ? Hence the first care of Demochares on his return from exile was to take charge of the committee on general administration (289/8 B.C.). Rigid economies were practised, and by a personal application he got from Lysimachus first thirty talents, and then, probably after the storming of the Museum, a second subsidy of one hundred talents. At the same time Antipater, Cassander's son, the ex-king of Macedon, to whom Lysimachus had given his daughter, and whom he professed to be supporting in his claim on the throne of his father, added twenty talents on his own account. Demochares, furthermore, had an embassy sent to Ptolemy which

---

261 B.C. The third can hardly belong to 318/7 B.C. if the Archippus of *IG.* ii. 5. 574e (Ditt. *Syll.*[2] 647) was the archon of this year, and not of 321/0 B.C., which is also possible ; besides, we have no record of Eleusis being separated from Athens at this time. Nor have we any certain evidence of a separation in 304 B.C. since Plutarch (*Demetr.* 23) mentions only Panacton and Phyle as being in the possession of Cassander during the siege. Still, there is no unlikelihood that he held Eleusis also. After 261 B.C. I know of no time when Eleusis was independent. Cf. below, viii. *ca.* 327 note.

It was in the winter of 290/89 or 289/8 B.C. that Poseidippus presented his first play. Suidas, *s.v.* "Poseidippus" ; cf. Wilhelm, *Urk. dram. Aufführ.* 117.

[1] Plut. *Demetr.* 46. There is extant a decree (*IG.* ii. 567 ; cf. *IG.* ii. 3. 1158) dated on the 5th of the eighth month (Elaphebolion) of the archonship of Isaeus, *i.e.* in March–April 287 B.C., or at approximately the same time that Philippides instituted an *agon* as an ὑπόμνημα τῆς τοῦ δήμου [ἐλευθερίας] (cf. Lattermann, *loc. cit.* 168, n. 1). It commends the senators of the *phyle* Aegeis for the conduct of their prytany in 289/8 B.C., and the Senate and *demos* of Athens, it seems, had crowned them previously. There is also mention of an *anathema* to be dedicated. Was it in the prytany of Aegeis that the revolt from Macedon took place ? The *agon* of Philippides was probably instituted on the first anniversary of the acquisition of liberty.

secured fifty talents.[1]   Another was despatched, on the
capture of the Museum, to announce the good news to
the ancestral friend of Athens, Spartocus, king of
Bosporus.   It effected its purpose, and in the early
spring of 288 B.C. fifteen thousand *medimni* of Pontic
corn reached the city.[2]   Audoleon, king of the Paeonians,
was likewise apprised of the good fortune of Athens, and
he too discovered what was needed, and started off seven
thousand five hundred Macedonian *medimni* of grain.   It
was despatched with all possible urgency, and succeeded
in reaching Athens early in July 288 B.C.[3]   Doubtless, it
was transported and unloaded under the protection of
Ptolemy's fleet, which had now relieved Zenon and his
cruisers of the onus of patrolling the islands of the
Aegean.   Supplies were thus rushed to Athens by all
who were solicitous for its welfare, or participants in
the league against Demetrius.[4]

Demetrius had not expected to be attacked in his
own country, and he had made a truce with Pyrrhus
with a view to getting a free hand for a great war of
conquest in Asia.   For this he had proceeded to make
extraordinary preparations.   A fleet of enormous battleships, one of which had thirteen banks of rowers, was
being constructed, partly in Demetrias, partly in Corinth,

---

[1] [Plut.], *Lives of the Ten Orators*, 851 E.   A reference to these embassies
(πρεσβείαις) is contained in *IG*. ii. 319, which was probably passed in the
archonship of Diotimus ; for within the period possible for this decree 301/0–
295/4 B.C. and 290/89–282/1 B.C. the name of only one other archon, viz.
Clearchus (301/0 B.C.), fills the space ; but 301/0 B.C. was an intercalary, the
year of *IG*. ii. 319 a common year.   Hence 289/8 B.C. is alone possible.
Accordingly, the gifts were received from Lysimachus before the end of
Elaphebolion ? (April) 288 B.C.   The πρεσβείαις are also mentioned in an
unpublished decree, for the text of which I am indebted to the kindness of
Professor D. M. Robinson.   It too belongs, apparently, to the month of
Elaphebolion of 288 B.C., and rewards a certain Artemidorus with citizenship
for services rendered in connexion with the embassies to Lysimachus.   [Dr.
A. C. Johnson very kindly informs me that in his judgment the archon-name
in *IG*. ii. 319 has one letter more than Koehler reports.   If this is so, the two
documents belong in 299/8 or 297/6 B.C.]   It is possible that the statue of
Lysimachus mentioned by Pausanias (i. 9. 4) was erected for this service.
[2] *IG*. ii. 311 (Ditt. *Syll.*[2] 194).   This decree was passed on the last day of
the 7th month of the year 289/8 B.C., which began at about the end of July
(*Class. Phil.*, 1908, p. 386).   This was accordingly about the 1st of March
288 B.C.
[3] *IG*. ii. 312 (Ditt. *Syll.*[2] 195).
[4] It was probably in this connexion that Demetrius of Phalerum sent τοῖς
᾿Αθηναίοις δωρεάς from Alexandria (Plut. *De exilio*, 7 ; cf. Wilamowitz, *Antigonus*, 340).

and partly in the Piraeus. His land army was said to number seventy thousand men. Demetrius felt himself to be a second Alexander, and now made it clear to the Macedonians that the kingship to which he laid claim was the despotic, inaccessible, consecrated, and showy office which the great king had devised for the government of the Graeco-Oriental world.[1] For two years an Athenian embassy was kept waiting for an audience,[2] and his Macedonian subjects, who had been accustomed to a patriarchal simplicity in the manners of their rulers, saw in his neighbourhood only degrading ceremonies and garments of purple and gold.[3] This they could not endure. His adversaries were Macedonians like himself, and the glamour of service with Alexander gave to Lysimachus, Seleucus, and Ptolemy a heroic stature which Demetrius lacked, while the gallant bearing of Pyrrhus won universal admiration. Accordingly, when Lysimachus and Pyrrhus invaded Macedon simultaneously in the spring of 288 B.C., the troops of Demetrius deserted in thousands, and he was happy to withdraw the remnant of his army to Cassandreia, and thence to the camp of his son, Antigonus, in Greece. It was there, in the great naval stations, Corinth, Demetrias, and the Piraeus, that he had his fleet, and even though Macedon was lost Greece might still be held.

It was in the fall of 288 or the spring of 287 B.C. that the situation of Athens became most serious. Demetrius might hurl all his forces, and his army was still eleven thousand strong, upon the rebellious city, and crush it before relief could come ; for help could reach Athens only through Boeotia, which Demetrius bound to himself by restoring to it its self-government, or from the fleet of Ptolemy, which even though it should vanquish the formidable navy of Poliorcetes, could not reach Athens because of the hostile garrison in the Piraeus.[4] Demetrius

---

[1] Duris, *Frg.* 31 (*FHG.* ii. 477) ; cf. above, ii. 64, n. 1 ; iii. 121.

[2] Plut. *Demetr.* 42 ; cf. Wilamowitz, *Antigonus*, 245, n. 1. The years were 290/89 and 289/8 B.C., two short years, to be sure, but the point of the remark consisted in the delay being as long as possible. The revolt of Athens probably gave to Demetrius a sufficient reason for detaining the ambassadors.

[3] Plut. *Demetr.* 42 ; Duris, *loc. cit.*

[4] Plut. *Demetr.* 44.

resolved to make the attempt.   He entered by the road
which led past Panacton and Phyle into Attica, and
leaving Eleusis to one side,[1] advanced upon Athens.
The wisdom of the attack was dubious, but the king's
indignation was strong, and a furious onslaught was
made.   The Athenians resolved to negotiate, and mind-
ful of the time when Xenocrates had tried to appease
Antipater, they turned to the Academy, and entrusted
Crates, the bosom friend of its head, with the conduct
of the embassy.   At the same time urgent messages
were sent to Pyrrhus to hasten his movements.[2]   The
eloquence of Crates and the approach of Pyrrhus were
together victorious—an excuse and a reason, what more
was needed?   The assault was abandoned and the
Athenians breathed more freely.   Pyrrhus shortly afterwards made his appearance, and there was great rejoicing
in the city when he proceeded in triumphal procession
to the Acropolis, and offered sacrifices to Athena.[3]   He
then withdrew, after advising the citizens to be more
careful for the future about admitting kings within
their gates.   His popularity in Athens was probably of
short duration, for in place of pushing matters in Greece
to a final issue, Pyrrhus made a treaty with Demetrius.[4]
Doubtless, the succession of Pyrrhus to the throne of
Macedon was acknowledged, and in turn Demetrius
was left in possession of Greece, and thereby given an
opportunity to use it as a starting-point for his
expedition against Asia.   The Athenians were safeguarded, but the garrisons of Demetrius still occupied
the Piraeus, and the forts Panacton and Phyle, and the
islands of Salamis, Scyros, Imbros, and Lemnos passed

---

[1] This we assume because Eleusis seems to have been Athenian from 289/8
B.C. onward, whereas Panacton and Phyle remained in the hands of Antigonus
till about 283 B.C.

[2] Plut. *Pyrrh.* 12 ; *Demetr.* 46.   For the justification of the report of the
mission of Crates—if one is needed—see Wilamowitz, *Antigonus*, 208 ff.   The
fleet of Ptolemy apparently kept out of the way during this crisis.

[3] It was at this time, perhaps, that the statue of Pyrrhus, mentioned in
Paus. i. 11. 1, was voted.

[4] The secret treaty alluded to by Phoenicides (Koch, iii. 333) is properly
referred by Beloch (iii. 1. 248, n. 2) to about a year later, since Antigonus, not
Demetrius, is said by Hesychius (*s.v.* δύνασαι σιωπᾶν) to have been one of the
parties to it.   The terms of the arrangement between Demetrius and Pyrrhus
have been inferred by Beloch (iii. 1. 240, n. 1) from the subsequent events.

out of Athenian control; for despite Ptolemy's fleet,
which apparently withdrew from the Aegean in the late
summer of 288 B.C.,[1] the sea remained in the possession
of Demetrius, who was thus able both to keep these
islands and to transport his army over to Miletus without
molestation (287 B.C.).   He therewith began his unfortunate enterprise in Asia Minor, while Antigonus, his
son, assumed the regal title and took over the management of Greek affairs.

The Athenians were rescued, and the democratic
government was safe, but the freedom of commerce and
the possibility of independent politics were limited
seriously by the presence of a foreign garrison in the
Piraeus.   The only potentate who at that time could be
expected to set aside an arrangement in which Pyrrhus
had concurred was Lysimachus, and negotiations, which
the intimacy of Philippides, the comedian, with the king
facilitated,[2] were carried on throughout 287 B.C. with
such effect that, relying upon assistance from Thrace to
carry them safely through a war, the Athenians attempted
in the winter or early spring of 287/6 B.C.,[3] at about the
same time that Ptolemy and Lysimachus, as will be
explained shortly, seized the insular and Anatolian
possessions of Demetrius, to repeat the performance of
two years earlier.   A plot was formed to surprise the
Piraeus, and in connexion with it an attempt was made
to win over Hierocles, a Carian, who was captain of the
mercenary division of the garrison, and, accordingly,
the chief lieutenant of the Macedonian commandant,
Heracleides.   Hierocles professed to sympathise with
the conspirators, but, in reality, betrayed them to his
superior, and when they were admitted within the fortifications they found the garrison ready to cut them to

---

[1] It was still in the vicinity of Athens in July (above, iv. 147). We can
readily understand that after the main object of the coalition was accomplished,
and Demetrius was expelled from Macedon, Ptolemy had no desire to fight it
out single-handed on the sea with the "son of Poseidon." It seems unlikely
that Lysimachus had a fleet before he obtained the remnant of that of
Demetrius in 287/6 B.C.   Besides, the general policy of Ptolemy Soter was "to
hit and run."

[2] *IG.* ii. 314 (Ditt. *Syll.*[2] 197. 31 ff.).

[3] Polyaenus, v. 17 ; Paus. i. 29. 10 ; cf. Beloch, iii. 1. 247, n. 5.   At the
time the plot failed Demetrius was περὶ τὴν Λυδίαν.

pieces. The deceit was so successful that it found a
place in the canon of ancient stratagems.[1] Few of the
party escaped, and the best that the Athenians could do
was to honour the general and four hundred and nineteen
men who were slain with a public burial in the Cerameicus,
where their tomb was seen by Pausanias four centuries
and a half later.[2] From their names we may judge that
they came from the best democratic families in Athens.[3]

So long as Demetrius was at liberty Antigonus had
no chance to act on his own initiative, but upon the
captivity and abdication of his father in 286 B.C. he
came into a position of independence. He now formed
a secret treaty with Pyrrhus,[4] and hence with Ptolemy,
the ally of Pyrrhus, by which he obtained a free hand
in Greece—the compensation being the isolation of
Lysimachus whose ambitions were dangerous to the
other monarchs. The disasters of Demetrius in Asia
Minor had been fatal to his authority both there and in
the Aegean; for his fleet, upon which this empire
depended, was lost in 287/6 B.C., so that in the autumn
of this year or the opening of the next Ptolemy's admiral
—apparently Philocles, king of the Sidonians—re-entered
the Aegean, and, on mastering the Cyclades, aided in
forming among them a League of the islanders, of
which Delos was made the centre. Bacchon, a Boeotian,
but in the naval service of Egypt, was deputed to act as its
chief executive with the title *nesiarch*.[5] At the same

[1] Polyaenus, v. 17.   [2] i. 29. 10.   [3] Wilamowitz, *Antigonus*, 230 ff.
[4] Koch, iii. 333 ; cf. above, iv. 149, n. 4.
[5] For the time see *JHS.*, 1910, p. 191. In 290 B.C. Zenon appears alone
(see above, iv. 142, n. 3), and in *ca.* 268 B.C. (Ditt. *OGIS*, 43 and 773 ; cf. *ibid.*
67, which is published more completely in *BCH.*, 1907, p. 341, and dated in
280/79 B.C.) in subordination to Bacchon, who, in turn, is under the admiral
Philocles in 280/79 B.C. (Ditt. *Syll.*[2] 202).   Ptolemy doubtless acquired the
southern islands (Thera and others) along with Cyprus in 295/4 B.C., and, on
the withdrawal of his admiral at that time before the superior power of
Demetrius, he left a squadron of quick-sailing, undecked triremes (Ditt. *OGIS.*
773) to operate under the command of Zenon in the Aegean. The fleet which
came from Egypt in 288 B.C. also withdrew after July of that year, but returned
in 287/6 B.C., after which in all probability Bacchon was appointed *nesiarch.*
Bacchon appears in a Delian inventory of the year 282 B.C. (*BCH.*, 1890, p. 403).
His superior Philocles accompanies him (*ibid.* 409). It seems probable that the
soteria alluded to in Ditt. *Syll.*[2] 209 (cf. *BCH.*, 1907, p. 373) as sacrificed on
his account in Delos and in Athens have something to do with the liberation
of Athens and the Cyclades, which was effected definitely on the reappearance
of Ptolemy's fleet in 287/6 B.C. At that time also, possibly, Philocles made the

time Lysimachus rounded out his territory in Asia Minor by seizing the cities subject to Demetrius,[1] and safeguarded the heart of his kingdom by occupying the islands in the Thracian archipelago.[2] Accordingly, his realm, extending as it now did from the Axius River or thereabouts in Macedon round the Aegean to southern Asia Minor and the Taurus Mountains, was a menace by its very size, population, and resources to all its neighbours. Pyrrhus came first in peril geographically, but Egypt was also vitally concerned, seeing that Lysimachus, as the heir of the fleet and ambitions of Poliorcetes, became the chief rival of Ptolemy. Hence these two, as already mentioned, made a treaty with Antigonus and arranged to let him consolidate his dominions in Greece. At this he set to work energetically, and in 285 and 284 B.C. he established his authority in the Peloponnesus, and forced even Sparta to acknowledge his suzerainty (285/4 B.C.).[3] The Athenians came next in line, and since the attack they had made on the Piraeus in the winter of 287/6 B.C. gave him ample ground for a war, and since he could enter Attica at any moment through having in his possession Panacton and Phyle, as well as the harbour,[4] the position of their city was

dedication in Athens of which the inscription is published in *IG.* ii. 3. 1371. At any rate, it is not likely that such friendly relations as these amenities imply existed between the Ptolemies and Athens from 286 to 276 B.C.

[1] For Samos see *Inscriptions of the British Museum*, iii. 403 (*CIG.* ii. 2254).

[2] See below, iv. 155.

[3] Euseb. (Schoene) ii. 118 ; Justin, xxiv. 1. 3 ; cf. Beloch, iii. 1. 248 and iii. 2. 304.

[4] The evidence adduced by de Sanctis (33) and Beloch (iii. 2. 379 ff.) is conclusive that the Piraeus was in the hands of Antigonus after 276 B.C. The Piraeus and the forts were not yet Athenian in October 287 B.C. (*IG.* ii. 314) ; and despite the encouragements of Lysimachus, the effort made in the following winter to capture the harbour town failed dismally. The only question open, it seems to me, is whether the Athenians captured the Piraeus after 286 B.C. and handed it back to Antigonus in 276 B.C. This is possible, and, indeed, is suggested by the following statement of Pausanias (i. 26. 3) : Ὀλυμπιοδώρῳ δὲ τόδε μέν ἐστιν ἔργον μέγιστον χωρὶς τούτων ὧν ἔπραξε Πειραιᾶ καὶ Μουνυχίαν ἀνασωσάμενος. The last word Unger and Beloch have changed to ἀνασωσόμενος "trying to recover." But the context makes it incredible that the achievement in deference to which Pausanias makes the reservation failed of its purpose. Since the incident is mentioned out of its chronological order, it seems to me possible that it refers to the recovery of the Piraeus and Munychia in either 307 B.C. or 295/4 B.C. Olympiodorus was a prominent man in 305 B.C., and in 294 B.C. he was designated archon ; so that he can well have been conspicuous in both enterprises.

That Phyle and Panacton were in the hands of Antigonus in 283 B.C. is

in the highest degree perilous.   From Egypt, the lord of
the adjacent seas, nothing but evil could be expected ;[1]
for the friendship of Lysimachus to the Athenians was
now the worst possible recommendation to the court
at Alexandria, seeing that Ptolemy Ceraunus, on being
excluded from the throne by his father, had found a
protector and prospective champion in the Thracian
monarch (285/4 B.C.).   Still, nothing was done till the
death of Soter, in the early spring of 283 B.C., paralyzed
for a time the strength of Egypt.[2]   Then Lysimachus
and Antigonus struck at one and the same moment.
The former attacked Pyrrhus and drove him headlong
out of the part of Macedon which had fallen to him in
287 B.C., and also out of Thessaly.   The latter invaded
Attica, but encountered a stout resistance.   Olympiodorus repulsed the attack which he made upon Eleusis,
mainly with the aid of the Eleusinians themselves ;[3]
so that his attack upon Athens did not get properly
started.   Meanwhile the ephebes, drawn into service by
the extremity of the danger, had garrisoned the Museum,
and thus held the city end of the Long Walls against
the Macedonian garrison which occupied the Piraeus at
the other end.[4]   Strombichus and the detachment of
mercenaries under his command remained faithful, and

perhaps the reason why Eleusis, which was recovered by the Athenians in 288 B.C.,
was the centre of the military operations of that year.   That the Piraeus was
then hostile to Athens is perhaps indicated by the fact that the Museum had
to be guarded on the same occasion, while it argues against this war being
opened by any such achievement as the capture of the Piraeus that Strombichus
was not credited with part in it, when in 282 B.C. he was given the citizenship
for past services.   Furthermore, there is no evidence of a struggle in 276 B.C.
after which the Piraeus was in the hands of Antigonus, and, finally, Hierocles,
the Carian, was an officer in the Piraeus both before 286 and after 276 B.C.

[1] This does not imply the like for all the islands.   Thus Tenos rendered
such services to Athens that in 285/4 B.C. its citizens were given again the
isoteleia which they had received at some time between 350 and 300 B.C. (*IG.*
ii. 97c, ii. 5. 345c).   What these services were we do not know ; nor do we know
the relations at this time existent between Tenos and the League of the Islanders.

[2] We have evidence of the presence of Philocles in the Aegean Sea in
282 B.C. (*BCH.*, 1890, p. 409), and again in 280/79 B.C. (Ditt. *Syll.*[2] 202 ; *BCH.*,
1906, p. 93 ; cf. *Musée belge*, xii. 19).   This implies the maintenance in this
region of the main Egyptian fleet during the crucial period.   Philadelphus,
however, seems to have had it take no part in the central struggles.

[3] Paus. i. 26. 3 ; Ditt. *Syll.*[2] 505.   Dion, secretary to the treasurer of the
sitonica for the year 283/2 B.C., rendered valuable services in keeping the
Athenians stationed at Eleusis supplied with food during the crisis.

[4] *IG.* ii. 316 (Ditt. *Syll.*[2] 520) ; cf. ii. 3. 1350, which, however, was not
voted till 281 B.C.

the city was preserved.[1] The attack was not repeated, for at this point the advance of the frontiers of Lysimachus to Thermopylae demanded the attention of Antigonus, and forced him to postpone the conquest of Attica; so that Soteria could be sacrificed at Eleusis in February 282 B.C. in connexion with the Little Mysteries;[2] and, whereas in the preceding August the Great Eleusinia had been of necessity omitted,[3] in July 282 B.C. the Great Panathenaea was celebrated with perhaps more than the usual display.[4]

At this point, when a struggle between Antigonus and Lysimachus seemed imminent, Seleucus, who had been for some time on unfriendly terms with both Lysimachus and the coalition opposed to him, interfered decisively in the action. In the spring of 282 B.C.[5] he crossed the Taurus mountains and invaded Asia Minor in full force. His advance was accompanied by a general falling away to him of the cities dependent upon Lysimachus, who, though obviously unprepared for the attack, crossed the Hellespont and advanced to Lydia to meet his assailant. At Corupedion the two armies met, and in the battle which ensued Lysimachus was defeated and slain (fall of 282 B.C.).[6] This great victory put Thrace, Macedon, and Thessaly within the grasp of the ruler of all Asia, but the murder of Seleucus by Ptolemy Ceraunus seven months later unsettled everything again, and in particular reopened the whole question of the Macedonian succession. No one had a better claim than Antigonus, and in 281 B.C. he left Greece with his fleet to make it good;[7] but on being beaten decisively by

[1] IG. ii. 317, 318 (Ditt. Syll.² 198, 199). It was possibly at this time that the Athenians voted to erect upon the Acropolis a statue of Olympiodorus, the military hero of the preceding generation (cf. above, iv. 145, n. 3).
[2] IG. ii. 315 (Ditt. Syll.² 649).
[3] For the time and the omission of the Great Eleusinia see Kolbe, op. cit. 69; P.-W. v. 2332.   [4] Klio, 1908, p. 345 ff.
[5] The friendly relations of Seleucus and Antigonus in the spring of 282 B.C. were manifested in their co-operation to do honour to the body of Demetrius Poliorcetes (Plut. Demetr. 52; cf. JHS., 1910, p. 193). The hostility of Lysimachus with Pyrrhus and Antigonus is attested by Paus. 1. 10. 2.
[6] de Sanctis (Storia dei Romani, ii. 390, n. 2) has given the best treatment of the chronology of these events.
[7] Memnon, 13; Justin, xxiv. 1. 8; cf. Beloch, iii. 1. 257 ff., who, however, dates all these incidents a year too late.

Ceraunus he returned to Boeotia.[1] In the spring of
280 B.C. he started out again, and leaving his half-brother,
the faithful Craterus, to represent him in Greece, he
sailed across the Aegean to assert his rights as grandson
of Antigonus Monophthalmus to Asia Minor, which after
the death of Seleucus seemed also a fair prize for any
claimant. This brought him into collision with Antiochus,
the son of Seleucus, with whose enemies, Bithynia,
Heracleia, Byzantium, and Chalcedon, he allied himself,
and for more than three years an indecisive struggle was
carried on.[2] He might have extricated himself from it
sooner had there been any advantage in doing so. But
he was now almost a king without a country, since his
defeats and absence, together with the intrigues of
Antiochus, were fatal to the integrity of his kingdom in
Greece, where, in consequence of a movement headed by
Sparta, practically everything was lost (281/79 B.C.)
except Corinth, Piraeus, Euboea, and perhaps a few
other places. It was at this time that Athens recovered
her cleruchies in the Thracian Sea, and probably also
Panacton and Phyle. The islands of Lemnos and Imbros
had been in the hands of Lysimachus since in 287/6 B.C.
he had taken them from Demetrius. The Thracian
monarch, in order to make his possession more secure,
had set aside the democratic institutions, and subjected
the Athenian colonists on Lemnos to what they felt to
be a harsh government. Accordingly, their first action
after the defeat of Lysimachus was to turn to his
vanquisher, Seleucus, with a request for the restoration
of their autonomy. Comeas of Lamptrae, an Athenian

---

[1] Memnon, 13 ; Justin, xxiv. 1. 8 ; cf. Beloch, iii. 1. 257 ff.

[2] Trogus, *Prolog.* 17 ; Justin, xxiv. 1. 8 ; cf. Beloch, iii. 1. 259 ; Memnon
15. 18 (*FHG.* iii. 534 ff.) ; Trogus, *Prolog.* 24 ; cf. Beloch, iii. 1. 579 ff. ;
A. J. Reinach (*Revue celtique*, 1909, p. 56, n. 2) finds this war still in progress
in 277 B.C. This is probably correct, but he gives no reason sufficient to prove
that it did not begin in the spring of 280 B.C. before the death of Ceraunus.
Memnon (18) says that it dragged along for a long time. Antigonus was
operating with his fleet in the Hellespont when he fell upon the Celts at
Lysimachia. Since the Celts were invited across the strait, apparently
(Reinach, *loc. cit.*) after the victory of Antigonus at Lysimachia, and they
crossed, according to Pausanias, in the year 278/7 B.C., the battle of Lysimachia
probably took place in the early part of 277 B.C. Antiochus then offered
Antigonus peace and his daughter, when he became king of Macedon (fall of
277 B.C.) ; but in the meantime the Celts had entered Asia Minor.

of a cleruch family,[1] was the mediator. Seleucus granted their petition, and in return they erected temples in his honour. After his death Antiochus went a step further. For, probably in order to win Athens as an ally in his struggle with Antigonus, and to the great joy of the cleruchs, which they expressed by electing him to a post of special honour among their gods, he gave them permission to rejoin their mother-country,[2] which thereupon stretched a point and elected Comeas *hipparch* of Lemnos for the following year (279/8 B.C.). At the expiry of his term he was voted a laudatory decree and a statue by joint action—as was proper—of the Lemnians and the Athenians.[3] Scyros and Imbros, doubtless, came into the possession of Athens at the same time. It was possibly in gratitude to Seleucus for liberating the cleruchs that the Athenians erected a statue of him before the Stoa Poicile.[4]

The reacquisition of their colonies, the embarrassments of Antigonus, and the simultaneous catastrophe which befell Macedon and Thrace through the Celtic migration, filled the Athenians with the belief that they had now achieved their lasting independence; that their long struggle with their northern neighbour had come to a successful termination, and that the policy of military resistance had been vindicated. The inaugurator and great martyr of this cause was, of course, Demosthenes, and it was therefore with some appropriateness that his nephew, Demochares, chose this moment (280/79 B.C.) to ask the Athenians for the canonization

---

[1] See Kirchner, *PA.* 8956, 15,348; *BCH.*, 1885, 49.

[2] Phylarchus (*FHG.* i. 341) in Athen. vi. 254 F. Beloch (iii. 1. 580) has seen the connexion of this action with the general development.

[3] *IG.* ii. 5. 318c. The archon-name to be restored is doubtless Δημοκλέους, not Τηλοκλέους, as Köhler intimates (p. 296). The island was allowed to join Athens by Seleucus, perhaps, but it was only under Antiochus that the fact was completed. This was in 279 B.C. at the earliest; hence, 279/8 B.C. was the year of service of Comeas, and the year following, the natural one for the enactment of his honours. How long the island remained Athenian we do not know; for the inferences of Shebelew (*Klio*, 1902, p. 36 ff.) are unproven though probable.

[4] Paus. i. 16. 1. But there are several possibilities. Thus Seleucus sent a tiger to Athens much earlier (see above, ii. 69, notes 3 and 4). Still the reference in Koch, Antiphanes, frg. 187, seems to establish a connexion between Athens and Seleucus after 306 B.C. Cf. Wilhelm, *Urk. dram. Aufführ.* 56.

which they had not yet granted to the great orator. Naturally the request was acceded to, and the bronze statue with the famous inscription, from which have come the extant likenesses of Demosthenes, was erected in the market-place. The state, furthermore, undertook to maintain at the public expense the oldest member of the family to which he belonged in all subsequent generations.[1] This benefited, in the first instance, Demochares himself, so that for the next ten years we have to think of the old agitator as dining in the town hall with the magistrates, prytanes, and other public pensioners. His time of active political life was past, and the same was true of Olympiodorus—if he was still alive—and of Phaedrus of Sphettus,[2] so that new men now took the lead in Athenian affairs. Conspicuous among them were Glaucon[3] and Chremonides,[4] the sons of Eteocles of Aethalidae, as yet young men—Glaucon known to us as a sportsman, horseman, and patron of dramatics,[5] Chremonides as one of Zeno's circle;[6] the first, however, who seems to have been the older, sufficiently matured to command the army of Athens and to exert the political influence of this office.[7]

New claimants had now appeared for the possession of Macedon. Finding all further advance into Italy checked by Rome's unification of that peninsula into one state and its crushing defeats of the Senones and Boii in 283 and 282 B.C., the Celts, whose loosely confederated tribes had been encircling the Alps for more than a century, now discovered in the Balkans the point of

---

[1] [Plut.], *Lives of the Ten Orators*, 847 A; cf. Kirchner, *PA*. i. p. 244. The tendency of this period to look back and sum up is attested by the compilation of the *didascaliae* and record of victors at the Dionysia and Lenaea, which, as Reisch (*Zeitsch. f. d. österr. Gymnasien*, 1907, p. 303), following the lead of Capps and Wilhelm, has shown, was made in the year 279/8 B.C. The theatre archives of Athens were put upon the interior walls of a hexagonal agonothetic monument.

[2] Olympiodorus disappears after *ca.* 282 B.C. Had he been alive in 279 B.C. he would, doubtless, have commanded at Thermopylae. The last specific service rendered by Phaedrus was in 282/1 B.C. *IG.* ii. 331; cf. Kirchner, *PA*. 13,963.   [3] Kirchner, *PA*. 3019; cf. *Klio*, 1908, p. 345 ff.

[4] *Ibid.*, 15,572. For their two sisters see *IG.* ii. 3. 1369 and Wilhelm, *Beiträge*, 75 ff. Their father Eteocles, who was obviously a man of wealth, had been *agonothetes* of the Dionysia (Wilhelm, *loc. cit.*).

[5] *IG.* ii. 3. 1291, *Inscr. von Olympia*, v. 178; Paus. vi. 16. 9.

[6] Diog. Laert. vii. 17.   [7] *IG.* ii. 3. 1291.

least resistance for an advance into the cultivated lands of the Mediterranean world.   The defenders of Macedon and Thrace had gone with Lysimachus to Corupedion, and such of them as had survived the death of their king were now employed on one side or other in the struggle for his kingdom.   Hence the Celts were able to push their way forward into the heart of Macedon. Ptolemy Ceraunus, rid for the moment of Antigonus, who had just opened his campaign in Asia Minor, put himself hurriedly in their way, but lost his army and his life.   In the following year Belgius, at the head of one Celtic horde, devastated the open country, while Brennus led another south upon Greece.   The way seemed open and the land defenceless, for Antigonus was absent in Asia ; Pyrrhus was absorbed in his colossal struggle with the Romans ; Antiochus was none too secure on the throne of Seleucus his father, and, besides, he had Antigonus to watch, so that the most that he and his rival felt able to do for the protection of Greece was to send five hundred men each.   Otherwise the Greeks were left to their own resources.   Aetolia was the chief military power in central Greece, and Boeotia was next in importance and first in danger.   A complete levy of these two nations went to Thermopylae to block the passage of the Celts out of Thessaly.   The Peloponnesians held aloof, but the other states in central Greece sent detachments according to their abilities.[1]   The Athenians co-operated manfully.   A corps of cavalry five hundred strong and a division of one thousand infantry joined the national forces at the pass, and its commander, Callippus, son of Moerocles,[2] took at least nominal control of the whole army.[3]   The project was

---

[1] Paus. x. 19–23 ; Justin, xxiv. 4–8 ; Diod. xxii. 3–4 ; *IG.* ii. 323 (Ditt. *Syll.*[2] 205, 206) ; *Acad. inscr. C.R.* 1904, p. 164.

[2] Paus. i. 3, 5. 4, 2 ; x. 20. 5.

[3] The report of Pausanias that Athens sent ships to Thermopylae, which carried off the Greeks when Brennus turned their position in the pass, has been rightly rejected by Beloch (iii. 1. 581, n. 1 ; iii. 2. 379), because the harbour of Athens was at this time still in the possession of Antigonus, and hence Athens had no fleet.   Besides, the ships are not mentioned in *IG.* ii. 323, where they could not have been missing had they really taken part in the affair.

The inscription from Cos, published by Herzog in *Acad. inscr. C.R.*, 1904,

unsuccessful, for Brennus, after being beaten back on a frontal attack, drew off the Aetolians by sending a detachment to ravage their homes, and then forced his way with part of his army over Mount Oeta. He entered by the path which Ephialtes had shown to Xerxes, and appeared in the rear of such Greeks as remained. The main army doubtless withdrew in time, but the Celts entered central Greece. Their repulse at Delphi, their fearful losses while retreating from this place and from Aetolia, their permanent occupation of Thrace and central Asia Minor, and their long three years [1] of murder and plunder in Macedon can only be mentioned here. In the spring of 277 B.C., however, Antigonus came in contact with a marauding army of them near Lysimachia on the Thracian Chersonese, and in the battle which ensued Pan fought on the side of the Macedonians and the barbarians were dispersed.[2] The victory was decisive. It established the military reputation of Antigonus, and opened the way for his entrance into the kingdom of Macedon. There was no one in a position to dispute seriously his succession to the throne. Antiochus, indeed, formally renounced his claim, and entered into an alliance with Antigonus, the

p. 164 ff., and commented on by Sal. Reinach (*ibid.* 158 ff.), has given a new starting-point to the long discussion as to the circumstances and results of the Celtic attack on Delphi. It seems now evident that the repulse of the Celts occurred in a blinding snowstorm (*BCH.*, 1894, p. 359) under such circumstances that the Greeks imagined that they had the god Apollo fighting with them in physical presence. We are, accordingly, bound to treat less cavalierly the report of Pausanias (x. 23) and Justin (xxiv. 8) in regard to the matter. None the less it is likely that the Celts were caught with some plunder in their possession rather than prevented from entering the precinct ; since otherwise the report of Livy, Appian, and Diodorus that they sacked Delphi, and certain pictorial scenes in which the Celts are represented with spoils in their possession when overwhelmed by the Greeks, are unintelligible (cf. von Bienkowski, *Die Darstellungen der Gallier in der hellenistischen Kunst*, 100 ff.). (This whole question is to be dealt with shortly by Pomtow ; see below, iv. 164, n. 1.)

[1] Diod. xxii. 4 (Syncellus, 266). Ceraunus became king in the winter or early spring of 282/1 B.C. He ruled one year and five months. Then in *ca.* May 280 B.C. the first Celtic invasion took place. Meleager ruled for May and June ; Antipater, the Etesian, in July and August—the time of the Etesian winds. Then when the Celts were gorged with booty, Sosthenes took hold of affairs and managed to keep out of their way till the fall of 279 or 278, when he too succumbed. An anarchy of one or two years followed. Beloch has worked this all out carefully, except that, as de Sanctis has shown, he begins a year too late.

[2] Usener, *Rhein. Mus.*, 1874, 25 ff. ; cf. Wilamowitz, *Antigonus*, 214 ff., *JHS.*, 1910, p. 196, n. 36, and below, v. 189, n. 1.

rights of the two families being combined by the marriage of Phila, daughter of Seleucus and Stratonice, to her uncle, Antigonus.[1]   Pyrrhus was at this moment in Sicily, and his return was doubtful, so that he could be left out of account with perfect safety.   Macedon, accordingly, came completely under the control of Antigonus, and in a moment the desperate adventurer of 280 B.C. became one of the most powerful monarchs of his age.

The siege of Cassandreia detained him for ten months, but in the spring of 276 B.C. he set about re-establishing his ascendancy in Greece.   Thessaly at once submitted. The Boeotian League remained independent, but, doubt-less, accepted his friendship.   The Aetolians were already his allies.[2]   Euboea was entirely in his hands, and Corinth had been all along the headquarters of Macedonian operations in Greece.   Athens was thus isolated, and isolated in a more dangerous way than ever before ; for not only was Ptolemy still bound to Antigonus[3] by the "secret treaty" of 286 B.C., and hence was unable to aid Athens, but, in view of a threatening attack on the part of Cyrene and Syria acting in concert, he was compelled to avoid all occasion of offending him.   Indeed, he probably thought it wise to lend a hand in smoothing out difficulties in Greece, if it be true, as it seems to be, that his ally Areus, king of Sparta, came to an immediate understanding with Antigonus, whose suzerainty he had not long since thrown off.[4]   Moreover, there was now no one to play the part which Lysimachus had played between 287 and 282 B.C., seeing that Antiochus, the prop of Athens between 281 and 277 B.C., had just become Antigonus's brother-in-law.   On the

[1] *Life of Aratus* (Westermann, 53, 60).   A boy born of this marriage was not a mere child in 262/1 B.C. (See below, iv. 181, n. 1.)   The marriage must have taken place in 277/6 B.C., or immediately after.

[2] They are called *socii eius* in Justin, xxiv. 1, 3.

[3] Schol. Callim. *Del.* 175 Ἀντίγονός τις φίλος τοῦ Φιλαδέλφου.   Wilamowitz, *Antigonus*, 215, n. 37.   The 4000 Celtic troops sent by Antigonus to Egypt were probably the remnants of the horde defeated at Lysimachia. Cf. A. J. Reinach, *Revue celtique*, 1909, p. 56, n. 2. ; *Rev. d. études anc.* 1911 ; cf. *Athenaeum*, 1911, i. p. 340.   Hence they were received in 277/5 B.C.

[4] This was explained satisfactorily for the first time by Lehmann-Haupt, *Klio*, 1905, p. 375 ff. ; cf. also below, iv. 171, n. 1.   I doubt, however, the com-plicity of Ptolemy in the attack of Areus upon Antigonus in 280-278 B.C.

other hand, the king of Macedon had a good reason to
make a speedy end of his difficulties with Greece, seeing
that, whatever the issue of the struggle then in progress
in the West, he had to anticipate trouble for himself on
the return of Pyrrhus to Epirus.[1]   Accordingly, he was
ready to come to terms with Athens.

The crisis in the foreign relations of Athens brought
about a crisis in her domestic politics also, since the
democratic leaders could not escape responsibility for
the grave danger of the city.   They were too deeply
compromised to extricate the state from its trouble, for
between them and Antigonus no sincere understanding
was possible.   The time was again favourable for the
men of conservative politics, for those who in 301 B.C.
had rescued Athens from the great wars going on round
about.   The consequence was that before July in the
year 276 B.C. peaceful tendencies and moderate men
became uppermost in Athenian public life.[2]   A limited
democracy was thereupon introduced.   Some of the
practices of 301 B.C. were restored, such as the tenure of
the superintendency of the general administration by a
single magistrate.[3]   At the same time this office was
relieved of various tasks through their transference to
the treasurer of military funds,[4] who was thus in a fashion
transformed into a treasurer of the *demos* now that
Athens ceased to have need of him to raise and hold
money for war.   Henceforth, as between 321 and 307
B.C., one skilled magistrate was to oversee the entire
administration and, in particular, to control all receipts

[1] Hence also his inability to crush the Achaean League, which, refounded
in 281/0 B.C., now (276/5 B.C.) added Aegium to its membership, and continued
to expand farther during the invasion of the Peloponnesus by Pyrrhus.

[2] *Klio*, 1905, p. 166 ff.   The new government authorized the drawing up of *IG*.
ii. 835 (*Priests of Asklepios*, 148 ff.)—a catalogue of dedications to Asclepius
made in the past forty-five years—in order that the priest in charge for 276/5 B.C.
might be in a position to hand over to his successor a complete statement of the
existent ex-votos, and that a similar accounting might be demanded from each
subsequent priest.   The decree in which the purpose is outlined was passed in
the second prytany of the archonship of Eu[bulus], August 276 B.C.   Accordingly,
the new government was already in power at this time.   The changes noticed
in this year were doubtless made, as usual, at its beginning.   For at the end
of 277/6 B.C., if Glaucippus was archon in that year ('Εφ. 'Αρχ., 1910, p. 19),
as seems probable, they had not yet been made.   Hence the influence of
Antigonus became predominant prior to July.

[3] *Klio*, 1905, p. 170.   [4] *Priests of Asklepios*, 149, n. 33.

and expenditures. In other respects reforms made in 301 B.C. were carried still further; for example, the judicial scrutiny required to consummate the conferring of citizenship was now made obligatory for the grant of other civic honours—such as statues and crowns.[1] These are, doubtless, simply samples of the alterations made. A general discarding of worn-out forms, and a general governmental house-cleaning certainly took place.[2] An amicable settlement with Antigonus was then possible. He did not insist on stationing troops within the city, to which the moderates were opposed on principle; in fact, he seems to have left Phyle and Panacton in the possession of the Athenians,[3] but the retention of the Piraeus was of essential importance to him, not simply as a general guarantee of Athenian fidelity, but also as a safeguard of the limited government.[4] Accordingly, the Macedonian garrison remained in the harbour town of Athens, and, to place it beyond the reach of treasonable overtures on the part of the democrats, its command was now or earlier entrusted to Hierocles, the Carian, whose hands were stained with the blood of hundreds of Athenian patriots. Athens remained outwardly independent, but during the following ten years Antigonus had access to it as to a Macedonian town, and it was treated by him as the capital of his Greek kingdom.[5] Sacrifices were offered on public occasions for his welfare as well as for that of the *demos* and its advisors [6]—*for* the welfare of the king,

---

[1] *Klio*, 1905, p. 167. This scrutiny was abandoned, probably in 266 B.C.

[2] *IG.* ii. 835 ; cf. above, iv. 161, n. 2. *IG.* ii. 324 ; cf. *Priests of Asklepios*, 166. In this connexion belongs the determination of the precise status of the Dionysiac artists. Challenged, probably, to justify its privileges the synod of the *technitae* appealed to the Amphictyonic League in the archonship of Hieron at Delphi (*IG.* ii. 551 ; cf. for the date Beloch, iii. 2. 325 ff., 350), which belongs between 278 and 276 B.C., and probably to 276 B.C. precisely. The answer was favourable to the association, and relieved its members of civic obligations. See below, v. 214, ix. *ca.* 369.

[3] Panacton and Phyle appear in the possession of Athenian garrisons between 276 and 266 B.C., 'Εφ. 'Αρχ., 1896, p. 33 ; cf. *Priests of Asklepios*, 159, n. 75.

[4] This results clearly from Diog. Laert. ii. 127, and the circumstances of the Chremonidean War, de Sanctis, 33 ; Beloch, iii. 2. 380. See above, iv. 152, n. 4.

[5] See below, iv. 168 f., and the inscription published in 'Εφ. 'Αρχ., 1896, p. 33, for the date of which see *Priests of Asklepios*, 159, n. 75. See also *JHS.*, 1910, p. 196, n. 36.

[6] *Priests of Asklepios*, 155 and note 55 ; cf. Beloch, iii. 2. 380 ff.

observe, not, as in the cult of the Soteres (Antigonus Monophthalmus and Demetrius Poliorcetes), *to* him ;[1] for Gonatas stood as king of Macedon under the institutions of public life,[2] not over them ; and hence he was in a position to make treaties and to accept the obligations they imposed, whereas his father as a god had viewed all arrangements as dependent for their maintenance simply upon his pleasure and convenience.   The ideas of Antigonus thus agreed in all essentials with those of the Athenian moderates whom he brought into power ;[3] and so long as they held the government, and the foreign situation did not force the king to coerce them to take action directly opposed to the wishes of the majority of the people, the situation—though not wholly to Antigonus's liking, since he preferred from experience and philosophic conviction to see the government in the hands of a " tyrant "—could be regarded as tolerably settled.

The year 275 B.C. was a time of peace in the Greek world—a lull before the coming storm.   The moment seemed, therefore, propitious for the Aetolians to secure general acceptance for the new games which they had determined to establish in thanksgiving for the preservation of Greece and the whole Hellenistic world from the storm of barbaric invasion which had swept over the greater part of it, but which had now happily spent its force.   The repulse of the Celts from Greece, and particularly the rescue of the Delphian oracle of Apollo, they regarded rightly as peculiarly their own achievement.   Moreover, they now controlled the shrine at Delphi, and the initiative for the establishment of an appropriate memorial thus devolved upon them. Accordingly, the matter was probably brought up at the October meeting of the Amphictyony in 275 B.C., and in consequence of the favourable reception accorded to the plan, ambassadors were despatched in all directions[4] to invite formally the participation of the Greeks in the

---

[1] *Klio*, 1908, p. 487 ff.   [2] See below, v. 190.   [3] See above, iii. 124 ff.
[4] *IG.* ii. 323 (Ditt. *Syll.*[2] 205, 206).   Cf. Kirchner, *GGA.*, 1900, p. 440 ff., and below, iv. 164, n. 1.

new musical and gymnastic contest—the Soteria. Then,
in connexion with the Pythia of 274 B.C.,[1] the festival
was celebrated for the first time. The old national
contest was expanded, and its first or more probably its
final part was devoted exclusively to the commemoration
of the pan-Hellenic victory over the Celts. Among the
Greek cities which sent a sacred delegation to the Soteria
was Athens. Was not Antigonus, the suzerain of the
city, an ally of the Aetolians? At the same time,
perhaps, the partisans of the Macedonian king took care
that his services were not forgotten, and Heracleitus of
Athmonon made a donation of paintings in the temple

---

[1] Kolbe, *op. cit.* 33. It is now obvious, as Herzog remarks in connexion
with the inscription from Cos published in *Acad. Inscr. C.R.*, 1904, p. 164 ff. and
especially 172, that the Soteria was not celebrated at the preceding Pythia in
278 B.C. ; cf. Beloch, iii. 2. 416. A new work on the Celtic attack on Delphi
and the events which followed is announced by Pomtow (*Berl. phil. Woch.*,
1910, p. 1096). He adheres to the conclusion reached by him thirteen years
ago, that the Soteria was first celebrated in a year in which there was no
Pythia. This he has done mainly on the basis of the well-known Sotion grave
inscription from Alexandria, which he dates, not with Pagenstecher in 239/8 B.C.
but with Merriam in 277/6 B.C. Sotion accordingly announced the Soteria in
Egypt in that year, the ninth in the reign of Philadelphus. Pomtow finds
239/8 B.C., the ninth in the reign of Euergetes—our one condition is that it
must belong in the ninth year of some Ptolemy—excluded, because in what is
apparently the year of Sotion's death the first day of the twelfth Macedonian
month Hyperberetaeus coincided with the seventh of the eighth Egyptian
month Pharmuthi (*Amer. Jour. Arch.*, 1909, Pl. xii.), whereas in 239/8 B.C.,
the year of the Canopus inscription, the seventh day of the second Macedonian
month Apellaeus coincided with the seventeenth of the fifth Egyptian month
Tybi. It seems impossible for Pharmuthi to have coincided with the fourth
and the twelfth Macedonian months of the same year—unless, as Strack once
maintained, there were two series of Macedonian and two series of Egyptian
months in progress at once. This view, however, Grenfell and Hunt have
shown to rest upon no sure foundations (*Hibeh Papyri*, Appendix I.). Nothing
clearly decisive, so far as I can judge, prevents Hyperberetaeus of 277/6 B.C.
from coinciding with Pharmuthi. If Rubensohn's contention were acceptable,
that Hyperberetaeus in 284/3 B.C. coincided with some month before Tybi (5th)
(*Papyri Elephantine*, 27), it must have suffered a violent wrench to coincide
with Pharmuthi (8th) seven years later. The contention in question, however,
has been disputed by Bouché-Leclercq (*Rev. de phil.*, 1908, p. 131 ff.). Beloch
(iii. 2. 23.) and Grenfell and Hunt (*loc. cit.*), moreover, have rejected 277/6 B.C.
for the Sotion inscription on the basis of the calendar alone ; and Pagenstecher
and Zahn (*Amer. Jour. Arch.*, 1909, p. 415) have rejected it because in their
judgment the vases of the Sotion group are later in style than those which
belong to 271–249 B.C. This being the state of affairs, and in view of the
difficulties in the Athenian chronology which Pomtow's view involves, I prefer
to await his entire brief before making changes in the text. These would not
be considerable in any case. It may perhaps be added that, if Bouché-Leclercq
is right (*loc. cit.*), the second year of Philadelphus was, on one computation,
283/2 B.C. ; hence the ninth ran from November to November 276/5 B.C. It
seems to me possible that the *theori*, of whom Sotion was one, were sent to
Alexandria in the fall of 275 B.C., and to Athens and Chios in the following
spring (cf. Boesch, Θεωρός, 133 ff.).

of Athena Nicé, in which was delineated the great victory of Antigonus over the Celts at Lysimachia.[1] Eighteen years later this zealous friend received his reward.

In 274 B.C. the storm broke. We refrain from following the course of the First Syrian War,[2] which the matrimonial and political alliance of Magas of Cyrene with Antiochus of Syria (*ca.* 275 B.C.) had precipitated, and the simultaneous conflict between Pyrrhus and Antigonus for the throne of Macedon and the overlordship of Greece. We note simply that in 273 B.C. Pyrrhus was apparently sweeping everything before him, and that many Greek cities, and among them Athens, sent ambassadors to interview him.[3] It is unlikely that the Athenians sought more than the acknowledgment of their neutrality—a policy which Pyrrhus himself had urged upon them at an earlier time. They did not break relations with Antigonus ; at any rate, after his victory in 272 B.C. they remained on the same intimate terms with him as before. The Piraeus was made a starting-point for the re-subjugation of Greek cities, and on one occasion Hierocles, its commandant, tried to secure the co-operation of Menedemus in an attempt on Eretria ; but the philosopher replied that he dealt with kings, not with adventurers.[4]

The period between the liberation of Athens from Demetrius and the Chremonidean War was a brilliant one in Athens. The creative work of Zeno and Epicurus had been accomplished mainly in the preceding two decades, but these remarkable men were now at the height of their influence. Straton, who in 288/6 B.C. had taken the place of Theophrastus as head of the Peripatos, was making marvellous discoveries in physical science,[5] and Polemon, Crates, and Crantor, the three grey-haired gentlemen of the old school who taught in the Academy, served as foils for the aggressive and

---

[1] *IG.* ii. 5. 371*b*. For the date see Kirchner, *PA.* 6496, and *Klio*, 1908, p. 349.

[2] Lehmann-Haupt, *Berl. phil. Woch.*, 1892, p. 1465 ; *Klio*, 1903, p. 496 ff.

[3] Justin, xxv. 4. 4.   [4] Diog. Laert. ii. 127.

[5] Gomperz, *Griech. Denker*, iii. 389 ff.

powerful intellect of Arcesilaus. Hundreds of young men, mostly foreigners, were engaged every year in the professional study of philosophy, history, literature, and natural science in the four schools. Nor was the dramatic activity less remarkable that the philosophic. Menander's career had come to an untimely end in 292 B.C., before his manner had ceased to be seductive or had become popular, but Apollodorus of Carystus and Poseidippus were now at their best, and Philemon, Diphilus, and Alexis were producing new plays annually, their vigour undiminished by the sixty years and more of creative effort which lay behind them; while they had keen and often successful rivals in scores of younger though less well-known comedians.[1] The Great Dionysia required five new comedies of conspicuous excellence every year, and still others were needed for the Lenaea, so that there was no lack of stimulus to productivity. Despite the marvellous development of Alexandria, Athens was still the recognized centre of Greek culture, and many an ambitious literary man sought to get into touch with its society.[2] The group of tragedians known as the Pleiades wrote for the Attic stage,[3] and Callimachus studied philosophy in an Athenian school, while his college acquaintance, Aratus, published his *Phaenomena*, one of the most influential poems in all Greek literature, in Athens,[4] and was a resident there, for the most part in the school of Zeno, till called to Pella in 277/6 B.C. Antagoras of Rhodes, a graceful and accomplished poet, stayed and went with Aratus. The most distinguished historian of this age, Timaeus of Tauromenium, lived and wrote in Athens in the 'seventies; while Philochorus, who was engaged on his valuable *Annals* of Athens, Demochares, who was publishing his entertaining

[1] The inference made by Reisch (*Zeitsch. f. d. österr. Gymnasien*, 1907, p. 300) from the cessation at about 285 B.C. of the list of Lenaean victors, which was inscribed on the agonothetic monument of 279/8 B.C., that the contest of new plays at the Lenaea ceased at about this time is shown by Capps (*Berl. phil. Woch.*, 1908, p. 637 ff.) to be fallacious.

[2] Thus, besides those mentioned below, Antigonus of Carystus was there in the early 'seventies (Wilamowitz, *Antigonus*, 127).

[3] Beloch, iii. 1. 437 ff. ; cf. Wilamowitz, *Griech. Literatur*, 128.

[4] See Knaack, P.-W. ii. 392. For Callimachus, *ibid*.

Histories, and Diyllus, author of a general narrative covering the period from 357/6 to 297/6 B.C,[1] worthily sustained the reputation of the local school of historians. Epoch-making works of art were not produced in Athens at this time, for the city had no such wealth as formerly ; still it was perhaps the Athenian school from which came the Ludovisi "Juno" and the "Aphrodite"of Melos,[2] and every year witnessed the erection of some new monument[3] or statue characterized by genuine Attic restraint and freshness.   The temperament of the age was scientific.   Men took pleasure in the collection and accurate description of plants and animals, and in the isolation and delineation of constitutions ; hence also in literary and artistic portraiture.   It was at this time that biography came to be added to the long series of literary types created by the Greeks,[4] and it was at this time too that marble and bronze portraits came first to please.   The statues erected in Athens of Demosthenes, Demochares, Theophrastus, Zeno, Seleucus, Ptolemy, Arsinoë, Pyrrhus, Phaedrus, Comeas, Philippides, Olympiodorus, and of many another, were no longer beautiful incorporations of a single idea, not yet grossly realistic.   The universal was still potent to guide the chisel towards something with which all mankind could have sympathy, while the individual or personal came to lend its infinite variety, its co-efficient of historic interest, to the creations of the imagination. The new departure in art was thus made in the old Greek way, the imperious dictation of the past and the harsh radicalism of the present being equally avoided.[5]

It is true that foreigners contributed very largely to these achievements in art, letters, and science ; but this had been the case at every period, and

[1] Schwartz in P.-W. v. 1247.
[2] Beloch, iii. 1. 539 ; the Nicē of Samothrace may be Rhodian rather than Athenian.
[3] For the agonothetic monuments see *IG.* ii. 3. 1289 ff. ; cf. Reisch, *loc. cit.*, and for the Thrasycles monument, Judeich, *Topographie von Athen*, 281.
[4] Leo, *Griech.-römisch. Biographie*, 85 ff.
[5] Furtwängler, "The Supremacy of Greek Art," *International Quarterly*, xii. 108 ff.

the very fact that writers and artists sought the inspiration and sympathy of the Attic public is one of the strongest testimonials to the breadth and depth of high culture there. And it is equally true that many Athenians went to foreign lands to spread abroad the qualities and methods of Athenian work. Demetrius of Phalerum was not the only exile who kindled with an Attic torch the sacred fire in rough Macedonian palaces.[1] Athens was no longer the imperial city agitated by the strong ferments of new ideas and proud hopes, nor yet the free city ennobled by the agony of a vain struggle for the preservation of liberty and by the severe criticism of social and political doubt. Indeed her life-blood was being steadily sapped, for trade and commerce were now ceasing to force wealth into the arteries of her body ;[2] but she was a great city still, and it is only in making a comparison with her own past that we may venture to speak disparagingly of the contribution which this little town of less than forty thousand free males was then making to the spiritual life of the world.

Antigonus did not misbehave himself in Athens as his father had done, and he also knew how to appreciate its rich culture ; but like Ptolemy Soter a generation earlier, and perhaps in conscious imitation of his own predecessor Archelaus, the patron of Euripides,[3] he at first sought to detach from Athens for the adornment of his own court at Pella a cluster of the distinguished men with which that city was thronged. Then, when Athens became his, he made it his Greek capital and came to visit it frequently. At one time we find him greeted by the Athenian troops stationed at Eleusis,[4] more often he appears as the auditor of Zeno, his friend

---

[1] Serapis was made presentable to the Greek world by Demetrius of Phalerum, who composed the hymn-book for his service ; by Timotheus of Eleusis, who organized his mysteries ; and by Bryaxis of Athens (Kirchner, *PA.* 2930 ; cf. Beloch, iii. 1. 541, n. 1), who gave him artistic interpretation. See Cumont, *Religions orientales,* 92 ff.

[2] At the time the *Histories* of Demochares were written the wealth and business activity of Athens, under Demetrius of Phalerum, had probably come into strong relief because of the subsequent decay.

[3] Wilamowitz, *Antigonus,* 215, 340.

[4] Ἐφ. Ἀρχ., 1896, p. 33 ; cf. above, iv. 162, n. 5.

and teacher.[1] Halcyoneus, the son born to him by Demo, the Athenian courtesan, was being educated in Athens under the watchful care of Persaeus, Zeno's favourite pupil.[2] Craterus, the half-brother of Antigonus, was at home in Epicurean circles, and it was probably at this time that he made his famous collection of the Athenian decrees.[3] Another half-brother, who had inherited the name, good looks, and disposition of Poliorcetes, was likewise a student at Athens, and enjoyed a much talked of intimacy with Arcesilaus, the noted Academician.[4] The commandant in the Piraeus too was a man of liberal interests, and was particularly devoted to Arcesilaus.[5] The city, doubtless, was flattered by these royal attentions, and the presence of the princes brought money to Athens and prestige to her philosophic schools. But the Macedonians were too much at home there to please the radical democrats who wished to play an independent rôle in public life. Here was the point at which a new political movement might gain a foothold in Athens.

This started in Egypt, or, to be more precise, with Arsinoë, sister and queen of Ptolemy Philadelphus.[6] Ptolemy Soter had laid much stress upon Athenian friendship, and had given a cordial reception to Philemon the comedian,[7] and to Demetrius of Phalerum, who, far from bearing a grudge against his fellow-citizens, used his new position to send subsidies of money to them.[8] He would have entertained Menander also had the poet been willing to leave Athens,[9] and he had summoned Straton, the most distinguished of the pupils of

---

[1] Diog. Laert. vii. 6 ἀπεδέχετο αὐτὸν καὶ Ἀντίγονος καὶ εἴ ποτε Ἀθήναζε ἥκοι, ἤκουεν αὐτοῦ. πολλά τε παρεκάλει ἀφικέσθαι ὡς αὐτόν.

[2] Diog. Laert. vii. 36. Persaeus went to Pella in 277/6 B.C. (Life of Aratus, Westermann, 60). Possibly Halcyoneus came into the charge of Hieronymus subsequently (see below, v. 233). He probably stayed in Athens for his ephebate (ca. 275 B.C.), and then joined his father, with whom he fought against Pyrrhus in 273/2 B.C. (Plut. Pyrrh. 34).

[3] Crönert, Kolotes, 14. 174 τούτωι δὲ ὅτι καὶ πέρ[υ]σ[ι]ν ? ἐγένετο χρήσιμος ὁ ἀνὴρ Φ[ί]λαι τε τῆι μ[η]τρὶ τῆι Κρατερ[ο]ῦ καὶ αὐτῷ Κρατερῶι. Cf. Usener, Epicurea, 410.

[4] Diog. Laert. iv. 41.   [5] Ibid. iv. 39.

[6] Lehmann-Haupt, Klio, 1905, p. 375 ff.

[7] Dietze, De Philemone comico, Diss. Gött., 1901, p. 4, n. 6.

[8] Plut. De exilio, 7.   [9] Alciphron, Epist. ii. 3, 4.

Theophrastus, to become the tutor of the Crown princes.[1]
He had aimed to make Alexandria a new Athens, and
had gone so far in this direction as to introduce tribes
on the Attic plan, to establish a Sunium and an Eleusis
in its neighbourhood, and to import a *hierophant* from
Attica, to perform the mysteries in due form.[2]   But,
as has been explained already, he was forced by the
general situation to abandon Athens to the tender
mercies of Antigonus between 286 and his death in
283 B.C.   Nor did Philadelphus have the power, even if
he had the will, to befriend the city till he had beaten
off the attack of his adversaries in the First Syrian War.
Hence for the first ten years of his reign (283-273 B.C.)[3]
there is no evidence that he helped Athens in any way,
and at the end of this period his friendly overtures
are represented as a consequence of the attitude of
his father and his wife.[4]   Arsinoë had been queen of
Macedon, and her son by Lysimachus, Ptolemy by name,
was, or was held to be, the rightful heir to this throne,
but between him and his inheritance stood Antigonus.
He must be driven from Macedon, and allies must be
won for that purpose.   Accordingly, as soon as the
First Syrian War came to an end, Arsinoë, part of whose
fierce energy seems to have been transmitted to the
highly intelligent, but sensuous, unwarlike, and weaker-
willed brother whom she had made her husband, bound
Sparta and its league of Peloponnesian states more
closely to Egypt, and also opened negotiations with
Athens.   Her scheming was the easier in that Egypt
and Macedon were still good friends, and Athens could
thus show enthusiasm for the Ptolemies without being
disloyal to Antigonus.   Enthusiasm she certainly dis-

---

[1] Diog. Laert. v. 58.

[2] See "Alexandreia" in P.-W. ; cf. Cumont, *op. cit.* See, moreover, Schiff
in P.-W. *s.v.* "Eleusis," and recently Pagenstecher, *Amer. Jour. Arch.*, 1909,
p. 390, n. 2.

[3] We have recently learned that 284/3 B.C. was the last year of Soter's reign.
He died before the 23rd of Tybi (March 24th) 283 B.C., Bouché-Leclercq,
Revue de philologie, 1908, p. 131 ff.   Philadelphus did not supersede him in
285/4 B.C. ; at most he became his father's co-regent.

[4] *IG.* ii. 332 (Ditt. *Syll.*[2] 214), 267/6 B.C. ὅ τε βασιλεὺς Πτολεμαῖος ἀκολούθως τεῖ τῶν προγόνων καὶ τεῖ τῆς ἀδελφῆς προ[α]ιρέσει φανερός ἐστιν σπουδάζων
ὑπὲρ τῆς κοινῆς τ[ῶν] Ἑλλήνων ἐλευθερίας.

played.   Thus Alexis in his *Hypobolimaeus*,[1] which was
produced between 276 and 270 B.C., proposed a toast to
Philadelphus and his wife and sister, Arsinoë, and also to
the *entente cordiale* at that time existing between them
and Athens.   It was doubtless at this same time that the
Athenians erected statues of Philadelphus and Arsinoë in
their market-place,[2] and gave a permit to the devotees of
Serapis to establish a mission in the city.[3]   The trend
of public sentiment was thus patent to any one who
chose to observe, and it was clear that the policy of
neutrality would be in grave peril the moment Egypt
was ready to show its hostility to Antigonus.   But
in the meanwhile the friends of Macedon and the
friends of Egypt met on terms of apparent cordiality,
and agreed to ignore differences of opinion as to the
internal government of the state.

This was the condition of affairs when Demochares
of Leuconoë, now upwards of eighty years of age,
breathed his last.   He had retired from public life in
280/79 B.C., and his later years had been spent in
literary work.   There passed down to subsequent generations, in addition to some of his orations,[4] a notable
history of his own times in more than twenty-one books.
It was frankly partisan and highly rhetorical,[5] but
valuable through its vivid details, and its presentation

[1] Koch, ii. 386, 244 (quoted at head of Chapter IV.).   This is the last
datable fragment of Alexis, and since he was born in *ca.* 372 B.C. (Capps,
Amer. Journ. Phil. xxi. 59), it was probably written not later than 274/3 B.C.
The relation between Athens and Ptolemy is designated ὁμονοία, not συμμαχία.
The proposal of a συμμαχία was probably rejected (cf. Diog. Laert. vii. 24).
These two passages serve to confirm the results obtained by Lehmann-Haupt
(*Klio*, 1905, p. 375 ff.), who shows that Ptolemy and Antigonus were friends
prior to 274 B.C.   From the way in which Antigonus recovered his position in
Greece in 276 B.C. it seems to me likely that they were friendly then (see above,
iv. 151, 160 for their earlier relations).   We have no date for the overtures of
Egypt to Athens; we know only that they belong after the marriage of
Philadelphus with his sister.
    In 277/6 B.C. we have a triangular alliance, Ptolemy-Antigonus, Antigonus-
Antiochus.   This was, doubtless, the diplomacy of the peaceful Philadelphus.
Since Arsinoë was the soul of the later aggressive foreign policy of Egypt, I am
inclined to put her marriage with her brother in the year of the change, 275 B.C.
[2] Paus. i. 8. 6.
[3] *Ibid.* i. 18. 4.   The *Sarapiastae* appear in the archonship of Hagnias
(*IG.* ii. 617).   The date is uncertain ; cf. Rusch, *De Serapide et Iside in Graecia
cultis*, Diss., Berlin, 1906, p. 4 ff.
[4] Cic. *De orat.* ii. 23 ; cf. Kirchner, *PA.*, 3716, and for some dialogues (?),
Wilamowitz, *Antigonus*, 194, n. 16.
[5] Cic. *Brutus*, 83 ; cf. Beloch, iii. 1. 492.

of contemporary politics from the standpoint of one
actively and honourably engaged in them.　He had been
a hard fighter all his life, and could not leave out of
his literary controversies the animus more natural to
political strife.　And he got as good as he gave.　Thus
Timaeus of Tauromenium, who was probably writing
his history in Athens at this time, found a chance some-
how to abuse him so roundly that over a hundred years
later Polybius was constrained to come to his defence;[1]
and the difference of estimate current in antiquity has
been reproduced in modern times.[2]　He prided himself
on his unswerving loyalty to democratic principles,
and the doctrines to which he had subscribed in his
youth and middle age were of the most uncompromising sternness.　But advancing years had mellowed his
temper somewhat, and the fierce democrat, who had
argued in 307/6 B.C. for the abolition of the schools of
philosophy, came in 275 B.C. to cultivate the acquaintance of the great Stoic teacher.　He could not, however,
rise to the latter's political detachment, and by sug-
gesting that Zeno should abuse the absolute confidence
of Antigonus for the personal advantage of Demochares,
he lost the respect of the philosopher altogether.[3]　The
incident reveals a disposition on the part of the democrat
to come to terms with Antigonus such as he would not
have displayed towards a Macedonian king thirty years
earlier.　It is likely that Antigonus was tactful in his
treatment of the old man; at any rate, after his death,
when Laches, the son of Demochares, sought for his
father the same honours obtained by him for Demosthenes
nine years earlier, the dominant party, despite its
Macedonian sympathies, did not prevent his request
from being granted.　In the preamble of the decree[4]
by which the honours were conferred the public services
of Demochares were recited.　The memorial throws an

---

[1] Polybius, xii. 13 ff. ; cf. Suidas, ᾧ τὸ ἱερὸν πῦρ ; Wilamowitz, *Antigonus*,
193, n. 14.
[2] Wilamowitz, *Antigonus*, 189 ff.　He is omitted altogether in the *Griech.
Literatur*.　On the other hand, see Holm, *History of Greece* (Engl. transl.),
iv. 77.
[3] Diog. Laert. vii. 14.　　　　[4] [Plut.], *Lives of the Ten Orators*, 851 D.

interesting light upon the political situation in Athens in 271/0 B.C. First are detailed his strenuous exertions at the time of the Four Years' War against Cassander. His exile was the work, not of the moderates, not of Stratocles and Demetrius Poliorcetes, but " of those who destroyed the democracy." [1] The period of exile is, curiously enough, left eventless. [2] Then follows the record of his financial activity after his return in 290/89 B.C.—the embassies to Lysimachus, Antipater, and Ptolemy, and the recovery of Eleusis. Finally, his political steadfastness is emphasized—his exile for the sake of democracy and his refusal to hold office on the ascendancy of an oligarchy. No mention is made of anything done by him during the last nineteen years of his life, so that there is no reference in the whole document to Antigonus, nor does the name of his father Demetrius appear in the earlier portion. There is nothing in it to give offence to a government which regarded itself as a moderate democracy. There is, perhaps, an intentional emphasis of his somewhat indirect connexion with Ptolemy. [3] On the request being granted, a statue of Demochares was erected in the agora which, transferred to the *prytaneum*, was to be seen there over four hundred years afterwards.

Another distinguished Athenian died in this same year (271/0 B.C.), the venerable and lovable autocrat of the Garden, and within three years he was followed by Straton and Polemon. Epicurus had lived and taught for thirty-five years in his retreat just outside the Dipylon gate of Athens. Though inactive in public affairs he was not indifferent to them, and he had shared all the vicissitudes of his native city. [4] As an ephebe from the Samian cleruchy he had fought in the Hellenic

[1] See *Klio*, 1905, p. 174.   [2] See above, iv. 137, n. 6.
[3] The memorial of the services of Phaedrus of Sphettus (*IG.* ii. 331), as dated and analyzed above (iv. 142, n. 1), betrays identically the same situation in Athens in 275/4 B.C., when account is taken of the fact that Phaedrus was a moderate (Demades-Phocion) democrat (see above, i. 13, iii. 120), Demochares a radical (Demosthenes) democrat.
[4] Diog. Laert. (x. 10) speaks of his πρὸς πατρίδα φιλία ; cf. also Crönert, *Kolotes*, 174 [κ]ατὰ τὴν ἅλωσιν τῶν ['Αθην]ῶν κτλ. This refers to 295/4 B.C. See above, iii. 133.

War,[1] and had become a wanderer when his father was driven out of Samos in 322 B.C. For propertyless persons such as he there was no place in Athens between 322 and 307 B.C., but as soon as the Macedonian régime came to an end and the law of Sophocles was declared unconstitutional,[2] Epicurus settled in Athens. During the blockade of 295/4 B.C. he left the Garden and took his school to his town house in Melite,[3] and he seems not to have been disturbed subsequently; but after such experiences it is natural that he should dislike the Macedonians. Friendship, rather the careless pursuit in the company of friends of intellectual pleasures, he thought the best means of happiness, and this the object of life; and in the midst of a devoted circle of friends he spent the rest of his days, leaving it only two or three times to visit a similar group at Mitylene.[4] Straton died in 270/69 B.C., or the year after, and Polemon in 268/7 B.C.[5] The Peripatetic gave way to Lycon, a young man who proved to be a mere lecturer; the Academician first to his respectable old friend Crates, and then, a few years later, to Arcesilaus,[6] the man who was to transform the Platonic doctrines in the same thorough way in which Theophrastus and Straton had transformed the Aristotelian.[7] He was already a man of fifty, and had made his influence felt

[1] Strabo, xiv. 638; cf. Clark, *Class. Phil.* i. 319, and Wilamowitz, *Griech. Literatur*, 130. For the place of his school see Wilamowitz, *Antigonus*, 288, n. 23; cf. Wachsmuth, *Stadt Athen*, i. 265, who puts it in the city, but Cicero locates it on the road to the Academy. [2] See above, iii. 107.

[3] Plut. *Demetr.* 34. The other suburban schools had to do the same more than once in the third century B.C. After 200 B.C. they retired into the city permanently. Wilamowitz, *Antigonus*, 267, n. 4.

[4] Diog. Laert. x. 10; cf. Usener, *Epicurea*, frg. 176 and 189. He is said to have abused his predecessors and contemporaries in philosophy with the manners of a fishwife, and Timon (Diog. Laert. x. 3) speaks of him as "the most ill-bred of mortals," but Diogenes himself refuses to believe his own report and defends him manfully (x. 9 ff.). Crönert (*Kolotes*, 16 ff.) points out that those alleged to have been attacked did not reply, and tries to show that all the venom attributed to Epicurus was derived from one forged letter. A. Körte (*GGA.*, 1907, p. 255 f.) dissents, and explains that the spite was found in letters published posthumously. For Epicureans in the New Comedy see Hegesippus, frg. 2 (Koch, iii. 314); Damoxenus, frg. 2 (Koch, iii. 349), and the work of Ranke cited above, ii. 73, n. 2.

[5] In the archonship of Philocrates; cf. *Cornell Studies*, x. 27.

[6] For the school heads see especially Beloch, iii. 2. 466 ff.

[7] A good account of Arcesilaus is given by von Arnim in P.-W. ii. 1164 ff.; cf. also Beloch, iii. 1. 452 ff., and for Theophrastus, Gomperz, *Griech. Denker* iii. 360 ff.

both upon the general public and upon the scientific world, and had added new lustre to his school, which of late had been eclipsed by both the Stoa and the Peripatos. He was the first foreigner to lead the Academy since the patriotic agitation against the philosophers had broken out in Athens.[1]

The year in which Athens lost Demochares and Epicurus had not yet come to a close when the world was stirred by the news of the death of the remarkably enterprising and shameless sister-queen of Egypt; for Arsinoë Philadelphus died in May-July of 270 B.C.,[2] leaving many plans unfinished and a lasting impression upon the more plastic mind of her royal consort. The foreign policy of Egypt was not indeed reversed by this event, for in 269 B.C. Philadelphus adopted as his son, associated with himself in the government of Egypt, and thus gave the strongest possible recognition to the child of Arsinoë and Lysimachus whom the sister-queen had put forward as the rightful heir to the throne of Thrace and Macedon. The project of Arsinoë thus lived after her, but by her death the personal animus and interest were taken from the foreign policy of Egypt, and the rupture with Pella, already imminent in 270 B.C., was deferred till the drift of events brought it about. Athens accordingly remained passive under the suzerainty of Antigonus for four years longer. This is the period of the " tyrants " in the Greek cities subject to Macedon. Ambitious citizens, preferred by the favour of Antigonus to despotic power in their native places, kept their fellow - townsmen under

---

[1] Unless it be that Socratides, the obscure person to whom Crates left the school, was a foreigner—for which no evidence exists and against which the [nick]name protests. Polemon and Crates were Athenians. On this point see Wilamowitz, *Antigonus*, 178 ff., especially 196 ff., 207 ff. The Academy was patriotic, anti-Macedonian, and Arcesilaus came to his aversion to Antigonus naturally (Diog. Laert. iv. 39).

[2] Mahaffy, *Ptolemaic Dynasty*, 78 ; cf. Beloch, iii. 2. 130 ; Kaerst, *op. cit.* ii. 1. 416. Her name was impressed upon many cities—nine at least are known to us—scattered throughout the empire. It seems probable that the admiral Patroclus and the nesiarch Hermias, who succeeded Philocles and Bacchon at *ca.* 275 B.C., were *her* men. Patroclus was eponymous priest in Alexandria in 270/69 B.C. (*Hibeh Papyri*, i. 272). For his relation to Arsinoë see Hegesander in Athen. xiv. 621 A. The interest of Hermias in Arsinoë is well attested (*JHS.*, 1910, p. 191).

Macedonian dictation. "Wise men," according to the Stoic creed to which Antigonus subscribed, were thus vested with the authority to which they were entitled by training and attainments. It is a fundamental misconception, as Wilamowitz pointed out,[1] to think of the early Stoa as a stronghold of republicanism. Zeno, its founder, lived quietly in Athens, and refused to migrate to Pella; but he sent his favourite pupils, Persaeus and Philonides,[2] and his ideas were put to the practical test in many parts of Greece.[3] They were not received with enthusiasm. Indeed, dislike of the tyrants helped the intrigues of Egypt more than any other single thing, and these speedily pushed the antagonism with Macedon to open rupture. Sparta feared the consolidation of Macedonian influence in the Peloponnesus, and hence Areus, its king, strengthened by his alliance with Ptolemy, headed the opposition to the local tyrants. The movement reached Athens in 267 B.C., when Philadelphus proffered assistance in a war of independence against Macedon. The government of the moderates could not defend its policy of neutrality against so attractive an offer. The time seemed come for the expulsion of Hierocles and his garrison from the Piraeus, and with this in view Athens entered into alliance with Ptolemy.[4] It at once became the rallying point for anti-Macedonian agitation. A proclamation was issued calling upon the Greeks generally to take up arms for their liberties, and in August of 266 B.C. the coalition

---

[1] Antigonus, 217 ff. "Die Stoa ist die Philosophie des aufgeklärten Absolutismus; sie geht durchaus vom einzelnen Menschen aus und gipfelt im Weisen, für den die Vereinzelung notwendig ist."

[2] Life of Aratus (Westermann), 60. This mentions only Persaeus. Epicurus knows of Persaeus and Philonides being together at Pella between 276 and 271/0 B.C. Crönert (Kolotes, 28-30) doubts that Zeno sent Philonides, but on insufficient grounds.

[3] von Arnim, Stoic. vet. frag. i. 102, 460; Diog. Laert. ii. 143. Persaeus prevented the restoration of democracy in Eretria. Polybius (ii. 41. 10) says of Antigonus, πλείστους γὰρ δὴ μονάρχους οὗτος ἐμφυτεῦσαι δοκεῖ τοῖς Ἕλλησι.

[4] Lehmann-Haupt, Klio, 1905, p. 383 ff. It is not without significance in this connexion that an Arcadian died in Alexandria in 267 B.C. while present there as presbeutes (Pagenstecher, Amer. Jour. Arch., 1909, p. 406, n. 3). For as Pomtow (Berl. phil. Woch., 1910, p. 1095) points out, it is a mistake when Pagenstecher (p. 409) and Boesch (Θεωρός, 135) think of a presbeutes as a religious agent alone.

was completed,[1] when Sparta and Athens, inspired by the memory of their common action against the Persians, bound themselves by solemn oaths to co-operate as good friends of Ptolemy in the vindication of Greek freedom. We cannot doubt the strength and sincerity of the sentiment which called forth this union ; nor is it to be supposed that Areus, who controlled the policy of Sparta, and Chremonides, who made the decisive motion in the Athenian assembly, were conscious tools in the subtle statecraft of Philadelphus. It is even doubtful whether the leaders in the revolt were under any delusions as to the position they must occupy in the Ptolemaic empire in the event of success. They were probably content to exchange overlords, to get as their patron the distant, pleasure-loving, rich, and generous enthusiast for Greek institutions and culture instead of the persistent, austere man, who made it a matter of conscience to attend in person to the details of government. Alexandria exercised a great fascination upon the imagination of the Greeks at this time. It was there that people went to obtain riches.[2] The court welcomed men of capacity to its political and military service, and large salaries and comfortable employments awaited scholars and *littérateurs* who chose to settle in Ptolemy's capital. The Egyptian recruiting officers were omnipresent with tempting offers of pay and adventure. The enormous wealth of the monarch, the brilliant pageantry of the court, the wonderful processions and fêtes, the profusion of all things provocative

---

[1] *IG.* ii. 332 and 333, and ii. 5. 510*d* (Wilhelm, *GGA*, 1903, p. 789). This document belongs to 266/5 B.C. The only alternative is 265/4, but this is to be rejected because Areus was killed in the second year's campaign, yet his death belongs in 264 at the latest. Nor is it conceivable that the preliminaries to a formal declaration of war—which followed *IG.* ii. 332 by we know not how great an interval—and the long drawn-out first campaign (see below, iv. 179) could have taken place in the months of August, September, October of 265, *i.e.* in the part of the military year still remaining after the passing of the Athenian decree. Rather, the preliminaries took place in the fall and winter of 266/5 B.C., and the first campaign began in the spring of 265 B.C.

[2] Teles, 39 (Hense[2]) εἰ βούλει τὸν υἱόν σου τῆς ἐνδείας καὶ σπάνεως παῦσαι, μὴ πρὸς Πτολεμαῖον πέμπε ὅπως χρήματα κτήσεται· εἰ δὲ μή, "ἀλαζονείαν προσλαβὼν ἀπελεύσεται," περαινεῖς δὲ οὐδέν, ἀλλ' εἰς Καδμείαν ('Ακαδημείαν MSS.) πρὸς Κράτητα. Cf. Wilamowitz, *Antigonus*, 300, n. 10. Though this was spoken some thirty years later (see below, v. 202, n. 2), the reference to Crates throws the time of the action back to this very epoch (Hense,[2] xxxiv.).

of appetites and lusts were subjects of common talk in contemporary Greece.[1] From almost any headland along the coast the magnificent fleets of Egypt could be seen patrolling the Aegean Sea, suppressing piracy, and restoring runaway slaves.[2] At Crete, Thera, Melos, Ceos, Methana (Arsinoë), Samothrace, and elsewhere stood Egyptian garrisons.[3] The islanders swore by Ptolemy, and held it to his credit that he had lightened their taxes and promoted their internal harmony and welfare. There were no tyrants in the cities of the Cyclades.[4] In short, the strength of Egypt seemed overwhelming, the devotion of its ruler to Greek institutions assured—what more was needed? Should Ptolemy prove insincere, there was the danger of secession to Macedon to hold him to his promises.

The situation at the opening of this, the so-called Chremonidean War,[5] was really full of danger for Antigonus. Doubtless, it did not surprise him or find him unprepared, and his plans were matured with rapidity and decision. By occupying Corinth and Megara he blocked the passage from the Peloponnesus into central Greece, and by keeping the Piraeus strongly garrisoned, he closed all approach to Athens from the side of the sea. Then, in the spring of 265 B.C., he led a powerful army into Attica and began the siege of the

---

[1] Theoc. *Idyll* 15 ; Athen. v. 196–203 ; cf. Niese, ii. 104 ff. ; Beloch, iii. 1. 293 ff., 334 ff. ; Mahaffy, *Empire of the Ptolemies*, § 74, *Greek Life and Thought*, 200 ff. ; Bouché-Leclercq, *op. cit.* i. 155.

[2] Teles, 23 (Hense[2]) ; cf. Wilamowitz, *Antigonus*, 302 and n. 14 ; Ditt. *OGIS.* 773 ; cf. iv. 151, n. 5. The naval superiority of Philadelphus is still clearly recognizable in the ὕβρις of Patroclus in the Chremonidean War (Athen. viii. 334), and the well-known anecdote which makes Antigonus Gonatas ask a doubter before the battle of Cos ἐμὲ δὲ αὐτὸν παρόντα πρὸς πόσας (ναῦς) ἀντιτάττεις; Plut. *On Self-praise*, 16. 545 : *Apophthegmata*, 183 ; Pelopidas, 2. Phylarchus obviously made out of the pride and fall of Philadelphus a catastrophe in the style of Herodotus. See also Callimachus, *Hymn on Delos.* A few years earlier (278-270 B.C.) Theocritus wrote his striking glorification of the Ptolemaic empire (*Idyll* 17. 85 ff.).

[3] Ditt. *OGIS.* 44, 45 ; *BCH.*, 1900, p. 225, 1906, p. 96 ; *IG.* xii. 3. 466 (Ditt. *OGIS.* 102 ; cf. 115) ; Niese, ii. 103, n. 1 ; Beloch, iii. 2. 271 ff.

[4] Ditt. *Syll.*[2] 202. In Arsinoë on the island of Ceos, however (*IG.* xii. 3. 320), an *epistates*, who amounted pretty nearly to the same thing, was stationed.

[5] Paus. i. 1. 1, 7. 3 ; iii. 6. 4 ff. ; Trogus, *Prolog.* 26 ; Justin, xxvi. 2. Cf. de Sanctis, 39 f., 55 f. ; Droysen, iii. 1. 225 ff. ; Wilamowitz, *Antigonus*, 219 ff. ; Beloch, iii. 1. 608 ff., iii. 2. 424 ff. For the chronology, *Priests of Asklepios*, 153 ff. ; cf. Lehmann-Haupt, *Berl. phil. Woch.*, 1906, p. 1265 f. The name is given to the war by Hegesander in Athen. vi. 250 F.

city.   The advantage of position thus rested with the
Macedonians.   To relieve Athens, Areus had first to
force the passage of the Isthmus.   Patroclus, the Egyptian
admiral, could join hands with the besieged only when
in control of the Piraeus, but there a Macedonian
garrison lay, and it was beyond his power to dislodge it.
Accordingly, the Peloponnesian army lay inactive before
the lines at Corinth.   The soldiers were desirous of a
conflict, but the prospects of success seemed to Areus
doubtful.   Patroclus urged him to try to force a passage
through, in which event he agreed to co-operate by
landing troops in Antigonus's rear.   He represented
that the Spartan king must take the initiative, since he,
with Egyptian sailors, could not attack Macedonian
hoplites.   But Areus persisted in his hesitation, and,
when supplies ran short in his camp, he led his army
home.   The best that Patroclus could do was to seize
and fortify a small island near Sunium on which to pass
the winter.[1]   By virtue of his control of the sea, he
could help in forwarding provisions through the lines to
the Athenians, and at the same time impede the free
entrance of supplies for the army of Antigonus.   During
the winter[2] the Celts stationed at Megara in the employ
of the Macedonian king mutinied, but Antigonus was
equal to the emergency.   He left a small garrison to
watch Athens and fell with full force upon the insurgents
The Celts were completely annihilated, the women and
children being slain by their relatives, the men by the
enemy.   In 264 B.C. Areus took the field again, and this
time ventured an attack upon the force defending the
isthmus of Corinth.   It was beaten back with loss and
the king himself was among the slain.[3]   This failure,
which had as a consequence the re-establishment[4] of
Macedonian preponderance in the Peloponnesus, was
doubtless due in part to the lack of co-operation between

---

[1] See also Phylarchus in Athen. viii. 334 A.

[2] This event was mentioned by Trogus (*Prolog.* 26) before the death of Areus
and after the description of the conditions in Greece which led up to the
Chremonidean War.   Moreover, Justin in his epitome (xxvi. 2) states that it
occurred simultaneously with the war against Sparta and Ptolemy.

[3] Plut. *Agis*, 3.   For the time see Diod. xx. 29. 1 ; cf. Beloch, iii. 2. 113 f.

[4] Beloch, iii. 1. 610 f.

the two relieving forces. Patroclus was in command of the sea. The anecdote that he sent fish and figs, prince's and peasant's fare, to Antigonus to symbolize the alternatives, sea power or poverty, discloses, at the least, a general belief in his naval superiority.[1] But with the Piraeus in the hands of the enemy a victory on the land was necessary for the relief of Athens. Accordingly, he could do nothing after the defeat and death of Areus, and he appears no more in our meagre records of the war. Athens had been well provisioned for a siege, and, doubtless, the neighbourhood of the Egyptian fleet rendered the blockade ineffective. At any rate, the second winter passed and the city showed no signs of capitulating. A respite now came to it from a new quarter. The son of Pyrrhus, Alexander, king of Epirus—another pawn, doubtless, in the hands of the Egyptian statesman—invaded and ravaged the upper portions of Macedon, and Antigonus, who knew from experience the danger of an Epirote attack, took part of his army with him,[2] and marched north to defend his kingdom. Most inexplicably, his troops deserted him, and all the highlands of Macedon submitted to Alexander, whereupon Antigonus fell back upon his Greek possessions and continued the struggle from this quarter. The conquest of Athens now became of minor importance to him. Hence at the opening of the next military season he made a truce with the Athenians, and withdrew his whole army of attack from Attica. The decisive thing, however, was the loyalty of the Macedonian people, who, in 262 B.C., rallied round

---

[1] Phylarchus in Athen. viii. 334. For Patroclus, see above, iv. 175, n. 2, and Ditt. *OGIS.* 45. 44 ; *BCH.*, 1900, p. 225, v. 35, 1906, p. 96. He probably succeeded Philocles, king of the Sidonians, in *ca.* 275 B.C.

[2] Lehmann-Haupt (*Berl. phil. Woch.*, 1906, p. 1266), who makes the war continue both in Macedon and Athens during 263 B.C., and puts the negotiations for a peace in 262 B.C.—after the expulsion of Alexander. The negotiations, moreover, are represented as a failure. This contradicts the report of Polyaenus and is done obviously with reference to Diog. Laert. iv. 39 ; cf. *Klio*, 1905, p. 391, n. 1. Had the battle of Cos taken place during the siege of Athens, it could hardly have been omitted in Justin and Pausanias. See also *JHS.*, 1910, p. 196, n. 36. The view taken in the text satisfies the conditions stated below, iv. 181, n. 1 and 2, and also the text of Polyaenus, which makes the truce last only from one summer to the spring next following.

Demetrius, the king's son, a lad of fourteen years,[1] and, under the leadership of competent officers, defeated Alexander, drove him from their country, and, then, from his own throne in Epirus. This episode occupied the best part of two military seasons, and during the summer and autumn of 262 B.C. the Athenians had been relieved of the blockade. The devotees of Ammon in the Piraeus were able to make an addition to their temple, and public and private business generally resumed its normal course.[2] Then, when the planting time came, in the fall of the year, and the conflict between Macedon and Epirus dragged on, the Athenians drew from their slender stock of provisions, and furnished seed grain to the country folk. It was a serious blunder, for in March of 261 B.C. Antigonus reappeared in Attica in full force, and the people, shut within their walls, viewed with chagrin and dismay the destruction of the ripening crops from which they had expected to replenish their stores.[3]

[1] "Puer admodum" in Justin xxvi. 2 and, therefore, not the brother of Antigonus, as Kärst suggests (P.-W. i. 1411). Demetrius the Fair must have been upwards of 24 at this time. Justin, moreover, says "son" of Antigonus, which is correct. Antigonus summoned Persaeus in 277/6 B.C. (Knaack, P.-W. ii. 391 ff.), and he arrived εἰς τὸν 'Αντιγόνου καὶ Φίλας γάμον. There was no need for Antigonus to remain at Cassandreia during the ten months of its siege. Hence we may put his marriage in the year 277 B.C., and the birth of Demetrius in 276 B.C. From the report of Justin (xxvi. 2. 9 ff.) certainty as to the exact time of this incident cannot be obtained, and Beloch (iii. 2. 427) disassociates it from the Chremonidean War altogether. This seems to me unwarranted. Justin seems to have thought of the invasion of Alexander as occurring while Antigonus was absent in Greece dealing with the revolt of Athens. "Adversus quem cum reversus a Graecia Antigonus esset," he was defeated and driven back. Then came the intervention of the prince in Macedon "absente patre reparato exercitu." The soldiers of Antigonus were, apparently, faithless, but the heart of the kingdom, to which the king did not have access, proved loyal. Beloch dates the incident in ca. 258 B.C. This leaves unmotived the absence of Antigonus with the Macedonian army and the occasion of Alexander's attack; for we know of no serious embarrassment of Macedon at this time. As Beloch himself admits, the extreme youth of Demetrius in 262 B.C. is an inadequate reason for making the transfer. All we can say as to the time at which Alexander recovered Epirus is that it preceded the peace with which the war ended.

[2] IG. ii. 5. 616b. (Passed on the 28th of Hecatombaeon in the archonship of Antipater: July 262 B.C. Ol. 129. 3, i.e. at the time of the Great Panathenaea.) IG. ii. 310; cf. Kirchner, Hermes, 1902, p. 436, and Berl. phil. Woch., 1906, p. 985.

[3] Polyaenus, iv. 6. 20; cf. Paus. i. 30. 4. Since Polyaenus is in general reliable, and since he (or his source) obviously had at his disposal detailed accounts of the wars of the third century B.C., I see no reason whatever to doubt the correctness of this report. The division of dedications to Asclepius in IG. ii. 836. 36 ff. between Phileas and Calliades, the priests of Asclepius before and after the fall of Athens in 262/1 B.C., suggests that the capitulation took place at about this season of the year; cf. Priests of Asklepios, 154.

Since no further prospect of relief existed, they now decided to capitulate.[1]

It was not the time for clemency. The city had used its freedom to rebel, and must not be left the chance to do so again. Accordingly, Antigonus placed a garrison within the ring-wall of Athens, and gave it the fortified position on the Museum from which his father's troops had been expelled in 289/8 B.C. Another remained in possession of Sunium, which it had probably held against Patroclus during the war, a third occupied the island of Salamis, and still others held the frontier posts, Panacton and Phyle. Of course, the Piraeus

---

[1] Polyaenus and Pausanias agree that the city surrendered — was not taken by storm. Philodemus says: ἀπὸ Κλεάρχου γὰρ ἐπ' ['Αρρ]ενε[ί]δην ἐφ' οὗ σημ[ειωθ]ῆναι [τε]τελευτηκένα[ι] Ζήνωνα ἔτη ἐστὶν ἐννέα κα[ὶ] τριάκο[ντα] καὶ μῆνες τρεῖς. Upon this I can only repeat what I have written in the *Priests of Asklepios*, 153 : "The sequence of Antipatros and Arrheneides is thus clearly established. Klearchos was archon in 301/0 B.C. Thirty-nine years bring us to the beginning of 261/0. Three months can carry us as well into the year 261/0 as into that of Klearchos. Hence Beloch's calculation is not the only one possible." Kolbe, on the other hand, affirms (*op. cit.* 41) that "wenn man die inklusive Zählung, die bei Ordinalzahlen am Platze ist, anwendet," we reach only the beginning of 262/1 B.C. But we are not dealing with ordinals, but with cardinals, in which case we are free to compute exclusively, if we want to. I cannot understand the positiveness with which Kolbe affirms that ἀπὸ Κλεάρχου necessarily includes in the school term of Zeno some, or, let us say, more than one or two months, of the year of Clearchus. I can find it easily credible that in 261/0 B.C.—to say nothing of the time of Philodemus or of his source—no one knew the precise month in which Zeno began to teach, or, knowing it, chose to make, let us say, the abolition of the ephebate at the end of the year 301/0 B.C., when Zeno first got a considerable number of hearers, the time of the founding of the school. Of course, the exact time of his death was known definitely. It may well have been the third month of 261/0 B.C. But if Kolbe insists that the length of the term is given with pedantic precision, why cannot he put one of the three extra months in 301/0 B.C. and the other two in 261/0 ? The only consequence would be to increase by one month the interval between Zeno's death and the erection of a public tomb in his honour. Certainly, Kolbe's interpretation of the phrase 'Αντίπατρος ὁ πρὸ 'Αρρενείδου is wrong. If the words occurred in an official list or document, the idea that the two archons shared the year between them would be permissible, though even then we should expect it to be expressed by 'Αντίπατρος καὶ 'Αρρενείδης, as in the case of the two archons for the year 124/3 B.C. But since it occurs only in Philodemus, its purpose is plainly to determine the position of Antipater with reference to Arrheneides, or the surrender of Athens with reference to the death of Zeno. It is with precisely the same purpose that in the Schol. on Aristoph. *Frogs*, 694 the phrase 'Αντιγένης ὁ πρὸ Καλλίου occurs. Antigenes was archon in 407/6 and Kallias in 406/5 B.C. The *Frogs* was put on the stage in the latter year, while the battle of Arginusae, which called for the scholium, took place ἐπ' 'Αντιγένους τοῦ πρὸ Καλλίου. Clearly Antipater belongs to the year before Arrheneides, and when the change of magistrates took place in the course of Antipater's year, the eponymous archon was re-elected, as in 319/8 and in 296/5 B.C., in order to avoid the confusion which was almost certain to arise through having two *eponymi* for one year.

and Munychia remained Macedonian, and the faithful Hierocles was entrusted with the command of all the Antigonid forces in Attica.[1]   At the same time, prob- ably, the Athenian generalship for home defence was abolished ; rather it was divided into two offices, one for the defence of the Paralia, and the other for the defence of the Eleusinian frontier, and soldiers in the employ of Athens were stationed along with the Macedonian garrisons in these districts.[2]   There re- mained not much for the civil authorities to do, and, in fact, it seems likely that the popular assembly ceased for the following five years (261–256 B.C.) to pass decrees except at the request of the Macedonian king or his agent.[3]   Antigonus, furthermore, discharged the magis- trates elected before the capture of the city,[4] and put in their places others whom he could trust.   One of the new *thesmothetae* was Demetrius, the grandson of Demetrius of Phalerum, from which we may conclude that the new government was constituted from the oligarchic faction.[5]   Antigonus, doubtless, had had enough of the democrats by this time.   The personnel of the administration was changed from the top to the bottom, even the politically insignificant priesthood of Asclepius being given to a new individual.[6]   The only exception, perhaps, was made in the case of Antipater, the eponymous archon, who, as in 319/8 and 296/5 B.C., was kept in office to designate by his name the entire year.   The lot was retained for the election of magistrates, and the old system of rotation of offices appears after 262/1 B.C. as before.   This being so, the conclusion is hardly evitable that a property qualifica- tion for candidacy was introduced.

[1] Paus. iii. 6. 6. For the garrison in the Museum see Eusebius (Schöne), ii. 120 f. ; for the one in Munychia and Salamis see *IG*. ii. 5. 591*b* ; for those in Eleusis, Panacton and Phyle, see *IG*. ii. 5. 614*b* ; for the one in the Paralia (Sunium and Rhamnus) see Kirchner, *Ath. Mitt.*, 1907, p. 470, and 'Εφ. 'Αρχ., 1892, p. 147 ; cf. Wilhelm, *ibid.*, 1902, p. 142.

[2] *Klio*, 1909, p. 318.

[3] At any rate the only decree of which we have knowledge for this period is that in honour of Zeno which was passed at the request of the king. See below, iv. 187.

[4] Beloch (Crönert), iii. 2. 424 ; cf. *Priests of Asklepios*, 153 f.

[5] Hegesander in Athen. iv. 167 F.

[6] *Priests of Asklepios*, 133, 139.

Whether public property, such as the silver mines, was diverted in whole or part to the Macedonian crown, we cannot affirm with certainty. At any rate, Athens lost the right of issuing money, and the Macedonian tetradrachms, the so-called Antigonids, took the place in Athenian circulation formerly held by the Attic "owls."[1] They were probably made in the Athenian mint, but belonged to the Macedonian monetary system.[2] This change advertised abroad the humiliation of the city, but it hurt more than the pride of the people: it was a disastrous blow to the foreign commerce of Athens, for the integrity of Attic money had given it a wide circulation, and its general use gave the place of issue an advantage over business rivals. To maintain this circulation the Athenians had preserved with great conservatism the rude processes and devices of their antique coins. Zeno still contrasts the purity and crudeness of the Attic tetradrachms with the beauty and impurity of the new coins of the successors of Alexander.[3] There was, therefore, we may be sure, regret elsewhere than at Athens when the reliable old pieces, which had once dominated the money market, ceased to be issued, and more than one generation passed before those already in circulation ceased to be used.[4]

An epoch in the history of a city is seldom so clearly defined as that which the Chremonidean War ended in Athens. With the "owls" disappeared her commercial supremacy—diverted to the coast of Asia by the opening up of the East—and with the Long Walls, which Antigonus let fall in ruins,[5] vanished her political importance, which had been maintained of late only by the most heroic sacrifice and courage. The old belligerent Athens was now no more, and her loss of pride, freedom, and prosperity showed how essential

[1] *IG.* ii. 836. 45, 80, 86, 93. For the dates of these τέτραχμα 'Αντιγόνεια see *Priests of Asklepios,* 147 f. For the maintenance of an Attic mint after 322 B.C. see Köhler, *Sitzb. d. berl. Akad.,* 1896, p. 1089 ff., and *Numis. Chron.,* 1905, p. 1 ff.

[2] Köhler, *loc. cit.* This issue has the *calathus* like the Attic bronze money and like the gold coins of Attica in Köhler's new series (*Zeitsch. f. Numis.,* 1898, p. 10). See *JHS.,* 1910, p. 196, n. 36.

[3] Diog. Laert. vii. 18. [4] See below, vi. 247, n. 4.

[5] See below, v. 211, n. 2.

these blessings had been for her spiritual life. The creative impulse, which the Persian Wars had given and the loss of empire had not checked, and which in the last fifty years had produced in rapid succession no less than sixty-four notable comedians,[1]—some of whom wrote as many as two hundred plays,[2]—seems to have spent its entire force upon the generation which witnessed the fall of Athens in 261 B.C. In the midst of this struggle the great comedian Philemon, the idol of the Athenian people, died verging upon his hundredth year. He was living in the Piraeus, perhaps to escape the hardships of the siege, and the story[3] goes that on the night before he died, he saw in a dream nine maidens leaving his house. They were the Muses, forced by their divine nature to flee all contact with death; and they went forth not from his house alone, but from the city in which they had made their home for over two hundred years.

Six months after the troops of Antigonus entered Athens, Zeno of Citium died,[4] and the city was poorer by the founder of the last of her great schools of philosophy. Plato, Aristotle, Epicurus, and Zeno—a mighty procession, all names to conjure with still.[5]

---

[1] Anonymous, Περὶ κωμ.; cf. Wilhelm, Urk. dram. Aufführ. 118 f. This author makes Philemon, Menander, Diphilus, Poseidippus, and Apollodorus the most distinguished of them.

[2] Menander wrote 105; Philemon 97; cf. Dietze, op. cit. 6; Alexis 245; Suidas, s.v.; cf. P.-W. i. 1469.

[3] Aelian, Var. hist., frg. 11; Diod. xxiii. 6. His deme was Diomeia (IG. ii. 1289; cf. iii. 948)—an exclusive city quarter or suburb (see P.-W. s.v.), and since he was made a citizen, he certainly lived where he was registered. Hence his being in the Piraeus was exceptional.

[4] In the archonship of Arrheneides (261/0 B.C.), for which see above, iv. 182, n. 1. He probably died in one of the early months of the year (July–Sept.), since Antigonus asked for a public tomb for him in the fifth month.

[5] See von Arnim, Stoic. vet. frg. i. 3 ff., where all the biographical data regarding Zeno is collected. He died in 261/0 B.C., at the age of 72, according to his own pupil Persaeus (Diog. Laert. vii. 28 : in von Arnim, p. 7); therefore he was born in 333/2 B.C. He came to Athens aged 22 (ibid.), i.e. in 311/0 B.C., and was with Crates (MSS. Xenocrates), who wrote, seemingly in Athens, at the time of Demetrius of Phalerum (above, iii. 129, n. 1), Stilpon, and Polemon for 10 years (Diog. Laert. vii. 2, where the 10 is erroneously made to refer to his apprenticeship with Xenocrates alone). Then, in 301/0 B.C. (archonship of Clearchus) he opened his own school (Philodemus, Περὶ τῶν Στοικῶν, col. 4; cf. Beloch, iii. 2. 39) under the circumstances set forth above, iii. 129. He was head of the school for thirty-nine years and three months (Philodemus, loc. cit.; cf. Priests of Asklepios, 153 f.), i.e. to the third month of 261/0 B.C.—reckoning exclusively in that last case, as in all the other computations in this note.

Zeno had come to Athens on business in 311 B.C. when the general peace of that year had opened the sea to commerce, and on being converted to philosophy by reading Xenophon's *Memoirs of Socrates*, he joined the ragged group which followed the Cynic Crates, but in a few years he abandoned it to learn from Polemon in the Academy the orthodox doctrines of Socrates and Plato. He was not an acquiescent pupil, and Polemon seems to have suspected his motives. At any rate, as already related, he left the Academy in 301/0 B.C. and founded his own school. He gave his lectures in the Stoa Poicile, a public place, and seems to have been disturbed considerably by the loungers.[1] The proximity of the lecture hall to the agora brought him pupils from among the ephebes of Athens, and his hold upon this fashionable clientele was strengthened by the fact that he won the love and admiration of Antigonus, the Macedonian crown prince (*ca.* 294 B.C.).[2] When the pupil succeeded to the throne of his father, and made Athens his Greek capital, Zeno became the best-known philosopher of the city. For ten years he stood in the centre of her intellectual life, and we have a suggestion that he was often the political adviser of the people.[3] Though of an ascetic temperament, and the expounder of a stern ethics, he was not unsocial in his habits, and took part, though with some reluctance and unusual moderation, in the gay parties of his friends.[4] Altogether, he was a most admirable personality, and his influence with

---

Beloch (iii. 2. 471) and Kolbe (*op. cit.* 40 ff.) err in computing inclusively. In the fifth month of 261/0 B.C., *i.e.* after time for a reference of the matter to Antigonus had elapsed, came the honorary decree given by Diog. Laert. vii. 10.

[1] Diog. Laert. vii. 14. His early following was none too respectable ; cf. Timon, *Frg.* xx. (von Arnim, i. 10. 21) :

ὄφρα πενεστάων σύναγεν νέφος, οἱ περὶ πάντων
πτωχότατοί τ' ἦσαν καὶ κουφότατοι βροτοὶ ἀστῶν.

[2] Diog. Laert. vii. 13 ; Philodemus, *loc. cit.* col. ix. (von Arnim, i. 10. 24). Antigonus Gonatas said that he τὸν δ' ἄνδρα θαυμάζειν καὶ τι[μᾶ]ν καθ' ὑπερβολήν.

[3] Diog. Laert. vii. 6 ; cf. vii. 14 ; Aelian, *Var. hist.* vii. 14 πολλὰ δὲ καὶ Ζήνων ὑπὲρ Ἀθηναίων ἐπολιτεύσατο πρὸς Ἀντίγονον. Had we no such intimations, we might have concluded as much from the relations between him and the king.

[4] Diog. Laert. vii. 13. The countenance of Antigonus obviously brought him into touch with the best Athenian society—with the set in which Demochares and Chremonides moved (*ibid.* 14, 17). Zenon, however, shrank from notoriety of every sort. He occupied such a position as to be approached for subscriptions (*ibid.* 12).

young men was undeniably wholesome ; hence the Athenians honoured themselves by honouring him with a crown and a statue.[1] As a partisan of Antigonus, and one indifferent to Egyptian courting,[2] he doubtless lost his dominant position in 266/5 B.C., not simply in that Arcesilaus, who had a strong antipathy to the Macedonian king, and, hence, an additional ground for popularity in Athens, became head of the Academy at about this time,[3] but in that Athens revolted from Macedon and began the unfortunate Chremonidean War. Zeno was, apparently, in the city during the long siege, and it was barely finished when he died aged seventy-two years. Two months later, in Maemacterion (November) of 261 B.C., when Thrason of Anacaea came to Antigonus on an embassy from the Athenians,[4] the king requested that Athens give to Zeno a public tomb in the Cerameicus, which was, accordingly, done. He had never wished for Athenian citizenship,[5] and had ordinarily kept aloof from public affairs ; he had professed monarchical principles, and had been intimate with the conqueror of Athens. Hence the honour could not be motived by any of the ordinary services. But "he had been a noble man ; had turned the youth towards virtue and *sophrosyne*, and had exemplified in his own life the doctrines which he taught," [6] and for this there was a place of honour in the public graveyard of Athens for the Semite from Citium.

---

[1] Diog. Laert. vii. 6 ; cf. Wilamowitz, *Antigonus*, 343 f. ; Wachsmuth, *Stadt Athen*, ii. 403, n. 1 ; Beloch, iii. 1. 466, n. 3.

[2] Diog. Laert. vii. 24. See above, iv. 171, n. 1.

[3] See von Arnim, *s.v. Arkesilaos* in P.-W. ii. 1164 ff.

[4] Diog. Laert. vii. 15 ; cf. Wilamowitz, *Antigonus*, 344.

[5] In fact he prided himself on being a native of Citium (Diog. Laert. vii. 12).

[6] See Wilamowitz, *Antigonus*, 232 "das haben sie ihm in das Psephisma gesetzt, kein Wort zu viel noch zu wenig : es gab damals nicht viel Psephismen derart. Wer die Athener liebt, wems ans Herze geht, wenn er sie in diesen Zeiten ihres Verfalls oft verachten muss, dem tut es wohl hier zuletzt, in der furcht-baren Not, einen Zug des alten wahren Atheneradels zu finden. Es ist doch noch die eine Eintracht auf Erden : Athen und die Philosophie, und in anderem Sinne, als die Volksschmeichler meinten, bleibt es eine ewige Wahrheit, τἄλλα πάντα κοινὰ εἶναι τῶν ἀνθρώπων, τὴν δ' ἐπὶ τὸν οὐρανὸν ἀνθρώπους φέρουσαν ὁδὸν Ἀθηναίους εἰδέναι μόνους."

CHAPTER V

A GENERATION OF MACEDONIAN RULE

ὁρῶ τὴν ἀκρόπολιν καὶ τὸ περὶ τῆς τριαίνης ἐκεῖ σημεῖον·
ὁρῶ τὴν Ἐλευσῖνα καὶ τῶν ἱερῶν γέγονα μύστης·
ἐκεῖνο Λεωκόριον· τοῦτο Θησεῖον.
οὐ δύναμαι δηλῶσαι καθ' ἓν ἕκαστον·
ἡ γὰρ Ἀττικὴ θεῶν ἐστι κτίσμα καὶ προγόνων ἡρώων.

Hegesias in STRABO, ix. 1. 16 (396).

UPON the capture of Athens in 261 B.C. there was a general scattering of the democratic leaders. Glaucon and Chremonides escaped in time and entered the service of Ptolemy, in which they later on obtained the highest official distinction.[1] Philochorus, the old seer and antiquarian, stayed in Athens, but shortly afterwards was executed for treasonable correspondence with the Egyptians.[2] It is unknown upon whom the blame rested, upon the oligarchs, upon the king, or upon Philochorus himself. In any case we can pardon Antigonus for being strict, seeing that he had to expect unrest in Athens, so long as there was any prospect of a successful revolt, and the hope of liberating themselves could not fail to present itself to the Athenians so long as the war continued and the naval supremacy of Philadelphus was unbroken. It was perhaps in *ca.* 259 B.C. that hostilities between Macedon and Egypt ceased, when, possibly, a peace was concluded,[3] the essential condition of which, from Antigonus's point of view,

[1] See below, v. 197. Several other Athenians appear subsequently in the employ of Euergetes: Epicrates (Kirchner, *PA.* 4864), Philinus (*ibid.* 14311), various persons mentioned in the *Flinders Petrie Papyri* (ii. n. 39e, ii. 6; iii. 21g 37, 54 Bd. 5, [110. ii. 6]), and, if P. M. Meyer is right (*Das Heerwesen der Ptolemäer*, 9), a number of the soldiers stationed on Thera (*IG.* xii. 3. 327, of which the date is uncertain; cf. Beloch, iii. 2. 25, n. 1).

[2] Suidas, *s.v.* Φιλόχορος.

[3] See *BCH.*,|1908, p. 57, n. 10, and Tarn, *JHS.*, 1910, p. 224. [Cf., however, *BCH.*, 1911, 36.]

being that Philadelphus abandoned Arsinoë's son Ptolemy, ousted him from the co-regency in Egypt (259/8 B.C.), and sent him to Ephesus, to which he had a valid claim on his mother's side. The honours and the profits of the Chremonidean War rested at its termination with Antigonus; but, since it was obvious that Macedon must continue to have trouble in Greece while Ptolemy held the adjacent islands and thus threatened it at every point, Antigonus devoted his energies during the next few years to the construction of a powerful fleet. Money coined in Athens with the head of Antigonus, thinly disguised as Pan, on the one side, and Athena Promachus on the other, doubtless, helped to finance the undertaking;[1] but an opportunity for the successful use of the new navy did not come till Philadelphus was drawn into a war, the so-called Second Syrian, which Antiochus II. declared against him and his allies[2] probably in *ca.* 256 B.C., and which was rendered doubly serious by the simultaneous rebellion of Ptolemy, son of Arsinoë, formerly co-regent of Egypt and pretender to the Macedonian throne, now practically exiled as governor of Ephesus. This defection carried with it not simply other Egyptian commandants in Ionia,[3] but also a considerable part of the fleet of Egypt, and required the concentration of the rest in the south-east corner of the Aegean, where it could both menace Ionia and protect Caria and Cilicia. The denuding of the Cyclades, which was involved in the detention of

---

[1] *JHS.*, 1910, p. 189 ff., to which a general reference must be given for the views taken as to the order and connexion of events between 261 and 241 B.C. "Provisional truth" is all that is possible where the evidence is so scanty. I believe, however, that my synthesis takes account of the facts more satisfactorily than does that of Tarn (*JHS.*, 1909, p. 264 ff.). Professor Dürrbach, as he very kindly informs me, thinks it possible to maintain unchanged Homolle's Delian archon-list from 301 to 225 B.C., regarding Lysimachides as of the period prior to 314 B.C., and Agatharchus I. and Mantitheus II. (Schulhof) as spurious. I do not see, offhand, how we can accept this solution, though, as Professor Dürrbach remarks, it does not vitiate my historical combination.

[2] Eumenes of Pergamum in particular. It is possible that the establishment of Philetaereia on Delos in 265 (266/5) B.C., being coincident in time with the outbreak of the Chremonidean War, designates the point from which the understanding between Pergamum and Egypt dates.

[3] Timarchus of Miletus, for example. Ptolemy, who was by adoption the son of Philadelphus, apparently thought himself entitled to the place assigned to Euergetes. His name, Ptolemy, indicates that he claimed and had been granted the oldest son's rights; hence his revolt.

the navy of Philadelphus in the vicinity of Cnidus, now gave Gonatas an opportunity to strike a decisive blow. Putting to sea with his new fleet in *ca.* 256 B.C., he occupied the Cyclades one after another, the Egyptian *aphracta*, or cruisers, being quite incapable of checking his advance. Then, despite a marked inferiority in the number of his ships, he boldly sought out the admirals of Philadelphus,[1] and, finding them at Leucolla near Cos, he attacked and routed them completely. This victory enabled him to join hands with Antiochus; and to give greater permanency to their union a marriage was arranged between Stratonice, sister of the Seleucid king, and Demetrius, the Macedonian crown prince. Antigonus then returned in triumph through the Aegean; and on stopping at Delos to effect the transfer of the League of the Islanders from Ptolemy's suzerainty to his own, he established on the island Stratonicia and Antigonia —fêtes indicative of sovereignty as well as piety. The usages of Hellenism had by this time become so well fixed that the position of Gonatas toward his new dependencies was capable of definition in only one way: he must be one of their gods. Accordingly, he was deified not only by the Delians, but also by the League of the Islanders, which instituted in his honour biennial games to be celebrated on Delos, probably in conjunction with the local Antigonia.[2] Within Macedon, however, Antigonus, warned perhaps by the fate of his father, continued to refuse apotheosis. He wore the diadem, of course, for that had become a conventional symbol of royalty, and to the Pan on his coins the engravers gave his features;[3] but he remained a Macedonian among Macedonians, a king who was rather the chief executive of a nation than a being with inherent right to rule and inherent power to enforce obedience.[4] By thus definitely

---

[1] The plural probably indicates that two or more Egyptian squadrons had united.   [2] *JHS.*, 1910, p. 200, n. 51.

[3] Seltman, *Num. Chron.*, 1909, p. 268, n. 5. For the deification of Antigonus in Arcadia see Persaeus in Athen. xiii. 607 c; Polybius, xxviii. 19. For the temple of Phila Aphrodite in Attica see above, iii. 57, n. 11.

[4] Tarn, *JHS.*, 1909, p. 268, § C. I can, however, see no further difference in the usage by Gonatas of the *ethnicon*, Μακεδών, and by Doson of the addition καὶ Μακεδόνες (*BCH.*, 1907, p. 95), than that in the first instance we have a private,

renouncing a position at once offensive to the usages of
his own people and, through the significance given to it
by his father and grandfather, menacing to the other
kings, he firmly secured the Macedonian throne for
himself and his dynasty.[1]

The stationing of the garrison on the Museum and
the suspension of republican government in Athens were
doubtless war measures, represented, as in 322 and 317
B.C., to be revocable at the end of the struggle.[2] This
had, of course, not been reached in 256/5 B.C., but to all
appearances Athens, hitherto on the border of two rival
empires, was now well in the centre of Macedonian
territory ; so that there seemed no further warrant in
the political and military situation for the abolition of
local liberties there.   Hence " after the sea-fight many
Athenians went to Antigonus or wrote to him suppli-
catory letters," with a view, apparently, to the restoration
of their autonomy.[3]   They had long since formed the
habit of choosing the head of the Academy for such
missions, so that they now sought Arcesilaus, who
enjoyed, moreover, the goodwill of Hierocles, governor
of the Piraeus, to intercede for them with the king.   But
Arcesilaus refused.   Aristodamus, the tyrant of Argos,
was less ungracious, and lent the weight of his influence
to their petitions.[4]   Antigonus's position was sufficiently
secure for generosity to be now sound policy, and in
256/5 B.C. he withdrew his troops from the Museum
and left the ·city to arrange its internal affairs as it saw
fit.[5]   The fact was that, with the Piraeus, Salamis,
Sunium, and the frontier forts garrisoned, the seas and
islands all about held by a victorious fleet, and Chalcis,
Megara, and Corinth governed for Antigonus by his

---

in the second a public, donation. The instances noted are too few to prove that
the phrases could not be interchanged.

[1] It is probably an effect of the victory of Antigonus at Cos that in 255 B.C.
the Achaean League strengthened its executive by substituting one general for
the two it had hitherto possessed. Unity of command was thereby secured
for the struggle for independence which must have seemed imminent after the
"elimination" of Ptolemy.

[2] See above, i. 27, 37.   [3] Diog. Laert. iv. 39.   [4] IG. ii. 371c.

[5] Eusebius (Schöne), ii. 120 f.   For the date see Priests of Asklepios, 147 and
n. 29.   The first decree extant after the restoration is IG. ii. 336 (256/5 B.C.).
For the resumption of a dedication by the demos to Asclepius in the same year
see Priests of Asklepios, 147.

half-brother Craterus, Attica was helpless. Hence, too, the need was past of putting the Athenian garrisons in charge of a foreigner. Hierocles, who besides being unpopular was now an old man, was accordingly succeeded by Heracleitus of Athmonon, an Athenian citizen whose zeal for Antigonus had been manifest eighteen years earlier, and who had been in his service once before, possibly while an exile at the time of the Chremonidean War.[1] His position in Athens was approximated to that of Demetrius of Phalerum, the most notable difference being that he had in addition the command of the Macedonian troops.

The victory of Cos gave Antiochus II. an opportunity to round out his dominions in Asia Minor, and he made such good use of it that at the end of three years he was in possession—quite precarious to be sure, since acquired by destructive concessions—of everything that had ever been Seleucid in this region with the exception of Pergamum, Caria, and Lycia. The whole fabric of the Ptolemaic empire was thus torn into shreds, and by 252 B.C. it was clear to Philadelphus that the resources of Egypt did not suffice to put it together again. Hence the crafty statesman in Alexandria determined to buy off the Asiatic enemy, by leaving him in momentary possession of his spoils, in order to regain from Macedon the control of the sea upon which all other action depended. Hence, in the winter of 252/1 B.C. he offered in marriage to Antiochus his only daughter Berenice, and gave her such a dowry that subsequently she was known in history as *Phernophorus*, and the conviction was established among contemporaries that with her Ptolemy had in fact purchased peace. Then he took up with new vigour the war against Antigonus.

He had already secured an opening for an intervention in Greece by giving Aratus of Sicyon one hundred and fifty talents, and thus confirming him and the Achaean

[1] *IG.* ii. 5. 371*b* (Ditt. *Syll.*[2] 207); cf. above, iv. 165, n. 1; *IG.* ii. 5. 591*b* (Ditt. *Syll.*[2] 220). His appointment was of recent date in 250/49 B.C. That it was made in 256/5 B.C. is Beloch's conjecture (iii. 2. 383). That Lycinus of Italy was governor of Megara, not of Athens, has been shown by Wilamowitz (*Antigonus*, 300 ff.; cf. Hense,[2] xxxvii.). For Diogenes's status see Wilhelm, *Beiträge*, 81.

League in a wavering hostility to Antigonus (252 B.C.). Aratus at once tried to seize Corinth and failed; but Alexander, its governor, the son of Craterus who was now dead, possessed the ambition of turning his province into an independent kingdom; so that, on being tempted by Philadelphus, he entered into his plans and made an alliance with the Achaeans also. Consequently, when the navy of Egypt entered the Aegean again in the spring of 251 B.C.,[1] Alexander, whose authority extended over the Antigonid possessions in Greece generally, refused to put the Macedonian war-ships, for which Corinth and Chalcis[2] were the most important stations, at the disposal of Antigonus; so that Philadelphus mastered Delos and the Cyclades without serious resistance. The Egyptian attack absorbed so completely the attention of Macedon during 251 and 250 B.C. that "King" Alexander got a chance to fall with his full weight upon Argos and Athens, the two chief cities in Greece which remained faithful to Antigonus, and which were needed to round out the new kingdom. These offered resistance. How the war against Aristomachus, the tyrant of Argos, was carried on, we do not know, but we see that Salamis, as was natural both because of its proximity to Megara and because of the superiority of the enemy on the sea, received the brunt of the attack upon Attica. The walls of the town, which had fallen down, were put in repair by Heracleitus, soldiers were stationed within them, and measures were taken to protect the country and repel and avenge incursions.[3]

The generosity of Gonatas in 256/5 B.C. probably bore fruit now, since in this crisis, as in those which followed during the next twenty years, the Athenians fought stoutly on his behalf. Alexander, however,

---

[1] The date depends mainly upon the disposition of the Delian archons made in *JHS.*, 1910, p. 190 ff., but it will remain unchanged if, as may prove to be the case, the archons between 304 and 227 B.C. have all to be put one year later; for in that event the Ptolemaea and the other fêtes concerned appear in our record in the year after their endowment.

[2] Wilhelm has shown ('Εφ. 'Αρχ., 1892, p. 127 ff.) that Alexander held Chalcis.

[3] *IG.* ii. 591*b* (Ditt. *Syll.*[2] 220).

seems to have been stronger than the two cities, so that finally Aristomachus opened negotiations with him. The new king was ready to make peace with Argos, probably because he wished to secure a free hand with Athens, but for this very reason Aristomachus was unable to abandon his ally. He even went so far in loyalty—or in anxiety lest he be isolated—as to loan Athens five talents to help her in meeting Alexander's demands.[1] Since with this and what she raised herself, immunity from further attacks was purchasable and purchased by Athens in 250/49 B.C., as with a similar sum by Argos, Alexander must have been obliged to use his army and navy against a more dangerous enemy. This could only be Antigonus himself. In 250/49 B.C., as Beloch has shown,[2] Cyrene passed out of the hands of the friends of Egypt into those of Apame, the queen-regent, and of Demetrius the Fair of Macedon, the prospective husband of her daughter Berenice. Hence Philadelphus was probably compelled to bring his fleet nearer home, and in this way to liberate Antigonus for more energetic action in Greece. How he used his opportunity we do not know; nor do we know with any certainty how Demetrius spent the next three years in Cyrene. We only know that in 247 B.C. the catastrophe there occurred. Led by passion for Demetrius and love of power, Apame seems to have planned to continue her intrigue with her daughter's fiancé and her regency in Cyrene indefinitely, but she did not count upon the indignation and energy of Berenice, who, putting herself at the head of the partisans of Egypt, trapped and slew Demetrius in her mother's chamber, put an end to the regency, and offered herself and her kingdom to Ptolemy, crown-prince of Egypt. Cyrene was thus re-united to the Ptolemaic empire after a separation of about fifty-three years. This was a great gain in political and material strength for Philadelphus, and once more he turned his undivided attention to the Macedonian War. The moment was full of gravity for Antigonus, and it seems to have been at this time

---

[1] *IG.* ii. 5. 371c.   [2] iii. 2. 133 ff.

that he sought and obtained the help of the Aetolians ;[1] but before the storm broke a greater storm arose in Asia.

Antiochus II. on his deathbed repudiated his new wife, Berenice, took back Laodice, whom he had divorced four years earlier, and left the crown to her and her son Seleucus, thus passing over the two-year-old boy whom his Egyptian queen had borne him, and whose accession must have in fact united the kingdoms of Syria and Egypt for an indefinite period, and perhaps permanently. Almost immediately thereafter the death of Philadelphus occurred, and Laodice took prompt advantage of it to have Berenice and her infant murdered. Such an outrage Euergetes, the new king of Egypt, could not overlook, and, regardless of consequences in Greece, he threw all the energies of Egypt by land and sea into the Laodicean War. After three years of fierce struggle a basis for an accommodation was reached. Seleucus had by that time regained his kingdom, which he had all but lost in 246 B.C., but Euergetes had recovered in Cilicia, Pamphylia, Ionia, and the Hellespont everything that Philadelphus had been forced to abandon in the Second Syrian War. Hence in 242 B.C. Egypt and Syria came to terms. Regard for the threatening attitude of his mother and Antiochus Hierax, his brother, actuated Seleucus in agreeing to such humiliating terms : regard for the situation in Greece forced Euergetes to relinquish the political advantages implicit in a great victory gained in Syria in 243 B.C. ; for in 246 B.C. Gonatas had once more put to sea with his fleet, and reoccupied Delos. Furthermore, during this and the following year he had re-established his suzerainty over the Cyclades. At the same time (245 B.C.) the Aetolians had overwhelmed

---

[1] *Priests of Asklepios*, 155 f. ; cf. also Beloch, iii. 2. 334 ff., and *JHS.*, 1910, p. 106, n. 35. In 247 B.C. Delos was Ptolemaic, and the Ptolemaea was celebrated there. In this year a new fund for the annual dedication of *phialae* became available. Tarn suggests (*JHS.*, 1910) that the Ptolemaea of the Delians, the Ptolemaea of the League of the Islanders, and the Ptolemaea of Alexandria are three distinct fêtes coming at possibly different intervals. No proof of this proposition is, however, offered. A direct connexion between the Ptolemaea in Alexandria and in the League of the Islanders is proved by Ditt. *Syll.*[2] 202.

Boeotia;[1] so that the kingdom of Corinth, which, on
Alexander's death (ca. 246 B.C.), had passed to his widow
Nicaea, was divided into two parts, communication being
impossible by land or sea. She had the option of joining
one of the two Leagues—the Achaean being the one most
natural by position and past friendliness—or of reaching
an understanding with Antigonus. In the first case,
she would have to abandon her regal position and
ihfluence; in the latter, as Antigonus presented it, she
might by marriage with his son Demetrius become queen
of a still greater kingdom. How the old king seized the
citadel while a fake marriage fête was being celebrated
in Corinth is well known; equally well how Aratus in
243 B.C. surprised and retook it, and brought Corinth,
together with Megara, Epidaurus, and Troezen, into the
League. Macedon and the Aetolians thereupon made a
pact to divide the Achaean territory between them. It
was at this point that Euergetes was forced to intervene;
for the anxious Achaeans chose him commander-in-chief
of their League on land and sea for 242/1 B.C., and thus
impelled him to render aid. On the land Aratus had to
shift for himself, which he did by making an alliance
with Agis of Sparta, and conducting a defensive
campaign against the Aetolians and their allies, the
Elians and Messenians. On the sea the defence was
conducted by Antigonus, but not alone; for presumably

---

[1] A settlement of disputes between citizens of Boeotia and Athens was then
made by means of arbitrators from Lamia (*IG*. ii. 308, ii. 5. 308*b*; Ditt. *Syll.*[2]
227, 228; cf. also *IG*. ii. 5. 373*h*; *Priests of Asklepios*, 155 f.). For other
relations between Athens and Aetolia see Mekler, *Acad. phil. index Hercul.* 75;
and for an Athenian dwelling in Aetolia in the late fifties, Kirchner, *PA*. 7919, and
Beloch, iii. 2. 334. It is possible that the archon 'A- in *IG*. ii. 5. 373*g* belongs in
245/4 B.C. or in one of the years between 243/2 and 240/39 B.C. At the time of
the Dionysia in 'A-'s year, Aetolians resident in Athens received special consideration from the *agonothetes*. An excision shows that the king of Macedon was
mentioned in connexion with some tripods. An ἐπίδοσις was made in the same
year, εἰς τὴν φυλακὴν τῆς χώρας. These conditions are best met when we put 'A-
in 243/2 B.C.,—the year of the pact between Antigonus and the Aetolians
to divide Achaea;—and connect the "subscriptions" for the defence of Attica
with the raid of Aratus, which was probably made in the spring of 242 B.C.
Shebelew (*op. cit.* 68 ff.; cf. below, 207, n. 1) tentatively restores 'A[ντίφιλος]
(224/3 B.C.), but both the excision and the way in which *the agonothetes* is
mentioned date the document before 229 (232/1) B.C. The Russian scholar (14,
n. 1) suggests 229 B.C. as the approximate time of the acceptance by Athens
(*IG*. vii. 1735*b*) of the Museia, which Thespiae and the Boeotians had just
reorganized; but 245 B.C. is an equally good period.

out of a dispute as to Caria, where the ambitions of
Rhodes and Egypt collided, and which Euergetes may
have occupied in 245 B.C.[1] without much discrimination
as to claimants, a war had arisen between Rhodes and
Ptolemy which the peace with Seleucus had not ended.
Hence the Rhodians were Antigonus's allies in this
crisis, and most valuable allies they proved themselves
to be.

One of the Ptolemaic admirals for 242–241 B.C. was
Chremonides ; and Glaucon, his brother, may have been
another.[2] These were now old men ; hence their choice
was probably dictated by the thought of a possible
revolt of Athens from Macedon. The actions, too, of
Aratus in 243/2 (probably in March–June 242[3]) B.C.
disclose the hope—based doubtless on realities and the
conditions of party strife in Athens—that the citizens
would try to regain their entire liberty at the first
opportunity. He marched through a corner of Attica,
but refrained apparently from ravaging the country,
and liberated without a ransom the citizens whom he
captured, thus displaying at once his power to injure
and his disposition to render service. His military
objective was the island of Salamis, which he invaded,
devastated, and made a serious effort to capture,[4] thus
indicating clearly that he counted on the naval
superiority, and possibly on the co-operation of Egypt.
In neither this nor in his political project was he
successful. Nor does it seem likely that Chremonides
fared better, despite the number of his ships and the

---

[1] Ditt. *OGIS*. 54. Part at least of Caria was Egyptian in 247 B.C. That
any acquisitions made by Euergetes in 245/4 B.C. were lost in 242/1 B.C. is, of
course, obvious. Hence nothing results from the absence of Caria in the list of
districts gained by Euergetes, since the Adulis inscription must be dated after
241 B.C. For friendly intercourse between Astypalaea and Alexandria in
244/3 B.C. see *Amer. Jour. Arch.*, 1909, p. 407, No. 12. For the date see above,
iv. 164, n. 1.

[2] Ditt. *Syll.*[2] 224 ; Teles, Περὶ φυγῆς (Hense[2]), 23 ; cf. Kirchner, *PA.*, Nos.
3019, 15,572. The only alternative for the expedition of Chremonides is that
chosen by Beloch (iii. 1. 615, n. 4), *ca.* 260 B.C. ; but Teles, who wrote between
239 and 235 B.C., expressly states that he is dealing with something that
happened quite recently : ἵνα μὴ τὰ παλαιά σοι λέγω, ἀλλὰ τὰ καθ' ἡμᾶς. 260 B.C.
would have seemed to an audience of boys (τὰ μειράκια ταυτί) a far remote past.
See *JHS.*, 1910, p. 199, n. 44.

[3] See *JHS.*, 1910, p. 203, and above, v. 196, n. 1.

[4] Plut. *Aratus*, xxiv.

abundance of his money.[1] There was in Athens no disposition to repeat the performance of 265–61 B.C. Besides, the issue was not even as clear now as then; for obviously the only way to escape the remote consequences of a revolt in these circumstances was for Athens to join the Achaean League, which meant simply to change masters; while the immediate consequences would be alike inevitable and disastrous—to make Athens the centre and Attica the arena of a great war. That their hesitation was well considered, the events of the next year (242/1 B.C.) proved; for Gonatas met one Ptolemaic fleet under Sophron off Andros, and Agathostratus, the Rhodian admiral, met Chremonides with another in the harbour of Ephesus, and each won a complete victory. Therewith the sea power of the Ptolemies was broken, as it proved for ever.[2]

It might now have gone hard with Egypt had not the strength of Asia been abused in a long-drawn-out struggle between Seleucus Callinicus and his brother Antiochus Hierax, which enabled Euergetes to retain his dominions in Palestine, Phoenicia, Syria, and all along the coast from the Gulf of Issus to Maroneia in Thrace.[3] It might also have gone hard with the Achaean League but for a disagreement which arose between Macedon and the Aetolians, and the death of Antigonus Gonatas in the winter or early spring[4] of 239 B.C. The Aetolians had long coveted the part of Acarnania which was not theirs already—which had fallen to Epirus when the country was dismembered some twenty years earlier—but till the death of Alexander of Epirus in about 246/5 B.C. they had kept quiet. But first in 244–2 B.C., and again in 240–39 B.C., they assailed

---

[1] Teles, Περὶ φυγῆς (Hense[2]), 23.

[2] See my article, "Egypt's Loss of Sea Power," in *JHS.*, 1910, p. 189 ff.

[3] For the measures taken by Euergetes to secure his transmarine possessions after these defeats, see *JHS.*, 1910, p. 201, n. 53. That henceforth Egypt lacked ships altogether is, of course, not affirmed (Polybius, v. 35. 11). What she lacked was a great navy, dominion of the sea, and control of the islands. What she possessed, as Polybius puts it (v. 34. 6-8), was a girdle of towns and harbours by which she menaced the islands as well as the Hinterland. Both islands and Hinterland belonged to others.

[4] For the date see *JHS.*, 1910, p. 191, n. 11. Beloch puts the change a year too late.

Olympias, his widow, who, after losing two sons in the struggle and making a vain appeal to Rome (243/2 B.C.), was left in 239 B.C. with three helpless daughters. One of them, Phthia by name, she now offered to Demetrius II., the new king of Macedon. He succumbed to the prospect of dominating Epirus, and at once divorced his wife, Stratonice, who had borne him no son, and whose brother in 252/1 and nephew in 242 B.C. had in turn left Macedon in the lurch, and took the Epirote princess in her stead. He thus assumed responsibility for the protection of Acarnania against the Aetolians.[1] Anger in their case, fear in that of the Achaeans, now brought the two Leagues — whose earlier amalgamation might have changed the whole course of Greek history—to form an offensive and defensive alliance (239 B.C.),[2] obviously against Macedon, though Macedon had warded off its point for the moment by coming to terms with the Achaeans,[3] and probably also with Euergetes. Since at the same time Aetolia and Rhodes established friendly relations with Egypt,[4] there was a truce in Greece and Greek waters during the year 239/8 B.C.

A truce meant for Aratus the suspension of regular warfare only. It afforded all the better opportunity for

[1] For the order of events here see Niese, ii. 264, and, against Beloch, iii. 2. 105 ff., Pomtow, *Berl. phil. Woch.*, 1909, p. 286.

[2] After the death of Antigonus, according to Polybius, ii. 44. 1; cf. Beloch, iii. 1. 653, n. 3; Plut. *Aratus*, xxxiii.

[3] This arrangement is implied in the indictment of Aratus for attacking Athens in 239/8 B.C. and also from the reported outbreak of a new war in 238/7 B.C. (*IG.* ii. 5. 614*b*). That there was peace in Attica in December of 239 B.C. (Charicles's archonship) has been observed in *Priests of Asklepios*, 158. Aratus's attack on Argos (before June 240 B.C.) was a breach of international law, for which he was condemned to pay a fine of thirty minae; but the complainant was the free city, not Macedon. Hence Argos may have had a separate peace with the League. The attack on Corinth in 243 B.C. was made during a time of peace (Beloch, iii. 1. 645); but obviously this outrage was followed by war with Macedon in 243, 242, and 241 B.C. After 241 B.C., however, we have no knowledge of further hostilities between the League and Antigonus. Hence the peace with Argos may have formed part of the general arrangement with Macedon which came to an end in 238 B.C. Fear of a rupture with Antigonus may thus have led to the condemnation of Aratus. The settlement of the struggle between Aratus and Gonatas in the autumn or winter of 241/0 B.C. left Sparta isolated. Hence the great Aetolian raid of the spring of 240 B.C. Then came the renewal of the attack of the Aetolians on Acarnania, 240/39 B.C., which had been interrupted by the war in the Peloponnesus in 242/0 B.C.

[4] *Theori* from Boeotia and Delphi, and *presbeutae* (see above, iv. 176, n. 4) from Rhodes, were in Alexandria in 239/8 B.C. (*Amer. Jour. Arch.*, 1909, p. 407 f., Nos. 21-23). For the date see above, iv. 164, n. 1.

the surprises which he planned with the morals and skill of a brigand. Erginus, a Syrian, who had aided him greatly in the capture of Acrocorinth, now (239/8 B.C.) led a night expedition against the Piraeus. The assailants had reached the walls and had planted their scaling ladders before they were discovered, but discovery even at this point was fatal, and Erginus and his men had difficulty in effecting their escape. The inference is mandatory that the attempt was made in concert with a party within the walls; so that if it had succeeded the revolt would have been attributed to Athenian initiative. As it turned out, it was equivalent to a breach of the peace, and in view of the protests of the Achaeans, Aratus tried to disown Erginus; but no one seems to have doubted his complicity, if not his actual participation, in the attempt.[1]

This wanton disregard for the usages of nations doubtless contributed to the renewal of hostilities, for in 238/7 B.C. the war broke out afresh,[2] but under different conditions in that the Aetolians now fought with the Achaeans against Macedon, while Euergetes, content with the embarrassments of his enemies, remained an idle spectator, neglected to rebuild his fleet, and did not attempt even to regain control of the Cyclades; so that, despite the efforts of the Rhodians, pirates—chiefly from Crete, Aetolia, and Illyricum—had an opportunity to multiply, and to paralyse commerce on the seas both east and west of Greece.[3] The struggle in this country had many side-issues. Thus in the Peloponnese the Macedonian possessions were subject to incessant attacks both from within and without, in consequence of which Lydiades of Megalopolis, the main prop of Macedonian authority in the centre of

---

[1] Hence Aratus was general at the time, which dates the incident in 239/8 B.C. It is placed after the conclusion of the truce with Macedon by Plutarch also, though the point at which he enters the death of Antigonus in his narrative makes it seem to have occurred before 240/39 B.C. The only alternative is 241/0 B.C., but Aratus was otherwise employed in this year.

[2] In the archonship of Lysias (*IG*. ii. 5. 614*b*); Plut. *Aratus*, xxxiv.; cf. Kolbe, *Festschrift f. Otto Hirschfeld*, 315 ff.; *Priests of Asklepios*, 159; *Klio*, 1907, p. 213.

[3] See below, v. 204, 209.

the peninsula, at length laid down his tyranny, and in
235 B.C. entered the Achaean League.   In Central
Greece the situation was not generally dissimilar.
Through controlling the passes at the isthmus of Corinth,
Aratus was able to make repeated efforts to take the
Piraeus by surprise, its possession being of essential
importance to him, since he had no chance of winning
Athens so long as the Macedonian garrison held the
harbour.   He was always unsuccessful, however, and
on one occasion he was hurt badly in the hurry of the
escape.[1] Demetrius had to fear the effects of these
attacks upon the spirit and loyalty of the Athenians;
hence, though he seems ordinarily to have given his
chief attention to the Aetolians, he sent his general,
Bithys of Lysimachia, to meet Aratus, probably in
235 B.C., and at Phylacia an important engagement was
fought.   Bithys was the victor, whereupon Opus, Phocis,
and Boeotia became or remained Macedonian,[2] and the
Achaean leader was thought to be among the prisoners or
among the slain.   Upon the receipt of this report the
Athenians were jubilant.   They crowned themselves with
wreaths, instituted a public thanksgiving, and conferred
citizenship and other honours upon Bithys.[3] Diogenes, a
foreigner who had obtained Athenian citizenship, and
had married into the clan of the Eteobutadae, was at
this time commandant of the Piraeus, for Heracleitus
of Athmonon had disappeared in or about the year
245 B.C., and Glaucon, his successor, of whom we know
nothing except that he was a teetotaller, had been
succeeded by Diogenes, perhaps on the accession of
Demetrius in 240/39 B.C.[4] Diogenes sought to get a
further advantage from the victory of Bithys and the
discouragement of the Achaeans, and, to this end, sent
an envoy to request the garrison in Corinth to lay down
its arms.   Aratus appeared in person to dismiss the

---

[1] Plut. *Aratus*, xxxiv.
[2] Polybius, xx. 5. 3, where it appears that Demetrius came in person to
Boeotia, but this may have been at the opening of the war when, perhaps,
Boeotia deserted the Aetolians of its own free will.   According to Plutarch
(*Aratus*, xxxiv.), he sent a ship to convey Aratus to him.
[3] *IG*. ii. 320 (Ditt. *Syll.*[2] 201); cf. Wilhelm, *GGA.*, 1903, p. 788 f.
[4] See Beloch, iii. 2. 384.

legates;[1] and to convince the Athenians that the
League was still a factor in the war he straightway led
a plundering expedition into Attica, and had it in his
power to sack the buildings and pleasure-grounds in the
Academy, and to otherwise despoil the suburbs of the
city. He was not a vandal, however, and contented
himself on this and other occasions with destroying the
crops in the Thriasian and Athenian plains.[2] To protect
them the Athenians had had to remain constantly on
guard, and they had all along kept garrisons stationed
at Eleusis, Panacton, and Phyle to co-operate with the
Macedonian mercenaries in this object. Their general
in 237 and 236 B.C. was Aristophanes of Leuconoë, who,
it appears, rendered meritorious service in providing for
the needs of his troops, in improving the fortifications

---

[1] The position of Phylacia and the time of the battle are both unknown;
but there can be little doubt that the place was south of Thermopylae (Beloch,
iii. 1. 657, n. 1), as the award of Athenian citizenship to the victorious general
suggests. It is apparent, moreover, from the rejoicing in Athens, that the
Athenians were relieved from great distress by the victory; so that it is likely
that it took place after the struggle had been in progress for some time, in one
of the generalships of Aratus, possibly in 235 B.C., the year in which Aristophanes of Leuconoë received commendation for his various services. Had it
taken place earlier, it is difficult to understand why Megalopolis should have
seceded to the League in 235 B.C.

[2] Plut. Arat. 34; Teles (Hense[2]), 46 f. ἢ πάλιν οἰκέται μὲν οἱ τυχόντες
αὐτοὺς τρέφουσι καὶ μισθὸν τελοῦσι τοῖς κυρίοις, ἐλεύθερος δὲ ἀνὴρ αὐτὸν τρέφειν οὐ
δυνήσεται; ἐπεὶ καὶ τῶν τοιούτων φροντίδων μοι δοκεῖ ὁ ἄβιος [Schwartz, GGA.,
1907, p. 258, n. 3, suggests ἀστεῖος: the MSS. have ασιος] λελυμένος πολὺ
εὐσχολώτερος εἶναι τῷ μηδὲν ὑπάρχειν. οἷον δήπου ἐν τῷ νῦν πολέμῳ περὶ οὐδενὸς
φροντίζει ἢ περὶ αὐτοῦ, ὁ δὲ πλούσιος καὶ περὶ ἑτέρων.
This passage, doubtless, gives us a glimpse of Athens at the time of the
war with Aratus; for we have no reason to place this discourse of Teles at a
different time than the one Περὶ φυγῆς, which Wilamowitz (Antigonus, 302),
following Droysen (iii. 1. 407, n. 2) on quite conclusive evidence, dates in
239/8 B.C. (see also JHS., 1910, p. 199, n. 44). Wilamowitz, however, makes the
war the Chremonidean War, but for no reason whatsoever, and the portion
quoted above suits the pillaging of Aratus better than the formal siege of
thirty years earlier. So also Hense,[2] xxxvi. The Περὶ φυγῆς was written in
Megara before the war of 238 B.C.: the Περὶ πενίας shortly afterwards in
Athens, which the peace of 239/8 B.C. opened to the Megarians, and where most
of the work of Teles was done (Wilamowitz, Antigonus, 300; Hense,[2] xxxvii.).
For a refutation of the reasons for which Beloch (iii. 2. 279) suggests 227 B.C.
as a terminus post quem for Teles, see Beloch's own argument. There is no
need to associate the measures taken by Hippomedon for the defence of
Samothrace with the alleged war between Doson and Euergetes in 228/5 B.C.
(Niese, ii. 169; IG. xii. 8. p. 45). See JHS., 1910, p. 201, n. 53. Besides, I
see no reason for believing that such a war occurred.
There was a close similarity between the conditions of 238 B.C. and those
of the Archidamian War, as is clear from the following passage of [Xenophon],
Ἀθην. πολ. ii. 14 νῦν δὲ οἱ γεωργοῦντες καὶ οἱ πλούσιοι Ἀθηναίων ὑπέρχονται τοὺς
πολεμίους μᾶλλον, ὁ δὲ δῆμος, ἅτε εὖ εἰδὼς ὅτι οὐδὲν τῶν σφῶν ἐμπρήσουσιν οὐδὲ
τεμοῦσιν, ἀδεῶς ζῇ καὶ οὐχ ὑπερχόμενος αὐτούς.

of the forts, and in guarding against the raids of the enemy.[1] The garrisons were still on active duty in 236/5, but, since the war in Attica was at an end in 235/4 B.C.,[2] it is likely that the battle of Phylacia and the conquest of Boeotia had brought this about. Thereafter Aratus must have been, for a time at least, more cautious about penetrating beyond the Isthmus of Corinth, while from Boeotia, Phocis, and Thessaly, Demetrius was able to carry the war into Aetolia. His successes in Central Greece were, however, more than offset by the loss of Epirus, where a republican revolution, aggravated by the intrigues of the enemies of the Macedonian alliance, had broken out, the upshot of which was that Queen Deidamia, Phthia's sister, and the only descendant of Pyrrhus left in Epirus, was deprived of her crown and her life (*ca.* 233 B.C.).[3] Epirus then established a federal league, and was numbered among the foes of Macedon, whereupon Acarnania sought by faithfulness to Demetrius to escape the fate otherwise inevitable—absorption by the Aetolians. These at once seized Ambracia and proceeded to subdue the entire country, while to its aid the Macedonian king despatched Agron, the king of the pirate state of Scodra, out of whose raid in 231 and that of Teuta his widow in 230 B.C. grew, as is well known, the first war of Rome beyond the Adriatic. Demetrius was unable to meet the Aetolians in person, because the enemies of the Illyrians, the wild Dardanians, threw themselves on his northern frontier. These new troubles for Macedon led, it seems, to a reopening of the struggle in Central Greece, so that in 232 B.C. we find the situation in Attica again unsettled. In the early summer of this year the crops in the Thriasian and Athenian plains had been damaged, and the rest were in peril. A call was, therefore, made upon the citizens to contribute

---

[1] *IG*. ii. 5. 614*b*. (Ditt. *Syll.*[2] 192). Aristophanes was *gymnasiarch* in 240/39 B.C., *i.e.* in the year in which the Demetria—the excision, together with the space, shows what the restoration should be—was first celebrated ; *phylarch* in 239/8 ; and in 238/7—the year in which the war began—the holder of some unknown *epimeleia.* Then, in 237/6 and 236/5 he was general ἐπ' Ἐλευσῖνος. What further proof is needed that Cimon was really archon in 237/6 B.C.?

[2] It it clear from *IG*. ii. 5. 614*b*, line 69, that the war in Attica was a thing of the past in July 235 B.C.

[3] For the chronology see Niese, ii. 265.

funds for their protection and harvesting. The need was, obviously, immediate, for the subscription list was to be closed within the month Munychion, and it was to be met by a popular movement; hence a maximum of two hundred and a minimum of fifty *drachmae* was imposed. The call was enthusiastically responded to, and Eurycleides of Cephisia, the military treasurer of the year, was able to give credit in his published accounts for subscriptions amounting to not less and probably much more than twenty thousand *drachmae*.[1] It is significant for the location of the exposed fields, and also for the section of the country where most wealth lay, and which was most prominent in Athenian affairs at this time, that the Mesogeia furnished the largest subscriptions, the greatest number of subscribers, and the leaders of the whole undertaking. Megara gave the Achaeans an unrivalled starting-point for border raids,[2] and for year after year they had ravaged the Eleusinian and Athenian plains. The Aetolians, moreover, under the leadership of Bucris of Naupactus, made landings all along the coasts, and carried off many people to Crete and sold them into slavery there.[3] The central uplands alone escaped economic prostration, and it was from them that the movement started which restored the self-confidence of the Athenians, and freed them from the Macedonian bondage.

During the long war the Athenians had learned to defend themselves. They did not disdain Macedonian assistance, of course, and so long as this was forthcoming they were content to do their part as Macedonian allies. But in 230 B.C.[4] a great calamity befell their suzerain. Demetrius was unable to withstand the fierce onslaughts of the Dardanians, and died shortly after a disastrous defeat in a great battle with them. The victors, thereupon, overran Macedon; and, what was apparently fatal

[1] *IG.* ii. 334; cf. *Priests of Asklepios,* 159 ff.
[2] For the Athenian exiles in Megara at about this time see Teles (Hense[2]), 29; cf. Wilamowitz, *Antigonus,* 301.
[3] *IG.* ii. 5. 385c. The ransom of the captives was fixed at twenty talents—part of which, as well as ἐφόδια, was provided by Eumaridas of Cydonia. See below, v. 209.
[4] For the time of the death of Demetrius see *JHS.,* 1910, p. 191, n. 11.

for the kingdom, the heir-apparent, Philip, the son of
Demetrius's concubine, Chryseis, was only about seven
years of age. Argos, thereupon, weighed the chances
of successful resistance to the Achaean League, found
them light, and, submitting, became a member of the
federation. Aegina, Phleius, and Hermione did likewise.
Boeotia made its peace with the Aetolians and Achaeans.[1]
What was Athens to do ?

Eurycleides of Cephisia was the prime minister of the
state at this time. He was possessed of great wealth—
how acquired we do not know, but after giving enough
for public purposes to impoverish even a rich man, he
left his family established in a substantial way for
several generations.[2] His influence had become paramount in 232 B.C., about two years before the death of
Demetrius,[3] and in 232/1 B.C. he was a most energetic
treasurer of military funds.[4] In the following year he
had the same office entrusted to his son, whom he
provided lavishly with money for the performance of the
duties attached to it. For some time the war had left
the Athenians free for no other cares, and both the
outlays required for it and the losses it entailed had
reduced the government to financial exhaustion. Hence
the fêtes had been perforce abandoned, so that for
several years the Dionysia, and doubtless also the

---

[1] See below, v. 208.

[2] Kirchner, *PA*. 5966.

[3] The narrow aristocracy established in 261 B.C. was obviously much
widened on the restoration of popular liberties in 256/5 B.C., but it seems likely
that the Macedonian governor in the Piraeus made his influence felt in Athens
by keeping a Macedonian party in control of the ecclesia. At some point the
ecclesia took a new lease of life through the impulse given to it by the agrarian
national leaders. Is this point determinable ? Everything points to 232 B.C.
as the time of the revival. Then a new catalogue of donations to Asclepius
was made on a democratic model (*IG*. ii. 836). In this year the old title
γραμματεὺς τοῦ δήμου reappears to designate the chief secretary (*IG*. ii. 334).
With this year an Attic club began a new list of its officials (*IG*. ii. 5. 618b).
In this year the treasurership of military funds, through which an energetic
movement of Attic defence was inaugurated, was held by Eurycleides of
Cephisia (for his "revival" of the Panathenaic vases see Wilhelm, *Beiträge*, 82),
whom an Athenian decree affirms to have done most μετὰ τοῦ ἀδελφοῦ Μικίωνος
μετὰ τοὺς ἀπ[οδόντας τὸν Πει]ραῖα for the restoration of complete freedom (Ditt.
Syll.[2] 233, n. 5). For these reasons I conclude that it was in 232 B.C. that
Athens, put upon its own resources through the Epirote and Dardanian troubles
of Demetrius, organized a new government under the leadership of Eurycleides
and Micion.

[4] *IG*. ii. 334 ; cf. Wilhelm, *Berl. phil. Woch*., 1902, p. 1100.

Panathenaea, had been omitted.[1] This neglect was now made good; for in 231/0 B.C. (?) Eurycleides became *agonothetes* of the Dionysia, and spent the enormous sum of seven talents in conducting the various contests connected with this fête;[2] and, not content with this outlay, he preferred his son to the *agonothesia* of the Panathenaea, and made liberal provision for the successful performance of the great gymnastic games of the next year (230/29 B.C.).[3] The situation in Athens in the autumn of 230 B.C. was almost hopeless. The land lay untilled, and the people had no seed grain. Again Eurycleides came to the rescue, and under his guidance the agricultural operations were resumed on the scale warranted by peace.[4] All these public-spirited acts brought it about that the decision as to what course Athens should pursue upon the death of Demetrius rested primarily with Eurycleides of Cephisia — and Diogenes, the commandant of the garrison. The Athenians resolved to secede from Macedon. In this conclusion Diogenes concurred, and he agreed to hand over the Piraeus and the forts, but only on receipt of the one hundred and fifty talents needed to pay off the soldiers.[5] This gave Aratus a chance to intervene in the interest of the Achaean League. Although not the chief executive of the confederation at the moment, and confined to his bed by a severe illness, so weighty did the matter seem that he had himself taken to Athens in his litter, and contributed twenty of the one hundred and fifty talents required.[6] All of the remainder was not raised in Athens. The citizens did their best, doubtless; but one hundred and thirty talents was a large sum to raise, and the crisis would not admit of delay. Hence

---

[1] Ditt. *Syll.*[2] 192, l. 31 (238–235 B.C.); cf. Dittenberger's note on this line and on 207, l. 1, where, however, the restoration is hardly correct.

[2] *IG.* ii. 379 (Ditt. *Syll.*[2] 233); cf. Wilhelm, *GGA.*, 1903, p. 790, *Beiträge*, 78, and below, Appendix II.

[3] *Klio*, viii. 348 f. Sundwall (*Acta*, 19 ff.) suggests that now for the first time several *agonothetae* were appointed.

[4] *IG.* ii. 379; cf. Kirchner, *PA.* 5966. If *IG.* ii. 335 belongs to 230/29 B.C., as Kolbe (*Die attisch. Archonten*, 67) suggests, *sitonae* were also appointed to relieve the grain famine.   [5] Plut. *Arat.* 34; Paus. ii. 8. 6.

[6] Before the end of May 229 B.C., since after that time Aratus was general of the League.

an appeal was made to the friends of Athens. It is often affirmed that Ptolemy Euergetes sent donatives, but of this we have no evidence. On the other hand, we know that Thespiae made a loan to the city, and that Thebes, whose walls the Athenians had done much to rebuild in 316 B.C., gave a gift of many talents to her neighbour.[1] Doubtless, assistance came from elsewhere also, and in this way the money was secured, so that in the early summer of 229 B.C. Athens was rid of a foreign garrison for the first time in sixty-five years. We can still read on a stone found at Thebes words, now half lost, in which was expressed the great sense of relief experienced by the Athenians on having the harbours once more under their own control.[2]

Athens had thus regained her liberty, but the question was still unsettled as to what she was to do with it. There can be no doubt that Aratus made the most strenuous efforts to induce the city to throw in its lot with the federation of which he was the guiding spirit; and we find that he was in Athens a second time in the year 228 B.C.[3] But all his endeavours were fruitless. The great past of the country was a silent protest against any surrender of local sovereignty. As already intimated,[4] the section of Attica now dominant was the Mesogeia, and the agrarian interests it represented, and which had everywhere become the more influential the more the shipping and trade of Athens had declined, were best promoted by securing peace. Had incorporation in the Achaean League brought with it immunity from devastation, Athens might have postponed sentiment to self-gain, but that was by no means the likely outcome. Rather, it was to be feared that Attica, if the

---

[1] For Thespiae see *IG.* vii. 1737, 1738. The month is Theiluthius (May–June) 229 B.C. For Thebes see *IG.* vii. 2405, 2406. The month is Prostaterius (March–April) 229 B.C. That these inscriptions belong to this year has been shown by Shebelew, *Hist. of Athens from 229 to 31 B.C.* (Russian), 7 ff. (In the footnotes of this work, which was published in 1898, most of the available sources are quoted. I have been able to use only parts of the text.) The alternative is 307/4 B.C.; but it is clear that Thebes, which was soliciting money for its own restoration at that time (Ditt. *Syll.*² 176), could not then aid Athens in this way.

[2] *IG.* vii. 2406.   [3] Plut. *Arat.* 35.

[4] Cf. *Priests of Asklepios*, 159 ff.

forepost of the League, would have to bear the brunt of
attack as often as the Achaeans came into conflict with
the Aetolians or the Macedonians. As the ally of
Antigonus and Demetrius, Attica had already been the
battle-ground of wars in which she was not directly
concerned, and she must inevitably continue to be so
if she joined the Achaean League. Devotion to old
traditions, self-interest, and also, let us add, the personal
ambition of Eurycleides of Cephisia and his younger
brother Micion, as well as the anti-Achaean sentiment
of Diogenes and the party which they led, thus coincided
in urging upon the Athenians the rejection of the proposal of Aratus, and the acceptance in its stead of a
policy of strict neutrality. The pure democracy had
thus come round to practically the same position as
that held by the moderate aristocracy in 301 B.C.

To be tenable the position taken required to be
conceded by the powers, and Eurycleides at once took
measures to have this done.[1] The Boeotians, the
nearest neighbours of Athens, had been friendly since
245 B.C., with a possible interval between 238 and 235
B.C., and at the same time that they rendered the
financial assistance already referred to, they renewed
their former friendship.[2] The difference of opinion
between Aratus and Eurycleides speedily hardened into
a violent antagonism,[3] but the Achaeans were unwilling
to take measures to coerce Athens for fear of driving
her into the arms of their enemies. The Aetolians made
peace with the city and thus substituted friendship for

---

[1] *IG.* ii. 379, with Wilhelm's restoration of 22 ff. (*GGA.*, 1903, p. 790, *Beiträge*,
78), runs as follows : καὶ πόλεις Ἑλληνίδας κ[αὶ συμμάχους προση]γάγετο
(Eurycleides), καὶ ὅσοι τῷ δήμῳ χρήμα[τα ὤφειλον, παρὰ τούτων] τὰ δίκαι᾽ ὅπως
γένητ᾽ ἐφρόντισ[εν - - - πο]ρίσας χρήματα καὶ τὰς ἀ - - - ησάμενος παρεσκευα - -
τῶι] δήμῳ χρήσιμα, προεισ[ήνεγκεν - -] εἰσήνεγκεν δὲ καὶ νό[μους συμφέροντας τῶι
δήμωι · ἐποίη]σεν δὲ καὶ τὰς θέας [τοῖς θεοῖς ὡς καλλίστας καὶ ἐπιθέτον] ἀγῶνα εἰσηγήσατο
ὁ[πλιτικὸν ὑπόμνημα τῆς ἐλευθερίας. η]ὔξησεν δὲ καὶ τὸν δ[ῆμον θεῶν ἱερὰ κατασκευάσας
καὶ τε]μένη καὶ στοὰν ἀνα[θεὶς ἐμ πᾶσιν ἀπόδειξιν ποιούμενος τῆ]s πρὸς πάντας
Ἀθ[ηναίους φιλοτιμίας - - For the renewing of the relations with various cities
see *IG.* ii. 386, 387 (ὁ δῆμος ὁ Κυμαί[ων]). The general policy of Eurycleides—
complete withdrawal from international affairs together with *pax et amicitia*
with everybody—is stated and caricatured by Polybius, v. 106. 7.

[2] Part of Boeotia was unfriendly to Macedon in 228/7 B.C. (Polybius, xx. 5.
7-11 ; cf. Beloch, iii. 1. 662, n. 2). For their past and future friendship to
Athens see *IG.* vii. 2405, 2406 ; ii. 388.

[3] Polybius, v. 106. 6 ; cf. Plut. *Arat.* 41.

enmity. The new regent of Macedon, Antigonus Doson, had the good sense, moreover, to recognize the *fait accompli*, and granted Athens his friendship at the same time that he asked the Aetolians for theirs.[1] This tactful act probably did its part in frustrating the plans of Aratus to annex Attica. It mitigated the animosity of the people against their ancient lords—if any such feeling existed—and made it possible for Antigonus I. and his son to continue among the eponymous heroes of the city.[2] The three powers most likely to endanger seriously the independence of Athens were thus disarmed, but from the sea there had come, if not danger, at least trouble. Danger depended upon the attitude of Rhodes, of which we know only that later it was friendly. The trouble came from Crete, which was the nurse of a troublesome brood of pirates. Hence an embassy was sent at once (228 B.C.) to establish friendly relations with the Cretan cities which had recently co-operated with the Aetolians and Achaeans in attacking Attica. The ambassadors went first to Cydonia, where Athens had friends, and used the good offices of Eumaridas, son of Pancleus, to effect its object with Polyrrhenia and Cnosus. For the rival league of Cretan cities—that having its head in Gortyn —no mediator was needed, and *all* the Cretans agreed not to molest Athens in the future.[3] The Athenians had already received many substantial testimonials of the interest of Attalus of Pergamum in their city,[4] and in May of 228 B.C. they had him to thank for still another.[5] There are extant to-day in various European

---

[1] The φιλία καὶ εἰρήνη referred to in *IG.* ii. 619*b*. These were renewed with both Aetolia and Macedon at the outbreak of the Social War (220 B.C.) ; see below, vi. 248. Antigonus arranged a peace with the Aetolians immediately after his accession to the throne (Beloch, iii. 1. 661).

[2] See below, vi. 242.

[3] *IG.* ii. 385*c*. Kolbe's assumption (*op. cit.* 51 ff.) of a second archon Heliodorus and his transfer of this document to 217/6 B.C. are unwarranted. Both are considered and rejected by Cardinali (*Riv. di storia ant.*, 1904, p. 81 ff.) for decisive reasons. We owe it to the Italian scholar also that we have ceased to read Polybius into this document.

[4] See below, vi. 240, n. 1. Diog. Laert., iv. 60, says : ὁ γοῦν Λακύδης ἐσχόλαζεν ἐν Ἀκαδημίᾳ ἐν τῷ κατασκευασθέντι κήπῳ ὑπὸ Ἀττάλου τοῦ βασιλέως, καὶ Λακύδειον ἀπ᾽ αὐτοῦ προσηγορεύετο. Lacydes retired in 216/5 B.C. at the latest. Hence the Lacydeum was built earlier than that date.

[5] *IG.* ii. 384 (May 228 B.C.) has [παρὰ] τοῦ βασιλέως Ἀ[ττάλου], not Ἀ[ντιγόνου],

museums ancient copies in marble of some little bronze statues which Attalus sent to Athens, possibly on this occasion, and which were erected on the top of the south wall of the Acropolis. Their subject was the contest of gods and giants, Lapiths and Centaurs, Greeks and Amazons, and—a rather audacious innovation on the theme of the struggle of the personalities making for law and order with all wild undisciplined things—his own war with the Celts. It is possible that recognition of their neutrality was also sought and secured from the Seleucids. At any rate, the city of Seleucia on the Orontes despatched an embassy headed by Aristocreon, the nephew of Chrysippus, who was head of the Stoic school at this time, to renew and extend the friendly relations pre-existent between the two cities. The Athenians thanked the legate and the city by the vote of a crown to each.[1] With Ptolemy Euergetes, too, they were bound by many personal and family ties, and on renewing them they found the Egyptian king ready to meet them more than half-way.[2] An unsolicited token of goodwill came to them finally when Rome, after having crushed the Illyrian pirates and brought its confederation across the Adriatic Sea, sent an embassy to crave the gratitude and friendship of the Athenians.[3] The whole ancient world seemed ready to recognize the independence of Athens.

Nevertheless, Eurycleides did not trust everything to the goodwill of his neighbours. Athens, he knew,

since in that case the name would have been excised in 199 B.C. Hence Attalus had the regal title and a connexion with Athens as early as the early summer of 228 B.C. Hence, too, his war with the Gauls had come to an end at least in 229 B.C., since it was after its completion that he took the regal title ; and both the *Prologue* of Trogus (*JHS.*, 1910, p. 201) and the establishment of the Basileia in the first year of Attalus's reign (A. J. Reinach, *Revue celtique*, 1909, p. 61) show that the struggle belongs in 241/0 ff. B.C., as our literary tradition affirms. For the time of the donation to Athens see Beloch, iii. 1. 706, and Reinach (*loc. cit.* 61, 71). Cardinali (*Il Regno di Pergamo*, 27, 202, n. 2) still puts their donation in the last years of the life of Attalus.

[1] *IG.* ii. 5. 407e and f. ; cf. Wilhelm, Ἐφ. Ἀρχ., 1901, p. 52.

[2] *IG.* ii. 381 (August 226 B.C.)—a decree passed in honour of Castor, a friend of King Ptolemy. *IG.* ii. 383 (date uncertain, possibly 224 B.C.) has mention of a stoa, and then of King P[tolemy] ; also, of talents for a wall, and of an Athenian from Phlya.

[3] Polybius, ii. 12. 8. Zonaras (viii. 19) misrepresents the incident as follows : οἱ δὲ Ῥωμαῖοι διὰ ταῦτα . . . καὶ πρὸς Ἀθηναίους δὲ φιλίαν ἐπεποιήκεσαν, καὶ τῆς πολιτείας σφῶν τῶν τε μυστηρίων μετέσχον. See below, vi. 256, n. 2, 270.

must be prepared to defend herself. Accordingly, we observe that an unusual interest was devoted to military affairs during the following period. Detachments of troops were kept constantly under arms and stationed as garrisons in all the forts—in Eleusis, Panacton, Phyle, Salamis, Sunium, Rhamnus. The distinct corps of foreign mercenaries which had been employed by the Macedonian kings disappeared with the Macedonian commandant, and men prevailingly of Athenian birth took their place.[1] The defences of Athens and the Piraeus were taken in hand by Eurycleides and Micion, and the ring-walls of both these places were repaired and improved. The Long Walls, however, were too far gone to be restored with the resources at this time available.[2] Their usefulness, too, was at an end now that Athens had ceased to be a sea-power. Hence they were left out of the defence system of the city and fell more and more into decay. Thus the Piraeus became to all intents and purposes a separate fortress, and, accordingly, it was at this time probably that a special general was detailed to take the place of Diogenes and attend to the military stores and preparations of the harbour. The work on the walls was expensive. So, too, was the strengthening of the sea-board defences, which was necessary as never before, now that a naval attack had to be repelled by the land forces alone. To get the needful funds the two brothers had to resort to direct taxation, and more than once the citizens and foreign residents were requested to make subscriptions of from ten to forty dollars apiece. One levy was made specifically for the protection of the little harbour Zea.[3]

No free state could exist without its own money. For this reason one of the first acts of the new government was to reopen the mints ; rather, to require the mints henceforth to coin Attic, not Macedonian, pieces.

[1] See below, vi. 251, notes.

[2] *IG.* ii. 379. The Long Walls are not mentioned in connexion with the repairs made at this time. This contrasts markedly with the way in which they figure in 307/2 B.C. (cf. *IG.* ii. 5. 371c, 6 ff.). They were evidently in ruins in 200 B.C. Livy, xxxi. 26. 8, and Wilcken, *Genethliakon*, 222. See also *Klio*, 1909, p. 319 f.

[3] *IG.* ii. 380.

A new series of Athenian coins was accordingly made,[1] not simply to meet the local needs, but also to bid for the circulation which the "owls" had enjoyed, and, above all, to express clearly the fact that Athens was once more a sovereign state. A new epoch in the life of the city had begun, and to proclaim its true character was the work not of the statesman alone but also of the artist. The world must be taught that the Athenian democracy had ceased to nourish imperialistic ambitions; that the old waspish, jingoish, fickle man of the Pnyx had changed his nature. He had come back to rule in Athens, for that was his right; but he had come, not with pride and covetousness in his heart, but full of gratitude and kindliness to all the world. Henceforth his monitor was to be Aphrodite. Eurycleides accordingly dedicated a new precinct to the *Demos and the Graces*, in which was placed an altar of the goddess of love, whose·epithet, Ἡγεμὼν τοῦ Δήμου, proclaimed her office. The priesthood of the new cult he made hereditary in his own family.[2] Thus was consummated the internationalizing of Athens.

The epoch just closed had been one of profound change. For the time of a whole generation the city had been a Macedonian municipality. During part of it the political activity of the citizens had been suppressed entirely, and during the rest it had been restricted to domestic concerns. In purely local affairs, moreover, the real decision often rested with Heracleitus, Glaucon, or Diogenes, the tyrants to whom the Macedonians had given commissions. With foreign affairs the Athenians had nothing further to do, so that the content of public life, in the narrow modern sense of this term, had become so slight that it was no longer possible for the ideal interests of the citizens to be satisfied wholly by it. Nor did public life, in its comprehensive ancient sense, mean for men now what it had meant in the fourth century B.C. The suppression, for example, of tribal

---

[1] Head, *Hist. Num.* 316 ff. ; cf. Sundwall, *Untersuchungen über die attischen Münzen*, 3.

[2] See the articles *s.v. Demos* by Haussoullier in Daremberg et Saglio, by von Schoeffer in P.-W., and specially Wilhelm, *Beiträge*, 79.

activities [1] had done more than destroy a training school
for national politics; it had been followed closely by
the atrophy of many amateur musical fêtes which had
been maintained, in part at least, by the stimulus of
tribal competition. The dithyrambic contests between
five choruses each of fifty men and as many of fifty boys,
each chorus being representative of a tribe, which had
thus involved the annual participation of five or six
hundred Athenians in the rendering of new musical and
literary productions, had been discontinued, apparently
before 280 B.C. [2] When required to justify their existence
on purely aesthetic grounds they had been unable to do
so, for despite the unusual talent of the average Athenian
for music, the professional artists, who had made their
appearance in the fourth century B.C., set a standard of
excellence which amateurs could not reach, while at the
same time the artistic elaboration of Greek music tended
of itself to create a chasm between the few and the
many. The result was that by the middle of the third
century B.C. the Athenian citizens generally had become
merely auditors where they had once been the performers,
and public life, in the Greek sense of this term, became
less rich by an invaluable ideal interest.

Music thus went the way which athletics and war,
oratory and dramatics had already gone. They had
once been spontaneous, popular, and natural; they
were now specialized, exclusive, and artificial. In place
of native vigour had come high technical excellence.
Speaking generally, we may say that Greek athletics
called for individual, not team work, and it was for this
reason, perhaps, that permanent associations of athletes
were not formed till Roman times. [3] The desirability of
co-operating was not great among the orators, hence
the schools of rhetoric were the nearest approach to a
permanent organization which appeared among them,
and their cohesion was due in each case to the personality
of the teacher alone. On the other hand, soldiers,

---

[1] See above, i. 23, ii. 55, iii. 98.
[2] See Wilamowitz, *GGA.*, 1906, p. 614, n. 2.
[3] P.-W. ii. 2056 ; Poland, *Gesch. des griech. Vereinswesens*, 147.

ephebes, and artists in the two generations prior to the Chremonidean War came to form little commonwealths for the transaction of their peculiar business. The artists, in fact, had established a gild sacred to Dionysus, and on the score of their religious function—the providing of musicians and actors for the Dionysiac contests both in Athens and in the *demes* of Attica[1]—they had obtained from the Delphian Amphictyony a guarantee of their special privileges[2] (276 B.C.), as well as exemptions from ordinary civic obligations. They were, indeed, citizens of many different Greek towns, and hence of none. They were absorbed in their profession, and, accordingly, superior to municipal distractions.

Philosophy had had a similar development. A prime object of the schools was still to train men for right living; indeed, this had never been so seriously their aim as now, but they had come to entertain a very different ideal of life from that which had animated Socrates and Plato. These men had regarded a philosophic training as the best preparation for citizenship. They aimed to take citizens individually, and to prepare them for a more intelligent performance of their civil duties. The schools did not all deny their founders. Thus Lycon, while head of the Peripatos, took an active part in Athenian politics;[3] but this was an exceptional case, and the arena of public life was no longer necessary, in the view of the third century B.C. philosophers, for healthy living. The schools now taught their disciples how to live a full and complete life without participating at all in public affairs. The Garden called men to the quiet reposeful life of a group of congenial spirits. The Stoa lifted its votaries to a high-minded indifference to power, distinctions, wealth, and the other objects of vulgar ambition. The Academy and the Peripatos

[1] There were to our knowledge theatres at the Piraeus, Thoricus, Acharnae, Aexone, Eleusis, Icaria, Collytus, Phlya, Salamis, and Myrrhinus. A. Mommsen, *Feste der Stadt Athen*, 350 f.

[2] Set forth in *IG.* ii. 551 (*ca.* 276 B.C.; cf. above, iv. 162, n. 2). For the general subject see Poland, *op. cit.* 129 ff.

[3] Diog. Laert. x. 16. One of the heirs of Epicurus, Amynomachus, son of Philocrates of Bate, was *rogator* of a decree of the Mesogeia in 250/49 B.C. (*IG.* ii. 602).

inculcated a scholarly ideal of life-long devotion to speculation and investigation. None of the great schools upheld the classic Greek doctrine of the complete equivalence of the best life and the life of a citizen in the midst of citizen cares and obligations; so that, whereas Plato and Aristotle had constructed ideal city-states for the promotion of right living, Zeno and Epicurus presented, as their model, the perfect wise man —a type for imitation, an exponent of the true theory of life. To be sure, the philosophers were all teachers, but their public lectures aimed to make converts for their doctrines, while the regular instruction was intended to train up philosophers like themselves. The clientèle of the schools thus came to draw more and more away from Athenian politics, and their isolation from the life round about them became the more necessary and obvious the more the student body and the teaching staff were recruited from aliens; for in the course of the third century B.C. the schools of philosophy became, like many other private associations, essentially nests of foreigners.[1] This was by no means an accident. Rather, the dissatisfaction of the philosophers with the narrow conditions of life in the city-states had led them to fix their attention primarily upon the elements of the population which served to bind the urban communities together into a larger polity. These were the voluntary or involuntary exiles resident in each centre—the obscure missionaries of cosmopolitanism. It was, accordingly, from the conditions of *their* life, rather than from those of the citizens in the old sense, that the ethics of the new philosophies were abstracted, the Epicureans being thoughtful of the individual group, the Stoics of the common bonds. Nor did the intellectual curiosity which the old philosophies inculcated concern in any special sense, as in the time of Socrates, the problems presented by the experience of citizens of one city. On the contrary, it found materials in the ideas and experiences of men and peoples generally. Hence there

---

[1] See the lists of pupils given in Meckler's *Acad. phil. index Hercul.*, *passim*.

was nothing parochial in the appeal of the third century B.C. schools, and what they taught was of universal application.

There had been a time in Athens when private associations were indispensable for safe and respectable living. The earliest of these, the primordial *phratries* or brotherhoods, had, indeed, meant more to men than citizenship itself, but on being brought into relation with the four Ionic tribes, they were annexed by the state for its own purposes. At the same time, moreover, they had been disrupted by the crystallization of numerous *hetaeriae* formed among their most important members into socio-political organizations, or clans (γένη), and by the power of individual nobles. These clans were shut to all except lineal descendants; hence among the plebeians somewhat analogical associations arose, but with a more pronounced religious purpose, to which were given the name *orgeones*. Cleisthenes found these institutions existing, and did not molest them; he merely enacted that both *orgeones* and *gennetae* should have the right of access to the brotherhoods, thus sanctioning the exclusion of such Athenians as were neither the one nor the other. This he could permit through making citizenship dependent, no longer upon registration in a brotherhood, but in one of the *demes* which he had created. During the fifth and early fourth centuries B.C., moreover, the state came to include so completely the ideal interests of the citizens that many found it a useless expense to enter a brotherhood. Hence the very poor dispensed with fraternal affiliations of this kind altogether. Admission to them was confined strictly to Athenian citizens, and upon the legitimate offspring of members each brotherhood was dependent for recruits, so that from them were excluded not simply the sons of citizens and concubines and the sons of Athenians and foreigners, but also the sons of all those who for one reason or another were once dropped from the rolls.[1] The Athenian democracy had aimed to secure universal participation in governing and being governed,

[1] See *Class. Phil.*, 1910, p. 257 ff.

but only on the part of the citizens; and while it had
attracted and welcomed strangers from all parts, it had
excluded them rigidly from its public life. These had
therefore to shift for themselves. What they missed
most in their adopted home was probably their native
religion, and to secure it they formed clubs, and, after
an interval of obscure national worship, they obtained
permission to erect a chapel, and, if they so desired, to
proselytize among the Athenians. This was done to our
knowledge by the Thracians resident in the Piraeus as
early as the time of Pericles, and these, the worshippers
of Bendis, were allowed, moreover, to become *orgeones*.[1]
That is to say, their religion was admitted into the list
of authorized Athenian cults, and men of Athens were
at liberty to worship Bendis without associating with
the Thracians in their club. Accordingly Bendis became
the patron deity of a circle of Athenians who co-operated
with the Thracians in the torch-light race, which was
the most striking public feature of the worship of
Bendis. The case of Asclepius was similar.[2] On his
transfer to Athens in 420 B.C., the healing god of
Epidaurus not only became associated with Amynus in
the homage of an existing association of *orgeones*, but
new clubs of *orgeones* were established in his honour.
A considerable interval, however, elapsed before other
foreigners were permitted to associate publicly for
religious purposes in Attica, and then it was as *thiasotae*
that they were allowed to organize. It was in this new
form—the use of the name *orgeones* was forbidden, and
the reservation of the abstract *thiasus* for a subdivision
of a brotherhood caused it to be avoided also[3]—that the
Phrygian worship of Sabazius and Magna Mater, who
had votaries in the Piraeus as early as the time of the
Peloponnesian War, made their noisy and offensive
propaganda among the lower classes. Then, at some
time prior to 333/2 B.C., the Egyptians in Athens
became incorporated as the club of Isis, and in this

[1] The special privilege of the Thracians is affirmed in the interesting
inscription published by Wilhelm, *Österr. Jahreshefte*, 1902, p. 127 ff.

[2] Koerte, *Athen. Mitt.*, 1896, p. 306 ff.

[3] Poland, *op. cit.* 20.

year the metics from Citium as the club of Aphrodite. Not long afterwards we find the Salaminians already organized; the Sidonian club appears later still, and, doubtless, all the *ethne* in Attica acquired similar associations. Moreover, individuals of different cities and nationalities joined themselves together round some Athenian or foreign deity, and thus the number of clubs was multiplied.[1] This involved the frequent importation of new deities, and Magna Mater, Tynarus, Ammon, Serapis, Zeus Labrandius, Men the Tyrant, and many other outlandish gods and goddesses secured their circles of worshippers at the Piraeus or in Athens. Nor was membership in them restricted to foreign men, but women were admitted also, not necessarily courtesans,[2] as was hastily assumed from certain names which appear in the extant rolls of members, but usually slaves or women of low station. Indeed, it is inconceivable that the wives and daughters of citizens of the upper classes mingled with men in the intimate life of the *thiasotae*; for besides performing religious rites, the clubs gave frequent opportunities for social intercourse, and a monthly dinner seems to have been a feature common to most of them. The clubs were also profitable in a business way, and some of those on Delos had, in addition to a chapel, rooms for the display of wares, and probably also sleeping apartments.[3] Migratory traders were thus relieved of many of the perplexities incident to their profession, but both they and the resident aliens obtained still more substantial benefits from the associations. By the constitution of a club of

[1] The private associations are treated by Foucart : *Assoc. relig. chez les Grecs* ; Lueders, *Die diony. Künstler* ; Schaefer, *Fleckeisens Jahrb.*, 1880, p. 417 ff. ; Wachsmuth, *Die Stadt Athen*, ii. 1. 157 ff. ; Ziebarth, *Das griech. Vereinswesen* ; Oehler, *Zum griech. Vereinswesen* ; Osborne, *A History of the Ancient Working People*, ii. 169 ff. ; Poland, *Gesch. des griech. Vereinswesens*. The last-named work contains (pp. 548 ff.) the most complete collection of the materials. A few new data are found in Robinson, *Amer. Jour. Phil.*, 1907, p. 430, and Tod, *Annual of the British School at Athens*, 1906/7, p. 328 ff. I have discussed the relations of the private associations to the semi-public *thiasi*, *phratries*, and *gene* in *Class. Phil.*, 1910, p. 257 ff.

[2] See Wilhelm, "Die sogenannte Hetäreninschrift aus Paros," *Athen. Mitt.*, 1898, p. 409 ff. That the patroness of the groups in 'Εφ. 'Αρχ., 1905, p. 239, and *IG.* ii. 5. 618*b* was Artemis is against their being courtesans. It is not known to whom the clubs in *IG.* ii. 987, 988, 989 were sacred.

[3] See below, ix. 356, n. 1.

thiasotae organized in about 300 B.C.[1] all the members
bound themselves to join in redressing wrongs done to
any of their comrades, and to move all their "friends"
to like action; so that to molest a stranger was not by
any means to deal with a helpless man.   The constitution
also required the officers of the association to superintend
the burial of deceased members, and to notify fathers,
sons, relatives, or "friends," while upon all the members
it placed the obligation to attend the funeral.   In fact,
to provide the assurance of decent obsequies for lonely
men, living or wandering far from those near and dear
to them, was a common motive for the formation of
these clubs;[2] and not infrequently they had their own
churchyards.[3]   To the aliens the associations were thus
indispensable.   "They emphasized the pleasant features
of their life," says Heracleides the Critic, who visited
Athens at about 205 B.C., "and by supplying to each
what he most craved, caused him to forget that he had
none of the rights of a freeman."[4]   To the "genuine
Athenians" they had less to offer, but it was inevitable
that a number of citizens should use their privilege of
entering them.   Still it was a surprisingly small number
—in many clubs none at all—and prior to 166 B.C.
Athenians took practically no part in their management.[5]   To citizens exclusively belonged the *gene* and
the associations of *orgeones*,[6] and during the last third

[1] Tod, *op. cit.* 328 ff.
[2] Ditt. *Syll.*[2] 727.   This feature appealed also to citizens, *ibid.* 731.
[3] *Ibid.* 746, 747, 748, and notes.
[4] See below, vi. 262.
[5] No citizen appears among the 21 mentioned in *IG.* ii. 987 (3 are here
women); none among the 23 mentioned in *IG.* ii. 988 (13 are here women);
and it is doubtful whether any of the 36 or so names of women mentioned in
IG. ii. 989 were those of the wives or daughters of citizens.   None of the 12
(5 women) in *IG.* ii. 5. 618*b* was an Athenian; nor were there any citizens
among the 58 listed in 'Εφ. 'Αρχ., 1905, p. 239.   *IG.* ii. 986 and 986*b* contain,
doubtless, divisions of the *phratries* (*thiasi*).   All the names are those of
citizens (Poland, 18 ff.).   They, therefore, do not belong in this connexion.
   In the business affairs of the associations one citizen appears in *IG.* ii. 5.
623*b* (archonship of Dionysius μετά (?) Nicophon; end of third or beginning of
second century B.C.), and two among the *hieropoei* in *IG.* ii. 3. 1333 (archonship of Philippides); none in the other documents prior to the middle of the
second century B.C.   For a later time see below, x. *ca.* 422, note.
[6] The only exception appears among the *orgeones* in *IG.* ii. 621 (178/7 B.C.),
where a certain Ergasion — apparently a foreigner—is listed among the
epimeletae of the association.   Ziebarth (36) refers this document to the club of
the Mother of the Gods, and its provenience favours this determination; but the

of the fourth century B.C., and particularly during the middle third of the one following, these assumed again some of their long-lost prominence in Attic life. The renascence of the private associations, since it affected aliens from all parts as well as natives, is a general Hellenistic,[1] not a specifically Attic phenomenon. It is attributable in largest part to the new cosmopolitanism which the conquests of Alexander had promoted;[2] for to be cosmopolitan meant, in Greece at least, to break old civic ties and to form no new ones—a deprivation against which the tense social sense of the people rebelled. The alternative was to join a club, and this presented itself forcefully, not to exiles alone, but to those also who were no longer able to employ their talents freely in home politics. That is to say, the relaxation of the imperious interest in state or municipal affairs was accompanied in Athens, as in the Roman empire, by the growth of private associations.

It can hardly be accidental that the *orgeones*, which were most active in the period after the Chremonidean War, had, as their patrons, deities like Bendis[3] and Asclepius;[4] for in the last quarter of the third century

patron deities are θεοί, not as in *IG.* ii. 622 θεαί, and in all the other decrees of the Mother of the Gods, ἡ θεός. Still, this is not decisive, since it seems most probable that by θεαί are meant Cybele and Attis, for whom θεοί would be the more natural designation were it not that the feminine deity predominated so decisively in the pair. The hypothesis of Foucart (98 ff. ; cf. Schaefer, 420, and lately Poland, 10 ff.) that an amalgamation took place between *orgeones* of Magna Mater and *thiasotae* of the Syrian Aphrodite is incapable of proof and improbable. It loses its main support when it is seen that *orgeones* of Magna Mater were first organized after 229 B.C., whereas there were *thiasotae* of this goddess from the early part of the third century B.C., and probably from the fourth. The only other argument for the amalgamation alleged is the use of θεαί. The admission of a foreigner to the *orgeones* simply shows how completely the *phratries* had disappeared, and how little citizenship was involved in membership in one of these associations.

[1] All the documents relating to the *thiasotae* and *orgeones* belong after 350 B.C. Poland determines the time of their greatest activity to within a few decades on either side of 300 B.C. (518 f.).

[2] See Percy Gardner, *New Chapters in Greek History*, 440 ff. ; Wendland, *Die hellenistisch-römische Kultur*, 13 ff. ; Dill, *Roman Society from Nero to Marcus Aurelius*, 256 ff.

[3] See the work of Oehler cited above, v. 218, n. 1, and especially Wilhelm, *Österr. Jahreshefte*, 1902, p. 127 ff.

[4] The following documents relating to clubs of Asclepius in the third century B.C. may be cited here : *IG.* ii. 620 (*Österr. Jahreshefte*, 1902, p. 130, n. 1 ; Lysitheides, archon. End of third century B.C.) ; *BCH.*, 1899, p. 370 ; *IG.* ii. 617*b*, p. 422, and ii. 5. p. 162 ; *IG.* ii. 5. 988*b* ; *IG.* ii. 5. *Add. Nov.* 617*c* (for date see Kirchner, *PA.* 7652 ; cf. *Athen. Mitt.*, 1896, p. 303) ; *IG.* ii. 990 (end

B.C. two new *orgeones* of the same character were added,
one for the worship of the Mother of the Gods and
another for the worship of Dionysus.   The god of
healing was a regular visitant at his shrine on the south
flank of the Acropolis in this century.[1]   His priest was
chosen by lot, and, in fact, the duties of the office did
not demand special knowledge of any kind, for they
involved simply the offering of sacrifices for the health
of the people, the appointment of a table and couches
for the communion service, the management of a
pannychis, and the maintenance of order and decorum
in the shrine.   The public physicians, however, were,
in a sense, the agents of Asclepius, and they had to
render thanks to him twice every year for the cures they
had effected.[2]   The patients were equally grateful, and
again and again the shrine became cluttered with the
little images of the parts of the body which had been
healed and with other thankofferings.   We need no
further explanation than this for the prominence of
Asclepius in club life.   Perhaps, however, the *pannychis*
was accompanied by orgies, by ecstatic trances; that is
to say, by some of the emotional excesses which rendered
the worship of Bendis, Dionysus, and Magna Mater
especially attractive.   We have already seen that
Athenians of good standing were able to worship
Bendis from the fifth century B.C. onward without
entering the association of the Thracians.   Sabazius[3]
and Magna Mater also had come to the Piraeus and to
possess votaries there at an early date, but the good
taste of the Athenians generally had been offended by

---

of second century B.C., according to Kirchner, *PA.* 23.   The only possible name
identification, however, is with *IG.* ii. 307, 246/5 B.C.; Wilhelm, *GGA.*, 1900,
p. 100); cf. also *IG.* ii. 352*b*, 373*b*, 477*b*, 567*b*, 453*b*, 639 (*Österr. Jahreshefte*,
1898, Beiblatt, p. 45); ii. 5. 178*b*.   For the rise of Asclepius see Gruppe,
Griech. Mythologie, especially ii. 1458, n. 4, from which it appears that the Attic
artists Phyromachus, Niceratus (Boethus), Timocles, and Timarchides made
famous idols of Asclepius.   A temple and *temenos* of Asclepius were constructed
at Sunium in 222/1 B.C. ('Εφ. 'Αρχ., 1900, p. 141, and *IG.* ii. 3. 1195).   This
god, as is well known, was first introduced into Rome in 293/1 B.C. (Wissowa,
Religion d. Römer, 253 ff.).   Cf. also Wilamowitz, *Nordionische Steine*, 42 f.

[1] See the lists of ex-votos, *IG.* ii. 835, 836.

[2] *IG.* ii. *Add. Nov.* 352*b* (252/1 B.C.).

[3] Besides the literary references (Aristophanes, *Lysistrata*, 387; *frg.* 478;
Cic. *De leg.* ii. 15; Dem. *De cor.* 259-60; Theophr. *Char.* 27, 18) see *e.g.*
IG. ii. 3. 1326 (342/1 B.C.).

the extravagances of these worships, and it was not till the end of the third century B.C. that citizens of repute became interested in them. Sabazius was not admitted to the list of Athenian deities, but that was hardly necessary, for Dionysus was his equivalent, and Dionysus was now perhaps the most Attic of deities. Hence it was quite a simple matter for Agathocles of Marathon and a group of influential men living in the Piraeus, but enrolled in other Attic demes, and thus, in a sense, exiles in their own country, to worship Sabazius by constituting themselves as *orgeones* of Dionysus.[1] The case of the Mother of the Gods was almost parallel. She had had a pale counterpart in Attica from time immemorial,[2] but the real Magna Mater, with her lover Attis, her emasculated priests, and her shameful orgies, was a denizen of Pessinus in Galatia, and a special introduction was necessary before she could enter polite Greek society. She now obtained a powerful advocate. Attalus of Pergamum became lord of Pessinus and interested himself in Magna Mater. He was, indeed,

---

[1] The *Asclepiastae* (*IG*. ii. 5. 988*b*; cf. *Ath. Mitt.*, 1888, p. 340)—an old association of which the headquarters were in Athens, where, too, the documents relating to it were found—were drawn largely from the city or neighbouring *demes*; and this was the natural arrangement, and the one which the lapse of time must inevitably produce. The same condition prevails in the case of the *orgeones* of Amynus Dexion and Asclepius.

On the other hand, none of the 15 *Dionysiastae* whose names are listed in *IG*. ii. 5. 623*d* (185/4 B.C.) belong to the *deme* Piraeus, where the ἱερόν of the patron god was located. Their *demes* were scattered all over Attica. In this case the evidence of *IG*. ii. 5. 623*e*, cf. ii. 3. 1336 (Ziebarth, *Neue Jahrb*. xiii. 568 ff. Dionysius here refers to πάντα τε σὸν θίασον), is conclusive that the association in *ca*. 180 B.C. had just entered upon the second generation of its life; so that its founding belongs to *ca*. 229 B.C. Hence also its use of the new titles σύνοδος and Διονυσιασταί (Poland, *op. cit*. 65). The members were thus doubtless new arrivals in Piraeus—men taken out of *orgeones* in their home villages, like the club in Prospalta, of which the membership is given in *IG*. ii. 990, and who sought a substitute by forming a new club in their new home. The same inference applies to the *Sabaziastae* of *IG*. ii. 626*b* (102/1 B.C.), where none of the 36 Athenians listed belong to the *deme* Piraeus; and also to the votaries of the Mother of the Gods, among whom the only Πειραιεύς appears in 175/4 B.C. (*IG*. ii. 5. 624*b*)—perhaps 50 years after the forming of the club. Of course, one or two may have been admitted from the *deme* in which the shrine was located, but in this case too the great majority were for two or three generations non-Πειραιεῖς. The late origin of the *orgeones* of Dionysus, Magna Mater, and Aphrodite Hagne is also proved by the fact that the term κοινόν, which is not applied to any of the old gentile associations, is used in their connexion (Poland, *op. cit*. 165).

[2] First mentioned in the inscriptions in *IG*. ii. 614 (283/2 B.C.), but the literary references date from the fifth century B.C. See Foucart, *op. cit*. 64; Livy, xxix. 10 ff.; Varro, vi. 15.

forced to withdraw from Galatia within a few years, but he took with him the aniconic idol of the goddess—a meteoric stone—and set it up in a new temple, the Megalesium, which he built in Pergamum.[1] The Mother of the Gods at once started upon a triumphal career through the world. She reached Athens in about 220 B.C.,[2] and a number of the richest citizens, who were residents but prevailingly not *demesmen* of the Piraeus, became her *orgeones*. Attideia were celebrated, collections were taken, a special priestess appointed, and her orgies duly performed.[3] Fifteen years later she was solemnly convoyed into Rome, where a religious association was likewise formed in her honour among the noblest citizens.[4]

We may easily overestimate the religious influence of the *orgeones*, for it is clear that they did not make serious demands upon the consciences of their members. They did not require them to subordinate their human activities to a one-sided religious ideal, nor did they require the denial of all other gods. It was inconceivable that duty to Magna Mater should be incompatible with devotion to Athena. There is as yet no shadow of priestly influence upon the pleasant social life of the *orgeones*. Those of the Great Mother chose and supervised their priestess, and like the priest of Asclepius, she had no special calling for her task. The founders of the club may have chosen their deity because of some personal preference, but their successors could not do so. They were born *orgeones* of the god or goddess of their parents, and none besides were admitted to the circle. Women were excluded altogether[5]—a fact which makes clear, as nothing else, how

---

[1] Showerman, *The Great Mother of the Gods*, 225 ; Cardinali, *Il Regno di Pergamo*, 83 ; Wissowa, *op. cit.* 263 ff. ; Bloch, *Philol.*, 1893, p. 580 ff.

[2] The date results from what is said above, v. 222, n. 1.

[3] *IG.* ii. 622 (211/0 B.C.) ; Wissowa, *op. cit.*, 263 ff., and especially Cumont, *Relig. orientales*, 57 ff.

[4] Livy, xxix. 10 ff. ; Cic. *Cato maior*, 45 ; cf. Showerman, *loc. cit.* ; Wissowa, *op. cit.* 57,264.

[5] It goes without saying that no women were *orgeones* of Dionysus ; so that their absence in the catalogue *IG.* ii. 5. 623*d* (185/4 B.C.) has no significance. Nor has that in the catalogue *IG.* ii. 5. 988*b*, since this too has a male deity. On the other hand, we have no catalogue of the *orgeones* of Bendis or the

little religion had to do with the life of the *orgeones*.
Still it was an event of grave religious significance when
distinguished Athenians banded themselves together to
conduct a ceremony at which the initiates crouched
while a boy read to them sections of holy script, whereupon, on being rubbed with mud and meal by a consecrated priest, they arose and exclaimed, " I have escaped
the evil, I have found the better." [1] It could not lack
import that they lent dignity to the shocking and
outlandish exercises (Attideia) which the votaries of
Magna Mater celebrated at Easter (22-27 March) of
every year. A pine tree was cut, bound with fillets of
wool like a corpse, covered with violets, furnished with
a bust of Attis, the lover of the goddess, and brought
in solemn procession to her shrine. There the death of
the god was mourned (22nd March); throughout the
23rd trumpets were blown, and on the 24th the pine
tree was buried with the wildest ecstasies of grief.
Maddened by the shrill music and the dizzy dances, the
priests beat their bodies with whips, cut their flesh with
knives, and sprinkled the altar of the goddess with their
blood; while at the same time, probably, those about
to consecrate themselves henceforth to the service of
Cybele attained the utmost of communion with her by
the supreme sacrifice of their masculinity. This was
the day of blood. Afterwards came the assembly by

Mother of the Gods. Still, in Ditt. *Syll.*[2] 439, it is provided that only sons be
admitted to the Demotionidae, and it is clear that women could not take part
in the procession and torch race which was the characteristic part of Bendis
worship.   Cf. Wilhelm, *Österr. Jahreshefte*, 1902, p. 127 ff.   Naturally the
priestess of the Mother of the Gods was a woman, and not unnaturally the wife
or daughter of one of the *orgeones*.   There is no evidence that she was herself
a member of the club.   Only males are listed in *IG*. ii. 990 among the *orgeones*
of Asclepius, nor are any women mentioned in the extant catalogues of *phrateres*.
The facts seem to be, as Ledl (*Wiener Stud.*, 1907, p. 173 ff. ; 1908, p. 1 ff.)
holds, that girls were acknowledged by their fathers as legitimate in the year
of their birth, and wives were introduced by their husbands as lawfully
wedded directly after marriage, by simple presentation to the *phrateres*.   On
the other hand, fathers were wont, not simply to present their sons in the
year of their birth, but also to prove that they were legitimate ; whereupon
the *phrateres*, if satisfied, voted to accept them, and the officials of the association registered them on the phratry roll.   Hence only males, and, in fact,
only males of citizen age, took part in the meetings.   A boy appears in *IG*. ii.
986 (cf. *Class. Phil.*, 1910, p. 270 ff.) simply because this is a list of subscribers
among whom it was possible for a wealthy minor—whose father perhaps was
dead—to be found.
[1] Dem. *De cor.* 259.

night in the shrine to await the resurrection of Attis. The grave was opened, a light inserted, the lips of the votaries anointed by the priests with holy oil, and the solemn assurance given : " Courage, *mystae*, since the god is rescued, to you also shall there be salvation from your afflictions." The day which followed was the day of rejoicing (Hilaria).[1] It must have been a powerful aid to public confidence when grave and respectable *orgeones* gave their active support to the periodic soliciting of alms for the goddess. The *Metragyrtae* issued forth through the streets carrying an image of Cybele in a little chapel, and after performing the dances and mutilations already described, took a collection from the bystanders. Nor can the *orgeones* themselves have been unmoved by the emotions kindled, the purification achieved, and the hopes inspired. They thus obtained without loss of caste the religious satisfaction secured by others in the foreign clubs which worshipped sensuous, non-Greek deities, but into which, as already pointed out, only Atticans, as they were called, that is to say, obscure persons of doubtful purity of race, entered before the last half of the second century B.C. The city of Athens was still a stronghold of conservatism at the end of the third century B.C., but the admission of Bendis, Asclepius, and especially of Magna Mater had sapped her fortifications. For every Attican who entered a foreign club, and every Athenian who combined with others to form a union of *orgeones* in honour of a new deity, struck a blow at the ancient national religion. He separated himself by an act of his own volition from his fellow-citizens. Without, perhaps, being conscious of it, with the real purpose often of obtaining helpful or congenial friends, or of gaining some social distinction, he in fact chose his own gods. He had been born into his state which had been also

---

[1] Cumont, *op. cit.* 69 ff. ; Eisele, "Die phrygischen Kulte und ihre Bedeutung für die griech.-römische Welt," *Neue Jahrb.*, 1909, p. 635. While it is true that the details here given are not drawn from contemporary, but, in the main, later sources, it is also true that these rites are very old (Ed. Meyer, *Gesch. d. Alt.* i. 2. 644 ff.), and that Attideia (*IG.* ii. 622), στρώσεις, and ἀγερμοί (*IG.* ii. 5. 624b) are mentioned in the Attic inscriptions of this time.

his church.　Into a religious association he went because
he wished to do so.　In other words, religion pressed
itself anew upon the attention of the poor and the
thoughtless as well as upon the rich and the cultivated
as a problem of great importance which every one had
to think about and to solve for himself.　It no longer
came to everybody with his parents and his city.
Depth of conviction was often lacking as yet, and the
world was far from ready for one god, but men were
already looking abroad for new deities, and their gaze
was ordinarily turned towards Asia.

The old deities were doomed to die with the city-
states, for whose protection they had been chiefly
valuable, of whose social life they were the incarnation,
and with whose public life their worship was identical.
They had, it is true, become in the thinking of the
educated the upholders of a moral, not a political
régime; so that civic devotion was less what they
craved than the proper kind of sociability, and as the
deities of private associations they continued to live on
in Attica; but the idea soon found acceptance that they
had no existence apart from the order in which they
manifested themselves—that they were, in fact, mere
abstractions of the activities of men and the processes
of nature.　A king was thus implicit in his work in the
same sense in which a god was revealed in his; therefore he too was a god.　In fact, since he created cities
and made laws, the inference was natural, and was made
in Athens in 290 B.C., that he was the only true god;
that he had deposed the Olympians.　Had he not taken
from them their chief office?　At his death his acts
could rarely be rescinded.　They had come to be too
deeply imbedded in the structure of society for that;
hence it meant simply his transference to Olympus,
whence he watched over the work he had done while
in the flesh.　Thus gods and kings were blended in
thinking, and on the establishment everywhere of the
cult of the rulers, in worship also; so that Euhemer-
ism, which made all gods past kings or benefactors,
became the fit expression of the popular conviction

that the old deities, being once men, were all alike touched with the frailty of humanity, and, hence, were powerless to solve the mysteries of life and death.

It was thus under the guidance of present and departed gods of human origin that Hellenic culture, which was in the main Attic culture, started in Alexander's time and afterwards to include in ever-widening circles the entire civilized world. In its advance into the East, however, it was met, not by national resistance—for the nations had died out there during the Persian time—but by the religions into which national feeling had been transmuted. These had long since dissociated themselves from the people to which they had once been peculiar, just as the culture of the Greeks had long since transcended the limits of the Greek race, but they had retained for the purposes of religious propaganda the organization which the nations had perfected for political expansion; and, making not race or birth the test of conformity, but recognition of the power of their gods, belief in certain doctrines, and performance of certain rites, the only condition of membership, they had, under Persian favour or toleration, sought by proselytizing to include in their congregation the entire world.[1] The Orient was thus strong where the Occident was weak. The one presented to the suffrages of the many a religious interpretation of the world, the other a scientific. Upon the voting was to depend the future of European culture. The vote of the Athenians in the third century B.C. was adverse to the Oriental deities; that of the Atticans was favourable. The lapse to a foreign deity was easy for those who felt the need of a really superhuman power, and there was no doubting the eternity of Isis, Cybele, or Atargatis. Behind them was the vast antiquity of the East. Their contact with humanity they made not through having been once men, but through coming down to earth and embodying themselves in human beings who might thus prophesy or work miracles or teach the

[1] Ed. Meyer, *Gesch. d. Alt.* iii. 93 ff.

means of salvation.[1] Their masculine mates had been
weakened by the destruction of the nations in which
deities of this sex had lived and moved and had their
being, but *they* had been exalted even by the decline of
their comrades. They had had from of old as their
peculiar care the fructification, birth, and decay of all
natural objects. Theirs was the province in which
the Greek gods—with the exceptions of Demeter,
Dionysus, Asclepius perhaps—had no sway : the great
mystery of life and death. Emancipated from local ties,
though not from a past in which were set many gross
myths and many grosser rites, the goddesses of Alexandria,
Bambyce, and Pessinus were able to make a universal
appeal, for precisely the same reason that Jahwe, the
great god of the Jews, succeeded during this period in
making converts to Judaeism in many parts of the world[2]
as well as in holding the allegiance of those who were
Israelites already. Over Jahwe they had what at first
proved an advantage, but was eventually their undoing
—the possibility, which the monotheism of Judaeism
precluded, of identifying themselves with the old deities
of Greece, whom they represented as their imperfect
manifestations, and winning by fatal concessions, not
individuals merely, but whole communities. Their progress throughout the Hellenistic world was accordingly
marvellously rapid. It could be stayed only by opposition of a political, social, and scientific character ; and it
was this opposition which Athens had presented to it
from the beginning. There is no evidence till relatively
late for a change of its attitude towards the Syrian
goddess. Isis, however, was associated along with the
babe Harpocrates and the jackal-headed Anubis in the
cult of the new deity Serapis whom Ptolemy Soter
introduced into Egypt and subsequently into his Egyptian
dependencies. In this powerful dynasty she obtained
a political and social coefficient which increased manifold the effectiveness of her religious propaganda.
Hence, as we have seen, a club of *Serapiastae* appears

---

[1] Reitzenstein, *GGA.*, 1908, p. 785.
[2] Ed. Meyer, *op. cit.* iii. 216 ff.

in Athens, in addition to the club of Isis in the Piraeus, as early as the reign of Ptolemy Philadelphus;[1] but even thus the cult was unable to secure public acceptance. Cybele was later in securing like political and social prestige, but, as we have also seen,[2] she was so distinctively the deity of Asia Minor that the moment the astute kings of Pergamum became the paramount power there, they transferred to their capital the black stone in which she resided, and sought in this way to identify with their own dynasty the sentiment which animated her worshippers. The consequences of this recognition were at once apparent in states friendly to Pergamum, such as Athens and Rome. The Ptolemies and Attalids were thus apostate to the Hellenic interpretation of life. Hence the attitude of the Seleucids, in itself remarkable, comes by contrast into all the stronger relief; for they made themselves to such a degree the champions of Hellenic civilization that they came eventually into hostile conflict with the native religions, which they thereupon sought to extirpate. This perhaps serves to explain why the Syrian goddess was the last to receive official recognition in Athens.[3]

The activity of the Athenian private associations in the third century B.C. is paralleled by a similar activity in the local centres of Attica, which was perhaps even more dangerous to the integrity of the state. The local associations had been largely suppressed by Cleisthenes, whose municipal organization of Attica had broken up the larger local groups, and subordinated the smaller under the new tribes which he had created. His scheme for composing the tribes of an equal portion from the city, coast, and uplands inevitably gave the control of the government to the third which lay nearest to the place of meeting. The assemblies, however, were held only in the city or the Piraeus, and this advantage, together with the growth of industry and commerce during the fifth and fourth

[1] See above, iv. 171; v. 217; cf. Rusch, *De Serapide et Iside in Graecia cultis*, Berlin, *Diss.*, 1906; Kaerst, *op. cit.* ii. 1. 269 ff.
[2] See above, v. 222.
[3] See below, vi. 260; ix. *ca.* 385 f.

centuries B.C., established so firmly the supremacy of
Athens in Attica that for two hundred years the local
interests could not venture to assert themselves. But
in the first forty years of the third century B.C. Athens
sank rapidly from the business metropolis of the world
to a second-rate town, and the decline was accompanied
by a shrinkage in the population of the city, and
especially of the Piraeus.[1]   At the same time the dilapidation of the Long Walls made Athens and the Piraeus
two separate cities, and this cleavage was accentuated by
the fact that, except for an interval of thirteen years,[2] the
harbour town remained in the hands of Macedon between
322 and 229 B.C.   At particular times during the same
period Salamis, Sunium, Rhamnus, Panacton, and Phyle
were likewise held by foreign garrisons, while Eleusis
had been on three occasions so far independent that it
had issued copper money of its own.[3]   Under these
circumstances the city ceased to fascinate and control the
minds of the people in the old imperious way.   The
change manifested itself in two particulars still visible to
us :—First, in the inability of men resident in Athens to
worship deities resident in the Piraeus, and the consequent duplication in the city of the harbour cults.   Thus
the Thracians in Athens found it necessary to establish
a club of *orgeones* of Bendis distinct from that in the
Piraeus ;[4] and Zeus Soter, the chief deity of the Piraeus,
was given appointments in both places.[5]   Secondly, in
the revival of activity in the Marathonian tetrapolis.
The four *demes* belonging to the tetrapolis, Marathon,
Tricorynthus, Oenoe, and Sypalettus, had formed the
Coast *trittys* or third of the Aeantis tribe in the
Cleisthenian system, and had thus maintained their

---

[1] This, however, should not be overestimated. The decline was probably
confined to the city proper and its harbour town. The absence of men from
the Piraeus in the public documents of the Macedonian era has been noted in
Priests of Asclepius, 157. A decline of population there results also from the
influx noticed to the Piraeus after 229 B.C.

[2] 307–294 B.C.

[3] See above, iv. 183, n. 1, and 145, n. 4.

[4] *Österr. Jahreshefte*, 1902, p. 127 ff.

[5] See *Priests of Asklepios*, 156 ff. For the date of *IG*. ii. 325, however, see
ibid. 152, n. 42, and Kolbe, *op. cit.* 150, and for the date of *IG*. ii. 305 see
'Εφ. 'Αρχ., 1910, p. 19.

federation and their own archon[1] during the following two centuries. Then, in the middle of the third century B.C., for the first time in our record the tetrapolis appears in legislative activity.[2] Its chief deity was Dionysus, but the district was perhaps the oldest centre of Apollo-worship in Attica. Athens, however, had absorbed the local religious customs, and had itself sent to Delphi the solemn religious procession (*Pythais*), which tradition held to be one of the prerogatives of Marathonian independence. In the third century Macedon was excluded from Delphi, and this disability extended to its dependency also,[3] so that Athens could no longer send the *Pythais*. The possibility of approaching once more the great shrine was gained by the liberation of the city in 229 B.C., but while Athens was forgetful of its former piety, the citizens of the tetrapolis were more devoted. By sending embassies on their own account they renewed their relation with Apollo, and obtained important privileges for themselves.[4] Such independence of action was the effect of the decentralization of Attica produced by the events of the third century B.C.

The influence of men from the Mesogeia, who, wherever resident, had property and votes in the upland *trittys* of their tribes, was paramount in Athenian politics in the last third of the third century B.C., as has been pointed out already.[5] This part of Attica, through having been less exposed to devastation, was most prosperous, and hence more able and inclined to provide funds for self-protection than were the walled towns or the districts already ravaged. Moreover, the agrarian interests which it represented became relatively more important through the decline of Athenian

---

[1] *IG.* ii. 1324. The name archon, used to designate the officer of the association, is restricted to the tetrapolis and the Mesogeia. That is to say, it is a survival from the time when these were political entities.

[2] Wilhelm, 'Εφ. 'Αρχ., 1905, p. 228 ff (*IG.* ii. 601). It belongs to the third century B.C., according to Wilhelm.

[3] Beloch, iii. 2. 324 ff.

[4] Colin, *BCH.*, 1906, p. 217, Nos. 33 (shortly after 229 B.C.), 34 (*ca.* 204 B.C.), 35 (178/7 B.C.). In 35 the legates of the tetrapolis are called πρεσβευταί; cf. above, iv. 176, n. 4.

[5] See also *Priests of Asklepios*, 160.

commerce and the foreign control of the Piraeus. The Mesogeia had once possessed a central organization, and a faint trace of it survived still in a club of city folk which met in the temple of Hercules at Cholargus;[1] but the district of the Mesogeia was too extensive, and too much pre-occupied by village activities for it to think of trying to serve its interests by giving new life to this old institution, especially since the means existed near at hand for bringing the whole people into line with its policy. The Mesogeia became thus the bearer of the national idea, not the stronghold of a particularistic movement, and the league of the Mesogeia remained a city club, which was prominent in the third century B.C. simply because of the widespread contemporary interest in religious associations. The integrity of the state was maintained, but the leadership in it passed from the city to the country. Athens, too, obtained its liberty, but it was not the old Athens with its wonderfully homogeneous culture, and its joyous and passionate public life, agitated ceaselessly by a strong democratic ferment : it was a new Athens with a narrower economy and narrower politics, with a loyalty divided between an anaemic state and hundreds of religious, professional, and social organizations of a semi-public or private character, with a culture broad and refined still, but no longer shared with the great mass of the population, and eminent in one department only—philosophy.

The Stoa had become the Macedonian court philosophy because of the dominating influence of Zeno with Antigonus Gonatas, but upon Zeno's death in 261 B.C. Persaeus took his place as the king's adviser, and the Stoa, under the leadership of Cleanthes of Assus (261–

---

[1] See Wilhelm, 'Εφ. 'Αρχ., 1905, p. 230 ; cf. *IG*. ii. 604, and P.-W. iii. 2367. The ἱερόν of the Mesogeia was in Cholargus, which belonged to the city *trittys* of Acamantis, and lay in the north-west from the city (*Abh. d. Berl. Akad.*, 1892, p. 24 ; cf. *Ath. Mitt.*, 1892, p. 393 ; 1893, p. 298 f.). Those whose names appear in the extant decrees of the association were from Bate (city *trittys* of Aegeis), Cerameicus (city *trittys* of Acamantis), and Cydathenaeum (city *trittys* of Pandionis), *i.e.*, from city *demes*. This shows what the name " archon " (see above, v. 231, n. 1) confirms, that the club was a very ancient one, which, through lapse of time, had lost all personal contact with the Mesogeia district.

[2] See *IG*. ii. 602, 603, and 604 ; cf. Wilhelm, 'Εφ. 'Αρχ., 1905, 232 ; *IG*. ii. 5. 623c.

231 B.C.),[1] at once lost its pre-eminence in Athens. In fact, it became divided against itself,[2] and the heretical branch, that founded in Cynosarges by Ariston of Chios, was by far the more influential and popular of the two.[3] Lycon also failed to hold the Peripatos together, and Hieronymus of Rhodes opened a school for himself. This secession was all the more formidable in that Antigonus Gonatas, after Halcyoneus, his son, had fallen in battle, and perhaps from some predilection of the deceased, chose Hieronymus to manage the funds which he appropriated to defray the cost of a regal celebration of the lad's birthday.[4] Lycon could not attend the memorial banquet, for obvious reasons, but it served to bring about famous gatherings of the other Athenian schoolmen. We hear no word of Epicureans being present, but Arcesilaus was there and seems to have received a large measure of rather savage banter from both Ariston and Hieronymus.[5] He was too conspicuous a figure to escape criticism, and too large a nature to resent it, and he apparently maintained the best of relations with Hieronymus and with Cleanthes;[6] in fact, all these philosophers were gentlemen, and hence able to be in earnest without being enemies. Except in Ariston, Arcesilaus had no serious rival between 261 B.C. and his death twenty years later. To the Academy he gave a fresh impulse by returning to the methods of Socrates and Plato; for by subjecting the doctrines of his contemporaries to a searching destructive criticism, he

---

[1] For the date see *Priests of Asklepios*, 153 ff. ; cf. Crönert, *Kolotes*, 192.

[2] Bion died in Chalcis while the city was under the control of Antigonus. Chalcis seceded with Alexander in *ca.* 251 B.C. Before Bion left Athens for Chalcis, Eratosthenes came there to study, and while he was a student there Ariston was already a famous lecturer. Hence Ariston set up for himself some time prior to *ca.* 251 B.C.—perhaps in 261 B.C., on the death of Zeno. A philosophic school seems ordinarily to have had branches. What the relations of the several teachers to the titular head were depended largely upon personalities and circumstances (see below, vi. 258 f., and viii. 337). They need not have been always unfriendly (see below, x. *ca.* 414, note).

[3] Strabo, i. 15 ; cf. P.-W. ii. 957.

[4] Plut. *Consol. ad Apoll.* 33, p. 119 ; Aelian, *Var. hist.* iii. 5 ; Diog. Laert. iv. 41.

[5] Diog. Laert. iv. 40 (von Arnim, i. 77, 345). Ariston of Chios charged him with corrupting the youth and nursing silly social ambitions. For Lycon see Diog. Laert. v. 68.

[6] Diog. Laert. iv. 42, vii. 171.

reopened many questions which seemed settled, and thus forced philosophy to make a new start.[1] Rather, since the work of Chrysippus which he inspired was subtle rather than original, defensive rather than constructive; and, after Carneades had shown this to be the case, philosophy made, not the quest for ultimate truth, but the education of the Romans its chief task, the new beginning was at the same time an ending : the scepticism of Arcesilaus and Carneades was never overcome in antiquity, except by the faith to which it drove men of serious purpose—faith in a traditional system of thought, or in a revealed religion.

Arcesilaus might have won the patronage of Antigonus had he been willing to conciliate him, but not even Hierocles, his friend, could induce him to pay court to the king.[2] He was accused, moreover, of being more interested in his native than in his adopted home ; and while he refused to solicit Antigonus for the removal of the garrison from the Museum, he went to Demetrias at about the same time to sue in the interest of Pitane.[3] This town now became a dependency of Pergamum, and the kinsmen of Arcesilaus were thus subjects of King Eumenes. A bond was soon forged between Arcesilaus and the court; in fact, between the Academy and the Attalids ; for not only did Eumenes subsidize the school, but his successors gave it their special interest for over a hundred years. The sole literary legacy of Arcesilaus consisted of letters addressed to Eumenes, and an epigram is extant in which he foreshadowed the lustre which Attalus I. was subsequently to bring upon Pergamum.[4] The latter, for his part, provided a new hall

---

[1] von Arnim, *Kultur der Gegenwart*, i. 5. 250 ff.

[2] Diog. Laert. iv. 39.

[3] *Ibid.* ; cf. Strabo, xiii. 614 (von Arnim, *Stoic. vet. frg.* i. 8, 10). From Ditt. *OGIS.* 335. 141, we learn that Pitane was acquired by Eumenes I. after having been practically independent, under the suzerainty of Antiochus I. for a number of years. This was doubtless during the war which broke out in *ca.* 262 B.C. between Antiochus and Eumenes (Niese, ii. 84). It was probably because of the subjection of Pitane at this time that Arcesilaus went to Antigonus —the ally of Syria—for aid against Eumenes, or at least in the interest of Pitane. Antigonus refused to meddle, and Arcesilaus soon yielded to the courtesies or money of Eumenes. Droysen (iii. 1. 192) refers the mission to *ca.* 278 B.C., but see Niese, ii. 23, n. 2.

[4] Diog. Laert. iv. 30. The epigram is attributed by A. J. Reinach (*Revue*

for the successor of Arcesilaus, which was named from its occupant the Lacydeum.[1]   The fact that three natives of the Troad were school-heads in Athens probably attracted the notice of Eumenes.   The second of these was Lycon, whose home had been in Alexandria Troas, and it is particularly noted that Eumenes and Attalus sent large sums of money to him.[2]   The third, the sturdy, unpretentious plebeian from Assus, seems to have evoked the admiration of the Athenians alone ; at any rate we hear of no subsidies being sent to him from either Pergamum or Pella.   There may have been some political motive in the gifts of Eumenes and Attalus, for they stand in marked contrast to the policy adopted by the other dynasties.   Whereas the Attalids helped to endow the Athenian institutions, the Antigonids, Ptolemies, and Seleucids[3] endeavoured to hurt them by inducing the most distinguished philosophers to leave Athens and settle in their capitals.   They did not succeed ; rather, they succeeded only partially.   The Museum, which Demetrius of Phalerum had inspired, and which the first three Ptolemies subsidized lavishly, drew to Alexandria the great scientists of this age,[4] but the philosophers stayed in Athens.   They could not leave the spots hallowed by the memories of Plato, Aristotle, Epicurus, and Zeno ; nor could they abandon without reluctance the endowments of the four schools. But stronger than either of these two motives was another.   The beauties of the Athenian *demi-monde* might, and did,[5] seek international reputations at the royal courts.   That was their business.   They had to advance themselves by pleasing the kings and their courtiers.   The philosophers had a different ideal, and to its realization absolute freedom of speech and thought

celtique, 1909, p. 58) to Attalus, the father of King Attalus († *ante* 261 B.C.), but without sufficient reason.   The line Πέργαμος οὐχ ὅπλοις κλεινὴ μόνον would have been ridiculous prior to the war with Antiochus Soter (cf. p. 234, n. 3).

[1] See below, vi. 240.
[2] Diog. Laert. v. 67.
[3] See above, iv. 168, 169.   Antiochus II. tried to obtain Lycon (Diog. Laert. v. 67).
[4] Ptolemy Euergetes took Eratosthenes from Athens, Suidas, *s.v.*
[5] Wagner, Reinh. *Symb. ad comicorum Graec. hist. crit. capita quattuor.* Diss., Leipzig, 1905 ; cf. A. Körte, *Berl. phil. Woch.*, 1906, p. 900 ff.

was necessary. They had been molested by Athenian laws, but that was before the legal status of their schools had been determined;[1] and besides, subjection to laws was a different thing from personal dependence upon the moods of a king, however kindly disposed he might be towards their profession. An independent Athens—one reverenced by the great powers, and hence left alone, an Athens which abandoned all political initiative, was the ideal place for the location of a cosmopolitan university. Hence Chrysippus of Soli, the rising hope of the Stoa and the most important philosopher of the coming generation, refused to leave Athens to go to Ptolemy.[2] Hence Academicians, Peripatetics, and Stoics all[3] sympathized with the movement for Athenian independence which came to a head in 229 B.C.

[1] See above, iii. 104.

[2] Sphaerus went instead (Diog. Laert. vii. 177, 185 ; Athen. viii. 354 E).

[3] Aristocreon, nephew of Chrysippus the Stoic, aided in the crisis of 230/29 B.C. See Ditt. *Syll.*[2] 481 ; Wilhelm, 'Εφ. 'Αρχ., 1901, p. 52. Lycon's name appears in the list of subscribers *IG.* ii. 334 (232/1 B.C.) ; while the interest of the Academicians is evidenced by *IG.* ii. 385.

CHAPTER VI

THE RÉGIME OF EURYCLEIDES AND MICION

δέσποιν' ἁπασῶν, πότνι' 'Αθηναίων πόλι,
ὡς πάγκαλόν σου φαίνεται τὸ νεώριον,
ὡς καλὸς ὁ Παρθενών. καλὸς δ' ὁ Πειραιεύς.
ἄλση δὲ τίς πω τοιάδ' ἔσχ' ἄλλη πόλις ;
καὶ τοὐρανοῦ γ', ὥς φασιν, ἐστὶν ἐν καλῷ.

Comic Fragment, Koch, iii. p. 471, No. 340.

BUILDING activity had ceased almost entirely during the Macedonian régime. The people had not the courage to begin any large work, the depression of the moment being fatal to public enterprise. Even the necessary repairs had been omitted, and on every side were speaking evidences of neglect[1] in tumble-down shrines and tottering walls and porticoes.[2] That was changed in 229 B.C. The enthusiasm of the citizens was directed in the first instance to the military needs of the state, and the walls and harbours were, accordingly, strengthened. This done and peace secured, the government turned to other public works. It seems fairly evident[3] that in the course of the third century B.C. Athens came to look less towards the Piraeus and the sea, more towards the north-east and the Mesogeia. The roads along which

---

[1] Symptomatic of the new start is the settling once more of a boundary-stone in 228/7 B.C. It was subsequently again restored at or after the time of Augustus (*IG.* ii. 2. 1102).

[2] 'Εφ. 'Αρχ., 1909, p. 271 ff., where, in an inscription of the outgoing third or beginning second century B.C., we are told in regard to the shrine of Amphiaraus in Rhamnus that τόν τε οἶκον ἄθυρον εἶναι καὶ τὸν κέραμον κατεαγέναι, καταπεπτωκέναι δὲ καὶ τοῦ τοίχου τὸ μέρος τοῦ κατὰ τὸν ὄλμον καὶ τὴν τράπεζαν τοῦ θεοῦ κατεαγέναι καὶ τὸ πρόστωιον κινδυνεύειν καταπεσεῖν. If this condition were the result of the wars of 200–197, or 192/1 B.C., in the event of the inscription being later than the struggle with Antiochus, the cause of the dilapidation could hardly fail to have been mentioned. Cf. also *IG.* ii. 982.

[3] See above, v. 204, 207, 231.

commodities were brought into the city were now less
markedly those which passed through the walls at the
Dipylon gate. Those which converged upon the Diochares
gate,[1] and forwarded wares and passengers into the
thinly-housed quarters of Athens which lay to the north
and east of the agora, exhibited a relative increase of
traffic. This gave an enhanced value to the property
situated in this vicinity, and a movement in this direction
of population and of buildings began, which, continuing
throughout the Hellenistic and Roman periods, led to an
extension of the city's walls at the time of Hadrian, and
accounts for the landward site of the modern city.[2] The
first clear sign of the shifting of the city's centre, rather
of the change of its back-yard into its front-yard, was
given when Eurycleides and Micion placed the public
improvements begun under their régime on the north-
east and east of the market-place, and in the adjacent
parts of Athens. Among those the most noteworthy
products of domestic enterprise were the *Precinct of
the Demos and the Graces*, and the *Diogeneum*, the
former a religious enclosure or park which also served as
a depository for the statues of state benefactors; the
latter a *gymnasium* and a shrine, a "Union" for the
Athenian cadets and a chapel to the memory of Diogenes,
the liberator of Athens from the Macedonians. The
precinct was finished not long after 229 B.C., at any rate
prior to 211 B.C., and a priesthood, which was probably
hereditary in the family of Eurycleides and Micion, was
established to keep it in order, and to attend to the cult
of the dual godhead.[3] It was a fitting symbol of the
devotion of the Athenian people to the two ideals of
democracy and the beautiful. The Diogeneum was
surrounded by a wall, and within it were placed public

---

[1] See P.-W. v. 656, *s.v.* "Diomeia."

[2] This movement is independent of the alleged shifting of the *agora* (Curtius,
Stadtgeschichte von Athen, 169 ff.), for which there is insufficient proof (Wachsmuth, *op. cit.* i. 156, 465 ff. ; Judeich, *Topographie*, 294). That it was followed
by the erection of a new prytaneum in this quarter (Judeich, *op. cit.* 266, n. 11)
is current doctrine ; if this is the case, the new edifice must have been built after
200 B.C. (Kirchner, *Klio*, 1908, 488).

[3] *IG.* ii. 5. 385*c* (see above, v. 208, n. 1, v. 212, n. 2); ii. 5. 1161*b* ; Wilhelm,
Beiträge, 76 ff.

testimonials to the merits of the ephebe officials.[1] The
older and greater *gymnasia* had been located in the
suburbs, one at each of the three corners accessible from
the city. They were now found to be inconveniently
distant from the civic centre. Moreover, they had been
monopolized by the new colleges. Accordingly, new
ones were desirable, and since the walls contained in all
probability a considerably smaller number of people
than in the Periclean days,[2] it was easy to secure lots
large enough for them well within the best wards of
the city. The position and time of construction of
the Diogeneum are not definitely determinable.[3] The
gymnasium presented by Ptolemy Euergetes in 224 B.C.[4]
—" the first great (Attic) edifice of Hellenistic times"—
was erected on the agora. It served to partially enclose
the east side of the *piazza*, and provided at the same
time a pleasant and quiet retreat from the bustle of
politics and business. It was named from its founder
the Ptolemaeum, and in it were lecture rooms and a
library. With it began the long series of public buildings
which, unlike those of earlier days, Athens owed to her
past greatness, and to the generosity or policy of foreign
princes. To be sure, Attalus, in addition to sending

---

[1] Judeich, *op. cit.* 337.

[2] Accepting the estimate of Ed. Meyer (*Forsch. zur alten Geschichte*, ii. 149 ff.),
Wilamowitz (*Aristoteles und Athen*, ii. 201 ff.), and Cavaignac (*Études sur
l'histoire financière d'Athènes au Ve siècle*, 161 ff.) for the population of Athens
at *ca.* 430 B.C.

[3] Wachsmuth (P.-W. v. 734) conjectures that the Diogeneum was not
constructed till the death of Diogenes, at the beginning of the second century
B.C. (*IG.* ii. 3. 1669, 1670). See Wilhelm, *Beiträge*, 80. For the location of
Cynosarges see Dörpfeld, *Ath. Mitt.*, 1895, p. 507. His placing of it has been
defended by Robinson (*Amer. Jour. Phil.*, 1907, p. 425 ff.) on new evidence against
Milchhöfer (P.-W. v. 830 f.), who put Diomeia and Cynosarges farther north—
near the Lyceum.

[4] For the date see *Priests of Asklepios*, 158, and *Klio*, 1908, p. 341 ; cf. 1909,
p. 339 ff., *JHS.*, 1910, p. 191, and below, vi. 241, n. 1. The Athenians had relations
with the court of Ptolemy as early as the summer of 226 B.C. (*IG.* ii. 381). The
Ptolemaeum was in existence in 208/4 B.C., since a statue of Chrysippus, who
died at this time, was placed in it (Paus. i. 17. 2). It is not mentioned by
Heracleides the Critic (see below, vi. 262), but he mentions only the things of
historic interest. Besides, a building like the Ptolemaeum—a new building—
could be seen anywhere in Greece in those days. It was not to be thought of
in the same group with the grassy, wooded parks, and the large complex of
buildings found in Academia, Lyceum, and Cynosarges. In 200 B.C. the
suburban *gymnasia* were ravaged, and though subsequently replanted and
otherwise set in order, it is doubtful if they were reoccupied by the philosophers
(Wilamowitz, *Antigonus*, 267, n. 4, and Judeich, *op. cit.* 91).

statues to commemorate his victory over the Gauls, had
already constructed the Lacydeum,[1] but that was a
tribute to Plato rather than to Athena. Euergetes, on
the other hand, addressed himself to the whole people ;
rather, the Ptolemaeum was the pledge given on his
part of a close political understanding now reached with
Athens. This was, doubtless, an abandonment by the
Athenians of the policy of strict neutrality embraced in
229 B.C., but changes in the political constellation had
made this necessary. Antigonus Doson, the son of
Demetrius the Fair, who had seized the regency in
Macedon, proved himself a man of tact and energy, and,
after ejecting the Dardanians and coming to terms with
his Greek neighbours, he assumed the regal title and
proceeded to re-establish the shattered suzerainty of
Macedon over the Aegean islands. This he did with
ease, and he even re-conquered Caria, thus bringing into
relief the weakness of Egypt.[2] For the thirteen years
which followed his second peace with Seleucus Callinicus,
in 237 B.C., Ptolemy Euergetes, as already intimated,
confined his attention to Egypt, made no serious efforts
to restore his navy, and let matters in Asia and Europe
take their course. At most he continued to pay Aratus
the pension of six talents per year arranged by Philadelphus, and to keep other suitable agents in his employ.
Since, however, the rebirth of Sparta (227 B.C.), the
decisive victory of Cleomenes, its king, over the
Achaean general Hyperbatas at Hecatombaeon (226
B.C.), and the subsequent negotiations of the League
with the victor and with Macedon (226/5 B.C.), led him
to foresee the elimination of the Achaeans from Greek
politics ; and since the effort which the young king of
Syria, Seleucus Soter (226–223/2 B.C.), was able to make,
now that the dynastic war had ended, to drive the king
of Pergamum out of Asia Minor, and thus restore the
integrity of the Seleucid Empire,[3] led him to foresee

---

[1] It was donated prior to 224/3 B.C., if Apollodorus is right that in this
year Lacydes resigned his position as school-head (see below, vi. 258).

[2] Beloch (iii. 2. 428 ff.) claims that Antigonus defeated the fleet of
Euergetes under Sophron in a battle off Andros at this time, but see above,
v. 198.

[3] Beloch, iii. 1. 725 ff. for Cleomenes ; *ibid.* 708 ff. for the war in Asia Minor.

further trouble for Egypt from that quarter, he set to
work in the style of his father to build up a combination
of powers capable of checkmating the two traditional
foes of the Ptolemies. Accordingly, he gave to the
Attalids his moral and such military support as the
condition of his army and navy made possible, without,
however, being able to stop the advance of the Seleucids,
and at the same time he entered into an arrangement
with Cleomenes and provided him liberally with money
(225/4 B.C.). It was to the interest of Euergetes to
have the Achaeans recognize the hegemony of Sparta,
but for Aratus this was impossible. To resort to Doson
for assistance was almost equally repugnant to him.
Hence he hesitated ; and, then, taking the only third
course open to him, he applied to the Aetolians and
Athenians for support against Cleomenes (225/4 B.C.).
Here also he found himself opposed by Egypt, so that
he was rebuffed in both places—in Athens through the
intervention of Eurycleides and Micion against a popular
movement in his favour.[1] This was decisive for Aratus.
He refused to humble himself before Cleomenes in order
to serve the purposes of Euergetes, and instead entered
energetically into the project of Doson. The Macedonian
king at once proceeded to revive the Hellenic Confederation in the way so frequently employed by his
predecessors for the subjugation of Greece (224 B.C.).
It was the fear that Macedon would respect their
neutrality only so long as it was powerless to do otherwise
that induced the Athenians to yield to the seductions
of Euergetes, while the Aetolians had equal reason to
apprehend danger from the growing strength of Doson.
Still, the gifts of Ptolemy were not despised by either
of them.

To the alliance thus formed the Athenians attached the
utmost importance. Friendship with Egypt remained
the pivotal point in the foreign policy of Eurycleides
and Micion for their entire lifetime. Polybius censures
them for it.[2] The two brothers, he alleges, conciliated

---

[1] Plut. *Arat.* 41 ; cf. Niese, ii. 331 ; Kirchner, P.-W. vi. 1328 ; Holleaux,
BCH., 1907, p. 98, n. 6.   [2] v. 106. 6 ff.

the Ptolemies by unworthy flatteries ; but, since Polybius
looked at these incidents through Achaean spectacles,
and with an inbred dislike of Athens, his judgment is
untrustworthy.[1]   Naturally, favours of the sort rendered
deserved gratitude, and the Aetolians showed their
appreciation for Ptolemy's backing by erecting statues
of himself and Berenice, his energetic wife, as well as of
their seven or eight children, at Thermon, their capital.[2]
The Athenians, for their part, made Euergetes the
eponymous hero of a new tribe, set up his statue,—the
thirteenth in the series,—and appointed a priest to
administer the cult which they established in his
honour.[3]   Nor did they forget his wife.   Ptolemy
received a tribe, the Ptolemais ; to Queen Berenice
was given a *deme*, and her name was thus substituted
for another in the legal designation of every family in
an Attic village, while at the same time she was associated in the cult of her husband.   The Ptolemaea too
was, it seems, established in Athens at this time.   This
festival had existed intermittently since 280/79 B.C. on
Delos and among the Islanders of the Aegean Sea, but
it was not till Ptolemy became an Athenian hero that
the fête for the worship and honour of his family could
be admitted with full propriety into Athens.[4]   A hero
more or less made no difference in the Attic religion,
but it was otherwise with a tribe.   There were twelve
tribes already, and this was the reasonable number,
though it had been avoided by Cleisthenes in 508 B.C.,
so as not to establish a coincidence between his new
tribes and the old *trittys*.   Thirteen were excessive,
not so much, perhaps, that they caused an increase of
the senate by fifty members, as that, for all except leap

---

[1] See below, viii. 315, 324.

[2] Ἐφ. Ἀρχ., 1905, p. 90 f.

[3] Bates, *Cornell Studies*, viii. 27 ff. ; Wilhelm, *Beiträge*, 77, where a man—
probably Eurycleides of Cephisia, certainly either he or his son Micion—was
at the same time priest of the *Demos and Graces*, and Ἱερε[ὺς Πτο]λεμαίου
Ε[ὐεργ]έτου καὶ [Βε]ρενίκης.   The absence of the regal title and the presence of
the cult-name are here equally noteworthy ; but the word Εὐεργέτης is used in
the same sense as in the inscription on one of the seats of the theatre—
Διογένους Εὐεργέτου.   In each case, it indicates a status decreed by the
Athenians themselves.   Cf. below, vii. 310.

[4] See *Klio*, 1908, p. 340 f. ; 1909, p. 339 f. ; *JHS.*, 1910, p. 191 f.

years, the extra tribe perpetuated two distinct divisions
of the year—the calendar year of twelve months, and the
civil year of thirteen prytanies.   Conceivably there was
no other way of honouring Ptolemy, but what was the
need of retaining the two Macedonian tribes?   The
simplest thing would have been to rename one of them
Ptolemais, and have done with it.   Of course this was
unprecedented, but so are all innovations.   The real
reason was that Athens in 224 B.C. was studious of
avoiding all occasion of offending Macedon.   She wished
to have the support of Egypt, and wished to have the
fact of her backing from that quarter known; but she
did not desire to provoke Antigonus Doson, who had
become her friend and well-wisher about four years
earlier.[1]

The course thus pursued, as the outcome proved, was
the best possible one for Athens to take in the circumstances.   It led to the alignment of the city with the
party in Greece which was unpatriotic in the great crises
of national affairs, but which secured the friendship of
Rome and the benefits of victory; and since Antigonus
Doson did not resent the Egyptian alliance, or did not
live long enough to mature his plans, and since Ptolemy
did not come in person, or call upon his allies, to support
Cleomenes,—in fact, abandoned him himself rather than
risk a war with Macedon,—it caused no momentary
troubles.   Athens remained a spectator in the fierce
struggle (222 B.C.) which put an end for all time to
the imperial aspirations of Sparta, and upon the death
of the victor of Sellasia (221 B.C.) she maintained
the same friendly relations with his ward and heir,
Philip V.

It was well understood abroad that Eurycleides, who
was probably hoplite-general for year after year,[2] and
Micion, his brother, dominated Athenian politics during
this entire epoch.   The personalities of these men are
no longer definable, but their methods and aims are
still sufficiently clear.   They took the view that the
people should sanction all their measures, and thus

---

[1] See above, v. 209.   [2] *IG.* ii. 858 ; 'Εφ. 'Αρχ., 1900, p. 145.

stimulated popular government, but they did not regularly take the initiative themselves. It was usually more expedient to have confidential friends in the Senate and Assembly make the necessary motions; but the veil assumed was a thin one, and it sometimes happened that a petitioner strengthened his request by alleging the support of the two brothers.[1] There was, accordingly, a scrupulous adherence to democratic forms of government, and this trait was not exhibited by them for the first time after 229 B.C. Eurycleides and Micion had, apparently, come into prominence and power as popular leaders. Thus in 232/1 B.C., when a catalogue was made of the objects dedicated to Asclepius since the sorting in 276/5 B.C., the work was completed, not as it had been done on the last occasion, but in the fashion of the cataloguers of about 330 B.C.[2] Similarly, the attempt was made to reform the title of the public secretary[3] in accordance with earlier democratic precedents, and after the restoration in 229 B.C. an attack was made upon institutions as well as names, and a committee was appointed instead of a single magistrate to take charge of the general administration.[4] Neither of these revivals, however, was permanently successful, and shortly after 229 B.C. they were again abandoned, but they disclose the ambition of Eurycleides and his friends to be historically correct in their reorganization of the government. This tendency is also shown in the searching out and citing the texts of important enactments. Thus the entire law is quoted in 228 B.C. in support of the claim put forward by a certain Timosthenes for the special privileges due to the

---

[1] *IG.* ii. 5. 385c, 41.

[2] *IG.* ii. 836 compared with *IG.* ii. 835 (see *Priests of Asklepios*, 149) and *IG.* ii. 767; *Add.* 766b, and ii. 766.

[3] The title γραμματεὺς τοῦ δήμου, which had been in vogue for a time at the end of the fourth century B.C. (*Cornell Studies*, vii. 63, and Pendorff, *Leipz. Stud.* xviii. 185), reappeared in 232/1 B.C. (*IG.* ii. 334), and is found occasionally thereafter (*IG.* ii. 5. 385c, 229/8 B.C.). *IG.* ii. 415, however, belongs to *ca.* 306 B.C. (Wilhelm, *GGA.*, 1903, p. 792); 'Εφ. 'Αρχ., 1903, p. 69, is Lemnian, and *IG.* ii. 5. 535d is dateless. For the time of this democratic movement see above, v. 205, n. 3.

[4] See *Priests of Asklepios*, 152, n. 42; cf. *Klio*, 1905, p. 170 f.; Kolbe, *op. cit.* 150; above, iv. 136, 161, and below, Appendix II.

descendant of a state benefactor.[1]   It was, accordingly, held that on starting anew Athens must not deny the obligations handed down to her from the past; nor yet accept illegal claims which imposed financial or other burdens upon the state.   At the same time the two brothers did not hesitate to make timely innovations. Those in the war department—the abandonment of the Long Walls, the designation of a new general for the Piraeus, and the strengthening of the defences of the harbour—have been referred to in another connexion,[2] but serve also to prove that Eurycleides and Micion were not slaves of tradition.   More radical action, however, was taken in the matter of the coinage, and the old coin types were definitely abandoned.   The new issues were made in the wider but thinner patterns which had come into use in the course of the third century B.C., with devices inoffensive to modern taste, and with marks to fix the responsibility for purity and weight upon mint officials and the various mines.[3]   A revision of the laws was also made,[4] and it appears that alterations were effected in the law of property by which the old prohibition against immigrants owning land within a certain distance of the frontier was extended,[5] and a maximum was imposed upon the value of real estate which a naturalized foreigner might acquire in Attica. It differed in different cases, on what principle we cannot ascertain.   In one instance the amount fixed was two talents, in another one thousand *drachmae* only, and in still another three thousand *drachmae* for house and two talents for land.   Conceivably the state granted simply the request which accompanied each petition for citizenship, and no longer gave *carte blanche* for future acquisitions.[6]   At any rate, we have an interest-

---

[1] *IG*. ii. 5. 385*b* (Ditt. *Syll.*[2] 467).   The state benefactor was also named Timosthenes, and his privileges were granted by *IG*. ii. 249 (Ditt. *Syll.*[2] 180) ; cf. Wilhelm, *GGA*., 1903, p. 785.

[2] See above, v. 211.

[3] Head, *Hist. Num.* 316 ; Hill, *Handbook of Greek and Roman Coins*, 121 ff. ; Sundwall, *Untersuch.* 110, n. 2.

[4] *IG*. ii. 379 (see above, v. 208, n. 1).

[5] *IG*. ii. 186 ; cf. Wilhelm, *Wien. Stud.* 1907, p. 1.

[6] A phrase κατὰ τὸν νόμον appears in the formula regarding the property rights involved in the grant of Athenian citizenship from the time of Lycurgus

ing sign of local jealousy of foreign enterprise. Doubt-less, there was a feeling of annoyance in the city at the tendency of landed property to fall into the hands of wealthy foreigners, for in addition to a relatively large number of grants of citizenship there is distinct evidence in the guide-book written at this time by Heracleides the Critic of a disposition on the part of many Greeks to choose Athens as their place of business or residence.[1] Part of the same movement to safeguard Athenian privileges is to be seen in the fact that the judicial scrutiny, which in 301 B.C. was instituted upon applica-tions for citizenship and in 276 B.C. was extended to petitions of citizens for public honours, was now made applicable to grants of *proxenia*.[2]

The ambition of Athens on acquiring her independ-ence was directed, in the words of a contemporary document, " to a restoration of her pristine happiness."[3] In so far as this object was identical with material pros-perity, there were not wanting some features of its realization. To the traveller on the Athenian high-ways well-cultivated lands presented themselves in all directions. The gains incident to unusually extensive building operations were distributed to contractors and artisans of all kinds; and that the money involved came from foreigners was an additional economic advantage. Athenian sculptors and contractors under-took commissions, not always with success, in cities near and remote.[4] The commerce of this age was enormous,

---

onwara (Köhler, *Ath. Mitt.*, 1883, p. 220; Wilhelm, *Hermes*, 1889, p. 328; Larfeld, *Handbuch d. griech. Epigraphik*, ii. 794), but Thalheim (P.-W. v. 2584) is doubtless right in referring it to the restriction mentioned in *IG.* ii. 186, that new citizens must not occupy land near the frontiers (Wilhelm, *Wien. Stud.*, 1907, p. 1). A regulation which required the definition of a maximum which differed in each case could not be summarised in any formula. See Larfeld (*loc. cit.*) for a complete list of the documents with a fixed maximum. See also *Class. Phil.*, 1907, p. 406. They belong, so far as they can be dated, between 229 and 200 B.C. After 200 B.C. we meet the formula γῆς καὶ οἰκίας ἔγκτησιν αἰτησαμένῳ κατὰ τὸν νόμον (*IG.* ii. 423), which supports the view of the requirement taken in the text.

[1] See below, vi. 262.

[2] Schubert, J. G., *De proxenia Attica*, 40 f., and Wilhelm, *Hermes*, 1889, p. 330. See also above, iii. 130; iv. 162.

[3] *IG.* ii. 5. 619*b* - - ὅπως ἂν μηδ' ὑ[φ]' ἑνὸς περι[σ]πωμένη ἡ πόλις [ἀ]ποκατα-σταθεῖ εἰς τὴν ἐξ ἀρχῆς εὐδαιμονίαν.

[4] I have noted the names of over fifty Athenian sculptors of the third and

and though its main arteries no longer centred in
Athens, its old courses were not entirely abandoned.
The Piraeus had dwindled away during the Macedonian
régime, but promptly after the departure of the foreign
garrison citizens from all parts of Attica had flocked
down to settle in it.[1] They came for business reasons
primarily, and there were obviously men of wealth and
enterprise among them with whose arrival the industrial
life of the place took a new start. In the last decades
of the third century B.C. over a score of Athenians
received patents of *proxenia* in the town of Oropus
alone,[2] and despite the vexatious tariff regulations of
the Oropians it is clear that the road which led thence
past the temple of Zeus Amphiaraus into Attica was
a busy thoroughfare for goods and travellers. In fact,
the Oropians were at this time in a fair way to be
Atticized, the demoralization of Boeotia being, perhaps,
an asset for the Athenian cause in this somewhat neutral
country. Plataea also hung now, as always, rather on
Athens than on Thebes,[3] so strong was the magnetic
force of the peace, freedom, and orderliness which prevailed to the east of Cithaeron. The new money of
Athens soon obtained the widest circulation :[4] that
Attic pottery, honey, figs, olives, did not is an unwarranted hypothesis. In fact, the exportation of such
articles is deducible from the existence of a prolonged

second centuries in Kirchner's *Prosopographia*. Of these, approximately 11
were active in Delos, 18 in Athens, 4 in Pergamum and Epidaurus each, 3
in Megara, 2 in Rhodes, Rome, Delphi, and Oropus each, and 1 in Argos,
Pherae, Euboea, Hyampolis, Thebes, Troezen, Acraphia, Elatea, and Tanagra.
A fair proportion of them belong to the end of the third century B.C., and
in *IG*. iv. 1509 (Kirchner, *PA*. 1264 c) we have a record of one who got into
difficulties in Epidaurus. Two others executed in the commission of τὸ κοινὸν
τῶν Ἀσιναίων, between 229 and 224 B.C. seemingly, a statue of Apia, daughter
of Aristippus of Argos, which was set up along with that of her uncle or
nephew Aristomachus II. in the shrine at Epidaurus (Wilhelm, *Beiträge*,
110 ff.). For an Athenian contractor who moved and rebuilt a temple in
Peparathos shortly after 197 B.C., see *IG*. xii. 8. 640.

[1] See above, v. 222, note.
[2] *IG*. vii. 301, 302, 304, 308, 310, 312, 314, 317, 319, 325, 329, 335, 339,
345, 346, 347, 353, 354, 358, 371.
[3] Heracleides the Critic, 7. 11.
[4] It is, however, a little surprising that in the two lots of coins which were
hidden in the last twenty years of the third century B.C.—one in Laconia
(*Annual of the British School at Athens*, 1907/8, p. 149 ff.), and the other in
the sea near Epidaurus (*Jour. int. d'arch. num.*, 1907, p. 35 ff.)—quite a large
proportion of old Attic coins, but none of the New Style, are found.

period of peace. On the other hand, the corn produced was now, as always, inadequate for home consumption, and it was only by selling its dainties that the country was able to buy its necessary food.

The revival of Athens was dependent absolutely upon the maintenance of peace. In this the Athenian statesmen were ultimately successful, but only by constant watchfulness. Within twelve months of the death of Antigonus Doson (221 B.C.) the Social War broke out. Philip V. of Macedon, and the Hellenic Confederacy of which he was the head, became involved in a fatal struggle (220–217 B.C.) with the Aetolians and their allies, the Eleians and Spartans. The Aetolians were notorious pirates and freebooters, and they had provoked the war by pillage and brigandage, but none the less they received the sympathy[1] of the neutral powers —Egypt, Pergamum, Rhodes, Chios, and Byzantium. Athens was secretly of the same way of thinking, for the Aetolians alone stood between them and dependence upon Macedon; but to take sides, as they wished, might involve them in disaster without saving their friends. At any rate it would make Attica, not Aetolia, the battle-ground of the war. Hence Eurycleides determined to preserve the strictest neutrality. Demaenetus of Athmonon was sent to the Aetolians and to Philip (220/19 B.C.) to make the necessary explanations and to obtain assurances that Attica would not be molested during the struggle.[2] His mission was successful in each case. The Aetolians had enemies enough already, and had no reason to add another in Athens. Philip, moreover, was found quite willing to renew the friendship and peace negotiated by Doson. In other words, he ignored the alliance between Athens and Egypt, which on grounds of general policy

---

[1] After the assurances given by Euergetes in 224 B.C., they probably had reason to expect more than sympathy; but Euergetes had died in 222/1 B.C. (Holleaux, *Mél. Nicole*, 273 ff.), and Philopator was fully employed till 217 B.C. in the Fourth Syrian War—that with Antiochus III.

[2] *IG.* ii. 5. 619*b*. The date of the embassy is necessarily the opening year of the war. That it is mentioned just prior to the first generalship of Demaenetus at Eleusis is a confirmation of the date (219/8 B.C.) assigned to this office and the archonship of Chaerephon by Kolbe (*op. cit.* 68 ff.).

he could not but resent, and to such a degree won the gratitude of the Athenians that they voted to him a statue and other honours.[1]   As the war proceeded, and the superiority of Macedon was increasingly demonstrated, the need for absolute correctness in the attitude of Athens became still greater.   Macedonian troops were constantly passing along the Attic frontiers, and Macedonian ships occasionally sailed past the Attic coasts on their way to and from the southern battlefields. There was always the danger that detachments would fail to discover the boundary till they had foraged Athenian territory.   Hence the city was obliged to keep men under arms in the frontier posts and wherever there were roads leading into Attica.[2]   Between the Attic guards and the Macedonian foraging parties conflicts were hard to avoid, and a skirmish might drag Athens into the war.   A still greater danger appeared in 218 B.C.   Philip, the young Macedonian king, was at this time much under the control of Aratus; so much so, in fact, that Apelles, the most powerful of the Macedonian nobles, and other leading officers, stood to lose their influence altogether.   They first plotted against Aratus, but when this move failed, they stirred up the soldiers against Philip himself.   Philip made concessions to the troops, but by publicly snubbing Apelles made clear that those who trusted in him to get them safely out of the conspiracy had leaned upon a broken reed.   Among these was Megaleas, who had been one of the ringleaders in the mutiny of the soldiers.   He perceived his danger in time, and fled to Athens.   The city was placed in an embarrassing position.   To refuse him admittance was to be false to one of the noblest traditions of the state, for in times past Athens had been the England of Greece,

---

[1] Which were done away with in 199 B.C.   See below, vi. 276.

[2] *IG.* ii. 1216 (225/4 B.C. ; cf. *BCH.*, 1888, p. 78, and *IG.* ii. 5. p. 251) ; Ἐφ. Ἀρχ., 1897, p. 43 (220/19 B.C.) ; *IG.* ii. 5. 619*b* (219/8–211/0 B.C.)=Ditt. *Syll.*[2] 246 ; Ἐφ. Ἀρχ., 1900, p. 141 (222/1 B.C.) ; *ibid.* 143 (after 229 B.C.). The two last mentioned refer to Sunium.   The ὕπαιθροι are mentioned in Ditt. *Syll.*[2] 246, a frg. published in Ἐφ. Ἀρχ., 1897, p. 39, dated by an archon whose name ended in -τος or -της, and in *IG.* ii. 1216,—all of which belong to this general period.

the kindly protector of the political exiles of less liberal countries. But the risk was too great. Should Philip demand the surrender of the traitor, Athens must, beyond a doubt, yield him up, and the only result would be to convince Philip of the hostility of the city. Consequently the Athenian generals refused to receive Megaleas, and he went to Thebes, where he anticipated execution by taking his own life.[1]

It is not stated that Athens was among the neutral states which in 218 and 217 B.C. brought pressure to bear upon Philip and the Aetolians to end the fratricidal struggle, and it is nowhere recorded that the Athenians contributed anything to the peace arranged in the latter year—the year in which Egypt, on ending the Fourth Syrian War by the great victory at Raphia, was free to exert a greater influence in Greece. But it can hardly be doubted that those who intervened had the goodwill of Eurycleides and Micion, not through sympathy with the purpose which actuated Philip in abandoning the struggle—the expulsion of the Romans from the Greek side of the Adriatic Sea—nor yet through the alarm to which Agelaus of Naupactus[2] gave expression at the conference of the contestants when he urged the imperative need of Greek unity to face the storm-cloud rising in the west, and the certain danger of an irresistible advance towards the Orient should either Rome or Carthage be victorious in the great Hannibalic War then in progress. The point of view of the Athenians was that of Ptolemy. They wished to preserve Aetolia as a thorn in the side of Macedon. They made a fetich of the balance of power in Greece, and, intent upon their own immediate interests, they shut their eyes to the great armaments which would be at the disposal of the victor in the western struggle; but, doubtless, they saw no end to the strife between Rome and Carthage, and viewed the Second Punic War as merely the current phase of a gigantic conflict which had been waged for centuries. At any rate, the

---

[1] Polybius, v. 26-27 ; cf. Niese, ii. 451 f.
[2] Polybius, v. 104.

indecisive end of the Social War came to them as a
relief from pressing danger.

Between 217 and 212 B.C. there was no war in
Greece which menaced the safety of Athens. The
times, however, were unsettled. The disposition of
Philip towards Greece was changing, and in his mind
the conviction was taking shape that the way to make
her harmless in the imminent Roman War was, not to
conciliate her, but to hold her in subjection by a policy
of blood and iron. The death of Aratus in 214/3 B.C.
disturbed the relations of parties and cities in the
Peloponnesus, which had been determined for over
thirty years by the personality of this great politician.
In Boeotia, moreover, conditions were altogether anarchic.
Hence Athens was compelled to keep troops constantly
under arms.[1] Of the volunteer force the cavalry alone
was put into requisition, the mercenaries being sufficient
for the ordinary needs.[2] They were probably ragged
regiments, for it is apparent that the soldiers were not
always adequately clothed. They were provided with
part of their food by the state,[3] but the greater part of it
they had to purchase from their wages ; and it is clear
that the regularity with which they received supplies
depended largely upon the energy, thoughtfulness, and
generosity of their generals. These mercenaries were
now four-fifths Athenian by birth. Earlier it had been
different. Athens at the beginning of the third century
B.C. was still a rich community, which paid good wages

---

[1] From *IG.* ii. 5. 964*b* it appears that the Eleusinian division had about
seventy-five men in *ca.* 205 B.C. The date results from the relation of this
document to *IG.* ii. 5. 619*b* (211/0 B.C.) : for among the five soldiers chosen in
this year to erect a statue of Demaenetus appears - - -]νδρος Τυρμείδης ; while the
hegemon at the time of *IG.* ii. 5. 964*b* was . . ε . . α . . ρος Τυρ(μείδης). The
two are obviously the same, and each name should be restored Σπεύσανδρος
(cf. Kirchner, *PA.* 12841). The prominent soldier in 211/0 B.C. was the captain
in the later document. See 'Εφ. 'Αρχ., 1899, p. 194, No. 14, for soldiers at Eleusis
for several years after the archonship of Antimachus (208/7 B.C.), and *IG.* ii.
5. 619*c* (archon Philinus, *ca.* 200 B.C.) for services rendered to them by the
treasurer of military funds. For the period prior to 211/0 B.C. the references
are given above, vi. 249, n. 2.

[2] At any rate there is no mention in our documents of ἐπίλεκτοι. στρατιῶται,
or mercenaries, alone appear. Nine foreigners are listed among the 75
in *IG.* ii. 5. 964*b*. Hence ξένοι would not have been a descriptive term for
the corps.

[3] Cf. *IG.* ii. 5. 619*b* and 614*c*.

and attracted recruits from the ends of the earth even
after Alexander had overrun Asia and the fever to be
gone to the east had seized hold of the adventurous youth
of Greece. Cyrenaeans and Cassandrians, Thracians and
Bithynians, Carians, Lycians and Pisidians, men from
Heracleia and Phaselis, and from all the islands between
Crete and Samothrace, as well as from Thessaly, the
Peloponnesus, and Central Greece had been in the
service of Athens at that time.[1] Now only a few
stragglers found their way into the Athenian con-
tingents. The troops fell into two divisions, one with
its headquarters at Eleusis, the other stationed in the
Paralia, and each of them was organized as a miniature
state, capable of passing decrees and conferring honours.
At the same time, moreover, that they were dependent
upon charity for their clothing they did not hesitate to
authorize taxes in order with the proceeds to reward
popular generals with bronze statues or gold wreaths—
facts equally significant for a grave weakness of Greek
character, and for the civic relation which, to the
disadvantage of the service, always existed between the
Athenian soldier and his commander. The moneys
appropriated by the state for army purposes were under
the supervision of the treasurer of the military funds,
and in the period next after 229 B.C. a close co-operation
existed between this official and those who had charge
of the general administration.[2] The unity of the
financial administration doubtless lay, as in the days
of Pericles and Cleon, Eubulus, Lycurgus, and Demetrius,
in the person of the dominant politician. One of the
services put to the credit of Eurycleides was his activity
in collecting for the state the sums due by recalcitrant
debtors.[3] The restoration of 229 B.C. was thus not
accompanied by a cancelling of at least public debts. In

---

[1] *IG.* ii. 963. The date of this list is after the founding of Cassandria in
316 B.C. The soldiers are not those of 257/6 B.C. ('Εφ. 'Αρχ., 1892, p. 147);
nor those of 240 B.C. (*IG.* ii. 5. 618*b*); nor those of 205 B.C. (*IG.* ii. 5. 964*b*).
There are no Celts among them, and no western Greeks.

[2] See *IG.* ii. 5. 385*c*, 407*e*, where the two offices co-operated for the
payment of the cost of publishing documents. A similar co-operation is attested
for the year 209/8 B.C. (?) by Kern, *Insch. v. Magnesia*, 37. This was as in the
year 277/6 B.C., 'Εφ. 'Αρχ., 1910, p. 19; cf. *IG.* ii. 327.

[3] See *IG.* ii. 379; cf. above, v. 208, n. 1.

fact, we have no reason to believe that the internal
peace of the community was broken by any such re-
missions of obligations or delays of justice as brought
ill-repute upon contemporary Sparta and Boeotia.   The
public credit of Athens was good, as we may judge from
the fact that she was called upon to act as arbitrator in
executing a treaty between Troezen and Hermione,[1] and
from the fact that foreigners sought and obtained redress against Athenian citizens from her jury courts.[2]
Certainly, abundant records are extant of the piety and
honesty of her senate and its officials.[3]   Foreigners were
still excluded from participation in her public life, but
this was less of a disability than in the earlier days,[4]
and citizenship began now to be conferred with increasing frequency.   The Hellenistic monarchs were
less illiberal with their favours than were the city-states,
for the same reason that new countries are always more
hospitable than old ones.   At their courts all Greeks
were welcome, and for the hundreds of outsiders who
came and settled in quiet Athens, as many Athenians[5]
went into their kingdoms to seek their fortunes.   They
are, of course, difficult to trace, for upon taking up
residence in any one of the scores of Greek cities
founded in this century, they lost their right to be
designated Athenians, and their services are reckoned
to the credit of their adopted home.   At a king's court,
however, men might maintain their national identity.
Thus Glaucon and Chremonides are still known as
Athenians while in the service of Egypt,[6] and the

---

[1] *IG.* iv. 752.

[2] *IG.* xii. 5. 1. 528 ; cf. Sonne, *De arbitris externis*, 29, and for the date
Hiller von Gärtringen in *IG. loc. cit.*

[3] *IG.* ii. 431 (212/1 B.C.), 390, 391 and 393 (*ca.* 202 B.C.), 392 (*ca.* 201 B.C.),
394 ; 'Εφ. 'Αρχ., 1903, p. 63 ; cf. Kirchner, *Rhein. Mus.*, 1904, p. 294.   This
whole group probably precedes 199 B.C., since in the invocation formula there
is no reference to the maledictions on Philip, which were prescribed by the
decree of this year (see below, vi. 277).   Otherwise, some of them may follow
the partial reconciliation with Macedon in 197/6 B.C.

[4] It is, however, called δουλεῖα by Heracleides the Critic (see below,
vi. 262).

[5] We shall do well, perhaps, not to magnify the exodus from Athens.   Apart
from the few who appear in the *Flinders Petrie Papyri* (see above, v. 188, n. 1),
I have noticed only one Athenian in the *papyri* from Egypt (*Hibeh Papyri*,
243 ; *ca.* 300 B.C.).

[6] Teles (Hense[2]), 23 ; cf. Polyaenus, v. 18 ; Ditt. *Syll.*[2] 224, n. 2.

same is true of Demetrius, the diplomat in the employ of Ptolemy Epiphanes.[1] Thus Xenophanes, son of Cleomachus, was rated an Athenian in the court of Philip V. when he was sent as ambassador in 216/5 B.C. to form the famous alliance with Hannibal. He had the misfortune to fall into the hands of the Romans : so much is indisputable.[2] Livy gives him other adventures. Captured while making his way through Apulia to Capua, he boldly informed the Roman general that he came from Philip to make a treaty with the Romans, whereupon he was let go and forwarded on his journey. Thus he reached Hannibal, concluded the negotiations, and took with him three Carthaginians to receive the oath of Philip. On the way back he had the bad luck to be captured a second time. He tried to escape by telling the same falsehood, but the presence of the Carthaginians betrayed him, and it was necessary for Philip to send a second embassy before a complete understanding was reached with Hannibal. Livy is probably romancing, for on the treaty actually concluded stands, as representative of Philip, the name of the Athenian Xenophanes.[3] Of the man we know nothing further. He appears at this critical moment of the world's history to usher the traditional enemy of his mother-country into its fatal struggle with Rome, and immediately passes from our view.

Athens was not drawn into the war[4] which in 212 B.C. Rome incited in Greece against Macedon. But she was too near the scene of operations not to be affected by it. In 210 B.C.[5] she was an eye-witness of the melancholy sack of Aegina, and among the captives made in this campaign were some Athenians. Attalus of Pergamum now joined zealously in the struggle as the ally of Rome, and when Aegina was put on the market he bought it. In the fall of 210 B.C. he was

---

[1] Polybius, xxii. 3. 5.
[2] *Ibid.* vii. 9. 1; cf. Livy, xxiii. 33 ; Niese, ii. 467.
[3] Polybius, *loc. cit.*
[4] Polybius alludes to the neutrality of Athens in commending that policy to Sparta (ix. 40).
[5] Cardinali, *op. cit.* 49.

chosen general of the Aetolians for the ensuing year,[1] and during 209 and 208 B.C. he commanded his fleet, which was operating in Attic waters, from its base in Aegina. There can be no doubt that he courted the Athenians. Thus to his fourth son he gave the name Athenaeus,[2] and in the winter of 210/9 B.C. he gave a favourable answer to the mediation of an Academic philosopher in the interest of the Athenian captives.[3] But there is no evidence that the Athenians sympathized with his policy. In fact, their effort in 209 B.C. to induce the Aetolians to end the struggle was probably distasteful to the king. The political advisers of Athens had been and remained the kings of Egypt, and the effort just mentioned was made in conjunction with Ptolemy Philopator, and the neutral states, Rhodes and Chios.[4] It failed of success, for the Romans had too much at stake in this year to let the war die out in Greece. They accordingly encouraged the Aetolians to continue it, and foiled a second attempt to effect a reconciliation in the spring of 208 B.C.,[5] so that peace was attained only when the neutrals intervened a third time in 207 B.C.[6] Athens is not mentioned among the peacemakers of 208 and 207 B.C., but this is probably due simply to the inadequacy of our sources, and her goodwill, doubtless, accompanied their work. Thus in the late fall of 208 B.C.[7] we find the city in amicable correspondence with Rhodes, the leader seemingly in the intervention,

---

[1] Cardinali, *op. cit.* 49 ; cf. Livy, xxvii. 29. 10, 30. 1.

[2] Attalus, the second of the four sons of Attalus I., was born in 220 B.C. Hence Athenaeus, the fourth son, was born in *ca.* 215 B.C. at the earliest, and perhaps some years later. His mother need not have been over thirty in 209 B.C. His father was sixty. He himself appears for the first time in our records in 189 B.C.

[3] *IG.* ii. 385. Crönert (*Kolotes*, 78 f., 180) has not helped the interpretation of this decree. It was in this same general period that *IG.* ii. 5. 451*b* i. was passed conferring *proxenia* upon a courtier named Apollodorus (*Class. Phil.*, 1907, p. 406).

[4] Livy, xxvii. 30.

[5] Livy, xxviii. 7. 13 ; cf. Niese, ii. 489 f. Livy speaks here only of Ptolemy and Rhodes, the two most important mediators.

[6] Polybius, xi. 4 ff., where, in addition to Ptolemy, Rhodes, and Chios, there is mention of Byzantium and Mitylene also. Cf. Appian, *Maced.* 3.

[7] *IG.* ii. 304 ; Kolbe, *Ath. Mitt.*, 1905, p. 76 ff. ; cf. *Priests of Asklepios*, 155, n. 52 ; Niese, ii. 571, n. 3.

and whose point of view they probably shared—that it was foolish for the Aetolians to seek to drive out Beelzebub with Satan, foolish and monstrous, since the expulsion of Philip from Greece meant, according to the treaty with Rome, that the Greeks of captured cities should be sold as slaves by the Italians, and that Aetolians should migrate into the lands and homes thus vacated.[1]

A short interval of peace followed, during which only one event of importance took place in the political history of Athens[2]—the death of the two brothers, Eurycleides and Micion. They died apparently within a short time of one another, for the rumour spread and got credence that they had been poisoned by Philip.[3] We

---

[1] Polybius, *loc. cit.*

[2] The Aetolians made peace with Philip in 206 B.C., and in the following year Rome did likewise. The allies of each were included in the treaty, and among those of Rome Livy (xxix. 12) mentions Athens. This does not harmonize with the tradition represented by Zonaras (viii. 19 ; cf. above, v. 210, n. 3) as to the relation entered into between Rome and Athens in 229 B.C., since the term he uses is φιλία, not συμμαχία. We have already seen that a formal alliance for defence and offence, such as inclusion in the treaty of 205 B.C. presupposes, was also quite out of keeping with the whole foreign policy of Eurycleides and Micion. The same is true of the years prior to 205 B.C. Certainly nothing occurred in the course of the war to indicate that Athens was bound to Rome rather than to Macedon. The city appears among the neutrals in 209 B.C., and Polybius (ix. 40. 1) expressly affirms its neutrality during this period. Philip did not molest Attic territory, nor did the fleets of Attalus and the Romans make their rendezvous in the Piraeus, as during the wars after 200 B.C. Niese, moreover, has suggested a reason for the inclusion of Athens among the allies of Rome (ii. 502, n. 4) ; *amicitia*, not *societas*, expressed the relation existent between Athens and Rome prior to 200 B.C. See Matthaei, *Class. Quart.*, 1907, p. 182 ff.

[3] They were still alive in 212/1 B.C. (Kirchner, *GGA.*, 1900, p. 453). On the other hand, they were already dead in 201 B.C. Pausanias (ii. 9. 4) simply mentions their reported poisoning after that of Aratus, who died in 214/3 B.C. (cf. Niese, ii. 472). The only clue for a closer determination of the time of their death is that involved in the tradition of their assassination by Philip. Their death would hardly have been accredited to him before his quarrel with Athens occurred. On the other hand, their place was already taken by Cephisodorus in 201 B.C. This being the case, we may, I think, venture to put the two archons, Nicophon and Dionysius, who, as Kolbe has again pointed out (*op. cit.* 90), precede 200 B.C. rather than follow it, and who, as Kirchner has shown (*GGA.*, 1900, p. 455 f.), are closely associated with Phanarchides (202/1 B.C. ?) in two of the three years vacant after 206/5 B.C. (*Priests of Asklepios*, 134), and preferably in the last two. Since Micion, the son of Eurycleides, has already succeeded to the priesthood of the *Demos and Graces* (Wilhelm, *Beiträge*, 79) in the year of Dionysius (203/2 B.C.?), his father's death had occurred previously. We may now make the further conjecture that it was in the first year of Micion's priesthood that the senate of Athens erected the altar to Aphrodite, the *hegemon* of the *demos* and to the Graces, of which the dedicatory inscription dated in the archonship of Dionysius was found in the *temenos* of the *Demos and Graces* (*IG.* ii. 5. 1161b). This would put the death of Eurycleides and Micion in 203 B.C.

have already given and discounted Polybius's appreciation of them.[1]   His is the only judgment of their work
that has come down to us from antiquity; for the
remark of Pausanias[2] that they were orators of some
influence with the people is begotten of ignorance.
Men who in this unsettled century obtained for their
country thirty years of liberty and peace, deserved a
better verdict.

It was inevitable that they should be misrepresented
in the *Memoirs* of Aratus, upon whose judgment of
their policy Polybius was dependent; and they were less
fortunate than the Spartan rivals of the Achaean in
that the history of Phylarchus on the period 273/2-220
B.C. has given us in Plutarch's *Lives* a sympathetic
account of Agis and Cleomenes, but has not impressed
itself upon our tradition in so far as it deals with Athens
and Athenian affairs.[3]   Since Phylarchus was an Athenian
by birth and probably a citizen of Naucratis by
adoption,[4] it is unlikely that he expressed disapproval of
the alliance of Athens with Euergetes; for he wrote
with candid partisanship and a direct appeal to the
emotions in the style which Duris of Samos had learned
of the Peripatetics.   He was not a scientific historian,
but he was apparently an interesting and an influential
one; and the same characterization may be made of his
contemporary, Ariston of Ceos, the representative of the
school of Theophrastus in the age of Eurycleides and
Micion.   Like his predecessor Lycon (†226/4 B.C.), he
was at best a popular scientist; for with him the
dominating interest was what had been the recreation
of the earlier masters.   He wrote a pamphlet entitled
Tithonus on Old Age, which Cicero embodied in his
Cato maior.   He developed to high perfection the art
of lecturing, in which he took Bion of Borysthenes as
his model; and he made a compilation of *Lives* of the
philosophers in the form of notes, documents—such as

---

[1] See above, vi. 241.   [2] ii. 9. 4.
[3] For Cleochares, the son of Bion of Cicynna, a melic poet honoured in Delphi
at the end of the third century B.C., see *BCH.*, 1894, p. 71.
[4] Köhler, *Rhein. Mus.*, 1898, p. 491, n. 1; Beloch, iii. 1. 493; iii. 2. 7, 8;
Wilamowitz, *Griech. Literatur*, 107.

the wills of the school-heads—and above all, anecdotes and gossip thrown together without regard to style or coherence.[1]

The Epicureans were of little significance at this time. For, apart from other drawbacks, the dissensions which had already hurt the other schools now infected the Garden, where individual ambition had been suppressed for a long time by the authority of the revered founder; and Hermarchus of Mitylene (271/0–*ca.* 240 B.C.) and Polystratus (*ca.* 240–*ca.* 210 B.C.) had been spared, apparently, anarchical competition from their pupils and colleagues. Now, however, the leadership of Dionysius of Lamptrae (*ca.* 210–180 B.C.) was contested by a certain Diotimus of Semachidae, and legal proceedings were necessary before his title to the school—and, what seems to have interested him more, its property —was recognized. The dispute was apparently grounded in the will of Polystratus and settled to the advantage of Dionysius, but of its details we know little or nothing, as is also the case with the subsequent fate of the disputants. They were seemingly all obscure natives of Athens, and it is doubtful whether the school—as distinct from the doctrines of its founder—had much public influence either at home or abroad at this time.[2] The Academy also suffered through the disadvantage of ineffective management followed by a long interregnum. For Lacydes, head since 241/0 B.C., withdrew from active service because of ill-health, according to one report in 224/3 B.C., but according to another in 216/5 B.C.[3] The school was, accordingly, left in charge of the *presbyters,* of whom Evander and Telecles were the most eminent members. What ensued we cannot determine precisely; but it seems probable that since the illness of Lacydes prevented him from really directing the institution, and his continuing to live prevented the appointment of a successor, at least both

---

[1] Gercke in P.-W. ii. 953 ff.

[2] Crönert, *Kolotes,* 81 ff., 181. Dionysius was at one time shut up in prison.

[3] For this incident see now Wilamowitz, *Hermes,* 1910, p. 406 ff., whose treatment has superseded the earlier literature.

Evander and Telecles and, perhaps, also other Academicians developed what were practically schools of their own.[1] Nor was this condition altered when Lacydes finally died in 206/5 B.C., for he simply left the Academy in charge of those who had conducted it during his retirement.[2] Why this was done and what subsequently happened we cannot say, but we have a hint that there was a schism in the school with which the name of Telecles has been connected.[3] In any case it was not till about 165 B.C. that Apollonius, the last of the *college* which took the management of the Academy in 206/5 B.C., died. Then, however, if not earlier, the long-lacked unity was restored to the school through the domination in it and accession to its headship of Hegesinus's brilliant pupil Carneades.[4] Up to this point we have been obviously dealing with a lot of petty men to whom it is no injustice to ascribe material motives. Hence it was doubtless not an accident that both Evander and Telecles were natives of Phocaea and that Hegesinus was born in Pergamum. In all probability the favour and subsidies of Attalus, the ruler of these cities, now formed the chief asset of the Academy, and a man's position in the school depended largely upon his ability to secure them.[5]

The weakness of the other schools served thus to elevate the Stoa, of which the head during this entire period was a man of indefatigable industry, unusual

---

[1] Thus in *IG.* ii. 385 (210/9 B.C.) we have reference to Εὐάνδρου σχολάς, while a certain Apollonius is defined by Apollodorus as Τηλεκλέους ἀκηκοώς (*Hermes*, loc. cit. 412).

[2] Philodemus, Column M (*Hermes*, loc. cit. 407), says: διαδόχους δὲ τούτους καταλιπὼν θν[ήσ]κει (Lacydes), whereupon follows a list of the *college*—Leonteus and Demon of Cyrene, Phaetes of Phocaea, Eubulus of Erythrae, and Eubulus of Ephesus, Moschion of Mallos, Evander and Telecles of Phocaea, and two or three others. The interregnum apparently involved two generations of scholars, since the *college* included later Hegesinus, a pupil of Evander, and Apollonius, a pupil of Telecles, whose names were apparently not in this list.

[3] Crönert, *Kolotes*, 75 ff.; Wilamowitz, *Hermes*, 1910, p. 408. The insertion of a side list of pupils in Philodemus's work, as well as his remark that somebody did not give the school to somebody else at his death because the latter had drawn off his pupils while he was alive, suggests a schism. The connexion of Telecles with it seems to me likely, though unproven.

[4] As Wilamowitz points out, Carneades may have been head in fact long before. Through the death of the last member of the *college*, he acceded to it formally. See below, vii. 300.

[5] It is possible that the progress of Carneades even was accelerated by the favour of Attalus and Ariarathes. See below, vii. 300.

power of work, and conspicuous logical endowment—
Chrysippus of Soli (231/0–*ca.* 206 B.C.).[1] He was not
meant for a court philosopher; hence he disdained a
call to Alexandria, refused to dedicate any of his many
writings to contemporary kings, and left it to the
Academicians to conciliate Pergamum. On the other
hand, he maintained and strengthened the tendency of
his school to work by example and precept upon the
youth of Athens; for he did not confine his teaching
to the regularly registered students, as his predecessors
had done, but gave free lectures in the open air in the
Lyceum.[2] In this way, perhaps, he brought it about
that an unusually large number of native Athenians
became his pupils.[3] Certainly he did not lack honour
in Athens; for the Athenians conferred upon him the
citizenship, which he also accepted, whereas Zeno had
refused it, and on his death they gave him a public
tomb in the outer, and a statue in the inner Cerameicus
beside those of Zeno [4]—an honour accorded, so far as we
know, to no other philosophers. In addition, another
statue of him was erected in the Ptolemaeum,[5] the new
rendezvous of the ephebes, which the Athenians were
decorating with plastic monuments at this time. Greater
recognition he could not have obtained from a king.
His interest in Athenian education, however, did not
make the Stoa less attractive to foreigners. Pupils
came to him from every quarter, but in particular from
Cilicia,[6] Syria, and Mesopotamia, where the superior
attractiveness of a philosophy was speedily perceived,

---

[1] von Arnim in P.-W. iii. 2502 ff.

[2] See above, iv. 185; Diog. Laert. vii. 185 πρῶτος ἐθάρρησε σχολὴν ἔχειν ὕπαιθρον ἐν Λυκείῳ.   [3] Crönert, *Kolotes,* 81.

[4] See above, iv. 186; Paus. i. 29. 15; Cic. *De fin.* i. 11. 39; Diog. Laert. vii. 7 (182); Wachsmuth, *Die Stadt Athen,* ii. 1. 261, n. 2; Judeich, *Topographie,* 319. The statue was a bronze statue by Eubulides II. It represented him *digitis computans.* Pliny, xxxiv. 88; cf. Milchhöfer, *Arch. Stud. H. Brunn dargebracht,* 37; Robert, P.-W. vi. 872 ff. The statue of Carneades erected subsequently in the inner Cerameicus was donated, not by Athens, but by King Attalus of Pergamum and King Ariarathes of Cappadocia (*IG.* ii. 3. 1406).

[5] Paus. i. 17. 2.

[6] The two following school-heads were Zenon of Tarsus and Diogenes of Seleucia on the Tigris, the so-called Babylonian—pupils of Chrysippus. The third was Antipater of Tarsus, and he had as his chief comrades, besides Mnesarchus and Dardanus of Athens, Boëthus of Sidon, Panaetius of Rhodes, and Apollodorus of Seleucia.

which, like that of Epicurus also,[1] satisfied the experiences of Greeks living in the Graeco-Oriental municipalities of the Seleucid Empire.

It was in these circumstances that Chrysippus, without whom, as the ancients said, there would have been
no Stoa, by fortifying the doctrines of Zeno against the
destructive criticism of Arcesilaus, made out of them
a logically defensible systematic philosophy, and by
emphasizing their popular basis and the cultural mission
of the school, qualified the Stoa to become the creed of
uncompromising republicanism.   It was henceforth the
intellectual support of men of political, moral, and
religious convictions.[2]

We are fortunate in possessing a description of Athens
under Eurycleides, broken and sketchy in character,
but unique, not only in the directness of the impressions
recorded and in the point of view taken—that of an
educated and intelligent stranger—but also in the
purpose subserved, which is to give a concise survey
of its attractions and drawbacks for the guidance of
prospective tourists and immigrants.   This description
is found in the sections devoted to Attica in the *Notes
on Greek Cities*, published by Heracleides the Critic
at about 205 B.C.[3]   Translated, it reads as follows :—

"Thence to Athens.   The road is pleasant, the land
all cultivated, the prospect inviting.   The city is everywhere dry, water being scarce ; and because of its age
the streets and blocks are irregular.   Most of the

---

[1] It is probably not an accident that Danaë, the daughter of Leontium and
Metrodorus, was the *confidante* of Laodice, the virile sister-wife of Antiochus II.
(Phylarchus, xii. *FHG*. i. *frg.* 23 in Athen. xiii. 593 B).   Other Epicureans high
in the service of the Seleucids were Philonides of Laodicea, and his son of the
same name, whose βίος has been recovered by the patience of Crönert from the
Herculanean rolls (*Sitz. d. Berl. Akad.*, 1900, p. 942 ff.).   He is said to have con-
verted Antiochus Epiphanes to Epicureanism.   He has been identified by
Köhler (*ibid.* 999 ff.) with the man of that name who received honours in
Athens both from the state and from the Eleusinian priestly *gene*.   Both
father and son and the latter's brother were given the Athenian citizenship.
For Epicureans with Alexander Balas see Crönert, *loc. cit.* 957.

[2] von Arnim, *Stoic. vet. frg.* ii. 1 ff. ; cf. P.-W. iii. 2502 ff. ; Kaerst,
op. cit. ii. 1. 136, notes.   It is hardly an accident that it was Chrysippus who
brought into prominence in Stoic thinking the political tendencies of man's
nature.

[3] For the text see *FGH*. ii. 254 ; *Geog. Graeci minores*, i. 97 ff., and
especially Kaibel, *Strena Helbigiana*, 143 ff.   For the date see below,
Appendix I.

houses are mean, the nice ones few. A stranger would doubt, on seeing it first, if this were really the renowned city of the Athenians. After a little, however, he would be convinced. An Odeum, the finest in the world; a notable theatre, large and excellent; a costly temple of Athena, far-visible (?) and well worth a visit, overhanging the theatre, the so-called Parthenon. It makes a great impression upon the spectator. An Olympieum, half finished but displaying the general plan. It would be the best if it were completed. Three gymnasia—Academia, Lyceum, Cynosarges—with grounds thickly wooded and grassy, schools of philosophers of every shade of opinion. . . . Banquets of all sorts, many snares and recreations of the spirit, unceasing shows. . . . But the living of strangers in close intimacy with one another (or with citizens) under the bond of common interests, by bringing into prominence what is pleasant, produces forgetfulness of their bondage : hunger[1] also is obscured by the shows and entertainments open to the public which cause forgetfulness of the taking of food. When strangers have brought their own supplies with them, there is no place like it for pleasure. . . . And the city has many other attractions besides; in fact, the towns near by are suburbs of Athens. . . .

" Its inhabitants, through throwing open its opportunities to any who happen along, are kind and helpful to all artists in acquiring a wide fame. The city is an admirable school of sculptors (?).

" Some of the inhabitants belong to Athens, others are Athenians. The Atticans are inquisitive gossips, insincere, prone to blackmail, and to pry into the private affairs of strangers. The Athenians are great-souled, simple in their manners, reliable custodians of friendship.[2] Some informers run about in the city, harassing wealthy visitors; but should the people catch them, theirs would be a hard fate. The genuine Athenians are keen art critics, and unwearying patrons

---

[1] See above, iii. 98, n. 1.

[2] For the distinction between 'Αττικοί and 'Αθηναῖοι—the *ktetikon* and the *ethnikon*—see Dittenberger, *Hermes*, 1907, p. 19.

of plays, concerts, and lectures. In a word, Athens
surpasses other cities in all that makes for the enjoyment and betterment of life, by as much as other cities
surpass the country.

" Be on your guard, most especially, against the
courtesans, lest you unwittingly meet a pleasant
destruction. As Lysippus says :

> "If you haven't seen Athenae, you're a stump.
> If you've seen, but not esteemed, you're an ass.
> But if, pleased, you hurry off, you're a mule.

"Thence to Oropus *via* Aphidna and the temple
of Zeus Amphiaraus, about a day's journey for a
pedestrian without baggage, uphill all the way ; but the
abundance of inns permits of frequent refreshments
and rests, and thus prevents the journey from wearying
travellers."

We find in this extract no hint of the existence in
Athens of judicial intimidation, or of danger from
bandits, such as we find in the *Notes* of Heracleides
on the Boeotian towns. There are no oddities in
Attica, like the veiled ladies with white robes and
coquettish purple sandals, golden hair, tall graceful
figures, and elegant Sicyonian manners, whom he met
at Thebes ; nor any of the mystery which already
haunted witch-ridden Thessaly. Athens is neither
lawless, provincial, nor romantic. She has high-
minded gentlemen and a waspish populace ; a constant
round of gaiety and ever-threatening hunger ; mean,
dusty streets and noble public buildings ; good taste
and critical acumen ; crowds of foreigners, busy schools
of philosophers, and, implicit in all else, the blessings
of peace.

Heretofore we have not met a single Roman in the
Athenian documents ; nor can a resident of Rome be
identified with any certainty in the Delian inscriptions
of the third century B.C.[1] But this does not imply

---

[1] Homolle, *BCH.*, 1884, p. 80 ff. A Ῥωμαῖος, Serdon by name, makes his
appearance as a wonder-worker at Delos (θαυματοποιός ; cf. Wilhelm, *Österr.
Jahreshefte*, 1900, p. 49b for a ῥωμαϊστής in 172 B.C.) in the archonship of
Phillis (262 B.C.). See *BCH.*, 1883, p. 114, and below, p. 264, n. 2.

that the Romans were unknown personally in Greece. We learn by chance of a Roman ship touching at Andros on its way to Syria in the middle of the third century,[1] and before it came to a close six or seven Italians[2] had made their appearance to our knowledge on the island of Delos. This means that citizens of Rome plied their business far beyond the limits of the Tyrrhenian, Ionian, and Adriatic Seas long before 200 B.C.—a clear warning that there was no restricting the political expansion of the Latin city to Italy and the Italian islands. Moreover, many exiles, especially from Magna Graecia and Sicily, had come to Greece to escape the Roman power,[3] while of their oppressors Hannibal had sold into slavery in Greece over two thousand during his stay in the peninsula.[4] Greece had thus ample opportunity to observe the characteristics of its subsequent masters. Nor did it lack instruction as to their political qualifications. The struggle with Pyrrhus was not carried on in secret, but, while it brought Roman patriotism, arms, and honesty into respect, it did not awaken Greece generally to the power of the Italian Confederation. Had not Pyrrhus been beaten by Carthage also? Had he not failed in repeated attempts to conquer Macedon? Still, the government in Alexandria had been impressed by the possibilities of diplomatic advantage to be gained by friendship with Rome, and in 273 B.C. Ptolemy II. sent an embassy to Rome and received one thence in turn, so that henceforth friendship (*amicitia*) existed between the two powers.[5] But few statesmen in the East were

---

[1] Plut. *Arat.* 12.

[2] Homolle, *BCH.*, 1884, p. 80 f. ; cf. *BCH.*, 1908, p. 81, where it is noted that a certain Minatus, perhaps an Oscan from Cumae, appears on Delos as early as *ca.* 220 B.C. He was probably a 'Ρωμαῖος, though not from the city of Rome ; and the same was, perhaps, the case with the two 'Ρωμαῖοι mentioned by Homolle, *Archives*, lxxiv. and li. (240–230 B.C.). See generally the article by Pernier, *s.v.* "Delus" in Ruggiero, *Dizionario epigrafico*.

[3] *IG.* ii. 5. 373e ; Teles, Περὶ φυγῆς (Hense[2]), 23.   [4] Livy, xxxiv. 50.

[5] Zonaras, viii. 6. 11 ; Dio Cass. *Frg.* 41 ; Eutrop. ii. 15 ; Livy, *Ep.* xiv. ; Justin, xviii. 2. 9 ; Val. Max. iii. 4. 9 ; Dion. Hal. xx. 14 ; cf. Niese, ii. 66, n. 2 ; Beloch, iii. 1. 686, n. 1 ; Lehmann-Haupt, *Klio*, 1902, p. 347 ; Colin, *Rome et la Grèce*, 32 ff. It was on the score of "friendship" with Rome that Philadelphus refused to loan two thousand talents to Carthage in the course of the First Punic War (Appian, *Sicel.* 1), and that Rome got grain from Egypt in 210 B.C. (Polyb. ix. 11 A ; Livy, xxvii. 4).

so calculating and far-sighted as Philadelphus; nor did
any other monarch adopt as a system the practice of
having others ready to pull the chestnuts from the fire
for him,[1] or need to watch Carthage as did a king who
had a hostile and covetous neighbour in Cyrene.[2]
There can be no thought that Rome and Alexandria
acted in concert in the diplomacy of 265 B.C.; still it
was not without significance that while the First Punic
War was being fought out in the West (264–241 B.C.),
Philadelphus and, after his death, Euergetes were engaged
continuously from 265 to 239 B.C. in a great struggle
with Syria and Macedon; for no Greek state was free
to intervene to prevent Sicily from falling a prey to
the barbarians. Nor shall we err if we assume that
the issue reached in the West had some effect in ac-
celerating the peace of 239 B.C. in the East. At any
rate, the threat of a Roman intervention in Acarnania
may have had something to do with bringing Demetrius
II. to its rescue even against his old allies, the
Aetolians;[3] while Euergetes seems to have had some
satisfaction in informing the Romans when in 241 B.C.
they proffered assistance against Seleucus Callinicus
that he had made a peace with him the year before.[4]
The East, moreover, could not fail to view with concern
the pretentions advanced by Rome of a right to protect
Ilium and the alleged colonies of the Trojan city.[5] These
incidents were all clear warnings that Rome had ceased
to be an Italian and had become a Mediterranean power,
warnings which could not be despised, since after 241 B.C.
Italy possessed the only first-class fleet on the entire
Mediterranean. Then followed the rapid and decisive
subjugations of Illyria in 229 and 219 B.C., which were
beyond a doubt timed with reference to the inability

[1] Cf. the remarks attributed to Antigonus Gonatas à propos of Aratus's visit
to Alexandria in 251/0 B.C. (Plut. *Aratus*, 15).

[2] Lehmann-Haupt, *Klio*, 1905, p. 384.

[3] See above, v. 198.

[4] Eutrop. iii. 1; Beloch, iii. 2. 453, n. 1. Whether this incident is a fact
or, as Niese (ii. 281) holds, an invention of the Roman annalists, the report of
it suffices to date the peace between Seleucus and Euergetes in 242 B.C., in
which year it also falls, according to Beloch's masterly treatment (iii. 2. 450 ff.)
of the entire problem.

[5] Suet. *Claud.* 25; cf. above, n. 4.

of Macedon to interfere, but which aimed simply to
safeguard the east coast of Italy by making Rome the
preponderant power in the Adriatic. The stress of
events was, however, stronger than the will of the
Senate; and what was a defence of Italy was at the
same time a limitation and a menace to Macedon, so
that the First Macedonian War ensued. Not this,
however, but the struggle in Italy revealed the great
vitality and vast resources of the Romans. By the
summer of 214 B.C. Philip expressed to the people of
Larisa in a letter, what his conduct of the war
abundantly disclosed, how profound was the respect
he entertained for the city on the Tiber "which had
increased its population, by taking up all elements
into its citizen body, to such a degree that it was able
to scatter almost seventy colonies up and down the
peninsula."[1] What was involved in the existence of
a state which could raise a navy of three hundred and
fifty ships of war, which could keep over one hundred
thousand unexcelled soldiers under arms for many
years at a stretch, and which held all Italy by a net-
work of forts despite the great victories of Hannibal,[2]
was immediately apparent to everybody in the East,
and subsequently all action there was taken in the
shadow of the war cloud which was gathering in the
West. The negotiations which were carried on between
209 and 207 B.C. show the horror which the brutality
of the Roman warfare had created in the minds of
the Greeks. It was even a greater asset for Pan-
hellenism than the Roman advance beyond the Adriatic
had been, but was powerless to destroy the particularism
which centuries of experience had ground into the Greek
character; and those who used the atrocity of a Roman
victory in 207 B.C. to draw the Aetolians from the flank
of Philip were the first to forget it when the king of
the Macedonians used his liberty to turn his army
against themselves.

Philip had made peace with Rome in 205 B.C., but
he could not be ignorant that at the end of the Second

[1] Ditt. *Syll.*[2] 239.　　　　[2] Beloch, iii. 1; Abschnitt ix. pp. 330 ff.

Punic War another settlement would be demanded. The crisis must not find him unprepared, and, accordingly, he seized with avidity an opportunity, which came in 203 B.C., of strengthening his position. The power of Egypt had long been on the wane. Its great empire had not been built up by diplomacy and money alone, as Euergetes found to his sorrow when his inability to send a fleet into Greek waters left Doson free between 224 and 222 B.C. to destroy the last vestige of Ptolemaic influence in the Peloponnesus. Without an invincible navy the empire of the Ptolemies was a mere shell incapable of withstanding any strong pressure, and had not the rebellion of Molon given Philopator time to raise an ample army from at home and abroad, the campaign with Antiochus III., which ended with victory at Raphia in 217 B.C., would probably have cost him his throne. As things went, his characterless reign, dissolute and extravagant life, and neglect of all the vital problems of national defence evoked native rebellions and brought Egypt into general contempt; so that when he died in 203 B.C.,[1] leaving the crown to his six-year-old son, his kingdom was ready for the spoilers. Accordingly, Philip and Antiochus formed a compact for the division of the Ptolemaic empire between them. Henceforth the eastern world was to have two great powers, not three, and the project entered into Philip's plans of crushing at the same time the Greek states and principalities which had leaned on Egyptian support—a more difficult undertaking, and, as it proved, impracticable without a much stronger fleet than Macedon possessed.

Athens came thus to suffer the consequences of the alliance negotiated with Euergetes in 224 B.C.; for the Acarnanian incident, out of which her war with Macedon issued, served merely to give Philip a decent pretext. Two young Acarnanians entered with the crowd into the hall of initiation at Eleusis. It is said that they did so unwittingly, but who can believe that any Greeks

[1] For the date see Holleaux, *BCH.*, 1906, p. 473, n. 2.

were ignorant of the place or of the profanity involved?
They were detected by the officials, haled before the
tribunals, and, after condemnation, were executed
according to the prescription of the sacred, but almost
obsolete, law of the Mysteries.[1] This harsh act created
great indignation in Acarnania—an ally of Macedon.
An expedition was organized, and Philip, on being asked
for assistance, sent a detachment of troops. The way
lay open through Thessaly and Boeotia, and the party
devastated Attica, and carried off booty of every kind.
Had the Acarnanians been alone the incident might
have closed at this point. The presence of the
Macedonian soldiers, however, showed the Athenians
that Philip was no longer ready to respect their
neutrality, and since the Macedonian fleet at about the
same time seized their ships of war,[2] they could not
regard the raid as an unauthorized act of reprisals. At
the moment they could not declare war; for Athens
was too weak to enter rashly into a struggle with
Macedon. There was much abasement and little
advantage, however, in maintaining domestic institutions which glorified the house of their enemy. The
most offensive of these was, doubtless, the pair of tribes,
Antigonis and Demetrias, which, because of convenience
in 289 and 266 B.C., and because of political considerations in 229 and 224 B.C., had outlived similar periods
of hostility to Macedon. Now they were abrogated,[3]
and a strange chance has preserved for us fragments of
the tablet published to make clear how the *demes*,
which had entered into these tribes, were redistributed
among the eleven *phylae* which were left.[4] This act

---

[1] Livy, xxxi. 14. 6 ; Polybius, xvi. 34. 5.

[2] Polybius, xvi. 26. 9. It is this incident to which, perhaps, Appian
(*Maced.* 4. 1) alludes when he makes part of Philip's army raid Attica and
besiege Athens in 201 B.C.   [3] *Priests of Asklepios*, 142 ff.

[4] *IG.* ii. 991 ; cf. von Schöffer, P.-W. v. 32, 38 ff. ; Tod, *Annual of the
British School in Athens*, 1902–3, p. 173 ff. ; *Priests of Asklepios*, loc. cit. Curiously
enough the abrogation of Antigonis and Demetrias is nowhere mentioned in the
ancient authorities. This is due, of course, to the loss of large portions of
Polybius. The two occasions on which it is natural to think that the disestablishment took place are (1) the reception of Attalus in 200 B.C. (Polybius, xvi. 25 ;
Livy, xxxi. 15 ; (2) the proscription of Philip in 199 B.C. (Livy, xxxi. 44).
The account given by Polybius of the occurrences of 200 B.C. is, however, most
explicit (see below, vi. 271), and no allusion whatever is made to an act of this

did not tend to conciliate Philip, but it did not constitute a *casus belli*, and it was still possible, in case of satisfactory explanations, to adjust matters amicably.

Before facing a war with Philip Athens needed to be sure of the support of her friends. Accordingly Cephisodorus, the successor of Eurycleides, and a convinced opponent of Macedon, at once called upon the Aetolians, Rhodians, Cretans, and upon Attalus and Ptolemy Epiphanes.[1] From Egypt most was expected, not simply because of the alliance which had been contracted with Euergetes, of which the present outrage was a consequence, but also because Egypt was itself face to face with a struggle against Philip. The Athenians in 201 B.C. still looked to Alexandria for the historic champion of Hellenic freedom. Only once in the course of the third century had a Ptolemy failed them altogether, and the financial or diplomatic support which Aratus, Cleomenes, and the Aetolians had received in their recent wars with Macedon was still fresh in their memory. Accordingly, trial must be made of Egypt, and if Egypt could not herself send assistance, Egypt had powerful friends to whom a word was sufficient. All the states approached by Cephisodorus guaranteed their aid, but particularly reassuring were the promises of the worried regents of Egypt, who were

---

sort. The report in Livy of the action taken in 199 B.C. is a free reproduction of the Athenian decree authorizing the proscription. Here, too, the absence of any reference to the setting aside of the two Macedonian tribes is very striking. Hence we conclude that they were abrogated on neither of these occasions. This conclusion is substantiated by the analysis of *IG*. ii. 991 ; for it is thereby made clear that Antigonis and Demetrias were set aside before Attalis was created. The only thinkable occasion prior to the declaration of war on Philip for such an act is the raid of the Acarnanians and Macedonians, and the seizure of the Athenian warships, crews and all, in 201 B.C. ; for Antigonis and Demetrias existed well down to the end of the century (they are still found in 208/7 B.C.; cf. Kolbe, *Ath. Mitt.*, 1905, p. 78). That they were actually abolished in 201 B.C. is finally demonstrated by the fact that the official order of the secretaries' tribes was broken at this point and first place in a new series given to Ptolemais, Ptolemy's tribe. Cf. also Kirchner, *Rhein. Mus.*, 1904, p. 297, and *GGA.*, 1900, p. 451, n. 1.

[1] Paus. i. 36. 5 f.   The ultimate source of Pausanias is obviously the Athenian laudatory decree for Cephisodorus ; cf. Niese, ii. 590, n. 1.   The communities in Crete were at this time all friendly to Athens.   This is obvious from *IG*. ii. 5. 385c, where as late as the fall of 202 B.C. (?) they are referred to in such a way as to imply their continued friendliness to Athens.   See above, v. 209.   In Cnosus, Gortyn, Cydonia, Hierapytna, Polyrrhenia, and Praesus coins on the Athenian pattern were issued in *ca.* 200 B.C.   Head, *Hist. Num.* 390 ff. ; cf. Hill, *Historical Greek Coins*, 134 f.

really too much embarrassed by their own domestic and
foreign affairs to give more than a passing thought to
the danger of Athens. Livy[1] tells us, however, that
they informed the Romans that they were willing to
assist the Athenians, in case the Romans were not.
What this meant was clear, seeing that at the same
time they implored Rome to save Egypt from the
attacks of Antiochus.

The course pursued by Athens was that followed by
the other states whom Philip menaced. They defended
themselves against him as best they could in 201 B.C.,
but, deprived of all hope of Egyptian assistance by
the great victory of Antiochus at Paneium[2] (spring of
200 B.C.), and unable to stand alone for any length of
time, they preferred to call in the western barbarians
rather than submit to the domination of one of their
own race ; and for that matter, there seemed to be
reason for the belief that the Romans were not
barbarians after all. Did they not claim Ilium as their
metropolis? As from the Aetolians, Rhodians, and
Attalus, so too from Athens, an embassy was despatched[3] to Rome to invite Roman interference.
Naturally, Cephisodorus was the leader of the Athenian
delegation.[4] The Aetolians were rebuffed—they had
deserted Rome in 206 B.C., but the request of the others
found ready acceptance. For since Philip and Antiochus
had formed their compact the battle of Zama had been
fought and Hannibal vanquished. Rome was full of
veterans, and, though the commons hung back, the
Roman senate was eager for action. Hence Athens was
assured of Roman assistance,[5] and a Roman embassy

---

[1] xxxi. 9.

[2] For the time see the careful determination of Holleaux (*Klio*, 1908, p. 267
ff.). The defeat of Egypt explains why Athens asked help of Ptolemy in 201,
and of Rome in 200 B.C.

[3] Livy, xxxi. 2.   [4] Paus. i. 36. 5 f.

[5] When the war was declared upon Philip the Athenians became σύμμαχοι
of Rome as well as φίλοι. It was, however, the relation of συμμαχία, as that
was understood in the Hellenistic world, rather than that of *societas* as this
was applied in Italy, which was contracted at this time by Rome and Athens.
The latter involved necessary military co-operation for ever, and by reserving
to Rome all diplomatic intercourse with foreign states, put the *socii* in the
position of the native principalities in British India. συμμαχία involved
co-operation for a specific enterprise, and was thus merely an intensified form

was sent in the early summer of 200 B.C. to deliver an ultimatum to Philip. He must leave Ptolemy and the neutral states alone, or count Rome among his enemies.

It was in Athens that the great war was finally begun. For the king of Pergamum, in person, and ambassadors from Rhodes met the Roman legates in the Piraeus, and from them learned that the Senate meant business. "Next morning," says Polybius,[1] "in company with the Romans and the Athenian magistrates, Attalus began his progress to Athens in great state. For he was met not only by all the magistrates and the knights, but by all the citizens with their children and wives. And when the two processions met, the warmth of the welcome given by the populace to the Romans, and still more to Attalus, could not have been exceeded. At his entrance into the city by the gate Dipylon the priests and priestesses lined the street on both sides : all the temples were then thrown open ; victims were placed ready at all the altars ; and the king was requested to offer sacrifices. Finally they voted him such high honours as they had never without great hesitation voted to any of their former benefactors : for, in addition to other compliments, they named a tribe after Attalus[2] and classed him among their eponymous heroes.

"They next summoned an ecclesia, and invited the king to address them. But upon his excusing himself, on the plea that it would be ill-bred for him to appear before the people and recount his own good services in the presence of those on whom they had been bestowed, they gave up asking for his personal appearance, but begged him to give them a written statement as to what he thought was the best thing to do in view of the existing circumstances. On his consenting to do

---

of *amicitia.* It might be renewed again and again on different terms (Ditt. *Syll.*[2] 930). It did not impair diplomatic freedom. It did not require general military assistance. See especially Matthaei, *Class. Quart.*, 1907, p. 182 ff.

[1] Polybius, xvi. 25, translated by Shuckburgh.

[2] Called *Attalis* and given the twelfth place in the official order. At the same time a *deme* was renamed *Apollonieis*, after Apollonis, the wife of Attalus. Suid., Steph. Byz., and Hesych., *s.v.* ; cf. Bates, *Cornell Studies*, viii. 52. Doubtless the priest (*IG.* ii. 1670) was common to the two new deities. See above, vi. 242, n. 3.

this, and writing the document, the magistrates produced the dispatch to the ecclesia. The contents of this written communication were briefly these : he recalled the good services he had done the people in the past ; enumerated the things he had accomplished in the existing war against Philip ; and lastly exhorted them to activity in this war, and protested that, if they did not determine resolutely to adopt this policy of hostility [1] to Philip in common with the Rhodians, Romans, and himself, and yet afterwards wished to share in the benefits which had been secured by others, they would miss securing the true interests of their country. As soon as this dispatch had been read, the people, influenced both by its contents and by their warm feeling towards Attalus, were prepared to vote the war : and when the Rhodians also entered, and argued at great length to the same effect, the Athenians at once decreed the war against Philip. They gave the Rhodians also a magnificent reception, and honoured their state with a crown of valour, and voted all Rhodians equal rights of citizenship at Athens, on the ground of their having, besides other things, restored the Athenian ships which had been captured with the men on board them."

As was proper, the Romans kept in the background in the Athenian assembly, since for them to publicly urge Athens to declare war would have been, at this stage in the proceedings, a breach of international law. That they lent their influence to the demands of Attalus and the Rhodians is, however, unquestionable. Nothing could make their quarrel with Philip seem more just than for them to appear in Greece as the champion of Athens. The Athenians, however, though they had received ample notification of Philip's hostile intentions, were still loath to abandon the policy of neutrality which had approved itself by thirty years of peace and prosperity. But the arguments of Attalus were unanswerable. The hesitation, moreover, concerned chiefly

[1] At this point, apparently, Athens was not yet a Roman ally. The decision to become such was under consideration at the moment.

the time of the declaration of war, and that the Athenians
had good reasons for holding back was obvious before
the year 200 B.C. came to an end.   For their country
lay fair in the midst of Philip's garrisons and allies,
and his answer to her challenge was to send Nicanor
with an army to ravage Attica.[1]   The Macedonian
troops advanced as far as the Academy, but there they
stopped ; for the Roman ambassadors came forth and
communicated to Nicanor the ultimatum of the Senate.
It daunted Nicanor to such a degree that he withdrew
from Attica : but upon Philip it had less effect ; for
to accept Rome's dictation would have been to abandon
without a struggle all that a disastrous defeat could
force from him.   Hence he preferred to fight with
Rome.   Athens he hoped to crush before the Roman
legions came to her assistance, but in this he was
mistaken.   The consul Sulpicius, who had crossed the
Adriatic in 200 B.C., planned to remain over winter in
Illyricum, but despatched his fleet and one thousand
soldiers to the Piraeus, where they were joined by four
Rhodian ships and troops sent from Pergamum (late
summer of 200 B.C.).[2]   The reinforcements were
urgently needed ; for not simply had Attica been
a prey to raids made from the land side, which was
entirely hostile, but the three open vessels which
formed the sole Athenian fleet[3] were quite unable to
protect the coasts from piratical expeditions organized
in Chalcis.   The allied forces had come simply to
defend Attica,[4] but during the late summer a squadron
was equipped and despatched stealthily to seize Chalcis
itself.   The surprise was complete, and the city was
taken and burned, but the fortress, although it commanded the Euripus, and thus had a great strategic
value, could not be held.   The attacking force, in fact,
was needed for the defence of Attica ; for when Philip,

[1] Polybius, xvi. 27.   Livy (xxxi. 16. 2) calls the general Philocles—a confusion, doubtless.

[2] Livy, xxxi. 14. 3 ; xxxi. 22. 4 ff.

[3] *Ibid.* 22. 8.   We are not told what happened to the four vessels (*naves
longae*) restored by the Rhodians to Athens, according to Livy, xxxi. 15. 5 ;
cf. Polybius, quoted above, vi. 272.

[4] For what follows see Livy, xxxi. 23-26.

who had started in person to the aid of Chalcis, arrived too late to catch the enemy, he crossed at once to Boeotia, and set out straight for Athens. With him were five thousand light troops and three thousand cavalry. He hoped to find the city unguarded, but a scout had warned it of his approach, and all through the night the generals and Dexippus, captain of the mercenaries, were busy making preparations for his reception. The troops from Pergamum were also in the city. Philip approached along the road which led from the Academy to the Dipylon gate, and, on seeing that his *coup* had failed, he drew up his forces and offered battle. The Athenians did not refuse. They pushed their men forward to the gate, and made a bold sally, but were repulsed with slaughter. Philip, thereupon, passed round to the south-east side of the city and encamped in the *gymnasium* and grove of Cynosarges. This was the part of Attica into which an invader seldom came, and near it were situated, besides Cynosarges itself, the Lyceum in which the Peripatetic school had its home, and many beautiful grave and other monuments both secular and religious. Philip had learned a lesson from the Roman way of waging war. The thing was a serious business, not a pleasant pastime, and every advantage must be pushed to the bitter end. Besides, he had lost all patience with the Athenians. Again and again Macedonian rulers had had Athens at their mercy, and every time they had stayed their hand. For twenty years Philip himself had done Attica no injury, though he could not have been unaware that her feelings were hostile. Now he showed no mercy,[1] and let his troops burn and destroy without religious or aesthetic discrimination. What did his wild Thracians know of the polite usages of Greek warfare? In the meantime, soldiers of Attalus from Aegina and Romans from the Piraeus succeeded in entering Athens. This

---

[1] Diod. xxviii. 7.   For the sack of the *gymnasia* see Wilamowitz, *Antigonus*, 267, n. 4.   After 200 B.C. the graveyard by the Eridanus seems not to have been used (Brueckner, *op. cit.* 26).

made an assault impracticable. Accordingly, Philip withdrew his camp three miles from the city, and, after making a futile effort to surprise Eleusis, in which Athenian soldiers were stationed, and to the rescue of which the allied fleet came, he evacuated Attica, and went to the Peloponnesus to attend the fall meeting of the Achaean League. He hoped to be able to induce the Achaeans to join him in the war, but, on failing to move them, he determined to make still another effort to master Athens. He ordered Philocles, his most distinguished general, to bring three thousand reinforcements from Euboea and meet him in Attica. Philocles entered over Mount Cithaeron and sent part of his men to devastate the open country, while with the rest he lay hidden near Eleusis, hoping to surprise the fort while its defenders were out protecting the fields. The stratagem failed, and an attack which he made on the walls was repulsed with slaughter. Philip now joined him, and the assault on Eleusis was renewed. But, when the allied fleet arrived bringing reinforcements from the Piraeus, Philip withdrew from Eleusis. He next despatched Philocles to engage the attention of the Athenians while he himself made a dash for the Piraeus. But he found the Romans from Eleusis there before him, and now joined Philocles before Athens. As he drew near to the city the defenders made a sudden sally with both infantry and cavalry, and a battle took place in the narrow space between the ruins of the Long Walls. The advance of Philip was, thereby, checked, and his project of capturing Athens had to be abandoned definitely. But the open country lay at his mercy, and Philip was in no merciful mood at the moment. He divided his army into two divisions, and proceeded in the most thorough fashion to burn and to destroy. All throughout Attica lay the little villages which had been for centuries the centres of an active and generous municipal life. They were adorned both with temples, shrines, altars, and sepulchres, and with statues, choregic monuments, and theatres. Many of them had seen no enemy in the lifetime of existing men, and on all sides, in olive and fig groves, in grain-fields and vineyards, were the evidences of a generation of peace. The crops and orchards were destroyed, of course : that was a good Greek custom. But Philip, as on the earlier occasion when he sacked the suburbs of Athens, destroyed the marble monuments also, not simply by tearing down the edifices, but also by breaking the stones into fragments. It was, in fact, a merciless act of vandalism, and hurt the cause of Macedon throughout the whole civilized world. Having thus vented his impotent rage on the priceless monuments of a time which comes only once in the life of a people Philip withdrew, and left the Athenians alone. Athens was saved. The approach of the Romans [1] had driven the king from his prey (fall of 200 B.C.).

In the summer of 200 B.C. Attalus and the Rhodians had been missionaries in winning over Athens to the war against Philip. The events of the autumn made the Athenians proselytes in their turn, and in the winter of the same year [2] they sent an embassy to urge the Aetolians to do as they had done. The Aetolians, however, had seen the consequences of the action of Athens, and were not much moved by the accusations of vandalism and sacrilege brought against Philip, for they were not wont to be over nice in such matters themselves. Accordingly, they preferred to await the movements of the Romans before attacking Philip, and the Athenian ambassadors had to return home without accomplishing their mission. At the same time the Athenians showed their hostility to Philip in a less worthy way. They solemnly decreed [3] that " all statues and pictures as well of Philip as of all his ancestors in both the male and the female line should be taken and destroyed ; that all holidays, *sacra*, and priesthoods instituted in his honour or that of his forefathers should

---

[1] An Athenian gentleman called a son born in those days Marcus (*IG.* ii. 446)—a tribute alike to the Italian republic and to Marcus Sulpicius, its consul for 201/0 B.C. A son of this Marcus was a boy of fourteen or fifteen in 153/2 B.C.

[2] Livy, xxxi. 29 f.   [3] *Ibid.* 44. 4-8.

be disestablished; that the places, too, in which a dedication or an inscription of this import had been placed should be accursed, nor should anything be erected or dedicated subsequently in them which by sacred right belonged in an undefiled spot; the state priests, moreover, in all prayers[1] for the people of Athens, its allies, armies, and fleets, should curse and execrate Philip and his children, his kingdom and all his forces on land and sea, the whole race and name of the Macedonians. An amendment was added that should any one subsequently propose a measure aimed at the public branding and infamy of Philip, the people of Athens would adopt it unanimously, but should any one move or put to motion a resolution against his ignominy or for his honour, he might be slain without redress. A final clause made valid against Philip all the decrees formerly voted against the Peisistratidae."[2] The Athenians thus carried farther the mutilation of public monuments begun by Philip; for the decree was at once put into effect. What value pertained to the works of art which were destroyed in this way we cannot say, but we are ourselves witnesses of the havoc wrought among the historical documents; for men were at once sent to chisel all allusions to the house of Antigonus the One-eyed from the tablets on which the chief memorials of Athenian public life during the third century B.C. had been inscribed. The act was symbolic of the passing of an old order; for at the same time the Macedonian age, with all its humiliation, suffering, and terror, was erased from the scroll of Athenian life. Henceforth the palimpsest was inscribed " Rome."[3]

---

[1] This act was probably rescinded in 197/6 B.C., since imprecations on Philip are lacking in the formulae of *IG.* ii. 417 (188/7 B.C.), cf. *IG.* ii. 440 (185/4 B.C.), where we should have expected them had they been still existent.

[2] For the obliteration of memorials of the Peisistratidae see the remarks of Wilhelm, *Beiträge*, 111 f.

[3] Of the following statement of Pausanias (i. 29. 14) nothing whatever can be made: φασὶ δὲ Ἀθηναῖοι καὶ Ῥωμαῖοις ὅμορόν τινα πολεμοῦσι πόλεμον στρατιὰν οὐ πολλὴν πέμψαι, καὶ ὕστερον ναυμαχίας Ῥωμαίων πρὸς Καρχηδονίους γινομένης τριήρεις πέντε Ἀττικαὶ παρεγένοντο.

CHAPTER VII

ATHENS UNDER THE TORY DEMOCRACY

Λητοΐδη, σὺ μὲν ἔσχες ἀλίρρυτον αὐχένα Δήλου,
κοῦρε Διὸς μεγάλου, θέσφατα πᾶσι λέγων·
Κεκροπίαν δ' 'Εχέδημος, ὁ δεύτερος 'Ατθίδι Φοῖβος,
ᾧ καλὸν ἀβροκόμης ἄνθος ἔλαμψεν "Ερως.
ἡ δ' ἀνὰ κῦμ' ἄρξασα καὶ ἐν χθονὶ πατρὶς 'Αθήνη,
νῦν κάλλει δούλην 'Ελλάδ' ὑπηγάγετο.

ARTEMON, *Anth. Pal.* xii. 55.

THE repeated invasion of Attica in 200 B.C. was only an anticipation of the main struggle. The great war itself swept across Greece at some distance to the north of Athens,[1] and the troops of the city seem not to have taken part in it. They doubtless had enough to do in defending their own frontiers; for until the winter of 197 B.C. the Boeotian League, to which Megara also belonged, as well as Corinth and Euboea, was fighting on Philip's side. Of course, there was no longer any question of conquering Athens; but the patrolling of a country exposed on so many sides was in itself a difficult task. Thus in the war on land Athens contributed little or nothing to the ultimate issue, and Livy[2] (Polybius) rather unkindly remarks that the Athenians fought with words, the Romans and Attalus with swords. The open vessels, moreover, which Athens sent to serve in the Rhodian squadron did nothing noticeable.[3] They dealt at best with pirates and plundering expeditions. The Piraeus, however, was the naval station of the allied fleets during the whole course of the war. Regularly, at the opening

---

[1] Niese, ii. 595 ff.; Kromayer, *Antike Schlachtfelder im Griechenland* ii. 3 ff.
[2] xxxi. 44.   [3] Ditt. *Syll.*[2] 264.

and close of every season,[1] the splendid harbour of
Athens was crowded with great battleships, and for
two winters a large part of the Roman or allied fleet
remained there. There were thousands of foreign
sailors to be found in Attica for months at a stretch ;
and, despite the admirable commissariat arrangements
of the Romans, it is not doubtful that the city was
obliged to make contributions to the support of the
crews. The Athenians were thus kept conversant with
all phases of the struggle, and the sense of direct
participation was enhanced by the presence in the city
at various times of the king of Pergamum, and the
Rhodian, Byzantine, and Roman commanders. Thus
in September of 199 B.C. Attalus was in Athens, and
had himself initiated into the Eleusinian Mysteries ;[2]
in the spring of 198 B.C. the Roman admiral, Lucius
Quinctius, the brother of Flamininus, came in person
to the Piraeus,[3] and at another time Erin of Byzantium
and three of his officers received the thanks and
hospitality of the Athenian state.[4] The Athenians,
furthermore, took an active part in all the diplomatic
business of the period. In 198 B.C. they sent an
embassy to the Achaeans to urge them to abandon
Philip and join the Romans.[5] They doubtless were
represented at the conference which was held at Nicaea
in the late fall of 198 B.C. ;[6] and to the fruitless peace
negotiations which were conducted at Rome in the
following winter they sent as agent their leading
politician Cephisodorus.[7] When Flamininus, incensed
at the assassination of five hundred Romans in Boeotia,
led a punitive expedition into that country in the
winter of 197/6 B.C., he announced his intention in
advance to the Athenians and the Achaeans, and, later,
these two peoples used their good offices to effect a
reconciliation.[8] During this same winter,—the battle
of Cynocephalae (197 B.C.) having forced Philip to

---

[1] Livy, xxxi. 45, xxxii. 16, xxxi. 47 ; cf. Niese, ii. 619.
[2] Livy, xxxi. 47.   [3] Ibid. xxxii. 16.   [4] IG. ii. 414.
[5] Livy, xxxii. 19-23 ; Appian, Maced. 6 ; Zonaras, ix. 16. 3.
[6] Niese, ii. 621, n. 4.   [7] Polybius, xviii. 10. 11.
[8] Livy, xxxiii. 29 ; Polybius, xx. 7. 3 ; Niese, ii. 646 ff.

yield,—like the others who had taken part in the
war, the Athenians placed their demands before the
Roman senate by a special embassy.[1] What they
claimed and how their claims were treated are equally
unknown, but it is probable that they asked for
damages and the restoration of their former insular
possessions, and obtained neither. Lemnos, at any
rate, was given its freedom,[2] not returned to Athens;
and to all appearances Delos, Imbros, and Scyros were
independent of the metropolis during the following
thirty years.[3] Roman diplomacy took a sharp turn at
this moment, and hence made the position of Rome's
sympathizers in many Greek states extremely difficult.
Not only did she grant favourable terms to Philip, but
she did so at the expense of the Aetolians, her most
valuable allies. The Greeks wished to reap the fruits
of the victory over Macedon : the Romans sought to
alienate Philip from his alliance with Antiochus of
Syria, with whom they had still to settle scores. The
aims of the two peoples were, in fact, quite different, and,
since the Romans had their way, and acted rather
cavalierly towards their allies, the parties in individual
Greek states which had used the existent hostility to
Philip as the means of bringing their cities into the
Roman alliance, were now required to turn face about,
or to abandon Rome. They did not abandon Rome,
for their domestic enemies forestalled them in seizing
upon that policy, but they lost credit with their con-
stituents, and the opposition leaders acquired more and
more influence. Thus is explained the zeal of the
Athenian government for Rome during the next few
years, and the strong popular sympathy several times
evinced for her adversaries.

The Aetolians and the Athenians had maintained

[1] Polybius, xviii. 42 ; cf. Livy, xxxiii. 24. The Athenians are not
mentioned specifically.
[2] Polybius, xviii. 48 ; cf. Livy, xxxiii. 35, xxxiii. 30.
[3] See Kirchner, *Berl. phil. Woch.*, 1909, p. 851 f. For Imbros see *IG*.
xii. 8. 51-53, and Fredrich, *Ath. Mitt.*, 1908, p. 109. For Scyros see *IG*. ii.
983, i. 67 (183/2 B.C.), and especially Fredrich, *IG*. xii. 8, p. 4. The islands
of Lemnos, Imbros, and Scyros were apparently in the hands of Antiochus III.
and Philip V. or Perseus during the greater part of this interval.

cordial relations with one another since 229 B.C., but when the former quarrelled with the Romans and the latter eulogized them and reproved their detractors, the representatives of the two peoples got into a sharp controversy (195 B.C.). Athens was accused publicly of abandoning the national cause, and of flattering the Romans with a view to her own profit.[1] As time passed, the situation became more and more critical. Rome had ostentatiously given the Greeks their freedom in 196 B.C., but she retained the "shackles of Greece," Demetrias, Chalcis, and Acrocorinth till 194 B.C. Their evacuation at that time, moreover, was a compromise which weakened seriously her military position, but which came two years too late to please the Greeks. All the while, the Aetolians carried on an agitation against the Romans, gave a head to the dissatisfaction which manifested itself in Greece, and negotiated with Antiochus of Syria with a view to breaking the ascendancy of Rome in the internal affairs of the nation. Differences of opinion on political matters were accentuated by grave differences of national character. The Roman and the Greek were at this time poles apart in customs and ideals. The one was self-repressed, rather haughty, and puritanical in his moral outlook; the other was expansive and cordial in manner, and discussion and controversy were to him the breath of life. The Greek was a born salesman. He loved to bargain, and held lying to be as integral a part of the game as bluff is of poker. To the blunt, practical Roman he appeared a talkative fellow. The Roman could not follow the niceties of his subtle dialectic, and wished to settle things without interminable speeches. To him, moreover, the Greeks were dishonest and untrustworthy, while his antique morality was equally offended by the emotional excesses of the masses and the free-thinking of the gentlemen. Accordingly, closer acquaintance did not tend to improve the

[1] Livy, xxxiv. 23. From *IG.* ii. 413 the conclusion has been drawn that Athens took part in the war waged by the Achaeans and Flamininus against Nabis of Sparta, but Wilhelm (*GGA.*, 1903, p. 793) has shown that this document belongs a century earlier.

relations between Greeks and Romans. Thus it happened
that in 192 B.C. Greece was seething with discontent,
and the Roman senate found it advisable to despatch
an embassy to answer the charges of the Aetolians,
discount the hopes put on Antiochus, and aid its
partisans in maintaining control of the government.[1]
At its head was Flamininus, the victor of Cynocephalae,
whose generous enthusiasm for Hellenic things did
much to lessen the shock occasioned by the clash of
two so divergent cultures. Among the Achaeans the
ambassadors found little to do, and they went in turn
to Athens, Chalcis, Demetrias, and Thessaly. Their
work in Chalcis and Demetrias[2] is significant for the
purpose and activity of the mission. Upon their
arrival, the Roman party gained a complete ascendancy,
and drove into exile the leaders of the opposite faction.
Thus Euthymidas was expelled from Chalcis and
Eurylochus from Demetrias. In Athens the opposition
had become dangerous, but Flamininus did not attempt
to break it up. At any rate, it was to Athens that
Euthymidas went, and it was from this city that he
started on the attempt made in the same year to regain
control of Chalcis. He could not have done this had
there not been a strong anti-Roman sentiment in Athens.
The government, however, was in safe hands. It was
made up of men who had been trained in the school of
Eurycleides and Micion. Micion, the son of Eurycleides,
belonged to it, as did Diocles of Erchia, Echedemus of
Cydathenaeum, and Leon of Aexone.[3] That is to say,
the families of wealth and social standing which had
taken hold of affairs in 232 B.C., and had formed
the new democratic party at that time organized,
sympathized with Rome. Accordingly, at the instigation of Flamininus, Athens sent a delegation to
the Panaetolicum of 192 B.C.[4] to make still one last

---

[1] Livy, xxxv. 31 ; cf. Niese, ii. 682.   [2] Livy, xxxv. 31. 37.
[3] Micion (Kirchner, *PA.* 10,186) heads the list of subscribers published in
IG. ii. 983. 8 (183/2 B.C.). His grandson of the same name appears in a
similar list nearly sixty years later (*IG.* ii. 1047. After 128/7 B.C.). For
Diocles see the *stemma* in Kirchner, *PA.* 4023 ; for Echedemus, *ibid.* 6165
and 6168 ; for Leon, *ibid.* 9108 and 8445.
[4] Livy, xxxv. 32.

effort to dissuade the Aetolians from their agitation in favour of Antiochus.   It prevented the Aetolians from declaring war without giving the Romans a hearing; but neither Flamininus nor the Athenians could delay long the rupture of relations between the two states.

Meanwhile, the opposition in Athens had become more dangerous.   The expectation that Antiochus would come to Greece to meet the Romans became gradually a certainty.   He must have a landing-place, and none was more suitable than the Piraeus; and, should his armament appear in its vicinity, it was to be feared that the anti-Romans would overpower the government and place this magnificent harbour at his disposal. The Roman senate had already sent a second com- mission [1] to aid Flamininus and his colleagues in their negotiations in Greece, and among them was Cato the Elder.   "Cato," says Plutarch, "spent a good deal of time at Athens. [2]   There is also," he continues, " an oration of his said to be extant which he spoke in Greek to the people; in which he expressed his admiration of the virtue of the ancient Athenians, and signified that he came with a great deal of pleasure to be a spectator of the beauty and greatness of their city.   But," remarks Plutarch, "this is a fiction; for he spoke to the Athenians by an interpreter, though he was able to have spoken himself; but he wished to observe the usage of his own country, and laughed at those who admired nothing but what was in Greek. . . . The Athenians, he says, admired the quickness and vehemence of his speech; for an interpreter would be very long in repeating what he expressed with a great deal of brevity; but on the whole he professed to believe that the words of the Greeks came only from their lips, whilst those of the Romans came from their hearts."   Certainly, there was much for the Roman ambassadors to do in Athens; for a certain Apollodorus [3] was making a determined effort to oust the friends of

---

[1] Plut. *Cato maior*, 12.   [2] *Ibid.* (Clough's translation).
[3] Probably not, as Niese suggests (ii. 694 n. 5), the κηποτύραννος (Diog. Laert. vii. 181; x. 25), whose headship seems to have fallen between the dates *ca.* 150 and *ca.* 120 B.C. See Crönert, *Kolotes*, 88.   It is, however, possible

Rome from the government. He doubtless spoke in the name of Antiochus, and in addition to exploiting the political situation and enlarging upon the injustice done the Aetolians, the hatred of the Greeks for Rome, and the imminence of a general secession to the Seleucid king, he inflamed the city population by holding out the prospect of their receiving magnificent gifts from Asia.[1] A tumult thereupon arose, and the government, finding itself unable to master the situation unaided, summoned the commissioners—not only Cato,[2] but also Flamininus. Their coming, which probably coincided with the arrival of king Eumenes of Pergamum[3] and an imposing fleet, overawed the opposition, and, on the suit of Leon of Aexone, Apollodorus was condemned and driven into exile. Still, the pro-Romans had been found in a minority, and further precautions were shown to be necessary. Hence a garrison of five hundred Achaeans was placed in the Piraeus.[4] Athens had thus been drawn against her will into the vortex of the world's politics, and with the same result as on every earlier occasion since Chaeronea — the loss of political initiative and the imposition of a foreign will upon the domestic activity of the people.

Notwithstanding the precautions taken by the Romans, it is clear from the facility with which Antiochus became master of Chalcis when he came to Europe, that, had he chosen Athens as his base of operations, he might have possessed himself of it without difficulty. He preferred Chalcis, however, and Athens suffered from his proximity in 192 B.C. until the Romans arrived. The fleets of the king were in command of the sea, and interrupted the commerce of the Piraeus; and probably the seeding operations were

that he is referred to in the following epigram of Phaedimus (*Anth. Pal.* xiii. 2; cf. below, 287, n. 2):

Καλλίστρατός σοι, Ζηνὸς ὦ διάκτορε,
ἔθηκε μορφῆς ξυνὸν ἥλικος τύπον·
Κηφισιεὺς ὁ κοῦρος· ᾧ χαριείς, ἄναξ,
'Απολλοδώρου παῖδα καὶ πάτραν σάω.

[1] Livy, xxxv. 50; cf. Niese, ii. 694.
[2] Accepting Niese's conjecture; ii. 694 n. 4.
[3] Livy, xxxv. 39.
[4] *Ibid.* xxxv. 50.

suspended in many parts of Attica.[1]   Relief came in the
spring of 191 B.C., when the arrival of the Roman consul
in Thessaly forced Antiochus to concentrate his troops
at Thermopylae; and the appearance of Aulus Atilius
with the Roman fleet in the Piraeus reopened the
adjacent waters to Athenian enterprise.   At this time
the Roman admiral was too weak to attack the fleet of
Antiochus.   When, however, the rout of the Syrian
army at Thermopylae paralyzed for a moment the naval
operations of the enemy, Atilius was able to surprise a
fleet of transport ships, sink some of them, and bring
others of them back with him into the Piraeus.   The
stores thus acquired were used to relieve the distress of
the Athenians and the other allies of Rome in these
parts.[2]   Later in the same year (191 B.C.), the successor
of Atilius, Gaius Livius, and the whole armament of
Rome arrived, and eighty-one great decked ships and
innumerable small craft and transports anchored in the
Piraeus.[3]   Athens had seen no such fleet since the time
of Antigonus Gonatas.

With this fleet the war was carried into Asia, and
Athens remained only a half-way station for the line of
transport ships which brought provisions from Italy and
Sicily for the thirty thousand Roman sailors in service
against Antiochus.[4]   It was sometimes a port of rendezvous for detached squadrons of the allied fleet, and
on one occasion[5] the Athenian undecked vessels were of
service in forwarding the third Roman admiral Lucius
Aemilius Regillus, to his command in Samos; and after
the war was over, the Roman fleet under Quintus Fabius
was concentrated in the Piraeus before returning to Italy.[6]
In Europe the war with the Aetolians detained the
Romans, and, accordingly, Athens despatched Echedemus
to solicit the two Scipios, who had been chosen by Rome
for the decisive campaign of 190 B C., in the interest of
their old friends and allies.   The Scipios welcomed the
intervention, and through Echedemus arranged for an

---

[1] This results from the need of distributing grain noted below, n. 2.
[2] Livy, xxxvi. 20. 7; Appian, *Syr.* 20.
[3] Livy, xxxvi. 42. 7-8.   [4] Niese, ii. 728 f.
[5] Livy, xxxvii. 14.   [6] *Ibid.* xxxviii. 39.

interview with the Aetolians. The terms proposed by
Rome being unacceptable, Echedemus talked matters
over with the council of the League, and the Romans
were asked for better conditions. When, however,
it appeared that the right to modify the demands
rested with the Roman senate, not with the Scipios,
Echedemus persuaded the Aetolians to beg for a truce
of six months. The Scipios at once acquiesced.[1] It
was an advantage to the League ; for the terms could
hardly be made worse, and in the meantime the war in
Asia must end in one way or the other. It was an
advantage to the Romans, in that they got a free hand
to fight in Asia. The real harm fell upon Antiochus,
who in the crisis found himself unaided by his most
zealous allies. In this way, then, the intervention of
Athens proved a valuable service to Rome, and it was
rendered without discredit to the city, seeing that
Athens was under no obligations to Antiochus. The
calculations of the Aetolians were faulty. They had,
indeed, respite from war till the battle of Magnesia
(190 B.C.) destroyed the power and prestige of the
Seleucids ; but the Roman senate would not abate one
jot or tittle of its former demands, and in 189 B.C. the
new Roman consul and all his Greek allies made fierce
and uninterrupted assaults upon Aetolia. The defence
of the League was not the least worthy among the
military achievements of the Greeks, and the Roman
consul, after a long and fruitless siege of Ambracia, had
come to respect fully the prowess of his foemen when
the Athenians, supported by the Rhodians,[2] again intervened to save their friends from destruction. The
consul agreed to a peace on very reasonable conditions,
but the Roman senate had to ratify it, and to effect
this the Athenians and Rhodians joined the Aetolians
in an embassy to Rome. We do not wish to over-
emphasize the influence of the speech delivered by the
Athenian, Leon of Aexone,[3] before the Roman senate ;
for with the same merciless logic displayed in all its

[1] Polybius, xxi. 4-5 ; Livy, xxxvii. 6. 4 ff.   [2] Polybius, xxi. 29 ff.
[3] *Ibid.* xxi. 31, 6-16. For the name, which is corrupt in the MSS., see
Kirchner, *PA.* 9108. Polybius gives a summary of Leon's speech.

dealings in Greece the Roman aristocracy had come to the conviction that their next struggle must be with Macedon, and that the Aetolians might serve them again as they had served them in their first two wars in Greece. There were thus reasons of policy in favour of clemency towards the League; but we need not on that account disbelieve the affirmation of Polybius that it was Leon's eloquence which finally convinced the Roman senators.[1]

The decisive victory of the Romans, both at Cynocephalae and at Magnesia, secured to the Athenian government a long and altogether unprecedented tenure of power. The men in charge of affairs, as we have already seen, came from the rich agricultural class. Country squires with excellent studs, they yet had a taste for polite literature, and patronized Phaedimus,[2] Artemon, and others of the fashionable epigrammatic poets. Aristocrats in feeling, they revived the ancient practice of decorating their family grave-plots with expensive monuments,[3] and used the quasi-monarchical privilege of putting their names upon the coins of the city.[4] They were, beyond doubt, the most wealthy men

---

[1] ὁ μὲν οὖν Ἀθηναῖος ταῦτ᾽ εἰπὼν ἔπεισε τὴν σύγκλητον διαλύεσθαι πρὸς τοὺς Αἰτωλούς.

[2] *Anth. Pal.* vi. 271. This is an epigram written by Phaedimus on the birth of a son to Leon and Themistodice, his wife. The identification is due to Kirchner, *Hermes*, 1893, p. 143, n. 2. The verses, which are worth quoting, if for nothing else, because of the rarity of Athenian poetry extant for this time, are as follows :—

"Ἄρτεμι, σοὶ τὰ πέδιλα Κιχησίου εἵσατο υἱός,
    καὶ πέπλων ὀλίγον πτύγμα Θεμιστοδίκη,
οὕνεκά οἱ πρηεῖα λεχοῖ δισσὰς ὑπερέσχες
    χεῖρας, ἄτερ τόξου, πότνια, νισσομένη.
Ἄρτεμι, νηπίαχον δὲ καὶ εἰσέτι παῖδα Λέοντι
    νεῦσον ἰδεῖν κοῦρον γυῖ᾽ ἐπαεξόμενον.

For *Anth. Pal.* xiii. 2, which is also by Phaedimus, see above, vii. 283, n. 3. It is misdated by Kirchner, *PA.* 8169. Echedemus of Cydathenaeum appears in *Anth. Pal.* xii. 55—an epigram attributed to Artemon which is quoted in the title of Chapter VII. (cf. Kirchner, *Hermes*, 1893, p. 143, n. 2), and also in xii. 124, which is likewise attributed to Artemon (Reitzenstein, P.-W. ii. 1446). See also in this general connexion the epigram from the base of a statue of Philtera published in *IG.* ii. 3. 1386.

[3] See Schrader, *Jahrb. d. Inst.*, 1906, p. 75. Holleaux (*Acad. inscr. C.R.*, 1904, p. 732) mentions the discovery in Delos of a grave-monument, like those of the fourth century B.C. from the Dipylon cemetery, which was left unfinished in the artist's studio, possibly in 88 B.C.

[4] Sundwall, in his *Untersuchungen über die attischen Muenzen*, has given us the most thorough treatment of the Attic coins inscribed with the names of

in the state. So far as they had opposition at all, it came from the proletariat, but the advocacy by the mob of the cause which had lost in 190 B.C. guaranteed to its opponents the support of the Roman senate. Consequently, the families which dominated Athens at 190 B.C. were still most influential there fifty years later. Leon of Aexone was prominent in public matters in 171 B.C., and twenty years afterwards we find his grandson occupying a conspicuous charge conferred by popular election.[1] The documents of this whole period fairly bristle with names which were hereditary in certain of these families: Diocles and Dromeas, Draco and Habron, Leon and Cichesias, Echedemus and Mnesitheus, and Eurycleides and Micion.[2] As a matter of fact, Athens was governed by an aristocracy, but it was a liberal aristocracy; and its ascendancy was due to its astuteness, not to special privileges; to its popular spirit, not to foreign assistance. Its traditions were purely democratic, not, as in 301 and 276 B.C., derived from an aristocratic *milieu*. This is demonstrated most clearly by a decree of the year 140 B.C. The man who moved it, in urging the claims of a magistrate of Troezen upon Athenian courtesy, cites the fact that the state had granted its citizenship to one of his ancestors. He had been crowned in the time of a democracy, and no less a liberal than Stratocles of Diomeia had presented the petition for citizenship to the popular assembly.[3] The inference is thus manifest that the political ideals of the people in 140 B.C. were found in radical governments of the days of the *diadochi*. This democratic spirit was an

---

mint magistrates. Prior to *ca.* 196 B.C. the Peisistratids alone had put their names on the Athenian coins (*Corolla numismatica* in honour of Head, 1 ff.). The innovation of *ca.* 196 B.C. was lessened by the use of monograms during the preceding thirty-three years.

[1] *IG.* ii. 448, 1047; cf. Kirchner, *PA.* 9109.

[2] See Kirchner, *PA.* 4023, 8445, 6165, 5966, and the new data in Sundwall's *Nachträge zur Prosopographia Attica.*

[3] *IG.* ii. 5. 458*b* [καὶ] διὰ [τ]αῦτα ἐν τῇ δημοκρατίᾳ στεφανωθεὶς - - ὑπὸ τοῦ δήμου χρυσῷ στεφάνῳ καὶ πολιτεία[ν λαβὼν κατὰ τὸ] ψήφισμα, ὃ Στρατοκλῆς Εὐθυδήμου Διομεεὺς εἶπ[εν, ἑαυτῷ τε] καὶ ἐκγόνοις διεφύλαξεν βεβ[α]ίαν καὶ ἀληθινὴ[ν τῷ δήμῳ] τὴν εὔνοιαν· ἐπέδειξεν δὲ ['Ονασος τὸ ψήφισμα τοῦ δήμου] ἐν τῷ μητρῴ ω(ι) κατ[ατεθειμένον τὸ περὶ αὐτοῦ].

important heritage for an aristocratic government, and it distinguished that which Eurycleides and Micion had established from all its predecessors. The institutions of democracy remained pretty much as they had been determined in 229 B.C. The civil offices were given by lot, yet the gentry ordinarily filled them. The military and *leiturgical* officers were elected by show of hands, yet the successful candidates were regularly men of means and social standing. The terrors of a judicial audit remained, but they did not deter the rich from accepting public charges, nor is there anything in the documents of this entire period to suggest a tendency to regard state offices as anything but a distinction. The situation in Athens was in these respects like that in the Roman municipalities in the first and second centuries A.D., unlike that of the long age which followed the murder of Alexander Severus. And the resemblance goes farther still. The offices were honourable, and were coveted by the ambitious, but they were costly to their incumbents, and hence were ordinarily out of the reach of the poor.[1] Of this we have abundant evidence, not simply in the names of wealthy men found in the lists of magistrates—the same parties head subscription lists —but also in the general expectation that officials should use their private fortunes for the conduct of sacrifices, shows, and embassies, in the repair of edifices[2] and the payment of subscriptions, and, in fact, in meeting the fees which were attached to the tenure of certain magistracies. Of course, the burden did not fall with equal weight upon all the offices. The petty magistracies, which brought little or no distinction, doubtless required no expenditures, and the salaries paid more than compensated for the time spent. This was true of the senate, whose members, six hundred in number, received pay at the rate of one *drachma* per

[1] Stob. 84. 7=iv. 27. 6, p. 657, from which appears the financial burden involved in the *gymnasiarchia*. For the time of the incident see Wilamowitz, *Hermes*, 1910, p. 393. Since the *gymnasiarch* was at this time an elected magistrate, not, as prior to 310 B.C. (?), the administrator of a *leiturgy*, the explanation of the passage given by Wilamowitz is incorrect.

[2] To this time in all likelihood belong the repairs referred to in *IG*. ii. 982 ; cf. 'Εφ. 'Αρχ., 1909, p. 271, and above, vi. 237, n. 2.

day,[1] and also of the jury courts. Juries were still
impanelled of as many as five hundred and one persons,
who, doubtless, were paid like the senators. But the
archons, generals, *hipparchs, phylarchs, epimeletae,
gymnasiarchs*, and, above all, the *agonothetae* had to
make large personal outlays in order to perform their
duties creditably. This was the way in which the
aristocracy paid for the honours it enjoyed almost as
special privileges.

The expenses were nowhere so great as in connexion
with the games, which were now, as ever, the most
brilliant occasions in the social life of the city. The
most important festivals were four in number: (1) the
Dionysia, celebrated annually, though comedies were
put in the contest only once every third year; (2) the
Eleusinia, accompanied by games every second year
only, and by notable games, like (3) the Panathenaea,
and (4) the Ptolemaea, only once in every four years.
The Dionysia had been under the charge of the archon
until 310/9 B.C., but it was now, as were the Panathenaea
and the Eleusinia,[2] under that of specially elected
agonothetae, while commissioners, over sixty in number
in the only known instance, conducted the Ptolemaea.
The uniqueness of these four festivals consisted in that
they were international in their patronage, the first
three from inherited right, the fourth because of the
political and commercial relations of Athens with the
dynasty in whose honour it was instituted. To them
came visitors from every corner of the world, and there
was no Attic honour more coveted, and no greater
distinction in the gift of Athens than the announcement
at these four festivals of services rendered to the
commonwealth.

The most important part of the Dionysia was the
contest of new tragedies. The comic contest was now
triennial,[3] and the cyclic choruses had disappeared long
since.[4] Old plays, a tragedy of the fifth century B.C.

---

[1] *IG.* ii. 444. 15, 445. 10, 446. 12. The *agonothetes* gave καθέσιμον to the 600
senators for one or both days of the Theseia.   [2] *IG.* ii. 985.
[3] See Reisch, *Zeitschr. f. d. österr. Gymnasien*, 1907, p. 299, n. 2.
[4] Wilamowitz, *GGA.*, 1906, p. 614, n. 1.

and a masterpiece of the New Comedy, preceded the presentation of original compositions. How often the tragedies were put in competition and how many poets competed, we do not know, but the comedies were five or six in number. The strife was not between play and play, but between poet and poet and actor and actor; and for the dramatist who composed the plays, and the actor who performed his part best, the state, or the *agonothetes*, provided prizes. Many names of actors and playwrights have come down to us, but of their work, little or nothing.[1] From the titles of the plays, however, the inference is warranted that this period of dramatic activity was reminiscent.[2] Accident has acquainted us chiefly with the celebrities of the comic stage, but to contemporaries the greater interest attached to the tragedians—to the fresh productions of living nobodies, moreover, and not to the nobler creations of an age and spirit gone past recall.[3]

The Dionysia recurred annually, and it was the musical contest *par excellence*. The others were first of all athletic. The Ptolemaea came in the first year of every Olympiad,[4] the Eleusinia in the second and the fourth, and the Panathenaea in the third, so that the Athenians had two international festivals every year. We know nothing about the composition of the Ptolemaea, and next to nothing about that of the Eleusinia.[5] The Great Panathenaea included a musical fête at this time also,—contests among rhapsodists, soloists accompanied by the lyre or the flute, lyrists, flute-players,—but this we know by inference,[6] not by positive evidence. On the other hand, chance has brought it about that we are better acquainted with the athletic contests at the Panathenaea in the second century B.C. than at any other time—chance, and the unusual brilliancy lent to the celebrations by the participation in them of foreign

---

[1] Wilhelm, *Urk. dram. Aufführ.* 68 ff., 134 ff.

[2] Foucart, *Jour. des Savants*, 1907, p. 550.

[3] It was at the contest of new tragedies that public proclamations were made.

[4] See the references given above, vi. 242, n. 4.

[5] See *BCH.*, 1907, p. 435, for a few new details.

[6] From *IG.* ii. 965 ; cf. above, ii. 57.

kings and noblemen.[1]   The gymnastic events preceded
the *hippic* and alone consumed two days.   Boys, youths,
and men competed in succession.   To the boys were
open long-distance and short-distance races—the one
and one-half mile run and the sprints of four hundred
and two hundred yards—as well as boxing and wrestling,
and a contest in which these two arts were combined.
The youths substituted for the long run an event in five
parts—race, long jump, and contests in spear-throwing,
discus-throwing, and wrestling.   The men had all those
of the boys and youths, and, in addition, the one-half
mile run and the race in heavy armour.   There were
thus twenty events in all.   The competitors were
entirely professionals, men from all quarters who went
from one field-day to another, and made their living
from the prizes.   These consisted in each case at the
Panathenaea of a beautiful vase,[2] and, in addition,
amphorae of oil, which differed in number according to
the importance of the event.   Few first prizes went to
native Athenians, and of these the majority were secured
in the rough and tumble fight, in which the catch and
the strike were both permissible.   There was, doubtless,
little that was edifying or ennobling in the gymnastics
of the second century B.C.[3]

Just as the entire festival had its consummation in
the magnificent procession, in which the whole people
went through the city to the Acropolis bearing a rich
new robe for the goddess Athena, so the games reached
their climax in the horse and chariot races, to witness
which the populace streamed forth from the city, the
Piraeus, and the country villages to the flat, low-lying
tract east and north of the harbour where the *hippodrome* was located.[4]   This was the occasion when the

---

[1] *IG.* ii. 966 ff. ; cf. Wilhelm, *Ath. Mitt.*, 1905, p. 219. For the interpreta-
tion of these documents see A. Mommsen, *Feste d. Stadt Athen*, 69 ff. ; Martin,
Les Cavaliers athéniens, 228 ff. ; E. N. Gardiner, *Greek Athletic Sports and
Festivals*, 229 ff.

[2] The archaizing, black-figured vase of clay was not given after 310/9 B.C. (see
above, ii. 56, n. 4) ; but there seems to have been some kind of a substitute for
it (*Klio*, 1908, p. 348).

[3] E. N. Gardiner, *Greek Athletic Sports and Festivals*, 146 ff.

[4] The *hippodrome* is mentioned in connexion with the *hipparch* for 222/1
B.C.—the Panathenaic year—in 'Εφ. 'Αρχ., 1897, p. 43.

kings of the East and the princes of the West displayed
to the admiring gaze of the assembled multitude their
magnificence and their enthusiasm for Hellenic sport.
In *ca.* 178 B.C. the Attalids—not King Eumenes alone,
but his three brothers as well—emphasized the *acme* of
their wealth, power, and culture by entering horses and
winning prizes in four distinct events.   Twelve years
later Mastanabal, the son of King Massinissa and father
of the infamous Jugurtha, gained a victory with a pair
of colts; and at the same time the colt entered by
Ptolemy Philometor I., the older of the two brothers at
that time ruling Egypt, won first place in its class.   A
melancholy interest is lent to the "Derby" of 162 B.C.
in that two victories were won by the boy-king of
Syria, Antiochus, the son of Antiochus Epiphanes, at
about the time that his cousin Demetrius, freed from
detention in Rome by the help of the historian Polybius,[1]
was planning his dethronement and murder.   These are
the most illustrious among the known victors.   Others
came from Athens, Cyprus, Cyrene, two Antiochs and
two Laodiceas, Sidon, Alexandria, and Myndus in
Caria.   The most frequent victors of all were Polycrates
the Argive, and his daughters Zeuxo, Eucrateia, and
Hermione.   The man, like a Hebrew patriarch, had
betaken himself with his family and all his possessions
to Egypt at about 222 B.C.   He had contributed to
Philopator's victory over Antiochus III. at Raphia in
217 B.C., and in reward had obtained a prominent
position in the Egyptian court, and later the governor-
ship of Cyprus.   In 196 B.C. he returned to Alexandria,
and shortly afterwards became practically grand-vizier
of the kingdom.   From 190 to 178 B.C. the name of
Polycrates (or of his daughters) is never absent from our
list of Panathenaic victors.

The gentlemen of Athens who had stables of their
own were completely outclassed in the general competition.   They were not, on that account, prevented
from making a display of their horsemanship.   They
simply arranged to give the great event an appropriate

---

[1] Polybius, xxxi. 11 ff.

setting. They placed before it a contest open, in part
to all citizens, in part to cavalry officers, and in part to
knights alone, and after it a great half parade, half
contest of citizens with race horses, war horses, war
chariots, and race chariots. The most distinctive feature
of the opening exercises was the double race of chariot
and sprinter. The owners of the horses, often elderly
squires, held the reins; the sprinters leaped in and out
of the chariots, and at the end ran in competition to the
goal. The larger the number of foreign entries, the
more the Athenians strove to display their local versa-
tility and pomp; and when events were once admitted
it was difficult to dislodge them: hence the tendency
was for the fête to grow more and more elaborate as
time went on. Probably no Athenian official had more
arduous, expensive, and distinguished functions to
perform at this time than the *agonothetes* of the Great
Panathenaea.

Horse racing was expensive, and the prizes were
never sufficient to enable any one to maintain a stud.
Hence this was the sport of the rich. Ordinary athletics
had fallen into the evil hands of professionals, and
whenever the competition was thrown open to all,
amateurs had little or no chance to win. This was the
case at the Panathenaea, and, in a minor degree, at the
Theseia also. This was one of the annual parochial
Athenian festivals to which foreigners rarely came.[1]
Yet the events open to adults were won by persons
whose insignificance proves their trade. However, the
main interest of the Theseia was not fixed in their strife.
The festival belonged to the young gentlemen of Attica,
and through it a healthy interest in manly sport was
fostered among the good families of the country. The
field-day was, doubtless, a great fashionable event. The
aristocracy went to it to see their sons run, box, leap,
wrestle, ride, and fence with boys and youths of their
own age and station. The ephebes turned out and
entered the competitions, and had rôles of their own
to play. The Theseia was, furthermore, the occasion of

[1] *IG.* ii. 444 ff. ; cf. A. Mommsen, *op. cit.* 295.

athletic competition among the cavalry and the cavalry officers.   Besides the chariot races there were races of mounted horses, and the richly caparisoned chargers gave colour and animation to the scene.   In addition, there were combats with arms of various sorts—mock duels between lads of twelve, fifteen, and eighteen years of age, not youthful gladiators, but scions of the noblest Athenian families.   Nor was the double race of chariot and sprinter lacking.   Such were the games proper. They were preceded by events not less important.   On the preceding afternoon came a review of the troops. Detachments of the Athenian volunteers, of the foreign residents organized in national units, and of the cavalry competed for prizes, both for general appearance, and for military equipment.   This was followed by contests between rival heralds and rival trumpeters, and, then, when the night drew on, by the wonderful torch races for which Athens was famous.   Boys from fashionable *palaestrae*, detachments of ephebes, groups of young men from the Lyceum, and, after 154/3 B.C., squadrons of regular or light-armed cavalry raced in the darkness from the Academy to the Dipylon gate—a distance of two-thirds of a mile—each individual carrying a torch which he strove to bring still lighted to the goal.[1]   The one who arrived first was victor, but he was counted out if his torch was extinguished.   It was a fascinating spectacle, which the populace enjoyed from the walls and exits of the city.

Some ancient festivals had been abandoned,—at least they appear no more in our documents,—but others had come to take their place.   Thus Philippides had introduced one to commemorate the freedom obtained by Athens in 289 B.C., and Eurycleides another with the same purpose in 229 B.C.   Ten years earlier, too (240/39 B.C.), the Demetria, a similar ephemeral *agon*, had been instituted.   Probably none of these three[2] was repeated often.   On the other hand, the Diogeneia (229 B.C.)[3] and

---

[1] See Daremberg et Saglio, *s.v.* "Lampadedromia," p. 912.
[2] See above, iv. 146, n. 1; v. 203, n. 1, 208, n. 1.
[3] See P.-W. v. 734.   That this was the *agon* instituted by Eurycleides is possible.

the Romaea (*ante* 153 B.C.),[1] like the Ptolemaea (224
B.C.),[2] were permanent recurring fêtes, and, when added
to the old ones still preserved, absorbed much of the
time, energy, and interest of the citizens.   But this was
characteristic not of one city, but of the age and people.[3]
The establishment of the Soteria in Delphi, the Asclepieia
in Cos, the Museia in Thespiae, the Didymeia in Miletus,
the Posideia in Tenos, the Ptoia in Acraephia, the
Hiacynthotrophia in Cnidus, the Leucophryena in
Magnesia, the Nicephoria in Pergamum, the Athenaea
in Sardis, the Coreia in Cyzicus,[4] not to mention the
numerous games named in honour of kings and peoples,
shows the increasing fondness of all the Greeks for this
kind of pleasure.   It betrays also the progress of cosmopolitanism ; for all that the Olympia, Nemea, Isthmia,
and Pythia had done for classic Greece in the matter of
breaking down local prejudices, stimulating widespread
interest in athletics, unifying literary and musical taste,
and promoting social intercourse among men of different
cities, that and much more was now accomplished for
the vast world of Hellenism by scores of similar fêtes.
For not only did they draw crowds as of old, but the
programmes, at any rate so far as they were literary
and musical, were now arranged by travelling troupes
of Dionysiac artists, who, in their migration from city
to city, like the rhapsodists and sophists of earlier days,
spread ideas abroad, and promoted uniformity of culture.
Their movements were facilitated by an international
organization, which also acted as a stimulus to the
establishment of new fêtes and the maintenance of old
ones.   How it arose we cannot say definitely ;[5] but by
the middle of the second century B.C. we find gilds of
artists located here and there over the Peloponnesus
and Central Greece united in a comprehensive League,
which had its headquarters in Thebes and Argos, and
an avowed connexion with the Isthmian and Nemean

---

[1] *IG.* ii. 953.   [2] *Klio*, 1908, p. 341 ; cf. above, vi. 242, n. 4.
[3] For the honours gained in thirteen different places by an Athenian athlete
of this age see *BCH.*, 1907, p. 433 f.
[4] For the time and circumstances of these foundations see Boesch, Θεωρός, 14 ff.
[5] See Poland, *op. cit.* 129 ff.

games. Outside the League stood the Athenian gild, the oldest of all, and obviously one of the most powerful, since it dealt on equal terms with the general syndicate. From both the League and from Athens, as well as from a similar association of Anatolian gilds, with its centre in Teus, troupes of artists were despatched to minister to the needs of the international contests.[1]   It is hard to imagine a more effective agency for unifying dramatic taste and technique, and for securing general familiarity with the masterpieces of ancient tragedy and comedy as well as with contemporary compositions. In the Athenian gild a circle of epic poets and connoisseurs was also maintained. There can be little doubt that the literary repertories of all the Dionysiac artists were composed largely of works of Attic origin.

The expenses connected with the Athenian games were met in part by the magistrates elected to conduct them, but only in part. The grain for the prizes at the Eleusinia, and the oil for those at the Panathenaea were, doubtless, still furnished by the farmers of Attica; and the state, perhaps, gave subventions from its regular revenues for other prizes, and for the entertainment of representatives sent by foreign states. The gild of Dionysiac artists, moreover, seems to have controlled funds of its own. But the entire outlay was, beyond doubt, inconsiderable when compared with the profits incident to the residence in Athens of so many foreigners; for the fête was also a great bazaar,[2] a time of interchange of commodities, and the Athenians got the advantage which the natives always have on such occasions. The games were thus profitable to the Athenians as well as entertaining, and their further elaboration was facilitated by the pretext of religious conservatism, political enthusiasm, or reviving piety. But what advantage was to be derived by contemporary monarchs through participating in them? What need had Egyptian, Seleucid, Attalid,

---

[1] There was, of course, a certain division of territory. Thus the Magnesians secured the services of the Teian syndicate alone for their new games—the Leucophryena (*Inschr. v. Magnesia*, 54). For the conflict between the Athenian gild and the Theban-Argive syndicate see below, ix. *ca.* 370.

[2] What Strabo (x. 485. 4) says of Delos was true generally : ἥ τε πανήγυρις ἐμπορικόν τι πρᾶγμά ἐστι. Cf. *e.g.* Plautus, *Menaechmi*, 24 ff.

and Numidian kings to conciliate the Athenians? Political strength Athens no longer possessed. Her commerce was relatively unimportant, and her trading privileges inconsiderable. Yet we find that not simply did these rulers patronize the Athenian festivals, but they frequently sent their sons to Athens to be educated,[1] and actually sought to outbid one another in the favour of this city by making donatives of all sorts to it.

The Ptolemies had now a mere shadow of their ancient strength. Rome had saved their dynasty in 200 B.C., but had not restored to them their maritime possessions. Hence they were no longer a European power, and the maintenance of political ties in Greece was not now a life and death matter for Egypt. Moreover, the Macedonian line had conjured up the demon of Egyptian national feeling, and till Physcon re-entrenched his house in native sentiment, the Ptolemies were much embarrassed by domestic uprisings. None the less, both Ptolemy Epiphanes and Ptolemy Philometor I. found repeated occasion to extend courtesies to Athens. In 182 B.C. Epiphanes competed at the Panathenaea, and showed the people the delicate attention of entering as an Athenian citizen. Twice in 188 B.C., and again in 184 and in *ca.* 170 B.C., the Athenians publicly thanked Egyptian courtiers and officials who stood high in the favour of their kings for services rendered to citizens travelling to Cyprus, Alexandria, Cyrene, and elsewhere in the empire of Egypt.[2] An Athenian embassy in regard to a gift,[3] headed by an unknown Demaratus and two *theoriae*, one in regard to the approaching Panathenaea, headed by Callias the pancratiast, and another in regard to the Mysteries, headed by a certain Cleostratus, were at the court of Ptolemy Philometor when Antiochus Epiphanes mastered Egypt in the early half of 170 B.C.[4] As has been already

---

[1] See *Class. Phil.*, 1907, p. 401 ff., and *Klio*, 1908, p. 353.

[2] *IG.* ii. 966*a*, ii. 5. 417*b* and *c*, ii. 439, ii. 5. 432*b* and *c*, ii. 377(?).

[3] Polybius, xxviii. 19.

[4] For this date, which the imminence of the Panathenaea in July 170 B.C. (Ol. 152. 3) confirms, see Wilcken, P.-W. i. 2471 f. Niese (iii. 168 ff.) puts the decisive campaign a year too late. See also Bouché-Leclercq, *Histoire des Lagides*, iv. 319.

mentioned, Philometor won a victory at the Athenian national games in 166 B.C.,[1] and for benefactions received, but not specified, an equestrian statue of a Ptolemy, probably this one,[2] was erected on the Acropolis beside the old temple of Athena Polias.   The importance of the Ptolemaea at this time is further evidence of the kindly disposition of Egypt towards Athens.

The Attalids, however, were the greatest regal bene-factors of Athens in the second century B.C., as they had been in the latter part of the third.   Eumenes II. (197–159 B.C.) constructed a spacious, two-storeyed portico five hundred and thirty-five feet long by fifty-eight feet broad along the south flank of the Acropolis just below the precinct of Asclepius.[3]   It could be entered from the theatre, so that it was particularly serviceable when the rain suspended, temporarily, the dramatic contests or the popular assemblies, which were now regularly held there.   This consideration probably determined its site, since in the second century B.C. a promenade of this size would otherwise have been located more advantageously on the opposite side of the citadel.

The Athenians in their turn set up colossal statues of Eumenes and his brother Attalus, which, after having been rebaptized in the name of Mark Antony, were hurled down by a storm shortly before the battle of Actium.[4]   The people had given their affection to the strange genius of Antiochus Epiphanes, and when the Attalids established him on the throne of the Seleucids, they voted to Eumenes, and to his father, mother, and three brothers the highest mark of distinction they were able to confer.[5]   They had already granted the citizenship to Attalus ; now they conferred it upon Philetaerus as well, and erected a statue of him at Olympia.[6]   To the friends of Eumenes they voted honours on several occasions, in the archonship of Achaeus (166/5 B.C. ?) to Menander, his physician,[7] and in December of 172

---

[1] *IG.* ii. 968.   [2] *Ibid.* 464 ; cf. *Klio*, 1908, p. 338 ff.
[3] Vitr. v. 9. 1 ; Dörpfeld, *Ath. Mitt.*, 1888, p. 100 ff. ; Judeich, *Topographie von Athen*, 290.   [4] Plut. *Ant.* 60.   [5] Ditt. *OGIS.* 248.
[6] Ditt. *Syll.*[2] 299 ; *IG.* ii. 435 ; cf. Ditt. *OGIS.* 248, l. 5.
[7] *IG.* ii. 433. For the date see Sundwall, *Klio*, 1909, p. 370. Kirchner (*Sitz. d. Berl. Akad.* 1910, 986) prefers 190/89 B.C.

B.C., in the year in which the agents of Perseus attacked and almost murdered Eumenes, they rewarded one of his friends who had rendered favours to Athenians at Pergamum.[1] Eumenes thus retained the popularity in Athens which he had lost elsewhere in Greece through stirring up Rome against Macedon; and even the manifest hostility of Rome towards him after 167 B.C. did not break the cordial relations which joined Athens to his family, for an exchange of courtesies was made in 166 B.C.[2]

The glory of the Athenian schools in the second quarter of the second century B.C. was Carneades, the head and third founder of the Academy. He had the honour of being the teacher of two princes, who were severed by a difference in age of twenty years, but united by a mutual affection for Stratonice, queen of Pergamum (the one was her brother, the other her brother-in-law and lover),[3] and by common college days in Athens—Attalus, subsequently the second king of that name, and Ariarathes who, later, as king of Cappadocia acclimated Greek culture, and especially Greek philosophy in his boorish and ill-reputed country. They joined in erecting a statue of their brilliant teacher, and, upon receiving Athenian citizenship, had themselves enrolled in the upper Cephisus *deme* Sypalettus. This was perhaps in 178 B.C.,[4] and the connexion thus established was maintained both with one another and with Athens for their respective lifetimes. Attalus had thus the goodwill of the city before he came to the throne in 159 B.C. During his reign he donated to the Athenians a magnificent public building,[5] the great stoa which was situated in the eastern side of the northern half of the market-

[1] *IG.* ii. 436 ; cf. Kirchner, *Berl. Phil. Woch.*, 1909, p. 851.
[2] *IG.* ii. 5. 441*d* ; cf. also Ditt. *Syll.*[2] 299.
[3] See *Class. Phil.*, 1906, p. 231 ff. Cardinali (*Il Regno di Pergamo*, 129 ff.) discusses the relations of Stratonice and Attalus anew, and escapes the conclusion that Attalus III. was the son of Attalus II. by a very forced interpretation of the passage of Polybius which comes into the question (xxx. 2). His criticism is much stronger than his construction. Cf. also *Klio*, 1907, p. 454 f. ; 1908, p. 354.
[4] *Klio*, 1908, p. 351 ff. ; cf. *Class. Phil.*, 1907, p. 401 ff.
[5] *IG.* ii. 3. 1170 ; cf. Judeich, *Topographie von Athen*, 315 ff.

place. It lay near the quarter towards which, as already mentioned, the business activity of later Athens tended to shift, and was designed to provide for Athenian trade the greater protection against sun and rain which these permanent Hellenistic bazaars afforded, as well as to embellish the central *piazza*, and indelibly associate the name of Attalus with the metropolis of Greek culture. Ariarathes was the Dion of the third Plato, and the only writings left behind by the philosopher were his letters to the Cappadocian king. The goodwill of Ariarathes, however, was not confined to Carneades.[1] Later, along with Nysa, his queen, he gave gifts to the club of Dionysiac artists in Athens. In return the artists erected his statue in their shrine, celebrated his birthday and that of his queen with sacrifices, and voted him other honours besides. It seems that Queen Nysa conferred some favour upon the people of Athens directly at the same time.[2] Less an honour to Ariarathes, her brother, or to Attalus III., her son, than a tribute to the recipient herself, was a statue of Stratonice erected at Delos, apparently after the death of Attalus II., when she was now dowager-queen of Pergamum.[3] Doubtless she had earned this distinction by more than a general goodwill to Athens.

There were at this time, apart from Commagene and Armenia which freed themselves from Seleucid control only in 165/4 B.C.,[4] two other Asia Minor kingdoms, Bithynia and Pontus. We have no direct evidence of a connexion between Bithynia and Athens, but this does not mean much, since we were, until recently, equally without proof of the Atticizing of the Pontic dynasty. Lately, however, we have learned that

[1] It has long been affirmed that Ariarathes was a mint magistrate in Athens like Antiochus Epiphanes (Kirchner, *PA*. 1608; Sundwall, *Untersuch*. 19 f.). Cf., however, Weil (*Berl. phil. Woch.*, 1909, p. 1475), who infers from the unworn condition of coins of this issue when they were hidden in 88/6 B.C., that they could not have been long in circulation. That the mint magistrate was not the king, but a private citizen, is doubtless the reason why his colleague Eurycleides has precedence on the coins. He is probably the Ariarathes, son of Attalus, dealt with in *Klio*, 1908, p. 353 f.

[2] Ditt. *OGIS*. 352; cf. *Class. Phil.*, 1907, p. 401 ff.

[3] Ditt. *OGIS*. 350; cf. *BCH.*, 1906, p. 46 f., 1910, p. 431 f.

[4] Niese, iii. 220.

Pharnaces was substantially interested in having a good repute in Athens, and that at some time prior to 171 B.C. he had agreed to pay to the city a sum of money in annual instalments. Owing to unfavourable circumstances, however, the subsidies had ceased. Hence Athens ventured to remind the king of his promises. Pharnaces paid the quota due, and renewed the agreement previously made, whereupon Athens decreed him her highest honour, and, not to miss an occasion for keeping in touch with his court, gave a similar distinction to Nysa, the young woman whom he had just received as his bride from her uncle, Antiochus IV. of Syria. They, moreover, decided to erect statues of the pair at Delos, and to send an ambassador to notify the court of Pontus of what they had done.[1] Pharnaces was an ambitious monarch. Twelve years previously he had seized the Greek city of Sinope, and in spite of the efforts of Eumenes to oust him, he had maintained himself in it as his capital. The lord of Amisus and of Sinope had inherited filial obligations which, it may be, compelled him to pay tribute to Athens. Perhaps, too, his matrimonial alliance with Epiphanes had something to do with bringing him into the roll of Athenian benefactors. For there existed no greater lover of the city than this versatile prince. He had made its acquaintance in 176 B.C., before he became king of Syria; for on his way back to Antioch after a detention of thirteen years in Rome, he stayed for some time in Athens,[2] received the Athenian citizenship and an Athenian commission, and donated an *aegis* of gold to Athena.[3] In return, Athens erected more than one statue of him in the agora.[4] It is commonly asserted, moreover, that he was made commander-in-chief of the Athenian army, but this is a mistake.[5] The office he held was that of joint superintendent of the mint. It was an honorary charge, and was given almost exclusively to members

[1] Ditt. *OGIS.* 771 ; cf. *BCH.*, 1910, p. 429 ; below, ix. 352, n. 2.
[2] Appian, *Syr.* 45. [3] Paus. v. 12. 4.
[4] Ditt. *OGIS.* 248. 55.
[5] See especially Sundwall, *Untersuch.* 14 f.

of the Athenian aristocracy. The great distinction it conferred was that it entitled its occupant to put his name and emblem on the annual coinage of the city, to usurp in Athens what was in Hellenistic thinking almost a royal prerogative. Hence it was that Antiochus stamped his name and his national symbol, the elephant, upon the issue of a year, probably 176/5 B.C.

Antiochus was still in Athens when his brother, Demetrius, was murdered. The murderers put his baby nephew on the throne. This gave Antiochus his chance. He secured the co-operation of the Attalids, in what way we do not know, and to their support he owed it mainly that he obtained possession of the kingdom; for Eumenes and Attalus escorted him to the frontier, provided him with funds, and fitted out his military expedition. The Athenians may have been helpful in bringing him into sympathetic relations with the Attalids; and, indeed, it seems probable that Philetaerus, the third of the sons of Attalus I., had been a resident of Athens along with Epiphanes,[1] and the two, we may think, became intimate in this way. At any rate, the Athenians regarded the Attalid champion-ship of Antiochus as a personal favour, and at once extended to the family the thanks and rewards already mentioned.[2] The devotion of Athens to Epiphanes was not altogether personal or mercenary. It was based on a cordial appreciation of his general policy. During his residence in Rome, where he had kept open house for the Roman aristocracy and made many friends,[3] he had observed closely the sources of Roman power. The superiority of the Roman army he was candid enough to recognize, and he sought to re-organize the Syrian on its model.[4] He had seen the impressive dignity of the Roman magistrates, and the knowledge and confidence which they acquired through obtaining office by the vote of a popular majority. Hence curule chairs were in-troduced into Antioch, and the king set a new example

---

[1] *IG.* ii. 435 ; cf. Ditt. *OGIS.* 248, n. 4.
[2] See above, vii. 299, n. 5.
[3] Asconius, *in Pison.* 12 (*Or.* p. 13, Clark).
[4] Polybius, xxx. 25. 3.

by canvassing for municipal posts clad in a white toga,
Roman fashion.[1] Like Philip V. of Macedon, he
estimated at their proper value the methods employed
by Rome for welding Italy into one great state—the
assimilation of all elements into the city body, and the
scattering up and down the peninsula of colonies,
organized as separate cities and hence locally free, but
animated with Roman patriotism and bent on impressing
their ways and speech upon the peoples round about.
To effect similar results in Antioch and its empire was
the supreme ambition of Antiochus ; to Hellenize Asia
as the Romans were Latinizing Italy was his ideal.
Hence he cultivated the Greeks assiduously,[2]—for these
he preferred to Macedonians, since the latter were
inclined, even though resident in Syria, to give their
first loyalty to their own old homes and kings,[3]—threw
his empire wide open to immigrants, and both
strengthened his interests in the old cities by new
liberties and new settlers, and founded new colonies
wherever practicable. For him, moreover, Greece had
its consummation in Athens. From Athens, accordingly, came in all probability settlers to give the desired
tone to the new quarter which he added to Antioch ;
the Attic calendar was acclimated in the Syrian
capital ; cavalry on the Attic pattern was organized,
and Athenians had special privileges in the empire.[4]
For Antiochus, moreover, Greek culture was consummated in the Olympian Zeus,[5] and it was to make way
for him that Jehovah was dethroned in Jerusalem.   At

---

[1] Polybius, xxvi. 1. 5 ; Livy, xli. 20.   [2] Niese, iii. 94.

[3] Justin, xxxv. 1 ; Livy, *Perioch.* 49 ; Diod. xxxi. 40a ; cf. Niese, iii.
260.   The incident here described helps to explain the generally friendly
relations existent between the Seleucids and Antigonids. There was a very
strong Macedonian element in the Greek-speaking population of the Seleucid
empire (Beloch, iii. 1. 264, 269, n. 4). It is probable that after the first
generation of Macedonian rule Egypt (Alexandria) drew its immigrants mainly
from Greece and Asia Minor (Polybius, xxxiv. 14 ; P. M. Meyer, *Das Heerwesen
der Ptolemäer*, 12 f. 93 f. ; cf. below, ix. *ca.* 380 n.).

[4] Niese, iii. 95, and the authorities there cited ; cf. ii. Macc. ix. 15, and for
earlier settlers from Athens above, iii. 112, n. 1. Josephus, *Antiq. Jud.* xii.
264 ; Polybius, xxx. 25 ; Bevan, *The House of Seleucus,* ii. 151. Attic influence is thus attested even if we regard Ditt. *OGIS.* 248 as from Athens, and
not from Antioch.   That it is really Attic has been made probable by
Dittenberger.

[5] Livy, xli. 20 ; cf. Bevan, *loc. cit.*

Athens there was no temple of this deity, but beside the Ilissus stood the foundations and the unfinished structure of an edifice begun in his honour by Peisistratus, the tyrant, but planned on so vast a scale that it had never been completed.   As it stood it had doubtless produced a profound impression upon the king while he was sojourning in Athens.   The great rough columns were over seven feet in diameter,[1] and the massive proportions of the building carried the imagination back to the days of genuine feeling for the ancient deities, when, as Eduard Meyer has happily remarked,[2] the Doric temples expressed the religion of the Greeks as accurately as the Gothic cathedrals embodied the spirit of the Middle Ages of Europe.   Still, the style did not satisfy the taste of a new age.   Hence, when Epiphanes determined to build for the Olympian Zeus—the Greek equivalent in his thinking of the Capitoline Jupiter, and the prototype of his own divinity [3]—worthy temples, he located one of them [4] in Athens, and chose the old site, indeed, but the edifice which he built was essentially a new structure.   It happened that at the time of his residence in Rome that city was in the midst of the constructive period *par excellence* of the republican era. The Second Punic War had left a less melancholy legacy than the conflict with Macedon.   It had handed down many vows of temples and shrines for the next generation to fulfil.   Hence it was that in the twenty-six years between 194 and 168 B.C. no less than sixteen temples were dedicated.[5]   In no city in the world was there such activity among masons, contractors, and architects.   It was there that the most recent experience of building large modern temples was to be found.   Moreover, the work was practically complete

---

[1] Penrose, *JHS.*, 1887, p. 273.   [2] *Gesch. d. Alt.* ii.[1] 603.

[3] The sovereignty of Rome over its Latin and Italian allies was acknowledged in the *foedus* struck with each : that of Antiochus over the cities in his Empire was expressed in their admission of him among their gods—not as a new deity, but as Zeus, "revealed" in this king's person—*Epiphanes*.   This is a clear mark of the orientalizing of Hellenic religious conceptions.   See above, v. 226 ff.   The king's insistence upon his divine rights shows that he had learned to appreciate the centralization of Italian power in Rome.   See above, i. 11.

[4] The other—others ?—was in Antioch.

[5] Wissowa, *Religion und Kultus der Römer*, 518.

on the accession of Antiochus, so that the best talent was free for work elsewhere. Hence Antiochus chose as his architect, not a Greek, but a Roman, Decimus Cossutius, son of Publius. The disciples were thus early called in to succeed their masters;[1] and it probably does not lack significance that it was a Roman who first gave the Corinthian order the most prominent place in a work of this kind erected in Greece.[2]

The Olympieum stood on a platform six hundred and seventy-six feet long by four hundred and twenty-six feet broad. The building itself was over half the length of St. Peter's in Rome (three hundred and fifty-four feet), and was nearly fifty feet wider (one hundred and thirty-five feet) than the nave of that huge church, while the height of its columns was within ten feet of that of the portico of the Christian edifice. It was, therefore, no wonder that Livy[3] called it the only temple in the world worthy of the majesty of Zeus, and that the reign of Epiphanes proved too short and checkered for its completion. Built with over a hundred columns of the Corinthian type it did much to establish the vogue of that order in subsequent antiquity.[4] It stands to-day in its ruins "by far the most imposing in scale of all the remains of ancient Athens."[5] The state immortalized the architect by putting his name, ancestry, and nationality upon a tablet of stone.[6] What specific honours it conferred upon Epiphanes we do not know. Private individuals, however, have left evidences of their gratitude for his public benefactions. At Delos two men, both Athenians in all probability, erected statues of Antiochus IV.[7]

---

[1] The architects employed by Ariobarzanes II. Philopator (63/2-52/1 B.C.) for the restoration of the Odeum were C. and M. Stallius and Menalippus (Vitr. v. 9. 1 ; *IG.* iii. 541).

[2] Penrose and E. A. Gardner in Whibley, *A Companion to Greek Studies*, 213.

[3] xli. 20 ; cf. Polybius, xxvi. 1. 11 ; Strabo, ix. 396 ; Velleius, i. 10. 1 ; Vitr. vii. *praef.* 15 ff. ; Paus. i. 18. 6.

[4] *Loc. cit.* above, vii. 306, n. 2.   [5] Frazer, *Pausanias*, ii. 178 ff.

[6] *IG.* iii. 561 ; Vitr. vii. *praef.* 15.

[7] Ditt. *OGIS.* 249, 250. The inference made by Homolle and Dittenberger from the use of 'Aθηναῖos, instead of the *demotikon*, that the dedication was made prior to 166 B.C. is not cogent. The Athenians on Delos often treated themselves as foreigners. See below, ix. 407.

Antiochus V., as we have already seen, won a Panathenaic victory in 162 B.C.

We have now presented the long list of regal benefactions and benefactors of which our records give
knowledge. The instances quoted are often in themselves of little historical value, and might be multiplied
indefinitely if all the documents in the Athenian
archives had been preserved; but the inferences
suggested as to the regard in which Athens was held
are important. Why, we repeat, did Egyptian, Attalid,
Seleucid, Cappadocian, Pontic, and Numidian rulers
think it worth while to conciliate, adorn, and subsidize
a city of less than twenty-five thousand citizens[1]—a
place, moreover, devoted to Rome whom they all feared
and secretly hated, and which had sent relatively few
colonists to reinforce the Hellenic element in their
kingdoms?[2] A bronze statue, a memorial tablet, a
gold crown possessed no intrinsic value for a Ptolemy
or an Attalid; yet such was the only material return
which Athens could give.

The answer is unquestionably this : that Athens was
recognized now no less than in the time of the *diadochi*
as the cultural centre of the world. Despite the marvellous rise of Alexandria, Antioch, and Pergamum,
despite the commercial and political prostration of
Attica, and the fierce competition of Rhodes, she still
made the same irresistible appeal as of old to the
imagination of the Greeks. "In a word," said
Heracleides in about 205 B.C., "Athens surpasses other
cities in all that makes for enjoyment and betterment
of life by as much as other cities surpass the country."
Nor was the distinction thus acknowledged without a
foundation in fact. Athens was undeniably different
from the other culture centres of the world. These
had welcomed immigrants from all quarters.[3] They had
no choice, since their growth and prosperity depended

---

[1] It seems that Athens presumed to ask for gifts, if Polybius (xxviii. 19.
4) does not misrepresent through excessive brevity.

[2] Cf., however, above, iii. 97, n. 2, v. 188, n. 1.

[3] See, for example, the list of natives of Asia Minor in possession of citizenship in Alexandria which Wilhelm has published in his *Beiträge*, 224 ff. ; cf.
below, ix. 381, n. 2, and the articles by Schubart there cited.

largely upon their attractiveness to foreigners. Athens, on the other hand, had preserved purity of blood and language for over a century after Alexander's death. Even in 205 B.C. its foreign residents could be designated slaves, so inferior was their status to that of aliens elsewhere. As already stated, the great movement of social and religious change which set in from the East at the end of the fourth century B.C. was met in Athens by a fierce counter-movement which aimed to preserve, together with the city-state, its old usages and its old deities and cults. The spirit which brooded over Attica during the third century B.C. was that of Lycurgus of Butadae, whose pietism and fanaticism for archaising had created an artificial glow of sentiment on behalf of the ancient order. In Athens there was no emancipating of women, no enthusiasm for a religion of redemption. There, too, the classic simplicity and restraint in art had lived on, undefiled by the taste for pomp and magnificence, for striking effects in size, movement, and feeling, and for truth to nature in all its hideousness as well as in all its beauty which pervaded the Hellenistic monarchies. To its conservatism Athens was indebted for a real distinction ; but this alone did not make it the cynosure of the world at the opening of the second century B.C. There came to be added a powerful tradition which worked to produce the same result. The loss of empire in the Peloponnesian War had forced the Athenians of the fourth century B.C. to fall back upon the great solace of their cultural superiority ; and it was on account of it that Isocrates had affirmed in his *Panegyricus*[1] the right of Athens to political leadership in Greece. To prove his point he had presented the stately array of services attributed by local tradition to his native land. By the second century B.C. the list had grown in extent and assertiveness. Athens now claimed to have been the "inaugurator of all human blessings, the guide of men from the life of beasts to gentle culture, the establisher in fact of the social organism altogether. This service

[1] § 28-51.

she had rendered through the dissemination of her Mysteries, which proclaimed abroad the sovereign value of mutual aid and confidence among men ; and also through passing on to others the education and laws with which the gods had dowered her. She claimed too that though grain had been given to her as her special property, she had made it everybody's heritage. She was, besides, the originator of music and dramatic art, the founder and developer of tragedy and comedy, and the first to introduce *thymelic* and histrionic contests."[1]   And not merely did Athens make these claims, but she got them accepted.   The Amphictyonic Council itself by a series of solemn decrees confirmed and promulgated the supreme services which Athens had rendered to humanity, and credence in their actual performance became so deeply grounded in the common belief of men that they appear subsequently as paramount and unquestionable facts.   Diodorus the Sicilian, Cicero, and the rhetoricians of the second century A.D. meet in reaffirming them.[2]

The real distinction of Athenian culture was thus reinforced by an accepted tradition in its favour.   The internationalizing of the city, moreover, which had been effected in 229 B.C., had consecrated it to Aphrodite and the Graces, just as Delos and Delphi were sacred to Apollo ; so that henceforth Greek rulers were able to render homage to it without regard to political consequences.   Its political insignificance was, in fact, a source of strength, for in recognizing the leadership of Athens the kings struck a blow at the pretensions of their rivals.   Pergamum could thus injure the prestige of Alexandria, and the new half-Greek courts in Asia Minor could worship Hellenism without being drawn into the orbit of either Pergamum or Antioch.   To foster Hellenism, however, was a prime necessity for the rulers of Asia, since it was the sympathy between the dynasty and the Greek elements in their kingdoms

---

[1] *BCH.* 1900, p. 96—an Amphictyonic decree of *ca.* 117 B.C., by no means the first of its kind.

[2] See also the *Anonymus* quoted by Wilamowitz, *Class. Phil.*, 1908, p. 232. Cf. Aelian, *Var. hist.* iii. 38 ; Diod. xiii. 26-27 ; Cic. *Pro Flacco*, 26, 62 ; *De orat.* i. 4. 13 ; *Verr.* ii. v. 72. 187.   Cf. Colin, *BCH.*, 1900, p. 110 ff.

that enabled them to maintain their position over against the native populations. The veneration in which Athens was held by the Hellenistic monarchs, finally, reacted in its turn upon the rest of Greece. It was a coefficient by which the excellence of the Attic schools and the esteem for Attic literature and culture were raised in consideration in the home land.

In view of the position which recognition of this sort implies, it is not to be wondered that the Athenians came to believe in the value of their own favour—to imagine that they alone had the key to immortality; that just as the memory of great and noble deeds in the time of Alexander and his successors would have been forgotten if not lauded in Athenian books or on Athenian monuments, so too the names and achievements of a Pharnaces or an Ariarathes could be preserved for posterity solely by the medium of Athenian commendation. Accordingly, they prepared resolutions which were " to fix the noble actions " of those whom they praised " in deathless memory," "constitute a monument in their honour to be seen for unending time," or " duly arrange everything for their glory and further reputation." [1] They felt that they were giving in these phrases a full equivalent for the favours they received, and were able to meet the Hellenistic kings on a plane of complete equality. Thus they did not follow the subjects of Ptolemy or Seleucus in adding to the regal titles of their rulers crown-names indicative of their office in the realm of the gods, an exception being made only, as in the case of Ptolemy Euergetes, when they had themselves conferred the deification. Otherwise, they addressed the monarchs in the style in which these designated themselves in their edicts and on their coins; so that it was not till Antiochus IV. started a new custom by assuming for his personal use the crown-name Epiphanes that the Athenians admitted these tokens of servility into their public documents. [2] So, too, when the Athenians

---

[1] Ditt. *OGIS.* 248 τὰ καλὰ τῶ[ν] ἔργων εἰς ἀΐδιομ μνήμην ἀνάγων καὶ νῦν καθάπε[ρ] καὶ πρότερον, *ibid.* 771.

[2] Strach, *Dynastie der Ptolemäer*, 120 f. ; Beloch, iii. 1. 376 ; *IG.* ii. 969a.

honoured a courtier they called him not "kinsman," "great friend," "friend," or "comrade," according to his position in the order of precedence then coming into general vogue,[1] but simply by his personal, paternal, and ethnic name, just as if he had been an ordinary Greek citizen. Accordingly, in these points they were slow in making a compromise with republicanism, but, with the purpose of speaking a language effective in the royal courts, in using the phrases already quoted from honorary decrees, they made a compromise with their literary taste. Nor was the incipient contamination of language there evidenced the only symptom of the collapse of Brahminism in Athens. Internationalization under the *aegis* first of Egypt and then of Rome meant peace and security. The city had no longer to stand on guard for the preservation of its political and cultural identity. Hence a war programme of defence was an anachronism. That Cybele was formally admitted to Athenian worship in about 220 B.C. has been already noted. That in the first half of the second century B.C. a new liberality was practised in conferring citizenship and civic offices upon foreigners is attested by individual instances and the general report of Polybius.[2]

Thus was marked the inception of a movement which was to destroy what was most distinctive in Athenian life, to bring the living Athenians into the contempt eventually felt by the Romans for all Hellenistic peoples, and, since the Athenians of classical times were undeniably great, to mark *them* off as alone deserving of honour. But in 170 B.C. the changes ultimately productive of loss of civic character strengthened rather than impaired the prestige of Athens; so that the Romans on coming to the East could not fail to succumb to the high estimate of the Athenians current in the world of culture. From this circumstance the Athenians drew a notable advantage, as will be explained in the next chapter.

[1] It was different elsewhere. In Delos, for example, the titles were in vogue almost as soon as in Egypt (*BCH.* 1908, p. 266). For titles in Thera see Ditt. *OGIS.* 136.   [2] See below, viii. 315.

CHAPTER VIII

ATHENS AND ROME

Quibus consulibus Carneades et ea legatio Romam venerit, scriptum est in tuo annali; haec nunc quaero, quae causa fuerit? de Oropo, opinor, sed certum nescio, et, si ita est, quae controversiae? praeterea, qui eo tempore nobilis Epicureus fuerit Athenis, qui praefuerit hortis? qui etiam Athenis πολιτικοί fuerint illustres? quae te etiam ex Apollodori puto posse invenire.—Cicero, *Ad Attic.* xii. 23. 2.

IT was, doubtless, a common thing for Romans to visit Athens during the first third of the second century B.C. We can readily believe, however, that they did not exhibit the same enthusiastic admiration for Athenian culture and the same regard for Athenian goodwill that the kings of the East did. They had too much pride of race to worship Greeks, and their victories were too recent for them to court anybody. No Romans appear in our broken lapidary records as victors in the Athenian chariot races, or as the recipients of Athenian commendation, or, indeed, in any capacity, before the outbreak of the Third Macedonian War. There is no doubting the steadfastness of Athens to her friend and protector. She had, indeed, ceased to publicly execrate Philip and all his race and people, but she still refused to admit Macedonians within her boundaries,[1] and gave her favours and her offices to staunch Roman partisans like Leon of Aexone. Probably her attitude toward Rome was much the same as that of the Dominion of Canada towards England to-day—one of affection for Rome and her political ideals, but of dislike for Romans individually. Accordingly, the state was not misled by the anti-Roman feeling in Greece to enter into negotiations with Perseus,

[1] Livy, xli. 23.

312

the son of Philip, who came to the throne of Macedon in
179 B.C., and sought to form a coalition against Rome.
Hence the Roman emissaries, sent in 172 B.C. to sound
Greek opinion and to secure the fidelity of the Greek
cities, found it unnecessary to visit Athens; nor did the
city hesitate a moment to take her place by Rome's side
when the war with Perseus began.   None the less, she
was treated harshly by the generals whom Rome sent to
open the campaign.   The Athenians despatched to their
aid such men and ships as they could, but the Roman
officers did not accept them, and made in their stead a
requisition of one hundred thousand *medimni* of grain.[1]
Athens at this time, as during the three preceding
centuries, was unable to provision herself from her
native resources, and was dependent upon importation
for a large part of her food supply.   Even the country
population had to buy grain.   Hence the demand seemed
unjust.   None the less she acceded to it, but on sending
an embassy in 169 B.C. to announce her continued
devotion to Rome, she took care that the Roman senate
should know what she thought of this treatment.   Her
case was not an isolated one; from all sides came complaints of outrageous conduct on the part of the generals
in the field.   Hence the Roman Government was obliged
to declare demands illegal which did not originate in a
senatorial decree.[2]   All the Roman officers were, it seems,
not as inconsiderate of Athens as those of the year 171
B.C.   Thus a decree [3] is still partially extant which granted
proxenia to Lucius Hortensius, the admiral of 170 B.C.
—the first and last Attic decree in favour of a Roman
which has come down to us from the pre-Christian

---

[1] Livy, xliii. 6 ; Niese, iii. 132, 136, n. 6.   The amount seems incredibly
large, for at least 85 talents worth of grain were demanded.   Still, an Athenian
metic might put as much as 4 talents into single oil and grain transactions at
this time (*Ath. Mitt.*, 1911, p. 75).   He brought the grain from Pontus to the
Piraeus, and collected the oil from the Aegean towns to make the return cargo.

[2] The process by which Rome's *amici* were being at this time subjected to
all the disadvantages—without any of the compensations—of the Italian *socii* has
been well sketched by Matthaei, *Class. Quart.*, 1907, p. 182 ff.   The autocratic
position assumed by Rome was not conferred by treaty stipulation.   It had to
be legalized, however.   For the way in which this was done see below, ix. 366,
383, n. 1.

[3] *IG.* ii. 423.   *IG.* ii. 424, in which Gaius Laelius, who was Consul in 160
B.C., is mentioned, is a decree of a Lemnian cleruchy.   Cf. below, viii. 317, n. 2.

era. This man, however, did not deserve much praise for his military achievements; nor did those who preceded or followed him in 171, 170, and 169 B.C. make any real progress with the war. Hence when the third campaign ended, and the strength of Macedon was still unbroken, there came an anxious moment for the Greek friends of Rome, above all for Eumenes of Pergamum and the Rhodians—the most deserving of the Senate's *amici* in Greece. What would be their fate if Perseus were victor after all? On the other hand, were Macedon destroyed, what would prevent Rome from treating them, not as friends, but as dependents? Roman faith? But what had its value been to the Aetolians after Cynocephalae, to Philip after Magnesia? Besides, there opened out to Eumenes and the Rhodians the brilliant possibility of utilizing the equilibrium between Rome and Macedon to control the situation to their own advantage. In short, they sought by intervention to put an end to the war for the same reasons as those which had actuated the neutral states, Athens among them, in trying to arrange a peace between the Aetolians and Philip. It was a natural impulse, and the Aetolians and the Achaeans were quite of the way of thinking of Eumenes and the Rhodians. Accordingly, the war with Perseus threatened to assume colossal dimensions. Hence the Romans put forth their strength in 168 B.C., and crushed Perseus completely. Italy was decisively stronger than Macedon, and all that the momentary wavering of the Greeks had accomplished was to give the Senate an excuse to treat its friends as enemies, and thus break the back of the next strong powers in the Orient.

Athens had remained unswerving in her loyalty to Rome during the crisis. In fact, it seems unlikely that a change of policy ever came up for formal discussion, since otherwise some noise of it would have got abroad. Probably the ships which had been rejected in 171 B.C. were accepted in 168 B.C., since Attic vessels[1] are

---

[1] The text of Livy (xlv. 10) reads *adticis navibus*. Weissenborn objects to *Atticis* because there has been hitherto no mention of Athenian vessels; but the passage in which the reference should have been found, if made, is corrupt

mentioned among those which lay at Delos at the end of
the war, and which had served to guard commerce against
the light *limbi* of the Macedonians.   Her zeal was thus
unimpeachable.   Hence the city found itself almost alone
in Greece in the favour of Rome, and proceeded to make
the most of the opportunity.   An embassy was despatched to consult with the Senate as to the disposition
of the spoils.   At first the ambassadors petitioned in
the interest of Haliartus,[1] which had been captured and
plundered most outrageously by the Romans in 171 B.C.
But when it appeared that the Senate was inexorable
toward the vanquished, and those who had shown the
least sympathy for the vanquished in the course of the
war, the Athenians changed their tune, and demanded
for themselves not simply Haliartus, but also Delos and
Lemnos.   Polybius, who is throughout harsh in his
judgment on Athens, blames them for augmenting the
misfortunes of Haliartus ; for Rome granted them their
entire request, and Athens took possession of her new
territory by sending settlers to occupy the lands of
those whom she had so recently championed and to drive
the Delians out of their island.   Possibly she sent others
to Lemnos to strengthen her old colony there, but of
this we have no record.[2]   No fault could be found with
the Athenians, according to Polybius, for coveting Delos
and Lemnos, since these islands had once formed part
of their empire ; but Haliartus was one of the most
ancient Boeotian cities, and for Athens to seize its lands
was, he thought, outrageous, and, like her newly adopted
prodigality in the granting of her citizenship, out of
keeping with the traditions of the city.[3]   Two other
islands, Imbros and Scyros, were, like Lemnos, Athenian
in population, and they were spoils of Macedon to boot,
but Polybius does not mention them in this connexion ;

(xliv. 29). The Athenian squadron was similarly employed at Delos in the
Second Macedonian War (see above, vii. 278, n. 3), and yet not mentioned in
the historians. It was suited for chasing pirates, not for sea fights. Niese,
iii. 155.

[1] Polybius, xxx. 20.   [2] See, however, below, viii. 317, n. 2.

[3] This is perhaps the sense of the passage in Polybius : τὸ γὰρ τὴν μὲν
ἰδίαν πατρίδα κοινὴν ποιεῖν ἅπασιν, τὰς δὲ τῶν ἄλλων ἀναιρεῖν, οὐδαμῶς οἰκεῖον ἂν
φανείη τοῦ τῆς πόλεως ἤθους. See above, vi. 245 f.

and, though they appear subsequently in the possession of Athens, we do not know for certain whether the restoration took place in 166 B.C. or a few years later. The probability is that they became Athenian almost immediately.[1]

Athens was again a state of considerable extent and population. The free and franchised inhabitants of Attica we may set down at from seventy-five to one hundred thousand.[2] The resident aliens were, of course, less numerous than at the time of Demetrius of Phalerum, but there existed groups of Thracians, Egyptians, Cyprians, Tyrians, and other foreigners, organized in ethnic associations, which were now recognized in the public games as constituent parts of the community.[3] Especially numerous were the metics from Heracleia on the Pontus, Miletus, and Antioch, of whom there seem to have been regular colonies in Attica.[4] Seemingly, too, there was now quite a group of non-resident and honorary citizens scattered about the world. There were, moreover, foreign students attached in varying numbers to each of the great schools of the city, and a straggling body of important young foreigners registered in the Attic ephebe corps. Altogether there must have been some thousands of foreigners in either permanent or temporary residence in Athens. The slaves were as ever a large element in the total population, but we have now no comedians and no orators to show them to us on the streets and squares, in the factories, banks, shops, and ships of Athens. We have, furthermore, no long lists of dedications to native and foreign gods, no accounts of committees on public buildings to enable us to determine their nationalities, employments, and wages. But they were there all the same, and

---

[1] Our hesitation arises through the failure of Polybius to mention them along with Lemnos and Delos.

[2] This, of course, is merely a rough approximation. The possibility of obtaining 650 or 600 new senators, *i.e.* citizens over thirty years of age, every second year presupposes some such total.

[3] *IG.* ii. 444, 445, 446 ; cf. Wilhelm, *Osterr. Jahreshefte*, 1902, p. 130.

[4] *IG.* ii. has the names of 81 *Heracleotae*, *IG.* iii. has 72. The Milesians number in the former 30, in the latter 262 ; the Antiochans 29 and 89, the Alexandrians 5 and 22, the Ephesians 10 and 2, the natives of Pergamum 4 and 3. See Brueckner, *op. cit.* 64. These numbers must be increased because of inscriptions recently published ; cf. Robinson, *Amer. Jour. Phil.*, 1910, p. 380 ff.

at a later time we shall find them displaying a spirit and audacity such as they had never exhibited to our knowledge in the fifth and fourth centuries B.C. While all the data for an accurate estimate are lacking, it is perhaps admissible to hazard the guess that there were some tens of thousands of slaves in Attica still. Perhaps there were from one hundred to one hundred and fifty thousand people within the old limits of the Athenian state, or from one hundred to one hundred and fifty to the square mile. The new territory brought perhaps fifty thousand more. To be sure, Haliartus and Delos were taken over, the former almost, the latter, apart from the foreign traders, quite, destitute of inhabitants, but Lemnos, Imbros, and Scyros, with a total area of three hundred and thirty square miles, were beyond a doubt more thickly populated than they are at the present time ; yet now they support about forty thousand [1] people, or approximately one hundred and twenty to the square mile.

The new territories were organized as cleruchies, like Salamis and the colonies sent out by Pericles in the fifth century B.C. In general they all had the same form of government. Their inhabitants were Athenian citizens. The old settlers had preserved their *deme* names during the one hundred years of foreign control, and thus could re - enter the body politic without trouble.[2] The new settlers, who were taken from all the tribes perhaps in about equal numbers,[3] carried

---

[1] Lemnos has about 27,000 inhabitants (Fredrich, *Ath. Mitt.* xxxi. 243, n. 1) ; Scyros 3512 (Philippson, *Petermann's Mitt.*, *Ergänzungsheft*, 134. 123, 164) ; Imbros from 4–10,000, or, according to Blau und Schlottmann (*Monatsberichte d. Berl. Akad.* 1855, p. 635), 9000. Possibly the Athenian citizenship was given to such citizens of Haliartus as remained. See above, viii. 315, n. 3.

[2] This is obvious from *IG.* ii. 494. 424, 593 ; *Add.* p. 422, No. 593, which, as Wilhelm informs me, all belong to the same *stele*. See below, viii. 323, n. 1. The matter is still clearer in the case of Imbros. Thus in *IG.* xii. 8. 72, a certain Achaeus, son of Achaeus [Beren]icides, appears. Either a *deme* was renamed Berenice in Imbros in 224 B.C. as well as in Athens, or this inscription belongs after 166 B.C., and the author of the *ex-voto* is a new immigrant to the island. It belongs after 224 B.C. in any case. Between 314 and 307 B.C., while separated from Athens, Imbros maintained the Attic *demes* (see above, ii. 50, n. 4).

[3] The institution of prytanies in the cleruchies presupposes a certain equality in the number of men from each tribe. In Imbros, for example, each tribe was represented in the Senate by two men (*IG.* xii. 8. 63). For a case where each tribe was equally represented in magistracies, see Carl Curtius, *Inschr. und Stud. zur Gesch. von Samos* (Progr.), Lübeck, 1877, No. 6.

over with them their domestic rights and classification.
When free of all foreign control the cleruchies had been
in the habit of replacing the Athenian magistrates, with
whose aid their government was normally carried on,
by officers of their own choosing—the model of Athens
being followed wherever practicable.[1] Since, however,
the islands had been Macedonian dependencies of late,
the probability is that such extra local officials had
been unnecessary, their work having been done by
agents of Perseus. Hence the reunion with Athens
interfered in no way with the existing cleruch institutions, which were in broad outlines the same in all the
settlements. Everywhere there was the general assembly
of all the citizens, with a large committee, the Senate,
to prepare proposals and supervise the administration.
The Senate was divided into prytanies like those in
Athens. The prytanies chose their chairman and *proedri*
to preside at meetings of the council and general assembly,
and took charge of affairs in an order fixed by lot. The
cleruchies were thus replicas of Athens itself. They
had their central administrative offices,[2] their assembly
and council halls, their jury courts and their judicial
auditing of the accounts of the magistrates. Some of
their local magistrates were chosen by lot, others by
popular election,[3] the mode being determined, doubtless,
by Athenian practice. Every cleruchy had its public
secretary and its state treasurer.[4] There were *agonothetae*, *gymnasiarchs*, heralds, and for the various
temples priests. The colonists took or had taken their
gods with them, and adopted liberally the deities of
the natives among whom they came or whom they
dispossessed.[5]

The cleruchies were self-governing communities of

[1] See especially *IG*. xii. 8. 47, 51, 666.
[2] For the *prytaneum* in Delos see *BCH.*, 1905, p.198 ; in Imbros see *IG*. xii. 8.
50 ; in Lemnos see *IG*. ii. 592 ; cf. Foucart, *Acad. inscr. mémoires présentées
par divers savants*, 1ère série, ix. 1878, p. 373 ff.
[3] Thus the lot was used in Imbros, as in Athens, for the election of the
archons. *IG*. xii. 8. 47 (314–307 B.C.).
[4] Except at Delos, where the place of the treasurer was taken by the
custodians of the sacred treasures.
[5] *IG*. xii. 8. 52, 74, 26, 642 ; 'Εφ. 'Αρχ., 1903, p. 67. See in general Foucart,
op. cit. 381 ff. ; Gilbert, *op. cit.* 448 ; and for Scyros, Graindor, *Hist. de l'île de
Skyros*, 74 ff.

Athenian citizens transplanted out of Attica, but they were not on that account exempt from the control of, or obligation towards, Athens. In fact, they were subject in a very marked degree to the supervision of the home authorities, though no more, perhaps, than were the *demes* or *trittys* of Athens itself. In the first place, the most important officials in the cleruchies were sent from Athens, not taken from the colonists, and though they were very sensitive to the praise or blame of the latter, they rendered an account of their acts and expenditures only to the whole Athenian community, of which they were magistrates. In other words, the cleruchy neither elected nor controlled its chief executive. It was equally restricted in legislative authority. Local concerns the cleruch assembly could, of course, attend to with full powers to act, but all important decisions, even the public commendation of the officials sent from Athens, were valid only upon acceptance by the assembly in Athens. After decreeing a crown or a statue to a well-deserving magistrate, the cleruchs sent an embassy of from three to ten members —ordinarily five—to secure the ratification of their vote in the capital.[1] In the three particulars of having local legislatures with a lesser executive, high imperial magistrates with little local responsibility, and legislative dependence upon the central parliament, the Athenian cleruchies were precisely on a par with the British colonies in North America prior to the granting of responsible government in 1841. Their status was even worse, in that like the thirteen states of the American Union prior to 1776 they were obliged to pay taxes to the mother state. This is expressly vouched for by Vitruvius in the case of Lemnos. He tells us that the two cities of this island, Myrina and Hephaestia, were required by the Roman Government to pay *stipendia* to Athens.[2] What form these took we do not know. At any rate, the Lemnian Athenians were obliged to contribute toward the support of the games celebrated in Athens, of the Dionysia, Pana-

---

[1] See Francotte, *Musée Belge*, 1900, p. 115 ff.   [2] Vitr. vii. 7.

thenaea, and other athletic and literary fêtes.[1]   To them
they sent *theori*, and, since the Delians did likewise,[2]
it is probable that this obligation was imposed upon
all the cleruchies.   Of course, it was not technically
taxation without representation, for the cleruchs could
probably vote in Athens if they cared to visit the city
for that purpose.

There was, then, a general resemblance between the
seven cleruchies both in their organization and in their
constitutional position.   They were, in fact, all crown
colonies.   They were not, however, alike in every
particular.   Differences were created by the fact that
Salamis had remained Athenian throughout ; Myrina,
Hephaestia, Imbros, and Scyros, though inhabited by
Athenian settlers without intermission, had been
separate communities for a long time,[3] and had
come to possess traditions and customs of their own
which had to be reckoned with ; Haliartus and Delos,
on the other hand, were essentially new settlements.
Thus it resulted that the Athenian archon was
eponymous in Delos (and Haliartus), while Salamis,
Scyros, Imbros (and later Peparethos) had each a local
archon as eponymous magistrate, and probably also an
Athenian general as chief imperial official,[4] just as in
the fourth century B.C.   Lemnos, too, like Salamis, was
the seat of an Athenian *hipparch*, as in the time of

---

[1] See *IG*. ii. 592, which is republished by Mylonas in 'Εφ. 'Αρχ., 1903, p. 67 ff.
The formula, which prescribes the places of advertisement of the honours conferred by this decree, is not as complete as is usually the case with similar
documents in contemporary Athens.   Still, the addition to the Dionysia and
the Panathenaea of καὶ τοῖς ἄλ]λοις γυμνικοῖς ἀγῶσιν shows that we have to deal
with the time when proclamations were made at the Eleusinia and the Ptolemaea
(224–146 B.C.).   Hence this decree belongs between 166 and 146 B.C.

[2] *CIG*. ii. 2270.

[3] They were lost to Athens possibly in 276 B.C., but more probably in 262/1
B.C.   Thereafter their fate was not different, apparently, from that of the
other Aegean islands.   The date of *IG*. ii. 592, on the basis of which it is sometimes affirmed (Fredrich, *IG*. xii. 8. p. 4) that they were regained by Athens in
229 B.C., is, however, 166–146 B.C. in all probability.   The last editor ('Εφ.
'Αρχ., 1903, p. 67 ff. ; cf. above, 320, n. 1) admits that it may belong to the
second century B.C.

[4] For Salamis see *IG*. ii. 469. 83 ; for Scyros, *IG*. xii. 8. 666 ; for Imbros,
IG. xii. 8. 47.   (This last reference shows that the archon was local, but
the inscription belongs to 314–307 B.C., when the island was independent.)   For
Peparethos see *IG*. xii. 8. 645.   For an archon at Samos in the fourth century
see Carl Curtius, *op. cit.* No. 6.   For the general in Scyros, Salamis, and
Imbros see Gilbert, *op. cit.* 451, n. 3 ; in Lemnos, see below, viii. 321, n. 2.

Demosthenes, Aristotle, and Demochares,[1] but it had benefited in the interval by securing a general in addition.[2] The latter was now, doubtless, the most influential official on the island. The administration of Lemnos thus preserved its military character or appearance. The chief official in each town was a general,[3] and the financial agent was not simply treasurer, or state treasurer, as was generally the case elsewhere, but treasurer of the military funds.[4] About Haliartus we know only that its chief executive was called, as in Delos, superintendent.[5] In Delos a cleruchy was established for the first time in 166 B.C.[6] The natives, through being essentially pensioners of the temples,[7] and certain to prove competitors of the incoming Athenians in trade, labour, and spoliation of pilgrims, were bound to be seriously in the way of the new owners. The island was small, and the arable land trifling in extent. The Delians, moreover, were in possession of the sites conveniently accessible from the sacred precinct and the harbour. They would have to be dislodged anyway : why not expel them from the

---

[1] Dem. iv. 27 ; Arist. *Constit. of Athens*, 61. 6 ; *IG*. ii. 5. 318c. ; cf. above, iv. 156, n. 3. Had there been a general in Lemnos as well as a *hipparch* at this time (cf. Ditt. *Syll.*[2] 587, n. 184) he should have appeared in this document.

[2] *IG*. ii. 593, which may belong to 165/4 or 164/3 B.C. The *hipparch* appears here as the subordinate of the *strategus*. In *IG*. xii. 8. 26 he is omitted altogether. Local archons appear on Lemnos, but only when the island was independent (*IG*. xii. 8. 19).

[3] For the general of each town see Ditt. *Syll.*[2] 587. 275 ; *IG*. ii. 593 ; *IG*. xii. 8. 26. Whether he was an Athenian or a local official cannot be decided with certainty. In Imbros (Ditt. *Syll.*[2] 659 ; *IG*. xii. 8. 65) an Athenian general is mentioned, but he is the counterpart of the *strategus ἐπὶ Λῆμνον*.

[4] For the ταμίας τῶν στρατιωτικῶν see Ἐφ. Ἀρχ., 1903, p. 67 ff. The treasurer in Scyros was ταμίας τοῦ δήμου (*IG*. xii. 8. 666) ; in Imbros (*IG*. xii. 8. 50) and in Salamis (*IG*. ii. 469) simply ταμίας. For Delos see above, viii. 318, n. 4, and below, ix. 354, n. 1.

[5] *Epimeletae* were sent by Athens to the cleruchies for a short time after their recovery in *ca.* 387 B.C. : *IG*. xii. 8. 5 ; Busolt, *Griech. Staatsalter.*, 89.

[6] For the time see *JHS.*, 1910, p. 190, n. 9. Dürrbach writes me that he also puts the last Delian archon a year later than Homolle does.

[7] Criton, whose *Aetolian* gained the victory in 168/7 B.C. (*IG*. ii. 975, col. iii. 19), writes in his *Philopragmon* (Koch, iii. p. 354, No. 3) as follows :

> Φοίνικα, μεγάλου κύριον βαλλαντίου,
> ναύκληρον ἐν τῷ λιμένι ποιήσας ἄπλουν,
> καὶ φορμιῶσαι ναῦς ἀναγκάσας δύο,
> εἰς Δῆλον ἐλθεῖν ἠθέλησ᾽ ἐκ Πειραιῶς,
> πάντων ἀκούων διότι παρασίτῳ τόπος
> οὗτος μόνος τρί᾽ ἀγαθὰ κεκτῆσθαι δοκεῖ,
> εὔοψον ἀγοράν, παντοδαπὸν θυτῶν ὄχλον,
> αὐτοὺς παρασίτους τοῦ θεοῦ τοὺς Δηλίους.

island altogether ? This was accordingly done, and
the cleruchs, at the same time that they occupied the
public buildings of the Delians, moved into their shops,
residences, and farms. They did so, apparently, at the
beginning of the Athenian year 166/5 B.C., and, since
outstanding loans, unexpired leases, and temple administration generally demanded that there should be
as little rupture of continuity as possible, the Athenian
Government simply replaced the Delian officials by
Athenians, and let everything go on as before. Thus
the superintendent superseded the Delian archon as
governor-general of the island. In the place of the
four *hieropoei* who, during the thirteen years prior to
166 B.C., had co-operated in managing the temples and
the sacred moneys,[1] came a commission of four Athenians
composed of two sections of two officials each—the
committee on religious matters and the custodians of
the sacred treasures. Three Athenian *agoranomi*, market
overseers, took the place of three Delian market overseers. An Athenian *gymnasiarch* came and took
charge of the Delian *gymnasium*. To each of the
temples came an Athenian priest instead of a Delian
priest, the *cleiduchs* and *canephori* becoming Athenian
where such subordinates were needed. The priests
were designated by lot—in Athens probably, though
candidates from the island were so often successful as
to suggest a doubt.[2] The others were chosen by popular
election in Athens.

Polybius tells us that in Lemnos and Delos the
Athenians seized wolves by the ears.[3] Delos, he affirms,
was a great trouble to them, and from Haliartus they
received more abuse than fruit. This was probably
written within thirty years after 166 B.C.,[4] before the
remarkable development of Delos had taken place, and
while the unpleasant incidents which accompanied the
establishment of Athenian authority in their new
possessions were still fresh in his mind. It is quite

[1] See below, ix. 347, p. 2.
[2] See for this section *Klio*, 1907, p. 234 ff. ; 1909, p. 334 ; and below, ix. 351, n. 1.
[3] xxx. 20. For the proverb cf. Koch, iii. p. 286, No. 18.
[4] Bury, *The Ancient Greek Historians*, 191 ff.

intelligible that the colonists at Haliartus, isolated in
the midst of a resentful and utterly demoralized country
like Boeotia, where brigandage was rife and the government powerless or indifferent, were exposed to frequent
incursions, and unable to enjoy in comfort the product
of their labour. What difficulties were encountered in
Lemnos we do not know. Myrina, at least, rejoiced for
the moment in exchanging the yoke of Macedon for
incorporation in her own mother state.[1] She sent a
thank-offering to Athena Archegetis and Soteira for
the re-establishment of Athenian authority over the
islands; offered sacrifices for the fame and safety of
Athens; congratulated its council and assembly on the
favourable issue of the decision of the Roman senate, and
sought by a public monument to perpetuate the memory
of her own gratitude and zeal. It is hardly doubtful that
the sentiments of Hephaestia were similar. The constitutional position of a cleruchy, however, tended to provoke
differences of opinion and authority between the local
and the central government, and we have records, though
of a much later date, of disputes in regard to the ownership of land. They are too fragmentary to admit of an
opinion as to the parties or circumstances, but difficulties
had to be referred more than once to Athens for settlement.[2] Possibly, land troubles such as these may be those
of which Polybius had knowledge prior to 134 B.C.

The Delians were required to withdraw from their
island by Rome. The same authority, however, permitted them to take their belongings with them.[3] This,
apparently, they were unable to do. Perhaps it was
difficult to determine what was movable and what was
unmovable property, and since the Athenians executed
the Roman terms, it is possible, as has been surmised,[4]
that strife arose between the two parties at the evacua-

[1] *IG.* ii. 494, 424, 593; *Add.* p. 422, No. 593. The date of this document is still
undetermined. It cannot be 167/6 B.C., since the Athenian *hipparch* is already
holding office a second time. It may, however, be 166/5 or 165/4 B.C. It is
hardly conceivable that such an ado would be made over anything else than the
restoration of Lemnos to Athens in 166 B.C. Hence the allusion in line 7 of 593
must be to the assignment of Lemnos and Delos to Athens in that year. Cf.
Polybius, xxxii. 7.
[2] *IG.* ii. 488, 489; ii. 5. 489*d*.　　[3] Polybius, xxxii. 7.　　[4] Niese, iii. 191.

tion itself. However that may be, the Delians went to Achaea, and had themselves enrolled as citizens there. This done, they laid claims against the Athenians for damages under the commercial treaty by which Achaeans and Athenians settled property disputes arising between citizens of the two countries. It was, perhaps, the only way of redress open to the exiles, but the application of this treaty to transactions which took place before the granting of Achaean citizenship was, doubtless, unwarranted, and the Athenians accordingly declined to adjudicate the claim. Thereupon the Delians obtained from the Achaeans rights of reprisals against Athens, and, on seizing property of Athenians in compensation for what they had lost, they brought it about, seemingly, that reciprocal pillage of Achaean and Attic commerce and territory was normal for a period of some years. Both the Achaeans and Athenians then sent ambassadors to obtain a final decision from the Roman senate. This affirmed the equity of the arrangements made by the Achaeans for the benefit of the Delians in so far as they were the result of legal action; this latter reservation, and, indeed, the whole report of Polybius on the matter, implying that uncommendable violence had also occurred. At any rate, it was not till about 157 B.C.[1] that the quarrel provoked with Athens by the Achaean League on the count of the Delians was settled by the Roman senate, and already a new strife had arisen in which Athens was the defendant, and in which the Achaean League became again the sponsor of the aggrieved party. Obviously, the relations between Athens and the Achaeans were strained during this whole period, and since the leaders in both states stood well with the Romans, it was natural that third parties should solicit the aid of the one against the other. The new *imbroglio* originated in the attempt of the Athenians to seize Oropus, continental territory to which they had claims on the score of former ownership, and which belonged to Attica through geographical location as decisively as

---

[1] Niese, iii. 191, n. 6. Büttner-Wobst, *Polybius*, vol. iv. p. 370, puts this section of Polybius in Ol. 155. 2 (159/8 B.C.).

it was Boeotian by language and history. We have already seen that Oropian *proxenia* was showered upon Athenians in the latter part of the third century B.C., and that Heracleides notes the tendency of the Oropians at this time to become Atticized.[1] Whether this intimacy led to a practical ignoring of the boundaries, or to an eventual estrangement, we do not know. Perhaps the Senate's award to Athens of her former dependencies was sufficiently vague in its wording to give the city a pretext for annexing Oropus. At any rate, an incident occurred which Athens represented as simply the collection, by peaceful means, of no more than equable tolls and tribute, but which the Oropians maintained to be a violent pillage of their property.[2] The Sicyonians, to whom the Roman senate, when appealed to, referred the complaint of the Oropians, took the view of the latter, and assessed the damages, in the absence of the Athenians, at five hundred talents. That was an enormous sum—about three times the annual harbour revenues of Rhodes in the time of her commercial greatness, about sixty times the maximum fixed by a contemporary Roman senator, with the purpose of giving an example of austere frugality, for the cost of his funeral.[3] Athens was, indeed, not a poverty-stricken city at this time. She was, in fact, entering upon a

[1] See above, vi. 247.

[2] Pausanias (vii. 11. 4) believed that Oropus was an Athenian dependency before the Oropian incident occurred. This view has been generally held to be inaccurate (Wilamowitz, *Hermes*, xxi. 102 ; Niese, iii. 319 ff.). The assumption that Oropus was Attic, however, underlies the Athenian explanation of their conduct, as that was set forth by Apollodorus (Philodemus), a contemporary of the incident : [εἰς Ῥώμην Ἀθην]αῖ[οι] τ[ὸν Καρνεάδην πρε]σ[βευ]τ[ὴν μετὰ Κριτολάου τ]ε [καὶ] Διο[γένους ἔπεμψαν ὡς ἐ]ξ ᾿Ω[ρωπ]ί[ων π]ό[λεως τέλ]η σπά[νια] καὶ [φόρ]ους [ὀλίγους] ἐν[εγ]κόν[τες] οὐ[δὲ βιασάμενοι· ὃ δ]ὲ [διη]γησά[μενος ὅσα πολέμ]οις ἀ[ει]μ[νήστοις ἡ πόλις ἔκα]με ?, τ[ὸ] τῶ[ν βουλευτῶν πάθος οὕτως] ἐκίν[ησεν ὥστε καί]πε[ρ] ? ἐρή[μην ὠφληκό]των [᾿Ω]ρω[π]ίοις [ἐμείωσαν τ]ὰ πεντα[κόσια τάλαντα] εἰς ἑ[κ]ατόν. Cf. Mekler, *Acad. phil. index Herc.* p. 82.

The contention of the Athenians was obviously out of accord with the facts, since otherwise the Romans would probably have quashed the fine altogether, and the contention of the Oropians would have been ridiculous.

[3] 1,000,000 asses ; Livy, *Epit.* xlviii. ; cf. Colin, *Rome et la Grèce*, 547. On the whole affair, and especially the visit of the philosophers, see Paus. vii. 11. 4 ; Hitzig und Blümner, ii. 2. 793 f. ; Plut. *Cato maior*, 22 ; Gellius, *N.A.* vi. 14. 8-10 ; Polybius, xxxii. 11. 5 ; Cic. *De orat.* ii. 155, *Tusc.* iv. 5 ; Pliny, *Nat. Hist.* vii. 112 ; Macrob. *Sat.* i. 5. 14 f. ; Aelian, *Var. Hist.* iii. 17 ; Ditt. *Syll.*[2], 308. See also Niese, iii. 319, n. 2 ; Toepffer, P.-W. i. 183 ; Wilamowitz, *loc. cit.* ; Colin, *op. cit.* 504 ff. ; Dürrbach, *De Oropo et Amphiarai sacro*, 64, 76 ; Koehler, *Ath. Mitt.* iv. 262 ff.

new era of material prosperity. Still, the fine was extravagantly large even for a verdict *in contumacia*, and Athens made a great effort to have it annulled. The crisis was hardly of sufficient magnitude to warrant recourse to the head of the Academy, but such was the action taken, and not only did the Athenians commission Carneades to plead for them in Rome, but they gave him as colleagues Diogenes, the head of the Stoa, and Critolaus, the head of the Peripatos. The other school, that of Epicurus, was apparently of less repute. The misrepresentation of Epicurean doctrines had attached to it the stigma of immorality, and robbed it of its good name. It was severely compromised in Rome, moreover, by the bad behaviour of its adherents, and not long before the Oropian incident the Roman senate had expelled the Epicurean teachers.[1] There were thus good reasons, quite apart from the personality of Basileides, the contemporary head of the Garden,[2] why the Athenians should pass him by and send only the other three. These were the living exponents of systems of thought which obtained the adhesion and actuated the conduct of men of culture all the world over. From Cappadocia to Carthage, from Damascus to Massilia, people in all classes of society looked to the heads of the Stoa, Academy, or Lyceum for inspiration and guidance. Thus the institutions which they represented, as well as the eloquence and charm of the schoolheads themselves, served to win a hearing for their cause, however intrinsically weak it might be. It was not the first time in Athenian history that an eminent scholar was chosen as a foreign ambassador[3]—nor the last in the experience of democratic states. In an age which had no ecclesiastical organization to throw its authority over peace-bearing priests, the apostles of philosophy were fitting mediators between states and princes. They took the place in later antiquity which the prelates of the Church sometimes occupied in the Middle Ages of Europe.

---

[1] Athen. xii. 68 ; cf. Colin, 570, 369 f.   [2] Crönert, *Kolotes*, 88.
[3] Mahaffy, *The Silver Age of the Greek World*, 94 ff.

The three philosophers were partially successful in
their mission.   The fine was reduced to one-fifth of its
former amount, but the Athenians declined to pay even
this, and adhered to the contention that Oropus was
theirs.   They even went so far as to despatch a cleruchy
to occupy a portion of Oropian territory.   The colonists
drove out the irreconcilables, and came to an understanding with the rest of the inhabitants, who, pending
a final settlement, were obliged to conciliate their more
powerful neighbours.   As a pledge for the safety of the
persons and property of the immigrants the Oropians
gave hostages, while the Athenian Government, for its
part, agreed to see to it that the cleruchs did not
maltreat the people among whom they were settled—
a promise easy to give, but difficult to keep.[1]   For some
years the cleruchy remained in control of the country.
It coined its own money,[2] and, apparently, felt securely
established ; but before long cases arose of alleged
wrongs done the natives by the Athenians, and the city
refused to punish the accused.   The people of Oropus,
thereupon, requested the Achaean League to come to
their rescue and rid them of the Athenian tyranny.
They pointed out that Rome could not object to such a
proceeding, being herself injured in that Oropus had been
a Roman *amicus*, and was consequently entitled to
Roman protection.   The most energetic advocate of
Oropus was Hieron of Aegeira.[3]   He befriended its
magistrates and refugees, and pled its case at a full
meeting of the Achaean senate which took place at
Corinth.   This body, however, did not have power to
act, and, accordingly, referred the matter to a general
assembly of the whole people, to be convoked at Argos,[4]
and at which the Athenians and other states, which

[1] This seems to be the only reasonable interpretation of what Pausanias
says about the Athenian occupation of Oropus and the treaty struck with its
people.
[2] *Ath. Mitt.* iv. 262 ff., and for the issuing of money by the Athenian
cleruchies, *ibid.* vi. 238, vii. 146 ; cf. above, iv. 145, n. 4.
[3] For the part played by Hieron see Ditt. *Syll.*[2] 308, and Wilamowitz,
Hermes, xxi. 102 ff.
[4] We owe it to the new Theopompus (?) and the keenness of Gaetano de
Sanctis (*Riv. di filol.*, 1908, xxxvi. 252 ff.) that the character and relations of
the Achaean σύνοδος or βουλή and σύγκλητος are now pretty clearly understood.

supported the claims of the Athenians, might be represented. Hieron entertained the refugees in his house in the interval, " offered sacrifices to Zeus Soter on their behalf," and appeared as their spokesman when the meeting took place. What actuated the Achaeans in deciding against Athens we do not know. The Athenians believed, and Pausanias [1] reports the matter as a fact, that the Oropians gave a bribe of ten talents to the general of the League, the Spartan Menalchidas, who, by promising the half to Callicrates, at that time the most influential man in Achaea, won his support for the Oropians, and that through these underhand means the League was led to send an army to reinstate the people of Oropus in their country. This is probably a bit of Athenian gossip.[2] Certainly the Oropians attributed their success, not to Menalchidas and Callicrates, but to Hieron of Aegeira, and it was to him that they voted public rewards after they were re-established in their homes. This followed closely after the dispersion of the assembly, for upon receiving word of the approach of the Achaean army, the Athenians plundered Oropus unmercifully, and withdrew to Athens. The Achaeans did not follow them.

Common talk in Athens, again reported by Pausanias,[3] derived from the Oropian incident the pitiful Achaean War with Rome. The Macedonian Menalchidas, it was asserted, wrested the ten talents from the Oropians, but refused to share it with Callicrates. This dishonesty among thieves caused a row between these politicians, out of which was revived the latent antagonism of their two states. Rome was called in, and, in despair of effecting a reconciliation, finally permitted Sparta, Corinth, Argos, Orchomenus, and Heracleia on Oeta to secede from the League. This meant the dissolution of the confederacy. In their indignation the Achaeans insulted and defied the Romans, refused all reparation, and in the war which their senseless conduct provoked they sustained utter defeat, and involved in their ruin the

[1] vii. 11. 7-8.   [2] See Niese, iii. 319, n. 2.
[3] vii. 12 ff. ; cf. Niese, iii. 337 ff.

leagues which existed in Boeotia, Phocis, Locris, and
Euboea, and which had joined them in the struggle.
This was an important gain for Roman policy, inasmuch
as it enabled the Senate to dissolve the Achaean and
the other confederations, and to put the cities composing them individually under the supervision of the
Macedonian proconsul—the Roman official who now sat
in the throne of the great Alexander. For Roman
commerce it was even more important, since the
conquest of Achaea was accompanied by the complete
destruction of Corinth—a wanton outrage, but remarkable chiefly because it was the last of the long series of
sacks and massacres which marked the progress of Roman
arms in the Greek world. It has been affirmed by
Mommsen[1] that the burning of Corinth was deliberate ;
that it betrays the ascendancy of the business interests
in Rome's councils ; that the merchants of Corinth—
and of Carthage—had to be outrooted for the aggrandizement of the merchants of Rome. This may, indeed,
have been the case, but probably the Romans were not
actuated by one motive alone.[2] The destruction of the
city may have been meant as a warning to the rest of
Greece, and hence may be explained on political grounds.
At any rate, there is no doubting the fact that its
destruction *did* benefit greatly Roman business. It
explains in large part the rise of a new commercial
metropolis—Delos—and the domination there, not of
Greek middlemen, but of the agents of Roman capital
and Roman capitalists themselves.

The acquisition of Delos in 166 B.C. had not been an
unmixed blessing for Athens, since out of it had come a
disastrous struggle with the Achaean League, and the
final payment of compensation to the dispossessed
Delians. Moreover, the Romans had given the island
to the Athenians subject to one condition—that the
port was to be a free port.[3] That is to say, the new
owners were not to levy any harbour dues. They were
to abrogate the innumerable petty tolls upon incoming

---

[1] *History of Rome* (Eng. trans.), iii. 69 f.   [2] Holm, iv. 411, 424.
[3] Polybius, xxx. 31 ; Strabo, x. 5. 2-4 (485 f.).

and outgoing commerce,[1] which had been a source of profit to their predecessors, and of exasperation to foreign merchants. This was an important restriction, and its effect upon competing places was disastrous. For Athens and the cleruchy it was a serious disability, in that it left them almost without revenues, and thus deprived them of the means of meeting the expenditures necessary for the equipment of the port and the administration of the island. Of course, the colonists who received houses, shops, and lands were benefited to this extent, and also in that they came thereby into an advantageous position to profit from the development of trade and commerce which was implicit in the creation of a free port. Nor did Athens take over an undeveloped site, since from time immemorial the shore in front of the sacred precinct was provided with docks, and protected from the north winds and seas by a great mole artificially constructed of blocks of granite sunk in the strait,[2] between Delos and Rheneia; while during the last two generations the dock space had been doubled towards the south,[3] the agora furnished with stoas such as became the mode for public and private business and pleasure during the Hellenistic period,[4] and reservoirs constructed to store and control the waters which the Inopus poured down from the slopes of Mount Cythnus into the central valley of the island.[5] But for all that it is doubtful whether the Athenian state, through the munificence of private citizens mainly, did not have to give out for a long time more than it received. Polybius, indeed, goes further, and intimates that Delos was a positive disadvantage to it.

The removal of harbour dues, doubtless, helped to increase the commerce of Delos; but only to increase, not to create it. Had it been possible for the Piraeus or Chalcis to attract business by a similar exemption, the example of Delos would have been speedily followed.

---

[1] See, for example, the regulations in regard to the import and sale of wood and charcoal published in *BCH.*, 1907, p. 46 ff.; cf. Homolle, "Comptes des hiéropes du temple d'Apollon délien," *BCH.*, 1882, p. 66.

[2] Holleaux, *Acad. inscr. C.R.*, 1909, p. 400.   [3] *Ibid.* 401.

[4] *Ibid.* 415; cf. below, ix. 363 and n. 3.

[5] *Acad. inscr. C.R.*, 1909, p. 403 ff., and especially 406.

The island possessed the additional advantage of an
admirable location.   There is, apparently, nothing
inherent in a point to make it for ever the meeting-
place of men who go down to the sea on ships. Without
a suitable harbour, of course, the thing cannot happen,
but with it the most has still to be done.   The
determining matter is situation at an advantageous
point on the main line of the world's commerce.   The
route of traffic by sea, however, is dependent upon
various factors, such as the seat of maritime empire,
the advance of civilization, and progress in shipbuilding.
These are the forces which made Athens, Rhodes, and
Delos in turn the *emporia* of the world's trade.   So
long as Athens ruled the sea, Hellas was the civilized
market, and the ebb and flow of trade was between
continental Greece and the rest of the Mediterranean
littoral ; the Piraeus was the great mart of European
business. When, however, the destruction of the Persian
empire by Alexander transferred the main scene of Greek
activity from Europe to Asia, and the Greek cities
between Sinope and Alexandria were enabled to forward
goods into, and receive commodities from, not a mere
fringe of territory, but an almost measureless continent
with a vast and industrious population ; when, moreover,
prior to 256 B.C., the friendly Ptolemaic, and thereafter
no single state, was in lasting political control of the
coasts of the eastern Mediterranean, such wares as were
not carried directly in the huge ships, then constructed
for the first time,[1] from the Asiatic Greek cities to their
destination in Sicily, Carthage, Italy, Greece, Macedon,
Pontus, Bosporus, and elsewhere, were brought in the
old-fashioned small vessels to Rhodes. The central
location of this island,[2] its prudent political neutrality,
enlightened commercial policy and laws, and energetic
sea-faring people, qualified it rarely both for carrying
the trade of the world and for the work of interchange

---

[1] Beloch, iii. 1. 306 f. ; Tarn, *JHS.*, 1910, p. 209 ff.
[2] See Philippson in *Petermann's Mitt.*, *Ergänzungsheft*, 134, pp. 159, 164,
and the remarks of W. T. Arnold, *Studies of Roman Imperialism*, 203. Cf.
also Francotte, *L'Industrie dans la Grèce ancienne*, i. 49, n. 2, and Dessau,
Hermes, xviii. 153.

—the buying and selling of commodities, and the exchange, borrowing, and loaning of money. But when Italy conquered the world, the Romans became the chief buyers, and the streams of commerce changed their currents towards the West; when, moreover, the Romans turned their political supremacy to profit, and took the banking, mercantile, and trading business into their own hands,[1] they could handle the goods which went to and fro in big bottoms at Tarentum or Puteoli; but for the concentration of the coast trade, the direct dealing with men from the Pontus, Bithynia, Asia Minor, Cilicia, Phoenicia, Egypt, and Greece, they needed a forepost in the East, and they found it at Delos. They had been in the habit of going there before the transfer of the island to the Athenians. As early as 200 B.C. an occasional Italian name appears in the Delian documents, and after the establishment of Roman supremacy they became more numerous; and not simply did men who called themselves Romans visit the island for trade, but some became permanent residents there.[2] Delos was a holy place, and its inhabitants enjoyed the benefits of religious protection. Thus even in the death struggle between Rome and Macedon we find the warships of both nations lying peaceably at anchor in the roadstead of Delos, and only engaging in battle when they put out into the high seas. Here was a place where the detested Italians could do business without constantly risking their lives. Here, too, at the annually recurring festivals, they could find the peculiar products of many different towns and countries. Here they had only the presence of a demonstratively hostile republic of contemptible "parasites of Apollo" to disturb them. The place would be ideal if the Delians were removed and their successors were friendly to Rome, and prohibited from collecting tolls from the Italians or from those with whom the Italians did business. Thus it came that in 166 B.C. the

---

[1] See especially Parvan, *Die Nationalität der Kaufleute im römischen Kaiserreiche*, 6 ff., Breslau, Diss., 1909.
[2] The main lines in the development of the Roman colony on Delos were perceived by Homolle and sketched in his well-known article in *BCH.* viii. 75 ff. Naturally, the details are now altogether unreliable.

Roman senate conferred a favour upon the Athenians, and a much greater one upon its own men of business through restoring Delos to Athens. Thus it was that Delos became a free port. Naturally, the Rhodians were hit hard, and the blow was all the more severe in that it did not come alone; for at the same time Rome broke up their empire, put their government into the hands of a compliant and reactionary oligarchy, and humiliated the proud republic before the eyes of the world in such a way as to make it conspicuously clear that Rhodes could no longer protect her own business interests, and that men who trusted their goods to Rhodian ships or their money to Rhodian banks did so at great risk of complete loss. The spirit of the Rhodians was speedily crushed, and already in 164 B.C.[1] Rhodian ambassadors complained to the Roman senate that their annual harbour dues had sunk from one million to one hundred and fifty thousand *drachmae*. Of course, Delos did not immediately reap a corresponding benefit. The sudden prostration of Rhodes, doubtless, occasioned a general paralysis of commerce and a dissipation into many ports of the business she had alone handled. Corinth, probably, received a large share of it. But when the Romans appeared in the East in still larger numbers, when Mummius burned the Isthmian city and laid a curse upon its site, and when the annexation of the kingdom of the Attalids and its surrender by C. Gracchus to the tender mercies of the *equites* made Asia Minor the most important sphere of Roman business, the great days of Delos came.

The visit to Rome of Carneades, Diogenes, and Critolaus came in a crucial moment of its development. From time immemorial the ideas and customs of the Greeks had been quietly transforming the life of the Roman people; so that no one could realize the extent

[1] Polybius, xxx. 31. The change of the MSS. of Polybius, by which the reduction of revenues is made to amount to only 150,000 *drachmae*, or from 1,000,000 to 850,000 *drachmae* (van Gelder, *Gesch. der alten Rhodier*, 156, n. 1; Niese, iii. 196), is unwarranted. Had the Rhodians lost only twenty-five talents they would not have complained so bitterly. A fluctuation of that amount might have occurred at any time. The political factor explains the sudden paralysis of Rhodian commerce.

to which commerce, architecture, art, religion, and political and military organization had been developed under Greek influence, exerted directly or indirectly. The Greek games had been introduced, and in time the Dionysiac artists came also. They brought with them, in particular, the Athenian comedies, which playwrights translated and adapted to the Roman stage. Thus between 240 and 167 B.C. Livius Andronicus, Naevius, Plautus, and Caecilius acclimated the New Comedy in the Italian capital. This meant an enormous extension of the influence of Athenian culture; and when in the next seven years Terence completed his work, it could be said that the diction and technique of Menander had been fairly reproduced in Latium. During this same period Ennius established the Greek versification and manner in the use of the Latin Epos; so that the national rhythms and the national comedy suffered an early death. But it was clearly demonstrated that the Latin language was a fit instrument for high poetry. The case was by no means so clear for prose. In the Senate men were long since wont to express their thoughts in terse and vigorous speech, and the Roman laws, decrees, and edicts had probably obtained the precision and clarity for which they were subsequently noted; but no one could as yet attain grace and elegance in Latin prose. Hence, as well as for the sake of reaching the world of letters, which did not know Latin, the Roman annalists of the early second century B.C. wrote in Greek. There was in Rome a circle of influential men who made a cult of things Hellenic, patronised Ennius and Terence, and gave their friendship to distinguished Greek men of letters who visited their city; but it was a small circle, and its very zeal brought into prominence the rapidity with which Rome was being denationalized; so that of late there had been a reaction against Greek culture—that is to say, against culture altogether. The military and political weakness of the Greek people, the differences of their national character from that of Rome, and the menace which Greek institutions and habits presented to the traditional customs and beliefs of the

Romans, had dispelled the illusions with which the
Romans first came to Greece, and led many to believe
that their own rough and simple living, doing, and
thinking were far superior to the wide and polite culture
of the older people.   It was a revelation to the Romans
to see the great school-heads face to face, to attend the
public lectures they gave, and experience upon themselves the matchless persuasiveness and charm of their
Hellenic speech.   High society, not merely the Scipionic
circle—the friends of things Greek—but also Cato, the
leader of the reaction, went to listen to the philosophers,
especially to Carneades, admittedly the greatest debater
of his age, and the most conspicuous of living scholars.
He made a profound impression upon his hearers ; so
impressive was he, in fact, that Cato caused the Senate
to get the business of the embassy settled and the
ambassadors out of the state as speedily as possible.   The
visit of Carneades marked an epoch in the intellectual
development of Rome, and his eloquence was a living
memory long after the most enlightened had ceased to
know for what he came ; and the retorts he made and
the topics he discussed were well known in literary and
philosophic circles five hundred years after his death.
Lucilius, Cicero, Plutarch, Gellius, and Lactantius, to
say nothing of the ancient historians of Rome, testify
to the lasting effect produced by his lectures and those
of his colleagues.[1]   Their visit to Rome became fixed in
tradition as the formal introduction of Greek philosophy
to the Italian people.

The heads of three of the four Athenian schools of
philosophy had travelled in company to Rome in 156/5
B.C., and had not been prevented by differences of creed
or personal rivalry from making a joint representation
to the Senate.[2]   This does not mean that the Academicians, Stoics, and Peripatetics lived harmoniously together while at home.   In fact, so far from this being
the case, Carneades, the chief of the schoolmen who
visited Rome, devoted his great abilities chiefly to a

[1] Constant Martha, Études morales sur l'antiquité : le philosophe Carnéade à
Rome, 1896, p. 61 ff.   See also the questions of Cicero prefixed to this chapter.
[2] Mahaffy, The Silver Age of the Greek World, 97.

refutation of the teachings of his colleague, Diogenes the Stoic—to a vindication of the open mind as a general attitude of thought as against the claims of a dogmatic summarization of truth,[1] such as Chrysippus had recently made. He was by far the most striking figure in academic circles during the middle of the second century B.C., and to his young Roman contemporary, the poet Lucilius, he stood out as the classic example of brilliancy and resourcefulness in discussion. Carneades is the pragmatist *par excellence* among the ancient philosophers. The inability of man to attain to absolute truth he upheld with Arcesilaus, but he felt and acknowledged the need of a working scheme for the conduct of life, and formulated it in his doctrine of probabilities. He distinguished between what was merely probable, what was probable by universal assumption, and what by universal assumption after circumspect criticism. Hence he assailed the Stoics not only because of their general dogmatic attitude, but also because of the improbability of many of their doctrines; but at the same time it was open to him to find his probabilities in specific articles of their creed, or of that of the Peripatetics and Epicureans, as well as among the tenets of the earlier Academicians. Indeed, the determination of values, in the absence of an absolute criterion of truth, had to be made on the basis of experience and general agreement;[2] so that a sharp line could not be drawn henceforth between the results of science and the postulates of tradition and superstition. Philosophy thus ceased to uphold the convictions of educated men, and subsequently religious belief was equally possible with religious disbelief. On the other hand, the teaching of Carneades was fundamental for eclecticism, " the creed of weary minds," which enjoyed so much vogue in Roman times. This was tantamount to an abandonment of the essential differences between the various systems of thought; and it led eventually to the formation of a

---

[1] Hirzel, *Untersuchungen zu Ciceros philosophischen Schriften*, ii. 256 ff., iii. 149 ff. ; Susemihl, *op. cit.* i. 83 ff., 127 ff. ; Martha, *loc. cit.* ; Zeller, *Phil. der Griechen*, iii. 1⁴. 507 ff.

[2] von Arnim, *Kultur der Gegenwart*, i. 5. 252 ff.

mosaic-like structure, made without much regard to the derivation of the component parts. But the immediate effect of the surrender of characteristic doctrines was the over-emphasis of the outward and non-essential differences, and the conversion of a struggle for truth into what was, in fact, little more than a contest for influence and pupils. The pupils of Carneades came from all parts of the known world. Thus in the year after his fame was carried dramatically into the West by his mission to Rome, a young man named Hasdrubal had come to Athens from Carthage (155/4 B.C.), who, upon devoting himself to philosophy, entered the school of Carneades under the Greek name of Cleito-machus (151/0 B.C.). The Semite never deviated much from the doctrines and methods of his teacher, but he was an energetic fellow, who knew how to bring himself before the public, as his work, written to console the Carthaginians for the destruction of their city in 146 B.C., and the dedication of one of his books to L. Censorinus, consul in 149 B.C., and another to Lucilius the poet, shows. Hence when it appeared that there was no place in the Academy for a young man beside its old head, he left it (140/39 B.C.), and moving to the suburb of Agrae beyond the Ilyssus, he opened a new college in the Palladium.[1] He had the advantage of comparative youth—a rare quality in a profession which, in the third and second centuries B.C., produced an unusual number of nonagenarians, and which was represented ordinarily in its high places by men of advanced years[2]—and soon attracted a large group of pupils. He conducted the new institution for eleven years. In the meanwhile Carneades, incapacitated by old age and blindness, had retired (137/6 B.C.), and given the management of the Academy first to a name-sake, and six years later (131/0 B.C.) to a certain Crates of Tarsus. Crates was, apparently, a small personality, and it was possible for Cleitomachus to exist beside him

---

[1] It is probably an echo of an attempt to explain away this desertion that in Cicero, *Acad.* ii. 98, we read : *a Clitomacho sumam, qui usque ad senectutem cum Carneade fuit.*

[2] Mahaffy, *op. cit.* 87 ff.

once the imperious old master was no more. Accordingly, when this occurred, he abandoned the Palladium and returned to the Academy (129/8 B.C.), bringing with him his large clientèle of pupils, one of whom was Philon of Larisa, who afterwards succeeded him. We do not know with what feelings Crates saw him arrive. Perhaps his health was failing; at any rate he died two years after Carneades (127/6 B.C.), and Cleitomachus now became, in name as well as in fact, head of the Academy.[1] Occurrences such as this were not uncommon within the schools,[2] and naturally the interscholastic feuds were productive of more lasting bitterness; but these dissensions were weakened in their power to create general disorder by the fact that the school-heads and the majority of the pupils were not Athenians by birth or citizenship. Still, such disputes raised feeling in the city, and in one particular at least the public authorities took sides.[3] They refused to countenance the teachings of the fourth of the schools—that of Epicurus. The other three were incorporated in the school system of the state, and the ephebes were required to round off their military education by attending indiscriminately the lectures of the Academicians, Stoics, and Peripatetics, but no rector dare take his charges to the Garden.[4] The disability thus imposed threw the Epicureans into opposition to the government, and since the government was pro-Roman and the Roman authorities were persecuting the Epicurean teachers also, the Garden became anti-Roman in its influence.

The two schools which enjoyed the patronage and sympathy of high society in Rome were the Stoa and the Academy. Cleitomachus made himself known and appreciated in the Scipionic circle in Rome, and both he and, after his death (110/9 B.C.), Philon, his successor,

[1] For the details of this incident see *Cornell Studies*, x. 74 f., corrected by Jacoby, *Apollodors Chronik*, 385, and Mekler, *Index Hercul.*, 100; also, Kirchner, *GGA.*, 1900, p. 465 f., and *PA.*, 1641, *Add.* The results have been restated by Kolbe, *Die attischen Archonten*, 121. Cf. Hirzel, *op. cit.* iii. 162 ff.

[2] See above, v. 233, vi. 258 f.

[3] For the gilds of the college students see Athen. v. 186 A πολλῶν γοῦν εἰσι φιλοσόφων ἐν ἄστει σύνοδοι, τῶν μὲν Διογενιστῶν, τῶν δὲ Ἀντιπατριστῶν λεγομένων, τῶν δὲ Παναιτιαστῶν. Cf. Crönert, *Sitzb. d. Berl. Akad.*, 1904, p. 482.

[4] *IG.* ii. 471. 19 ff. ; cf. Capes, *University Life in Ancient Athens*, 30.

were repeatedly honoured by having Roman magistrates or noblemen among their auditors,[1] while Panaetius of Rhodes, who between his student time in Athens (152/1 B.C.) and his succession to the headship of the Stoa had paid a visit to Rome,[2] was received there with enthusiasm. He became an intimate associate of Scipio Aemilianus, and the teacher of most of the men of worth and honour in Roman public life during the following generation.[3] No such attentions were paid to the Peripatetics. The Epicureans eschewed politics on principle, but the followers of Aristotle were traditionally active in public affairs, and we have some evidence for the belief[4] that they resented the partiality of the Romans for their rivals.

Despite the brilliancy of Carneades, it seems probable that the Stoa, under Diogenes of Babylon ($\dagger$ *ante* 152 B.C.) and Antipater of Tarsus ($\dagger$ *ca.* 140 B.C.), attracted the most active and original students at the middle of the second century B.C. The importance of the Stoics in Attic life is evidenced by the fact that over a dozen of them were among the commissioners who administered the Ptolemaea in 152/1 B.C.;[5] while the presence in the school of Blossius of Cumae, the intimate and adviser of Tiberius Gracchus, and Panaetius of Rhodes, argues sufficiently for their historical influence. It has been mentioned already[6] that the Stoa made a special appeal to the Athenian youth, and that Mnesarchus and Dardanus of Athens were among the most distinguished pupils of Diogenes. He had also the far greater honour of starting Apollodorus, the son of Asclepiades, on his

---

[1] The *praetor* Crassus attended the lectures of Cleitomachus. Cic. *De orat.* i. 11; Homolle, *BCH.*, 1893, 149 f. Cichorius (*Untersuchungen zu Lucilius*, 40 ff.) makes the poet Lucilius his pupil also, but the social standing of Lucilius and the official position of Cleitomachus explain their relationship as well as the other data adduced by Cichorius. No one of the senatorial aristocracy who was born at Suessa Aurunca, died at Naples, and belonged to the Scipionic circle could fail to be saturated with Greek ideas, and to sprinkle his pages with Greek phrases. I see no reason for thinking that Cleitomachus did not justify, or at least condone, the destruction of Carthage.

[2] Crönert, *Sitzb. d. Berl. Akad.*, 1904, p. 475 ff. ; Cichorius, *Rhein. Mus.*, 1908, p. 197 ff. ; Kolbe, *op. cit.* 115 ff. ; *Klio*, 1909, p. 337 ff.

[3] Mahaffy, *op. cit.* 101 ff.   [4] See below, x. 441.

[5] Crönert, *Sitzb. d. Berl. Akad.*, 1904, p. 471 ff. ; Cichorius, *Rhein. Mus.*, 1908, p. 197 ff. ; cf. *Klio*, 1909, p. 337 ff.

[6] See above, vi. 260, n. 3.

scientific career. This man, according to Schwartz,[1] one
of the three greatest philologists of Greece, was an
Athenian by birth—an asset of considerable value in an
age when to be an Athenian established, in the case of
literary or scientific men, *prima facie* evidence of the
possession of finer qualities of mind and manners than
were to be found in newer centres of culture.[2] The
Stoa was his college; the Museum of Alexandria his
university, and he is said to have collaborated for many
years with Aristarchus (*ca*. 151(?)–145 B.C.). The accession
of Euergetes II. to the throne of Egypt probably cost
both of them their positions, and Apollodorus went to
Pergamum, where, prior to 138 and probably in 144 B.C.,
he published his metrical *Chronicle*. Subsequently he
returned to Athens, and died there after having brought
this work down to a date later than 120/19 B.C.[3] He
combined in his own person the training of the three
great centres of learning of his time—an eclecticism
being thus practised which implies in the case of a
philologist the possession of the highest scientific ideals.
His *Chronicle*, which, for mnemonic purposes, was
written in iambics, was based largely on the work of his
predecessor Eratosthenes; and it was sound in method,
accurate in results, and a standard authority for several
following generations. This was perhaps the least of
his books. His commentary on the catalogue of the
ships in Homer's *Iliad* and his history of Greek religion
(Περὶ θεῶν) were apparently of much more intrinsic value
—the first a sensible, well-informed treatment of
Homeric geography, to which Strabo is much indebted;
the second a scientific, but not unsympathetic, inquiry
into the phenomena of religious life. Apollodorus was
the last of the great Athenian scholars.

Antipater's most distinguished pupil was the Rhodian
Panaetius, who succeeded him as head of the Stoa at
about 140 B.C. His youth had been spent in a free
republic ruled by a commercial aristocracy; in Athens

---

[1] P.-W. i. 2875 ; cf. Wilamowitz, *Griech. Literatur*, 115.
[2] Pseudo-Scymnus in Jacoby, *Apollodors Chronik*, 2 ff. ; cf. also below,
x. 458, n. 2.
[3] Jacoby, *op. cit.* 12 ff.

he had found a Tory democracy left in charge of the government by popular consent, while dominant in the world at large was the Roman senate—the élite of the Romans and potentially of mankind. The instruction of men for the realization of one of their primary instincts—political life—had been a fundamental ideal of Stoicism from the beginning;[1] and Zeno had set forward as a model for human imitation his ideal wise man, who could be converted into the sphere of real politics only as an enlightened despot like Antigonus Gonatas. Chrysippus had then taught the school to trust for the propagation of its creed mainly upon an intellectual appeal; but by the very fact of dispensing with a political agent he had been obliged to take the populace more into his confidence, and had emphasized the republican basis of Stoicism—its conviction that all men were naturally possessed of the qualities requisite for sound public life.[2] It remained for Panaetius to discard the vain intellectualism of Chrysippus, and both to soften the impracticable Stoic ideals in such a way as to make them capable of more general realization, and to designate an aristocracy as their fitting embodiment and their proper executive. The only aristocracy thinkable for such a task, however, was the Roman senate. To have brought Stoicism into direct contact with the Roman state, and to have furnished the best Roman senators with a worthy theory of their own rule, is the sufficient basis for Panaetius's claim to ecumenical importance.[3]

The year of the mission of the philosophers to Rome (156/5 B.C.) was also fixed by tradition as the point at which Greek art entered upon its Indian summer. Thus Pliny fixes in this year precisely the end of a long period of obscurity which began, he alleges, in 296 B.C.[4] It seems that no new *Richtung* appeared at this time, but

---

[1] Wendland, *Hellenistisch-römische Kultur*, 16 ff.

[2] φύσει πολιτικὰ ζῷα : von Arnim, *Stoic. vet. frg.* iii. p. 77, 314 ; cf. Kärst, *Gesch. des hellenistischen Zeitalters*, ii. 136 ff.

[3] Schwartz, *Charakterköpfe aus der antiken Literatur*, i. 85 ff.

[4] Pliny, *Nat. Hist.* xxxiv. 52: "cessavit deinde ars, ac rursus olympiade clvi. revixit, cum fuere longe quidem infra praedictos, probati tamen, Antaeus, Callistratus, Polycles Athenaeus, Callixenus, Pythocles, Pythias, Timocles."

that the renascence of sculpture, of which Pliny is chiefly
thinking, was occasioned by a change of taste on the
part of the public ; and since the style which now found
appreciation was that prevalent in Athens, the revival
was particularly noticeable there.   In the third century
B.C. Athens had been conservative in art as in everything
else.[1]   Her sculptors had turned to portraiture, but, as
already mentioned, they had done so with genuine
classic reserve.[2]   They had also developed in connexion
with the choregic and *agonothetic* monuments a decorative art which had much in common in lines and composition with the vase paintings of the fourth century
B.C., and which thus approximated to the well-known
Hellenistic reliefs ;[3] but they had shrunk from both the
colossal and the realistic-dramatic effects of the Rhodian
and Anatolian schools.   They had, accordingly, continued to make in the commission of the state what
seem to have been excellent portrait statues, and to have
executed the other tasks which the slender resources of
the city enabled, somewhat less skilfully, but in the
general style of Praxiteles, Scopas, and Lysippus.[4]
What they obtained in 156 B.C. was an enlargement
of opportunity.   For, in the first place, the renewed
wealth of Athens gave them more work to do at home,
where ample employment was afforded to Eubulides and
his son, Eucheir, of Cropidae—the representatives in the
early half of the second century B.C. of a distinguished
Athenian family of artists—in the execution of various
commissions, such as the statues of distinguished men,
the decoration of the new precincts of the *Demos and
Graces* and of the Dionysiac artists, and, doubtless, also
the plastic adornment of the stoas of Eumenes and
Attalus and of the Olympieum.[5]   Their contemporaries
Caïcosthenes and Dies, sons of Apollonides of Thria,
made many statues of Athenian men and women—eight
pedestals inscribed with the names of one or both of
them being extant—and in addition likenesses of athletes

[1] Collignon, *Griech. Plastik*, ii. 492 ff.   [2] See above, iv. 167.
[3] *BCH.*, 1907, p. 504 ff.
[4] See above, vi. 260, n. 4 ; Robert, in P.-W. vi. 875.
[5] P.-W. vi. 871 ; Collignon, ii. 672 ff.

and comedians. For his success in portraiture, as well as
for his modelling in clay, Caïcosthenes achieved a lasting
reputation.[1] There was so much, in fact, for artists to
do in Athens that foreigners of note migrated to it at
this time.[2] The third most distinguished Athenian
family of sculptors,[3] on the other hand,—that of Timarchides and his two sons, Polycles and Dionysius, of
Thoricus,—accepted a call to Rome, which was now
adorning with porticoes and statuary — the plunder
of Syracuse, Tarentum, Macedon, Ambracia, and many
other Greek places for the most part[4]—the temples
built in the preceding generation. These three artists
entered into the employ of Metellus Macedonicus, and
executed famous images of Apollo, Jupiter, and Juno,
which were subsequently to be seen in the portico which
bore his name.[5] The great wealth of the imperial people
was thus put at the service of the Attic school of art,
and from this time on there was a constant resort of
Athenian sculptors to Rome.[6] This was probably the
most important condition of the renascence of art in
Athens ;[7] and its origin at approximately the time of
the mission of the philosophers led to the view that
philosophy and art came to Rome from Athens in the
same year.[8] It was, however, supplemented by another
condition almost equally influential—the practical monopoly of sculpture on Delos by artists from Athens.
There numerous opportunities for the exercise of their
talents were presented ; and in the last half of the second
century B.C. the Attic style dominated on the island.[9]
It drew its strength from the past—from the master-

[1] Pliny, *Nat. Hist.* xxxiv. 87, xxxv. 155 ; *IG.* ii. 3. 1633, 1635, 1636, 1383, 1379, 1634, 1161 (ii. 5. p. 248), ii. 5. 1406b. In Appendix I., pp. 331 ff., Shebelew (*op. cit.*) deals with the family Eubulides-Eucheir ; in Appendix II., pp. 346 ff., with that of Dies-Caïcosthenes ; and in Appendix III., pp. 349 ff., with Polycles.
[2] From Pliny (*Nat. Hist.* xxxv. 135) we learn that Aemilius Paulus obtained from Athens a philosopher and painter named Metrodorus. He wished a tutor and painter in one. After 167 B.C. a Macedonian artist named Heracleides moved to Athens. *Ibid.*
[3] Kirchner, *PA.* 11992, P.-W. v. 1000.   [4] Collignon, ii. 660 ff.
[5] Pliny, *Nat. Hist.* xxxvi. 35 ; Collignon, ii. 674 ff.
[6] Collignon, ii. 684 ff.
[7] Overbeck, *Griech. Plastik,*[4] ii. 414, and especially 428 ff.
[8] M. Marcellus was consul, along with P. Scipio, in 156/5 B.C.
[9] See below, ix. 410, n. 1.

pieces of the fifth and fourth centuries B.C. It was
frankly eclectic, like the contemporary Attic philosophy,
and escaped from being purely imitative by combining
themes and methods of various old masters and various
old arts. In technical skill these anticipators of the
neo-Atticists of the Roman age were not much inferior
to their models, but they made their strongest appeal
because of their dependence upon others—because of the
conviction which grew in this age with each succeeding
generation that that was best which came nearest the
classic : a conviction which concerned not art alone but
also rhetoric, poetry, and culture in general. It was,
perhaps, but the recognition of the truth ; at any rate,
it was the deliberate opinion of the most eminent critics
of the time,[1] but it meant the negation of further progress. This was the beginning of the end. Not long
afterwards Polybius interpreted the preceding century
of Greek history to the disadvantage of Athens,[2] which he
represented as a nest of pampered parasites, and before
the next generation had passed its *akmé* the Roman
officials, whose practical sense made it difficult for them
to conceive how a people devoid of power could be
possessed of virtue, endorsed his judgment and made
manifest their contempt for the living Athenians by
words and actions. But for the present the future was
closed. In 166 B.C. the western nobles, whose rule over
the nations was now almost as undisputed as that of the
Olympians in the universe,[3] rendered homage to Athens

---

[1] Andron and Menecles in Athen. iv. 184 B. This doctrine was disseminated
particularly from Pergamum. Susemihl, ii. 483 ; Hauser, *Die neuattischen
Reliefs*, 180 ; Collignon, ii. 664. It was thought later that the scattering of
the scientists from Alexandria under Euergetes II. caused a revival of learning
in Greece generally. See below, ix. 368. That Apollodorus is our ultimate
authority for the doctrine as to the renascence of art in 156/5 B.C., though
asserted by Kalkmann (*Die Quellen der Kunstgesch. des Plinius*, 34 ff.), is doubtful;
cf. Jacoby, *Apollodors Chronik*, 30. That the date was fixed with reference to
the mission of the philosophers seems to me obvious.

[2] How inadequate an impression Polybius had formed of the political achievements of Athens is obvious from his remarks at vi. 44. His teachers (as interpreted by their followers, doubtless ; cf. Newman, *The Politics of Aristotle*, vol. ii.
p. xii.) had been the political theorists, Plato and Aristotle, whose conception of
Pericles Perrin (*Trans. Conn. Acad. of Arts and Sciences*, 1909, p. 219 ff.) shows
to have impaired the judgment of Plutarch also. Polybius's generalization
leaves out of account entirely Athenian experience after Aristotle's time.

[3] They were, in fact, rated with the Olympians ; see below, ix. 366, 383, n. 1.

as the cultural centre of the world by reuniting all the Athenians in one state, and by giving to them the custody of the new *emporium* of Mediterranean trade ; and for what they got in direct return ten years later— a far-working intellectual and aesthetic impulse—the best of them continued to be grateful for many a generation.

CHAPTER IX

ATHENS AND DELOS

ἀλλὰ σὺ Δήλῳ, Φοῖβε, μάλιστ᾽ ἐπιτέρπεαι ἦτορ,
ἔνθα τοι ἑλκεχίτωνες Ἰάονες ἠγερέθονται
αὐτοῖς σὺν παίδεσσι καὶ αἰδοίῃς ἀλόχοισιν.
οἱ δέ σε πυγμαχίῃ τε καὶ ὀρχηθμῷ καὶ ἀοιδῇ
μνησάμενοι τέρπουσιν, ὅταν στήσωνται ἀγῶνα.
φαίη κ᾽ ἀθανάτους καὶ ἀγήρως ἔμμεναι αἰεί,
ὃς τότ᾽ ἐπαντιάσει᾽, ὅτ᾽ Ἰάονες ἀθρόοι εἶεν·
πάντων γάρ κεν ἴδοιτο χάριν, τέρψαιτο δὲ θυμὸν
ἄνδρας τ᾽ εἰσορόων καλλιζώνους τε γυναῖκας,
νῆάς τ᾽ ὠκείας ἠδ᾽ αὐτῶν κτήματα πολλά.

Homeric Hymn to Apollo, 146 ff.

. . . ἡ Δῆλος, δυναμένη μυριάδας ἀνδραπόδων αὐθημερὸν καὶ δέξασθαι καὶ ἀποπέμψαι,
ὥστε καὶ παροιμίαν γενέσθαι διὰ τοῦτο, "ἔμπορε, κατάπλευσον, ἐξελοῦ, πάντα
πέπραται."—STRABO, xiv. 5. 2 (668).

THE interests both of Athens and of the Athenian cleruchy at Delos were bound up closely with those of the temple of Apollo. The sanctuary was not only the depository and recipient of many valuable dedicatory objects—of which an annual inventory was required from the custodians of the sacred treasures and the committee on religious matters [1]—but it was the owner of residences, flats, shops, market franchises, and farms on the island, and the possessor of a considerable capital, which it loaned, under the Athenian administration, at ten per cent per annum for the normal period of five years. [2] The same officials who made out the inventories were required to prepare an account of the financial transactions of the year, and submit both records to magistrates and jurors in Athens for audit. [3] The docu-

[1] BCH., 1905, p. 533, 554.
[2] von Schoeffer, "De Deli insulae rebus," Berl. Stud. ix. 1. 205 ; cf. BCH., 1903, p. 63.
[3] BCH., 1892, p. 371 ; 1889, p. 426 ; cf. 1905, p. 196, 532. The inventories for 157/6 B.C. and 151/0 B.C. are still unpublished. None of the accounts have

ments were then inscribed upon stone and published at Delos. The charge of the temple property fell primarily upon the shoulders of the custodians of sacred treasures,[1] but the committee on religious matters was associated with them in making the inventories. Perhaps the two sections worked as one body in investing the moneys, and managing the other properties of the temple—rather, temples, for the same officials had the care of all the religious establishments on Delos. It is possible that in the financial administration the functions of the two sections converged ;[2] for the specific and separate duties of the committee on religious matters were the maintenance and repair of the religious buildings, monuments, and precincts, and the construction of new sacred edifices.[3] Of course, both Boards were assisted in the details of their business by the nine priests,[4] who, attached, one to each building or precinct, dated by their names the statues, *exedras*, chapels, and other large objects dedicated during their years of office, looked after the several interests of their own temples, attended to the ritual and sacrifices requisite for worship, and probably defrayed a large part of the expense.[5] The four higher offices seem to have been held by young men of good families in Athens—a wise precaution, in view of the great value of the temple treasures committed to their care. These were apparently taken over by the Athenian authorities

been printed as yet. Small extracts from them appear in *BCH.*, 1880, p. 182 ff. (162/1 ff. B.C.). Homolle (*BCH.*, 1903, p. 63) has promised to edit some samples soon.

[1] The work was actually done by a δημόσιος selected by show of hands (*BCH.*, 1889, p. 426 ; 1905, p. 534).

[2] Until the last thirteen years of the Delian administration it is only occasionally that all four *hieropoei* were concerned with the treasures (Homolle, *BCH.*, 1882, 58 ; 1890, 417 ; P.-W. iv. 2486). Regularly only the two who correspond to the custodians of sacred treasures appear in the records. After 179 B.C., however, the four seldom fail.

[3] For their names upon edifices and dedications see *BCH.*, 1883, p. 338 ; 1882, p. 334 ; 1877, p. 88 ; 1892, p. 481 ; 1908, pp. 386, 442, 427, 429, and elsewhere.

[4] *BCH.*, 1907, p. 425, No. 17 (153/2 B.C.). In 137/6 B.C. a tenth was added —that of Serapis (see below, ix. 358), and in *ca.* 120 B.C. an eleventh—that of Aphrodite Hagne (see below, ix. 386) ; but in 88/6 B.C. these two deities were given but one priest between them, so that in *BCH.*, 1908, p. 438, No. 64 (*ca.* 84 B.C.), only ten priests are listed in all. See *Klio*, 1909, p. 333 ff.

[5] For a decree in honour of the priests for 153/2 B.C. see *BCH.*, 1907, p. 425, No. 17 ; and for a list of those in office for some year shortly after 86/4 B.C. see *BCH.*, 1908, p. 438, No. 64.

intact, and seventy-eight years after the Athenian occupation began, they were of sufficient importance to justify a struggle for the possession of Delos. They had probably increased enormously in the interval.[1] Certainly the conversion of Delos into a free port, and the consequent influx of foreigners, had an immediate effect on the character of the temple property and business. " Where there had been in 179 B.C.," says M. Homolle,[2] " only residences leased to a single tenant, there appeared in 157 B.C. large and small apartment houses, studios, and stores, which yielded much more ample revenues. Instead of Delians and Rheneians alone,[3] men from Athens, Myndus, Elaea, Naxos, Apollonia, Stratoniceia, Tenos, Antioch, Phaselis, Sidon, Eleutherna, Chalcis, and Italy leased the temple properties, or went as surety for the tenants. The amount of the income derived from rents had already tripled. A similar change had taken place in the clientèle of borrowers, but there the diversity of provenience was less marked." As with temple property, so with private property on the island—there was everywhere a rapid doubling and tripling of values.[4] The effects can be readily imagined. Many a poor cleruch of 166 B.C. must have become wealthy within ten years, simply through the advance of prices paid for real estate. And this was a gain which came to Athenians alone ;[5] for under the Attic law foreigners had no right to

[1] See below, x. 445. Only one or two of the inventories for the second Athenian period have been published up to the present (*BCH.*, 1905, p. 532 ff. ; 1910, p. 181 ff).

[2] *BCH.*, 1884, p. 93.

[3] Ziebarth (*Zeitschr. f. vergl. Rechtswiss.* xix. 283) cites the names of three foreigners who were tenants prior to 166 B.C.

[4] Fluctuations of values had occurred earlier. Thus between 253 and *ca.* 243 B.C. there was a notable advance of rents received for houses owned by the temple. In *ca.* 224 B.C., on the other hand, an extraordinary fall is noticeable. This is retrieved in 179 B.C., when Delos had already begun its second century B.C. career. See the table in Ziebarth, *loc. cit.* 278 f. ; cf. *BCH.*, 1890, p. 437. The farms owned by the temple, on the other hand, kept constantly declining in value during the third century B.C. (*BCH.*, 1905, p. 440). Hence when we speak of the increase in value of private property in the text, the town lots with their improvements are meant. We are not yet able to continue these investigations beyond 166 B.C., though the materials have been in the hands of M. Homolle for a quarter of a century. Hence all that remains is to quote his generalizations.

[5] It is sometimes affirmed (*e.g.* by Kornemann in P.-W. iv. 1197) that Romans had the rights of citizens in regard to property in the cities in which they were settled. Whether this was the case or not I do not know, but it is

hold real property,[1] and those to whom the citizenship was granted by special enactment were limited in the acquisition of it by the fixing of a moderate maximum. It is reasonably certain, in these circumstances, that many of the lots assigned to the cleruchs came before 157 B.C. into the ownership of the men of business in Athens,[2] and that the high rents received in Delos increased the incomes of many of those whom we find prominent in public life in the capital in this and the following generation. Here, then, was to be found a compensation for the public loss in Delian administration. For this reason the efficiency of the insular government became a genuine concern to the wealthy classes in power in Athens, and, accordingly, we find that great care was given to the supervision of the business affairs of Delos. Decency and order were maintained in the streets and market-places by three (after *ca.* 152 B.C.[3] two) *agoranomi*, men who combined the duties of market clerks, police inspectors, and police magistrates. A Board of three elected officials was sent to the island every year to superintend the *emporium*. What it had to do we are nowhere told, but judging from the title, and the fact that the name of one of them appears inscribed upon official measures,[4] we may venture to conclude that it was directly concerned with the regulation of foreign

clear that Romans in Athens did not have this sort of a *ius commercii*, since otherwise the special grant of γῆς καὶ οἰκίας ἔγκτησιν αἰτησαμένῳ κατὰ τὸν νόμον to L. Hortensius in 170 B.C. would have had no sense.

[1] For this reason, doubtless, foreigners form so large a proportion of the temple tenants (Ziebarth, *loc. cit.* 283, n. 18), especially since the Athenian tenants of the temple belonged largely to the cleruchy, not to the metropolis (see *Klio*, 1909, p. 334, and below, ix. 351, n. 1).

[2] Holleaux (*Acad. inscr. C.R.*, 1905, p. 774) calls attention to the paucity of rich men's houses in Delos.

[3] There were three *agoranomi* in the archonship of Zaleucus (*BCH.*, 1886, p. 33), but only two in 151/0 B.C. (*BCH.*, 1892, p. 371), as in 124/3 B.C. (*BCH.*, 1908, p. 419, Nos. 12 and 13 ; cf. 14 and 15), and in 100/99 B.C. (*IG.* ii. 2. 985, Col. i. E 36). Homolle (*BCH.*, 1889, p. 411) and Dürrbach (*BCH.*, 1902, p. 517, n. 3) err in affirming that in 102/1 and 98/7 B.C. there was only one *agoranomus.* In these years only one of the two contributed to the *Pythais* (*Klio*, 1909, p. 313 f.). Accordingly, Zaleucus must be dated earlier than 151/0 B.C., *i.e.* in 155/3 B.C. I conjecture that the reconstruction of this Board took place in 152/1 B.C., in the archonship of Lysiades, and that to an arrangement made at the same time there is reference in *BCH.*, 1892, p. 371, where it is prescribed that the secretary of the *epimeletes* inscribe a decree in honour of the *agoranomi* on a stone tablet, καὶ στῆσαι ἀκολούθως τοῖς ἄρξασιν τὸν ἐπὶ Λυ[σ]ιάδου ἄρχοντος ἐνιαυτόν. For the date of Lysiades see *Klio*, 1909, p. 337 ff.

[4] *BCH.*, 1905, p. 226 ; 1910, p. 409, No. 59.

trade, as well as with the provision of facilities for the weighing, measuring, and selling of commodities. To facilitate the changing of money—a most important transaction in a mart where hundreds of different coins circulated, some of which must have caused trouble even to experts [1]—and to gain for the state some of the profits of the banking business, the Athenians established a public banking counter at Delos, and every year appointed a manager to take charge of it. He was sometimes one of the most prominent men in the city.[2] Perhaps his business was rather to fix the ratios of exchange, and thus to prevent cheating, then to compete with private banking. It is difficult, moreover, to imagine how the new issues of Athenian silver, which were made at this time in large amounts, and with monthly regularity, were put into circulation at Delos, if not through his instrumentality.

Such were the officials appointed by the Athenians to attend to the civil and religious administration of Delos. There was a small committee or a single officer in charge of public order, trade and commerce, banking, the worship of recognized deities, religious dedications, and temple property and income. Each worked in practical independence of the other, yet the administration did not lack centralization; for associated with almost every department and ranking superior to all the officials was the annually elected governor-general of Delos,[3] whose position thus approximated closely to that of the superintendent of the administration in Athens, and owed its power over the other offices, possibly, to the example of bureaucratic government in the contemporary kingdoms. His name characterizes him as the chief executive official of the island; the habitual commendation of his fairness and regard for justice [4]

[1] *BCH.*, 1905, p. 569. As in Delphi, for which see Bourguet, *Administration financière du sanctuaire pythique*, 24, 107.

[2] *e.g.* Medeius of Piraeus (Kirchner, *PA.* No. 10098; Roussel, *BCH.*, 1908, p. 530, No. 401) was manager of the bank in 97/6 B.C. See also *BCH.*, 1910, p. 181 ff.

[3] The Athenian archon was eponymous on Delos, not the *epimeletes*; hence the habitual presence of the latter's name in dedications of temples, porticoes, and statues is traceable to his co-operation in their erection, *i.e.* his association with the priests and others immediately concerned.

[4] See, for example, *BCH.*, 1892, p. 150.

point to his being the enforcer of the law, the conductor of preliminary investigations, and the president of the insular courts; his family, station, and activity show his office to have been perhaps the most important of those at that time in the gift of the Athenian people.

All these magistrates were sent from or chosen in Athens. They were, moreover, designated by popular election, not by lot, the priests alone being excepted.[1] To the governor - generals, the custodians of sacred treasures, and, doubtless, all the elected magistrates, furthermore, the law was inapplicable that the same person could not hold a civil office twice.[2] That is to say, their positions were classified with the military offices where election by show of hands and repeated tenure were admissible—with those whose duties required a peculiar fitness in the candidate, a training or natural aptitude not to be found with certainty in a chance person. And since the same was doubtless true of the governor-general of Haliartus, as it was, of course, true of the general and *hipparch* sent to Lemnos and of the generals sent to the other cleruchies, it is clear that the ideas which had been influential in the reconstruction of Athenian administration at the end of the fourth century B.C. had been modified in the interval in at least one notable particular. For the preservation of the view that special fitness and interest should be considered in the choice of officials, the practice of the

[1] See *CIG.* ii. 2270. That the priest in this case, as in the case of the entire nine in *BCH.*, 1907, p. 425, No. 17, received the ratification of honours from the *demos* of Athens, indicates that he was an official of the whole people, not of the cleruchy alone. Accordingly my remark in *Klio*, 1907, p. 220, needs correction. It is still true, doubtless, that frequently, if not regularly, the priest was a cleruch. Thus, apart from the rare appearance of priests in contemporary Athenian documents—an argument of considerable importance—the demonstration can be made that various priests resided on Delos. Thus Staseas of Colone, priest of Serapis in 118/7 B.C., had a *palaestra* on the island. Gorgias of Ionidae, priest in 153/2 B.C., was *agoranomus* in the archonship of Zaleucus, and at another time *gymnasiarch*—both minor offices for which continual residence on the island was necessary; and Pylades of Perithoedae, priest in the same year, was chairman of the Delian *proedri* at about the same time (*BCH.*, 1907, p. 427). Moreover, men of the same families as the priests appear frequently in the business documents of the temple. For example: Roussel, *BCH.*, 1908, p. 306 ff., Nos. 74, 94, 251 and 252, 255 and 264, 261, 423 (and Kirchner, *PA.* 4667), 499, 570, 145, 335, 508. On the other hand, Roussel, Nos. 82, 84, 333, 373 are cases of men who held priestships in Delos and offices of one kind or another in Athens.

[2] 'Αθήν. iv. 459; *BCH.*, 1882, p. 334; *BCH.*, 1908, p. 424, No. 25; *BCH.*, 1910, p. 183, n. 2.

Hellenistic monarchies with their staffs of professional administrators was decisive; so that no return to election by lot was possible. It was in the matter of re-election that an innovation was made. That the colonial magistracies created in 166 B.C. should be opened to the same person for more than one term, whereas in 307 B.C. no one was allowed to offer himself as a candidate for the second time for the positions of superintendent of the administration, treasurer of military funds, *agonothetes*, and *gymnasiarch*, shows how, as in the kingdoms, experience had come to be regarded as an advantage for an important civil position. Still, the feeling of the Athenians was adverse to maintaining the same individual in the same office for a long number of years, so that a very sparing use was apparently made of the right to re-elect, against which, moreover, the example of Rome weighed heavily. Hence the benefit of experience, though admitted theoretically, was only in small measure gained in the government of the new dependencies.

However it may have been in the mother city, in Delos the democratic institutions were virile enough at the start. There the chief power was the *demos* of the Athenians dwelling on the island, the little republic whose organization has been described already. The scope of its activity was, of course, limited by its dependence upon the Athenian *ecclesia* and the entire delegation of foreign affairs to Athens; but the town meetings were held frequently and countless little matters were debated and settled at them. Ordinarily no lapidary records were kept, but decrees in favour of Athenian officials and of local professors were regularly cut upon stone.[1] Since the former required ratification in Athens and the latter were valid without it,[2] it is clear that

---

[1] *BCH.*, 1905, p. 199; 1886, p. 36=1889, p. 245 (165/4 B.C.); *CIG.* ii. 2270 (159/8 B.C.); *BCH.*, 1905, p. 198 (?); cf. above, viii. 318, n. 2; 1886, p. 33 (155/3 B.C.)=1889, p. 410 (153/2 B.C.); 1907, p. 425, No. 17 (153/2 B.C.); 1886, p. 38 (151/0 B.C.); 1905, p. 196 (151/0 B.C.); 1892, p. 371 (151/0 B.C.); 1889, p. 413 (150/49 B.C.); [1892, p. 372 (150/49 B.C.)]; 1889, p. 250 (133/2 B.C.); 1892, p. 375 (133/2 B.C.); [1892, p. 376 (132/1 B.C.)]. A few more fragments of decrees were discovered in 1906 (*Acad. inscr. C.R.*, 1907, p. 370).

[2] *BCH.*, 1886, p. 36=1889, p. 245; 1889, p. 250; 1905, p. 196.

education—apart from the instruction of the ephebes—
lay within the province of the cleruchy. On the other
hand, the Athenians on Delos were incompetent to dispose of land to aliens, at any rate for religious purposes
—this being a prerogative of the sovereign[1] *demos* in
the capital. To them belonged, however, full discretion
as to the distribution of new statues, tablets, and
similar monuments within the public areas.[2] We
are not in a position to define in other directions
the limits which separated matters in which the
imperial magistrates could act on their own authority,
with or without instructions from Athens, from those in
which a reference to the local assembly was obligatory.
Of course, certain broad definitions of the spheres of
each were made, for they were absolutely necessary ;
but it must have been impossible to say in advance
whether an unforeseen case should be settled by
executive or legislative action. This was the point at
which, on *a priori* grounds, it was to be expected that
disagreements and vexatious delays would arise, and
there is a possibility that deadlocks, produced in this
way, led ultimately to the breaking up of the whole
system. To be sure, the officials rendered an account
of their acts, not to the cleruchy, but to the *demos* in
Athens,[3] and since they were imperial, not local magistrates, the source of honours lay in their case solely
with the sovereign *ecclesia* ;[4] but, though this was true,
it was apparently necessary that the recommendations
for rewards of good service should come from Delos to
Athens in the form of a commendatory decree passed by
the cleruch assembly.[5] The Delian republic was, thereby,
given considerable control over administration, and to a

---

[1] See below, ix. 358.
[2] Permission to erect a statue at Delos might be taken for granted, now, as
at all times. Ditt. *OGIS*. 266. 16, 771. 35. Ditt. *Syll.*[2] 722 and 514 show
that at first the cleruchy, and after its dissolution the *epimeletes*, had the disposition of new monuments. In Ditt. *OGIS*. 771 the Athenian *strategi* and
military treasurer are required to erect the two statues voted. Had Delos been
Athenian at this time (archon Tychander), as alleged (Kolbe, *op. cit.* 151), the
local officials would have been requested to attend to the business.
[3] See especially *BCH.*, 1892, p. 375 ; cf. 1889, p. 414.
[4] Francotte, *Musée belge*, 1900, p. 115 ff.
[5] At any rate, no decree in honour of a Delian official is extant in which the
initiative was taken in Athens.

corresponding degree was enabled to interfere with the free action of the high officials. No special insight into human nature is required to see that these must have chafed at the restrictions thus imposed; but they had to be conciliatory. Otherwise, how could they ask the cleruchy to praise them for their services, and to designate five men or more to go to the capital and urge their merits upon the senate and people of Athens with a view to an honorary crown or statue? This was done, to our knowledge, half a dozen times between 166 and 131 B.C., and, beyond our knowledge, in scores of other cases. The cleruch assembly, on the other hand, could not afford to be too arrogant; for the funds with which it met the expenses of legislation came from the temple treasury, where they were under the control of the custodians of the sacred treasures—officials of the central government.[1]

The Delian cleruchy had been constituted originally, beyond doubt, from men to whom the prospect of an allotment of property outweighed the unpleasantness of expatriation. These were the poorer people. The assigning of land and buildings was, naturally, made on a fair basis of equality. Hence at the beginning the cleruchy exhibited good conditions for the success of democratic institutions. We have no means of estimating the number of the original colonists, but, if we equate it with that of Delphi, which had less than seven hundred male citizens,[2] we should probably shoot beyond the mark. This little settlement was quickly disintegrated, the rapid rise in the value of real estate being a sure cause for the concentration of property in the hands of a few Athenians, and the expansion of trade and commerce being a certain inducement for Athenian labourers and artisans to flock to Delos.[3]   It

[1] This is true of decrees which did not need the assent of the Athenians.
[2] Bourguet, *op. cit.* 44 f. The contention of Homolle that there was a *heliaea* on Delos prior to 166 B.C. composed of a total of 500 members shows the approximate number of citizens. In one important court only 31 jurors served (*BCH.*, 1890, p. 491, n. 3; cf. 1907, pp. 46, 75 f.; 1908, p. 45).
[3] See *Acad. inscr. C.R.*, 1905, p. 776, for the discovery on Delos of a potter's house (cf. *BCH.*, 1908, p. 160), and the house of a maker of ex-votos; *ibid.* 1904, p. 732, for the *atelier* of a sculptor, and *ibid.* 1905, p. 781 f. for four *caches* of Attic coins.

is, therefore, likely that the second generation of cleruchs was much less homogeneous in point of property and ideas than was the first; that, in fact, the majority in the Delian assembly was then quite as objectionable in aristocratic thinking as it was in contemporary Athens.[1] Nor was that all. At first the settlers from Athens probably outnumbered the rest of the island population,[2] but within forty years they were overwhelmed by the outlanders. Doubtless, the colonists had been reinforced by new arrivals from at home, but these can have been but a mere handful when compared to the large increase of the people from other lands. One epoch in the history of this influx we have already determined —the destruction of Corinth in 146 B.C., which was followed by the migration to Delos of the Roman trading population there resident, and of the Greeks and Orientals who had come to Corinth to meet the Romans. Their presence made itself felt speedily. The Italians formed a loose group[3] easily distinguishable from the other inhabitants. At its head stood, apparently, six[4] *masters* (*magistri*), who were sacral

---

[1] See above, ix. 349, n. 2.

[2] Thus as late as 153/2 B.C. the Delian priests offered sacrifices on behalf of Athens, Rome, and the Athenians resident on Delos, but not on behalf of the other Delian inhabitants; cf. below, ix. 382, n. 1.

[3] Kornemann (*Berl. Stud.* xiv. 58 ff.) gave the first approximately correct sketch of the Delian colony. It must now be supplemented by the use of Pernier's article "Delus" in Ruggiero's *Dizionario epigrafico.* The publication of the treatises by Pâris and Hatzfeld referred to in *Acad. inscr. C.R.*, 1909, p. 547 ff., will probably advance our knowledge of the subject considerably. The term *Italici* includes Greeks from Naples, Heracleia, Tarentum, and elsewhere, as well as Romans, as is now conceded by Kornemann (P.-W. iv. 1187) and demonstrated by Schulten (*De conventibus civium Romanorum*, 44), if any demonstration is needed of what is obvious. See below, ix. 402, n. 4. The name of the organization of the *Italici* is nowhere mentioned. Schulten and Kornemann call it a *conventus*, which it was in form, if not in theory (P.-W. iv. 1180). Hatzfeld, however, in a new *mémoire* entitled *Remarques sur les Italiens établis à Delos*, of which a résumé by Haussoullier has just appeared in *Acad. Inscr. C.R.*, 1910, p. 598 ff., deals in chapter iv. with *Le prétendu Conventus civium Romanorum de Délos*, and in chapter vi. affirms that the Italians on the island formed not one group but several. See, however, below, ix. 398, n. 4.

[4] *CIL.* iii. *Suppl.* 7217; cf. *BCH.*, 1884, p. 96; 1899, p. 58; 1896, p. 436. For the date of this document, which is now re-edited as a whole in *BCH.*, 1910, p. 402, No. 52, see below, ix. 356, n. 4. *BCH.*, 1884, p. 118 = *CIL.* iii. *Suppl.* 7212, is incomplete. *BCH.*, 1877, p. 284, No. 6 = *CIL.* iii. *Suppl.* 7218; *BCH.*, 1899, p. 56, No. 1. These lists of Hermaistae are old. For the date of the first see Kornemann, *Berl. Stud.* xiv. 59. Two of the *magistri* are said to appear in *ca.* 180 B.C. (*BCH.*, 1882, p. 45, ll. 147 and 148). For the date of the second see *BCH.*, 1889, p. 401, where Q. Pactumius M.f. receives the *proxenia* of Cierium between 178 and 146 B.C. This same man appears in this list.

officers of Hermes and Maea, the patron deities of the Italians, and hence were called in Greek the *Hermaistae*. The probability is that as early as 140 B.C. this association had a headquarters somewhere on the island, but whether it was located where later rose the splendid *statio* [1] of the Italians, or had an altogether different site, seems to be as yet unsettled.[2] It was at about this time, in any case, that, when the little cove to the south of the stoa of Philip was filled in with débris so as to enlarge the public agora of the city,[3] the *masters*, taking advantage of the additional space thus secured, built a small square chapel [4] of Hermes and Maea, to which then or not long afterwards certain public-spirited Italians added a small circular temple, an altar, and statues of Maea, Hercules, Athena, and other deities, including, doubtless, Hermes and the Lares.[5] The statues, altars, and chapels were all placed within an enclosure (*compitum*), which occupied what soon came to be the most central crossways in Delos—the opening of the thorough-

---

[1] The time at which this structure was begun is still uncertain, but it is impossible to date any of it as early as 140 B.C. The statue of Ofellius (*BCH.*, 1881, Plate xii.) which was located in it was made by two Athenian artists, Dionysius and Timarchides (below, ix. 410, n. 1), whose *akmé* is set by Kirchner (*PA.* 11993), on the basis of Pliny (*Nat. Hist.* xxxiv. 52 ; cf. xxxvi. 35), at 156 B.C. A freedman of Ofellius, however, appears among the *competaliastae*, none of whom belong earlier than the last part of the second century B.C. (below, ix. 400, n. 4). Moreover, in *IG.* ii. 5, *Add. Nov.* 1647 B, we find Τιμαρχίδης Πολυκλέους Θορίκιος defined as νεώτερος. This presupposes an older Timarchides, to whom in all likelihood Pliny refers when he places his *akmé* at 156 B.C. Dionysius is the son of the elder Timarchides, and uncle of the younger. Hence the statue of Ofellius was not made till the end of the second century B.C.

[2] For the foreign club-houses on Delos that of the *Posidoniastae* of Beyrout may be taken as typical. It consisted of an οἶκος, various στόαι with statues, and χρηστήρια, "dependances" ; cf. *BCH.*, 1907, p. 448 f., Nos. 39-42, and the editors' comments.

[3] See below, ix. 364, n. 4.

[4] *CIL.* iii. *Suppl.* 7217 = *BCH.*, 1910, p. 402, No. 52. One of the six *magistri* who erected the square temple, Marcus Lollius, is named in an unedited inventory of about 150 B.C. The date of the round temple, and of the whole enclosure, for that matter, is probably determined by the inscription published by Dürrbach in *BCH.*, 1902, p. 536, No. 8. That the archon Dionysius, by which it is dated, belongs shortly before 133/2 B.C., has been demonstrated by Roussel (*BCH.*, 1908, p. 404). That the document relates to the statue of Maea erected in the *compitum* suggests itself when it ("Maiam statuerunt iisdem aaram") is placed in juxtaposition with *BCH.*, 1899, p. 60, No. 5 (οἱ τὴν Μαία[ν ο]ἱ αὐτοὶ καὶ τὸν βωμόν), and with the other dedicatory inscriptions from the *compitum*: οἱ αὐτοὶ καὶ τοὺς θεοὺς [οἱ κ]αὶ τὸν ναὸν ἀνέθηκαν ; οἱ καὶ τὸν Ἡρακλῆν ; οἱ καὶ τὴν Ἀθηνᾶν ; οἱ καὶ τὸν περίβολον. The finding of *BCH.*, 1902, p. 536, No. 8 in the *thermae*, into which the group of porticoes falsely called by Homolle the *Tetragonus* was converted in later times, simply means that the stone was used in the new edifice.   [5] See below, ix. 399 f.

fare from the theatre and the southern quays into the agora. It was the place of the most distinctive worship of the Italians, and may have been the only head-quarters possessed by them. This was by no means an isolated occurrence. Thus in 137/6 B.C. the worshippers of the Egyptian circle of deities, Serapis, Isis, Anubis, and Harpocrates, who had been organized earlier as a *thiasus* of *Serapiastae* with inner synods of *melanephori* and *therapeutae*,[1] and who had possessed a little temple situated on a rocky niche on the east slope of the Inopus canyon, moved into a more commodious enclosure which was assigned to them a little farther up the ravine.[2] Here they began the construction of a new temple which was completed in 135/4 B.C., and formally dedicated by the *demos* of Athens.[3] They had as neighbours in this somewhat remote place—up to which, however, following the valley of the Inopus and the road to the summit of the mountain, houses now began to

[1] *Acad. Inscr. C.R.*, 1910, p. 524.

[2] I formerly affirmed that the Serapieum Anubieum and the Isieum, referred to in *BCH.*, 1908, p. 82, l. 15; 1882, pp. 20, 24, 27, 52; 1904, p. 159; cf. Ditt. *Syll.*[2] 588, 220, *ca.* 180 B.C., were located near the precinct of Apollo (*Acad. inscr. C.R.*, 1908, p. 186); but Roussel insisted that the first structures in the precinct on the Inopus canyon were thus designated (*Acad. inscr. C.R.*, 1910, p. 295). The finding of dedications to Serapis and Isis in this locality, which are dated on palaeographical grounds earlier than 137/6 B.C., was *prima facie* evidence that the precinct was older than the appointment of the Athenian priest, though evidence was not lacking from Delos for the movement of *anathemata* from one shrine to another (*BCH.*, 1910, p. 185). Consequently, what I had written in *Klio*, 1907, p. 226; 1909, p. 332, seemed to need modification. The latest excavations, however, have shown that the worshippers of Serapis and Isis did in fact move into a new precinct at *ca.* 137/6 B.C.; the only point in which my earlier view was incorrect is as to the place at which the *ancien sanctuaire égyptien* was situated (*Acad. inscr. C.R.*, 1910, p. 523 f.). These Egyptian deities were apparently not long on the island prior to 180 B.C. (Rusch, "De Serapide et Iside in Graecia cultis," *Berl. Diss.*, 1906, p. 39; *BCH.*, 1910, p. 179). The idol donated by Decimus Aemilius M.f., a Roman resident of the island, in *ca.* 135 B.C. (*BCH.*, 1884, p. 121 f.), was probably one of their earliest cult objects. The Egyptian statuette, of which the second portion was found in 1906 (*BCH.*, 1882, p. 313 ff.), and *Acad. inscr. C.R.*, 1907, p. 364 ff.), and on which is written a hieroglyphic inscription which Maspero dates between 250 and 150 B.C., may have been brought to Delos for the new temple of Isis Nemesis in 110/9 B.C.

[3] For the dedicatory inscription see *BCH.*, 1892, p. 481. For the architect see below, ix. 410, n. 1. It is true that Roussel (*BCH.*, 1908, p. 398) objects to the identification here proposed on the ground that the Ionic epistyle, on which the dedicatory inscription is engraved, is too slight for such a large temple. I am not able to judge of the validity of this argument. This much seems clear : that the main temple was erected before 117/6 B.C., when the steps up to it were donated (see below, ix. 388, n. 4). How long before, I see no means of determining. Certainly, the edifice of 135/4 B.C. is distinguished from all others erected in this precinct by having the name of the architect put in the dedicatory inscription.

creep [1]—other foreign deities, for sixteen years earlier (153 B.C.) a shrine of the Tyrian Hercules had been already located in this district,[2] while quite near, but on the opposite side of the Inopus canyon, some other foreigners had laid out, many generations before, a precinct and erected in it a sanctuary of the great deities of Samothrace, the Dioscuri, and the Cabiri. We have abundant evidence that traders from Egypt were settled at Delos before the Athenians came there, but it was only in 137/6 B.C. that, after having been strengthened by constant additions, they were able, not simply to obtain a new enclosure and begin a new temple, but to secure Athenian recognition and an Athenian priest, and to undertake a large scheme for the extension and beautifying of their precinct.[3] Their Tyrian predecessors were less ambitious or less fortunate. It apparently had not been easy for them to secure a *temenos* in the first instance ; for the matter was one in which, not the cleruchy, but the home government had jurisdiction, and resort had eventually to be had to Athens. Still, through the kind offices of an Athenian citizen the difficulties were overcome, and henceforth the devotees of Melcarth, under the presidency of their *archithiasites*, did not need to use the precinct of Apollo for their meetings, but could congregate in their own shrine. Beyond this they never got, however, and the Tyrian Hercules always lacked the distinction of an Athenian priest. In other words, his worship was confined to the members of the Tyrian colony, or to those whom it admitted to its *thiasus*. The Hercules of Tyre, like the Poseidon of Beyrout, was content to be a national deity : he did not, like Serapis and Isis, seek universal recognition. After 137/6 B.C., on the other hand, all the Delians were in a sense *Serapiastae*, and, accordingly, the special *thiasus* disappeared.

---

[1] *Acad. inscr. C.R.*, 1910, p. 302.

[2] A Heraclium existed on Delos as early as *ca.* 300 B.C. (*BCH.*, 1908, p. 41), but obviously not that of the Tyrians (*CIG.* ii. 2271, republished with corrections in Wilhelm, *Beiträge*, p. 163 f., and Schürer, *Gesch. des jüdischen Volkes*,[3] iii. 57). The Cabirium was also old (*BCH.*, 1908, p. 390, n. 1 ; cf. 391), but see below, x. 438.

[3] See *Klio*, 1907, p. 226 ff. ; 1909, p. 333 ff. ; cf. above, ix. 357, n. 2.

It has been remarked[1] that those who frequented Delos came mostly from the continental parts of Asia— Pontus, Bithynia, Syria, Phoenicia, and from Egypt and Italy; that none came from Rhodes or Macedon, and very few from Asia Minor, the Greek islands, or from Greece proper outside of Attica. The observation is probably correct for the period prior to 130 B.C. The provenience of the foreign traders, furthermore, has been justly taken as indicative of the general directions of Delian trade. We shall do well, however, not to insist upon this point too much, and not to jump to the conclusion that Macedon and the Greek mainland were unenterprising and impoverished.[2] Because they did not deal with Delos is no evidence that they did not deal with Athens, Rhodes, Alexandria, or Tarentum.[3] At any rate, the fewness of their representatives may be set down to their credit on the reflection that the dominating trade of Delos at this time was the slave trade; and, besides, it is clear that men from contiguous places could do business at Delos without making permanent settlements there, whereas to the merchants of the Pontus and Levant, as to the corporations in Rome, agents and headquarters on the island were indispensable. The great fêtes moreover, gave the near-by Greeks the opportunity to bring their goods to Delos when there was the best chance to sell them;[4] when they could combine with trade pleasant social intercourse, and with both the performance of religious duties. Thus, when the annual *panegyris* came round and the sacred delegations from far and near were congregating on the island, the long boats with curled prows, high square sails, and fifty or one hundred oars on either side,[5] started from

[1] von Schoeffer, *op. cit.*, 187 f. After 130 B.C. Asia Minor and the Aegean districts assume more importance. See the list of youths trained in the *palaestra* of Staseas (*BCH.*, 1891, p. 257), and of the men who subscribed for the restoration of the edifices destroyed in 88 B.C. (*BCH.*, 1884, p. 186).

[2] von Schoeffer, *loc. cit.*

[3] Holm, *op. cit.* iv. 508. Among the *Sabaziastae* in the Piraeus in 102/1 B.C. (*IG.* ii. 5. 626*b*) were two Macedonians and one *Maronite*.

[4] ἦ τε πανήγυρις ἐμπορικόν τι πρᾶγμά ἐστι. Strabo x. 485. 4.

[5] See the drawings of the boats on the Delian walls which are published in *BCH.*, 1906, p. 550.

the neighbouring islands and coasts, and pulled into the harbour of Delos, laden with wares and with pilgrims. The noise of Greek speech filled the ways, squares, porticoes, and broad waterfront; the gesticulation of Greek bargaining lent animation to the street scenes; the Greek temples in the plain were thronged with worshippers, and scattered groups made their way along the rough path past the precincts of the foreign deities to the grotto of Apollo, and the temple of Zeus and Athena, visible on the summit of Mt. Cynthus— the bare, cone-shaped hill up to which the island reaches from all sides. There were solemn processions and the chanting of hymns,[1] there were games,[2] and sacrifices, and feastings. We can imagine with what eagerness the visitors were welcomed by the Athenian residents. Some of these were, doubtless, educated gentlemen, instinct with pride of race and culture.[3] All about them were the evidences of foreign aggressiveness. There were Italians of harsh and overbearing manners, not the Roman nobles—for these did not live on the island—but their grasping freedmen and other dealers in human flesh. There were half-Greeks from raw Bithynia and Cilicia; men from Syria with wives of strange names and speech—Martha or Taosa, Ribu or Rumatha;[4] crowds of fat-pursed Phoenicians;[5] curious synods of black-robed communicants, and the fanatical priests of the eastern cults, who slept near the temples[6] and stirred up strange feelings and longings

---

[1] See BCH., 1902, p. 518 ff., 1905, p. 225.

[2] Those attested for this time are the Dionysia (BCH., 1892, p. 371; cf. 1889, p. 372), the Delia (BCH., 1907, p. 434; 1879, p. 378), the Apollonia (BCH., 1879, p. 378; CIG. ii. 2306), the Romaea (BCH., 1886, p. 33 f. = 1908, p. 439, No. 65), the Hermaea (BCH., 1891, p. 257 ff.; 1883, p. 370), and the Theseia (BCH., 1908, p. 416, No. 5).

[3] For rich Delian families see von Schoeffer, op. cit., 187. The monuments erected by various families prove their wealth; cf. Roussel, BCH., 1908, p. 360, Nos. 13, 205, 265. See, however, above, ix. 349, n. 2.

[4] BCH., 1892, p. 160 ff.; 1882, p. 345; cf. 1880, p. 129; 1882, p. 349; cf. 1904, p. 151; 1908, p. 397, n. 8; 1882, p. 490; 1909, p. 517, No. 38.

[5] Φοίνικα, μεγάλου κύριον βαλλαντίου (above, viii. 321, n. 7).

[6] The therapeutae, or sacred attendants, who were connected with the shrine of both Serapis and Aphrodite Hagne, and had their pastophorion, or furnished dwelling-house. See BCH., 1882, p. 323; CIG. ii. 2297; BCH., 1882, p. 489; cf. Klio, 1907, p. 228. For the therapeutae of Aphrodite see BCH., 1907, p. 335; 1908, p. 381 ff., and 1882, p. 500, No. 24 (cf. 1904, p. 152), where it is stated: ἀξιῶ δὲ καὶ δέομαι πάντας τοὺς θεραπευτὰς βλασφημεῖν αὐτὴν καθ' ὥραν.

among Greek men. On all sides the outlanders en-croached upon the Athenian quarters, and formed by their very numbers a menacing circle round about. At least during fête time there seemed to be some pure Greeks in the world.

In spite of the influx of foreigners the cleruchy dominated such public life as existed on the island for the first thirty-five years of its existence. If the Delian documents thus far published ceased at 131 B.C., we would have no conception whatever of the multitude of foreigners on Delos. If we had record of no monu-ments of art except those erected before 131 B.C., moreover, we must have concluded that the island was almost destitute of wealth and public spirit. Except the Heraclium,[1] opened by the Tyrians in 153 B.C., not a single temple was built to our knowledge within thirty years of the settlement of the cleruchy;[2] and apart from the few statues authorized by joint vote of the *demos* in Delos and Athens, we know of less than twenty works of art[3] which belong certainly before 135 B.C. Possibly the foreigners were somewhat repressed by the Athenian occupants of the island, but more probably the energy and capital of all alike were fully employed in developing the material resources of the place. It is not yet time to speak with any positiveness of the results of their labour, for the excavation of the city of Delos is still far from complete, and the excavators have been unable as yet to dis-tinguish sharply between the houses which preceded the Athenian occupation and those which followed it, much less to differentiate early and late work in the latter period. Still, the uniformity of plan,—rooms ranged round an upper and lower court; the similarity of internal finish,—stucco marked off in layers and

---

[1] *CIG.* ii. 2271.

[2] Unless the little chapels in the agora of the *competaliastae* be thought of as temples. See above, ix. 356.

[3] *BCH.*, 1892, p. 154; 1883, pp. 338, 340; 1877, p. 88, No. 37; Ditt. *OGIS.* 136 = *BCH.*, 1878, p. 398 (?); *BCH.*, 1879, p. 364; *CIG.* ii. 2280 = Ditt. *OGIS.* 350 (?); *CIG.* ii. 2329 (?); *BCH.*, 1905, p. 221; 1902, p. 515 (?); 1884, p. 96; cf. 1899, p. 58, and 1896, p. 436 = *CIL.* iii. *Suppl.* 7217; (as to the dates of these Roman dedications see below, ix. 396, n. 2); *BCH.*, 1899, p. 56; cf. 1889, p. 401; *BCH.*, 1908, p. 432, No. 46.

coloured, so as to resemble the exterior of marble buildings, and the identity of construction and materials, suffice,[1] perhaps, to show that the buildings thus far examined belong essentially to one epoch,[2] while their general location with reference to the Apollo precinct and the adjacent agora, that is to say, their aloofness from the centre of the town, indicate that this epoch is the one with which we are now concerned.[3] The old inhabitants had lived in a cluster round the harbour, precinct, and agora;[4] and the Athenian cleruchs on their arrival had scarcely built new houses while old ones were lying empty to receive them. But when the "boom" began, the property to the south on the water-front was developed, and, accordingly, the owners erected large warehouses upon their lots, and constructed granite docks in front of them, which, though private property, formed in their *ensemble* a public passage.[5] In the rear of the sea-board tier of houses, from the agora south-wards, ran a thoroughfare. Not far past its exit from the agora it forked, and another main street ran south-

---

[1] *BCH.*, 1884, p. 473 ff. ; 1896, p. 428 ff. ; 1905, p. 5 ff. ; 1906, p. 485 ff. ; 1907, p. 471 ff.

[2] See, however, Jarde's report on the *magazines* along the southern water-front, where two stages are recognized—one prior to *ca.* 200 B.C., and one for the second period of Athenian control (*BCH.*, 1905, p. 32 ff.).

[3] An *insula* in the theatre quarter is now dated in 138/7 B.C. ; for in or shortly after this year a certain Cleopatra erected statues of herself and her husband, Dioscurides, in the court in front of their house (*Acad. inscr. C.R.*, 1907, p. 365 ff. ; cf. *BCH.*, 1908, p. 432, No. 46). A reproduction of them is given in *BCH.*, 1907, p. 414 ff. The dates of issue of the coins found in these houses lead to the same time for their erection (*Acad. inscr. C.R.*, 1905, p. 781).

[4] This fact was demonstrated by the excavations of 1906 (*Acad. inscr. C.R.*, 1907, p. 358 ff.), which fixed an approximate limit to the circuit of the old town. The cemetery then found (*ibid.* 360) doubtless lay outside the earlier city limits. The circuit of the town, both before and after the period during which it transcended its natural boundaries, ran not very far inland from where the agora of the *competaliastae*—rather, the little cove in which this was subsequently constructed—was located. It included, however, the slope to the north of the precinct of Apollo (*Acad. inscr. C.R.*, 1909, p. 403), though the hill farther east on which the agora of the Romans was subsequently erected may have been unoccupied (*Acad. inscr. C.R.*, 1905, p. 764). Near the little cove there was the greatest congestion of population in the bloom time, and it was mainly there that the old houses of the classic time, and the houses which continued to be occupied in the Roman era, after the disaster of 88 B.C. (*ibid.* 768, 774), were located.

[5] *BCH.*, 1896, p. 439 ff. ; 1905, p. 23 ff. ; 1906, p. 640 ff. See the chart published in *BCH.*, 1906, Plate ix., and also in *Acad. inscr. C.R.*, 1908, p. 162. The first instalments of the definite publication on the excavations in Delos (*Exploration archéologique de Delos*), Bellot's *Carte de l'île*, and Leroux's *Salle hypostyle* have recently appeared.

east up the hill to the theatre. All around the theatre, and between it and the sea, houses and stores were built.[1] From the agora another thoroughfare passed along the south side of the sacred precinct, and, on dividing at the farther end of it, went in a northerly direction towards the sacred lake, and in a southerly up the Inopus canyon, past the precincts of the foreign gods, to the temple of Zeus and Athena on the summit of the mountain. To the north-east of the sacred precinct, and stretching to the eastern shore, lay the only arable land on the northern part of the island, and it is doubtful if the city encroached upon it much. On the other hand, a large settlement was formed on the hills to the north of the sacred precinct. The most central part of the town was the area to the south of the Apollo precinct, which we have called the agora.[2] It was there that Philip of Macedon in 221-179 B.C. had built a spacious portico to supplement one already existing—the so-called Little Stoa—and it was there that in *ca.* 173 B.C. two rows of one-roomed shops opening on porticoes, where the wares they held might be exposed for sale, had been erected to accommodate the business for which the Little Stoa, which was similar in structure and purpose, had become inadequate.[3] This was, then, the quarter in which crowds congregated, and near it, we may be sure, the best business properties lay. Certainly its only rival in commercial importance was the point at which the northern quarter debouched on the harbour; but there the water was shallower, docks were lacking,

---

[1] *BCH.*, 1906, p. 485 ff.

[2] It was thus designated on the plan, adapted from that of Nénot in the *Guide Joanne Grèce*, which is published in P.-W. iv. 2469, and has been identified with certainty by an inscription discovered in 1908 (*Acad. inscr. C.R.*, 1909, p. 415). This agora was then enlarged by redeeming the agora of the *competaliastae* to the south, and that of Theophrastus to the north. That the portico of Philip was built in an earlier agora is shown by Holleaux (*Acad. inscr. C.R.*, 1905, p. 767). This building was a pleasure resort—a promenade—and had no shops (*ibid.* 766).

[3] Dürrbach (*BCH.*, 1902, p. 544 ff.) has tried to show that the so-called Little Stoa was erected between 250 and 230 B.C.; the stoa of Philip—rather, the first half of it—in 203-197 B.C.—rather, between 221 and 179 B.C.; cf. *BCH.*, 1907, p. 50, n. 1; and the major part of the so-called *Tetragonus* prior to 112/1 B.C., and probably after 130 B.C.; but see *Acad. inscr. C.R.*, 1909, p. 415, where Holleaux shows by the aid of a new inscription that it was erected in 173 B.C. Roussel (*BCH.*, 1910, p. 110 ff.) has now shown that the name *Tetragonus* does not apply to a place or an edifice, but to a professional gild.

bazaars had in all probability not yet been constructed, and much needed still to be done to reclaim from the sea a space adequate for an agora.[1]   The need, too, for development in this direction was less urgent, since the northern quarter was slow in being settled; hence the energy of the Athenians was first directed towards meeting the requirements of the southern district, with which, moreover, the northern section had easy connexion both before and behind the sacred precinct. More market space was necessary, and additional facilities for the increasing transmarine commerce; hence a line of new piers was pushed out into the sea at right angles to the old ones, so as to enclose completely the southern side of the port, while in its rear on the land thus reclaimed a new agora was laid out.[2] This became at once the centre for the Italian shipping, and it was, accordingly, here, as already mentioned,[3] that the enclosure of the *competaliastae* was located.[4]

We can better imagine than demonstrate the activity which the building of the town evoked.   There was a constant hurrying with the quarrying, hauling, cutting, and placing of stones; the making and applying of stucco; the designing and painting of the interior walls; the digging and walling of wells and cisterns under the courts of the houses; the laying out of streets, each with its central sewer and lateral connexions, each plastered with slabs of slate, all sloping by easy gradients towards the sea.   Men were busied with the sinking and fitting of granite blocks along the water-front, and with all the subsidiary tasks which these various operations entailed. Practically everything was left to private initiative. The narrow, irregular streets—they were very much

---

[1] Holleaux, *Acad. inscr. C.R.*, 1909, p. 401 ff.   [2] *Ibid.*
[3] See above, ix. 356, and for the date, n. 4.
[4] For the evidence that the older shore-line passed to the north of the agora of Theophrastus (see below, ix. 385) and to the west of the *Oikos Porinos*; that it skirted close to the stoa of Philip, and bent in so as to make a little bay where the agora of the *competaliastae* later stood; and that a new shore-line, which redeemed the two agoras and an area in front of the stoa of Philip, *i.e.* one still considerably less advanced into the sea than at present, was established through the great "travaux de remblaiement qui datent du iie siècle avant notre ère," see *Acad. inscr. C.R.*, 1907, p. 362 ff.; 1909, p. 398 ff.   From the time of construction of the *compitum* (see above, ix. 356, n. 4) it is clear that the little bay was already redeemed at *ca.* 140 B.C.

like those of Venice in these particulars—were as broad
and as straight as the business convenience of the property
owners demanded, no broader and no straighter.[1]   The
docks were integral parts of the warehouses in their
rear, and aimed to maintain no greater uniformity than
an even surface.[2]   Both were hence an expense to those
to whom they were in the first degree an advantage.
Perhaps the sewage system was a municipal care, but
even of this we cannot be certain.   Since the state was
forbidden to collect tolls on commerce, and probably did
not dare to levy an income tax on the island, it is not
surprising that individuals were left to provide for themselves.   The island was the producer of much wealth,
but only a small part of it remained on the spot.   Hence
the residents were incapable of giving freely for religious
or ornamental structures or statues.   Nor could such
things be expected from the Roman and Asiatic capitalists,
so long as they had only a tenant's interest in the island.
Once, however, the material needs were adequately met,
the Delians could turn their attention to public buildings.
The religious obligations came first.   What work was
done in the Apollo precinct the state of our knowledge
forbids us to define; but, in general, it seems likely that
the native Greek gods were housed and comfortable when
the Athenians took possession, and that little was needed
in the precinct subsequently.[3]   It was different with the
foreign deities.   They had either petty shrines and modest
temples or none at all.   Hence, as we have seen already,[4]
a new temple of Serapis was formally dedicated by the
demos of Athens in 135/4 B.C.[5]   It was the opening
of a period of architectural activity in the precincts
of the Inopus region, but before the next temple was
ready for occupation an event occurred which changed
totally the situation on the island.

During this entire period, 150-130 B.C., we are ill

---

[1] Contrasting in this particular most markedly with Priene, which was
laid off with scientific regularity (*Neue Jahrb.*, 1910, p. 549).

[2] See the detailed reports in *BCH.*, 1906, p. 640 ff.

[3] This impression is strengthened by the cursory report given by Holleaux
of the excavations recently conducted within the precinct (*Acad. inscr. C.R.*,
1908, p. 164 ff. ; 1909, p. 409 ff.).

[4] See above, ix. 357.   [5] *Klio*, 1907, p. 226.

provided with information as to what was happening in Athens, but it is easy to see that the great progress in Delos was reacting upon the capital, and that Delian questions were often uppermost in the minds of the Athenian public. In April of every year, immediately after the grain harvest, the city was filled with the excitement of a general election, and a large proportion of the canvassers for office sought positions in Delos. Again and again an embassy bearing a decree of the local assembly arrived from the island and asked that the Athenians be pleased to ratify it; and innumerable were the requests for public works which came from the Delian priests and magistrates.

That the Athenians in the capital made special efforts to conciliate the low-class Italians who kept gathering in ever-increasing numbers in their colony is improbable, but with Rome and its governing aristocracy they had to use the utmost consideration. There could be no mistaking the fact that the relations between Athens and the Rupublic were not now of equal and equal— despite the *symmachia* formed in 200 B.C., which took this for granted—but of client and patron, of protégé toward benefactor and protector. The Roman government, moreover, had formed the habit of making demands of Athens, as of its other *amici* in Greece, which were not warranted by any treaty rights.[1] To accede to them was necessary, but humiliating and offensive to the ideas of a world accustomed to constitutional government. It had seemed, therefore, expedient to give Rome and its authorities a legal right to the powers which they actually exercised, especially since a simple form had long since been devised for this purpose. Accordingly, Rome was deified as the goddess *Roma*, and her worship was associated along with that of the *Demos*, which had been instituted in 229 B.C., in the precinct of the *Graces*. The fête, Romaea, was established as early as 152 B.C.[2] Senators and magistrates of Rome were at the same time classified as *Euergetae*, like Ptolemy III.

---

[1] See above, viii. 313.
[2] *IG*. ii. 953.   Cf. Ditt. *Syll.*[2] 521, n. 4; and below, ix. 383, n. 1.

and Diogenes ; so that they were henceforth entitled to
divine honours on coming to Athens.[1]   Magistrates and
ephebes turned out to meet them and they entered the
city in a solemn *pompe*, like to that in the midst of
which Attalus had entered Athens in 200 B.C.   For
their convenience a special stand was constructed before
the stoa of Attalus that they might, if they wished,
address the assembled multitude,[2] and for their suitable
entertainment a special residence, the Romaeum, was
set apart—an edifice under public control, to which a
portico was affixed.[3]   Athens was never so devoted to
Rome as during the sixties, fifties, and forties of the
second century B.C.[4]   It was thither that the ambassadors
of Metellus retired when the Achaeans threatened their
lives in Corinth in 146 B.C.[5]   The imperial city was at
this time almost the worshipper of Athens, and there
was a constant resort thither of Romans of the best
families to train with the ephebes, study with the
philosophers, and obtain the cultivation which came
from residence in the intellectual metropolis of the
world.[6]   Rome's sympathy, moreover, though it ex-
asperated Achaeans like Polybius, had too little that
was political in it to lead the eastern kings, who viewed
the Republic as a jealous tyrant, to transfer their favour
elsewhere.   Even because of Rome's attitude they could
all the less afford not to be known and appreciated in
Athens.   Nor had Athens any reason to avoid their
benevolences ; hence old understandings were generally

[1] *IG.* ii. 551. 94 ; Ditt. *Syll.*² 521. 15 ; *ibid.* 930. 46 ; cf. below, x. 417.
Especially significant is *IG.* xii. 8. 640—a decree of Peparathos dated not long
after 197 B.C.—where access to the Senate and *demos* is given to a certain
individual first μετὰ τὰ ἱερὰ καὶ τοὺς Ῥωμαίους.   See also Wilhelm (*Österr.
Jahreshefte*, 1905, p. 281 f.).

[2] Athen. v. 212 F ; cf. below, x. 442.

[3] *IG.* ii. 446. 29.   For τὸ Ῥωμαῖον built in Sparta in *ca.* 184–178 B.C. see the
Annual of the British School in Athens, xiii. 40 ; *CIG.* i. 1331, and especially
Ziebarth, *Rhein. Mus.*, 1909, p. 335.   Cf. the public residence with a temple-
like pediment assigned in Rome after deification to Julius Caesar.   Heinen,
Klio, 1911, p. 131.

[4] Thus Velleius Paterculus (ii. 23. 4) says, *a propos* of the events of 88–86
B.C. : "si quis hoc rebellandi tempus, quo Athenae oppugnatae a Sulla sunt,
imputat Atheniensibus, nimirum veri vetustatisque ignarus est ; adeo enim
certa Atheniensium in Romanos fides fuit, ut semper et in omni re, quidquid
sincera fide gereretur, id Romani Attica fieri praedicarent."

[5] Polybius, xxxviii. 13. 9.

[6] *IG.* ii. 953 ; cf. above, viii. 339, n. 1.

maintained.[1] With Egypt, however, an estrangement occurred. Ptolemy Philometor seems to have been particularly well liked in Athens, and he doubtless had its moral support against his brother, rival, and successor, Euergetes II. Moreover, the latter prince had espoused the cause of the native Egyptians in order to get a popular backing in his struggle for the throne. Upon his accession in 146/5 B.C. he did not forget who had been his friends and who his enemies. The Greeks in Alexandria seem to have generally helped Cleopatra, his brother's widow and sister, in her struggle against him ; so that, provoked by frequent revolts, he, in turn, let loose his soldiers upon them, and by repeated massacres almost broke up the Greek settlement.[2] The great Museum was neglected, and its scientific production was never of conspicuous value subsequently. The home of the epigram, the best poetry of this age, shifted from the banks of the Nile to those of the Orontes,[3] and the islands and cities of Greece were filled with penniless artists, scientists, and educators. These were evil days for the Greeks in Egypt, and the whole Greek world sympathized with them.[4] The Greeks everywhere felt the utmost indignation that one of their own race should do such things, and they visited their persecutor with a lasting punishment. Euergetes was bad enough in all reason, but the Greek writers made him a most atrocious monster. All the crimes in the decalogue were attached

[1] *IG.* ii. 3. 1170—the dedicatory inscription from the stoa of Attalus, which was donated after 159 B.C. It is not clear whether the Attalus of *IG.* ii. *Add.* 438*b* is the second or the third of that name. The document probably belongs after 146 B.C., and seems to refer to some commercial privileges given to Athens by Pergamum. For the education of a second Ariarathes of Cappadocia in Athens see *Klio*, 1908, p. 353. The daughter of Ptolemy Philometor, Cleopatra Thea, sent her son, afterwards Antiochus VIII., Grypus (125-96 B.C.), to Athens to be educated (Niese, iii. 307 f.). Both daughter and grandson helped to adorn Delos (Ditt. *OGIS.* 260 ; cf. 258 and 259, and *BCH.*, 1907, p. 444, No. 35). The name Cleopatra now becomes common in Athens (Kirchner, *P.A. s.v.* and *BCH.*, 1908, p. 432, No. 46).

[2] ἐποίησε [Πτολεμαῖος] πλήρεις τάς τε νήσους καὶ πόλεις ἀνδρῶν γραμματικῶν, φιλοσόφων, γεωμετρῶν, μουσικῶν, ζωγράφων, παιδοτριβῶν τε καὶ ἰατρῶν καὶ ἄλλων πολλῶν τεχνιτῶν· οἱ διὰ τὸ πένεσθαι διδασκόντες ἃ ἠπίσταντο πόλλους κατεσκεύασαν ἄνδρας ἐλλογίμους. Athen. iv. 184 c ; cf. *Klio*, 1908, p. 338 ff. ; *Sitzb. d. Berl. Akad.*, 1904, p. 471 ff. ; Mahaffy, *The Ptolemaic Dynasty*, 191 ; Cichorius, *Rhein. Mus.*, 1908, p. 197 ff. ; cf. *Klio*, 1909, p. 337 ff. See Jacoby, *Apollodors Chronik*, 8.

[3] Wilamowitz, *Archiv f. Papyrusforschung*, i. 223.

[4] For the attitude of Delphi see P.-W. iv. 2576.

to his name, and it was not till these very latest days that any one has tried to clear his memory.[1] Nor was the ill-will confined to the scientific world, but it was shared by men of affairs also, and had we records enough, we would probably find that the Ptolemaea, the great fête in honour of the Ptolemies, suffered an eclipse everywhere. In Athens, at any rate, where, as late as 152 B.C., over sixty commissioners, including Panaetius of Rhodes, and many students from the Stoa and the Academy, officiated at a single celebration, the Ptolemaea disappears from our records for about fifty years. If it was omitted altogether, as seems most probable, a rupture of diplomatic relations between Athens and Alexandria was doubtless involved.[2] The name of Euergetes, moreover, is never mentioned in an extant Athenian document, and in Delos honours were conferred upon his courtiers, to our knowledge, only by Alexandrian Romans and a company of Alexandrian merchants. To the king himself no monument of any kind seems to have been erected.[3]

There are many indications that the budget of Athens was at this time insufficient for the public needs. Not that the wealth of the citizens had diminished—it had probably increased enormously—but that the system of taxation was inadequate. One means employed to augment the revenues was for the government to engage in mercantile transactions : to buy grain and even oil at an advantageous figure—on occasion from one who wished to do the city a favour—and sell them at home or abroad at a profit.[4] Another was to have recourse to voluntary subscriptions, and long lists of names are still extant of men who gave funds for specific purposes.[5]

---

[1] Mahaffy, *op. cit.* 195 ; cf. Grenfell and Hunt, *Tebtunis Papyri*, i. 19 f., and for the other side of the case, Niese, iii. 272, n. 6.

[2] The living Ptolemy was thereafter no longer an Attic god. The divine *eponymus* of the tribe Ptolemais was, of course, the departed Euergetes I.

[3] For this section see *Klio*, 1908, p. 338 ff. It seems to me likely that the commissioners who managed the Ptolemaea in 153 B.C. were in the main the students of philosophy who had their *rendezvous* in the *gymnasium* Ptolemaeum (cf. below, x. 416, n. 1).

[4] A. v. Premerstein, *Ath. Mitt.*, 1911, p. 73 ff.

[5] *IG.* ii. 983 (183/2 B.C.) ; 984 (after 183/2 B.C.) ; 985 (102/1 B.C.) ; cf. also 1047, which belongs after 128/7 B.C.

The repair of public works, which, now that better days had come, was undertaken generally,[1] was likewise left to private initiative. The expensiveness of holding office was increased further through imposing upon magistrates tolls to defray the cost of public outlays.[2] Here are to be found already fully developed the methods of finance employed generally in the Roman municipalities under the early emperors, and the basic facts are in both cases the same—the presence of a group of rich and ambitious men in the midst of a majority of impecunious, but franchised, citizens. The greater the disparity in the ownership of property became, the stronger grew the tendency to augment the public burdens of wealth.

The efforts made to put in order the fallen or half-ruined edifices of the earlier time are only one of several signs of a re-awakening life. The prominence and enterprise of the Attic gild of dramatic artists is another. Shortly after the middle of the second century B.C. we find it in correspondence with the phil-Hellene king of Cappadocia, Ariarathes V., to whom it voted honours like an autonomous republic.[3] And at about the same time its competition became so serious to the general Dionysiac League that the latter sought to have its members excluded from participating in the international games. This led to an appeal to the Roman proconsul of Macedon, Publius Cornelius (138 or 134 B.C.), who tried to settle the dispute by ordering that the

---

[1] *IG.* ii. 421, and ii. 5. 421 : repairs on Acropolis, Odeum, Anacium, and a fallen stoa. The last decree on this *stele* was passed in 141/0 B.C.—the year after the Great Panathenaea of Ol. 159. 3, when a man from Butadae was secretary. The first—that in which the repairs are mentioned—was passed prior to 151/0 B.C. *IG.* ii. 594: repairs on the wall of a stoa in Salamis. *IG.* ii. 625, 1646 : improvements in the *temenos* of the Dionysiac artists ; cf. Milchhoefer, *Archäol. Stud. H. Brunn dargebracht*, 37 ff., and Robert, P.-W. vi. 873 f. It was at about this time probably that the Tower of the Winds (*horologium*) was constructed by Andronicus of Cyrrhus in Macedon, who also made a *horologium* for Tenos in the last half of the second century B.C. (Graindor, *Musée belge*, 1906, p. 353 ff. ; cf. Judeich, *op. cit.* 92, n. 11, 333 ; cf. also *IG.* ii. 1200-1202). The neglect of the Attic μνήματα in the preceding decades was noted by Heliodoros, if B. Keil (*Hermes*, 1895, p. 199 ff.) is right in attributing to him certain passages which the pseudo-Plutarch (*Lives of the Ten Orators*) found in Caecilius. For the repair of the theatre in the Piraeus see *IG.* ii. 984, Doerpfeld-Reisch, *Das griech. Theater*, 100.

[2] Koehler, *IG.* ii. 588 ; cf. 985.

[3] Ditt. *OGIS.* 352, and for the date *Class. Phil.*, 1907, p. 401 ff. For the autonomy of the *technitae* see Ziebarth, *Das griech. Vereinswesen*, 83 ff.

Athenians be admitted into the larger body. Henceforth Argos in the Peloponnesus and Thebes in Boeotia were to be the headquarters of the association. The amalgamation was equally advantageous to the Athenians and unsatisfactory to their competitors, who accordingly sought to keep their territory free from invasion by disputing the credentials of the Attic gild. Its members, however, called upon the Amphictyonic Council to settle the question as to its status, and in 130/29 B.C. this body decided in their favour and renewed to the club all the immunities which had been granted to it a century and a half earlier [1]—freedom from taxation and military service, and protection of life and property at all times and places,—immunities of which Athens was notified, but which, significantly enough, were subject to the approval of the Romans, to whom the regulation of international affairs belonged.[2] This was not withheld, but none the less, and despite repeated *pronunciamentos* from Delphi that not only was the Athenian a true club of Dionysiac artists, but the prototype of them all,[3] the League insisted on boycotting its members, so that further reference to Pella, and when this simply resulted in the splitting of the League into a Peloponnesian and a Central Grecian faction, ultimate resort to the Senate at Rome, were necessary before the Athenians obtained the recognition and the privileges claimed [4] (112/1 B.C.). In this way the Athenian section, aided by the prosperity of Athens and the favour of Delphi and Rome, as well as by the decay of Achaean wealth and influence, became the dominant partner in the League.

The verdict of the Amphictyonic Council was also a charter of rights to the gild as against the Athenian authorities, since, of course, the allegation of the Peloponnesians that its members were not Dionysiac *technitae* at all, imperilled their immunities everywhere. Hence Athens was carefully provided with a text of

---

[1] See above, iv. 162, n. 2.
[2] *IG.* ii. 551. 94 ; cf. Cardinali, *Studi storici per l' antichità classica*, iii. 33 ff.
[3] *BCH.*, 1900, p. 96 ; cf. 1906, p. 272, 288.
[4] For this entire incident see *BCH.*, 1899, p. 5 ff. ; Ditt. *Syll.*[2] 930 ; Poland, *Gesch. d. griech. Vereinswesens*, 131 ff.

the decision. The gild was thus recognized anew by Delphi and Rome as an independent organism. It was, in fact, a polity within a polity, and was not bound by the decrees of the Athenian assembly. When it took part in a public movement, it did so voluntarily, and was entitled to distinct gratitude. One of the occasions in which it co-operated with the Athenians was in reviving the abandoned custom of sending a *Pythais* to Delphi. This was not an ordinary *theoria* : it did not go to represent Athens at the international games. Its mission was to offer a sacrifice to the Pythian Apollo, obtain fire from the sacred hearth at Delphi, and hand over to the temple tithes presented by the Athenian office-holders in the name of the city. While Athens had been a Macedonian dependency, the *Pythais*, as already mentioned,[1] had been abandoned, and upon the recovery of independence in 229 B.C. the city had been unable to renew it, but the Marathonian tetrapolis, where the worship of Apollo was most vital in Attica, kept alive the memory of classic usage by an occasional act of homage. The acquisition of Delos, and the control of the temple on the island, then impelled the Athenians to emphasize the bond of union between the two great centres of Apollo worship. That was the procession, which, following the line of Apollo's mythical progression from his birthplace on Delos to Delphi, first received the delegates which represented the Paralia and the Marathonian tetrapolis, and then passed along the sacred way into Boeotia, and through it and Phocis to its destination. It was an almost pandemic exodus. For three days in going, and as many in returning, men, women, and children, to the number of five hundred or more, were on the road. The distance was over one hundred miles; hence provisions had to be carried, and sleeping-places arranged in advance.[2] First marched the ephebes, sometimes one hundred

---

[1] See above, v. 231.

[2] For the *Pythais* see the elaborate monograph of Colin in *BCH.*, 1906, p. 161 ff. ; cf. also *Klio*, 1909, p. 304 ff. For hotels in Greece, and the housing of pilgrims, see the interesting remarks of Ziebarth in *Zeitschr. f. vergleich. Rechtswissenschaft*, xix. 291 ff.

strong; then the *Pythais* proper, made up of *theori*,
pythaistae, and *canephori*—the élite of the city, under
the management of high officials—who were flanked on
either side by the Athenian knights and light-armed
cavalry, and attended by a great chorus of flute-players,
singers, poets, actors, and all the various gentry who
belonged to the gild of Dionysiac artists. In the rear
came a detachment of mercenary foot-soldiers. The
first *Pythais* was sent in 138/7 B.C., but its despatch
was an isolated act, and did not bind the city to a
repetition. But the authorities of Delphi had naturally
been pleased with the devotion and generosity of Athens,
and took pains that not only was a second one sent in
128/7 B.C., but that the Athenians were convinced, by
the joint persuasion of oracles and historical evidence,
of their obligation to send others at intervals of every
few years.[1]

The restoration of buildings in Athens, the growth
of the power of its Dionysiac gild, and the brilliancy of
the revived *Pythais*, present a strong contrast to the
picture of decline and depopulation of Hellas in this
century which we owe to a famous passage of Polybius.[2]
"In our time," it begins, "lack of children and lack of
men have become general throughout all Greece." This
wretched condition the historian traces, not to God or
to any marvellous visitation, but to the self-indulgent
habits of the people. Rather than deprive themselves
of the luxuries which they craved, or in order to leave
their offspring in comfortable circumstances, they tended
to restrict their families to one or two children, or to
avoid matrimony altogether. Children seem to have
been born as usual, but the vicious practice of exposing
those whom the father did not care to raise destroyed
the normal increase.[3] In other words, child murder
effected much the same object in the Hellenistic age
which deliberate childlessness does in modern times.

---

[1] *Klio*, 1909, p. 304 ff.

[2] xxxvi. 17 ; cf. particularly Ed. Meyer, *Kleine Schriften*, 138 ff.

[3] τῶν γὰρ ἀνθρώπων εἰς ἀλαζονείαν καὶ φιλοχρηματοσύνην, ἔτι δὲ ῥαθυμίαν
ἐκτετραμμένων καὶ μὴ βουλομένων μήτε γαμεῖν μήτ᾽, ἐὰν γήμωσι, τὰ γινόμενα τέκνα
τρέφειν, ἀλλὰ μόλις ἐν τῶν πλείστων ἢ δύο χάριν τοῦ πλουσίους τούτους καταλιπεῖν
καὶ σπαταλῶντας θρέψαι, ταχέως ἔλαθε τὸ κακὸν αὐξηθέν.

We should have expected the results of the customs
censured by Polybius to have been particularly manifest
among the super-refined Athenians of the later second
century B.C.   Such, however, was by no means the case.
On the contrary, we have no hesitation in affirming
that large families—families of three or four sons and
the usual complement of daughters—were normal among
the rich and fashionable people of Athens at this time.[1]
Since the upper classes were tolerant of many children,
it is not rash to assume the like of the masses.   The
social position and ambitions of women, obviously, were
such as did not interfere seriously with the duties of
matrimony and motherhood.[2]   There is involved in
these facts, however, no contradiction of what is said
by Polybius, for the historian is speaking of Greece
generally, we of Athens in particular ; he of the early
half of the second century B.C., we of the eighty years
after 166 B.C.   Athens in this period was exceptional
among the states of old Greece in that it enjoyed a
rapid and steady increase of its material resources.
Accordingly, since children were actually born, they
could now be raised without impoverishing the family,
and this circumstance reinforced the repugnance, always
entertained against exposure,[3] to bring about the education of large families.   There was, therefore, beyond all
doubt, a substantial increase of citizen population at
Athens in the two generations which preceded the
Mithradatic War.

An essential condition of Attic well-being was,
accordingly, economic improvement.   For this, however,
the circumstances were all favourable.   That the agrarian interests were promoted through the establishment
of a large market under Athenian control at Delos is
clear.   Attic grain was needed at home, but for its oil,

---

[1] See Sundwall, "Heiratsalter und Kinderzahl im alten Athen," *Klio.*   The
material for my observation is found in Kirchner's *Prosopographia Attica,*
supplemented by Sundwall's *Nachträge.*

[2] The birth of many children, of whom only one or two were reared, shows
how limited was the emancipation which women obtained in old Greece in
Hellenistic times.   Cf. above, ii. 85.

[3] See Glotz, *Études sociales et juridiques sur l'antiquité grecque,* 187 ff. ; cf.
above, ii. 81.

olives, figs, honey, and other similar products Delos was the natural purchaser, for Delos was practically a barren island. Still, that the prosperity of Athens was not produced by a revival of agriculture alone becomes apparent, when we note the proportional increase in the number of those registered in the Piraeus, and the proportional decrease of those registered in an opulent country *deme* like Erchia.[1] The matchless harbour of Athens had its natural effect, and just as the decline of Athens in the third century B.C. was accompanied by a falling off in the size and influence of the mercantile interests, so in the renascence of the second century the regrowth of the Piraeus is a prominent feature. There were foreign gilds of shipowners and commission merchants there,[2] just as in Delos. They did not come for nothing. Rather it is to be supposed that the friendship of Rome and the public confidence thereby inspired drew to the Piraeus at least part of the carrying trade which Rhodes and Corinth had lost, and that the close relation of Athens and Delos, and the

[1] The statistics are, roughly, as follows :—

	VI.	V.	IV.	III.	II.	I.	Undated.
Piraeus . . .	..	12	83	19 ?	77	17	13
Phalerum . . .	..	6	70	24	36	16	7
Cydathenaeum .	1	30	149	32	37	17	12 (5)
Eleusis . . .	1	17	100	24	17	5	10 (2)
Sunium . . .	..	2	71	17	39	5	11
Paeania . . .	..	22	187	40	67	12	25 (2)
Erchia . . .	..	9	98	57 (11 ?)	29	7	2

The argument involved is strengthened by the fact that the up-country *demes* are credited with those who had migrated to the Piraeus. In this matter there was no fair reciprocity ; for there was, doubtless, a general disinclination to move from the city to the farm. Still, the *enktetikon*, or municipal tax levied on property owned by members of other *demes*, tended to keep Athenians in their home *demes*, or to lead them, by adoption or some other device, to change their registration with their residence. It discouraged the holding of property in more than one place, which, of course, was possible for only the rich in any case. Politics and business might induce men to take up residence in Athens ; they probably did not migrate in any considerable number elsewhither, except to the Piraeus, though we learn of settlements of Athenians without local rights in Eleusis and Rhamnus (Wilhelm, *Beiträge*, p. 61). Cf. Haussoullier, *La Vie municipale en Attique*, 68 f. ; Beauchet, *Hist. du droit privé de la république athénienne*, iii. 98.

[2] *IG.* ii. 3. 1339 ; ii. 475 ; *Rev. arch.* iii. 11 (1888), 5 ff. ; cf. Ziebarth, *Griech. Vereinswesen*, 27 ; and below, x. 436, n. 1 ; Francotte, *L'Industrie dans la Grèce ancienne*, ii. 204 ff. The foreign names on the tombstones found in Attica is evidence of the same thing. *IG.* ii. 3. 2723 ff. ; cf. Niese, iii. 19.

participation of Athenian shippers in the business which arose or was transacted on the island,[1] preserved this portion even after Delos had attracted the lion's share of Eastern commerce. The large fortunes made in trade in Delos, and those reserved for Athenian speculators in Delian real estate have been mentioned already. They must not be forgotten when we are considering the sources of Athenian wealth at this time. Doubtless, some of the vases and bronzes purchased by Roman connoisseurs as Delian[2] came from Athenian studios. Athenian sculptors and architects, at any rate, executed almost all the local commissions there.[3] Finally, the operation of the Attic quarries and mines yielded ample gains to their owners or lessees. Marble from Pentelicon and Hymettus was prized as never before, and long trains of oxen were constantly employed in hauling huge blocks of it to the Piraeus for shipment to Rome, Delos, and wherever sculptors and architects were at work. Nor was it sent away simply as raw material, for the practice existed for the local sculptors to cut or flute columns, to carve capitals according to the dominant styles, and to otherwise dress the marble, before exporting it. Ships loaded with these building materials, as well as with vases, bronze and silver lamps, beds, and other household furnishings, and statues of bronze and marble were constantly setting out for the West.[4] That they frequently carried works produced in earlier ages depleted the art capital of Attica, but increased the immediate gain; for the Romans, being constrained by fashion when not by taste to fill their houses with curios and works of ancient Greek art, paid freely for what

---

[1] See below, x. 426 ; and above, viii. 321, n. 7.

[2] Mommsen, *Hist. of Rome*, iii. 70 ; cf. Homolle, *BCH.*, 1884, p. 97 ; von Schoeffer, *op. cit.* 184.

[3] See below, ix. 410, n. 1.

[4] Merlin, *Journal des savants*, 1909, p. 374 ff., lists the cargo of a ship from Attica wrecked at Madhia, off the Syrtis (cf. 'Εφ. 'Αρχ., 1902, p. 145 ff., and below, x. 455). A still fuller account is given in *Acad. inscr. C.R.*, 1909, p. 650 ff., and from the style of lamp used by the crew at the time the ship went down—in the hold of which columns in consecutive heaps occupied a length of over one hundred feet—the inference is made that the disaster occurred between 150 and 50 B.C.—probably near the latter date. See further, *Acad. inscr. C.R.*, 1910, p. 585, and *Revue critique*, 1911, p. 260. For the dressing of the marble in Attica before shipment, see Plut. *Publicola*, 15.

they could not obtain by pillage or extortion. Thus new wealth was diffused in Athens and an appreciation for classic art in Italy. Many Athenians must have been enriched by the silver industry, for the demand for the metal for minting purposes alone was at this time large and insistent. Thousands of slaves were employed in the parts about Sunium mining and smelting the ore. The coins were made by hand in a public mint located in the shrine of the hero Stephanephorus, and if certain marks on the coins have been interpreted correctly in this sense, the mint used the output of thirty or forty separate mines.[1] The whole process was superintended by two gentlemen of means and position, who were responsible for each year's issue, and by a third, probably taken from the Areopagus,[2] who controlled the output for every month. It was a large business, and the mint worked under pressure. Hastily, and with little regard to elegance of form, the dies were made and the coins struck; for the Athenian money, being honest in weight and material, had secured a wide circulation, and silver and bronze pieces had to be ready to meet the growing needs of the immense commerce of Delos.[3]

The Athenians had at this time only three undecked war vessels, in addition, perhaps, to the sacred triremes. This Liliputian navy was, doubtless, maintained primarily for protection against pirates, and for ceremonial purposes. It was under the charge of three admirals, the generals, probably, to whom specific departments had not been assigned.[4] The Athenian army was now a small and, for the greater part, a purely ornamental affair. The ephebes, knights, *tarantini*, and picked volunteers (*epilecti*) made a brave show when the great games came round, or the city displayed its pomp

---

[1] Hill, G. F. (*A Handbook of Greek and Roman Coins*, 129 ff.), took the mint marks to designate the various workshops in the mint; but Sundwall (*Untersuch.* 110) dissents, and offers as an alternative the view expressed in the text. It is confirmed by a new document relating to the Attic silver mines (*Ath. Mitt.*, 1910, p. 296 ff.).

[2] Sundwall, *op. cit.* 69 ff.; cf. *Class. Phil.*, 1908, p. 395.

[3] The time of greatest monetary expansion was after 125 B.C. Sundwall, *op. cit.* 107, n. 1.

[4] See *Klio*, 1909, p. 314 ff.

abroad ; and the importance of the corps for purposes of
display, and the social distinction of the men who served
in them, gave their commander, the hoplite-general, an
enviable pre-eminence in the city. But the most of
such people could not be expected to stand on guard in
the frontier and coast forts to scare off the pirates with
whom the seas were infested, and to prevent freebooters
from raiding Attic territory. This duty fell upon the
paid troops, the small standing army, which was now
mainly, if not entirely, recruited in Attica. Considerable expense was incurred in paying and equipping this
force, but its maintenance was vital to the city, for with
it the slave population had to be kept in awe and
restraint. We are now dealing with the time in the
ancient world when slavery was most universal and
slaves most numerous. Moreover, the plantation system
of land culture, and the capitalistic organization of
industry had brought the slaves together in unusual
masses. The personnel of the slave class, too, was
different from what it had been formerly. The Roman
conquests, and the slave traffic which the Romans
licensed, brought into the servile condition men prone,
through high spirit or religious excitability, to question
the definiteness of their shackles. There came to be
added the fact that the Roman armies were far off on
the frontiers, and the government at home deeply embarrassed as well as careless and corrupt. Merciless
treatment could not hide the alarm which dictated it,
and thus the fearful slave insurrections broke out (136
B.C.), first, as was natural, in Sicily, where the plantation
system was most perfect and most odious. The uprising began with alarming success, seeing that the local
officers mismanaged it for two years ; and in 135 B.C. the
slave leaders, Eunus and Cleon, defeated the praetor
L. Plautius Hypsaeus, and in 134 B.C. the consul,
C. Fulvius Flaccus, to whom the Senate had in turn
specially entrusted the suppression of the revolt. This
gave the slaves in Italy the courage to emulate their
Sicilian comrades, and in 133 B.C. servile insurrections
occurred at Sinuessa, Minturnae, and even in Rome

itself. These were checked immediately and rigorously, and in 132 B.C. P. Rupilius, the consul, crushed the original movement ;[1] but already Aristonicus, the bastard son of Eumenes II. of Pergamum, had called the slaves of Asia to his standards in a fierce effort to keep his father's kingdom out of the clutches of the Romans. Obviously, the great under population of the Mediterranean world was seething with unrest, and by means of secret communications the agitation was carried from one slave centre to another. Thus it happened that probably in the early summer of 130 B.C.,[2] when the army of Aristonicus had slain the consul Crassus and routed his forces, the slaves in Delos and in the mining district of Attica, like those in Italy at the crisis of the Sicilian trouble, made a sympathetic outbreak. The Athenian general, Heracleitus,[3] speedily mastered the insurrection in Sunium, in which over one thousand slaves had participated, but inasmuch as the government of Athens was not in a position to spare soldiers for Delos, the cleruchs there had to act alone ; and since they were unable, apparently, to cope with the revolt unaided, the whole free population co-operated[4] in beating back the slaves into their quarters. This was completed quickly, and the slave business went vigorously on. From all

[1] Rathke, "De Romanorum bellis servilibus," *Berl. Diss.*, 1904.

[2] *Klio*, 1907, p. 238 f. Rathke (33 ff.) dates the outbreak in Italy in 133 B.C., which is probably correct, since the conspiracy there is referred by Obsequens (27, 86) to 134 B.C., the actual outbreak, however, to the year next following. The uprisings in Attica and Delos are mentioned by Diodorus (xxxiv. 2. 19) and Orosius (v. 9), together with those in Italy ; but they were all mentioned by Poseidonius, from whom Diodorus and Livy (Obsequens) depend, in connexion with the opening of the war in Sicily in 137/6 B.C. (Rathke, 35), so that we cannot judge from the place at which the reference occurs as to the exact time of their happening. Thus Orosius inserts the whole group after having mentioned the death of Tib. Gracchus, and Diodorus elsewhere (xxxiv. 3) puts the Sicilian and the Asiatic revolts at approximately the same time. Obsequens (Livy) alone mentions the Italian insurrections in connexion with a definite year, and he fails to remark upon those in Attica and Delos at all. The trouble in Delos must be dated by local evidence alone.

[3] Orosius, v. 9 "orta praeterea in Sicilia belli servilis contagio multas late infecit provincias. Nam et Minturnis quadringenti et quinquaginta servi in crucem acti, et Sinuessae ad quatuor millia servorum a Q. Metello et Cn. Servilio Caepione oppressa sunt. In metallis quoque Atheniensium idem tumultus servilis ab Heraclito praetore discussus est. Apud Delon etiam servi novo motu intumescentes, oppidanis praevenientibus oppressi sunt, absque illo primo Siciliensis mali fomite, a quo istae velut scintillae emicantes, diversa haec incendia seminarunt." Cf. Hertzberg, *Gesch. Griechenlands unter d. Herrschaft d. Römer*, i. 319 ; *Klio*, 1907, p. 237.

[4] As Orosius puts it : "oppidanis praevenientibus oppressi sunt."

the recesses of the archipelago and the Levant the
pirates steered for Delos with captives seized on sea and
land.[1]   Tens of thousands of slaves were exposed daily
on the market-place of the island, and so fierce was the
demand that a proverb arose : " Land, skipper, unload,
all's sold."   Still the warning was not unheeded.   The
little group of Athenians had been resourceless in the
crisis.   A new body, not politic, but capable of becoming such, had been created in the face of the deadly
peril.   Why destroy it and restore to the cleruchy all
its exasperating privileges ?   The Romans on the island
decided not to do so, and in their opinion the Athenian
magistrates and the governing class in Athens concurred.
Accordingly, the cleruchy was dissolved, and a new
assemblage took its place.   From this time forward the
public life of the island was incorporated, not, as before,
in the Athenian colony, but in the aggregate of Athenians,
Romans, Greeks, and others, both in permanent residence
on the island and frequenting it as merchants and
shippers.[2]   The control of Delos remained in the hands
of Athens, but the officials sent from the capital governed
Athenians and Romans, Greeks and Orientals, all alike.
We hear nothing further of the local legislature and its
complex apparatus for transacting public business.
Indeed, there is little evidence henceforth of any public
activity on the part of the people of the island in their
totality.   The possibility may have existed of convoking
all the inhabitants, but who called them together, what
matters were laid before them, how they expressed their
opinion, and how they deliberated, we cannot say.   We
simply know that the freemen on the island were able
to co-operate for the purpose of erecting monuments to
popular Athenian officials.

[1] Strabo xiv. 668 5. 2.   Cf. above, ix. 346.

[2] *Klio*, 1907, p. 234 ff.   The cleruchy was still in existence in February
131 B.C.   The new aggregate appears in our record in 126/5 B.C.   In the
interval the change occurred.   Its motivation, if not in the slave revolt, may
have been in the reduction of Asia to provincial status.   It seems likely that
the islanders of the Aegean were put generally under the new pro-magistrate ;
but Delos, of course, remained with Athens and the Macedonian governor.   [In
chapter v. of his *mémoire* (see above, ix. 355, n. 3), *Les Romains de Délos et le
gouvernement de l'île*, M. Hatzfeld seems to have reached generally the same
view of the situation on the island as that taken in the text, but to have
minimised unduly the weight of the changes made in *ca.* 130 B.C.]

There can be little doubt that the new importance which Delos acquired through the organization of the province of Asia (133-129 B.C.) and the disposition made ten years later of its public franchises, made it especially desirable to the Italian capitalists to have the island more directly under their control. The fierce energy they displayed in exploiting the region from which had come the fabulous riches of the Attalids, and the magnitude of the interests which they secured in Asia Minor need no emphasis here. Nor is more than a glance at the map required to discover the strategic importance of Delos for the new business. It lay directly on the line of trade followed by Asiatic products consigned to Italy ; so that natives of Asia Minor now found it desirable to settle there. It must of necessity become a port of call for the Roman proconsuls and the Roman knights while going and coming between Rome and their province. Hence both senators and equites in Rome were more than ready to ignore the change in the government of Delos, while their agents on the spot beyond doubt lent their aid in destroying the prerogatives of the Athenian colony ; for nobody profited by these changes more than they did. In the first place, they escaped thereby from what was in theory an inferior status into full legal equality with the proprietary people, for subsequently the aliens as well as the Athenians were " settlers " (κάτοικοι),[1] and the community in its entirety formed one of the *katoikiai* at that time numerous in the Hellenistic world.[2] Nor did

[1] See the *formulae* quoted in *Klio*, 1907, p. 236, n. 2. A new instance or two have since been added. *BCH.*, 1902, p. 539 (published in 1908) ; *BCH.*, 1908, p. 417, No. 7 (112/1 B.C.).

[2] What a *katoikia* was has been most clearly and concisely defined by Ed. Meyer in *Hermes*, 1898, p. 643 : " In der Tat ist angesichts der Ausführungen von Buresch, Aus Lydien (1898) S. 2 f. u.a. garnicht zu bezweifeln, dass κατοικία 'Ansiedlung, Ortschaft' in Kleinasien eine grössere Ansiedlung bezeichnet, die zwar fast völlig oder selbst vollständig städtisch organisirt ist, aber kein Stadtrecht hat, sondern von einer Stadt abhängig ist, und die sich deshalb auch nicht πόλις nennen darf."

It may perhaps be pointed out in this connexion that the subsequent organization of Delos coincided closely with that of the city of Alexandria, where, it seems, Ptolemy (or his *strategus*) and the imperial officials stood over an aggregate of quasi-public ethnic associations, each with its own regulations, organization, and privileges (Schubart, *Klio*, 1910, p. 63 ff.). There, as in Delos, registration in the *demes* and *phylae* belonged only to the original

the implication contained in the designation officially applied in the beginning to the new aggregate, that the Romans and non-Athenian Greeks were "foreigners," escape condemnation long; hence shortly after 118/7 B.C. the formula was revised and thereafter none of the elements was branded as alien. Nor was this change needed, in all probability, to give the right of ownership of land and houses on the island equally to all the free inhabitants, that having been, apparently, obtained in 130 B.C. This, however, was an economic gain for the "outlanders," on the importance of which it is unnecessary to enlarge. In the second place, the Italians had no longer the inconvenience of doing business with two sets of authorities — the petty officers of the cleruchy and the high magistrates from Athens. It was an advantage for them not to have to know and to observe the fine distinctions of Athenian constitutional practice. Of course, Athens was a free city, and hence entitled to exercise jurisdiction over all those settled within its boundaries,[1] but this required the Italians to carry their legal business before the court of the governor-general and his associates alone. Finally,

---

nucleus of the population and its descendants; outside this inner circle stood an outer circle of Ἀλεξανδρεῖς analogous in status to the Ἀθηναῖοι in Delos; while the majority of the population—in Alexandria made up largely of Ἕλληνες, in Delos of *Italici*, though in the former there were numerous Macedonians, Persians, Jews, Egyptians, Phrygians, etc., and in the latter many ξένοι from all parts of the Hellenistic world—was composed of those who in status were residents simply. Since political privileges were apparently not dependent upon civic registration, the lesser organizations—epicycles, so to speak, of differing magnitude moving in the circumference of the outer circle—πολιτεύματα, or ἔθνη, or σύνοδοι, or whatever they may have been called, satisfied the real political needs of the great body of the inhabitants (see the important article by Schubart, *Archiv f. Papyrusforsch.*, 1909, p. 35 ff.).

[1] Kornemann, *Berl. Stud.* xiv. 47, and P.-W. iv. 1173. The Italians in Delos were in a better position than a *conventus* in a free town, since the inhabitants of the free town in their case lacked free institutions, while the magistrates from Athens lacked the strength which they would have had if they were dealing with Italians in Athens among their own people. On the other hand, the Italians on the island did not have the advantages of the Italians resident in a provincial city, of recourse to the court of the proconsul and exemption from the jurisdiction of the local authorities. Kornemann, *op. cit.* 44 ff. The way in which the foreign settlement was earlier ignored is clear from the following passage of an honorary decree: ἐπειδὴ οἱ ἱερεῖς οἱ ἐν Δήλῳ οἱ [ἐπὶ Φαιδρίου ἄρχ]οντος τάς τε θυσίας ἔθυ[σαν τὰς καθηκ]ούσας ἁπάσας ὑπέρ τε τῆς [βουλῆς καὶ τ]οῦ δήμου τοῦ Ἀθηναίων καὶ [παίδων] καὶ γυναικῶν καὶ τοῦ δήμου Ῥω[μ]αίων καὶ τῶν κατοικούντων Ἀθηναίων [τ]ῶν ἐν Δήλῳ κτλ. *BCH.*, 1907, p. 425.

what was most important to Roman thinking in the period of reaction which followed the overthrow of the democratic tyranny of Tib. Gracchus (132 B.C.), the dissolution of the cleruchy strengthened the hands of the Athenian officials sent to the island. It rid them of the need to consider the goodwill of the Athenian populace there, and left them free to side with the Italians in cases of differences between residents of the two nationalities. The influence of the Romans is perceptible in another sphere also—in the introduction of new institutions and the gradual transformation of old ones. Thus in the years immediately following 130 B.C. we meet for the first time in Delos with the Romaea, and an elected priest of Roma, whose political function was proclaimed by her association, along with *Demos*, in the cult of Hestia,[1] the hearth goddess of the island. Thus, too, at this moment a notable reconstruction of the executive offices was brought to a termination. As has been pointed out already,[2] the Athenians left the magistracies undisturbed when they occupied Delos. But in *ca.* 152 B.C.[3] two *agoranomi* took the place of three, and in *ca.* 130 B.C. the committee of three superintendents of the *emporium* was dissolved[4] and a single superintendent of the *emporium* succeeded to it, but with powers almost co-ordinate with those of the superintendent of the island. There were

---

[1] *BCH.*, 1886, p. 34, No. 14 (129/8 B.C.); *BCH.*, 1886, p. 33, No. 12 (127/6 B.C.), and *BCH.*, 1905, p. 232, No. 90=*BCH.*, 1908, p. 439, No. 65. In this year the Romaea was celebrated by twenty-one officials, seventeen being Athenians, and four foreigners—Greeks, however (*BCH.*, 1908, p. 438, No. 64). From the nature of the case only foreigners could worship Roma (see, however, below, ix. 401, n. 4), and so it remained in the time of Augustus. Likewise, of course, no Hellenistic king could worship himself. The worship of Roma, doubtless, elevated the Roman state above the laws of the cities in which it was established. Hence its inauguration had most important *staatsrechtliche* consequences (cf. article "Roma" in Roscher's *Lexicon*, and Poland, *op. cit.* 225). Smyrna claimed to have been the first to build a temple to Roma (Tac. *Annals*, iv. 56). This was in 195 B.C. For the fact that the priesthood was triple, see *BCH.*, 1909, p. 525. It is, of course, possible that the priest and the Romaea existed earlier; but even so, their first appearance at this time is hardly accidental.

[2] See above, viii. 322.   [3] See above, ix. 349, n. 3.

[4] That there was only one superintendent of the *emporium* in the period after *ca.* 131 B.C. is shown conclusively by *BCH.*, 1908, p. 429, No. 40. This was the case in 97/6, 100/99 (*IG.* ii. 985, Col. i. E 34), and in 124/3 B.C. (*BCH.*, 1892, p. 152). That the two superintendents were associated in a pair is clear from the first reference. Cf. also *Class. Phil.*, 1907, p. 404.

thus from this time onwards two superintendents, two commissioners of religious affairs, two custodians of sacred treasures, two *agoranomi,* and two *paedotribae.*[1] This was not the old Athenian practice, for in Athens committees had been regularly composed of ten members, and though time had worked serious changes there, and though Boards, such as those of the generals and the *agonothetae,* had been dissolved for all practical purposes,[2] they had been dissolved into groups of two each only when, as in the case of the *agoranomi* and *astynomi,* the *college* had been divided for service in both Athens and the Piraeus. What we have in Delos is probably the application of the Roman collegiate principle—an early case of the imitation of the institutions of Rome which was, in time, to stud the Mediterranean world with an aggregate of Romes, all, big and little, moulded on the pattern of the great Italian mother of cities.

There is reason to believe that the change of 130 B.C. was not distasteful to the Athenian governing class, in which the men of business were coming gradually to displace the old landed aristocracy.[3] Certainly, the dissolution of the cleruchy was to the advantage of those who succeeded in winning Delian offices. At home the magistrates were limited to routine duties by the most precise definitions and the most jealous popular control. On the island they had henceforth a chance to decide questions on their own responsibility, to act with authority in the presence of the Romans and the Greeks from the great cities to the north and east, to conduct themselves, in fact, almost like Roman proconsuls, unconcerned except with a calling to account which came only at the end of a year's service. There is nothing more noticeable in the documents of the next forty years than the activity displayed by the Athenian officers, by the governor-generals in particular, unless it be the sudden burst of public enterprise which followed the disestablishment of

---

[1] For the *paedotribae,* see *BCH.,* 1908, p. 373 f.
[2] *Klio,* 1908, p. 347 ; 1909, p. 322 f.
[3] *Klio,* 1904, p. 10 ff ; and above, ix. 375.

the cleruchy. In all probability it was a little earlier
that two new porticoes—the western half of the stoa of
Philip [1] being one of them—were erected in the old
market.[2] But it was now that the circuit of the
artificial harbour, on which much labour and money
had been expended at intervals during half a millen-
nium, was completed, when Theophrastus of Acharnae,
governor - general in 126/5 B.C., faced its northern
shore with a stone embankment, and at the same
time finished off a *piazza* for the reception of public
buildings and monuments at the point where the pier
in front of the Sacred Precinct received the streets
which converged from the north and north-east.[3] It
served as a sort of an approach to the district which,
during the next few decades, came to possess the
most splendid foreign club-houses. Between 130/29
and 128/7 B.C. two chapels or temples—one to Anubis
in 130/29 and one to Isis in 128/7 B.C.—were solemnly
opened in the *temenos* of Serapis,[4] and during the four
years which followed 130/29 B.C. a large number of
altars, statues, statuettes, and other similar objects
were dedicated in this precinct, the dated bases of
many of them being still extant.[5] In 128/7 B.C.,
moreover, Achaeus of Hierapolis in Syria, a zealous

[1] *BCH.*, 1907, p. 50. At least three of the statues made by Hephaestion,
son of Myron, the most popular artist in Delos in the twenties of the second
century B.C., were apparently set up in the stoa of Philip (*BCH.*, 1880, p.
220; *ibid.* 221; *BCH.*, 1892, p. 152), and at the same time a work by Boethus
and Theodosius (*BCH.*, 1887, p. 263) was placed in conjunction with them.
Other dedications, however, date the new half at *ca.* 150 B.C. See *Acad. inscr.*
C.R., 1911, p. 221.

[2] Holleaux, *Acad. inscr. C.R.*, 1907, p. 356. The date is a mere approximation.

[3] The dedicatory inscription of a monument in honour of Theophrastus
is published in *BCH.*, 1884, p. 123. Three parts bearing the name of
Theophrastus are extant in *BCH.*, 1884, p. 123; *CIG.* ii. 2286; *BCH.*, 1887,
p. 257, No. 10. They all belong to one monument; cf. *BCH.*, 1907, p. 469, No. 77.

[4] *Klio*, 1907, p. 226. Roussel (*BCH.*, 1908, p. 384) has made it probable
that no temple of Aphrodite was erected in 127/6 B.C. The ναοί of Anubis
and Isis are distinctive in being dedicated by the *demos* of Athens. Besides
the main temple—that of Serapis—Roussel (*Acad. inscr. C.R.*, 1910, p.
294 ff.) has found the remains of five or six ναοί in the precinct of the
Egyptian deities. The identification of these with those mentioned in the
inscriptions he has not yet made.

[5] 129/8 B.C.: *BCH.*, 1886, p. 34, No. 14; 1882, p. 326, No. 19; 332,
No. 27. 128/7 B.C.: *BCH.*, 1882, p. 335, No. 32; 'Αθήν. iv. 459, No. 8, and
BCH., 1908, p. 424, No. 25; *CIG.* ii. 2296. 127/6 B.C.: *BCH.*, 1886, p. 33,
No. 12=*BCH.*, 1908, p. 439, No. 65; *BCH.*, 1882, p. 317, No. 1; *BCH.*,
1882, p. 341, No. 50; *BCH.*, 1882, p. 348, No. 73; *BCH.*, 1883, p. 370;
Lebègue, *Recherches sur Délos*, 163 (?).

worshipper of Hadad and Atargatis, the lord and lady of his native city, built with its sanction a little temple of these deities in a precinct abutting that of Serapis, a little lower down the canyon.[1] The cult was not accepted immediately by Athens, and Achaeus and at least three of his fellow-countrymen were elected in turn priests by the Hierapolitans on the island;[2] but this condition did not last long. The colony from Hierapolis was apparently large and influential,[3] and Atargatis an attractive deity; so that she was recognized by the Athenian state, and, as Aphrodite Hagne,[4] the lady of Bambyce received the honour of an Athenian priest within a decade after the gift made by Achaeus. Her consort was less fortunate. And though he continued to be associated with Aphrodite, it was now in the second instead of the first place,[5] except, occasionally, when the worshipper[6] was a Hierapolitan. The same problem thus presents itself here that presents itself in the migration of Serapis and Isis, Adonis and Astarte, and Attis and Cybele from the Orient into Europe—the precedence given in the home land to the male, and in the new land to the female member of the pair; and nowhere does it present itself more definitely. The solution is, perhaps, that in the East the precedence involved was merely one in the external action of the worship; that there, too, the real power[7] was not

[1] BCH., 1882, p. 495, No. 12. At about the same time, or possibly a little later, a certain Aristarchus, son of Isidorus, was chosen by the Hierapolitans to attend to repairs which had become necessary in the enclosure (BCH., 1882, p. 496, No. 13). For the place see Acad. inscr. C.R., 1910, p. 292.

[2] Cf. BCH., 1882, p. 496, No. 13; 497, No. 14; and especially 498, No. 16, with the other dedications made to this shrine.

[3] Thus prior to the acceptance of the cult by Athens a certain Diophantus had provided the precinct with a stairway leading up from the Inopus valley.

[4] von Schoeffer, op. cit. 194; Roussel, BCH., 1908, p. 380 ff. Atargatis was converted into Aphrodite before 118/7 B.C. (BCH., 1907, p. 335). Her naos has not yet been identified. It was obviously a small affair. See below, 389.

[5] Macrobius, Saturn. I. xxiii. 17-18, "hunc ergo ut potentissimum adorant deum, sed subiungunt eidem deam nomine Adargatin."

[6] BCH., 1882, p. 495 ff.; cf. 498, No. 16.

[7] Frazer, Adonis Attis and Osiris, 319 f.; Ed. Meyer, Gesch. d. Alt. i. 2. 394, 605, 636-656. In the new inscription published in Acad. inscr. C.R., 1910, p. 301, which belongs before the acceptance of the cult by Athens, Artargatis precedes Hadad. The theological question involved came, as is well

ATHENS AND DELOS

possessed by the lover of the goddess, however moving
he might be in his beauty, death, and revival, but by
the goddess herself. It was she who sought him out
and wooed, she who sorrowed at his untimely loss, but
not vainly and without hope ; for it was she who
restored him to at least transient life. She was herself
immortal. Serapis, Adonis, and Hadad had the frailties
of humanity about them : Isis, Astarte, and Aphrodite
had the omnipotence of the gods, together with the love
of women. There was once a time in the Semitic world
when Adonis and his comrades were the supreme gods of
their several cities ; when every action of their peoples
was a manifestation of their will and power ; [1] but this
time was long since past when Hadad and Atargatis
came to Delos, and only in the stereotyped *formulae*
of the ritual was there a reminiscence of it. The
insistence of Isidore, son of Numenius of Hierapolis,
even after the acceptance of the cult by Athens, to put
Hadad before Aphrodite Hagne in making his offering
shows how the ancient usage could have persisted for so
long a time. To the Greeks, however, such piety had
nothing to commend it ; hence it was to the goddess
that the Athenians rendered chief honour.

Once the temples sacred to the Egyptian deities
were finished, the care and further decoration of the
precinct were left to the synod of black-robed communicants, the sacred attendants, and the honorary
priests connected with the worship of Serapis and his
companions. It is easy to see that the cult was in
good hands. The priest was wont to make offerings,
obviously with the purpose of winning the commendation of the communicants and the attendants, who
thereupon, if satisfied, voted to him a statue which
was erected, of course, as a further embellishment of
the enclosure.[2] In general, the dedications made during

---

known, to a sharp issue in the fierce controversy which was waged between
Antioch and Alexandria in the fifth century A.D. as to the relation between
Christ and the Virgin-Mother, ἡ θεοτόκος.

[1] Ed. Meyer, *op. cit.* i. 2. 368 ff.

[2] 'Αθήν. ii. 134 ; *CIG.* ii. 2293 = *BCH.*, 1892, p. 483 ; *BCH.*, 1882, p. 318 ;
cf. *BCH.*, 1882, pp. 317, 334, 341.

the period 125-110 B.C. came from the temple officials,[1] but occasionally private persons lent aid, ordinarily of their own volition,[2] but sometimes in the execution of an order issued to them by the deities.[3] Notable among the dedicated objects were an *exedra* (118/7 B.C.), arcades, altars, steps[4] (117/6 B.C.), and a fountain (116/5 B.C.)—the gifts of three successive priests;[5] a monastery—the gift of two Romans,[6] and the furnishings therefor—the gift of Theophilus of Antioch (112/1 B.C.), while hardly a year passed without the presentation of one or more statues to the precinct. During this decade and a half others[7] were donated to the adjacent shrine of Aphrodite Hagne. This cult had obtained the power of extending far beyond the limits of the Hierapolitan colony through being accepted by the Athenian authorities; and those who entered into intimate relations with it were now of all nationalities and tongues.[8] Still, little attention seems to have been given for several years to the arrangement and

---

[1] Ἀθήν. ii. 134 (124/3 B.C.), synod of *melanephori*; *BCH.*, 1882, p. 320 (118/7 B.C.), priest; *BCH.*, 1883, p. 368, No. 18, and *BCH.*, 1908, p. 424, No. 27 (117/6 B.C.), priest and *canephorus*; *BCH.*, 1882, 347 (116/5 B.C.), priest; Ἀθήν. ii. 134 (116/5 B.C.), father of priest; *CIG.* ii. 2295 (115/4 B.C.), priest, *melanephori*, and *therapeutae*; *BCH.*, 1882, p. 339 (115/4 B.C.), *oneiro-crites* and *aretalogus*; *CIG.* ii. 2297 (112/1 B.C.), *melanephorus*; *BCH.*, 1882, p. 339 (112/1 B.C.), priest; *CIG.* ii. 2298 (110/9 B.C.), father of *canephorus*; *BCH.*, 1882, p. 326 (110/9 B.C.), father of the *cleiduch*.

[2] *BCH.*, 1908, p. 424, No. 26; *CIG.* ii. 2300; *BCH.*, 1882, p. 340; *CIG.* ii. 2302; *BCH.*, 1882, p. 324, No. 15; Ἀθήν. ii. 134.

[3] κατὰ πρόσταγμα, *BCH.*, 1882, p. 336; *ibid.* 339. προσαναφέροντες τῷ ὀνειροκρίτῃ, *BCH.*, 1908, p. 425, No. 28. With this agrees the Latin *ex iussu* (*CIL.* ii. 5521, xii. 403, *et passim*); *ex imperio* (*CIL.* xii. 4323, xiii. 7889, 8211, *et passim*); *ex praecepto* (*CIL.* vi. 406).

[4] It is natural to think of these steps as having led up to the elevated site on which the Serapium was located; cf. Plate xi. in *BCH.*, 1882, and better, *Guides-Joanne, Grèce*, ii. 461. Cf. also Roussel (*Acad. inscr. C.R.*, 1910, p. 299), who, however, cites only the pair of inscriptions mentioned in n. 9, p. 389, below. The steps seem to have been removed prior to 84 B.C. (Roussel in *BCH.*, 1908, p. 424, No. 27). That the inscription was put on two or more steps of the ἀνάβασις is clear from a comparison of *BCH.*, 1883, p. 368, No. 18, and 1908, p. 424, No. 27, with *BCH.*, 1882, p. 330, Nos. 24 and 25; cf. below, ix. 389, n. 9. It is possible that the chief temple—that of Serapis and his colleagues—was not built in 135/4 B.C. (see above, ix. 357, n. 3), but shortly before the steps in *ca.* 120–117 B.C. Still, the steps may have become necessary in 117/6 B.C. by some changes made in the lower terrace in 120–117 B.C. Roussel (*Acad. inscr. C.R.*, 1910, p. 295) says of the chief temple: "La construction en est tardive: il ne remonte sans doute pas plus haut que la fin du IIᵉ siècle." The reason for this conclusion is not yet published: hence we cannot control it.

[5] See above, n. 1, for the references.

[6] *BCH.*, 1882, p. 323.

[7] Cf. *BCH.*, 1907, p. 335 (118/7 B.C.).

[8] *BCH.*, 1882, p. 490 ff.

ornamentation of the enclosure. Accordingly, the *temenos* of the goddess became congested with dedications and monuments of one kind or another. Intimation after intimation[1] was given to the Athenian government that improvements were desired by Aphrodite, but it was not till 110/9 B.C. that relief came. Then, at the same time that a new temple of Isis Nemesis was built in the adjoining precinct of Serapis with funds donated in part at least by Nicomedes III. Euergetes of Bithynia,[2] a thorough overhauling of the shrine of Aphrodite was made. Stoas were constructed, statues were transferred from one place to another, repaired, and provided with new pedestals, the throne of the goddess was overlaid with gold,[3] and a monastery built or refurnished.[4] In the following years a little theatre capable of seating upwards of one hundred persons, two *exedrae* and a mosaic were constructed in the outer precinct,[5] and the temple was ornamented with pilasters and cupids.[6] The external effect was thus enhanced, while at the same time altars, and a new throne, on which in all probability the goddess sat with a lion on either side, improved the appearance of the interior.[7] In the meanwhile the temple of Isis Nemesis had been finished,[8] retaining walls being constructed, and a stairway built up to the terrace on which it was located.[9] Characteristic of the precinct of Aphrodite was, in addition to the theatre in which religious scenes were doubtless enacted, a vast inner court with a mosaic floor and at the rear

---

[1] *BCH.*, 1882, p. 491, No. 3.

[2] *Ibid.* p. 337, No. 39 ; cf. *Klio*, 1907, p. 227. Unfortunately for us, the reforms instituted in 110/9 B.C. led to the use of a new tablet for the registration of the names of the priests of Serapis. The old one alone has come down to us (*BCH.*, 1908, p. 396).

[3] *BCH.*, 1882, p. 494, No. 11 ; 1905, p. 223.

[4] *BCH.*, 1882, p. 489, No. 1. This may possibly be the edifice in the outer precinct marked P on the plan in *Acad. inscr. C.R.*, 1910, p. 289.

[5] *Ibid.* p. 497, No. 15 (109/8 B.C. ?) ; *BCH.*, 1883, p. 280 ; 1908, p. 387 f.

[6] 'Aθήν. iv. 460.

[7] *Ibid.* p. 461 f. ; cf. Cumont, *Dea Syria* in P.-W. iv. 2243 ; Ruggiero, *Dizionario epigraf.*, *s.v. Dea Syria* ii. 1467 ff. ; Wissowa, *Religion u. Cultus der Römer*, 301.

[8] *BCH.*, 1882, p. 346, No. 67 (106/5 B.C. ?).

[9] *Ibid.* p. 320, Nos. 24 and 25 ; cf. above, p. 388 n. 4.

little chapels, one of which, constructed perhaps between 105/4 and 103/2 B.C., belonged to Hadran, a Syrian colleague of Hadad;[1] also a cistern, possibly a fish-pond like the one which existed in the parent shrine at Hierapolis and in the branch later established on the Janiculum.[2] Peculiar in the precinct of the Egyptian deities was the scattered group of little chapels for the several divinities, and the main temple with a great altar in front of it, which, probably because there was but one Athenian priest, was shared by Serapis with Isis, Anubis, and Harpocrates; also, at a lower level than the chief shrine, a long-walled and paved avenue set on either side with statues and leading up to a little temple—the whole being situated in the middle of a court enclosed by stoas.[3] In both precincts the material used for the buildings and walls was ordinarily rough stone overlaid with stucco, and despite the copious dedications, the gilded thrones, and the multitude of chapels and altars, the impression of hasty and careless workmanship which is stamped upon almost everything Delian is accentuated here by the cheapness and flimsiness of much of the building materials used.

At about the same time that the two precincts on the right bank of the Inopus came to receive their equipment, the Samothracium, situated directly opposite them on the left bank of the stream, finally obtained attention. In 101/0 B.C. Helianax, priest of Poseidon and the Cabiri for life (since 103/2 B.C. possibly), dedicated to the gods whom he served and to Dionysus a fine new temple on the old site.[4] Inscribed shields placed inside connected the edifice with kings and

[1] *Acad. inscr. C.R.*, 1910, p. 302. It seems likely that the new archon Criton falls in one of the three years vacant after 106/5 B.C. The other possibilities are 114/3 and 93/1 B.C. In 99/8 B.C. another chapel was dedicated in this precinct (*BCH.*, 1908, p. 381). Another Syrian comrade of Hadad, Hydr(e)on, is mentioned in *BCH.*, 1882, p. 500, No. 23.

[2] *Acad. inscr. C.R.*, 1910, p. 380. Of the *temenos* of Atargatis on the Janiculum Gaukler here writes : "Comme tant de temples d'Orient établis sur les hauts lieux, il se composait d'un *temenos* à ciel ouvert autour d'un petit *adyton* ; mais de plus, comme à Hierapolis, il était accompagné d'un vivier où l'on nourrissait des poissons sacrés."

[3] See the new plan in *Acad. inscr. C.R.*, 1910, p. 289.

[4] *Acad. inscr. C.R.*, 1910, p. 308.

courtiers of Pontus, Cappadocia, Parthia, and Syria.[1]
The Cabiri had thus a vogue in Asia comparable to that
of Isis and Atargatis in Europe.

The Mother of the Gods and the Byblian Astarte
with their consorts seem to have made little impression
on Delos, though a community which had an altar to
Oddos, the national god of the Minaei in South Arabia,[2]
cannot have lacked votaries of these imperial deities.[3]
And in fact as the Palestine Astarte Aphrodite Urania,
and possibly as Pistiche or Aphrodite Pistiche, the
goddess of Byblus probably appears in Delian dedications recently discovered.[4] The god of Beyrout, to whom
Poseidon was the nearest Greek equivalent, was certainly
well known in Delos; for this city was in a fashion
continued on the island after its destruction by Tryphon
(145-138 B.C.),[5] and a colony of its merchants, shippers,
and commission merchants lived there organized on the
model of a Greek *thiasus*. From their patron deity
they got the name of the *Poseidoniastae*.[6] Like the
Hierapolitans, they make their first appearance in our
records after 130 B.C., and in 112/1 B.C. their handsome
two-storied *agora* and club-house was already in course
of construction. When finished, it was adorned with
stoas, frescoes, and sensuous, though carelessly executed,
groups of statuary. It was well situated on a hill to
the north-east of the sacred precinct.[7]

Naturally, the material progress of these eastern
cults presses itself most definitely upon our notice.
We can count temples, arcades, altars, and statues,

[1] Ditt. *OGIS.* 258, 353, 371–374, 430. See below, x. 426, n. 3.

[2] *Acad. inscr. C.R.*, 1906, p. 546 ff.

[3] 'Αθήν. iv. 458 ; *BCH.*, 1882, p. 500, No. 22 ; p. 502, No. 25 ; *Acad.
inscr. C.R.*, 1910, p. 524 ; 1908, p. 186 ; 1909, p. 307.

[4] *BCH.*, 1910, p. 411 ff.

[5] Strabo, xvi. 756 ; Niese, iii. 279, n. 1.

[6] This *thiasus* has nothing whatever to do with the *Poseidoniastae* who
appear in the title (Greek) of the *magistri* of the *Italici*. The members of the
thiasus were from Beyrout—the *magistri* from Italy.

[7] *BCH.*, 1883, p. 467 ff. ; 1907, p. 444 ff. ; cf. for the marble group of
Aphrodite attacked by Pan and defending herself playfully with her sandal,
BCH., 1906, p. 614 ff. and Plates xiii.–xvi. The first sharply-dated record
belongs to 122/1 B.C. (*BCH.*, 1907, p. 445), and since it alone of the inscriptions
relating to this club was not found in the neighbourhood of its agora,
Bizard and Roussel conclude that the agora was not in existence in 122/1 B.C.
(*BCH.*, 1907, p. 446).

but the progress of the habits and ideas associated with these worships, and the growth of their influence upon the lives of individuals, are more elusive developments. Should we judge from *ex-votos* alone, we must rate the Greeks of all times as a very pious, not to say superstitious people. But who can penetrate into the spirit of a religious offering? Who can ascertain with what differences of feeling an Athenian came to lay his gift on the altars of Isis and Demeter respectively?[1] The donor had in each case hopes of personal assistance, but there have come down to us none of the promises held out by the priestly attendants of the Egyptian and Syrian deities.[2] We may judge of the help expected simply by the attributes of the gods and goddesses. The dedications were regularly made to the entire Egyptian group, which was able, through combining the several powers of Serapis, Isis, Anubis, and Harpocrates, to perform the functions of the whole Greek hierarchy, or of a universal deity such as the Syrian goddess aspired to be.[3] Here was Zeus, Pluto, Hermes, Apollo, Hercules, Eros, Dicaeosyne, Tyche, Nice, Hygieia, Nemesis, Astarte, Aphrodite, all in one; here a divinity efficacious in all the undertakings and trials of life, as well as on the journey after death, and in the world to come, a divinity, moreover, recommended by the impressive practice and belief of Egypt.[4] Nor was it difficult to secure the attention

---

[1] Reitzenstein (*GGA.*, 1908, p. 786, n. 1) makes the possession of πίστις the difference. But how early a confession of faith was demanded or made we do not know. It *was* ultimately the chief difference, beyond a doubt.

[2] See the remarks of Cumont, *Les Religions orientales dans le paganisme romain*, xvii., 20 ff. ; and on the general subject, *ibid*. ch. iv. and v.

[3] Wissowa, *op. cit.* 302, and *BCH.*, 1882, p. 502.

[4] Rusch, *De Serapide et Iside in Graecia cultis*, Berl. Diss., 1906, p. 42 ff. Rusch's interpretation of the terms *therapeutae* and *melanephori*, the former of which he takes to mean worshippers generally, the latter priestly attendants, is also tenable. That the *therapeutae* were the professional servants is, however, suggested by the fact that the *pastophorium*, or monastery, was dedicated on their behalf and not on behalf of the *melanephori* (*BCH.*, 1882, p. 323, No. 12 ; cf. *CIG.* ii. 2297), which is true also of the monastery of the shrine of Aphrodite Hagne (*BCH.*, 1882, p. 489). The *melanephori* were numerous enough to form a synod ('Aθήν. ii. 134 ; *BCH.*, 1884, p. 121 ff.), but so were the *therapeutae* (*Acad. inscr. C.R.*, 1910, p. 524). Individual *melanephori* were rich men and able to make donations to the shrine (see above, ix. 388, n. 1), which is never done, to our knowledge, by individual *therapeutae*. The professional servants of Isis were branded and tonsured males : the *melanephori*, on the

and guidance of these deities. They heard a curse
pronounced upon an enemy;[1] they came in the night
to those who slept in the temples, and empowered
experts to interpret the messages then delivered in
dreams,[2] as well as others to expound their sacred story,
their miracles, and their healing and saving power.[3]
Nor were their demands impossible of fulfilment, since
they involved specific offerings to the shrines,[4] and, in
general, devotion acknowledged by purificatory rites,
and participation in peculiar ceremonies. Thus it came
that strange rites were witnessed on Delos. Every day
at dawn the inner temple of Isis was thrown open,
and the initiated waited in rapt attention for the
coming of the goddess. A priest lit the sacred fire and
made libations of Nile water; then called aloud the
name of the goddess, whereupon the statue, decorated
with rich robes and jewels, was presented for the adoration of the crowd. On every afternoon came a second
service and the closing of the temple. Thus it came
that novel processions were seen on Delos, at the
opening of each winter, of men and women—Italians

---

other hand, might be women (*BCH.*, 1908, p. 386). The name *therapeutae*
probably betrays the office ; cf. Lucian, *De dea Syra*, 31 οὐ μέντοι πάντες οἱ ἱρέες,
ἀλλὰ οἱ μάλιστα ἀγχίθεοί τέ εἰσι καὶ οἶσι πᾶσα ἐς τὸ ἱρὸν μέλεται θεραπηίη. They
are officiating and proselytizing priests—"des prophètes instruits dans la science
divine, des stolistes, ou ornatrices, chargées de vêtir les statues des dieux, des
pastophores qui portent dans les processions les chapelles sacrées, d'autres
encore" (Cumont, *op. cit.* 115 ; *BCH.*, 1902, p. 531, n. 2). The priest was
merely an honorary president designated by lot.

[1] One is extant, *BCH.*, 1882, p. 501; cf. Gruppe, *Griech. Mythologie u.
Religionsgesch.* ii. 1565, n. 2.

[2] ὀνειροκρίται, *BCH.*, 1882, p. 325, and especially the inscription found in
Athens which has been republished by Rusch, *op. cit.* 52, and *BCH.*, 1908,
p. 425, No. 28.

[3] ἀρεταλόγοι, *BCH.*, 1882, p. 327, and especially Reitzenstein, *Hellenistische
Wundererzählungen*, 9 ff., where the articles by Crusius in P.-W. ii. 670, and
Reinach in *BCH.*, 1885, p. 257 ff., are *überwunden*. Reitzenstein remarks, "Im
hellenistischen Kult ägyptischer Heilgötter ist ἀρεταλόγος Standesbezeichnung
für den von dem Gotte selbst berufenen Verkünder oder Deuter von Visionen
und Träumen." This latter seems to me rather the office of the ὀνειροκρίτης ;
that of the *aretalogus*, on the other hand, as stated in the text. The one
person might be both (*BCH.*, 1882, p. 339). What the *aretalogi* were supposed
to expound is set forth in the case of Athena Lindia in an inscription published
in Lindus at the order of the state, "contenant l'histoire légendaire de la
fondation du temple avec compte-rendu des diverses apparitions de la déesse et
liste des bienfaiteurs fabuleux et historiques du sanctuaire." Blinkenberg et
Kinch, *Bull. de l'Acad. de Danemark*, 1907, p. 45 f., as reported by Bourguet
et Reinach, *REG.*, 1908, p. 191.

[4] Frequently dedicated κατὰ πρόσταγμα τῆς θεοῦ. See above, ix. 388, n. 3.

and Greeks, as well as Orientals—clad in black robes,[1] and pure from the taint of wine and sexual intimacy,[2] engaged under the conduct of tonsured and branded[3] priests in helping Isis and Anubis in their hunt for the body of Osiris-Serapis, wild with grief during the search, ecstatic with joy during the days which followed the finding. At the end of each winter a congregation of the same persons might be observed bearing a ship to the sea-side as a symbol of the opening of a new season, for Isis was ruler of the sea and its traffic. Throughout the year, moreover, at various times the narrow streets were alive with the whirl and clamour of the castrated priests of Atargatis, whose obscene dances and self-mutilations evoked the indignation at a later time of conservative Romans.[4]

The priestly organization of these eastern cults was a powerful factor in their propaganda. How it worked, how the visions were sent and the orders issued, we cannot, of course, know; but that it worked successfully is indubitable. We have already seen that it was able to coerce the reluctant government of

[1] The congregation on Delos wore black robes. On the other hand, the white linen robes of the votaries of Isis are frequently mentioned (Wissowa, op. cit. 297, n. 2). We have mention of a sindonophorus on Delos (BCH., 1882, p. 323). The black robes were appropriate to the mourning of Isis while engaged in the search for Osiris-Serapis, which occupied the first day of the Isis fête (Abel, Orphic. Hymn. 42, and Plut. De Iside et Osir. 366 E, cited by Rusch, op. cit. 56). After the finding came the rejoicing (Wissowa, op. cit. 295), to which the white robes were suitable.

[2] As the inscription set in large letters over the sanctuary put it, ἀπ' οἴνου μὴ προσιέναι μηδὲ ἐν ἀνθινοῖς (BCH., 1882, p. 350). All who have seen Chinese prostitutes on the streets of San Francisco know what ἐν ἀνθινοῖς means ; cf. Janell, Ausgewählte Inschr. 152 A ; Ditt. Syll.² 564, 939, 6 ; Mau, P.-W. i. 2377. The prohibition of sexual intercourse is not mentioned at Delos in connexion with Isis—as in connexion with Aphrodite Hagne (Acad. inscr. C.R., 1910, p. 305) and Zeus Cynthius and Athena Cynthia (Lebègue, op. cit. 158, and better, 'Aθήν. iv. 456), but belongs to Isis worship elsewhere (Wissowa, op. cit. 297, n. 11). It was not an Oriental trait (Menander, Epitrep. 221-224 ; Diog. Laert. viii. 43 ; Strabo, xvi. 1, 20, 745, and Dittenberger's note on Syll.² 566 ; cf. Syll.² 567, 633 ; Wilhelm, GGA., 1900, p. 100 ; BCH., 1887, p. 257 ; Revue arch. sér. iii. tome 2, 1883, p. 181 ; and especially Kretschmer, Österr. Jahreshefte, 1902, p. 139 ff., and Wächter, Reinheitsvorschriften im griech. Kult, 1910).

[3] For the tonsure of the priests, and the cross branded on their foreheads see Dennison, Amer. Journ. Arch., 1905, p. 11 ff., and Hauser, ibid. 1908, p. 56 ff.

[4] These festivals are presumed for Delos because of the presence there of the cults with which they were subsequently connected (Wissowa, op. cit. 295 f., 300 ; Rusch, op. cit. 79 f. ; Gruppe, op. cit. 1560 ff.). We cannot be quite sure that some of the traits did not grow up after 100 B.C. See, however, Cumont, op. cit. 116 ff., and Otto, Priester u. Tempel in hellenistischen Ägypten, i. 114 ff.

Athens,[1] and, when it could do this, we may be sure that it spoke to individuals with uncommon persuasiveness. A dedication exacted by the deities from the *therapeutae* alone is unknown, but to the priest and the *therapeutae* combined the mandate might come. Thus it was in this way that the little theatre in the precinct of Aphrodite Hagne was constructed.[2] The outer precinct of the Syrian goddess was liberally provided with small rectangular alcoves, open to the court on one side—so-called *exedrae*. In these raised platforms were set, upon which worshippers slept. There they received the "visions" and "commands," the latter being probably self-explanatory, the former being read by the experts.[3] There was doubtless here, as in all incubation, a fusion of piety and imposture, aberrations due to tense nerves and excited imaginations, as well as 'to priestly hocus-pocus.

The worship of Atargatis and Isis was altogether divorced from Semitic or Egyptian nationality, and into relation with them men entered individually, not collectively; hence their temples stood open to all— to Romans as well as Greeks. We remark especially the zeal for these Oriental deities exhibited by the Aemilii,[4] a Roman family resident on Delos. A cult idol, and the house of the priestly attendants of Serapis, as well as an *exedra* in the precinct of the Syrian goddess, were their gifts. About a dozen others of their countrymen appear in our records as the authors of *ex-votos*, and scores of them besides, as well as of Italian Greeks, learned to worship Isis and Dea Syria at Delos, and to carry their new deities back with them to Tarentum, Naples, and Puteoli, whence the road to Rome was not long or difficult.[5]

---

[1] *BCH.*, 1882, p. 491; cf. *Klio*, 1907, p. 229, and above, ix. 389.

[2] The names of the priest and the *therapeutae* who dedicated the theatre are found in an unpublished inscription. *Acad. inscr. C.R.*, 1910, p. 304 f. From this list we shall learn much as to the organization of the association of Aphrodite on Delos.

[3] *Acad. inscr. C.R.*, 1910, p. 523; *Rh. Mus.* xix. p. 256; κρίνοντος τὰ ὁ[ρ]άματα Διονυσίου ’Αντιοχέως.

[4] *Klio*, 1907, p. 228, n. 2; cf. *BCH.*, 1908, p. 416, No. 5 (?).

[5] Wissowa, *op. cit.* 292, 301, n. 3, and *Acad. inscr. C.R.*, 1910, p. 306, 522 f.

The Romans figure individually at Delos also as the givers or recipients of statues, friends of Ptolemy Euergetes II. being among those honoured by them,[1] the recipients being, prior to 105/3 B.C., only three or four distinguished persons, mostly magistrates.[2] It is probable that, in general, the high Roman officials ignored their countrymen on the island until Delos became a stopping-place on their way to Asia and Cilicia.[3] They could do this the more easily in that the residents there were mainly freedmen not of themselves but of the *equites*. In many cases, too, the Latin names which these had obtained on emancipation obscured only thinly the fact that they were of Greek origin,[4] it being, of course, advantageous in a business way for the Roman capitalists to send as agents to Delos men who spoke Greek fluently. Still, they had been long enough in Italy to have learned Roman ways and to reflect Roman sentiment, so that their form of organization was quite different from that of any other association on Delos. The *masters* were not merely the professional ministrants of a cult like the servants of Serapis and Aphrodite Hagne, and the Italians were

---

[1] *BCH.*, 1884, p. 107 ; *CIG.* ii. 2285. In both cases the Roman dedicators were probably settled in Alexandria.

[2] Gnaeus Pap[irius] στρατηγὸν ἀνθύπατον Ῥωμαίων (*BCH.*, 1884, p. 105 = 1910, p. 395) (112 B.C. ?) ; Marcus ταμίαν καὶ ἀντιστρατηγὸν Ῥωμαίων (*BCH.*, 1884, p. 131), the same seemingly as M. Antonius M. f. ταμίας, ἀντιστρατηγὸς Ῥωμ., whose statue was erected by the city of Prostanna in Pisidia. Antonius was in Athens in 103/2 B.C. (Cic. *De orat.* i. 82 ; cf. below, x. 428, n. 2 ; Drumann-Groebe, i. 44, No. 9 ; Foucart, *Journal des savants*, 1906, pp. 569, 576). His *elogium* is given from Delos in *BCH.*, 1884, p. 133 (85/4 B.C.). Servius Cornelius Ser. f. Lentulus στρατηγὸν ἀνθύπατον Ῥωμαίων (*BCH.*, 1885, p. 380 ; 1907, p. 455, No. 53. After 110/9 B.C. For the title ἀνθύπατος cf. Mommsen, *Staatsr.* ii.[3] p. 647 ff. It appears only between 146 and 84 B.C. Foucart, *Revue de philologie*, 1899, p. 254 ff.). As to G. Ofellius M. f. Ferus see *BCH.*, 1881, p. 391, and above, ix. 356, n. 1.

For other Romans who appear in Delos earlier than Sulla's time see *BCH.*, 1884, p. 119 ; *CIG.* ii. 2285*b* ; cf. *BCH.*, 1887, p. 270, No. 34, and *CIL.* iii. *Suppl.* 7233. After 88 B.C., according to Graindor, *Musée belge*, 1908, p. 111, but, as Roussel shows (*BCH.*, 1909, p. 443), about 100 B.C. ; *BCH.*, 1887, p. 269 (97/6? B.C.) ; *BCH.*, 1884, p. 182 ; *BCH.*, 1880, p. 219 (*ca.* 102/1 B.C.) ; *BCH.*, 1887, 272 f. (*ca.* 97 B.C.) ; *BCH.*, 1899, p. 73 ; cf. 1905, pp. 18 and 229 ; *BCH.*, 1907, p. 457, Nos. 54 to 57 (prior to 88 B.C.) ; *BCH.*, 1905, p. 237, Nos. 97 and 98 ; *BCH.*, 1910, p. 398, Nos. 44 and 45. For the Romans on Delos in general see now Pernier *s.v. Delus* in Ruggiero, *Dizionario epigraf.* ii. (1907).

[3] None of the statues of Roman magistrates can be dated with any certainty earlier than 112 B.C.

[4] See *e.g.* the lists published in *BCH.*, 1899, p. 56 ff. ; *BCH.*, 1907, p. 441 f. ; *BCH.*, 1909, p. 493 ff.

neither a gild like the *Poseidoniastae* of Beyrout nor a congregation like the *melanephori* of Serapis; for admission seems to have depended not upon the payment of contributions or subscription to special forms, but upon the fact of Italian abstraction—of origin in a Greek or Latin community in Italy. They formed an incipient political community (*conventus*), and had the circumstances been propitious, they would eventually have developed into the Roman colony of Delos.[1] The organization at their head is more like a board of Athenian magistrates than any institution of Greek collegiate life, and for a parallel we have to go to Italy —to the twelve *magistri pagorum* of Campania, to the Roman *magistri Mercuriales*,[2] and *magistri collegiorum compitalicorum*, or to the various boards of *masters* appointed annually by the chief executive of the Roman colonies to attend to the religious and administrative duties attached to the care and use of each of the municipal temples.[3] The settlement tended by the *masters* grew very rapidly after 130 B.C., and a corresponding increase occurred in the responsibilities and importance of its officials. Hence at about the time that G. Gracchus gave the *decumani* licence to despoil Asia with impunity, certainly prior to 113/2 B.C., their number was doubled,[4] and the final size was thus given to the administrative board of the *Italici*. Simultaneously, in all probability, another change was made. Hermes and Maea, the divine patrons of the settlement, were humble traders' saints; whereas now that Delos had become a point of vantage to the *equites* for the plunder of Asia, it was the place of residence of many important people. Hermes was needed still, and was retained, though in a subordinate

---

[1] For the *conventus* see Kornemann, P.-W. iv. 385, 1180 ff., 1196 ff.; Mommsen, *Hermes*, vii. 322.

[2] For the possible relation between the *magistri Mercuriales* and the *sexviri Augustales* see Mommsen, *Staatsrecht*, iii.³ 456, n. 1.

[3] Marquardt, *Staatsverwaltung*, iii.³ 203 ff.; Mommsen, *Staatsrecht*³, ii. 1035 f. The officials, moreover, of a *vicus* (*katoikia*) were ordinarily termed *magistri*.

[4] *Acad. inscr. C.R.*, 1908, p. 185 (113/2 B.C.)=*BCH.*, 1909, p. 493, No. 15; *BCH.*, 1909, p. 496, No. 16 (*ca.* 100 B.C.); *BCH.*, 1884, p. 145 f. (74 B.C.); *BCH.*, 1877, p. 87 f., where one name has probably fallen out; and *BCH.*, 1910, p. 404, No. 54.

position; but Maea was abandoned,[1] and in her stead came, as chief guardians of the Italians, Poseidon, god of the sea, and Apollo. Henceforth *masters*, or, to give the title in full, *magistreis Mirquiri Apollinis Neptuni*, was expressed in Greek by *Hermaistae Poseidoniastae Apolloniastae*, the latter being six in number,[2] the *Hermaistae* two, and the *Poseidoniastae* four.[3] The twelve were the administrative committee of the *Italici*[4]—an office which devolved upon them through the lack of the civil executive which belonged to a Roman colony—and, where Apollo, Poseidon, and Hermes were not specifically concerned, they acted as a single corporation. The bodies of six, four, and two, which by union constituted the twelve, were the sacral

---

[1] Maea appears in *BCH.*, 1910, p. 402, No. 52, and *BCH.*, 1902, p. 536 (*ca.* 140 B.C.); cf. also *BCH.*, 1899, p. 60, No. 5, but not in the later dedications of the *masters*; cf. above, p. 397, n. 4.

[2] The only appearance of the *Apolloniastae* alone is in *BCH.*, 1907, p. 442, No. 33. The sculptor of the dedication they then made, Ammonius son of Zopyrus of Miletus, was active in Delos in 124/3 B.C. (*BCH.*, 1908, p. 419 f. Nos. 12 and 13. Here he collaborated with his brother Perigetes).

[3] The *Poseidoniastae* (*Neptunales*) appear alone only in *BCH.*, 1909, p. 501, No. 17, where they are four in number, two being *ingenui*. The *Hermaistae* appear alone in what is probably the post-reorganization period only in *BCH.*, 1910, p. 402, No. 53, where the stone is broken so that their number, two, has perhaps no significance; but they appear also in *BCH.*, 1907, p. 439, No. 30, where they are certainly two in number, both *liberti*. It is not a partial list, for if that were so, it is difficult to see why the *magistreis* were not *Poseidoniastae Apolloniastae*, as well as *Hermaistae*. Besides, the *Apolloniastae* being six and the *Poseidoniastae* four, the *Hermaistae* must have been two. In *BCH.*, 1909, p. 504, No. 19 (57/5 B.C.), the *Hermaistae* are mentioned, but their names are not given.

[4] We cannot determine sharply the relations existent between the Athenian *epimeletae* and the Italian *masters*; but the wishes expressed by the latter cannot have been ignored by the former. I see no reason for thinking that there was ever more than one *college* of *masters* on Delos—with subdivisions, of course. The alternate view (*Acad. inscr. C.R.*, 1910, p. 600), that there were three groups of *masters* which, by uniting, formed one *collegium*, involves the idea that it is the weakest and least important of them about which we hear most. Moreover, no reason is apparent why the *magistreis Mirquiri* should have shrunk from six to two simply because of an occasional co-operation with two other groups of *masters*. It is possible that the *magistreis Mirquiri* received their commission from only a fraction of the *Italici* on Delos, though this seems to me unlikely; in which case we can speak properly of a Delian *conventus* only when they assumed charge of the cult of Neptune and Apollo also. From this time on there is a clear relation between the *masters* and the *Italici* (*BCH.*, 1910, p. 406). They gave games, constructed public works, and donated porticoes and statues quite in the style of municipal magistrates. It is not denied, however, that from the point of view of Attic law the *conventus* was simply an aggregate of three *conlegia* (see below, x. 452, n. 1), though we never find the *masters* serving any but the *Italici* as a whole. Constitutionally there were no magistrates of the *Italici* except the Athenian officials.

ministrants of the three deities from whom they received their names, and whose cult we find subsequently united in the great *schola* of the Italians. The inclusion and pre-eminence of Apollo, which were not dictated by professional reasons, show now fully the Italians felt at home˙ on Delos. They had, in fact, adopted the local god as their own; and it seems probable that at the time of this reorganization of their association the erection of a permanent and worthy headquarters on the island was already contemplated, if not actually begun.[1]

The reduction in the number of *Hermaistae* from six to two is not adequately explained by the exclusion of Maea from their care. The chief reason is, undoubtedly, that they lost at the same time responsibility for the maintenance and religious use of the two little chapels by the market-place, whose establishment has been already alluded to. There had, of course, been no doubt hitherto as to the nature of the enclosure in which these *sacra* were situated. It was clearly a *compitum* sacred to the Lares of the cross-roads, such as was to be found in any settlement in Italy,[2] and by the door of almost every Roman house on Delos were to be seen, perpetuated in paintings on altars, niches, or panels, scenes of their worship taken direct from domestic life;[3] but as yet the care of the cult of the Lares was merely an incident among the duties of the *masters*. Hence a board of *ministri*[4] with this express duty was desirable. It was now created, the increased dignity and respectability of the settlement being a sufficient reason for relieving the *masters* of the duties connected with this humble plebeian office, and henceforth from five to twelve *competaliastae*, as the Greeks

---

[1] See below, x. 432, notes.

[2] In Italy the officers of the *compitum* were called *magistri* (Ascon. Pedian. in Cic. *Orat. in Pison.* 6 p. 7 (Clark) "solebant autem magistri collegiorum ludos facere, sicut magistri vicorum faciebant, Compitalios praetextati "). This name does not appear in Delos, but simply for the reason that the extant dedicatory inscriptions are all written in Greek.

[3] Bulard, "Peintures murales et mosaïques de Delos," *Fondation Eugène Piot*, xiv. p. 33 ff.

[4] The *magistri vicorum* in Rome also had humble *ministri* to assist them in managing the *Compitalia*. Marquardt, *Staatsverwaltung*, iii.[3] 204.

named them, were appointed annually for this purpose.[1]
From this time on, in the middle of each winter,
when the sea was rough and the island was isolated
from the rest of the world, the *competaliastae* summoned the Italian colonists, who remained over winter,
to put puppets and balls of wool upon the altars at
the cross-ways, and give more freedom and wine to
the slaves; for the Lares had their day of power,[2]
and clad in short tunics and holding wreaths or *rhyta*
aloft in the right hand and palm branches or *paterae*
in the other,[3] the twain now showed themselves to
spiritual eyes, and bade free and slave alike to join
them in the merry dance and drown their cares in wine.
The many freedmen on the island had an unforget-
able reason to maintain the *Compitalia*.

We do not know by whom the *competaliastae* were
appointed, but since the office was reserved for Italians
in the same way as that of the *Hermaistae*, from which
it had apparently branched off, the inference is permissible that the *Italici* formed their constituency. The
competaliastae named in the lists thus far discovered
were all freedmen or Italian Greeks,[4] and from the
general character of the fête they administered,[5] and the
active participation in it of slaves,[6] we may judge that
this institution appealed primarily to the humbler
elements of the Italian colony. The Lares were always

[1] The earliest dated occurrence of the *competaliastae* is as yet *BCH.*, 1899, p. 64 (99/8 B.C.), but they were doubtless instituted some time before.
[2] *Compitalicius dies* (Cic. *Ad Att.* vii. 7. 3); cf. Wissowa, P.-W. iv. 791.
[3] *BCH.*, 1899, p. 60, No. 6, where Jourguet has described from a relief—without being aware of its identity—the two dancing Lares so common in relief and bronze after the time of Augustus (Wissowa, *Religion d. Römer*, 148 ff., and *Gesammelte Abhandlungen zur röm. Religions- und Stadtgeschichte*, 63 ff.; Roscher's *Lexicon*, ii. 1891 ff.; Reinach, *Statuaire*, ii. 493–500, 812), differing, however, in that they hold in their hands *amphorae* and branches of laurel. Our example, which dates apparently from shortly before 133/2 B.C., is one of the earliest extant of a type which dates from at least the time of Naevius. See especially Bulard (*loc. cit.*), who has discovered a whole series of representations of the Lares in the mural paintings of Delos.
[4] *BCH.*, 1883, p. 12, No. 5 (97/6 B.C.)=Ditt. *Syll.*[2] 322; cf. *BCH.*, 1884, p. 490, n. 1; *BCH.*, 1899, p. 62 (*ca.* 97/6 B.C.); *ibid.* p. 63 f. (date uncertain. One of the five members was a freedman of G. Ofellius). *Ibid.* p. 64 (99/8 B.C.); *ibid.* p. 70 (93/2 B.C. 12 members); *ibid.* p. 66 (Aropus of Azenia *epimeletes* of Delos, *ca.* 91/0 B.C.). Cf. *BCH.*, 1896, p. 435 ff.; 1899, p. 56; 1907, p. 441. According to *BCH.*, 1906, p. 632, n. 2, a more extended treatment of this subject is to be expected soon.   [5] Cf. P.-W. iv. 791.
[6] Dion. Hal. iv. 14, cited by Wissowa, *Religion d. Römer*, 149; cf. 151.

dear to the common folk, and one went with the Italian family in all its migrations;[1] but as yet the *compitum* has been found nowhere else outside of Italy before the imperial age. Here, moreover, its chapel had been built by the chief officials of the entire Italian colony,[2] and a place was found in the *compitum* for Maea, Hercules, Minerva, *Roma*, and *Fides*, the two latter being, significantly enough, additions, made after the care of the enclosure had passed from the keeping of the *magistri* into that of the *competaliastae*;[3] for the worship of *Roma* and *Fides* belonged properly to foreigners, freedmen, and slaves—not to full citizens—just as, at a later time, the worship of Augustus in the Roman municipalities belonged to the rich freedmen (*Augustales*),[4] and the worship of *Roma et Augustus* to the provincials.

Within the semi-political association of the *Italici* the Romans formed by far the most influential, if not the most numerous, group. They were of two kinds, freemen and freedmen. In Rome, of course, the latter were disqualified for office holding, an exception being made, however, in that they might share in the management of the *compita Larum*.[5] In Delos they were as an aggregate placed on a precise equality with those of

---

[1] Samter (*Familienfeste der Griechen und Römer*, 105 ff.) has defended against Wissowa the old view that the household Lar was derived from the spirits of the dead members of the family; the Lares of the *compitum* being the aggregate of the household Lares of the quarter. That they appear as two is simply an artistic convention. Wissowa would localize the primordial Lares as guardians of agriculture in the corners of the farms, and would have one of the group transferred from the *compitum* to each house on the adjacent properties. As to origins, let the specialists argue. This is certain, that in *ca.* 140 B.C. the Lares of the *compitum* in Delos had nothing to do with the protection of land or crops, since we cannot think of the Italians as coming to Delos to farm. They are already the guardians of the Italian households on the island. See also Bulard, *loc. cit.*

[2] *CIL.* iii. *Suppl.* 7217, and *BCH.*, 1910, p. 402, No. 52. Here one is a freeman with an Italian name, and one a freedman, the rest of unknown status. No freemen with Italian names occur among the *competaliastae*; hence these six are the *magistri*. The bilingual dedication, moreover, shows them not to have been *competaliastae*.

[3] *BCH.*, 1899, p. 61, No. 10 ff. A Πίστις or *Fides* was added to the group of deities in 97/6 B.C. (*BCH.*, 1883, p. 13), and a *Roma* in 94/3 B.C. (*BCH.*, 1899, p. 68). A similar association of Πίστις and *Roma* is found on coins of Locri in Magna Graecia of the year 204 (274 ?) B.C. (Roscher's Lexicon, *Roma*, 146, 149), and in the hymn to Flamininus: μέλπετε, κοῦραι, Ζῆνα μέγαν 'Ρώμαν τε Τίτον θ'ἅμα 'Ρωμαίων τε Πίστιν (Plut. *Flam.* 16). See P.-W. *s.v. Fides* (vi. 2281).

[4] Mommsen, *Staatsrecht*, iii.[3] 454, n. 2.

[5] *Ibid.* iii.[3] pp. 451, 454.

free birth, and of the six *magistri* three were always freedmen.[1] So, too, when the number was doubled one half of the *magistreis Mirquiri Apollinis Neptuni* remained of servile origin, and the only change made later was to replace one of the Roman freemen by a freedman and another by a free citizen of Tarentum, Naples, Heracleia, or some other of the Greek cities in Italy.[2] It seems unlikely that this was done before the extension of the franchise to the Allies at the time of the Social War. It is obvious, accordingly, that the Italians of free birth on Delos were far outnumbered by those of servile extraction, since otherwise the latter would have been granted no such influence in the management of the affairs of the community ; and the same was doubtless the case in the other settlements made at this time by Italians outside of Italy.[3] On the other hand, the recognition ultimately given to the Greeks of South Italy proves that these were on Delos in considerable numbers. Prior to the Social War only those in possession of the Roman citizenship held office on Delos, but the position held by the *competaliastae* was opened to the Italian allies of Rome from its establishment, and as early as 97/6 B.C. a Neapolitan appears among the freedmen by whom the cult of the Lares was administered.[4] In other words, the distinctions drawn in Italy were so far as practicable observed in Delos, but it is significant for the growth of Italian nationality in this age that the Romans on the island did not draw themselves apart into an organization of their own, but regarded themselves rather as a privileged class among the *Italici*

[1] *BCH.*, 1899, p. 56, No. 1 ; 1877, p. 284, No. 6. In *CIL.* iii. *Suppl.* 7212 of the four names left, two are those of freedmen, one of a freeman, while the other is doubtful. In *BCH.*, 1910, p. 402, No. 52, one is a freeman, one a freedman, the others incapable of classification.

[2] *BCH.*, 1909, p. 494, No. 15 ; p. 496, No. 16 ; 1910, p. 404, No. 54, where the names of six freedmen and three freemen are alone capable of classification. In *BCH.*, 1884, p. 146 (74 B.C.), on the other hand, there are seven freedmen, four Roman freemen, and one citizen of Heracleia, while in *BCH.*, 1877, p. 87 f.—where one name is lost, doubtless—four are Romans, one a Neapolitan, and six freedmen.

[3] See for the relation in point of organization of the settlement on Delos to the general Roman scheme the excellent article by Kornemann in P.-W. 1187 ff.

[4] *BCH.*, 1883, p. 12, No. 5 (Ditt. *Syll.*[2] 322). Two appear among the ten in *BCH.*, 1899, p. 67, No. 14. For the admission of the lower classes to this office in Rome see Mommsen, *Staatsrecht*, iii.[3] 451 ; ii.[3] 1036.

than as a separate people. To the world at large they seemed in fact to form a single nation, and the Greeks in Mithradates' time confused them in an undiscriminating hatred. Whatever might be the case in Italy, abroad the Italians generally enjoyed in about equal measure the solid business advantages that followed the acquisition by Rome of world-empire ;[1] and secure in the possession of these, the settlers from the Italian allies were content to leave to the Romans among them the dignity and responsibility of holding the magistracies.

The existence of the *conventus* did not prevent, though it probably discouraged, the formation of *thiasi* or *collegia*[2] among the Italians. Business and religion were, in fact, largely international in this time and place ; so that the Italians could probably enter freely into the chief private associations. Their interest in these might be weak or strong, according to circumstances, but in one they dominated—that of the bankers (*trapezitae : negotiatores*).[3] Apart from the counters of the Athenian government,[4] and those of the temple of Apollo, only one bank[5] is demonstrable on Delos which was not owned by an Italian. That is to say, the private business of usury and banking there, as generally in the Roman Empire,[6] was subject to such conditions that few except Italians could engage in it with success. What advantages were reserved to Romans are, it seems, nowhere stated explicitly, but it is conceivable that they arose from the great accumulation of capital

[1] Hence the maritime allies of Rome, as well as Campania and Latium, remained loyal during the Social War. The revolt was confined mainly to the central agricultural districts, from which the Roman soldiers were largely recruited. Hence its success.

[2] See below, x. 452, n. 1. [3] *BCH.*, 1899, p. 78.

[4] Were these located in the temple of Apollo (cf. Wilcken, *Archiv f. Papyrusforschung*, 1909, p. 212)? Deposits made by the bank in the temple of Apollo are alluded to in the inventory published in *BCH.*, 1910, p. 181 ff.

[5] *BCH.*, 1877, p. 86, No. 29. The banker in question was a native of Ascalon ; no accident, as is clear from the fact that one other of the five Delian bankers known to us was a native of Ascalon before obtaining citizenship in Naples. Cf. also Cumont, *op. cit.* 132, and especially Parvan, *op. cit.* 110 ff.

[6] Kornemann, *Berl. Stud.* xiv. 5 ; Ernesti, *De negotiatoribus Romanis* in *Opusc. phil. crit.* 3 ff. ; Greenidge, *A Hist. of Rome*, i. 49 ff., esp. 52 ; and for the technique of Roman banking, Moritz Voigt, "Über die Bankiers, die Buchführung und die Litteralobligation der Römer," in the *Abh. der sächs. Ges. d. Wiss.* x. 513 ff.

in Rome; from the necessity—which was involved in the fact that Italy was largely the purchaser—of the constant transfer of coin from the banks in Italy to the provinces, and from the handling of most of the funds of the imperial government by the Roman bankers. To these must be added, however, the exclusive ability of the Italians to make loans to municipalities and to men resident outside their own towns, with the assurance that the Roman officials would permit or enable them to enforce their contracts. This being the case, it was inevitable that the temple should invest its limited capital in local property, or make loans for which local property was given as security;[1] that the Athenian state should engage primarily in putting its money into circulation by buying and selling coins, and that the commercial banking should thus become practically an Italian monopoly. About the bankers' gild we know only that it existed, but honorary statues attest the importance of the four Italian bankers whose names appear in our records.[2]

There was a multitude of associations of one sort or another on Delos, as was to be expected of so heterogeneous and disorganized a community. Some were permanent, as that of the merchants and shippers of Tyre,[3] that of the merchants and shippers dealing with Bithynia,[4] that of the makers of Herms,[5] and those of

---

[1] It might, of course, open accounts with the Italian bankers now, as earlier.

[2] *BCH.*, 1892, p. 154 (banker from Tarentum); *BCH.*, 1884, pp. 129 and 488; cf. *BCH.*, 1907, p. 438, No. 29 (from Naples); *BCH.*, 1887, p. 269, and *BCH.*, 1907, p. 456 ff., Nos. 54 and 55 (from Rome); *BCH.*, 1887, p. 267, and *BCH.*, 1910, p. 398 f., Nos. 44 and 45 (from Rome). In regard to the banker from Tarentum see the remarks of Roussel (*BCH.*, 1908, p. 408), who locates Demaratus, the *epimeletes* of Delos in the year in which the pertinent inscription was inscribed, not long after 166 B.C. The name of the artist proves this dating to be correct (Polianthes, see below, ix. 410, n. 1). The first-mentioned banker from Rome, Marius Gerillanus Marii f., received more than three statues at Delos. See also in regard to his family, *BCH.*, 1907, p. 464. The one mentioned second, Lucius Aufidius L.f., had a freedman in charge of his bank on Delos (*BCH.*, 1910, p. 398). The inscription from a monument erected in his honour by the dealers on the island mentions, as one of the constituent elements of Ἀθηναίων καὶ Ῥωμαίων καὶ τῶν ἄλλων ξένων (?), [οἱ ἐργαζόμε]νοι τῇ τραπέζ[ᾳ].

[3] See above, ix. 358; cf. *CIG.* ii. 2271; *BCH.*, 1879, 374.

[4] *BCH.*, 1880, p. 222.

[5] See Roussel, *BCH.*, 1910, p. 110 ff. If Roussel is right this gild was in the charge of an elected *epimeletes*. I see no reason for thinking that he was elected by the Athenian *demos* and not by the gild itself, however.

the wine and oil dealers;[1] others were chance and temporary.[2] They appear in our sight almost exclusively as the authors of dedications, but in spite of the practically entire absence of published resolutions we cannot doubt that at their meetings matters of national, professional, and other interest were considered and settled. They provided, in fact, all the various services and satisfactions which we have enumerated while dealing with the Attic associations.[3]

Trade was now of course the great magnet of Delos, not religion; but there as everywhere it is in regard to the ordinary daily activities of life that we are least informed. It is clear, however, that one quite important section of the Delians lived, not on land, but on the vessels with which the harbour was alive during the shipping season. The men who sailed to and fro between Delos and Bithynia, Syria, Egypt, Sicily, and Italy had, of course, no residences on the island, and needed only the inns and club-houses for their accommodation while in port. What their presence in the harbour meant no one who knows a modern waterfront of the frontier sort can doubt: it meant cookshops, brothels, quarrelling, and chicanery of every kind. Within the strait between Delos and Rheneia there was peace, but it must have been a sort of armed truce among the assortment of pirates, slave-dealers, traders, and adventurers which congregated there. A merchant with a cargo of spices or of Phoenician stuffs might reach the harbour in safety, thanks to the gods of his home, of his destination, and of the wind; or he might arrive in the hold of a lugger to be sold on the Delian slave mart. It was not well to be over-friendly with the ship berthed next on the dock, since it might be a pirate craft waiting to follow a rich galley out on the high seas. Every merchant vessel had

---

[1] *BCH.*, 1899, p. 75; cf. 1907, p. 465, n. 1; *BCH.*, 1908, p. 429, No. 40; *BCH.*, 1909, p. 491, No. 14.; *BCH.*, 1899, p. 73.

[2] *BCH.*, 1882, p. 349; 'Αθήν. iv. 457; *BCH.*, 1891, p. 265; *BCH.*, 1904, p. 138; *BCH.*, 1908, p. 430, No. 42—a society with the same kind of an official at its head as the merchants of Beyrout and of Tyre, but in honour of Hermes, and apparently in connexion with the cult of Aphrodite Hagne. Cf. *BCH.*, 1910, p. 401, No. 50.

[3] For titles conferred by a Delian club see *BCH.*, 1883, p. 470; 1907, p. 445 ff.

its crew of one or two hundred men, who were doubtless armed to the teeth when they were not slaves tied to the rowers' benches. It is likely that the traders sailed in company, and that the corsairs hunted in packs; so that the sea had its struggles and its mysteries in which the perils of the deep had no part, and a safe arrival at Delos was no slight occasion for a thank-offering to Poseidon, Isis, Zeus Urius, or Zeus Soter. Apollo, too, had to be remembered. This was followed by unloading and reloading by day and carousals by night. The goods might be simply transhipped, or sold on the dock, or stored in the warehouses of the commission merchants. The great staple was slaves—a commodity which did not need special buildings or contrivances for its handling, fetters, rooms, and food being sufficient; hence few traces of this business are now visible among the ruins of Delos. Yet the port was beyond doubt the centre of this horrible traffic which was depopulating Bithynia and flooding Sicily and Italy with lawless and desperate men. Food products were a second Delian staple; for apart from the Greek wines and oil, which as yet dominated the world's market, the grain of Asia, Egypt, and the Black Sea, the nuts and dried fruits of Cyprus and the entire Levant, fish and shell-fish of many varieties, and a hundred other articles of general or restricted use entered into the commerce which the island served. Moreover, a population of some tens of thousands, as well as the crews of many ocean-going ships, had to be provisioned almost entirely from imported food-stuffs. The probability is that imperial Rome was at no time more dependent upon the wind and waves for its supplies, and was never in greater danger of chronic famine, than was the multitude which now inhabited the almost barren island. The retailing of provisions on the market and waterfront of Delos must have been in itself a considerable business. The handling of art goods of various kinds, metal work and pottery, marble work and statuary, house furnishings of various kinds, added to the volume of Delian trade; while the reputation of the island in Rome and the resort to it of Syrians, Arabians, and

Alexandrians are ample evidence of the part it played in distributing spices, unguents, glass work, and woven stuffs of all materials and textures over both the East and West. It was with such wares as these, doubtless, that the rows of little shops in the agora and the *stationes* of the men from Beyrout and Tyre were stocked. The lubrication, as it were, of all this traffic was afforded by the Italian money-changers and money-lenders who had flocked to the island with such advantages and capital as to practically destroy competition. The money thus put in circulation, however, and the official currency, as well as the standard weights and measures, were Attic, so that the Athenian bank manager and market clerks had important functions to perform. The chief language was Greek and the chief costume was the tunic, but a little of everything might be heard and seen on Delos, and the second speech was undoubtedly Latin and the second dress the toga. Campania, in particular, furnished a large element of the Delian population—a fact to be called to mind, along with the similar dualism in language, race, and dress, and the similar absorption in local and foreign trade, when we observe that the Roman poet Lucilius in about 125 B.C. designated Puteoli, the first port of western Italy, a "lesser Delos."

There is some reason to believe that the Athenians resident on Delos tended to lose their national identity during the thirty years which finished the second century B.C. At any rate, they felt themselves to be living almost in a foreign country.[1] Probably they did not always take pains to register their sons in the Attic *deme* lists, for such a classification had no longer a purpose. There were, of course, rich men among them who were able to hold their own with the magistrates and traders from the capital, and who were as often rivals as friends of the foreign dealers;[2] but probably the majority of the ex-cleruchs found it hard enough to

---

[1] The frequency with which the *deme*-name yields to the *ethnicum* in Delos is evidence of this; cf. above, ix. 381, n. 2.

[2] Athen. v. 212 ff. quoted below, x. 442.

compete with the Italians, who, if not in themselves powerful,[1] had the prestige of powerful political and financial backing. The Athenians, moreover, seem to have lacked the capacity for union except as one element in the composite assembly,[2] while the Italians had their *conventus*, and the other foreigners their professional and religious associations. In business, particularly in the slave business, the Athenians had many equals, but in matters of education and of taste they were, however, masters still. The island had a theatre (it is preserved even to-day[3]) in which dramatic representations were given. The names scrawled on its ornaments and pillars are those of Athenians alone,[4] and probably the pleasure-seekers as well as the idlers were ordinarily of Greek and not of Italian extraction. The Romans had too much to do to waste time listening to plays which they could probably neither understand nor appreciate. Besides, they had their own amusements —the gladiatorial games. And what ideas of the fitness of things these Athenians had! An ex-governor-general of the island, a former priest of Apollo to boot, not only wrote satyric plays and lyrics, but, when his works gained first prize in a competitive exhibition, erected a

---

[1] The following is the tree of a Delian business family :

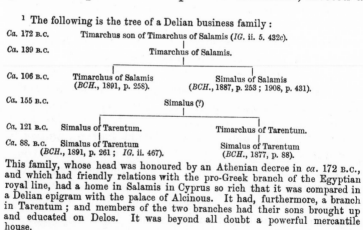

Ca. 172 B.C.	Timarchus son of Timarchus of Salamis (*IG.* ii. 5. 432c).	
Ca. 139 B.C.	Timarchus of Salamis.	
Ca. 106 B.C.	Timarchus of Salamis (*BCH.*, 1891, p. 258).	Simalus of Salamis (*BCH.*, 1887, p. 253 ; 1908, p. 431).
Ca. 155 B.C.	Simalus (?)	
Ca. 121 B.C.	Simalus of Tarentum.	Timarchus of Tarentum.
Ca. 88. B.C.	Simalus of Tarentum (*BCH.*, 1891, p. 261 ; *IG.* ii. 467).	Simalus of Tarentum (*BCH.*, 1877, p. 88).

This family, whose head was honoured by an Athenian decree in *ca.* 172 B.C., and which had friendly relations with the pro-Greek branch of the Egyptian royal line, had a home in Salamis in Cyprus so rich that it was compared in a Delian epigram with the palace of Alcinous. It had, furthermore, a branch in Tarentum ; and members of the two branches had their sons brought up and educated on Delos. It was beyond all doubt a powerful mercantile house.

[2] No *koinon* of the Athenians appears to take the place of the polity which was broken up in *ca.* 131 B.C.

[3] Doerpfeld und Reisch, *Das griech. Theatre*, 144 ff.

[4] *BCH.*, 1889, plates xii. and xiii. ; *BCH.*, 1905, p. 249.

monument to commemorate his victory.[1] To Greeks
music and dramatics were indispensable. They formed
one of the constituent parts of popular education, and,
doubtless, many a Roman too lost his indifference to the
stage through closer acquaintance with the theatre in
Delos. The island had a *gymnasium*,[2] located, as was
fitting for a place where young men exercised naked,
at some distance from the city. In it the ephebes made
their rendezvous, for Delos was a miniature Athens in
this respect also, that the systematic training of the
young men in manly sports, military duties, and civic
virtues was organized there as in the capital. The sons
of the wealthy men on the island had to be educated.
Hence several private *palaestrae* were instituted,[3] and
an ephebe corps was drawn up under public instructors.
In it Athenians predominated, but youths from Sidon,
Tyre, Laodicea, Damascus, Ascalon, Alexandria, Phaselis,
Alabanda, Sinope, Rome, Naples, Tarentum, and the
Aegean islands and cities were also enrolled. As was
natural, they tended to chum in ethnic groups, but the
intimacy of college life helped to cement friendships
between ephebes of different languages and nationalities,
and in time to create an *esprit de corps* among the
wealthy people on the island.[4]

The educational institutions of Delos were thus
Athenian in type and spirit. The same was true
of its art. The most eminent sculptors were almost

---

[1] *BCH.*, 1889, p. 372. His statue was erected in the Dionysiac theatre in
Athens among those of obscure dramatists which Pausanias (i. 21. 1) saw ;
cf. Wilhelm, *Urk. dram. Aufführ.*, 135 f.   [2] *BCH.*, 1891, p. 238 ff.

[3] *BCH.*, 1891, pp. 264, 257 ; *BCH.*, 1908, p. 415, No. 3.

[4] *BCH.*, 1908, p. 414, No. 1 (*ca.* 140 B.C.), a group of chums, probably
all Athenians.

BCH., 1908, p. 414, No. 2 (123/2 B.C.), ditto, all foreigners.

BCH., 1891, p. 252 (121/0 B.C.), ditto, all Athenians.

BCH., 1892, p. 159 (118/7 B.C.), ditto, all Syrians.

BCH., 1905, p. 229 (108/7 B.C.), ditto, a mixed lot.

BCH., 1891, p. 261 (102/1 B.C.), ditto, a mixed lot.

BCH., 1908, p. 415, No. 3 (95/4 B.C. ? or 118/7 B.C. ?) ; cf. *BCH.*, 1908,
p. 374, ditto, a mixed lot; *BCH.*, 1907, p. 436, No. 27. Re-edited with an addition
in *BCH.*, 1910, p. 418, No. 82, and assigned to the end of the second century
B.C. (It does not, however, belong to the archonship of Sosicrates 111/0 B.C.,
Kirchner, *Berl. phil. Woch.*, 1908, p. 883. It probably belongs to Echecrates,
101/0 B.C.). This, too, is a group of chums—a mixed lot. The groups were
ordinarily formed in the *palaestrae* out of which the young men passed into
the ephebe corps ; cf. *BCH.*, 1908, p. 415, No. 3.

exclusively Athenians by birth and citizenship,[1] and their patrons prevailingly Greeks. There was, doubtless, much crude work done at this time ; many statues erected whose heavy draperies, unfinished surfaces, and false proportions show their makers to have been careless artists, and apparently for the most part mere copyists;[2] many mosaics hastily pieced together, and many ugly buildings weakly constructed. But that is the prominent mark of hasty performance everywhere, and Delos was built in a hurry. We can judge of the prevailing taste only by observing the qualities of the best work, the evidences of amateur accomplishments, and the features of hack work there as compared with those of hack work elsewhere. But, unfortunately, of the best work nothing is extant unless it be the statue of Ofellius from the agora of the Romans, or the *Venus Defending Herself with her Sandal against Pan*, from the agora of the *Poseidoniastae*, in which case the best is not very good. But this latter group was ordered by a half Greek from Beyrout, and the statue is anonymous ; while the former, though signed by Dionysius and Timarchides of Athens,

---

[1] The only non-Athenian sculptors active to our knowledge between 166 and 103 B.C. were Polianthes, who had a studio on Delos before the Athenians came (Loewy, *Inschr. griech. Bildhauer*, Nos. 212-217) ; Boethus and Theodosius (*ca.* 120 B.C. ; cf. Robert, P.-W. iii. 606. These may be Athenians, though the probabilities are otherwise) ; Menophilus (*BCH.*, 1908, p. 433, No. 50 ; cf. *ibid.* 327, No. 192. His nativity is unknown) ; and Ammonius and Perigenes, the sons of Zopyrus, possibly of Miletus (*BCH.*, 1908, p. 419, Nos. 12 and 13, 124/3 B.C. ; cf. *BCH.*, 1884, p. 175, No. 10 ; Loewy, *op. cit.*, No. 257). The Athenians are the following : Apollodorus, architect of the temple of Serapis in 135/4 B.C. (*BCH.*, 1892, p. 481) ; Dionysius, son of Timarchides, and his nephew Timarchides, son of Polycles, of Thoricus (*BCH.*, 1881, plate xii., *ca.* 156 B.C., according to Kirchner, *PA.* 4181, 13620, 11992 ; but see above, ix. 356, n. 1.) ; Hephaestion, son of Myron (124/3–116/5 B.C., Kirchner, *PA.* 6553) ; Myron and Graphicus (*ca.* 140 B.C., *BCH.*, 1902, p. 537. This Myron may be the father of Hephaestion) ; Melanus (122/1 B.C. *BCH.*, 1883, p. 467) ; Adamas, Dionysodorus, and Moschion, sons of Adamas (111/0 B.C. *CIG.* ii. 2298) ; Eutychides, son of Hephaestion (117/6 B.C.–95/4 B.C.). Cf. *Klio*, 1907, p. 232, n. 2, where a correction has to be made because of the transfer of the archons Menoetes and Sarapion from 105/3 to 117/5 B.C. ; also *BCH.*, 1908, p. 409, and 1909, p. 490 (100/99 B.C.). Eutychides is rated an Athenian by Loewy, *op. cit.*, p. 180 ff., and by Robert, P.-W. vi. 1533, Nos. 3 and 4. He was the son of Hephaestion, according to an unpublished inscription (*BCH.*, 1908, p. 404, n. 7) ; Praxias (after 166 B.C., Homolle, *Mon. Grecs*, 1879, viii. 53) ; Demostratus, son of Demostratus (102/1 B.C., *BCH.*, 1880, p. 219 ; 1881, p. 463, No. 3) ; Zoilus, son of Demostratus (98/7 B.C., *BCH.*, 1905, p. 222).

[2] See the discriminating article by Mayence and Leroux in *BCH.*, 1907, 390 ff., and the plates which accompany it.

was probably made to suit conventional Roman taste.[1]
The *Delian Warrior*—a fine marble which has much
in common in pose with the famous *Dying Gaul*, and
in style with the art of Pergamum at its best—would
lend distinction to the work done on the island, if its
attribution to Agasias son of Menophilus were not
questionable, and its time of composition possibly the
third century B.C.[2] This sculptor, the contemporary,
kinsman, and namesake of the author of the wonderful
Borghese Warrior, came to the front in Delos at the
opening of the first century B.C., but nothing of his
work, nor of that of his predecessors, Hephaestion and
Eutychides, or of his contemporaries, Lysippus and
Menodorus,—to mention only the most popular among
them,—has been preserved to us. Still, enough of the
Delian sculpture of the last half of the second century
B.C. remains for us to note its general characteristics.
It is the product of men who are masters in the technique
of working stone,[3] and whose ideal is to reproduce the
classic as truly as possible; who are eclectics, but who
choose sparingly, if at all, from the styles and ideas of
the realistic school of the third century B.C. :[4] men, in
fact, who are working for patrons to whom the antique
is alone admirable, and who, moreover, lack the knowledge, taste, and discrimination necessary to impose
exacting demands upon those whom they employ.
They knew approximately what they wanted and they
wanted it quickly. Their patronage gave no stimulus
to sculptors to bring into play their creative faculties;
to labour indefatigably in the way that alone leads to
the highest and best. In Delos we, accordingly, see in
miniature what was going on in the world at large in

---

[1] *BCH.*, 1881, plate xii. ; *BCH.*, 1906, plates xiii.-xvi. Dionysius, if he
is the old man of this name (see above, viii. 343), had lived in Rome.

[2] *BCH.*, 1889, p. 113 ff., plates i. and ii. Wolters (*Ath. Mitt.*, 1890,
p. 188 ff.) tries to show that the *Delian Warrior* is not the work of Agasias,
the son of Menophilus of Ephesus, but possibly of the Athenian Niceratus.
Leroux, however, seems to have shown (*BCH.*, 1910, p. 478 ff.) that it has
nothing to do with either Agasias or Niceratus.

[3] The technical power of some of the Delian artists is emphasized by
Mayence and Leroux in the article cited above (ix. 410, n. 2), p. 416. See also
the bronze relief published and commented on by Holleaux in *Acad. inscr.*
C.R., 1909, p. 414 f. : "l'exécution," he says, "qui vaut mieux que le style,
en est exacte et soignée."   [4] See above, viii. 342 f.

the second century B.C.—the decline of culture simply through its diffusion among less cultivated peoples.[1]

When we study the mural paintings and the mosaics the same general observation has to be made. The style of the decorative art used on the walls of the houses on Theatre Street is the same as that employed in all Hellenistic edifices. It is still the work of men of high technical power. The mural decorations of Delos, says M. Chamonard,[2] the French *savant* who has made a special study of the subject, surpass those of Pompeii a century and a half later in simplicity of arrangement, harmony of the proportions of the subordinate elements, and restraint in the use and juxtaposition of colours. The same writer[3] notes the excellence of the Delian mosaics in point of colour effect and general technical execution, and their easy superiority over similar work in the later Italian town. The workmen do not shrink from the most ambitious designs—a Dionysus poised on the back of a tiger, Cupids mounted on dolphins which swim merrily from the corners of the *impluvium* to the centre, a Panathenaic vase with all its elaborate detail.[4] Still the drawing is at times faulty and the general proportions bad:[5] hasty performance and too easy satisfaction with the results; disinclination to invent and consequent uniformity of general effect,—these are the ominous vices of the professional artists of Delos.

Those who should have done the best work succumbed most quickly to the temptation of lower standards; for to them alone the temptation came. To amateurs there remained the need to satisfy their own taste. The amateurs on Delos who seem to have had artistic taste to satisfy were the Athenians;[6] and

[1] Beloch, *Hist. Zeitschr.*, 1900 (84), p. 1 ff. ; de Sanctis, *Per la scienza dell' antichità*, 244 ff.   [2] *BCH.*, 1906, p. 524 ; Bulard, *loc. cit.*, 91 ff.

[3] *BCH.*, 1906, p. 531 ff. ; cf. 540.   A work on the Delian mosaics promised by M. Bulard has now appeared as vol. xiv. of the *Fondation Eugène Piot*.

[4] *BCH.*, 1906, pp. 538, 540.   [5] *Ibid.*

[6] *BCH.*, 1889, plates xii. and xiii. ; *BCH.*, 1906, p. 550 ff.   The names accompanying the *graffiti* are those of Athenians, *e.g.* Staseas, Medeius, and Theodotus.   The last two appear coupled in both plate xii. of *BCH.*, 1889, and in *BCH.*, 1905, p. 249, and above their names in the latter case is written : ἀεὶ φίλοι.

in the Delian *graffiti* we have a striking monument of their artistic powers. The careless work of idle men and boys, they reveal, not the skill of individual draftsmen, but the artistic gifts of the people in general; yet in surety of touch, correctness of design, and spiritual charm they show astonishing merit, and surpass the *graffiti* of Pompeii and everything similar not found on Greek soil. "They possess the qualities," says M. Sal. Reinach, "which constitute the charm of so many of the vase paintings—products of obscure artists working in haste, but knowing how to be expeditious without being vulgar. Humble efforts, they yet bear the marks of a civilization for which we vainly seek an equal elsewhere."[1]

The forms of the dwelling-houses, the interior furnishings and decorations, and the conveniences of sanitation found in Delos are found in Pompeii a century and a half later;[2] and, indeed, the spread of Greek artistic and literary forms is no more marked a feature of Hellenistic development than is the spread of the Greek *oeconomy*, to use that word in an etymological sense. There can be no doubt that Delos was one of the most active centres of distribution for all the Hellenistic inventions which made for the comfort and refinement of domestic life in later antiquity; for the island was the scene of a long, though noiseless, conflict between Italian and Greek ideas on these matters. It had its take as well as its give, however; and if the traveller who spends a day among the ruins of Delos looks attentively, he will perceive writ small upon the stones of the island the story of the contact of two cultures — the subsidence of rough Italians in the embrace of a soft, but refining, Greek environment;[3] the swift onset of Roman political ideas and Roman religious[4] and commercial usages; and, afterwards, the

---

[1] *BCH.*, 1889, 376 f.

[2] Fr. von Duhn, *Pompeii, eine hellenistische Stadt in Italien*, ch. v.

[3] For the *Coae vestes*, or silken *himatia*, worn by the rich Delian ladies, see the portrait statue of Cleopatra, wife of Dioscurídes of Myrrhinutta, *BCH.*, 1907, p. 415, Fig. 9 and the commentary.

[4] Bulard (*op. cit.*, 205, cf. 88) says in summing up his work: "Il y a ainsi une opposition très nette, dans les habitations privées de Délos, entre

compromise upon a lower standard of art and morals. There are few battlefields in the ancient world like Delos. There Greek fought Roman, and, absorbed in the struggle, neither paid heed to the reaching out among them of the insidious ideals of the East. We may doubt whether Zeus and Athena, as they looked down from their vantage-point on the summit of Mt. Cythnus, took much pleasure in this new war of the Greeks and the Trojans. Win or lose, their chosen people must suffer in treasure and character, while the pawns, the victims of the fierce slave-trade, were often the bodies and souls of Greek men and women. But Serapis, Isis, and Atargatis, peering forth from their lowlier post on the Delian mount, could find much to please them in the spectacle; and the black-robed communicants and the fanatical priests took heart for wider efforts. Meanwhile, the Virgin on the Acropolis was the sad witness of another struggle—the fratricidal war of Athenian against Athenian; and, after a fight to the death, what she had never seen before—the wild rush by night through the streets, and, visible in the glare of the burning Odeum, the rising and falling of swords, and the new heaps of Athenian dead.

---

les peintures liturgiques, en rapports étroits et intimes avec les cultes domestiques italiens, et les mosaïques ou les revêtements décoratifs, d'un charactère exclusivement hellénique ou hellénistique."

CHAPTER X

BETWEEN ROME AND PONTUS

Post me erat Aegina, ante me Megara, dextra Piraeus, sinistra Corinthus ; quae oppida quodam tempore florentissima fuerunt, nunc prostrata et diruta ante oculos iacent.

Sulpicius, in Cic., *Epist. ad famil.* iv. 5.

Adsunt Athenienses, unde humanitas, doctrina, religio, fruges, iura, leges ortae atque in omnes terras distributae putantur ; de quorum urbis possessione propter pulchritudinem etiam inter deos certamen fuisse proditum est ; quae vetustate ea est ut ipsa ex sese suos cives genuisse dicatur et eorum eadem terra parens, altrix, patria dicatur, auctoritate autem tanta est ut iam fractum prope ac debilitatum Graeciae nomen huius urbis laude nitatur.

CICERO, *Pro Flacco*, 26. 62.

THE political history of Athens during the twenty-five years which followed the dissolution of its colony on Delos is almost a total blank. No incidents known to us occurred to connect the city or its dominions in any way with the affairs of the world in general. Nor do the individual internal happenings, of which we have knowledge, deserve much consideration. The sending of a *Pythais* to Delphi in 128/7 B.C.,[1] and of another twenty-two years later, evoked keen contemporary interest among the citizens, but for us they have no importance. Nor do we care that the ephebes, whose names, officers, and services now appear in our records in exasperating completeness,[2] preserved order at public meetings, escorted Romans into the city, learned to use their armour, bows, spears and catapults, to launch and dock the warships, and to sit patiently through the lectures of the

---

[1] Above, ix. 372 ff.
[2] *BCH.*, 1906, p. 237 (128/7 B.C.) ; *IG.* ii. **471 (123/2 B.C.)** ; **469 (119/8 B.C.)** ; 465 (117/6 B.C.) ; 470 (107/6 B.C.).

philosophers.[1] It does not interest us here that they gave several exhibitions of their military skill, marched occasionally to the frontier in order to see the forts and learn the roads, and held two boat races; that they were present at innumerable festivals and sacrifices and often sacrificed on their own account; for all this or something closely similar they had been doing annually for two hundred years. Occasionally, but only occasionally, something new happened. Thus at one time the state requested them to make an annual dedication to the Mother of the Gods, and at another to donate yearly some books to a public library; on one occasion a rector attracted attention by refusing to accept the gift of a gold crown and a statue from his charges, and on another a *cosmetes* of a military turn of mind won praise by having them fit up and learn to use an old and obsolete machine for hurling missiles. But generally only the routine things were done; so that the decrees passed by the Senate and people in honour of the ephebes and their officers were in large part couched in identical language year after year.

The death of Panaetius (before 110/9 B.C.), and of Cleitomachus (110/9 B.C.),[2] probably impresses us more than it did their contemporaries; for they were both far along in years at the time, and it was not then obvious that Athens was not again to have a thinker of ecumenical importance. In the place of the Academician came his pupil Philon of Larisa, who, after twenty-two years of service, fled from Athens to Rome and became there the teacher of Cicero.[3] Panaetius was succeeded in turn by Mnesarchus, Dardanus, and Apollodorus,[4] all of whom were Athenians—the first natives, in fact, to

---

[1] See above, viii. 338. In 123/2 B.C. (*IG.* ii. 471. 19) the lectures of the Stoic Zenodotus, a pupil of Diogenes the Babylonian (Diog. Laert. vii. 29), are especially mentioned. They were given in the Ptolemaeum and the Lyceum. From Apollodorus's *Chronicle* (Jacoby, 391) we learn that Charmadas also lectured in the Ptolemaeum, as did Antiochus of Ascalon (Cic. *De fin.* v. 1). It was, accordingly, shared by Stoics and Academicians (see above, viii. 339). Since Panaetius was head of the Stoa in 123/2 B.C., Zenodotus was either his rival, or a special lecturer designated by the school to instruct the ephebes.
[2] Cic. *De orat.* i. 11, 45; cf. *BCH.*, 1893, p. 149 f.; cf. *Cornell Studies*, x. 85.
[3] Below, x. 444. For his influence on Cicero see von Arnim, *Dio von Prusa*, 97, 104 ff. Wilamowitz, *Hermes*, 1900, p. 18 f.
[4] Zeller, *Phil. d. Griechen*, iii. 1⁴, 589, n. 3.

head the Stoa—and all of whom were apparently feeble persons. To us they are mere names. It was in Rhodes that the fresh life of the Stoic ideas was now to be found; for there taught Poseidonius of Apamea, the most gifted pupil of Panaetius. With this generation the scientific interest in philosophy ceased to be dominant and the educational to take its place. To impress the Romans with the value of learning and at the same time to lead them to take a more serious view of their public responsibilities was henceforth the great problem of the schools. Practical men of affairs were in the ascendant in the world then as now; and what they wanted was not a well-thought-out system of philosophy, but a satisfactory rule of life. What concern had they with the historic differences of the schools? The gist of the whole matter was sufficient, and this all the philosophers now strove to provide for them. For public activity in Rome, however, power to use general ideas readily in controversy was even more important than sound views on the chief social and ethical problems. But instruction in this art had belonged since the time of Plato and Isocrates to the province of the teachers of rhetoric, and for it the correct philosophic attitude was in general one of contempt. Now the subject was taken up by the Academy, and Philon of Larisa, as Cicero tells us, began the practice of handling in alternation the precepts of the rhetoricians and the philosophers.[1] By this eclecticism and apostasy he may have saved his science from utter neglect and enabled it to continue to be a force in the world. It was of course not his fault that the Romans proved such inapt pupils.

A Roman who came to Athens, if he belonged to the governing circles, was entitled to a special reception;[2] and, since we learn by mere chance that Crassus visited it in 110/09 and M. Antonius in 103/2 B.C.,[3] we may be sure that the city was often obliged to extend its hospitality to men of their class. Indeed, the ephebes

---

[1] *Tusc. disp.* ii. 9. The significance of Philon's innovation has been pointed out by von Arnim, *loc. cit.*

[2] The friends and allies whom the ephebes escort are always Romans.

[3] See below, x. 428, n. 2.

had to turn out to act as their escort frequently during every year. There were accordingly some disadvantages in having not one monarch as suzerain, but a whole aristocracy; and in possessing a famous and attractive city, not an obscure village; while, if there were any benefits, they came to the philosophers of the Stoa and the Academy, and the men of the highest social station with whom the Romans fraternized. To the rest of the population the visits of the Romans[1] were probably only unpleasant reminders of a foreign yoke.

This is a surmise for the confirmation of which we have to look to the sequel.[2] That Athens was generally prosperous in this generation is capable of proof: the rapid increase in the circulation of its money tells an unmistakable story;[3] also the prevalence of large families.[4] The making of repairs on public buildings and equipment was continued zealously[5]—a mark alike of well-being and of civic pride. This all went to promote a feeling of renewed strength and to revive old ambitions. In the year 122/1 B.C. the rector took the ephebes under his charge on an excursion to the shrine of Zeus Amphiarius in the territory of Oropus,[6] and on the spot told those whom he was training for patriotic citizenship the story of Athens's ancient lordship over the place. The incident is significant: it suggested a programme to youths whose pulse-beats had just been quickened by marching over the old road to Marathon and rowing down the famous strait to Salamis, in order on the spot to consecrate themselves to the service in which their heroic ancestors had fallen. The Athenians were at this time indulging in dangerous dreams.

The whole life of Athens in this generation was being stirred profoundly by momentous movements of a social and economic character, which speedily affected ideas

---

[1] Magistrates were, perhaps, already forbidden to bring their full complement of *fasces* and lictors into a free city (Tac. *Annales*, ii. 53. 3), though this restriction may have been of Augustan origin. Despite it, Piso made what Tacitus (*ibid.* ii. 55. 1) calls a *turbidus incessus* into Athens in 18 A.D.

[2] See below, x. 427, 444 ff. [3] Sundwall, *Untersuch.* 107, n. 1.

[4] See above, ix. 374. [5] The ephebe inscriptions *passim*.

[6] *IG*. ii. 471. 27, 70.

and eventually overturned institutions.   Of these the
most striking was the development of a class which
claimed privileges in public and private life on the
score of riches, birth, and special fitness for governing.
This development was probably promoted by several
factors : the accumulation of wealth in the hands of men
of business rather than of culture and traditions ; the
dissatisfaction of these *nouveaux riches* with the popular
forms conserved by the tory democracy ; the influence
upon sentiment and conduct of the timocratic example
of Rome, and the chafing of men habituated to
irresponsible power on Delos at the petty restraints
imposed upon the magistrates by Athenian custom.[1]
The political initiative in Athens was now largely in
the possession of the Areopagus, which had experienced
of late a notable increase in prestige and public importance.   This had come about, not through any
marked extension of its legal powers, but through the
reappearance of the conditions upon which its ascendancy in Greek mediaeval times had been based ultimately—the experience, wealth, and influence of its
members.   The corporation had never lacked a certain
dignity.   Thus, as we have seen, Demetrius of Phalerum
had thought it worthy of exercising once more the
vague censorial powers taken from it by Ephialtes and
Pericles.[2]   It was the only organ which ordinarily
weathered a severe constitutional storm ; for membership in it was for life, in the Senate and magistracies for
a year, or for even a shorter term at the pleasure of the
sovereign *demos*.   Hence it could congregate quickly in
the midst or at the end of a governmental crisis which
had put out of action or out of existence the ordinary
official leaders.   In this way, perhaps, we may explain
the rôle it played in finance during the Four Years' War,
and in raising the moneys needed in 230/29 B.C.[3]   Such
an intervention as this was not, however, without
precedent ; for throughout the fourth century B.C. the

---

[1] These conclusions are rather inferential than positively demonstrable.
[2] See above, ii. 46.
[3] See above, iii. 114, v. 207, n. 1.   Note also the rôle played by it in investi-
gating the disposition of the Harpalus money.

practice had existed for it, as for the Senate in Rome—
at the request of the popular assembly, however—to
serve as a general emergency commission and to conduct
investigations into unusual criminal or treasonable
offences ;[1] and, subsequently, on more than one occasion
during the third century B.C. it was requested to name
part of various extraordinary committees.[2] The commanding position which this distinction implies was due,
we believe, in part to its permanency, but only in part.
It arose from the personnel of the Areopagus also.
Ex-archons became Areopagites, and the lot designated
the archons. When people of all stations and attainments had sought the archonships, the average ability
of the Areopagites was low ; but when, as in the fourth
century B.C. to a certain degree,[3] and increasingly and
prevailingly in the third and second,[4] those who presented themselves for the allotment were men of some
distinction, the Areopagus came to present, if not the
ablest, at least the most influential aggregate of persons
among the Athenians ; and for several generations prior
to 130 B.C. it had been filled by men in sympathy with
the tory democracy. Being a body of about two
hundred and twenty-five members, it could act effectively only when divided into committees, and accordingly it consisted of sections, apparently twelve in
number, from which individuals were designated for
specific duties, such as the supervision of the mint—and
doubtless also the other magistrates.[5] Such a body was
constitutionally fitted to oppose new ideas, since the
advocates of change had to trust to chance to bring
their partisans into its midst. This condition made it
doubly necessary for aristocratic reformers to abolish
election by lot, which in the first place was objectionable to them as one of the impediments to the exercise
of political influence in elections and legislation by men
of wealth, and as the chief obstacle to the use of skilled

---

[1] Philippi, *Der Areopag und die Epheten*, 170 ff.
[2] *IG.* ii. 403. 836 B, a 9, 839.   [3] Sundwall, *Klio*, Beiheft i. 4, 68 ff.
[4] For the reason of the change see above, iii. 100.
[5] Cic. *Pro Balbo*, xii. 30 ; cf. *Klio*, 1909, p. 329, n. 8 ; *Class. Phil.*, 1908, p.
398 ; Sundwall, *Untersuch.* 104 ff.

and experienced men in the administrative service. But more than this was necessary. The magistrates must have greater power and freedom. Hence plans were made for the removal of the prohibition against repetition in the tenure of civil offices, and for the enlargement of the initiative and independence of the magistrates. Hitherto a man could hold an ordinary civil office only once, and a senatorship only twice in his lifetime. This put a premium upon inexperience, and since there were three hundred senatorships to be filled annually from a total of about twice that number of qualified citizens, it made the Senate necessarily a simple mirror of popular sentiment.[1] To enable a magistrate or a senator to secure frequent re-election to the same position must inevitably have the effect of increasing his influence, since knowledge obtained by experience could not be ignored. The same end would be promoted much more effectively, moreover, by abrogating the ordeal to which the magistrates were subject at the expiry of their term, namely, of giving an account of their transactions first to a series of specially appointed auditors—if these still existed— and finally to a panel of common jurors. The abolition of this accounting, however, was equivalent to the emasculating of the popular courts of justice, and the destruction of the institution by which the Athenian people had been able to give their offices to their rich and respectable citizens, and yet retain large control of the administration. To whom the magistrates were to be made responsible is not quite certain, but it seems probable that it was to the Senate of the six hundred.

At the head of this whole movement were Medeius of the Piraeus, Sarapion of Melite, Theodotus of Sunium,[2] Diodorus of Halae, Calliphon, and a number of kindred spirits, all ardent pro-Romans and closely identified with Delian affairs. It was their connection with Delos

---

[1] The maintenance of classic usage in these particulars throughout the third and second centuries B.C. is made probable both by the absence of any instances which prove the contrary, and by the practice after 88/6 B.C. Cf. *Klio*, 1909, p. 328 f.

[2] Coupled twice with Medeius in the Delian *graffiti*. See above, ix. 412, n. 6. For the entire group see *Klio*, 1904, p. 10 ff.

probably which caused them to be affected by the second of the two great movements which swept through Athens at this time. This had as its outcome to break down the uncompromising conservatism in social and religious matters of the upper classes in Athens; to bring Athens out of an eddy into the main currents of Hellenistic life. That the Athenians of the early third century B.C. had refused to alter the general scheme of their society to bring it into accord with the larger place then occupied in their lives and thoughts by their wives and daughters, or to recognize the emancipation of women which went on apace in the new Hellenistic world, has been explained at an earlier place in this book.[1] Conclusive evidence for a fundamental change in this respect is not adducible for the capital in the second century B.C., but when a lady in Delos could put a life-size statue of herself in the court of her new house [2]—not an idealized funerary or religious monument, but a portrait which disclosed to the passers-by her physical and spiritual individuality in a manner quite out of keeping with the old notions of what was fitting—we may surmise that on the island Athenian women now appeared in public with much new liberty. In Athens too, as in Alexandria at the time of Ptolemy Philadelphus, individual women of good standing were made the themes of courtly epigrams.[3] Public decrees, moreover, were published in which were set forth the names and praises of the maidens who spun the wool for the *peplos* of Athena.[4] Girls went on religious pilgrimages which required association with hundreds of young men and boys for over a week at a stretch.[5] This enlargement of liberties was, doubtless, promoted by the increase of religious rites which brought the sexes together; and, in particular, by the spread of the Oriental cults which divorced religion from citizenship and authorized congregations open to men and women alike. As already observed,

---

[1] See above, ii. 85.

[2] *BCH.*, 1908, p. 432, No. 46; cf. 1907, p. 414 ff. A portrait statue of a lady in Athens in the second century B.C. is described in the accompanying epigram as ζωῆς πιστότατον φύλακα (*IG.* ii. 1372).   [3] See above, vii. 287.

[4] *IG.* ii. 5. 477, 477d.   [5] *Klio*, 1909, p. 309.

the best Athenians of the third century B.C. had assumed
an attitude of chill conservatism towards the groups,
mainly of foreigners, which fostered these worships in
Attica.[1] Now their aversion to entering the foreign
clubs was overcome, and they came with ever-increasing frequency into intimate relations with aliens
in worshipping alien deities.[2] Moreover, in order to
enable intercourse between Athenians and outsiders, a
new type of private association, in which both classes
could mingle freely and without misconstruction,
appeared and multiplied rapidly in the city, while the
fact that civic privileges were now being granted to
foreigners with a liberality which violated all earlier
precedents[3] tended to obscure the old lines of social
cleavage. The point to which this development advanced
is indicated by the recognition now accorded to inter-
marriage between citizens and aliens of both sexes.[4]
Naturalization alone qualified foreigners for admission
to the *orgeones*, but it did as much for the foreign
deities; and it was not at Delos alone that Atargatis
was recognized as an Athenian goddess, but in Athens
also she became as Aphrodite Hagne the patron saint of
one of these aristocratic associations.[5]

At the same time changes were made in a matter so
markedly conservative as national nomenclature; and,
abandoning the traditional practice of giving their

---

[1] See above, v. 219.

[2] *Ath. Mitt.*, 1896, p. 438, where on a *stele* set up in *ca*. 135 B.C. by the
archeranistes Irenaeus of Antioch are enumerated in col. i. the names of 27
men, of whom one is an Athenian; in col. ii. the names of 29 women, all
foreign; and in col. iii. the names of 30 men and 5 women, 5 of the former
being citizens. The catalogue is broken at the bottom. The foreigners are
probably slaves—many apparently being from the Orient. The citizens, on the
other hand, were among the most distinguished in Athens (cf. Wilhelm, *loc.
cit.*). *IG.* ii. 475, where the treasurer of the shippers and merchants forming
the gild of Zeus Xenius in the Piraeus, whose need of a *proxenus* (*patronus* ?)
discloses their prevailing nationality in other countries, is an Athenian. *IG.*
ii. 5. 626b, 102/1 B.C., where only 17 out of 52 *Sabaziastae* are foreigners.
Since none of the members were from the Piraeus, where the club-house was
located, the association was probably of recent origin, and what we possess is
practically the list of charter members. See above, v. 222, n. 1.

[3] *Class. Phil.*, 1910, p. 228 f.; above, viii. 315.

[4] See *IG.* ii. 3, 2786, 2788, 2894, 2916, 2962, 3127, etc.; Robinson, *Amer.
Journ. Phil.* 1910, p. 377 ff., Nos. 13, 44, 58, 60; Brueckner, *op. cit.* 47, n. 2.

[5] *IG.* ii. 627 (95/4 B.C.). Since Aphrodite Hagne was not recognized in
Delos till *ca*. 120 B.C., this association was doubtless of recent origin. She
could hardly have been recognized by Athenians on Delos and not at Athens.

children family names, many citizens now used new
formations, of which the name of Isis or Serapis[1] or some
other foreign deity was one component—a clear sign
both of religious interest or conviction and of social dis-
integration.   This weakening of old traditions is also
betrayed to us by the custom frequently adopted in this
age of conferring upon children the names of Romans
or of famous Hellenistic kings and generals.   An Alexander, Attalus, Seleucus, Pyrrhus now appears in many
families which were high in Athenian society, and a
Byttacus, Ptolemy, Parmenion, Ariarathes, Archelaus,
Cleopatra, and the like were by no means of uncommon
occurrence.[3]   Athens in this way came soon to have the
appearance of being a *conluvies nationum*, without being
such in fact.

The honorary titles current generally in the Hellenistic world also found acceptance among the Athenians
of the out-going second century B.C.   The innovation
was made in Delos first.   There usages had long been
cosmopolitan, and on coming to the island in 166 B.C.
the Athenians had found everywhere about them *ex-
votos* and statues inscribed with the names and full
titles of Egyptian and Asiatic dignitaries.[4]   The colonists
had been unable to change the practice,[5] even if they
had wanted to; and in the metropolis titles were soon
given with care and discrimination.[6]   To obtain one it
was necessary to enter into the service of a monarch;
for they were apparently not bestowed upon foreigners
simply as badges of honour.   But the absence of any
common citizenship in the Hellenistic kingdoms brought
with it the condition that a man remained an Athenian,
if that was the place of his birth, however high he might
be in the service of Ptolemy or Seleucus, unless he had
been given citizenship in Alexandria or Antioch or some
other Egyptian or Asiatic *polis*.   Consequently men
soon appear in our records who are still Athenians

---

[1] Rusch, *op. cit.* 16.
[2] *BCH.*, 1908, p. 349, Nos. 386 and 387 ; 351, No. 407.
[3] *Klio*, 1908, p. 354 ; cf. *BCH.*, 1908, p. 345, No. 352 and elsewhere.
[4] Cf. Ditt. *OGIS.* 104, 247.
[5] *Ibid.* 249, 250, 251, 255, 256, *et passim* ; *BCH.*, 1907, p. 445.
[6] Ditt. *OGIS.* 352, 354 ff.

though loaded down with titles obtained in Egypt, Syria, Pontus, or elsewhere.[1] In Athens such nobility came to possess much social value in the period with which we are now dealing.[2]

The contamination of social and religious life proceeds so slowly and works so insidiously upon ideals that its effects are often achieved before men become conscious of its existence. It appeared in Athens as the inevitable consequence of the intimacy with Delos and of the business which Delos brought to Athens; and we may doubt whether the tory democracy did more than offer a passive resistance to its progress. The leaders of this party were probably infected with some of the virus. Still when a clear consciousness of its working was reached, and the issue was raised for the preservation of the old ways and the old culture, or the adoption of the modern ideals, we may be sure that the traditional here, like the traditional in politics, did not lack advocates among the aristocratic Athenian families, and that Medeius, Sarapion, Theodotus, Diodorus, Calliphron, and their associates were the champions of Hellenism in Athens as they were of a new up-to-date polity. None the less, Medeius, the Critias of the revolution, should revolution be the issue, belonged to an ancient and distinguished family. Its founder was in a sense Lycurgus, the orator. But the spirit of this fanatic had departed long since from the Eteobutadae, and the clan had not disdained to give the hand of one of its maidens to Diogenes, the captain of *condottieri*, who subsequently liberated Athens from the Macedonians. A like honour had fallen in the next generation upon Pausimachus, son of Philostratus of Pergamum, who, on marrying the daughter of Diogenes, entered into the service of Athens and became five times general under the tory democracy,[3] while the father of Medeius and Medeius himself had not lacked public recognition.[4] It was a family which owed much to the Athenian *demos*, but had acquired

---

[1] Ditt. *OGIS.* 173 ; *BCH.*, 1908, p. 430 ff., Nos. 43, 44, 45, 45a.
[2] See below, x. 441.
[3] *IG.* ii. 3. 1386 ; cf. Wilhelm, *Beiträge*, 81.
[4] Kirchner, *PA.* 10,096 ff.

the habit of looking abroad for new strength; so that, given the need, Medeius the younger was not an unnatural person to plan revolution. The personal moment in determining his action and that of his colleagues we shall never know. It was important, doubtless, then, as always. And the very name of Sarapion signified that he was one of a family to which the ancient traditions of Athens meant little or nothing;[1] while Theodotus of Sunium, the bosom friend of Medeius, was the son of a man who had not disdained to belong to a club of aliens, native mainly in the East and organized under a president from Antioch.[2] He is himself characterized, moreover, by the tenure of the priesthood of Aphrodite Hagne on Delos, and the reasons he gave in Athens for honouring John Hyrcanus, high-priest and ethnarch of the Jews, as an enterprising man of affairs, especially interested in establishing favourable conditions for Athenians engaged in public and private business in the Levant.[3] Diodorus of Halae, moreover, had been a capable superintendent of the Piraeus, and as such had made himself so popular among the foreign merchants and shippers there that an association of them chose him as their *proxenus* (*patronus*?), and applied to the Athenian senate for permission to erect his statue in his office.[4] These men were beyond doubt the equivalent in Athens of the *equites* in Rome, whose agents and partisans now dominated in Delos, and to whom the supremacy of similar elements in the metropolis—whence came the governor-generals and other officials of the island—could not fail to be a matter of concern. The interests of the Athenian merchants and of the Roman bankers and traders were not, of course, necessarily

---

[1] See, moreover, *BCH.*, 1899, p. 80, where a Tyrian, renamed Hellen, designates himself Σαραπίωνος, *i.e. Sarapionis libertus*, and calls Sarapion his πάτρων =*patronus.*

[2] *Ath. Mitt.*, 1896, p. 438; cf. above, x. 423, n. 2.

[3] *BCH.*, 1908, p. 430, No. 42. Josephus, *Antiq. Iud.* xiv. 149 ff.; cf. Wilhelm, *Philologus*, 1901, p. 487 ff. It is probably not without significance that his name as *epimeletes* of Delos in 101/0 B.C. appears in the dedicatory inscription of the temple of Poseidon, the Cabiri and Dionysus for the erection of which Helianax the priest secured in all likelihood the assistance of the kings and courtiers of Syria, Pontus, Parthia, and Cappadocia (see *Acad. inscr. C.R.*, 1910, p. 308, and above, ix. 390).   [4] *IG.* ii. 475.

identical; but to both, strong government, the provision of business facilities, and the good-will of the authorities in the chief regions of trade, were advantageous. Hence we shall probably not err in making concern for the maintenance of cordial relations between Athens and Rome—the Rome of Marius and the financial imperialists —the leading motive in the agitation begun by Medeius and his associates. The partiality of the Romans for an aristocratic government in their dependencies was notorious,[1] and the knowledge of this fact must have led many in Athens to wonder how long their democracy would be tolerated. Certainly, there was no more efficacious method of securing irrevocably the favour of the Roman governing circles than by bringing Athens into the firm grasp of the business men of the community. Moreover, there had not been wanting of late signs that the Athenian populace was becoming unmanageable; that the city was nourishing dangerous ambitions, and that hatred of the Romans, long since a passion with the masses and thoroughly deserved, was being mingled with contempt, bred largely on ignorance, yet not unnatural after the recent military fiascoes of Rome in Africa and Gaul, and the trouble with the proletariate and the slaves.[2] The achievements of Mithradates of Pontus were already appealing to the popular imagination of the Greeks.[3] To the intelligent business men of Athens, however, the loss of Roman favour meant irremediable disaster; an open rupture with Rome, the greatest of conceivable evils. Such an issue must be avoided at all cost.

What now remained was to seize a suitable occasion for a revolution. This was found in 103/2 B.C.[4] That was the time of the second insurrection of the slaves in

[1] Paus. vii. 16. 9; cf. Hertzberg, i. 309 f.; Pöhlmann, *Grundriss d. griech. Gesch.*[3] 295; Holm, iv. 424 ff.   [2] See above, viii. 388 ff., x. 418.

[3] Ditt. *OGIS.* 368; cf. below, x. 438, n. 2.

[4] *Klio*, 1904, p. 1 ff. The date cannot be fixed with quite such precision as is affirmed in this article. The revolution must have occurred prior to 100/99 B.C., and probably prior to 102/1 B.C. On the other hand, it occurred after 106/5 B.C., if we take the disappearance of a reference to a judicial audit in the ephebe documents as a criterion. The official order of the tribes of the prytany-secretaries was maintained in 108/7 B.C. (*Klio*, 1907, p. 224; *Berl. phil. Woch.*, 1908, p. 883), but it was out of use in 100/99 B.C. In the case of the priests of Apollo in Delos, where it probably coincided with that of the priests of Serapis and the prytany-secretaries, it had already ceased in 102/1 B.C. (*Klio*, 1909,

Sicily, and again the sedition was borne to Athens along mysterious channels. The slaves in the silver mines overpowered their guards, seized the fortress at Sunium, and with this as a base ravaged the country round about until eventually they were mastered and overwhelmed.[1] The refuge of escaped slaves was the sea, where the pirates now reigned—the agents of the slave trade, the pest of all other maritime occupations. After 108/7 B.C. the interests directing Rome's policy were no longer those of the great planters, whose greed for cheap slaves had been a charter of immunity to the corsairs, but those of the merchants, bankers, traders, and tax-gatherers, to whom the paralysis of commerce due to piracy was intolerable. Accordingly, in 103/2 B.C., M. Antonius was sent by the Roman government to restore order on the high seas and establish a permanent military district in Cilicia, the home of brigandage. It seems to have been while he was in Athens, which he visited while on his way to the East, that the revolution, long since brewing, occurred; and since the institutions adopted then are said in our only record to have been introduced by the Romans, it is probable that he lent his aid to the reformers.[2] All the oligarchic movements came to a head at that moment. The democracy was overthrown, and a government of business men took its place. Not simply was the constitution altered in that the judicial control of the magistrates was abandoned and, if any, senatorial control substituted for it; not simply was the lot discarded generally, and election,

p. 336, n. 1). The first *enneeteris* began in 102/1 B.C.; so did the term of Euodus as sacristan in the precinct of Aphrodite in Delos, in all probability. The first case of repetition of names in the archon list occurs in 97/5 B.C. Medeius became eponymous archon in 100/99 B.C. 103/2 B.C. is thus still the most probable year for the revolution.

[1] Poseidonius in Athen. vi. 272 F οὗτος δ' ἦν ὁ καιρός, ὅτε καὶ ἐν Σικελίᾳ ἡ δευτέρα τῶν δούλων ἐπανάστασις ἐγένετο· πολλαὶ δὲ αὗται ἐγένοντο κτλ. In the time of Athenaeus δευτέρα could designate only the revolt of 104 B.C. That the δευτέρα was taken without change from Poseidonius and that in his usage it designated the outbreak of Cleon which occurred shortly after that of Eunus in 137/6 B.C., or something similar, are hypotheses incapable of proof and unwarranted. They would be debatable only when we had some reason to doubt that a slave revolt occurred in Athens in 104 B.C. Th. Reinach, *Mithridate Eupator*, 137 f.

[2] See Cic. *De Orat.* i. 82; cf. P.-W. i. 2590. Appian, *Mith.* 39 καὶ νόμους (Sulla) ἔθηκεν ἅπασιν ἀγχοῦ τῶν πρόσθεν αὐτοῖς ὑπὸ Ῥωμαίων ὁρισθέντων.

probably on a limited franchise, put in its place ; not simply was the same person permitted to hold the same civil offices for an indefinite number of times or for life,[1] and the Areopagus reduced in size and in powers, though not in dignity ;[2] but the business men's government also took in hand the reform of administration[3] and the removal of administrative abuses.   It was settled that a *Pythais* should not be sent to Delphi in the old irregular fashion, but that, as the Delphian oracles and ancient records seemed to demand, it should go once every eight years, and should be financed by regular tolls collected from the magistrates and priests who held office during the period.[4]   At the same time Diodorus of Halae was appointed a commissioner to replace the old and mislaid or lost standard weights and measures.   His report is extant still.[5]   It provided for the safe-keeping of the new standards in four different places, the punishment of the public slaves in case the models disappeared or were injured, the classification of tampering with them as a criminal offence to be taken cognizance of by the Areopagus,

---

[1] *Klio*, 1904, p. 1 ff.   The *pythaistae* were κληρωτοί after 103/2 B.C. as before it ; cf. *BCH.*, 1906, p. 200 f.   By 101/0 B.C. Helianax had become priest of the Great Deities for life (see below, x. 438).

[2] Repetition in the tenure of the archonships, of course, reduced the size of the Areopagus automatically.   The herald of the Areopagus now ranks with the hoplite-general and the superintendents of Delos.   The earliest reference to him thus far known is in a document of the year 128/7 B.C. (*BCH.*, 1906, p. 184).   He appears more frequently and in more conspicuous places from about 110 B.C. onward.   In the catalogue of ἀπαρχαί he pays a toll of 200 drachmae—the highest toll, which only the hoplite-general and the governor-general of Delos equal.   It was not through a recent enlargement of its powers, as was affirmed in *Klio*, 1904, p. 9, that the Areopagus in 103/2 B.C. possesses jurisdiction in cases of κακουργία ; for it had possessed this authority since 322 B.C. (above, ii. 19).   Sundwall (*Untersuch.* 72, 105) has connected with the revolution the cessation of the so-called third mint magistracy, which reappears, moreover, in the year of the revived democracy 88/7 B.C.—properly, as the dates show.   That he was an Areopagite nominated to control the other officials in the issuing of money is also very probable.   The Areopagus was responsible for the weights used in minting ; hence, also, we may infer for the weight of the coins.   That the new magistrates were made responsible to the Senate of the 600 perhaps involved the abolition of the Areopagite control of the minting.

[3] For some change in the office of the ὑφιέρεια of Artemis on Delos made in the archonship of Medeius (100/99 B.C.) see *BCH.*, 1909, p. 490, No. 13.

[4] *Klio*, 1909, p. 311 ff.

[5] *IG.* ii. 476.   For the date see *Klio*, 1904, p. 8 f.   For the interpretation of the document see Boeckh, *Staatshaushaltung*,[3] ii. 318 ff.   For *sekomata*, or official measures, in Delos an article may be expected soon (*BCH.*, 1905, p. 18, n. 2).

and the designation of various officials with instructions in cases of neglect to flog the custodians, who were, of course, slaves. It furthermore arranged means for making the standards accessible to private persons, and for annual state supervision of the measures and weights actually employed in business. Nor did it stop there. It fixed the measures which must be used in the sale of certain commodities, such as walnuts, almonds, hazelnuts, chestnuts, pine-nuts, Egyptian beans, dates, lupines, olives, pine kernels,—a smaller measure for dried products, and a larger one for green almonds, olives, and figs. It established a simple method of converting the Aeginetan or commercial and the Solonian or mint systems of weights and coinage both into terms of one another and into terms of the Roman and the Phoenician systems, which were the two of foreign origin most commonly used in Delos.[1] It also enacted that in all cases where the unit of measurement was not specified the commercial system was to apply. The report is indicative of the earlier laxness of Athenian methods of trade, and of the motives which actuated the new government. Nobody who bought or sold in Athens was to be cheated henceforth by illegal weights or measures or by the ambiguity implicit in the existence of two metrical systems, or by inability to reckon the value of one coin, pound, or gallon in terms of another equally current. The city was to become a fair place in which to do business. And, in fact, it can hardly be an accident that in *ca.* 96/5 B.C. the Delphian Amphictyony prescribed the use of the Attic tetradrachm in all the territory over which it had jurisdiction.[2]

The new regulations doubtless applied to Delos as well as to Athens, for which, in fact, they may have been equally intended.[3] There no slave revolt

---

[1] *Klio, loc. cit.* ; cf. Gilliard, *Quelques réformes de Solon,* 255, n. 1.

[2] Information on this point I owe to the kindness of M. Th. Reinach, who will publish a paper on the matter in a coming issue of the *Mémoires de l'Acad. des inscriptions.*

[3] No regulation was issued for the keeping of copies of the standards in Delos, as in Athens, Piraeus, and Eleusis, but the status of Delos after *ca.* 130 B.C. was such as to make this inadvisable.

had taken place, but the hostile attitude towards
piracy now assumed by the Roman government had
important bearings upon its business.   Hitherto the
pirates had come to the island fearlessly and with the
assurance that no questions would be asked as to the
source of their supplies of slaves.[1]   This was changed
when the expedition of M. Antonius expelled them
from their base of operations in Cilicia.   Planting themselves in Isauria and Crete they continued their business
in open hostility to Rome;[2] so that in 100 B.C. action
was concerted by the government of Marius for ex-
cluding them from all the ports of the Mediterranean.[3]
Henceforth they were beyond the pale of the law
altogether.   Delos hitherto the host, now became the
enemy of the corsairs, and we may be sure that this
great mart was an important administrative point in
all the serious efforts made by the Roman magistrates
to segregate the pirates from the traders in order to
suppress the one and protect the other.   It seems that
already in 102 B.C. Antonius paid a visit to Delos, and
took such measures in its interest that he was made
a *patronus* of the local community.[4]   Subsequently the
islanders were able to greet a high Roman officer almost
every year;[5] to possess representatives (*patroni*), distinct from the *proxeni* of Athens, in influential Roman

[1] Diod. xxxvi. 3 ; cf. Rathke, *op. cit.*, 42, and above, ix. 380.   For close
relations between Crete and Delos see Ditt. *Syll.*[2] 722, 46 (before 131/0 B.C.),
514 (116/5 B.C.) ; between Crete and Athens *IG.* ii. 549 (111/0 B.C.).

[2] Cf. the dedication made on Delos by Damon, son of Demetrius of Ascalon,
to Zeus Urius, and the Palestine Astarte Aphrodite Urania, because of being
rescued from pirates while *en route* to Delos (*Acad. inscr. C.R.*, 1909,
p. 308).

[3] Foucart (*Journ. des savants*, iv., 1906, p. 569 f.) on the basis of a Delphian
inscription as yet unpublished ; cf. also Jardé-Cagnat in *Acad. inscr. C.R.*,
1904, 532 f.

[4] For statues erected to him at Delos by Dionysius, son of Dionysius of
Sphettus and the Pisidians, see above, ix. 396, n. 2.   The dedicatory inscription
of another is published in *BCH.*, 1884, p. 133 f.   This one was erected by the
Delii, *i.e.* when Delos was independent in 86/4 B.C., after the death of Antonius
(†87 B.C.) ; but of course the patronate had been conferred earlier, and 102 B.C.
is the most likely time.

[5] M. Aemilius M. f. Scaurus (*CIL.* iii. *Suppl.*, 7219) ; C. Rabirius, proconsul
(*CIL.* iii. *Suppl.*, 7239) ; G. Papirius, *strategus* (*BCH.*, 1884, 105) ; C.
Villienus C. f. *legatus* (*CIG.* ii. 2285 *b*) ; C. Cluvius L. f., proconsul (*BCH.*,
1884, p. 119) ; C. Julius C. f. Caesar, proconsul (*BCH.*, 1905, p. 18, 229 ; cf.
BCH., 1899, p. 73 ; *BCH.*, 1902, p. 541) ; *legatus* (*BCH.* 1884, p. 108 f.) ; L.
Cornelius S. f. Lentulus, *quaestor* (*BCH.*, 1880, p. 919).

circles;[1] and, by thus reaching the real sources of authority without having recourse to their nominal suzerain, to assert their independence of Athens and their citizenship in Italy.

An open avowal was now made of the Italian domination of Delos.[2] The dissolution of the Athenian cleruchy had given all those who frequented the island an even chance. This had meant, when the political supremacy of Rome and the great and increasing size of the Italian community were taken into account, a substantial elevation of the Italians above all others, and it was on behalf of the *demos* of Athens *and Rome* that public works had been dedicated subsequently. Now came the definite establishment of a government in Athens friendly to Rome and to the mercantile interests, as well as independent of popular outbursts, which brought with it to the Italians on Delos a feeling of complete present and prospective security. The new sense of ownership displayed itself in a number of ways. Italians and Italian organizations took the lead in honouring strangers and in beautifying public places.[3] Besides placing several new statues on the *piazza* of Theophrastus,[4] they now either built for themselves for the first time or remodelled fundamentally—if a beginning had been made earlier—a large and elaborate *statio* or *schola* on the hill to the north-east of the precinct of Apollo.[5] A quadrangular

---

[1] The two *patroni* of Delos thus far known are M. Antonius and C. Julius Caesar. For the difference between the patronate and the *proxenia* see Monceaux, *Les Proxénies grecques*, 241 ff. Athens had Roman *proxeni* in 170 B.C. (*IG.* ii. 423), and probably did not deign to have *patroni*. Delos could thus have its own, and probably a different kind of foreign, representatives. Rhodes, however, had both *proxeni* and *patroni* at this time.

[2] Holleaux (*Acad. inscr. C.R.*, 1908, 187) intimates that the entire agora of the Romans was built at this time. However that may be (see above, ix. 356 and 399, and below, n. 5), it is clear that an enlargement and a notable readornment of it took place at *ca.* 100 B.C. (see *BCH.*, 1910, p. 404 ff. ; *CIG.* ii. 2285 *b* ; cf. *BCH.*, 1884, p. 182=*BCH.*, 1884, p. 115, for a statue erected in it—the work of Agasias the son of Menophilus. Cf. *ibid.* 119).

[3] Thus it was a Roman, Spurius Stertinius Sp. f., who at this time embellished and probably repaired the well Minoe (*Acad. inscr. C.R.*, 1909, p. 414).

[4] *BCH.*, 1909, p. 472.

[5] *Acad. inscr. C.R.*, 1909, p. 547 ff. The articles by Pâris and Hatzfeld on this subject are not yet accessible. The former holds that part of the structure is older than the end of the century ; the latter, to whose view Roussel and Holleaux subscribe, that it was all built at the end of the second and the beginning of the first century B.C.

court was enclosed by a group of buildings, which was set within and without by a fringe of stoas designed primarily for the exposition of goods and works of art. Doubtless lodging rooms were also provided. Here the public and private life of the Italians on the island was henceforth focussed, and ampler opportunity was given to the Campanians and Latins to lessen the tedium of their exile by gladiatorial exhibitions; for the *masters* were now able to fit up the courtyard of the *statio* as an arena and to give in it at their own expense their national *ludi*.[1] The necessary equipment of a gladiatorial ring was also provided—the *Laconicum*, or sweat-bath, being a contribution of two freedmen of L. Orbius who were *masters* at the time.[2] The island naturally had its own corps of gladiators.[3] The *statio*, moreover, could serve in case of need as a defensible stronghold for the Romans in the midst of the town. As a matter of course they decorated it to suit their own taste, which, seeing that many of them were in reality Greeks from southern Italy or Oscans from Campania, had doubtless been formed in their home surroundings. Their initiative in these matters was, accordingly, fatal to the Italian monopoly of the art business on the island, and from this time forward the favourite sculptors were Agasias son of Menophilus of Ephesus,[4] Lysippus son of Lysippus of Heracleia in Magna Graecia,[5] and Menodorus son of Phaenandrus of Mallos in Cilicia.[6] The names of Athenian artists are rarely found on the pedestals which have been

---

[1] *BCH.*, 1910, p. 404, No. 54.
[2] *BCH.*, 1907, p. 439/40, No. 30.
[3] *BCH.*, 1910, p. 417, No. 81.
[4] *BCH.*, 1907, p. 458 n. 2. Thirteen signatures of Agasias have been found already. They date prevailingly after *ca.* 100 B.C. He was dead or had left Delos in 86/4 B.C., since his statues were then restored by Aristandrus son of Scopas of Paros (*BCH.*, 1907, p. 458 ff.). [All the signatures of Agasias are now collected and published by Picard in *BCH.*, 1910, p. 538 ff.]
[5] *BCH.*, 1883, p. 372 f. (Loewy, 312); *BCH.*, 1899, p. 67, No. 14. The *ethnicum* Ἡράκλειος belongs to Heracleia in Italy (Smith, *Dict. of Class. Geog.*, s. v.). That it is an Alexandrian *demotikon* has been conjectured by Crönert, but this is quite improbable (*Archiv f. Papyrusforsch.*, 1909, p. 110).
[6] Loewy, 306, 307. Another foreign sculptor of this time (*BCH.*, 1899, p. 66) is Sopatrus son of Archias of Soli, who did work in the *epimeleia* of Aropus son of Leon of Azenia (*ca.* 91 B.C., *BCH.*, 1908, p. 412).

preserved for the following period,[1] which is symptomatic, doubtless, of an alteration in the prevalent taste. At the same time the *competaliastae* proceeded to erect statues of *Roma* and *Fides* in the enclosure of which they had charge,[2] to set the names of the Roman consuls at the head of their documents along with those of the Athenian archons or superintendents, and before ten years were past to omit the Athenian eponymous magistrate altogether.[3] In other words, they now ventured to do what the more powerful *masters* of the *conventus* had done a decade and more earlier,[4] they introduced the Roman era into Delos. This shows how rapidly the island was being Romanized. The extent of Roman influence is, perhaps, brought out most explicitly by an epigram which was put upon the base of a statue erected by the inhabitants of Delos to the Athenian governor-general for the year 94/3 B.C. The donors were the Athenians, Hellenes, and the tens of thousands of Romans on the island. Aropus, the recipient, a relative of Medeius, had performed his duties with conspicuous merit; he had safeguarded the life and property of the Hellenes, preserved the excellent spirit of justice traditional to the Athenians, and stood loyally by the decisions reached by the Romans. In other words, the chief executive of the island is commended for having taken his orders from the Italian colony.[5] The Italians were thus acknowledged masters of Delos.

The establishment by the special commissioner of

---

[1] One work of Eutychides is dated after 102 B.C., viz. Loewy, 247 (95/4 B.C.). Of course others may be as late or later ; cf. *BCH.*, 1908, p. 409 ff., and *Acad. inscr. C.R.*, 1909, p. 417. The name of Demostratus son of Demostratus appears in 102/1 B.C. (*PA.* 3614 ; cf. *BCH.*, 1908, p. 321, No. 145). The man there mentioned may be the son of the sculptor, since the document may belong to 95/4 B.C. The name of Zoilus son of Demostratus appears in 98/7 B.C. (*BCH.*, 1905, p. 222). These three Athenian names are the only ones which appear on the bases of works dated after 103/2 B.C. See, on the other hand, above, ix. 410, n. 1.

[2] Pistis in 97/6 B.C. (*BCH.*, 1883, p. 13) ; Roma in 94/3 B.C. (*BCH.*, 1899, p. 68). [3] *BCH.*, 1899, p. 72.

[4] *BCH.*, 1909, p. 493, No. 15; *BCH.*, 1880, p. 190 (97/6 B.C.). In *BCH.*, 1884, p. 146 (74 B.C.) the *masters* also use the names of the Roman consuls alone. Cf. *CIL.* iii., *Suppl.* 7222 (74 B.C.).

[5] *BCH.*, 1892, p. 150 ; cf. *Klio*, 1907, p. 239.

an easy means of converting Attic coins, weights, and measures into Phoenician was not simply a convenience to the Oriental interests of Theodotus of Sunium. The system thus made commensurable with that of Athens was the one used in Alexandria and throughout the entire region of Ptolemaic influence.[1] With the Egpytian government Athens had of late been estranged, but for the ground of the quarrel—the sentimental championship of the Greeks in Alexandria against Euergetes II. —the new business government of Athens could not be expected to have much sympathy. Besides, on the death of Cleopatra Euergetis in 102/1 B.C. the anti-Greek movement came to an end ; and after its foremost opponent Soter II., now king of Cyprus, had given his daughter Berenice in marriage to his brother, Alexander —who had paved the way for a reconciliation by putting to death their imperious old mother—there existed no reason whatsoever for Athens to continue to antagonize the Ptolemies.[2]   Accordingly, the fête Ptolemaea was restored to its old dignity ;[3] statues of the second Ptolemy and his admirals and *nesiarchs* which had been mutilated on Delos, probably at the time of the establishment of the first Macedonian ascendancy in the Aegean, were rededicated ;[4] and in return for many favours received from Soter II. and for the opening given to many Athenians in his service, several statues of him were erected on the island, while in Athens bronze effigies of him and his daughter Berenice were voted and placed in front of the Odeum.[5]   Courtiers of Soter sent their sons from Salamis to be trained with the Athenian ephebes,[6] and no doubt the best possible opportunities were secured for Athenian merchants in Cyprus and the other Ptolemaic possessions.

For twelve years the government established in 103/2 B.C. remained in undisputed possession of affairs. It was a time, apparently, of commercial expansion and

---

[1] Beloch, iii. 1. 314 ff.
[2] *Klio*, 1908, 343 f.   [3] *Ibid.* 338, n. 4.
[4] *BCH.*, 1909, 480. The *nesiarch* Bacchon and the *nauarch* Callicrates of Samos suffered along with Philadelphus.
[5] *Klio*, 1908, p. 338 f.   [6] See above, ix. 408, n. 1.

enlarged material welfare,[1] of brilliant fêtes at home[2] and of unusual activity in Delos;[3] but it was also a period of political depression. As the years passed by men not in the confidence of the government tended to withdraw from public life altogether, and the inner circle grew narrower and narrower[4] till finally the initiative and also the financial burdens rested mainly with Medeius, Sarapion, and a score or two of others. They tended to monopolize the offices, perhaps voluntarily, but perhaps also because others refused them. Thus evidence is remaining still that Sarapion was not only governor - general of Delos and chief superintendent of the *Pythais*, but at least three times hoplite-general, and *agonothetes* of four separate fêtes,[5] and that Medeius was governor-general of Delos, chairman of the Areopagus, and manager of the public bank in Delos all in one year, as well as hoplite-general, twice *agonothetes*, and four times eponymous archon.[6] The administration secured by this cumulation of offices much of the permanency of a bureaucratic system, without, however, being open to talent wherever found, as was the public service in Alexandria or Antioch ; for it was simply unthinkable that an ancient city-state or municipality should substitute salaried officials for honorary ones. Only very rich men could shoulder the burdens which the repeated tenure of offices entailed ; for, as already noted,[7] the oligarchs had increased the contributions expected of magistrates. The wealth of the men constituting the government was, in fact, their chief strength, and its political value was greatly

---

[1] We learn from a bilingual inscription of 96 B.C., published in *Rev. arch.*, iii. 11 (1888), 5 ff. ; cf. Wachsmuth, *Die Stadt Athen*, ii. 161, n. 3, and *C.I. Semit.* i. 119, of the existence in the Piraeus at this time of a club of Sidonians —Bel being the patron deity—who vote to inscribe a list of their members on a gilt *stele*.

[2] For the *Pythais* of 97/6 B.C. see *BCH.*, 1906, 179 ; for the giving of the *peplos* to Athena in 102/1 and 94/3 B.C. see *IG*. ii. 5. 477 and 477d ; for the renewal of the Ptolemaea see *Klio*, 1908, p. 338, n. 4. The fête was due in Ol. 170. 1, 100/99 B.C. It also came in 104/3 B.C. Cf. *Klio*, 1909, 339 f.

[3] See above, x. 432, n. 2.

[4] Observe the falling off in the number of the subscribers to the ἀπαρχαί, which is noticeable as early as 99/8 B.C. ; cf. *Klio*, 1909, p. 312.

[5] Kirchner, *PA.*, 12,564.

[6] *Ibid.* 10,098 and *BCH.*, 1908, p. 350, No. 401.

[7] In connexion with the reform of the *Pythais* ; cf. *IG*. ii. 985.

enhanced through its being loaned to the poorer Athenians. The oligarchs stood thus in the relation of creditors to many to whom a change of government alone could bring release from obligations and embarrassments.[1] No such change was thinkable, however, except through the overthrow of Rome's hegemony in the East, whereupon private citizens, and probably also the state, could repudiate debts contracted on ruinous rates of interest with Roman and other bankers.[2] Of this there was now some prospect, first because of the secession of the Italian allies and the threatened internal collapse of the mighty republic, and, when this hope failed, through the power, aggressiveness, and success of an external foe, and a Greek to boot, Mithradates Eupator, king of Pontus.

The relations between Pontus and Athens had been intimate and of long standing.[3] There were citizens in Sinope and Amisus, the two Pontic capitals, who were proud to recall that their ancestors had been immigrants from Attica, and as late as the fourth century B.C. Amisus had been named for a time Piraeus. The Pontic dynasty traced its descent from a Persian nobleman to whom Athens had given its civic privileges in the days of Demosthenes, and many civilities had passed between the two countries before Pharnaces, as already mentioned,[4] sent subsidies of money in 171 B.C. His son[5] and grandson were likewise phil-Athenians. Thus an enlargement or endowment of the Delian *gymnasium* was facilitated by the generosity of Mithradates V. Euergetes;[6] and a similar benefaction was rendered by

---

[1] See below, x. 441. The debts to be cancelled were, doubtless, in part obligations to the richer Athenians (Sarapion was the owner of slaves and the patron of freedmen; cf. *BCH.*, 1899, p. 80); in part public and private loans made with Roman bankers.

[2] Atticus (Nepos, *Atticus*, 2) was doubtless not the first Roman banker to make loans to Athens. For a monument erected in Athens, probably between 105 and 90 B.C., to the Roman knight, Gn. Pompeius Strabo, see Groebe, *Ath. Mitt.*, 1908, p. 135 ff.

[3] Reinach, Th., *op. cit.* 138.   [4] See above, vii. 302.

[5] This is likely, though no evidence happens to be extant.

[6] *CIG.* ii. 2277*a*; cf. Kirchner, *PA.* 4122=*BCH.*, 1877, p. 86. This, like *CIG.* ii. 2276, was made by a *gymnasiarch.* Reinach (*BCH.*, 1906, p. 50) wrongfully doubts the genuineness of this inscription; cf. *BCH.*, 1908, p. 376, n. 1. See also *BCH.*, 1908, p. 431, No. 44.

Mithradates VI. Eupator shortly after the *coup d'état* by which he came to power. His kindly feeling was reciprocated, and prior to 110/9 B.C.[1] an Athenian magistrate dedicated a monument at Delos in his honour. His enterprise in the Crimea brought him dramatically into prominence as the champion of the Greeks—of those in Russia as well as of those who suffered through lack of Russian grain ; and on Delos an offering was made in the precinct of Serapis for him, and his mission, to Zeus Urius, the god whose temple greeted mariners as they sailed in and out of the Black Sea.[2] He was apparently among the most conspicuous benefactors of the island in 101/100 B.C., since Helianax, priest for life of Poseidon Aesius and of the Cabiri, placed the bust of the king of Pontus and those of five of his courtiers—of whom three were natives of Amisus—in medallions, which helped to adorn the interior of a new temple erected at this time in the precinct of the Samothracian deities.[3]

His victories in the Crimea had been achieved already ; Cholcis and Lesser Armenia had been subdued ; in conjunction with Nicomedes III. of Bithynia

---

[1] At the time of the dedication Dionysius, son of Nicon of Pallene (Kirchner, *PA.* 4237 ; Roussel, *BCH.*, 1908, p. 327, No. 192), was *gymnasiarch* of Delos. In 110/9 B.C. this man held the higher office of governor-general of Delos. The date of the *coup* of Mithradates is variously assigned by modern scholars. Ed. Meyer (*Gesch. d. Königreichs Pontus*, 85) puts it in *ca.* 115 B.C. Reinach (*op. cit.* 54 f.), who quotes Justin, xxxviii. 8, for the lapse of twenty-three years between the *coup* and the rupture with Rome, puts it in *ca.* 111 B.C. It took place in 111/0 B.C. or earlier—probably earlier.

[2] *BCH.*, 1882, p. 343, No. 57 = Reinach, *op. cit.* 457, No. 5. The terms of the dedication : ὑπὲρ βασι[λέως] Μιθραδάτου Εὐπάτορος καὶ τοῦ ἀδελφοῦ αὐτοῦ Μιθραδάτου Χρηστοῦ καὶ τῶν πραγμάτων αὐτῶν, are quite unusual, if not altogether unique on Delos, but the phrase τὰ πράγματα αὐτῶν appears, with the same implication of partisanship, in an Egyptian inscription which registers a vow made on behalf of Ptolemy Euergetes II. and Cleopatra, the niece-wife of this strangely polygamous monarch (*Archiv f. Papyrusforschung*, 1909, p. 160, No. 5). The reference here can hardly be to anything except the enterprises in Bosporus. Accordingly, these were in progress before the death of the younger brother of Mithradates, which occurred not long after the *coup* (*Memnon*, 30 : *FHG.*, iii. p. 541 ; Appian, *Mith.* 112 ; cf. Reinach, *op. cit.* 55, n. 2). Reinach (72) errs in putting them between 96 and 90 B.C. For the temple of Zeus Urius see Beloch, iii. 1. 106. This deity was identified with Jupiter Secundanus ; cf. Holleaux, *Acad. inscr. C.R.*, 1908, p. 186 = *BCH.*, 1909, p. 496, No. 16.

[3] *BCH.*, 1883, p. 346 ff. ; cf. Reinach, *op. cit.* 459, No. 9 ; Ditt. *OGIS.* 371. For the latest report of excavations conducted in the Cabeirium see *Acad. inscr. C.R.*, 1910, p. 306 ff. Why the temple was dedicated to Dionysus, as well as to the deities of which Helianax was titular priest, is not clear.

he had seized Paphlagonia and Galatia (103 B.C.), and when Nicomedes had annexed Cappadocia he had interfered in the interest of the ancient dynasty, and had put his nephew Ariarathes VII. on the throne.[1]   Moreover, he had not yet made a definite breach with Rome, for by a judicious employment of diplomacy and bribery he had overcome the suspicions which his ambition had aroused in various Roman circles.[2]   Not long afterwards, however, he murdered Ariarathes VII. with his own hand, and occupied Cappadocia for himself.   This roused the Romans to action.   They forced him to disgorge the territory he had annexed in Asia Minor (100-95 B.C.),[3] and subsequently the two powers were enemies.   The pirates sought from Pontus the licence which the Roman government had recently withdrawn, and after about 100 B.C. no honours to Mithradates were published on Roman Delos.[4]   It was not till 92 B.C., however, that the interests of Rome and Pontus clashed again.   Then Mithradates was driven out of Cappadocia a second time, and two years later he yielded once more, and evacuated peaceably Bithynia and Cappadocia, which he had again overrun in the meanwhile.   The Roman governor of Asia, M. Aquillius, was not content with this diplomatic success.   He pushed for open war, and in the winter of 89/8 B.C. he obtained it with interest.   Mithradates had been making preparations for a long time for such an eventuality.   He now drove the Bithynians, who had invaded Pontus at the instigation of Aquillius, out of his kingdom, and by a series of rapid victories became master of all Asia Minor.   The governor of Cilicia was captured.   Aquillius shared his fate, and the Roman province of Asia fell into the hands of Mithradates.

[1] *Ca.* 102/1 B.C., Meyer ed., *op. cit.* 103 ; cf. Reinach, *op. cit.* 98.
[2] Reinach, *op. cit.* 96 f.
[3] 95 B.C. according to Reinach, *op. cit.* 101, n. 1.
[4] Reinach, *op. cit.* 458, No. 7, probably belongs to 88 B.C. ; cf. Ditt. *OGIS.* 370, n. 2.   460, No. 10, is dateless.   It may belong to 88/7 B.C. There is, moreover, no evidence to connect the *Eupatoristae* of the latter inscription with Delos (Ziebarth, P.-W. vi. 1163), or with Athens (Reinach, *op. cii.* 288).   The vase on which it is engraved was found at Antium ; cf. Ditt. *OGIS.* 367.   No other Delian inscriptions dealing with Mithradates belong later than 101/0 B.C.

The long years of fiscal oppression and uneven justice
had engendered bitter feelings in the hearts of the
Greeks of Asia, and now that a deliverer had come they
took vengeance upon all the Italians in their power.
Eighty thousand of them were massacred throughout
the cities of Asia.   Nor did the revolt of the Greeks
stop there.   The pirate fleets of Mithradates ruled the
seas, and the agitation was thus transferred to Europe.

The Athenians had not waited for its coming.   The
narrowing down of the oligarchy had resulted in a
usurpation of power on the part of the office-holders,
if we may make this generalization from the fact
that for three years in succession (91/0-89/8 B.C.)
Medeius was eponymous archon,[1] and the same pair of
mint magistrates had charge of the coinage.[2]   This had
occasioned a violent reaction within the city, whereupon
the government adopted coercion[3] as the best means of
stemming it.   All gatherings of the people, whether for
educational, social and religious, or for judicial and
political purposes, were forbidden.   Naturally the situation thus established could not continue indefinitely;
hence at about the same time[4] a formal reference of the
matter was made to the Roman senate,[5] and the democrats

---

[1] The list of archons, after the capture of Athens, was made up by the
Roman party.   Hence the anarchy is entered for 88/7 B.C. (*IG.* iii. 1014 ; cf.
Kirchner, *GGA.*, 1900, p. 476 ff. ; *Priests of Asklepios*, 145 ; Kolbe, *op. cit.*
138 ff.).   It would be interesting to know where the Pontic party would have
placed the anarchy, had they been in a position to construct the official
list.   It is probable that all the magistrates held office continuously from
91 to 88 B.C.   This is not proved by the case of Philocrates ; for this man was
apparently priest of Serapis for the first time at *ca.* 84 B.C. (*Klio*, 1909,
p. 334).   Nor is it disproved by the case of the superintendents of Delos,
whom Roussel (*BCH.*, 1908, p. 412) places in this period ; for they are only
dated conjecturally.   For the evidence see below, n. 2.   It was probably at
this time that the *Pythais* became annual (*Klio*, 1909, p. 314).

[2] Sundwall (*Untersuch.* 110 f.) makes it clear that Xenocles and Harmoxenus
issued three consecutive annual series of coins at about this time, one of them
inscribed with a statue of the goddess *Roma.*   The same Harmoxenus reappeared
apparently in a mint magistracy right after March 1, 86 B.C. (Sundwall, 112).
For the discovery of a new inscription of the year 91/0 B.C. see *Acad. inscr.
C.R.*, 1909, p. 416.

[3] The suspension of the various public activities did not take place in
103/2 B.C., as the decrees from the following years show.   The last dated
decree thus far extant belongs probably to 94/3 B.C (*IG.* ii. 5. 477*d*.   Archon,
Demochares).

[4] This must have been in the winter or early spring of 89/8 B.C.

[5] Presumably an appeal was taken from the decision of the governor of
Macedon, to whose tribunal the matter in all probability was first carried.

quietly despatched a prominent Peripatetic philosopher,
Athenion by name, to Mithradates. The Senate
promised to make an investigation of the trouble in
Athens, but delayed doing so with the intention, doubtless, of deferring a crisis till a more seasonable time.
Mithradates received the legate with marked consideration, and it was not long till the receipt of a patent of
nobility disclosed the fact that Athenion had been
taken into his service and confidence. Henceforth the
philosopher could speak as an accredited *nuntio* of the
king. His letters were, accordingly, firebrands which
kindled the passions of the mob. The Roman hegemony,
they alleged, was overthrown; there would be a cancelling of debts, a restoration of the democracy, and
an uninterrupted stream of gold flowing from Pontus
into Athens.[1] An ambassador who forwarded such a
report need not fear for a cordial reception on his
return. The contemporary Stoic historian, Poseidonius
of Apamea, described the circumstances of his home-
coming with inimitable liveliness, and even at the risk
of preserving the malice, born of professional, political,
and class animosity, implicit in every line of his
narrative, we venture to quote it extensively.[2] " No
sooner had Mithradates overrun Asia than Athenion
set out for Athens; but, blown off by a gale, he made
Carystus instead. Upon learning of this mishap the
Cecropidae sent warships and a litter with silver feet
for his conveyance farther, and as he entered the city
almost everybody flooded out in a crush to receive him.
Some, indeed, went simply as spectators in amazement
at the chance which brought back to Athens in a silver-
footed litter and purple wraps an imposter who had never
before seen so much as a streak of purple in his beggars'
rags; for not even a Roman had ever paraded in such a
haughty fashion in Attica. Accordingly men, women,
and children thronged hastily to see the sight, naturally
expecting great things from Mithradates, seeing that
this pauper, Athenion, who had made his living by

---

[1] Poseidonius in Athen. v. 212 A δωρεῶν μεγάλων τυχεῖν ἰδίᾳ καὶ δημοσίᾳ.
[2] *Ibid.* v. 212 B and following; cf. Mahaffy, *op. cit.* 121 ff.

subscription lectures, had come back from his court in grand estate, lolling along at his ease through country and town. Out came the Dionysiac artists, too, with the request that the envoy of the new Dionysus (for such was the rank and title of Mithradates among the Olympians) should be their guest, and accept their vows and thanksgivings. And so it came that he who had departed from a mean little hired flat was entertained on his return in the house of the Delian nabob, Dies, a palace rich with rugs and paintings, statues and silver plate.

" After lunch he made his appearance with a brilliant cloak on his shoulder, and on his finger a gold ring set with the head of Mithradates. Before and after went many attendants. Upon his arrival in the *temenos* of the artists a herald issued a solemn proclamation, and sacrifices were offered and thanks rendered for the advent of Athenion. Next day throngs of people assembled at his house, waiting for him to come out, and the Cerameicus was packed with citizens and foreigners, who, without the formality of a summons, rushed pell-mell to hold a town meeting. Athenion had difficulty in making his way forward ; for around and in front of him was a bodyguard of politicians who wished to stand in with a popular movement, and who strove to touch though it were only the hem of his garment. At length he reached the platform which had been built before the stoa of Attalus for the use of the Roman generals, and mounting on it, he looked upon the multitude all about him, and then upwards, and said : ' Men of Athens, circumstances and the good of my country constrain me to relate what I know ; but the magnitude of the subject and the startling elements in it stand in my way.' A great cheer went up for him to take courage and speak on. ' Well, then,' he continued, ' I tell you things unhoped for, things beyond the fancies of a dream. King Mithradates is lord of Bithynia and of Upper Cappadocia, lord of all Asia as far as Pamphylia and Cilicia. The kings of the Armenians and the Persians march in his bodyguard, and with them are the princes of the Maeotis and of the nations which dwell about the whole Pontus in a circuit of thirty thousand stades. Of the Romans the governor of Pamphylia, Q. Oppius, has been surrendered into his hands, and follows after him in chains ; Manius Aquillius, an ex-consul and the hero of a Sicilian triumph, is tied by a long rope to a seven-foot Cossack and dragged behind his horse on foot ; others are prostrate before the altars of the gods, and the rest have doffed their togas and, renegades a second time, no longer deny the land which gave them birth. All the cities receive him with superhuman honours, and call him god and king. Oracles from every quarter promise to him the lordship of the world, and great armaments are now on their way to Thrace and Macedon with a view to their fulfilment. The eyes of all the European peoples are turned expectantly toward him, and ambassadors have come to him already not only from the nations of Italy, but also from the Carthaginians (*sic*), asking for his co-operation in the annihilation of Rome.' Then, after waiting a while and giving them a chance to talk over his astonishing budget of news, he rubbed his forehead and continued. 'Now for my advice. Let us not put up with the anarchy which the Roman senate is pro-longing till it has ascertained how we ought to be governed. Let us not stand by inactive while the temples are shut, the *gymnasia* foul through disuse, the theatre without the ecclesia, the jury-courts silent, and the pnyx taken away from the people, though consecrated to its use by the oracles of the gods. Let us not stand by inactive, men of Athens, whilst the sacred cry Iacchus is silenced, the hallowed sanctuary of Castor and Pollux is closed, and the conference halls of the philosophers are voiceless.' When the scullion had spoken at length in this strain, the mob talked it over, and hurrying into the theatre, chose Athenion hoplite-general. The Peripatetic then entered the orchestra, 'stepping daintily, like Pythocles' (as Demosthenes says),[1] and after congratulating the Athenians said : 'Now

---

[1] xix. 314.

you are your own generals, while I am your commander-in-chief. If you strike stoutly in unison with me I'll accomplish as much as all of you put together.' With this he suggested the names of the other magistrates, whom they forthwith elected."[1] At the same time the democratic institutions were restored in their entirety; and four silver tetradrachms issued by the *demos* of Athens in person during the last month or two of the year 89/8 B.C., still exist to bear witness to the event.[2]

Thus Athenion became dictator of Athens, and another was added to the many examples of a philosopher in supreme control of a state. He had in reality grown great on the hatred of Rome, but on obtaining power he professed to be the creature of a purely local movement. He studiously avoided a definite breach with the Senate; while on the one hand he consulted the people on all occasions, and on the other persecuted vigorously the adherents of the government which he had deposed. These had seen what was coming and had started to escape. Medeius, Calliphon, Philon the head of the Academy, and others made their way to Roman protection, and a general exodus of the propertied classes began. Athenion, however, posted thirty guards at each gate to prevent the passage of suspects and to

---

[1] Since 88/7 B.C. was a year of anarchy, no aristocratic archon was elected at its beginning; hence the nomination of Athenion took place prior to July 88 B.C. Weil (*Ath. Mitt.* vi. 315 ff.) makes the home-coming of Athenion coincide with the elections, which were due to take place at about May 88 B.C. At its time, if Poseidonius is exact in the speech he gives to Athenion, the Pontic expedition to Thrace and Macedon was already projected; hence, as is obvious from the report of Athenion, Asia Minor was already in the possession of Mithradates. He may have spent March and April in this conquest, and have been joined by Athenion during the advance. It was Athenion apparently—at least in Poseidonius's presentation of the matter—who brought to Athens the first news of the astonishing achievements of Mithradates.

Accordingly the reign of terror of Athenion in Athens, and the expedition of Apellicon to Delos, belong to the months of May and June. The crossing of Archelaus and the arrival of Aristion in Athens took place a little before July, since Aristion was mint magistrate for 88/7 B.C., and as such issued twelve series of coins—one for each month (Sundwall, *Untersuch.* 69). His coin symbol being a pegasus—the coat of arms of Mithradates—there can be no doubt as to the identification, the time, or the fact of Aristion's presence in Athens for the whole of 88/7 B.C. (Reinach, *op. cit.* 140, n. 1).

[2] Sundwall, *Untersuch.* 111 f. ; cf. *Woch. f. klass. Philol.*, 1908, p. 1356, also *IG.* ii. 3. 1672 Ἀθηνᾶς Δημοκρατίας.

seize such as let themselves down over the walls by
night; while by sending cuirassiers in pursuit of those
who had reached the open, he caused some to be slain
and others to be held in prison.   Many, too, he put
to death within the city on the pretext of treasonable
communications with the refugees.   No one could
enter or leave the city at pleasure, while a curfew law
was enforced within the walls, and guards demanded
passports of all who travelled in the country.   The
mountains, even, were searched for hiding aristocrats.
Imprisoning, torturing, and judicial murders were the
order of the day, and by general confiscation the tyrant
amassed "wells of gold."   "Nor was the property of
citizens alone plundered," continues Poseidonius, "but
that of foreigners as well, and he even stretched out his
hands to seize the sacred treasures at Delos."   The
lieutenant chosen for this mission was Apellicon of Teus,
a collector of old books and a purloiner of rare documents, a fellow Peripatetic and companion at wrangling
of Athenion, and like his leader a dubious character
(according to Poseidonius) and an Athenian by adoption
only.   Athenion stayed at home to put the citizens on
siege rations and prepare for the Romans, while Apellicon took one thousand troops and landed on Delos,
where the Romans had intimidated the ex-cleruchs, and
taken affairs entirely into their own hands.   The island
was protected by its sanctity only; hence Apellicon had
no difficulty in disembarking his troops.   He acted,
however (according to Poseidonius), as if he were the
head of a sacred procession instead of an invading army.
No fortifications were put about his camp: a lax guard
faced the city, and none at all watched his rear.   This
conduct is quite inexplicable; for the enemy outnumbered his soldiers ten to one, and were at a disadvantage
simply through the lack of arms and a leader.   A certain
Orbius [1] supplied the latter deficiency.   He was probably

---

[1] "Who was cruising with a squadron in Delian waters," according to
Reinach (*op. cit.* 141), but Mommsen (*CIL.* iii. Suppl. 7225 and 7234) called
attention to the presence on Delos of an important Roman of that name (*ibid.*
7224; see also *BCH.*, 1907, p. 440, No. 31; 1909, p. 399, No. 47; for a certain
M. Orbius L. f., *BCH.*, 1892, p. 160, No. 18, and for M. Orbius M. f., *CIL.*

one of the *masters* of the Italian *conventus*, and in this capacity he organized the Roman partisans on the island, and, making an attack on a dark night, he caught the Athenians asleep or drunk. The Athenians were slain like sheep. Some fled to the villas in the suburbs, which were thereupon burned over their heads. Four hundred prisoners were taken, six hundred were slain, and very few were as fortunate as their commander, who made his escape from the island. His siege machines were all destroyed by fire. The losses of Orbius were mainly incurred while trying to seize the Athenian ships.[1]

The expedition of Apellicon had been a complete failure, and it is not doubtful that the disgrace it brought and the heavy losses of life it occasioned undermined the position of Athenion in Athens. At any rate, there was a scattering of the Peripatetics, and we hear no more of Apellicon or his patron. In their stead a certain Aristion, whom Appian calls an Epicurean philosopher,[2] made his appearance, having been sent from Asia with

iii. Suppl. 7225. For the freedmen of L. Orbius see *BCH.*, 1907, p. 439, No. 30). L(*ucius*) *Orbius* M(*arci*) *f*(*ilius*) *Hor*(*atia*) *mag*(*ister*) appears on Delos after 88/6 B.C., *Musée belge*, xii. 111. Graindor (*ibid.*) suggests that the title *strategus* applied to him in Athenaeus is a mistaken interpretation of *magister*. The view of Schulten (*op. cit.* 56) that Orbius was *magister* in chief of the *Italici* has nothing to commend it. Had there been such a supreme Italian official on Delos we must have found *him*, and not the subordinate *masters* in the inscriptions. The epigram quoted below (n. 1) from the sepulchral monument of those slain at this time has been used to strengthen Reinach's interpretation. It mentions only losses incurred at sea ; but those who fell on land may have been buried elsewhere. Besides, the stiffest fight was probably fought on the water. It also mentions ξένοι, which can mean almost anything ; for practically all the non-Athenian inhabitants of the island were ξένοι, but it would hardly have been used for 'Ρωμαῖοι, if Romans alone were meant. Hence it is preferable to think of the fight on the sea as fought between the Athenians and the pro-Roman islanders. These can have had no difficulty in procuring boats in such a mart as Delos was.

[1] The epigram placed on the chief sepulchral monument reads as follows (Athen. v. 21f B) :—

τούσδε θανόντας ἔχει ξείνους τάφος, οἳ περὶ Δήλου
μαρνάμενοι ψυχὰς ὤλεσαν ἐν πελάγει,
τὴν ἱερὰν ὅτε νῆσον Ἀθηναῖοι κεράϊζον
κοινὸν Ἄρη βασιλεῖ Καππαδόκων θέμενοι.

The Athenians probably came in four or five trieremes or *naves apertae*.

[2] It may have been at this time, as Zeller (*Phil. d. Griech.* iii. 1⁴, 385. 1) conjectures, that Zenon the Epicurean secured the condemnation and execution of Diotimus, a Stoic, who had forged nasty letters to the discredit of the founder of the Garden (Athen. xiii. 611 B ; Diog. Laert. x. 3 ; cf. P.-W. v. 1150).

Archelaus, commander of the advance guard which Mithradates despatched to Greece in the early summer of 88 B.C.[1] Since he arrived with the Delian treasures in his possession which Apellicon had failed to secure, and with the report that they had left twenty thousand Romans dead on Delos and the neighbouring islands, and that of the arrogant Roman colonists the widows and orphans were slaves, the *schola*, where, perhaps, the last stand was made, was battered,[2] and the statues, with which the Italians had adorned the island, were thrown from their pedestals or into the sea; since, moreover, he could announce the restoration to Athens of Delos and other places,[3] and could count on the support of two thousand Pontic troops which he had brought with him, he had no difficulty in pushing Athenion aside, and making himself dictator of the city. They both shone with a reflected light, and the new star eclipsed the old.

During the fall of 88 B.C. Archelaus and Aristion won over the Achaeans and Spartans, and also the Boeotian cities, with the exception, however, of Thespiae. This they harassed during the winter, but upon the advent of Sulla in the summer of 87 B.C. with thirty thousand veterans of the Social War, they withdrew,

[1] The distinction drawn by Niese (*Rhein. Mus.* xlii. 574 ff.) between Athenion and Aristion has been generally accepted, but not by Mahaffy (*The Silver Age of the Greek World*, 121), or by Holm (iv. 546), who agree with Reinach (*op. cit.* 139, n. 1) in identifying them. The difficulties which Reinach finds in the report of the ancients have been disposed of in note 1 on p. 444 above. The suggestion of Mahaffy that Athenion is a nickname ironically applied to Aristion by Poseidonius, is too far-fetched to satisfy. Moreover, it is hardly credible that Athenaeus would have finished his extract from Poseidonius with the fiasco of Apellicon, if the story of Athenion had continued to the surrender of the Acropolis and the execution of its defenders by Sulla; for that would have been the very best grist for his mill. (The career of Aristion was too creditable to be cited against the philosophers.) Appian, it is true, contaminates his sources and gives to Aristion the experiences of Athenion as well as his own, but Appian is not of equal value with Poseidonius as an authority. Strabo (ix. 398) knows of more than one tyrant in Athens at this time. Cf. also Plut. *Sulla*, 11; Eutrop. v. 6; Orosius, vi. 2; Hertzberg, i. 347 ff.; Weil, *Ath. Mitt.* vi. 329; Paus. i. 20. 5; iii. 23. 3.

[2] The so-called basilica in Delos, to which *fasciculus* 2 of the *Exploration archéologique de Délos* (Leroux, *La Salle hypostyle*) is devoted, was likewise destroyed, probably at this time (*Acad. inscr. C.R.*, 1907, p. 620). Restorations in the agora of the Italians were made after 86/4 B.C. (See below, x. 452, n. 4.) For a sack of Tenos in 88 B.C. see *Musée belge*, 1906, p. 339 ff.

[3] Perhaps both *BCH.*, 1884, p. 103 = Reinach, *op. cit.* 458, No. 7, in which Mithradates is entitled Dionysus, and the club of the *Eupatoristae* (see above, x. 439, n. 4) belong to 88/6 B.C.

the Pontic general to the Piraeus, Aristion to Athens.[1]
The Long Walls had been abandoned for nearly one
hundred and fifty years, so that the city was isolated
from the harbour and the sea, and, being thus left outside the lines of Archelaus, was obliged to protect itself
as best it could. Famine was the most dreadful enemy,
and in anticipation of its arrival many Athenians
withdrew to their friends and kinsmen in Amisus.[2]

Aristion was made of better stuff than the Peripatetics, if the latter have not been slandered seriously
by Poseidonius; and so long as Archelaus kept the main
army of Sulla employed before the Piraeus, the detachment before Athens could do nothing but blockade the
city. Financial exhaustion came first, and gold coins,
the stormy petrels of Athenian finance, speedily made
their appearance.[3] In their rear came starvation. For
his part, despite decisive superiority in numbers,[4] Sulla
failed to take the Piraeus by storm. Siege machines
were then brought from Thebes, and others constructed
on the spot—the trees in the Academy and Lyceum
being cut down for this purpose. A ramp made of
stones from the ruins of the Long Walls, and of earth
and logs, was begun against the wall of the Piraeus,
which, built with classic solidity, rose, it is said, sixty
feet high of solid masonry.[5] Great towers were moved
forward to the walls and the assault was renewed, but
Dromichaetes arrived from Mithradates with reinforcements for Archelaus, and by a sally the defenders

---

[1] For what follows see Appian, *Mith.* 29 ff. and Plut. *Sulla*, 11 ff.; cf.
especially Kromayer, *Antike Schlachtfelder*, ii. 353 ff. Bruttius Sura came to
the rescue of Thespiae, and this place was the centre of interest throughout
the winter of 88/7 B.C. Appian's report that he retreated to the Piraeus after
an indecisive engagement with Aristion and Archelaus μεχρι και τουδε 'Αρχέλαος
ἐπιπλεύσας κατέσχεν, contains a false designation of the place. The attack on
Macedon and Thrace projected in April–May 88 B.C. was delivered probably
in that same year by Metrophanes, but failed of success. It was Metrophanes,
and not Archelaus, according to Pausanias (iii. 23. 3), who sacked Delos.
The army of Taxiles started in the spring of 86 B.C.
[2] Plut. *Lucullus*, 19, who names Aristion in connexion with the efflux.
Since they went to the capital of Pontus, they can hardly have aimed to escape
the tyranny of the Pontic agents.
[3] Koehler, *Zeitschr. f. Numismatik*, xxi. 15 f.
[4] Kromayer, *op. cit.* ii. 388.
[5] Appian, *Mith.* 30. This report as to their height is rejected by L. Ross,
Arch. Aufs. i. 230 ff., and by Wachsmuth, *Stadt Athen*, ii. 19 ff.

succeeded in burning the towers, tortoises, and battering-rams of Sulla. Emboldened by this success, Archelaus offered battle under the wall, but was defeated, and forced within the ramparts. It was now winter (87/6 B.C.), and Sulla withdrew to Eleusis, but left his cordon round Athens. He had correspondents within the Piraeus, and by means of letters which they inscribed on lead bullets, and hurled by the catapults from the walls, he received information which enabled him to intercept all supplies forwarded from the harbour by Archelaus. Then, upon renewing the siege of the Piraeus in the spring of 86 B.C., he threw a wall of circumvallation round Athens, and through stopping the efflux of citizens to Delphi[1] and elsewhere, increased the famine within the city. Athens was now in sore straits for food, and Archelaus renewed the attempt to break through the Roman lines with provisions for its relief, but the traitors in the Piraeus informed Sulla in time, and the supplies and their escort were captured. In the meanwhile operations had been resumed against the Piraeus. The ramp was completed, the mines of the defenders met by countermines, and the wall battered down in places; but Archelaus constructed a new crescent-shaped wall behind the breach, and upon venturing an assault, the Romans were over-whelmed by missiles from in front and both sides, and were repulsed with loss. Sulla was obliged to desist for the moment. He, accordingly, gave his chief attention to Athens, where the defenders were so weakened by starvation as to be unable to offer a pro-longed resistance. They had come to relish the juice of boiled leather and hides; grain cost one thousand *drachmae* per *medimnum*; herbs were eagerly sought

[1] Paus. i. 20. 7. The friendship of Athens and Delphi from about 140 B.C. onward is worth noting in this connexion. The goodwill of Athens is manifested most clearly in the *Pythais*: the influence of Delphi in its organization and reorganization. Delphi, as has been pointed out, assisted the Attic gild of Dionysiac artists against the general League, and ordered that the Attic tetradrachm be used throughout all Greece. It may be remarked also that Sulla robbed the temples at Delphi. After the Mithradatic catastrophe the repute of the Delphic oracle wanes. Was the Pythia on the losing side at this time, as four hundred years earlier? Or did the sack of the temple by the Celts in 85/4 B.C. (A. J. Reinach, *BCH.*, 1910, p. 320) destroy its prestige?

and devoured, and human flesh was in demand.[1]   There was, moreover, an influential party within the city which advocated surrender,[2] but Aristion met their representatives, when they came to interview him, with a hail of arrows.   He preserved a contemptuous and cynical attitude throughout both toward the Romans and the citizens, and stories are current of how his companions taunted the "mulberry faced dictator" from the walls, and showered vile names upon both Sulla and Metella, Sulla's "consular" wife,[3] while at one and the same time he lived in a constant round of eating and drinking,[4] and with a heartless jest repulsed the priestess of Demeter when she came begging for a half pint of wheat.   Finally, however, he was forced to open negotiations, but it was too late.   Sulla was inexorable.   He met the enumeration of the past services of Athens by the remark that he had not come to learn ancient history, but to punish rebels, and the blockade was continued.

The end came through a surprise.[5]   Sulla found the wall lying between the Piraeic and the Sacred gate unguarded, and scaled it by night.   Marcus Ateius was the first to reach the top.   He broke his sword over the helmet of the sentinel, but maintained his place till joined by others.   The wall was then torn down, and on the Calends of March 86 B.C. the Roman army entered the city.   A merciless slaughter followed; for Sulla ordered a general massacre of the inhabitants, and the soldiers, rushing through the narrow streets with drawn swords, slew without regard to age or sex.   The noblest did not await their fate, but, unable through the weakness of starvation to resist, took their own lives. The whole inner Cerameicus was heaped with dead.   At daybreak Sulla stopped the carnage, moved by the

[1] Plut. *Sulla*, 13 ff.

[2] The sacred lamp of Athena is said to have gone out through lack of oil; Plut. *Numa*, 9.

[3] She had fled from the Marians to join her husband before Athens; cf. Münzer, P.-W. iii. 1235; Fröhlich, *ibid.* iv. 1531.

[4] Suspiciously in keeping with the Epicurean character given to him by Appian.   Plutarch has the same report.

[5] Plut. *Sulla*, 14; Appian, *Mith.* 38.

entreaties of Medeius, Calliphon, and other exiles, and
also by the intercession of the Senators in his staff.   A
remnant of the Athenians was preserved, but it lost all
political privileges,[1] and for more than a decade [2] the
Athenians who had seceded to Mithradates were without the franchise in their own city.   The slaves were at
once sold, and the city was thoroughly pillaged, but on
Sulla's orders the houses, into which the inhabitants had
probably shut themselves, were not fired.[3]

Aristion and a small following had withdrawn to the
Acropolis when the Romans poured into the city, but
before doing so, they set fire to the Odeum, lest Sulla
should find in it timber ready at hand for use in
assaulting the citadel.[4]   Fortunately, Sulla did not
train his battering-rams against the Propylaea.   He
simply stationed guards, under the command of a certain
Curio, round about the Acropolis, and left famine to do
the rest.[5]   Now he hurled his storming parties once
more against the Piraeus, in what his adversary characterized as a frenzied and senseless effort, but, though
it should cost him half his army, Sulla must take the
place at once ; for the main army of Mithradates was
approaching by the land route through Thrace and
Macedon.[6]   The outer walls were, accordingly, carried
by sheer force, but Archelaus withdrew to Munychia,
which Sulla could not take.   This failure, however, had
no serious consequences, for shortly afterwards Archelaus
abandoned this post, and went to Thermopylae to take
command of the main army, which, after reducing Thrace
and Macedon (87/6 B.C.), was now on the point of entering Greece.   Thus the whole of the Piraeus became
again Athenian.   The Acropolis held out till Sulla's
victory at Chaeronea, but thereupon the besieged, half
dead through lack of food and water—for Curio had
seized the Clepsydra—and deprived of all prospect of
relief, surrendered unconditionally.[7]   Aristion with his

---

[1] Appian, *Mith.* 38.
[2] *Klio*, 1909, p. 327.   Longer still if Kolbe (*Die attischen Archonten*, 148 ff.)
is right in attributing the democratic restoration to Julius Caesar.
[3] Appian, *Mith.* 38.   [4] *Ibid.*
[5] Plut. *Sulla*, 14 f.   [6] Kromayer, *op. cit.* ii. 356.
[7] Paus. i. 20. 6 ; cf. Kromayer, *loc. cit.*

bodyguard and all those who had held offices under the
tyranny Sulla executed : the rest he pardoned. Then,
when his second victory at Orchomenus (86/5 B.C.) had
freed Europe of the invaders, the war was carried into
Asia, and Roman influence became at once preponderant
in the Aegean. Sulla was, however, far too busy to
take time for settling the status of the islanders. The
survivors on Delos were consequently left to shift for
themselves, and it is not surprising that they declined
to sail in the same boat with the disloyal Athenians.
Now that no magistrates came from the metropolis,
the *colleges*, that is to say, the *masters*, took the
initiative in managing the public business [1] of the
Delii,[2] and for a year and a half (85 to *ca.* July
84 B.C.) the island was free and autonomous.[3] There
was left on it only a handful of its earlier population : enough Italians to retain the organization under
masters, and to restore their agora ; [4] some Athenians

---

[1] *CIL.* iii. Suppl. 7235 "L. Cornelius L. f. Sulla pro cos. de pequnia quam conlegia incommune conlatam."

[2] *BCH.*, 1884, p. 133. This document is different from other Delian dedications in that it cites not the office held at the moment, but the *cursus honorum*
of the subject—M. Antonius, the orator. That is to say, it is his *elogium* set
up after his death. Since this occurred in 87 B.C., *BCH.*, 1884, p. 133 belongs
after that time. Hence, as is in itself obvious, the *Delii* belong after the
restoration of Roman influence in the Aegean, not in 88/7 B.C. Cf. below, n. 4.

[3] In the archonship of Apollodorus (*ca.* 80 B.C.) the organization of the island
was the same as that prior to 88 B.C. (*BCH.*, 1879, pp. 151 and 157 ; Nicanor
was *epimeletes* in Apollodorus's archonship, *BCH.*, 1879, p. 376). So too in
78 B.C. (*BCH.*, 1879, p. 147 : monument of Lucullus) the *Delii* have already disappeared. They were doubtless set aside by Sulla when he restored the island
to Athens in 84 B.C. In *BCH.*, 1883, p. 470, what is read, 'Ο δῆμος ὁ Δ[ηλίων]
should perhaps be changed to 'Ο δῆμος ὁ 'Α[θηναίων], which may easily have
been repeated. On the other hand, a reference to the sack of Delos occurs in
IG. ix. 1. 877–879—a grave-inscription, which, seeing that the dead man claims
Delos, not Athens, as his native land, may possibly be dated in 86/4 B.C.
BCH., 1882, p. 325, No. 18, where a Δήλιος is mentioned, certainly belongs to
this epoch ; cf. Roussel, *BCH.*, 1908, p. 397, n. 3.

[4] *Hermaistae, Poseidoniastae, Apolloniastae* in 78 B.C. (*BCH.*, 1884, p. 144 :
magistri) and in 74 B.C. (*BCH.*, 1884, p. 146). The subscription list for the
restoration is now extant (*BCH.*, 1907, p. 461, No. 68). Since two Δήλιοι appear
among the contributors, the moneys were perhaps collected during the period of
independence ; or the *Delii* may be the descendants of those expelled by Rome
and Athens in 166 B.C. ; or those born on the island since 166 B.C. who lacked
citizenship in any other state. Among the contributors are several Athenians
from the capital, among them a son of Sarapion and a certain Nicanor. This
man was *epimeletes*, but apparently not at the time of the subscription, since in
that case his title would have been mentioned. During the *epimeleia* of
Callimachus of Leuconoë the work of restoration was still in progress (*BCH.*,
1882, p. 346, No. 66). We are thus led to date him in 84/3 B.C. Nicanor
belongs in one of the following years. Part of the work of restoration was to

and other Greeks, but so few worshippers of Aphrodite
Hagne and Serapis that one shrine alone was reopened
and repaired,[1] and one priest alone attended henceforth
to the cultus of the two deities ; some slaves, doubtless,
but too few adorers of the Lares to equip anew the
compitum, and to establish once more the *competaliastae*.[2]
The rustic dances ceased, and most of the *therapeutae*
slunk away to more hopeful centres.

The remnant was ardently pro-Sullan, and it is
likely that Sulla visited Delos while on his way to the
Piraeus in the summer of 84 B.C.   At any rate, he put
his own signature and that of Q. Pompeius Rufus, his
luckless colleague in the consulship in 88 B.C., upon two
colossal monuments erected at this time ;[3] and used
money collected by the gilds on Delos to help in the
work of restoration.[4]   He also interested himself in
relieving the distress of the children of the slain traders,[5]
and was, doubtless, instrumental in having memorials
erected to those who had fallen in the struggle against
the Athenians and the Cappadocians,[6] and to M. Antonius,

---

set up again various statues by Agasias, the son of Menophilus of Ephesus, and
the artist employed in this work was Aristandrus, son of Scopas of Paros
(Loewy, 287-288 ; *BCH.*, 1907, p. 458, No. 58 ; *BCH.*, 1884, p. 143 ; Rayet,
Mon. de l'art ant. ii. Nos. 64 and 65, p. 10.   For the other restorations see
BCH., 1881, p. 462 ; 1884, pp. 143, 182 ; 1887, p. 270 ; 1889, p. 123 ; *Musée belge*,
1906, p. 340 ; *CIL.* iii. Suppl. 7227 and 7233).   It should perhaps be mentioned
here that in and after 85 B.C. was not the only time at which restorations
were made in Delos ; cf. *BCH.*, 1882, p. 496, No. 13 ; 1905, p. 223, No. 81 ; and
Acad. inscr. C.R., 1909, p. 416.

   [1] Roussel, *BCH.*, 1908, p. 385 ; cf. p. 425, No. 29, and *BCH.*, 1882, p. 346,
No. 66 ; *Klio*, 1909, p. 333 ff.   [See now also *Acad. inscr. C.R.*, 1910, p.
301, n. 1, and *Jour. des savants*, 1910, p. 569.   The precincts in the Inopus
canyon, as well as the *gymnasium*, were left outside the wall built round Delos
sixteen years later.]

   [2] *BCH.*, 1899, p. 73.

   [3] *CIL.* iii. Suppl. 7234 and 7238.   A plinth from the basis of a statue by
Agasias, son of Menophilus of Ephesus, was re-used in the monument of Q. Pompeius Rufus (Loewy, No. 289).   Since Pompeius was slain in 88 B.C., this
monument, though apparently dedicated by him in person, was obviously not
set up till after his death.   The lettering, moreover, is similar to that of the
Sulla monument (cf. *CIL.* iii. Suppl. 7238, note).   A new Delian monument to
Sulla is now published in *BCH.*, 1910, p. 399 f.

   [4] *CIL.* iii. Suppl. 7235.

   [5] *BCH.*, 1892, p. 158 = 1893, p. 202 :

   θν[άσκε]ιν εὐχέσθω τις ἀ[π]έχθεος ἄνδιχα μοίρας,
   τερπόμενος τέκνων ἐλπίδι γηροκόμῳ
   ἢ προλιπεῖν μὴ παῖδ[α]ς ἐν ὀρφανίησιν ἐρήμο[υς],
   ἢ Σύλλου θνάσκων ἀνθυπάτοιο τ[υχεῖ]ν.

   [6] See above, x. 446, n. 1 ; 445, n. 1.

the orator and patron of Delos, who had been slain by the Marians in 87 B.C.[1] None the less, he restored the island together with Lemnos, Imbros, and Scyros to Athens,[2] and for forty years after 84 B.C. affairs on Delos were managed by Athenian magistrates and a heterogeneous assemblage as between *ca.* 130 and 88 B.C.[3] During this interval pirates in the service of Mithradates sacked the defenceless island most unmercifully (69 B.C.), thus undoing the work of recuperation already completed and discouraging further effort. But, protected by a wall built for them in this year by C. Triarius round the district between the water-front and a line drawn north and south from the Roman *statio* to the theatre, and given immunity from tribute by a legislative act of the year 65 B.C.,[4] the foreign traders held out till Julius Caesar administered to their settlement the *coup de grâce* by planting a colony of Romans on the old site of Corinth. To this point the local trade of the eastern Mediterranean at once flowed, and Delos was abandoned even more rapidly than it was occupied. There was, apparently, no need for two such centres. Accordingly, at about that time the heterogeneous assemblage disappeared and Athens resumed complete control of the island.[5]

A provisional government of the business men had been re-established in[6] Athens before the surrender of Aristion, but despite its friendliness to himself Sulla

---

[1] See above, x. 452, n. 2.

[2] For Lemnos see *IG.* ii. 488, 489; xii. 8. 26. For Scyros see Graindor, *Hist. de l'île de Skyros*, 77; the cession of Sciathos, Icos, and Peparathos to Athens by Antony (Appian, *Civil War*, v. 7; cf. Wachsmuth, *Stadt Athen*, i. 664; *BCH.*, 1877, p. 82) presupposes that it possessed Scyros earlier. For Imbros see *IG.* xii. 8. 57, 64; *BCH.*, 1889, p. 431.

[3] *Klio*, 1907, p. 240. The restoration of the title in *BCH.*, 1908, p. 418, No. 10, is manifestly wrong.

[4] *Jour. des savants*, 1910, p. 569.

[5] von Schoeffer, P.-W. iv. 2499; *Klio*, 1907, p. 240, n. 3.

[6] The restoration took place in 87/6 B.C., *i.e.* after the 1st of March 86 B.C. and before the first of Hecatombaeon of the same year. This we know because of the appointment of an eponymous archon—Philanthes, the *hierophant* (?) (Sundwall, *Klio*, 1909, p. 365)—for the remnant of the year (*IG.* iii. 1014; cf. *Priests of Asklepios*, 137, 144 f.), and because of the reintroduction of the official order of the tribes of the priests of Asclepius, which took place in 87/6 B.C. To this provisional government are to be attributed two eccentric series of coins (Sundwall, *Untersuch.* 112). Significantly the inscription AΘE is omitted.

was in too urgent need of money to withhold his hand from the deposits of gold and silver found on the Acropolis. Forty pounds of gold and six hundred pounds of silver are said [1] to have been appropriated by him for his own uses. He can hardly have found time in the year 86 B.C. for impressing his ideas upon Athenian institutions, but on his return from Asia two years later he spent several months in Athens, and on this occasion, using a Roman victor's prerogatives, he took from the unfinished Olympieum columns [2] and from the stoa of Zeus Eleutherius and other public buildings of Athens statues and paintings to adorn his triumph and his city. One shipload of his spoils the sea engulfed off Cape Malea. The library of Apellicon of Teus, into which had come by a series of curious accidents the works of Aristotle and Theophrastus, Sulla likewise took from Athens.[3] In regard to the constitution of the city he seems then to have confirmed the arrangements already made, which amounted in substance to a restoration of the constitution of 103/2 B.C.,[4] though some new and important restrictions were put upon the populace, in that matters which prior to 91/0 B.C. had been reserved for the sovereign assembly were now put within the competence of the senate of six hundred; while others, such as the government of the dependencies, were transferred to the jurisdiction of the Areopagus.[5] There was thus a strengthening of senatorial at the expense of popular authority. It seems likely that the Areopagus was fostered by the Romans in the belief that it was the Athenian equivalent of their own council; but its supervision of the administration was not re-established.[6] It passed not a *psephisma*, like the senate of six hundred, but drafted a memorandum, which, however, seems to have been as imperative as the decree of the Roman senate. The chief executive power of Athens was vested from this time forward in the herald of the

---

[1] By Appian, *Mith.* 39.   [2] Pliny, *Nat. Hist.* xxxvi. 6. 45.
[3] Luc. *Zeuxis*, 3; Plut. *Sulla*, 26; Paus. x. 21. 6.
[4] Strabo, ix. 20. 398; Appian, *Mith.* 39.
[5] *IG*. xii. 8. 26; cf. *Klio*, 1909, p. 323 ff.; Kolbe, *Die attischen Archonten*, 148 ff.
[6] The third mint officials do not appear after 89/8 B.C.

Areopagus and the hoplite-general — the Athenian consuls, perhaps. The second of the two was particularly prominent, and overshadowed completely his colleagues and the other magistrates. The college of the nine archons was left as it was before 103/2 B.C. ; for no change was there possible without affecting the Areopagus. Nor did it conform with Sulla's political thinking to admit re-election to this or to the other purely civil offices; hence the old prohibition against the repeated tenure of the archonships, which had been repealed in 103/2 B.C.—inadvisably, as the events of 91/0-89/8 B.C. seemed to prove—was now re-enacted. These offices were chiefly valuable for what followed their tenure — admission to the Areopagus. Real power, doubtless, came still with election to the governorships of the dependencies, which seem to have been open in fact, if not in theory, to Areopagites alone, just as in Rome similar trusts were reserved to Senators.[1] The disfranchisement of the adherents of Mithradates reserved the offices for the friends of Rome, so that no further limitation of citizenship was necessary. The lot was still employed for the designation of certain magistrates, though hardly for the designation of those with political powers. It was still a useful means of reaching a decision, and its corollary, the mechanical rotation of office, was continued in at least various priesthoods. How justice was administered we do not know, but we may affirm that the jury courts ceased to be important in a political sense.[2] The division of the people into the twelve tribes was maintained, as was many another institution of old Athens; but the heart was taken out of the Athenian democracy by the disfranchisement of the rebels, as it was out of Athenian industry and commerce by the confiscation of the slaves.[3] The new

---

[1] Sundwall, *Untersuch.*, 71.

[2] For the status of Athens after 84 B.C. see *Klio*, 1909, p. 323 ff.

[3] Money was coined with some regularity after 86 B.C., but not in very large quantities (Sundwall, *Untersuch.*, 106). The poverty and demoralization of the city during the next few decades are manifest both from its dealings with Atticus (*Nepos*, 2) and from the fact that the cemetery by the Eridanus, which had not been used since *ca.* 200 B.C., was then converted into a stone quarry (Brueckner, *op. cit.* 26 f.). See in this connexion also *Klio*, 1909, p. 326.

hope of the city was gone. In less than two years the progress of a century and a half had been undone. During this period Athens had been brought—mainly because of Delos—into sympathy with the Hellenistic spirit, but henceforth she lived apart, a recluse in a troubled world. She had welcomed Cybele, Isis, and Atargatis, but to both Mithras and Christ she subsequently denied admittance.[1] From the sea the new life had come, but her harbour was now little more than a heap of smouldering ruins. The great walls had been torn down and the private houses burned. There remained the half-demolished docks, ship-houses, and bazaar, the temple of Aphrodite Pandemus—the patron saint of Sulla—and, prominent in the midst of the desolation, the temple of Zeus Soter and Athena Soteira. As time went by a little settlement gathered round the ruins, but the glory of the Piraeus was gone beyond recall.[2]

In 88 B.C. the Athenian democrats had leaned upon a broken reed, but their inclination had been in the right direction. A people which refused to jeopardize their material prosperity in an effort to rid the world of the pascha rule of the proconsuls and the shameless avarice of the Roman corporations, would not have deserved much sympathy.[3] Nor was oppression the only provocation of the Athenians. Their place in Delos had been usurped by the Italians, and into the house of Athena, and even into the shrine of the *Demos* and *Graces, Roma* had come as mistress, bringing with her new ways and new orders, and yielding her favours to a few renegades only. While seeking to cast out the foreign harlot and her favourites, the Cecropidae, as Poseidonius ironically calls them, had never been wont to consider nicely the question of power. And that was their misfortune. The city-state was a hapless survival of a greater but a smaller world. It was the

---

[1] Harnack, *The Expansion of Christianity*, ii. 373 ; Cumont, *The Mysteries of Mithra*, 79.

[2] Strabo, ix. 1. 15. 395 ; cf. Weller, *Class. Phil.* i. 351. Many restorations were apparently made between the time of Strabo and Pausanias.

[3] Beloch, *Hist. Zeitschr.*, 1900 (84), p. 19 : "Der Heldenkampf Athens blieb vergeblich ; aber er wirft wie ein blutiges Abendroth einen verklärenden Schimmer auf den Untergang der Nation."

plaything of the big, strong, modern nations, and it
would have been as well for Athens, perhaps, had her
proud spirit been broken, her walls cast down, and her
identity lost in a petty municipality when Alexander
destroyed Thebes. Still, who that knows the subsequent history of Boeotia—the economic stagnation, the
decrease of population, the demoralization of private
life, the general lawlessness and spasmodic outbursts
of ruffianism characteristic of that rich country—will
venture to affirm that the Thebans were better off than
the Athenians. However that may be, after 86 B.C.
resignation was the only policy for the Athenians;
meekness their cardinal virtue. The present was a
mean time. It produced a race of degenerate men;
the Romans thought so, and the fortune of war had
proved them right. But the past was undeniably great,
and it might revenge the present. From it had sprung
the ideas which seemed destined to rule eternally the
world of art and letters ;[1] and where should men learn
of them, if not in the grove where Plato had taught, in
the city where stood the matchless Parthenon ? Athens
had no future except as the seat of a great university,[2]
and this was but a modest one. High culture is a
delicate plant. It thrives only in the keen air of a free
country. In a hot-house it makes but a sickly growth.
After 86 B.C. the Athenian schools sent forth into the
world many Romans and Greeks who were finer and
nobler men for their influence.[3] Like Matthew Arnold's
Oxford, they manifested their "sentiment for beauty
and sweetness," and their "sentiment against hideous-

[1] Renan, *St. Paul*, 176, 187.

[2] "Athenis iam diu doctrina ipsorum Atheniensium interiit, domicilium
tantum in illa urbe remanet studiorum, quibus vacant cives, peregrini fruuntur,
capti quodam modo nomine urbis et auctoritate. tamen eruditissimos homines
Asiaticos quivis Atheniensis indoctus non verbis sed sono vocis, nec tam bene
quam suaviter loquendo facile superabit" (Cic. *De orat.* 3. 43 ; cf. Wilamowitz, *Hermes*, 1900, p. 1, n. 2).

[3] For example, the two sons of Ariobarzanes of Cappadocia, ephebes in the
archonship of Apollodorus (*ca.* 80 B.C.), for whose fidelity see Tyrrell and Purser,
Correspondence of Cicero, III. xxiii. f. Athens was the *alma mater* of Plutarch,
and it was an Athenian professor who, when some enterprising men sought to
introduce the gladiatorial games into Athens, bade them first cast down the
altar of Pity (Luc. *Demonax*, 57 ; cf. Dill, *Roman Society from Nero to
Marcus Aurelius*, 366).

ness and rawness," by their "attachment to so many beaten causes," and their "opposition to so many triumphant movements"; but, and we drop the parallel at this point, they gave to men few new and helpful ideas.

APPENDIX I

SOURCES AND GENERAL BIBLIOGRAPHY

THE extant literary sources for the period with which this history of Athens deals are at the same time exasperating and reassuring: exasperating because of their scrappy character; reassuring because of their general reliability. They carry us back to an extensive, detailed, and well-informed historical and biographical literature, in part contemporary to the events or persons described, in part based upon contemporary documents. The loss of this literature is irremediable.

As it is, Diodorus the Sicilian is our best guide for the period from 323 to 302 B.C. He deals, of course, with history in general, and refers only here and there to events in Athens. His chief ultimate authority, however, was well acquainted with Athenian affairs, and must have consulted original documents, such as the edict of Arrhidaeus and the Athenian decrees. He was undoubtedly Hieronymus of Cardia, who wrote a history of his own times at about 270-60 B.C., which Diodorus apparently found worked up with some other materials in a second century B.C. abridgement. The *Lives* of Phocion, Demosthenes, Eumenes, and Demetrius by Plutarch are valuable for particular portions of this same period, but in their case the line of transmission was longer and more broken. It had, moreover, its point of departure in a more miscellaneous body of materials—such as the published speeches, the comedies, the contemporary biographies and memoirs, and the more sensational histories. Plutarch's task was moral portraiture, or, to be more precise, comparative moral portraiture; hence, in so far as he had to do with incidents at all, it was with such as exhibited the character of each successive hero, or with such as by accident or constraint helped to establish the parallelism sought by Plutarch in the careers of each successive pair. He is concerned only secondarily with the public effect of a man and his work. The Hellenistic biography in general, or perhaps we should say, that into which the Hellenistic biography degenerated, ignored the historical

461

background too much to be of structural value to us in our work. Still, Plutarch preserves many details that would otherwise have been lost. What we have chiefly to be on our guard against is misunderstandings and miscollocations of the original reports.

The Hellenistic age was one in which men of political prominence felt called upon to justify their careers or to register their impressions of contemporary events; nor did Athenians resist this tendency. Thus Demetrius of Phalerum published in Egypt, along with various antiquarian and legal as well as philosophic works, an apology of his *decaëtia* of rule in Athens which has left a marked imprint upon our tradition. Thus Demochares of Leuconoe, his opponent, justified democracy in a lively history of his own times; and Philochorus of Anaphlystus stamped his quaint personality upon his *Atthis*, or chronicle of Athens, reaching from the earliest times to 262/1 B.C.[1] If these three works were extant we could not wish for more in regard to this period, unless it be the general history of Diyllus, son of the antiquarian Phanodemus of Thymaetadae, which extended, with constant reference to Athens, from the Sacred War to the death of Philip IV. in 297/6 B.C. The fact of the continued existence and use of these books in later antiquity compels us to give a fair hearing and general credence to much that would be otherwise suspicious.

The New Comedy was a mine of information of all kinds to the ancient students of the social life of early Hellenistic Athens, and to us also the quotations they made from it (Koch, *Frg. Com. Graec.*) have all along had some value; but seeing that they were taken from imaginative literature in the first instance, lacked a context, and were seldom serviceable to us for the point for which they were used in antiquity, their value has been always problematical. Nor was the case otherwise with the adaptations of these plays made by Plautus and Terence for the Latin stage, the difficulty there being to decide what belonged to Athens and what to Rome. Material assistance for the use of both these sources, as well as important new data, has now been obtained through the recent discovery in Egypt of considerable portions of five of Menander's comedies (*Georgus, Epitrepontes, Periceiromene, Heros, Samia*; cf. *Menandrea*, A. Koerte: Teubner, 1910). Every custom vindicated in them to Athens may now be used even when described with more detail in the Latin adaptations; while the interpretation of some at least of the old fragments is no longer disputable. The

---

[1] Whether Istros, the pupil of Callimachus, for whom see Busolt, *Griech. Gesch.* ii.[2] 11 and the literature there cited, brought his *Corpus Atthidum* down to his own time or not is uncertain.

point of departure, however, for the proper use of historical materials found in the New Comedy must always be taken from passages of the new plays, or of other plays which we may expect to turn up in the course of subsequent excavations. From the *Characters* of Theophrastus we may also obtain information as to the composition of Athenian society under Demetrius of Phalerum.

In the *Lives* already mentioned Plutarch carries us to about 280 B.C., and he becomes of some value again in his *Lives* of Aratus and of Agis and Cleomenes at about 250 B.C., but with still less direct reference to Athens. For the interval between 280 and 250 B.C. we are singularly devoid of literary help. Plutarch's *Life* of Pyrrhus, from which a stray item or two may be culled prior to 273 B.C., ceases at that point. The only continuous narrative, moreover, of general history for this period is the miserable epitome of Pompeius Trogus's *Universal History* made by Justin at about the time of Hadrian. The incompetence of the abbreviator is best gauged by a comparison of his work with the *Contents* (*Prologi*) of Trogus's own composition, which have been preserved to us through being incorporated in Justin's abridgement. This double narrative lacks precise chronological definitions, and since various contemporaneous series of events were arranged by Trogus one after the other, it can be used to determine only the order of events within each series, and not to fix the order of the series themselves except in a very general way. The sources of Trogus are uncertain. Trogus-Justin mentions Athens only incidentally both during the period 280-250 B.C. and during those which precede and follow.

Into the wealth of materials which once existed for the history of Athens during the third century B.C. the *Lives of the Philosophers* by Diogenes Laertius give us a tantalizing glimpse ; and now and then an anecdote or incident which they contain serves to illumine the social or political background. Similar in their revelation and serviceability for the entire period covered in this book are the biographical data preserved by Philodemus in regard to the Attic school-heads. These are now accessible in Usener's *Epicurea*, von Arnim's *Frg. Stoic. vet.*, Crönert's unhappy *Kolotes und Menedemos*, Mekler's *Phil. Acad. Index Hercul.*, and Jacoby's *Apollodors Chronik*. From this source much may still be drawn. For an orientation on the *Quellenforschung* of Diogenes and Philodemus see A. Koerte, *Gött. gel. Anz.*, 1907, p. 257.

The *Strategemata* of Polyaenus (and Frontinus) contain some instances taken from detailed and generally reliable narratives of the military history of the Hellenistic age ; but

they give only the tactical movements, rarely the strategic, and
never the political setting or occasion. For their value see
Melber, "Über die Quellen und den Wert der Strategemensamm-
lung Polyaens," *Neue Jahrb.*, Suppl. xiv. (1885), p. 599 ff., 657,
660. Pausanias, on the other hand, drew his few reports on
Athenian history, directly or indirectly, from sources of diverse
value. At times, as in the case of the careers of Olympiodorus
and Cephisodorus, his ultimate source was a public decree; and
in other cases, as in that of the tyranny of Lachares, the Gallic
invasion, the Chremonidean War, and the Oropian incident, his
authorities transmitted to him simply the orthodox Athenian
version of what happened. Pausanias himself shows little or no
acquaintance with the general course of events in Athens in
the Hellenistic period. His reports, accordingly, must be used
with caution.

For us Pausanias stands at the end of a considerable literature, that of the *periegetae* or *cicerone,* which the enthusiasm for
Athens in the Hellenistic, and for old Greece in the Roman,
world called into being (cf. Gurlitt, *Über Pausanias*, 1 ff.;
Frazer, *Pausanias*, i. p. lxxxiii. ff.). At its beginning, if priority
does not belong to the horribly mutilated *Attische Periegese von
Hawara* which U. Wilcken has recently republished in Robert's
Genethliakon, 189-225, stands Diodorus, seemingly an Athenian,
who wrote a description of the monuments and *demes* of Attica
at an unknown date, but after Alexander and certainly before 224
B.C. (P.-W. v. 662); and in its middle stand Heliodorus the
Athenian (cf. Keil, *Hermes*, 1895, 199 ff.) and Polemon of
Ilium, both contemporaries of Antiochus Epiphanes. The
former composed a work in fifteen books on the Acropolis, and
the latter, who anticipates the Romans in an archaising interest
in the whole of Greece, wrote a series of works on its monuments and curiosities, notably one each on the Acropolis, the
eponymous heroes of the Attic *demes* and *phylae,* and the Sacred
Way. The purpose of the *periegetae* was to explain the classic
monuments and the antiquities of Athens, and, subsequently,
of Hellas, to intelligent or curious tourists. This gives us the
reason why they help so little for the history of Hellenistic
Athens.

Most valuable and instructive is the brief but comprehensive survey of the attractions of Athens and the character
of its people made by Heracleides the Critic at about 205 B.C.
in his *Notes on Greek Cities.* That he was the author was
established by Carl Müller (*FHG.* ii. 232) through discovering
in the *Notes* a passage elsewhere (Apollonius, *Hist. mirab.* 19)
attributed to him. Hence also we know the title of the book.
The time is, however, disputed. Thus Wachsmuth (*Die Stadt*

Athen, i. 44) assigned it to *post* 175 B.C., because he thought the Olympieum, to which the *Notes* refer, to be the new edifice of Cossutius. And for the same reason Frazer, *Pausanias,* i. p. xliii, dates it between 164 and 86 B.C. Susemihl, following Unger (*Rhein. Mus.,* 1883, pp. 481 ff.), first assigned it to 192 B.C. (*Gesch. d. griech. Lit. d. Alexandriner Zeit,* ii. 1 ff.), but later, because of the arguments of Fabricius (*Bonner Stud. R. Kekulé gewidmet,* 58 ff.), he located it at *ca.* 250 B.C. (*ibid.* ii. 683). So Judeich (*Topographie d. Stadt Athen,* 10); and this is perhaps the date now generally accepted.

That it was written before 200 B.C. seems clearly established by Fabricius, and his reasons need not be repeated here; but his arguments for an earlier date than 229 B.C. are not equally convincing. That the Ptolemaeum is not mentioned along with Academia, Lyceum, and Cynosarges, falls far short of proving that it had not yet been built (see above, vi. 239, n. 4). Nor is it possible to construe the δουλεία of the following passage, ἀλλ' ἡ τῶν ξένων ἑκάστοις (Κ. ἐν ἀστοῖς) συνοικειουμένη ταῖς προθυμίαις εὐάρμοστος διατριβή, περισπῶσα τὴν διάνοιαν ἐπὶ τὸ ἀρέσκον, λήθην τῆς δουλείας ἐργάζεται, into a reference to Macedonian control of Athens; for how could ἡ τῶν ξένων . . . διατριβή bring forgetfulness of their δουλεία to Athenian citizens? The reference to ἐφόδια in what follows shows to whom the λιμός is conceived as present: it is an evil to the strangers; and it is also their condition in Athens which is defined as servitude—a servitude which their intimacy with one another in fraternal associations (*thiasi* ?) —or, if we accept Kaibel's conjecture, ἐν ἀστοῖς, their social intimacy with citizens—rendered tolerable. Elsewhere in the *Notes,* Heracleides is thinking not simply of travellers, but also of foreign residents—permanent tourists and others. Tanagra, he reports, was the safest place in Boeotia for strangers to live in; Thebes is recommended for summer, but not for winter. Athens gave an inferior legal status (δουλεία is a hard word, but see *Amer. Hist. Rev.,* 1910, 9), as did other old Greek cities, in marked contrast to the liberality in this particular of the new foundations in the Hellenistic kingdoms; still, in Athens strangers of all varieties of interests were so numerous that they had pleasant social groups of their own; or, if one prefers to accept Kaibel's conjecture, in Athens strangers lived on terms of social equality with citizens whose interests they shared. Plainly no chronological possibilities are involved in this reference.

Only one period prior to 229 B.C. will satisfy the general conditions, viz. 259/8-252 B.C. At that time Athens had peace and prosperity; Chalcis was a flourishing naval centre and a resort for philosophers, and there was seemingly no war in

Attica, Boeotia, or Thessaly. After 252 B.C. this condition did not recur till *ca.* 205 B.C. It is between these two dates that we have to decide.

Apart from the fact that in 259/8-252 B.C. Attica can hardly have recovered from the many years of war which preceded, three considerations favour 205 B.C. (1) At the time of the composition of the *Notes* two men named Poseidippus were of established international reputation ; for the one referred to in the *Notes* (i. 11, ii. 7) is mentioned each time as ὁ τῶν κωμῳδιῶν ποιητής, obviously to distinguish him from his contemporary, Poseidippus the epigrammatist, for whom see Susemihl, ii. 530 f. Lysippus, Xenon, Sophocles, Laon, Pherecrates, Philiscus, Euripides—the other authors named in the *Notes*—are named only, while Homer is simply ὁ ποιητής. Now, Poseidippus the comedian gave his first play in 290-88 B.C., and in 259/8-252 B.C. he may have been still alive. The dates of his namesake are uncertain. This *factum* makes 255 B.C. possible, but 205 B.C. better. (2) When the *Notes* were written Oropus was οἰκεῖα Θηβῶν. In 205 B.C. she was a member along with Thebes of the Boeotian League. We know nothing of either Oropus or Boeotia in 259/8-252 B.C., but this could probably have been said of Oropus at any time after 313 B.C. Still, the inns on the road from Oropus into Attica suggest a somewhat prolonged period of friendly intercourse such as is unthinkable for any stretch of time prior to 252 B.C., but which is demonstrable for 229-205 B.C. ; and the leaning of Oropus towards Athens commented on in the *Notes* is illustrated by the score of grants of *proxenia* known to have been made by Oropus in favour of Athenians at this time (see above, vi. 247, n. 2). This is, we believe, a mark of the ending of a considerable period of estrangement. Is it thinkable that Oropus and Plataea were anxious to throw in their lot with Athens between 259/8 and 252 B.C. ? (3) When the *Notes* were written suits had been dragging along in Thebes for thirty years—so great was the demoralization of justice in that country. Now, that is precisely the condition which Polybius (xx. 4-6, xxii. 4) affirms to have existed in Boeotia between 215 and 190 B.C., and in the last half of the third century B.C. generally. This *datum* is decisive for 205 B.C., since Polybius would have written very differently had thirty years of judicial disorder and intimidation preceded 250 B.C. also ; for he admits that the Boeotian claim of good government was well grounded prior to the generalship of Abaeocritus, and clearly dates the cessation of law and order there after his defeat and the establishment of the Aetolian suzerainty in 245 B.C. (Polyb. xx. 4).

We have thus confirmed the *dictum* of Wilamowitz (*Hermes,*

1886, 103, n. 1; cf. Antigonus, 165) that the *Notes* belong to the last quarter of the third century B.C. They probably presuppose the general peace of 206-203 B.C. The identification of the writer with Heracleides the Critic, that is to say, of the school of Pergamum, which the date of Fabricius made impossible, is thus beyond any reasonable doubt correct (Susemihl, ii. 1. ff.).

In the last third of the third century B.C. we reach the period which is dominated by Polybius; and it is either from him directly or from him through Livy that we learn of the part played by Athens in the Macedonian and Roman wars. Polybius formed his judgment of Attic policy and character at a time when Achaea, his native state, was hostile to Athens; and, moreover, he drew upon the *Memoirs* of Aratus, who had worked ardently but fruitlessly to persuade or constrain Athens to throw in her lot with the Achaean League, and who must, accordingly, have condemned the Athenians for preferring first to remain neutral and subsequently to rely upon Egypt rather than by joining him to fight it out for the independence of Greece. Consequently we are not surprised that Polybius misrepresented or belittled much that Athens did at this time.

The continuator of Polybius's *Histories* was Poseidonius. Poseidonius was likewise anti-Athenian; at least, as a pro-Roman (see Ed. Meyer, *Kleine Schriften*, 390 ff.), Stoic, and aristocrat, he had no sympathy with the anti-Roman, democratic movement turned by Peripatetic and Epicurean rivals to the service of Mithradates the Great; and for this reason the only extant fragment of Poseidonius which relates to our theme—that dealing with Athenion—is manifestly partisan and unfair. Poseidonius is also the ultimate source of our knowledge of the slave revolts of the last third of the second century B.C.

For the war in Greece between the generals of Mithradates and Sulla our record goes back to Sulla's *Memoirs*, which were used both by Plutarch, that is to say, his sources, in his *Life* of Sulla, and by Appian in his *Mithradatica*, but by neither with any real comprehension of the military movements involved. Still, we have in the two works, which supplement one another, a very complete picture of the siege and fall of the Piraeus and Athens. Remarks in Cicero's speeches and letters serve to add a detail or two.

.   .   .   .

Our most important sources have still to be considered—the inscriptions. Of them the most peculiar is the *Parian Chronicle*. This contained a record of literary and political events, dated in the successive years of the Athenian archons and by the time which elapsed between their happening and 264/3 B.C.—the point at which the *Chronicle* was compiled. Unfortunately, the items for the years between 301 and 264/3 B.C. are lost. The rest is now accessible in *IG.* xii. 5. 444, and in the *Marmor Parium* of Felix Jacoby. The inscriptions found in Attica prior to 1896 are published, with a few exceptions, in *IG.* ii. 1, 2, 3, and 5 ; those from Delos are still unpublished or scattered, mainly through the volumes of the *Bulletin de correspondance hellénique*, but Messrs. Holleaux, Dürrbach, and Roussel are busy editing or re-editing them for *IG.* xi. ; those from Lemnos, Imbros, Scyros, and the smaller islands in the north Aegean have just appeared in *IG.* xii. 8. The Attic inscriptions from Delphi are being prepared by Homolle for *IG.* vii. ; in the meanwhile they are for the most part accessible in the *BCH.* for 1906. The inscriptions of Attic origin found since 1896 are still scattered in the scientific journals, but Kirchner has been now at work for some time preparing them for a second edition of *IG.* ii. 2, 3, and 5. In this work he will incorporate many of the rereadings made by the master of Greek epigraphy, Wilhelm of Vienna ; others may be found meanwhile in this scholar's " Urkunden dramatischer Aufführungen " and "Beiträge zur griechischen Inschriftenkunde " (*Sonderschriften des österreichischen archäologischen Institutes in Wien*, Bande VI. und VII.).

On the appearance of *IG.* xi., and when Kirchner's work is completed, the inscriptional sources for Athens and its colonies during the Hellenistic period will be readily accessible. It is from them that we obtain our knowledge of the institutions of public and social life, of the families and persons influential at particular epochs, of the religious and economic currents—in fact, of the entire inner life of the people. Kirchner's *Prosopographia Attica*, or genealogical catalogue of all the Athenians known up to 1901, forms a mine of historical materials of the most variegated character. An *Appendix* prepared by Sundwall (*Nachträge zur Prosopographia Attica : Öfversigt af Finska Vetenskaps-Societetens Förhandlingar*, lii. 1909-1910. *Afd.* B, No. 1) brings this work up to date. It is to be regretted that as yet no *Corpus* of the Athenian coins exists, since it would help us very much in writing the economic history of the second century B.C., when the annual and even the monthly issues of coins can be distinguished with some precision (see Sundwall, *Untersuch. über die attischen Münzen des neueren Stiles : Öfversigt*, xlix. 1906-1907, No. 9). The ruins of ancient buildings, streets, parks, cemeteries, and plastic and other monuments, as unearthed and described by the archaeologists, form a useful source for historical inferences in regard to this period, as in regard to all epochs of Greek development. A convenient survey of the materials and sites in

Athens is given by Judeich in his *Topographie von Athen* (1905), 84 ff. Nothing similar exists as yet for Athenian Delos; but the definite report of the excavations conducted there first by Homolle, and latterly with conspicuous skill and success by Holleaux (*Exploration archéologique de Délos*), for which many preliminary studies have appeared already, particularly in the *Bulletin de correspondance hellénique*, has now begun to be made (see above, ix. 362, n. 5; x. 447, n. 2), and before long we shall be able to trace the material and artistic development of this great Hellenistic *emporium* with singular precision. In the meantime, however, the historian is dependent upon the provisional reports, which in their totality, to speak with Aristotle, are not εὐκατάληπτα.

Gaetano de Sanctis's "Contributi alla storia ateniese della Guerra Lamiaca alla Guerra Cremonidea" (in Beloch's *Studi di storia antica*, ii., 1893) begins with the death of Alexander the Great and extends to the end of the Chremonidean War (262/1 B.C). S. Shebelew's *History of Athens from 229 to 31 B.C.* (Russian), St. Petersburg, 1898, which I could use only in places and by the aid of a translator, reaches from the expulsion of the Macedonians in 229 B.C. to the time of Augustus. Apart from these two works, we are dependent for the history of Hellenistic Athens upon the general histories of Thirlwall, Droysen, Hertzberg, Holm, Niese, Poehlmann, and Beloch, each valuable in its way and time, but dealing with Athens only incidentally; upon the meagre outline of Athenian constitutional development given by Gilbert, Thumser, and Busolt; upon the materials arranged from a topographical or archaeological point of view in the books by Gardner, D'Ooge, and Judeich; upon the histories of literature and philosophy by Susemihl, Croiset, Mahaffy, Wilamowitz, Zeller, Hirzel, and von Arnim; and upon Wachsmuth's *Stadt Athen im Altertum*, i. (1874) 608 ff., and Curtius's *Stadtgeschichte von Athen* (1891), 219 ff., which furnish the most detailed treatments of the entire later development of Athens. For the period where the story of Athens is interwoven with that of Rome and Pontus Mommsen's *History of Rome*, Theodore Reinach's *Mithradate Eupator*, and Colin's *Rome et la Grèce* contain valuable discussions of Athenian topics.

The rest of the literature consists of special monographs and articles to which references are given in the footnotes. Special mention is, however, due to Wilamowitz-Moellendorff's "Antigonos von Karystos" (*Phil. Untersuch.*, iv. 178 ff.), and to the articles in Pauly-Wissowa's *Real-Encyklopädie*. A selected bibliography of later Athenian history will be found in Sundwall's pamphlet entitled "De institutis reipublicae Atheniensium post Aristotelis aetatem commutatis" (*Acta societatis scientiarum Fennicae*, 1907, tom. xxxiv. No. 4).

Various studies made by the author in the preparation of this book have been published in so many different or out-of-the-way places that it may prove serviceable to list the whole of them here:

1. The Athenian Secretaries, *Cornell Studies*, 1898, vii. 1-80.
2. The Athenian Archons of the Third and Second Centuries B.C., *Ibid.*, 1899, x. 1-99.
3. The Oligarchic Revolution at Athens of the Year 103/2 B.C., *Klio*, 1904, iv. 1-17.
4. Athenian Politics in the Early Third Century, *Klio*, 1905, v. 155-179.
5. The Priests of Asklepios, *Univ. of California Publications, Class. Phil.*, 1906 : reprinted 1907, i. 131-173.
6. The Death of Menander, *Class. Phil.*, 1907, ii. 305-312.
7. Notes on Greek Inscriptions, *Ibid.*, 1907, ii. 401-406.
8. The Athenian Calendar, *Ibid.*, 1908, iii. 386-398.
9. Researches in Athenian and Delian Documents, (i.) *Klio*, 1907, vii. 213-240 ; (ii.) *Ibid.*, 1908, viii. 338-355 ; (iii.) *Ibid.*, 1909, ix. 304-340.
10. The Athenian Phratries, *Class. Phil.*, 1910, v. 257-284.
11. Athens and Hellenism, *Amer. Hist. Rev.*, 1910, xvi. 1-10.
12. Egypt's Loss of Sea-Power, *Jour. Hell. Stud.*, 1910, xxx. 189-209.
13. The Laws of Demetrius of Phalerum and their Guardians, *Klio*, 1911, xi. 265-277.

APPENDIX II

THE INSTRUMENTS OF ATHENIAN GOVERNMENT

BETWEEN 323 and 294 B.C. serious changes were made in the Athenian administration. Then followed a long period of general stability. With the reacquisition of the colonies in 166 B.C. many new offices were created, but it was not till the end of this century that the ground-plan of the government which had come into being in 294 B.C. was radically reconstructed. The administrative service as it existed between 166 and 103 B.C. was in outline as follows.

The regular officers of the Athenian state—apart from those instituted for a special purpose, such as *presbeis, theori, pythaistae,* and the like — fall into four groups: (1) local officials, (2) those who are agents of the prytany, (3) those who are agents of the senate, (4) those who are agents or committees of the *demos.* Of these the first included, in addition to the local cleruch officials, the treasurer and, if they still existed, the three *epimeletae* of each *phyle,* the *trittyarchs,* in case they were not abolished after 294 B.C., and the hundred and seventy or so *demarchs* (*IG.* ii. and ii. 5. 570 ff., ii. 5. 477c, 614b. 79) with their secretaries, treasurers, priests, *hieropoei,* and heralds. The second included a treasurer τῶν πρυτάνεων: ἐπὶ τὰ πρυτανεῖα (*IG.* ii. 3, 1201), a secretary τῶν πρυτάνεων, an assistant secretary, a priest τοῦ ἐπωνύμου, and a flute-player (*IG.* ii. 391 ff.). The third included those who ministered to the Senate in its dual capacity of preparing business for the popular assembly and of supervising the executive committees. At this time there belonged to it the prytany-secretary (γραμματεὺς κατὰ πρυτανείαν : γραμματεὺς τοῦ δήμου), the public reader (γραμματεὺς τῆς βουλῆς καὶ τοῦ δήμου), the law clerk (γραμματεὺς ἐπὶ τοὺς νόμους), the auditor-general (ἀντιγραφεύς), the treasurer of the senate, and the herald of the senate and *demos* (*IG.* ii. 391 ff.). The fourth, which was by far the largest and most important, included the senate, divided into prytanies with temporary *proedri* and *epistatae* and a large standing committee of thirty-six (?) members

471

(are they the thirty-six *epimeletae* τῆς φυλῆς ?) to gather the people together for public meetings (Ditt. *Syll.*² 496, n. 10); the Areopagus with its annual herald and its twelve (?) subdivisions (*Klio*, 1909, p. 329, n. 8); and all the ordinary magistracies. These were : I. The ten generals (*Klio*, 1909, p. 314 ff.) —(1) ἐπὶ τοὺς ὁπλίτας, (2) ἐπ᾽ Ἐλευσῖνος, (3) ἐπὶ τὴν παραλίαν, (4) ἐπὶ τὴν παρασκευὴν τὴν ἐν ἄστει, (5-7) ἐπὶ τὸν Πειραιᾶ— ἐπὶ τοῦ Πειραιέως, εἰς τὴν Μουνιχίαν, εἰς τὴν Ἀκτήν, (8-10) εἰς τὸ ναυτικόν. II. The colonial generals — one each for Lemnos (also a *hipparch*), Salamis (also a *hipparch*), Imbros, and Scyros ; the two *hipparchs* and the *tarantinarch*, the twelve *taxiarchs* and the twelve *phylarchs*; the *trierarchs*. III. *Epimeletae*, one of springs, if he still existed, one of the *emporium* in the Piraeus, one of Delos, one of the *emporium* in Delos (after *ca.* 130 B.C. : three prior thereto), one of Haliartus ; *epimeletae* (?) of the mint, two annual and one monthly ; committees of *epimeletae*— one first of ten, later of twenty-four members for the Dionysiac *pompe* (*IG.* ii. 420, Ditt. *Syll.*² 636), a second of two members for the Eleusinian Mysteries (Ditt. *Syll.*² 647, 649, 650). IV. Two custodians of sacred moneys and two committee-men on religious matters in Delos. V. The *cosmetes* of the ephebes, together with his subordinates—the athletic instructor, four military instructors, a secretary and an assistant or two; two athletic instructors in Delos, and, doubtless, others in the other cleruchies. VI. A *gymnasiarch* in Athens (cf. *IG.* iii. 1. 1016) and a second in Delos. VII. The treasurer of military funds. VIII. The superintendent of the administration, together with twelve, perhaps occasional, *sitonae* (Ditt. *Syll.*² 505 ; *IG.* ii. 335) with a treasurer and a secretary. IX. The *agonothetae*—one each for the Dionysia, Panathenaea, Eleusinia, Theseia, Delia, and perhaps other similar *agones*. X. The nine archons, together with the *paredri* (six in number) of three of them (Ditt. *Syll.*² 636, 648) and a herald, flute-player, and *leiturgos*. XI. Priests and priestesses—eleven for Delos alone, at least as many more for Athens, others for Lemnos, Imbros, and Scyros; and as their assistants a corps of heralds, prophets, *hieromnemones*, *exegetae*, flute - players, *cleiducs*, *zacori*, etc. XII. *Hieropoei* for Athens and Eleusis and for specific fêtes, such as the Ptolemaea and Romaea. XIII. Two market clerks each in Athens and (after *ca.* 152/1 B.C. : three prior thereto) Delos, two *astynomi* in Athens. XIV. *Logistae* (Ditt. *Syll.*² 650). XV. *Poletae*, *practores* (cf. *IG.* xii. 8. 51) and *desmophylaces*. XVI. Subordinate officials of the jury courts. XVII. Hereditary priesthoods. XVIII. The public architects —one ἐπὶ τὰ ἱερά; the public physicians. XIX. The *demosioi* or public slaves.

Of these officials I. to IV. were chosen by popular vote, and the incumbents, with the exception, perhaps, of the *epimeletae* τῶν κρηνῶν, were eligible for re-election ; V. to XV. could in all probability hold office only once, and all but V. to IX. were designated by lot; XVI. to XIX., like the assistants of all the magistrates, were probably permanent appointees. In addition to the subordinate, permanent, and local officials, and the Areopagites, Senators and *hieropoei*, over one hundred and seventy-five magistrates were required annually.

That a man could not be an *agonothetes* a second time is proved by the absence of instances of repetition, and also by the means employed to evade the disability thus imposed, viz. by performing the duties in the name of a son (Ditt. *Syll.*[2] 213, l. 56. 233). The same conclusion holds in the case of the treasurer of military funds, since there, too, the same evasion is employed (Ditt. *Syll.*[2] 233). To our knowledge no man was *cosmetes* twice. We have no information as to ὁ ἐπὶ τῇ διοικήσει, or superintendent of the administration. It may be observed, however, that he and the *agonothetae* were the successors of οἱ ἐπὶ τὸ θεωρικόν, in regard to whom Aristotle reports as follows (*Const. of Athens*, 43. 1): τὰς δ᾽ ἀρχὰς τὰς περὶ τὴν ἐγκύκλιον διοίκησιν ἁπάσας ποιοῦσι κληρωτὰς πλὴν ταμίου στρατιωτικῶν καὶ τῶν ἐπὶ τὸ θεωρικὸν καὶ τοῦ τῶν κρηνῶν ἐπιμελητοῦ. ταύτας δὲ χειροτονοῦσιν, καὶ οἱ χειροτονηθέντες ἄρχουσιν ἐκ Παναθηναίων εἰς Παναθήναια. χειροτονοῦσι δὲ καὶ τὰς πρὸς τὸν πόλεμον ἁπάσας. The three offices thus specified were subject to all the conditions imposed upon the civil magistracies except as to term of office ; and from the statement with which Aristotle closes his description of the administrative service of Athens (*Const. of Athens*, 62. 3) we learn what the most weighty of these was : ἄρχειν δὲ τὰς μὲν κατὰ πόλεμον ἀρχὰς ἔξεστι πλεονάκις, τῶν δ᾽ ἄλλων οὐδεμίαν πλὴν βουλεῦσαι δίς. They could hold office only once. Whether the superintendent of springs existed after 294 B.C. or not, we do not know. The committee on theoric funds does not appear after 322/1 B.C., and since its work was done thereafter in part by the superintendent of the administration, who appears prior to 307 B.C., and in part by the *agonothetae* and the *gymnasiarch*, whom Demetrius of Phalerum created in 309/8 B.C., it seems likely that this board was abolished at the end of the Hellenic War. The alternative is that it was discarded by Demetrius in 309/8 B.C. In any case the superintendent of the administration doubtless appeared first when the theoric committee disappeared. Since the *agonothetae* and the *gymnasiarch* were subject to the restriction as to re-election earlier put upon the committee, it seems likely that the same was true of ὁ or οἱ ἐπὶ τῇ διοικήσει.

It had been generally assumed that in the phrase ἐκ Παναθηναίων εἰς Παναθήναια, Panathenaea means Great Panathenaea, and that the three magistracies thus segregated by Aristotle are different from all the other civil magistracies (except the *athlothetae*, of whom Aristotle, *Const. of Athens*, 60. 1, says, not that they served ἐκ Π. εἰς Π., but that δοκιμασθέντες ἄρχουσι τέτταρα ἔτη) in that their incumbents served for a four- instead of a one-year term. This assumption is, however, erroneous. In the first place, if Great Panathenaea were meant, ἐκ Μεγάλων Π. ἐις Μεγάλα Π. should have been said; for otherwise the Athenians distinguish the Great and the Minor Panathenaea. In the second place, when the phrase ἐκ Π. εἰς Π. is used to define the financial year of the *tamiae* of Athena and of the other gods, it means from one fête to the next without regard to its magnitude. For it is clear from the lists of the *tamiae* that each board served for a single year, the four-year period existing simply in that the accounts of the treasurers were published four at a time. The rubric for the collected accounts is as follows : τάδε παρέδοσαν αἱ τέτταρες ἀρχαί, αἳ ἐδίδοσαν τὸν λόγον ἐκ Παναθηναίων ἐς Παναθήναια · τοῖς ταμίασι κτλ. (*IG.* i. 117 ff.). Hicks and Hill (*Greek Historical Inscriptions*, 130) interpret : " Accordingly, the accounts of these Treasurers, although audited yearly, were inscribed for a πεντετηρίς at a time, ἐκ Παναθηναίων ἐς Παναθήναια"; with which I should agree entirely if the phrase ἐκ Π. ἐς Π. had been inserted after " yearly." For that it seems to me is the meaning of the following paragraph from the act constituting the board of treasurers of the other gods (Ditt. *Syll.*[2] 21): καὶ τὸ λοιπὸν ἀναγραφόντον οἱ αἰεὶ ταμίαι ἐς στέλεν καὶ λόγον διδόντον τόν τε ὄντον χρεμάτον καὶ τὸν προσιόντον τοῖς θεοῖς καὶ ἐάν τι ἀπαναλίσκεται κατὰ τὸν ἐνιαυτόν, πρὸς τὸς λογιστάς, καὶ εὐθύνας διδόντον. καὶ ἐκ Παναθεναίον ἐς Παναθέναια τὸλ λόγον διδόντον, καθάπερ οἱ τὰ τὲς Ἀθεναίας ταμιεύοντες. To me it seems arbitrary to distinguish the λόγος which οἱ αἰεὶ ταμίαι are to give κατ' ἐνιαυτόν from that which they are to give ἐκ Π. ἐς Π. Rather, the same account is meant in each case, the year being simply defined as running, not from the first of Hecatombaeon to the first next following, as did the civil year, but from the twenty-eighth to the twenty-eighth. So, too, in the following prescript, [τάδε τοῦ τόκου (?) ἐλογίσαντ]ο οἱ λογιστα[ὶ ἐν τοῖς τέτ]ταρσιν ἔτεσιν ἐκ Παναθηναίων ἐς [Παναθήναια ὀφειλόμενα ?] (*IG.* ii. 273), though it is perhaps more natural, if the restorations are accepted, to take the Panathenaea as the outside limits of the four-year period, still it is the phrase ἐν τοῖς τέτταρσιν ἔτεσιν which determines the time involved, not the phrase ἐκ Π. ἐς Π., which simply specifies the nature of the year : it is four financial, not four civil, years with which the *logistae* have to do. However that may be, it is evident that the *epimeletes* τῶν κρηνῶν, who, as we have seen, served ἐκ Π. εἰς Π., was elected for a single year only. Thus in *IG.* ii. 5. 110c a man is described as having been chosen ἐπ[ὶ Θ]ε[μιστοκλέους ἄρχοντ]ος (Ol. 108. 2; 347/6 B.C.) ἐπι[μελέσθαι τῶν κρηνῶν; and on the ninth of Metageitnion, and the thirty-ninth of the first prytany of the year Ol. 111. 4; 333/2 B.C., that is to say, at the first meeting of the ecclesia after the financial year ended with the Panathenaea, a certain Pytheas was commended for his management of this office, the vote being subject to the condition that he stand his audit successfully (ἐπειδὰν τὰς εὐθύνας δῷ). Had his period of service been defined by the great Panathenaea, Pytheas must have waited for a year and ten days before receiving his reward, and he must have had, even at this late date, to face an accounting for his official acts. This, however, is not only unthinkable, but altogether impossible, seeing that he had to present his accounts within thirty days of the date at which he went out of office (Harpocr. *s.v.* λογισταί; cf. Ditt. *Syll².* 580, n. 6). The conclusion is therefore obvious that all Aristotle tried to say of the three exceptional magistrates was that their year of office was defined by the Panathenaea not by the first of Hecatombaeon.

The view that the committee on the theoric funds and the military treasurer served for four years continuously is thus robbed of the support of Aristotle, while the inscriptions just cited prove that their companion, the superintendent of springs, was in fact an annual magistrate. The only other evidence available in favour of a four-years' term for a financial officer in the fourth century B.C. is the following passage from the decree in honour of Lycurgus transmitted in [Plut.], *Lives of the Ten Orators,* 852 B : καὶ γενόμενος τῆς κοινῆς προσόδου ταμίας τῇ πόλει ἐπὶ τρεῖς πεντετηρίδας καὶ διανείμας ἐκ τῆς κοινῆς προσόδου μύρια καὶ ὀκτακισχίλια καὶ ἐνακόσια τάλαντα κτλ. This, however, if construed strictly, proves the existence of a treasurership tenable for a twelve-year period. It cannot be made to mean that Lycurgus was either ταμίας τῶν στρατιωτικῶν or ὁ ἐπὶ τὸ θεωρικόν for three terms of four years each, for we have already seen that Aristotle clearly makes a repeated tenure of either of these offices, and in fact of any financial magistracy, for more than one term impossible. The fact underlying the approximate language of the paraphrased decree is that Lycurgus dominated Athenian finance from 338 to 326 B.C.: Ol. 110. 3, to Ol. 113. 3, or for three *penteterides* (Diod. xvi. 88: δώδεκα ἔτη τὰς προσόδους τῆς πόλεως διοικήσας). This means that in the coalition government then existing this department was handed over to him, so that his proposals were regularly accepted by the ecclesia. The total period of his control is not twelve years by accident simply, since four financial years were doubtless put together for certain purposes to form a *tetraëtia* in the fourth century B.C. as in the fifth.   Thus we have mention in a mutilated inscription of the time of Lycurgus (*IG.* ii. 162, 1. 17) of ο]ν ἐνιαυτοῦ ἐν τῇ τετραετίᾳ, etc.   The dates inscribed on the Panathenaic prize-*amphorae*, moreover, presuppose some such fiscal period, and, in fact, the *athlothetae*, who administered the Panathenaea, served for four consecutive years.

INDEX

ABYDUS, sea-fight of, 17

Academy, 214 f.; patronised by Attalids, 234, 448

Acarnania, in Hellenic War, 15; incident of, 267 f.

Achaeans, in Hellenic War, 15; alliance with Aetolians, 199; war with Demetrius, 200 f.; peace with Athens, 208; garrison Piraeus, 284; befriend Delians, 324; quarrel with Athens, 324; champion Oropus, 327 f.; expel Attic cleruchy from Oropus, 328

Achaeus, of Hierapolis, 385

Acropolis, siege and capture of, 451 ff.

Aegina, 205; sack of, 254

Aemilii, on Delos, 395

Aeschetades, general in Salamis, 117

Aeschines, in coalition government, 7

Aetolians, revolt from Macedon, 14; alliance of, with Athens, 114; seize Delphi, 141; plunder Attica, 142; found Soteria, 163; join Gonatas, 195; overwhelm Boeotia, 196; relations of, with Athens, 196 n.; alliance of, with Achaeans, 199; with Egypt, 199; war of, with Demetrius II., 144, 200; take Ambracia, 203; make peace with Athens, 208; renew it, 248; agitate against Rome, 281; make peace with Scipios, 286

Agasias, son of Menophilus, 411, 433

Agathocles of Marathon, 222

Agathostratus, Rhodian admiral, 198

Agis, king of Sparta, 196

Agonothetae, in Athens, 56, 99, 100, 290, 384, 436; in cleruchies, 318

Agoranomi, in Athens, 99, 322, 384; in Delos, 349, 383

Agron, king of Scodra, 203

Alexander the Great, deification of, 11 f.; restores exiles, 12; gifts of, to Athens, 69; death of, 14

Alexander, the young, murdered, 53

Alexander, the son of Polyperchon, in Athens, 31, 34

Alexander of Epirus, invades Macedon, 180

Alexander, son of Craterus, attacks Attica, 193 f.; death of, 196

Alexander, son of Cassander, 132

Alexandria, growth of, 66; a second Athens, 69, 170; influence of, 177 f.; government of, 381 n.

Alexis, comedian, 123, 166, 171

Ambracia, siege of, 286

Amici, of Rome, 313 n., 314

Amisus, 302, 437, 438, 448

Ammon, worshippers of, 181

Amorgos, battle of, 17

Amphictyonic Council, 309, 371, 430

Anagrapheus, 24

Andros, battle of, 198

Antagoras, of Rhodes, 166

Antalcidas, treaty of, 6

Antigoneia, established in Athens, 64; in Delos, 190

Antigoneia, city of, colonized by Athenians, 69, 112

Antigonis, established, 64, 96; abolished, 268

Antigonus I., war with Perdiccas, 21; seeks regency, 28; naval victory at Byzantium, 35; aims at universal empire, 49; gives autonomy to Greek cities, 49; regal title, 107 f.; deified in Athens, 108; gifts to Athens, 112, 114

Antigonus II., defeats Thebans, 139 f.; king of Greece, 150; secret treaty of, 151; masters Peloponnese, 152; attacks Athens, 152 f.; in Asia Minor, 155; king of Macedon, 159 f.; makes peace with Antiochus I., 159 f.; refuses deification, 163; paintings describing victory of, 165; in Athens, 168; fosters tyranny, 175; exponent of Stoicism, 176; besieges Athens, 179; captures it, 182; makes peace with Egypt, 188 f.; builds fleet, 189; deified at Delos, 190; but not in Macedon, 190 f.; withdraws garrison from Museum, 191 f.; takes Corinth, 196; dies, 198

Antigonus III., peace of, with Athens, 209; restores power of Macedon, 240; defeats Cleomenes, 243